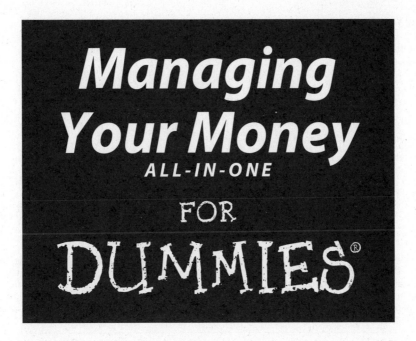

Managing Your Money
ALL-IN-ONE
FOR
DUMMIES®

by Ted Benna, Stephen R. Bucci, James P. Caher,
John M. Caher, N. Brian Caverly, Peter Economy,
Jack Hungelmann, John E. Lucas, Sarah Glendon Lyons,
Margaret A. Munro, EA, Brenda Watson Newmann,
Mary Reed, Jordan S. Simon, Kathleen Sindell, PhD,
Deborah Taylor-Hough, John Ventura

WILEY

Wiley Publishing, Inc.

Managing Your Money All-in-One For Dummies®

Published by
Wiley Publishing, Inc.
111 River St.
Hoboken, NJ 07030-5774
www.wiley.com

WILEY

About the Authors

Ted Benna is often called the "father of the 401(k)" because he created and gained IRS approval for the first 401(k) savings plan. Ted is a nationally recognized expert on retirement issues whose articles and comments have appeared in myriad publications. Ted has been profiled in *The New York Times*, *USA Today*, *Fortune*, and *Kiplinger*. During his career, Ted has helped thousands of employers establish, restructure, and administer their retirement programs. He is president and founder of the 401(k) Association. Ted is the coauthor of *401(k)s For Dummies*.

Stephen R. Bucci is currently the president of the Money Management International Financial Education Foundation, www.mmifoundation.org, which provides funds and materials for essential money management education. In addition, he is helping to build one of the nation's largest credit counseling services, Money Management International (MMI). MMI is not only accredited by the Council on Accreditation, but is also a member of both the Association of Independent Consumer Credit Counseling Agencies and the National Foundation for Consumer Credit — the umbrella associations for credit counseling nationwide. In addition, all of their counselors are certified — and trained to help you find the best way out of debt. Stephen is the author of *Credit Repair Kit For Dummies*, 2nd Edition.

James P. Caher is a practicing attorney with 30 years of experience, is a nationally recognized expert on consumer bankruptcies and authority on the Bankruptcy Abuse Prevention and Consumer Protection Act of 2005. Jim has published scores of articles for bankruptcy professionals and is frequently called upon to analyze and interpret the complicated provisions of the 2005 bankruptcy law. He also serves on the editorial board of the American Bankruptcy Institute. Jim graduated from Niagara University and then earned his law degree from Memphis State University Law School, where he was a member of the Law Review and recipient of the American Jurisprudence Award for Excellence in the field of debtor-creditor relations. He filed his first consumer bankruptcy case shortly after graduating in 1975 and lives and practices in Eugene, Oregon. James is coauthor of *Personal Bankruptcy Laws For Dummies*.

John M. Caher is a legal journalist who has written about law and the courts for most of his long career. He has been Albany bureau chief for the *New York Law Journal* and state editor and legal affairs reporter for the *Times*

Union of Albany, New York. His legal reportage has won more than two dozen awards, including prestigious honors from the American Bar Association, the New York State Bar Association, the Erie County Bar Association, and the Associated Press. John is coauthor of *Personal Bankruptcy Laws For Dummies*.

N. Brian Caverly is a practicing lawyer in Pennsylvania. He has practiced law since 1968, and in his practice emphasizes wills and estates, estate planning, and elder law. He holds an AB degree in economics from Bucknell University, and a JD degree from the Dickinson School of Law. He serves on the board of directors of the Angeline Elizabeth Kirby Memorial Health Center in Wilkes-Barre, a major charitable organization. Brian is also chairman of the Luzerne County Planning Commission. He presents lectures and writes articles and papers about various legal topics, including those related to estate planning. Brian is the coauthor of *Estate Planning For Dummies*.

Peter Economy lives in La Jolla, California and is a bestselling author or coauthor of more than 35 books, including *Managing For Dummies* and *Consulting For Dummies* with Bob Nelson, *Home-Based Business For Dummies* with Paul and Sarah Edwards, and *Writing Children's Books For Dummies* with Lisa Rojany Buccieri. Peter is also Associate Editor for the Apex Award-winning magazine *Leader to Leader*.

Jack Hungelmann's policy knowledge, problem-solving expertise, and coverage analysis was gained through more than 25 years in the insurance business as a claims adjuster, agent, and consultant. He has advised individuals and commercial enterprises on their insurance needs and has earned several distinguished designations. Jack graduated from the University of Minnesota in 1969 and has taught professional continuing education classes for both the CPCU and CIC societies. He has been published numerous times in *American Agent & Broker* magazine. He lives in Chanhassen, Minnesota with his wife Judy. Jack is the author of *Insurance For Dummies*.

John E. Lucas has been in the mortgage banking industry for over 40 years, actively originating mortgage loans in the Van Nuys, California area. When the Department of Housing and Urban Development (HUD) introduced the HECM reverse mortgage in 1989, he worked with one of the companies HUD chose to participate in the test program. He has lectured on reverse mortgages to a wide variety of organizations and groups such as senior centers, realtors, CPAs, financial planners, elder law attorneys, service clubs and university groups, and is a member of the National Reverse Mortgage Lenders Association. John is the coauthor of *Reverse Mortgages For Dummies*.

Sarah Glendon Lyons is a San Diego-based writer with a diverse portfolio of housing-industry experience. She holds a B.A. in English Language and Literature from the University of Arizona and studied at Australia's University of Wollongong before joining Hanley Wood LLC, publishers of over 75 consumer home magazines. As an editor for Pfingsten Publishing's *Mortgage Originator* magazine, she has written hundreds of articles for mortgage professionals. Although she has developed a wide scope of lending insight, her particular expertise is in the reverse mortgage field. Sarah offers reverse mortgage information to originators and consumers around the country. Her perspective as an unbiased researcher and consultant allows her to provide readers with both the benefits and challenges of reverse mortgages. Sarah is the coauthor of *Reverse Mortgages For Dummies*.

Margaret A. Munro, EA, is a tax consultant/advisor/writer/lecturer with over 30 years of experience in various areas of finance and taxation. She is an enrolled agent, licensed by the federal government to represent clients in the areas of tax and tax-related issues. She currently operates a widely diverse private practice that specializes in the financial concerns of families with school-age children, a group that is near and dear to her heart. She is a graduate of The Johns Hopkins University and has also attended University College Cork and the Pontifical Institute of Mediaeval Studies in Toronto. Peggy is the author of *529 & Other College Savings Plans For Dummies* and *Estate and Trust Administration For Dummies*.

Brenda Watson Newmann is a writer and editor dedicated to helping ordinary folks understand complicated topics. She was in charge of editorial content for the mPower Cafe, a leading educational Web site for retirement investors. Under her direction, the site won accolades including *Forbes* magazine's "Best of the Web." Brenda keeps attuned to the concerns of 401(k) investors through the emails she receives regularly from readers. She frequently writes articles on retirement investing and has been interviewed by media outlets, such as *USA Today* and *Investor's Business Daily*. Brenda began her writing career with The Associated Pres, and was a foreign correspondent in Germany and Switzerland. She is a graduate of Stanford University and the Johns Hopkins University School of Advanced International Studies. Brenda is the coauthor of *401(k)s For Dummies*.

Mary Reed is a personal finance writer who has coauthored or ghostwritten numerous books on topics related to consumer money matters and legal rights. Mary has also written for the magazines *Good Housekeeping*, *Home Office Computing*, and *Small Business Computing* and she has ghostwritten numerous articles that have appeared in national and local publications. She is the owner of Mary Reed Public Relations, an Austin, Texas-based firm that provides public relations services to a wide variety of clients, including authors, publishers, attorneys, financial planners, healthcare professionals, retailers, hotels, restaurants, and nonprofits. She received her MBA from Boston University and her BA from Trinity University in Washington, DC. Mary is the coauthor of *Managing Debt For Dummies*.

Jordan S. Simon is vice president of asset management at Venture West, Inc., a Tucson, Arizona-based investment firm, where he has worked since 1988. Jordan focuses on real estate investments. He received his BA from the University of Arizona and his MBA from the University of Southern California, where he was the recipient of the Quon Award for outstanding university and community service. He is the coauthor of *The Computer Professional's Guide to Effective Communications* and *Estate Planning For Dummies*.

Kathleen Sindell, PhD, is the author of numerous books on investing and Internet topics. She was contributing author to the *Encyclopedia of Computer Science* and online investing columnist for *Investor Direct* magazine. Dr. Sindell is an expert on electronic commerce and is an adjunct faculty member at The Johns Hopkins University MBA program. She is the former Associate Director of the Financial Management and Commercial Real Estate Programs for the University of Maryland, University College Graduate School of Management & Technology. She received her BA in Business from Antioch University, an MBA. in Finance from the California State University at San Jose, and a PhD in Administration and Management from Walden University, Institute for Advanced Studies. Dr. Sindell is the author of *Managing Your Money Online For Dummies*.

Deborah Taylor-Hough has been living the frugal lifestyle most of her life. Deborah is the editor/publisher of the Simple Times Newsletter, an email publication reaching tens of thousands of subscribers since 1998. She has authored several books on frugal living topics and has been featured extensively in television, radio, and print media throughout the United States and Canada. She frequently conducts workshops on frugal living, voluntary simplicity, and assorted homemaking topics for conferences, retreats, women's groups, and church functions. Debi is the author of *Frugal Living For Dummies*.

John Ventura is a best-selling author and board-certified bankruptcy attorney. He is also adjunct professor at the University of Houston Law School and Director of the Texas Consumer Complaint Center at the Law School.

John earned his JD degree from the University of Houston Law School. Later, he and a partner established a law firm in Texas, building it into one of the most successful consumer bankruptcy firms in the state. He subsequently began a successful consumer law firm in South Texas. He is also a regular speaker at law conferences around the country and serves on the Bankruptcy Council for the Texas Bar Association. John is the author of numerous books on consumer and small business legal matters, including *Managing Debt For Dummies*.

Publisher's Acknowledgments

We're proud of this book; please send us your comments through our Dummies online registration form located at www.dummies.com/register/.

Some of the people who helped bring this book to market include the following:

Acquisitions, Editorial, and Media Development

Project Editor: Corbin Collins

Acquisitions Editor: Tracy Boggier

Copy Editor: Krista Hansing

Assistant Editor: Erin Calligan Mooney

Technical Editor: Brian Richman

Senior Editorial Manager: Jennifer Ehrlich

Editorial Supervisor and Reprint Editor: Carmen Krikorian

Editorial Assistants: Joe Niesen, David Lutton

Cover Photo: © Creatas Images

Cartoons: Rich Tennant (www.the5thwave.com)

Composition Services

Project Coordinator: Katherine Key

Layout and Graphics: Carl Byers, Jennifer Mayberry

Proofreaders: Melissa D. Buddendeck, Dwight Ramsey

Indexer: Sharon Shock

Publishing and Editorial for Consumer Dummies

> **Diane Graves Steele,** Vice President and Publisher, Consumer Dummies
>
> **Joyce Pepple,** Acquisitions Director, Consumer Dummies
>
> **Kristin Ferguson-Wagstaffe,** Product Development Director, Consumer Dummies
>
> **Ensley Eikenburg,** Associate Publisher, Travel
>
> **Kelly Regan,** Editorial Director, Travel

Publishing for Technology Dummies

> **Andy Cummings,** Vice President and Publisher, Dummies Technology/General User

Composition Services

> **Gerry Fahey,** Vice President of Production Services
>
> **Debbie Stailey,** Director of Composition Services

Contents at a Glance

Table of Contents

Introduction

Welcome to *Managing Your Money All-in-One For Dummies,* a big one-stop shop designed to help you get control over your financial life!

This book tackles a lot of big topics, but we've tried to keep things simple, clear, and to-the-point. We've culled the best, juiciest information from a good sampling of *For Dummies* books on personal finance and compiled them into one fat volume. It's absolutely packed with easy-to-grasp advice on all things having to do with managing your money. Whether you're a home-maker, truck driver, burger flipper, or CEO — whether you're interviewing for your first job or you retired ten years ago — we bet you'll find scads of great tips and sound advice in these pages that will help you get a handle on every-thing from your credit cards to your health insurance, from your groceries to your taxes to your will.

If it has something to do with your personal relationship to your own money, it's a good bet we talk about it in this book. *Managing Your Money All-in-One For Dummies* offers money-management and personal-finance tips to help assess your true financial situation and take charge of your economic life. You'll find information on getting the best mortgage, saving for the future (whether for college or retirement), paying off debt, scaling back on expenses, managing home and personal budgets, repairing and improving your credit rating, planning an estate, banking online, saving and investing, and protecting your money and other assets.

The facts on the ground aren't pretty at the moment. Real wages have been stagnant or declining for nearly 40 years in America. And in the current cli-mate of economic uncertainty, skyrocketing home foreclosures, job cuts, bank failures, and unaffordable health insurance, many people feel more pow-erless than ever against mighty and faceless institutions that seem designed for nothing but to confuse and rip off. We're here to tell you: *It doesn't have to be that way.* By doing a little homework and taking a renewed interest in your own situation, you can reclaim many rights and advantages you probably didn't know you had.

If information is power, then this book is like a gigantic supervitamin.

Foolish Assumptions

In order to shovel so much material on such a wide variety of topics into a single book that's actually helpful and inviting, we make a few assumptions about you, the reader. See whether one or more of these shoes fit:

- ✔ You can't seem to get out from under credit card debt.
- ✔ You'd like to find ways to spend less money, but the idea of sitting down and setting up a budget makes you feel slightly ill.
- ✔ You've heard about how great it is to save for retirement in an IRA or 401(k), but the whole concept seems too complicated to deal with.
- ✔ When tax time rolls around, you feel frightened and uncertain.
- ✔ You can't seem to keep up with mounting bills and wonder where in the world your paycheck goes every month.
- ✔ You worry that you'll ever be able to afford college for your kids.
- ✔ You have a vague feeling that you should probably have certain kinds of insurance, but what they might be is a mystery.
- ✔ You have health problems and are afraid they are going to end up bankrupting you.

If we've hit the mark with any (or, God forbid, all) of these descriptions, this book is most definitely for you.

How This Book Is Organized

Managing Your Money All-in-One For Dummies is organized so that you can easily and quickly access the information you're looking for. We've arranged everything into seven "books," each of which focuses on one aspect of your financial life. Without further ado, here's how it's all set up:

Book 1: Taking Charge of Your Finances

We start at the very beginning and take a good, hard, honest — and yes, perhaps slightly painful — look at where you are now financially. (Sometimes pain leads to something good: Look at surgery, for example, or birth.) The chapters here ask that you be truthful with yourself and your habits when it comes to handling your own money. Only by seeing what you are actually, really, and truly doing with your cash now will you be able to make the most efficient and worthwhile improvements necessary to turn around your finances.

Before you know it you'll be tracking where your hard-earned dollars go, easily maintaining a household budget, trimming away unnecessary spending, finding ways to make extra money, and even tackling that ugly but important beast: your credit report.

Book II: Managing Home and Personal Finances

Here is where we delve a bit deeper into how you deal with the money that comes in and goes out every month. Your home is your castle, as they say, and here is where we explore concrete and detailed ways of turning your household into a strong financial fort. In recent years, the American dream of owning a home has suffered seriously from the popped housing bubble, the housing market slump, the credit crisis, and rising mortgage defaults nationwide. That's why it's more important than ever to understand how to find and maintain the right kind of mortgage for you and how to avoid trouble with it down the road.

Housing is usually the largest piece of your monthly financial pie, but another increasingly large slice goes to health insurance and other health-related expenses. We devote a whole chapter on health insurance and ways to reduce your medical costs. And we address ways of using the greatest information tool of all time, the Internet, to help you in your new quest for financial self-empowerment.

Book III: Dealing with Debt

"In the midst of life we are in debt, et cetera," sang one of the great bands of the 1980s (The Smiths, in case you have to ask), and truer words were never spoken. There's little you can do to totally avoid debt in your life, and in some ways that's not a terrible thing. You may be surprised to learn that some debts are a *lot* better than other debts. What you want to do is reduce your "bad" debts before worrying too much about your "good" ones.

The first step is to find out how much you owe and to whom. The next is to gain a little knowledge about what exactly credit is and how the different types really work. Remember: Knowledge is power. For those in need of a little bit more aggressive help credit-wise, we tackle the issues of debt consolidation (in which you bundle your debts into fewer payments), negotiating with creditors (yes, it is possible and in many cases very advisable), and seeking professional help from knowledgeable credit counselors who can size up your particular situation.

In the end, it may be that even after all that, you are still saddled with too much debt to keep your head above water. In that case, we give you the lowdown on whether, when, and how to declare bankruptcy and thereby give yourself a fresh start while protecting as much of your assets as possible. There *is* such a thing as a second chance, but if you need it, you need to do it the right way.

Book IV: Saving and Investing

Debt is only one side of the coin. We'll call it tails. Heads, then, is all about keeping some of the money you have worked so hard to earn. It's amazing how diligently people will work — only to unthinkingly fritter it away and have nothing to show for it at the end of the month. If you're like most people, you have to change your thinking about saving money, and this book lays the groundwork for how to become a saver.

There are lots of ways to save money, and some are easier and work out better for you than others. The classic and historically most successful method is to invest your money in stocks, bonds, and mutual funds, and now there are cutting-edge ways of doing that online. We also cover the smartest ways to save up for giving the next generation that most important arrow in the financial quiver: a college education.

Book V: Protecting Your Money and Assets

Once you do get a grip on your finances and manage to start your nest egg, you may notice that your egg attracts predators and has become vulnerable to new dangers. One growing danger is that of identity theft, and you need to know how to avoid falling prey to those who would use information against you in order to take away what's yours. And where do you keep your money? In the bank, right? Well, banking itself has gone through the online revolution, and it's a very good idea to know options and pitfalls in this area.

The main way most people avoid financial disasters in their lives is by buying insurance, which (knock on wood) pays things off when bad things happen. Besides health insurance, which we cover in Book II, there are three other main forms of insuring yourself against catastrophic losses: homeowner's insurance, auto insurance, and life insurance. We tell you what and what *not* to look for in all three categories.

There's one other "predator" out there that drools over the thought of your moolah: That would be the government, which seems to want a piece of everything you do. It's all very well and good, of course, to pay your fair share to enjoy the benefits of living in a modern society, but there's no reason to pay *more* than that out of ignorance, is there? That's why we include a chapter on how to deal intelligently with your tax bill and how to avoid tipping Uncle Sam unnecessarily.

Book VI: Retiring Comfortably

You see yourself laughing with friends on a boat, perhaps, a merrily clinking drink in your hand, with a little paper umbrella, recounting stories to captivated friends? Snapping photos of the Great Pyramid or strolling through some exotic, colorful bazaar? Or maybe you'd like to do nothing but play golf everyday and lunch in the sun? Well, we hope we're not the first to tell you that Social Security isn't going to cover that stuff. When it comes to clichés, we try to avoid them like the plague, but here's one that is most definitely true: *Failing to plan is planning to fail.*

To enjoy your Golden Years to their full extent, you absolutely have to prepare for them, and the sooner the better. Fortunately, retirement plans such as IRAs, 401(k)s, and 403(b)s are excellent vehicles for doing just that. Also, if you've been paying off that big house that got you through your full nest period, there's a way to make that house start paying you back: the reverse mortgage. The Internet is a great resource in these areas as well.

And once you *are* retired, that doesn't mean you can slack off on all the financial tricks and skills you've gained — or you could very well end up spending your "retirement" greeting people at your neighborhood supermegacenter. That's why we have a chapter on great ways of managing your money in retirement.

Book VII: Planning Your Estate and Will

It's just a fact that even if you follow every piece of advice in this book and end up wealthy and happy beyond your wildest dreams, when it comes time to head off into the sunset you'll have to leave your possessions behind. What will happen to your estate? Bad things, possibly, if you are careless.

The more you know about preparing for this eventuality, the more control you'll have over what happens to your stuff after you're gone. Here we give you lots of information on the best ways to gain and keep that control. And in many cases it's not just you that you have to worry about, which is why we include a chapter on taking care of aging parents.

Icons Used in This Book

You'll see a number of funny-looking little graphic elements sprinkled throughout this book. Here's what they are and what they mean:

Marks concrete tips and tricks that you can put to use in giving you more control over your financial life.

Highlights passages that are good to keep in mind when it comes time to make decisions.

Alerts you to common mistakes that can trip you up and cause trouble when managing your money.

Notifies you that something is a bit more complex than usual, and that you can safely skip it if you're in a hurry or only want to skim the surface of the topic.

Where to Go from Here

If you already have a specific interest in one particular area of managing your money, or have a sense of what you really need to tackle first, by all means flip to the Table of Contents or Index and zip straight to that section. You certainly are *not* expected to read this book cover to cover. On the other hand, if you're here because you are well and truly lost when it comes to handling your finances, you may as well begin at the beginning with Book I, Chapter 1 and go from there.

However you end up using this book, we hope you at least gain some insight into better and smarter ways of keeping more and wasting less of what you work so hard for. And we hope you find the determination to apply some of the ideas here to your life. You'll be very glad you did, we promise. Just keep in mind that even in tough times like these, there are a surprising number of things you can do to beat the system, even if it seems stacked against you.

The idea is to empower yourself. No one is going to stop you if you try, and no one is going to do it for you. So, buck up and steel yourself to look at your life more critically and honestly. We all have bad habits. Recognizing them is half the battle. Get ready to take charge of your life and get more out of it. Good luck! We know you can do it.

Book I
Taking Charge of Your Finances

The 5th Wave   By Rich Tennant

"We're trying to save money by buying in bulk. Caviar?"

In this book . . .

*W*e ask you to take an unflinching look at your financial life and your relationship to your own money. Don't be afraid! It's not like you are going to be *that* surprised, is it? No, you know deep down approximately how bad things are. So why not face them once and for all and begin repairing your economic standing? And maybe things aren't *quite* as bad as you suspect. In the end it's not only financially rewarding to face the music, it's also a tremendous load off your shoulders to feel that you are finally doing something about it. There's a ton of stuff you can do immediately to begin improving your finances. So, what are you waiting for? Starting at Square One is what this book is about.

Here are the contents of Book I at a glance.

Chapter 1

Assessing Where You Are Financially

*Y*ou've bought this book, so we assume you're probably at least a little worried — maybe *really* worried — about your financial health. Perhaps your debts have you biting your nails, and you're not sure what to do about them. We doubt you're reading this book for the fun of it! And you probably don't have a good handle on the true state of your finances. After all, it's human nature to try to avoid bad news.

We understand. Facing financial facts can be unsettling and even scary. When you know the state of your finances, it becomes hard to ignore the fact that improving your financial situation requires changing your lifestyle and making some big sacrifices. But no matter how scary it is, confronting the reality of your financial situation *is essential* — and the good news is that seeking out this book is a terrific first step to doing just that.

This chapter begins your next step: figuring out where you are so you know where you need to go. Until you come face to face with the actual facts of your finances, you may find it impossible to develop the resolve and self-discipline you need to implement your plan of action. That's why we begin with this series of fact-finding exercises to get you going.

The more bad news you get as you complete these exercises, the more critical it is that you get serious about dealing with your debts. The sooner you do that, the quicker and easier it will be to improve your finances and the less likely that your creditors will take some of your assets or that you'll have to file for bankruptcy. So let's get going!

Some Preliminary Questions

You can get a rough sense of your debt problem by honestly answering the following questions. The more "yes" answers, the more work you have to do.

- ✔ Are you clueless about how much you owe your creditors?

- ✔ Over time, is a growing percentage of your household income going toward paying your debts?

- ✔ Do you ever pay your bills late because you don't have enough money?

- ✔ Have you stopped paying some of your debts?

- ✔ Are you paying only the minimum due on some of your credit cards because you can't afford to pay more?

- ✔ Are you using credit and/or credit card cash advances to help pay debts and/or your basic living expenses, such as groceries, rent, or utilities?

- ✔ Have you maxed out any of your credit cards, or have any of your cards been cancelled for nonpayment?

- ✔ Do you have little or nothing in savings?

- ✔ Have you borrowed money from friends or relatives to pay your bills?

- ✔ Have debt collectors begun calling you, and/or are you receiving threatening notices from some of your creditors?

- ✔ Are you having a hard time concentrating at work because you are worried about money?

- ✔ Are you losing sleep because of your finances?

- ✔ Have you and your spouse or partner begun to fight about money?

- ✔ Are you drinking more or using illegal drugs to try to cope with your money worries?

- ✔ Are you an overspender? According to Debtors Anonymous, most compulsive spenders answer "yes" to at least 8 of 15 questions. Go to `www.debtorsanonymous.org/help/questions.htm` and take the Debt Quiz.

Your Relationship with Money

You may have the misconception that you are what you buy. You may believe on some level that the more you spend, the more successful and important you are. Developing that mindset is easy because all of us are constantly bombarded with messages that equate money and stuff with success. How often do you see ads promoting frugality, saving, or self-denial? If you're struggling to keep up with the Joneses, you may need to reevaluate your friendships. The Joneses may be driving you straight to the poorhouse.

Recognizing emotional spending

Maybe you spend money for emotional reasons. For example, think about what you do when you feel sad or disappointed, or when you want to celebrate a success. Do you head to the mall? Do you click on your favorite retail Web site? Do you treat yourself to an expensive meal or enjoy a weekend getaway even though you really can't afford it? If so, spending may have become a sort of addiction. Everyone likes to reward themselves from time to time, but doing so continually is a problem, and losing track of whether you can afford to treat yourself is a cause for real concern.

If emotional spending describes your behavior to a T, you need to get a handle on it fast. One option is to meet with a mental health professional; you may qualify for help from a low-cost/no-cost clinic in your area. Or get involved with Debtors Anonymous (www.debtorsanonymous.org or 781-453-2743). DA uses the time-tested methods of Alcoholics Anonymous to help people understand why they spend and to gain control over their spending.

Living for the moment

Maybe your problem is that you "live for today" and don't think about tomorrow. In some ways, living in the moment is great, sure — but not if you turn a blind eye toward your future. How do you know if you've got this attitude toward money? You probably

- ✔ Use credit too much.
- ✔ Don't try to pay off your credit balances as quickly as possible, telling yourself there will be plenty of time to do that later.
- ✔ Save little, if anything.
- ✔ Rarely, if ever, take time to balance your checkbook, check out your credit reports and credit score, or maintain a household budget.

Such money attitudes are self-destructive, and they do catch up with you eventually. Because you're reading this book, they may already have.

Checking Out Your Credit Reports

Three national credit-reporting companies operate in the United States: Equifax, Experian, and TransUnion. Reviewing the information in your credit report from each company is an excellent way to see your true financial picture.

Getting copies of your credit reports

For a comprehensive survey of your creditworthiness, order a copy of your credit report from each of the national credit-reporting agencies, not just from one. Each report may contain slightly different information about you, partly because not all creditors report all consumer account payment information to all three agencies.

You are entitled to one free copy of each of your credit reports every year. To order yours, go to www.annualcreditreport.com or call 877-FACT-ACT.

If you've already obtained free copies of your credit reports during the past 12 months, you must pay a fee to order additional copies. In most states, the cost is $10 per report (and some states also charge a sales tax), although the cost is less in some states. You can call your state attorney general's office to find out.

Also, you are always entitled to a free credit report if

- ✔ You are unemployed and intend to apply for a job within 60 days.
- ✔ You are receiving public welfare assistance.
- ✔ You believe that you have been the victim of identity theft.
- ✔ You have been denied credit, employment, insurance, or a place to rent within the past 60 days because of information in your credit report.

To order additional copies of your credit reports after you've obtained your free annual ones, you must contact each of the three credit-reporting agencies individually. You can order the copies by mail, by phone, or online.

- ✔ **Equifax:** www.equifax.com; 800-685-1111; Disclosure Department, P.O. Box 740241, Atlanta, GA 30374
- ✔ **Experian:** www.experian.com; 888-397-3742; P.O. Box 2104, Allen, TX 75013
- ✔ **TransUnion:** www.transunion.com; 800-888-4213; P.O. Box 1000, Chester, PA 19022

If you order additional copies by mail, put your request in a letter that includes the following information, and be sure to sign it:

- ✔ Your full name (including Jr., Sr., III, and so on)
- ✔ Your Social Security number
- ✔ Your date of birth
- ✔ Your current address and previous addresses for the past five years
- ✔ Your phone number, including area code
- ✔ The name of your current employer

Knowing why your reports matter

The credit report you get is the same one that your current creditors and potential future creditors use to make decisions about you. The more negative information is in your credit histories (such as past-due accounts, accounts in collection, accounts that your creditors have charged off as uncollectible, tax liens, and so on), the worse your finances are.

Your existing creditors may use the information to decide whether to raise the interest rates you are paying, lower your credit limits, or even cancel your credit. And whenever you apply for new credit, the creditors review your credit record information to decide whether to approve your application, how much credit to give to you, the interest rate you must pay, and so on.

Many insurance companies, landlords, and employers also review your credit record information. If they find a lot of negative information, insurance companies may not agree to insure you or may charge you higher-than-normal premiums; landlords may refuse to rent to you; and employers may not want to hire you or to give you the promotion you applied for.

The federal Fair Credit Reporting Act says that most negative information remains in your credit reports for 7½ years and that a Chapter 7 liquidation bankruptcy and a Chapter 13 reorganization of debt linger there for ten years. However, the three credit reporting agencies have a policy of reporting completed Chapter 13s for only seven years. A tax lien sticks around until you pay it.

For more detailed information about credit reporting, including advice on understanding your credit reports and correcting problems in them, pick up a copy of *Credit Repair Kit For Dummies,* by Steve Bucci (Wiley).

Finding Out Your FICO Score

A growing number of creditors, as well as insurance companies, employers, and landlords, use something called a FICO score together with (or even instead of) your credit history to make decisions about you. Your FICO score is a numeric representation of your creditworthiness and is derived from your credit history information. Like your credit history, the score is a snapshot of how you've managed credit in the past. As such, your FICO score is generally considered an indicator of how well you are likely to manage credit in the future.

Actually, a variety of different credit scores exist. Equifax, Experian, and TransUnion have developed their own credit scores. (Each credit-reporting agency sells its credit score on its Web site.) But the FICO score has become the industry standard. You can order your FICO score by going to www. myfico.com.

Your FICO score can range from 300 to 850. The higher, the better: A score of at least 720 is considered to be very good. If your score is well below 720, you may still qualify for credit from some creditors, but you'll be charged a higher interest rate and you may not qualify for as much credit as you would like. Likewise, insurance companies may be willing to sell you insurance, but you'll probably pay extra for the coverage and you may not be able to purchase as much insurance as you would like. When you have a low FICO score, some landlords will not rent to you, and you may not qualify for certain kinds of jobs, especially those that involve handling money.

You can raise your FICO score by improving the state of your finances. For example, your credit score will go up if you

- Pay down your account balances.
- Begin paying your debts on time.
- Build up your savings.
- Minimize the amount of credit you apply for.
- Correct problems in your credit histories.

Comparing Spending and Income

Now comes the *real* measure of the state of your finances: figuring out how your total spending compares to your total household income. You may be in for a shock. Are you ready?

Gathering the necessary materials

To complete this exercise, you need a pad of paper, a pen or pencil, and a calculator. You also need the following financial information:

- Check registers
- Bank statements
- Receipts for major purchases not made with a credit card
- Credit card account statements
- Other expense records for the past 12 months

You also need records of your income for the past 12 months, such as pay stubs and deposit slips or direct deposit information. If you're self-employed, you need your business records.

Your spouse or partner should gather the same information because the goal of this exercise is to give you as complete a picture as possible of how your *household* spending compares to your *household* income.

Categorizing your expenses

Creating a worksheet modeled after the one in Table 1-1 (at the end of this section) will help you organize your spending and income information and make sure that you don't overlook anything. This worksheet will also come in handy in Book I, Chapter 3, where we help you build a budget.

The worksheet in Table 1-1 divides your spending into three categories:

- ✓ **Fixed expenses:** These expenses stay the same from month to month. Examples are your rent or mortgage, car loan, home equity loan, and insurance.

- ✓ **Variable expenses:** These expenses tend to vary from month to month. Examples are your groceries, gas, utilities, restaurant meals, movies, CDs, and books.

- ✓ **Periodic expenses:** These expenses may be fixed or variable. You pay them just once in a while, such as quarterly, every six months, or annually. Tuition, some kinds of insurance, property taxes, and dues are examples.

Some expenses listed as *fixed* on the worksheet may actually be *periodic* expenses for you. For example, instead of paying your auto insurance every month, you may pay it every quarter.

After you've calculated total annual amounts for each of your debts and for all your living expenses, enter them on the appropriate worksheet lines.

Figuring out the fritter factor

It's *so* easy to fritter money away, isn't it? A latte here, a happy-hour drink or two there, lunch out with friends or colleagues, new clothes. Before you know it, it's the end of the month and you don't have any money left. Where did it all go? Most likely, you unconsciously frittered it away on unnecessary, miscellaneous items. Each purchase may not have cost much, but together over a month's time, frittering adds up to a significant amount. How much?

Let's assume that every workday you spend $3 on a latte. In a month, you spend $60, and in a year that small daily purchase adds up to $720! If you also spend $2.50 per day for a bagel or pastry to go with the latte, you're spending $110 each month and more than $1,300 per year! Scary, huh?

If you're like the vast majority of people, you get paid money much less often than you spend it. You probably get paid every week, every two weeks, or every month — but you spend money every day, don't you? This leads to a distortion in how you think about money and makes frittering all too easy.

To help you get a handle on how much you fritter away, for one month we want you to write down *everything* you purchase with cash, a debit card, or a credit card. Your spouse or partner should do the same. Carry a small notebook with you whenever you leave the house so you can record every expenditure right away instead of trying to remember it later. When the month is up, add up everything you spent on nonessential items. We bet you'll be shocked to see how much it amounts to. Multiply this number by 12, and put that number in your worksheet under "Other" in the "Variable Spending" section.

Totaling spending and earnings

Add up the numbers in each of the three spending categories in Table 1-1 to get a subtotal for each category. Then add up the subtotals. The final number represents the amount you are currently spending each year.

Next, add up all the income you received during the same 12-month period. Take into account not just your net household income (your *take-home pay*, which is gross income minus all deductions including taxes), but also any other income you or your spouse or partner may receive: government benefits, investments, royalties, child support or spousal support, income from a family business, and so on. Record that total on your worksheet.

If you are entitled to child support and/or spousal support but the payments rarely come, don't include those amounts when you calculate total annual income for your household. If it's unreliable income, you can't count on it to help cover your spending.

Calculating your financial bottom line

When you have a total annual income amount and a total annual spending amount, subtract your spending total from your income total.

If the final number you calculate is negative, you can probably guess what that means: The amount you are spending is more than your annual household income. You may be financing your lifestyle by using credit cards and cash advances, and/or you may be falling behind on some of your obligations. Furthermore, you may not be paying some of your bills at all, which means that if you add the amount of those bills into your calculations, you have an even bigger deficit.

If you ended up with a positive number, your finances may be in better shape than you think. Or not. If the number is small, you may be just barely staying ahead. And if your bottom line is positive only because you're paying just the minimum due on your credit cards each month or because you've stopped paying some of your debts, you have no cause for celebration. If this describes your situation, you are treading water, at best, and a financial setback such as a job loss or expensive illness could be devastating.

Table 1-1	Annual Income and Spending Worksheet
Annual Income	
Your household take-home pay	$_____
Child support income	$_____
Alimony income	$_____
Other income (specify the source)	$_____
Other income (specify the source)	$_____
Other income (specify the source)	$_____
Total Annual Income	$_____
Annual Spending	
Fixed Spending	
Rent	$_____
Mortgage	$_____
Home equity loan	$_____
Condo or homeowners' association fee	$_____
Car payment	$_____
Other loans	$_____
Homeowner's insurance	$_____
Renter's insurance	$_____
Health insurance	$_____
Auto insurance	$_____
Life insurance	$_____
Other insurance	$_____
Childcare	$_____
Dues and fees	$_____
Cable/satellite service	$_____
Internet access	$_____
Child support obligation	$_____

(continued)

Table 1-1 *(continued)*

Alimony obligation	$
Other fixed expenses (specify type)	$
Other fixed expenses (specify type)	$
Other fixed expenses (specify type)	$
Other fixed expenses (specify type)	$
Total Annual Fixed Spending	$
Variable Spending	
Groceries	$
Cigarettes	$
Alcohol	$
Utilities	$
Cell phone	$
Gas for car	$
Public transportation	$
Tolls and parking	$
Newspapers, books, and magazines	$
Allowances	$
After-school activities for kids	$
Baby-sitting	$
Entertainment	$
Restaurant meals	$
Personal care products	$
Clothing	$
Body care (haircuts, manicures, massages)	$
Laundry and dry cleaning	$
Out-of-pocket medical expenses	$
Lawn care	$
Home repair and maintenance	$
Other (specify type)	$
Other (specify type)	$
Other (specify type)	$
Other (specify type)	$

Total Annual Variable Spending	$_____
Periodic Spending	
Insurance	$_____
Auto registration and inspection	$_____
Subscriptions	$_____
Charitable donations	$_____
Tuition	$_____
Dues and fees	$_____
Income taxes	$_____
Property taxes	$_____
Other (specify type)	$_____
Other (specify type)	$_____
Other (specify type)	$_____
Other (specify type)	$_____
Total Annual Periodic Spending	$_____
Total Annual Spending	$_____
Total Annual Income	$_____
minus	–
Total Annual Spending	$_____
equals	=
Your Bottom Line	$_____

Assessing Your Spending Habits

Congratulations! You just took the most important step on the road to financial recovery. To varying degrees, we all live in a self-imposed fog when it comes to spending money. Spending becomes a comfortable habit — just the way you go about your daily life — and habits are always hard to break. But you're on your way. Now that you've committed yourself to recovery, you can take a closer look at where your money is going, consider the possibility that overspending is a habit, and, if it is, examine ways to deal with it.

Okay, documenting your expenses has proven the obvious: You've wasted money and probably made some lousy financial decisions. Who hasn't? (If you haven't assessed your spending habits, see the section "Comparing Spending and Income," earlier in this chapter.) Now that you have a handle on the problem, you're in position to take control. With the right attitude, eliminating unnecessary expenditures can be a little like a treasure hunt. There's extra money out there — you just have to find it!

Although we don't presume to tell you how much to spend on any particular item — that's your call — here are a few things to zero in on:

- **Credit card payments:** If a big chunk of your monthly income is going to pay credit card bills (especially if you're paying minimum payments), bankruptcy may be the best solution by far (see Book III, Chapter 5). If this is the case, you're just spinning your wheels in the worst of all worlds — paying interest without significantly reducing the principal amount of the debts. For example, say you've got a fairly modest credit card debt of $3,000. At 17 percent interest — and a lot of times the interest rate is even higher — you'll be indebted to the credit card company for about 35 years if you just make minimum payments.

- **Daily dribbles:** We all live our lives amid daily patterns that eventually become habits. Many times, these habits include unnecessary spending that provides no real benefit or enjoyment. What seems like small stuff eventually adds up. Again, consider the latte on the way to work, the buck you put in the soda machine, and the $2.50 you spend for an afternoon snack — all without even thinking about it, right? Over the course of a year, you've blown $1,430. If you invested this money for 20 years at 10 percent interest, you'd end up with more than $80,000!

- **Extravagances:** True, one person's luxury is another's necessity, but you really need to think long and hard before plopping down $100 at a restaurant or $60 for a pay-per-view prize fight on TV. It's sometimes helpful — though painful — to figure out how much work you had to do to pay for a particular treat. If a night on the town costs you a day and a half of work, is it really a good return on your investment?

- **Impulse purchases:** In the section "Cataloging What You Own," later in this chapter, we ask you to list all your belongings; for now, just make a trip to your attic, basement, and garage. If you're like most people — and us — you'll see tons of stuff you've bought but rarely, if ever, use. Simplify. And go further: Sell.

- **Gifts:** Studies show that many folks spend lavishly on gifts they would never buy for themselves. Christmas, of course, is the granddaddy of budget-busters. Scale back gifting.

- **Overwhelming mortgage payments:** If you obtained your mortgage recently, most of your monthly payment goes toward the interest. You may not have much equity, and the home may not be worth keeping — especially if it's a second mortgage.

- **Killer car payments:** New cars are awfully pricey these days. If you're struggling to maintain payments on a new car, you may want to consider selling it and buying something more affordable. Plenty of reliable, moderately priced used cars are on the market.

Cataloging What You Own

When you know what your spending habits and your earnings are, you need to get an equally firm grasp on what you *own*. Documenting your assets

- ✔ Helps determine what property you may lose by filing bankruptcy.
- ✔ Lets you know whether selling things could head off bankruptcy.
- ✔ Demonstrates how little you have to show for credit card debt.

Use Table 1-2 to get a rough idea of what you own and how much it's worth.

Table 1-2	What You Own
Asset	*Value*
Real Property	
Your home	
Other real property	
Timeshares	
Motor Vehicles	
Bank Account Balances	
Household Goods	
Furniture	
Appliances	
Audio and video equipment	
Computers and accessories	
Other household items	
Art Objects and Collectibles	
Jewelry	

(continued)

Table 1-2 *(continued)*

Asset	Value
Firearms	
Hobby Equipment	
Stocks, Bonds, and Other Investments	
Cash Value of Life Insurance	
Interests in Any Trusts	
Business Interests and Inventory	
Money You Are Owed	
Alimony and support	
Bonuses at work	
Accounts receivable	
Claims where you can sue someone	
Commissions	
Tax refunds	
Money You Are Entitled to Because Someone Died	
Life insurance	
Distributions from an estate	
Patents and Copyrights	
Tools and Machinery Used for Work	
Cash Value of Pensions	

Asset	Value
Office Equipment Not Included in Household Goods	
Other Assets	

Adding Up What You Owe

Purveyors of consumer credit want you to think in terms of monthly payments instead of considering the total amount you owe. It's a lot easier to sell that new car when the customer focuses on a $400 monthly payment rather than on a $25,000 albatross. But when it comes to assessing your financial condition, knowing the total amount of your debts is critical.

Consider home and car loans separately from other debts, for two reasons:

✔ You can reduce or eliminate these loans if you sell the house or car.

✔ Bankruptcy affects home and car loans differently than other debts.

You can find out how much you owe on these loans by phoning the creditor. If you're behind in payments, also find out how much it will take to bring the loan *current* (that is, not behind anymore, as opposed to paid in full).

Filling the blanks in Table 1-3 helps you get a grip on what you owe.

Table 1-3	What You Owe on Mortgage and Car Loans			
	Total Balance Owed	Monthly Payment	Value of Home/Car	Arrearage (Amount You're Behind)
Residence				
Other real estate				
Cars				

Calculating how much you owe on other debts is a little tougher. Ordering credit reports is one place to start (see earlier in this chapter and Book I, Chapter 5). You can often determine the amounts owed on judgments, child support, alimony, fines, and restitution obligations from documents on file in the courthouse. You can get a rough idea of how much you owe on income taxes by looking at copies of your income tax returns, but this method doesn't give you the amount of penalties and interest that have accrued. Hopefully, you have a rough idea of how much you owe on student loans. If not, find out.

When you know what you owe, use Table 1-4 to help you keep track of it.

If creditors don't how where you live, or have given up on you, don't ring their bell by calling them. However, you may have to face the music about the money that you owe eventually because some types of debts will not go away. So use the time when creditors are not hounding you to plan how you will deal with your debts. Among other options, for example, you can try to increase your income and/or save more money so that you can eventually contact your creditors and offer to satisfy your debts by paying a percentage of their total amounts. You can also contact a reputable credit-counseling organization for help working out payment plans with your creditors; or you can look into bankruptcy as a possible solution to your financial problems.

Table 1-4	How Much Do You Owe on Other Debts?
Type of Debt	*Total Amount Owed*
Judgments	
Income taxes	
Child support and alimony	
Student loans	
Fines and restitution obligations	
Medical bills	
Credit card balances	
Loans to friends and relatives	

At this point, you should have a better idea of your particular situation. Feel free to scan the Table of Contents or Index to go straight to the area you need to address first. If you're like most folks, it likely involves debt. If that's your problem, run — don't walk — to Book III. If you want to continue your preliminary assessment and examine your relationship to money, turn the page to Chapter 2 and keep reading.

Book I

Taking Charge of Your Finances

Chapter 2

Improving Your Relationship with Money

. . . .

In This Chapter

▶ Achieving financial goals with your partner

▶ Staying positive

▶ Dealing with setbacks and seeking help

▶ Getting out of debt and budgeting

. . . .

*J*ust as you have relationships with the people in your life, you also have a relationship with money — how you earn it, spend it, lose it, waste it, save it. It's important to take a good, hard look at how you use and misuse money. Otherwise, you'll never really get a grip on what happens to it, and you'll always be left scratching your head, wondering what happened to your earnings.

In this chapter we help you analyze and improve your own habits and patterns regarding how you handle your love-hate connection to your cash.

Most people are not in the boat alone, and finding financial common ground can be difficult when one spouse is a spendthrift and the other's a miser. Being smart about money is a choice that's easiest to live with if both partners share the same general financial goals, even if their money styles are a bit different. If you both want to save money, get out of debt, live within your means, and attain mutual long-term goals, it's important to discuss your different approaches to money management and find some common ground. Otherwise your frugal efforts may be voided by your partner's poor spending habits.

Children can also be difficult to win over. If you listen carefully, you can probably still hear the echoes from the latest whine-fest: "But I want it *now!*"

Working with Your Partner to Achieve Financial Goals

Wouldn't it be nice if everyone were exactly the same? Well, actually not. You probably wouldn't want to live in a boring world of identical clones that look, think, and act exactly alike. Variety is the spice of life, and it's also the spice of relationships, even in the area of finances. Just like the ingredients in your favorite meal, the right amount of spice can make the mix of flavors absolutely perfect — but too much spice is almost unbearable. You don't need to do away with each and every difference; you just need to blend the flavors together.

Resolving (or at least discussing openly) any financial differences between you and your partner is important. In order to fully adopt many of the practices outlined in this book, everyone involved needs to understand the benefits of adopting a more frugal lifestyle and how important it is to control impulsive spending habits.

Recognizing your financial strengths and weaknesses

If you're currently involved with someone and considering a serious commitment, or if you've never discussed your spending habits with your spouse or significant other, take some time to talk about your financial mindsets. Identify your differences and spend some time planning how you want to handle them in your relationship. By dealing with your financial differences, you'll not only cut down on arguments later in life, but you and your partner will become a united front working for common financial goals.

Sit down together and share details about the practical aspects of your personal money style. If you're already married, use this opportunity to reevaluate your current financial situation. Ask yourselves, individually, the following questions and then compare answers:

- Do I carry credit cards? How many and what kind? Gas cards, department store cards, general credit cards? Do I pay the cards in full each month, or just the minimum payments?

- Do I carry cash with me? How much? What do I use it for? How do I keep records of cash spent?

- What does my credit history look like? Any debt problems, overdue bills, repossessions, bankruptcy filings, or late payments?

- What sort of insurance coverage and financial contingency plans do I have for medical expenses and other emergencies?

🠖 Do I have a system for paying bills? What is it?

🠖 How do I keep track of receipts and tax-related paperwork?

🠖 Do I buy lunch at work every day or bring it from home?

🠖 Is recreational shopping a favorite pastime? What sort of limits, if any, do I set for my personal shopping sprees?

🠖 How do I decide to make a major purchase such as a car, new furniture, large appliances, or a home?

🠖 How much of my income do I save each month, and what sort of system do I use for saving money?

🠖 What is my philosophy about financially assisting elderly, disabled, or cash-strapped relatives?

🠖 Do I want (or want my spouse) to stay home after we have children?

🠖 Is tithing or regular philanthropic giving important to me?

🠖 How far in debt can I go and still feel comfortable?

You may well find that your significant other is a spendthrift and you're a miser or vice versa — opposites tend to attract each other. One reason opposites attract may be that on some unconscious level, people are aware of their own weaknesses and shortcomings and know almost instinctively what they need to "complete" themselves. If you have trouble keeping to a written budget, you may choose a life partner whose greatest joy is keeping detailed written records of every flower growing in the yard or every penny spent on bubble gum by the kids — and imagine you balance each other out in the process. Having differences is healthy, but we also know from experience that these differences can test your limits of grace and reason.

If you are the spend-a-holic in the relationship and are already convinced of the need for financial change in your life, the road ahead is much easier. Unfortunately, reforming a loved one from *their* spendthrift ways can be difficult and requires a lot of sensitivity and tact. Don't allow yourself to become adversarial with the spend-a-holic in your life. Instead, be reasonable and show how adopting frugal habits can reduce outstanding debt, free up money for fun activities such as vacations, and help to finance large future expenses such as buying a house or paying for college tuition.

Identifying long-term goals

You've probably heard the old cliché, "If you don't know where you're going, how will you know when you get there?" Well, it holds true in the area of family finances, too. Establishing long-term goals for yourself and your family helps to keep your current financial picture in perspective. For example, if one of your goals as a couple is to have a full-time parent at home when the new baby arrives, you can start cutting back on spending now in order to get out of debt and establish some savings before that big day arrives. Keeping your long-term goals in mind will help keep you on track whenever you're tempted to spend money on extras.

A necessary step toward working together as a financial team is to establish your life goals and review them with your significant other. Ask yourself the following questions to help you determine your long-term financial goals:

- ✔ What hobbies do I want to pursue to add recreation and fun to my life?

- ✔ What place does education hold in my future or that of others in my immediate family?

- ✔ How important is home ownership in my future?

- ✔ What are my career goals? What further training, if any, do I need to reach those goals?

- ✔ How much time, money, and effort do I want to give in the near future to charity or church-related activities?

- ✔ What character traits do I value most and want to develop in my own life and the life of my children? Are my financial goals and decisions in line with those character traits?

- ✔ What are my retirement goals?

- ✔ How will I take care of future healthcare concerns?

- ✔ How soon do I want to pay off any outstanding consumer debt?

- ✔ At the end of my life, what things might I regret if I choose to spend my money on less-important pursuits?

Writing out your goals and the values that are important to your family can go a long way toward keeping your life and finances on track. But even if you don't write down your goals, thinking through your priorities and keeping them in mind as you make decisions (financial and otherwise) is an excellent habit.

Establishing savings goals

After you've discussed your financial desires and goals for life, set some savings goals. If you and your partner are not accustomed to working together toward a financial goal, start with something relatively small like saving for a new couch or your next short vacation. You can usually reach these goals within six months to a year, and so you get a fairly quick return on your savings investment — and an opportunity to reinforce the value of working together toward a savings goal. After you've seen that you can work together toward small goals, start working on long-term goals like retirement and the kids' education.

One way to set up a savings plan is to set aside a small amount of money in a special account from each paycheck until you've reached your short-term goal. Keep a big jar on the dresser, where you can empty your pockets and purse of loose change. It's entirely possible to finance a long weekend at the ocean with just the change you throw into a jar every day. Seeing a successful example of how easy it can be to reach a savings goal can be just the thing that many spendthrifts need to give second thought to their impulsive spending habits.

Finding peaceful solutions to differences

Above all else, it's important to discover the art of diplomacy when you identify significant financial differences between you and your partner. Money problems are the root of all sorts of marital discord and strife.

Even when you're in the middle of a major disagreement about finances or your savings goals, the relationship doesn't have to break down if you continue to treat each other with kindness and respect. You will never convince people to change their minds by yelling at them, calling them names, manipulating their emotions, or giving them the silent treatment.

The three checking account system

One way for partners who each have their own income to deal with differing money habits is to open three checking accounts: one joint account (for paying bills) and an individual account for each person. Note: It's important to first establish a workable budget before implementing the three-account system so each partner knows how much to deposit each pay period to cover the basics. See later in this chapter for more on budgeting basics.

When you receive your paychecks, you each deposit a predetermined amount into the joint account. The joint account is then used for paying bills and for short-term savings for future expenses. The individual accounts are for the money left after you both pay for the basic essentials. If one partner wants to fritter his money away on designer coffees and video rentals, fine. The other person can be happily saving for that nice vacation she's been dreaming of for years — whether she chooses to take the spendthrift spouse with her on vacation may be another story, though.

If you are beyond the talking stage and are in the yelling, crying, door-slamming stage, consider seeking help from a trained financial counselor with a local debt-counseling agency. You can contact the National Foundation for Credit Counseling, a nationwide nonprofit network of Consumer Credit Counseling Service offices, at 1-800-388-CCCS and www.nfcc.org. The NFCC can put you in touch with a counseling office near you. Even if you're not dealing specifically with debt issues, a financial counselor can help you work through financial planning decisions in a calm, reasonable fashion. Many religious communities and churches offer free counseling of this sort, too. Just having an uninvolved third party helping you think calmly through your financial choices can be tremendously helpful.

Pulling together with your spouse or partner

If you're the primary money manager in your family, you will probably shoulder most of the responsibility for turning your family's finances around. However, the cooperation of your spouse or partner and family is essential. Although you may pay the bills each month, you and your spouse or partner both spend your family's money, so he or she has a very direct effect on the success or failure of your financial program.

The support and cooperation of your spouse or partner is essential to getting your family's finances back on track. One of you can't be pinching pennies while the other is spending like there is no tomorrow. Both of you should be totally committed to getting out of debt and reducing or eliminating the use of credit.

You may find that talking about money is easier in a public place, such as a coffee shop or a park. If a change of venue doesn't improve your communication, consider scheduling an appointment with a marriage counselor or religious advisor so you can get at the root problems.

When you talk with your spouse or partner about your debts, try to stay focused on solutions to your financial problems instead of letting the conversation turn into a blame game. Both of you are probably responsible for your debts to some degree, and finger-pointing won't pay the bills. Keep in mind that no matter how hard you try to cooperate with one another, money problems create a lot of stress in a relationship. We can't offer easy solutions for getting through the tough times ahead. We can only encourage you to work hard at keeping your relationship amicable.

If your spouse or partner is unwilling to work with you to help your family get out of debt, and if you are concerned that his or her spending will condemn you to a life of financial troubles, you may have little choice but to reevaluate your relationship. Although ending your relationship at the same time you are trying to resolve your family's financial problems won't be easy, you may conclude that it's best. If you are thinking about divorce, consider *Divorce For Dummies* (Wiley), which explains how to prepare for it emotionally and financially.

Talking money with your children

You should be honest about your family's finances with your children. They don't need to know all the details, but if your children are old enough to sense money-related tension and anxiety in your household, you need to tell them what is going on and what you are doing to improve things.

If you're like a lot of parents, your initial instinct may be to protect your children from your family's financial problems. Usually, that doesn't end up a good idea. Even very young children are amazingly perceptive about negative changes in their environment. They may not know exactly how things have changed or why, but they can sense the change and may develop problems as a result unless you help your kids understand and deal with what is going on.

Help your children maintain a sense of security by explaining your family's financial situation and what they can expect in the months ahead. Take their ages and maturity levels into consideration when you decide what to say and how to say it. Tell them as much as you think they need to know and can process intellectually, being careful not to scare them.

You probably need to go into greater detail with a preteen or teenage child than you do with a younger child. Teen and preteen kids generally have more financial needs and wants than young children and are more subject to peer pressure, so they need a clear sense of how they may be affected by your efforts to get out of debt. For example, they may have to start bringing their lunches to school, or you may need them to get part-time jobs to help pay for their gas, auto insurance, or nonessentials.

Compared to younger kids, preteens and teenagers are most apt to have difficulty accepting the fact that they can't do and have all the things they have become used to. Peer pressure can be a powerful thing.

Regardless of the age of your children, reassure them that things may be different for a while, but you love them and everything will be okay. Help them feel safe by letting them know that you and your spouse or partner are putting a financial turnaround plan together, by keeping their day-to-day routines as unchanged as possible, and by doing fun things together.

Be alert to signs that your family's financial problems are creating a lot of stress in your children's lives or that they are becoming depressed. Signs of trouble include crying, angry outbursts, withdrawal, behavior problems at school, headaches, stomachaches, not wanting to go to school — just about anything out of the ordinary. Try to get your kids to talk about what is bothering them. If they won't, or if their symptoms get worse, they probably need to meet with a mental health professional. Contact the psychologist at their school and consider letting their teachers know what is going on so they can look for signs of trouble as well.

As you help your children cope with your family's financial circumstances, bear in mind that your money troubles offer you an opportunity to teach them important lessons about managing money and the dangers of too much debt. When they become adults, they may be able to use those lessons to avoid financial trouble. One good way to help them master these lessons is to involve them in creating a monthly household budget. We talk about budgeting later in this chapter.

Believing in Yourself

Getting out of debt can be no fun. We're the first to admit it because we've been there. Like countless other people, we've had our share of money troubles over the years, so we understand what a drag it is to pinch pennies, give up the things you enjoy, and work harder than ever. We've also counseled people whose finances were in such bad shape that getting out of debt meant having to take further steps such as consolidating their debts, negotiating with their creditors, and even giving up some of their assets.

Keeping family relationships a priority

Most people at the end of their life don't wish they'd spent more time at the office, but they do often regret not spending more time with their family, especially when their children were young. Unfortunately, people who find themselves with debt payments that exceed what they can reasonably afford usually cast about for ways to increase their income.

Instead of taking a part-time job, working overtime every week, or getting involved in a get-rich-quick scheme, look at your budget for ways to cut back your spending. Decreasing spending is usually a lot easier than increasing your income. Plus, you won't sacrifice time with your family in exchange for a paid-off credit card. By cutting back and tightening your money belt, you can pay off your bills *and* watch little Johnny's championship T-ball game on Saturday afternoon.

It can be daunting to owe a bundle to your creditors and to be faced with the change and sacrifices that are necessary to turn your finances around. Success may require every ounce of determination and self-discipline you can muster. It definitely requires that you be able to maintain a can-do attitude — a get-out-of-debt attitude — over a sustained period of time, because your finances are probably going to improve gradually, not overnight.

Book I

Taking Charge of Your Finances

A positive, *I-can-get-out-of-debt* attitude is key to turning your finances around. You have to believe that you've got what it takes. Here are some proven strategies for helping you believe in yourself and set your resolve:

- ✔ **Draw strength from tough challenges you've faced in the past.** Maybe someone in your family had a serious illness, you went through a divorce, a close relative or friend died, or you experienced a major disappointment in your career. Think about what you did to get through those tough times and use the memories to remind yourself of your strengths and abilities.

- ✔ **If you believe that you're largely responsible for your family's financial problems, don't beat yourself up about what you did or didn't do.** You can't change what happened, and letting feelings of self-recrimination and guilt bog you down makes it a lot harder to do what you need to do now. Benefit from your mistakes and move on. When negative thoughts come into your head, shrug them off, knowing they cannot control you after all.

  A negative attitude can be contagious. If you act bummed out all the time about your family's financial situation, your bad attitude is likely to spread to everyone else in your household. If you have kids, don't forget that they are observing how you behave in the face of adversity, so set a good example.

- ✔ **Remember that you're not the only person who has ever experienced financial problems.** Millions of people have been where you are and have had to do what you must now do to get out of debt. If they can do it, so can you!

- ✔ **Get inspired by reading a book or watching a documentary about someone who had to overcome something difficult.** These types of stories are plentiful, but if you need some suggestions, consider Franklin Delano Roosevelt, Nelson Mandela, Helen Keller, or Stephen Hawking.

- ✔ **Motivate yourself by visualizing your future.** Close your eyes and think about what life will be like when you don't have a lot of debt, you're not stressed out about money all the time, you've got a comfortable balance in your savings account, and you and your family can afford a few extras.

- ✔ **Don't stay silent about your money troubles.** You don't need to shout it from the rooftops, but let your close friends and family members know that you are going through some financially tough times, even if you have to swallow your pride and admit some mistakes. You may need their support and encouragement. If you've kept your financial problems a secret until now, telling people about them can take a huge load off your shoulders. And you just may discover that your friends or relatives have been in similar situations.

If some of your friends or family members are also experiencing money problems, create your own support group. Get together regularly to share ideas about getting out of debt, to give one another encouragement, and to celebrate your successes.

✔ **Boost your self-confidence by getting smarter about money.** Enroll in a basic personal finance class or read a good book on the subject (such as this one). Make regular visits to personal finance Web sites such as www.bankrate.com for practical information about all aspects of everyday money management.

✔ **Be realistic about how long getting out of debt will take.** Don't expect to pay off your high-interest debts, build your savings account, and have extra money in your pocket by next week. Depending on the specifics of your finances, tackling your debt could take months — or, yes, years. As long as you're serious about dealing with your debts, you'll see gradual improvement in your finances, but there's no quick fix for serious money problems — so don't get yourself down because you can't find it.

✔ **Rethink your definition of success.** It's easy to get caught up in the idea that success means spending a lot of money. After all, the more stuff you have, the happier you'll be, right? That's certainly what credit card companies and advertisers want you to believe! But there are other ways to define success: being a good parent, spouse, and friend; helping the less fortunate; living an ethical life; making a difference in your community; and so on. Money can't buy these things, yet they can bring you more profound and lasting happiness than more stuff ever could.

✔ **Stop making excuses.** Maybe you hear yourself saying, "Yes, but I don't have time to find cheaper insurance." "Yes, but living on a budget is too much work." "Yes, but I can't earn more money right now." You *can* make the necessary changes in your life. You *can't* afford to make excuses.

Handling Setbacks

When you begin down the path toward financial health, you may get off course occasionally. If you do, don't beat yourself up. Instead, refocus, steel your resolve to do better from now on, and move forward.

Okay, that's great advice, but is it realistic? Negative thinking can creep up on any of us, making it seem impossible to move forward. Maybe you're tired of living on a budget, having to say no to your kids, and working all the time. Maybe you've been hit with a financial setback such as a creditor who

refuses to negotiate with you or the loss of an asset you wanted to hold on
to. Of course you're going to feel blue once in a while. What can you do about
it? Well, lots.

- ✔ **Celebrate each get-out-of-debt success.** At a minimum, take time to
  acknowledge what you've achieved. Maybe you got one of your creditors to agree to lower the interest you are paying, or you landed a part-
  time job that will allow you to pay off your debts faster. Celebrating your
  successes, even small ones, can motivate you to keep moving forward.

- ✔ **Stay active.** Exercise is a great way to get rid of stress, frustration, and
  negative thoughts. So when you're feeling down, don't plop yourself in
  front of the TV. Go for a run or walk, take a bike ride, swim, or play your
  favorite sport.

- ✔ **Find things to laugh about.** Rent a funny movie, spend time with a witty
  friend, watch your favorite sitcom, read the funny papers, or check out
  a humorous Web site such as `www.theonion.com` or `http://swcbc.org/humor`. A good belly laugh is therapeutic.

- ✔ **Do something fun.** There are plenty of ways to have fun on the cheap.
  Read a good book, play board games, do puzzles with your kids, go for
  hikes, dig in the garden, invite friends over for a potluck meal, rent a
  movie, enjoy your local park, visit a museum. Go out and play!

- ✔ **Count your blessings.** Draw strength from the good things in your life.
  Volunteering at a food bank or homeless shelter is an excellent way to
  get rid of a "poor me" attitude and to keep your situation in perspective.

- ✔ **Accept what you can't change.** If your financial problems are the result
  of things you had no control over (maybe you lost your job in a downsiz-
  ing or had a bad accident that landed you in the hospital), railing against
  your fate is a waste of time. Accept what happened and move on.

- ✔ **Find peace through prayer or meditation.** Whether it's a church, syna-
  gogue, mosque, Buddhist retreat — or your house or nearby woods or
  beach — find a quiet place where you can recharge your spirit regularly.
  Use prayer or meditation to detach yourself from the negatives going on
  in your life. Tell yourself, "All this will pass." And it will, eventually.

If you're experiencing more than the occasional blues — if you can't shake
your negative feelings — you may be clinically depressed. Major Depression
will sap your energy and make it difficult, if not impossible, to move forward
(see the nearby "Signs of depression" sidebar). Get help by scheduling an
appointment with a mental health professional. We can hear you saying, "But
I can't afford that!" But if you really are depressed, can you afford not to?
Your local chapter of the Mental Health Association is a good resource for
finding the help you need at an affordable price. To get started finding local
help, ask your doctor or go to `www.nmha.org/go/find_therapy`.

Signs of depression

Major Depression can be a debilitating disease, and even fatal given its suicide rate, but in most cases it's also very treatable. If, after reading the following list of symptoms, you suspect that you may be depressed, schedule an appointment with a mental health therapist right away. Keep in mind that you don't have to have all these symptoms to be diagnosed as depressed.

Signs of depression include

✔ Sadness, all the time.

✔ Worthlessness, hopelessness, and/or guilt for no rational reason.

✔ Constant anxiety and/or irritability.

✔ Lethargy.

✔ Loss of interest in the activities you used to enjoy.

✔ A change in your sleep patterns: You want to sleep all the time, you are having trouble falling asleep, or you're not getting a full night's sleep.

✔ Difficulty concentrating and making decisions.

✔ A lot of headaches or stomachaches.

✔ Loss of interest in eating or a need to overeat.

✔ Alcohol and/or illegal drug use to avoid reality.

✔ Constantly thinking about death or even suicide. If you have these thoughts, get help immediately. The crisis hotline of the National Strategy for Suicide Prevention is a good resource: Call 800-273-8255. It will connect you immediately to someone with your local suicide crisis center who can help you deal with your feelings.

Asking for Help

You may find that you need more than pure willpower and resolve (coupled with the information in a good book like this) to help you handle your financial problems. If you are having trouble committing to a get-out-of-debt program and staying focused, or if you can't shake feelings of discouragement and hopelessness about your finances, take advantage of these resources:

✔ **Debtors Anonymous (DA):** Drawing on the time-tested principles and approach of Alcoholics Anonymous, DA chapters around the country help consumers with spending problems. DA meetings are free and open to anyone. Hearing other DA members talk about their own struggles and successes can be inspiring. And having a sponsor — someone to call when you feel discouraged or want to spend money that you shouldn't — can help you stay in control of your life and get out of debt. To find a DA chapter near you, use your local Yellow Pages, go to www.debtorsanonymous.org, or call 781-453-2743.

✔ **Mental health professionals:** Individual or group therapy can be invaluable when emotional problems are getting in the way of your get-out-of-debt efforts. If you have medical insurance but it doesn't cover mental health therapy, or if you don't have insurance, find out about low-cost/no-cost mental health resources in your area. A good place to start is the Web site of the National Mental Health Association, `www.nmha.org`.

✔ **Other books about money and your relationship with it:** Reading books like *Your Money or Your Life: Transforming Your Relationship with Money and Achieving Financial Independence* by Joe Dominguez and Vicki Robin (Penguin Books) and *Mary Hunt's Debt-Proof Living: The Complete Guide to Living Financially Free* by Mary Hunt (Broadman & Holman Publishers) can help you rethink your attitude toward spending and debt. They can also help you live a life that is simpler, more personally rewarding, and less focused on spending.

✔ **Your friends and family:** Don't let pride and embarrassment keep you from letting the people closest to you know that you're having financial trouble. You'll isolate yourself when you are most in need of their moral support and encouragement.

Digging Out of Debt

Excessive consumer debt can be a prison, holding you captive to past financial decisions and overspending. You need to pay off your debts to free up money for your current lifestyle and future plans and dreams. In addition to living an all-around frugal lifestyle, the following steps help you get debt free.

Step 1: Acknowledge the problem

The most important step is acknowledging the problem and realizing you need to actively do something about it. Make paying off your debt a high priority or you may face a major debt-related problem such as utility shut-off notices or even a personal bankruptcy. If any of the following statements are true, you have a consumer debt problem:

✔ You have little or no savings and are at your limit on most credit cards.

✔ You juggle bills each month, deciding which ones to pay and which need to wait until the next payday, even if it means paying after the bill's due date and incurring subsequent late fees.

✔ You've taken at least one cash advance from a credit card account or other line of credit to make payments on other debts.

✔ Your debt load (including car payments but not including mortgage) exceeds 20 percent of your income. Most budgets can reasonably handle a 10–15 percent debt load, but more than that is excessive.

If you use credit cards to finance your lifestyle, you're living beyond your means. It's time to remedy the situation.

Step 2: Cut the cards

Identifying the problem is the first step to digging out of debt. The second step is often difficult for hard-core credit card junkies: Cut up your credit cards. Yep, pull out the scissors and start snipping.

Some credit providers can't officially close the account until you've paid in full, but consider it closed to your usage. Do not, under any circumstances, use a credit card until your debts are paid in full. If you're deeply in debt, be aware that this can take several years. But after you're out from under the burden of excessive debt, the relief you experience more than makes up for the inconvenience of going without credit for a long stretch of time.

Sometimes you need a credit card of some sort for making airline reservations, buying items online, or renting a car. If so, get a *check card* from your bank. You are essentially paying cash because the money immediately comes out of your checking account. But this way you can take have a "credit card" without deepening your credit debt.

Step 3: Set a good budget and live within it

When planning your budget, be realistic about what you need to spend in each category, but don't be overly generous with yourself either. You need to cinch in your money belt if you're serious about repaying your debts so that you have the money to budget for your debt-repayment plan. Chapter 3 in this book and Book II's Chapter 1 contain a lot of tips on this process so you can get in shape to pay off those debts as quickly as possible.

Step 4: Contact your creditors

Communicate directly with your creditors and explain to them that you're having problems meeting your payments. Tell them about your frugal budget and ask whether they'd be willing to accept slightly lower payments for a period of time. Many creditors are more than happy to lower monthly payments if that prevents a customer from filing bankruptcy — after all, from their point of view, a smaller payment is better than no payment at all.

Some creditors, though, would rather play hardball and force you into bankruptcy before accepting a lower payment each month. If you have difficult creditors, contact a credit counseling agency. These agencies have experience communicating directly with creditors and working out solutions to debt-repayment problems. If you search online, you'll find a large number of credit counseling agencies, but we strongly recommend beginning your search with the National Foundation for Credit Counseling at 1-800-388-2227 or `www.nfcc.org` for help locating a counseling agency near you. This network of credit counseling agencies is nonprofit and doesn't have a vested interest in making money off the debt-ridden consumer.

Budgeting for the Future

Does the word *budget* send chills up your spine? We know it did for us for many years. But we've had a change of heart on this whole topic of budgets. Now we realize that budgets allow you to be organized and have some control over what you spend. They help you to decide how to spend your money, plan for your future, pay off existing debt, and save a few pennies each month by reducing wasteful and impulsive purchases. Book 1, Chapter 1 introduces budgets, and Book 1, Chapter 3 talks a lot more about budgeting, but the following is a refresher on what you will be doing when you start budgeting.

Step 1: Categorize your expenses

When you begin setting up a monthly budget, start with big categories before breaking down your budget into smaller expense categories. A good list of basic budget categories to begin with includes the following:

- ✔ **Housing:** Mortgage/rent, repairs, property taxes, cleaning supplies, homeowner's/renter's insurance, utilities, furnishings, décor

- ✔ **Food:** Groceries, meals out, pizza delivery, snacks and beverages at work

- ✔ **Transportation:** Car payments, insurance, gas, oil, parking, repairs/maintenance, public transportation fees

- ✔ **Medical:** Insurance, out-of-pocket expenses such as deductibles and noninsurance-covered medical services, pharmacy, eye care, dental

- ✔ **Clothing:** New purchases, dry cleaning, repair

- ✔ **Personal:** Cosmetics, haircuts, cleansers

- ✔ **Insurance:** Life insurance and any other insurance not covered under home, transportation, or medical expenses

- ✔ **Education:** Tuition, dues/fees, school pictures, yearbooks, school supplies, books

- ✔ **Credit accounts:** Payments on major credit cards, department store cards, lines of credit through your bank or other lender, or on any other outstanding debt

- ✔ **Gifts:** Holidays, birthdays, graduations, weddings, showers

- ✔ **Recreation:** Vacations, movies, books, magazines, newspapers, cable TV, restaurants, sporting events, sports equipment

- ✔ **Savings:** Long-term and short-term goals, as well as retirement

- ✔ **Donations:** Charities, churches

You need to set aside money each month for those yearly and quarterly payments that often sneak up on you when you least expect them. If you spend $1,200 on your yearly property taxes, divide that number by 12 and set aside $100 per month so that you aren't caught off guard by your property taxes, insurance payments, or any other periodic bills.

Within each general budget category, note that some items are essential (the mortgage or rent payment, the electric bill, and groceries), but other items are extra (new furniture, gifts, and pizza delivery). From your first list of general budget items, develop two separate budget lists, one for *essentials* and the other for *extras*. (We can't dictate what's essential and what's extra for other people, so we don't divide up the lists for you. Some people may have to eat out regularly because of work-related issues and so dining out is an essential item in their life rather than an extra. Others may consider charitable giving an extra, whereas their friends down the street consider it non-negotiable because of religious convictions.)

After you divide your expenses into two lists, look through both your essential and extra lists to find flexible budget items such as clothing, groceries, and other food-related expenses where you can cut back using the tips and advice throughout this book. Make a star next to flexible items in each of your lists to identify them easily.

Extra and flexible budget items are the main places to focus your frugal living tactics. You're always going to have to pay your water bill, but cable television may be an extra utility that can be done away with for awhile if money's needed in a more-essential budget category. Book II deals with many budget categories and helps you find lots of ways to cut back on the extras — and save a bit on the essentials, as well.

Step 2: Estimate what you spend

You can't control what you don't know. Go through your checkbook and any other receipts or records you've kept over the past few months so that you can track how much you actually spend on essentials. Then for one month, keep a detailed diary of all your extra purchases, even for cheap things like newspapers or coffee from the vending machine at work. Little expenses quickly add up to big money when they're made on a daily basis, and these smaller, out-of-pocket purchases that are frequently made with cash usually won't show up in your check register, so writing them all down helps make you aware of where the cash is dribbling out of your life.

After you've discovered exactly where your money goes throughout the month, you may need to reevaluate your written budget lists if you find your actual spending differed from your anticipated spending.

Step 3: Calculate and adjust

Now that you've made two lists of budget items (essentials and extras), use the two lists to see if your spending habits are keeping you in the red.

Add up the essentials list and the extras list separately. Subtract the essentials total from your monthly income. If you have money left over, subtract the extras total from that amount. If you still have money left over, great! Look into a savings or investing plan — talk to your bank or a certified financial planner for help in setting one up. But if your extras list takes you into negative numbers, start looking for places to cut back. For example, cancel your newspaper delivery or eat out once a month instead of once a week. You can also trim from the extras list in order to put more money toward debt repayment if that's a high priority in your financial picture. Much of this book is dedicated to helping you save money on various expenses, so don't give up hope if you find you need to drastically cut your spending in order to stick to your budget and live within your means. A lot more ideas are waiting for you in these pages.

The envelope system

The simplest budgeting plan is frequently referred to as the *envelope system*. You can revolutionize your financial situation by setting aside cash in envelopes labeled with the various expense categories that you pay for in cash: bus fare, gas and oil for the car, groceries, lunch money, toiletries, office supplies, and so on. (For things like utility bills that need to be paid with checks, you don't use the envelopes.) The envelope system can make all the difference in the world because you can visualize how taking a few dollars from the grocery envelope to pay for a movie is actually stealing money from a budget category. When your money is just a lump of abstract figures in your bank statement, taking a little bit here and there for nonbudgeted items is easier to do. But taking only cash to the grocery store makes you shop more carefully, plan meals more frugally, and put things back on the shelves if you go over the budgeted amount.

For keeping track of your budget, take a look at office supply stores for an easy-to-use, inexpensive family budgeting book. If you want something small that you can carry with you at all times, the Budget Map (http://budget map.com) is a specially designed ledger that fits in your personal checkbook and takes the fuss out of making and sticking to a budget. We've found it to be easy, effective, and relatively inexpensive ($30, with a 90-day money back, no-questions-asked guarantee). Give up one latte a month, and the Budget Map is paid for.

A simple tip for taking care of your budgeting woes for regular bills is to pay for a part of each budget item each time you get paid. Maybe your utility bill is due every two months, but your husband gets paid twice a month. Figure out what your average two-month utility bill is and then divide that number by four. That amount then comes out of each and every pay period for utilities. Sometimes you can plan for a small payment every two weeks easier than for one large payment once every other month. If you have a monthly mortgage payment and get paid twice a month, write a check for half the mortgage payment each pay period. If you have an insurance payment due every six months, write 12 small checks, one on each pay period.

We hope you've caught the budget bug! If so, the next chapter is up your alley.

Chapter 3

Building and Sticking to a Budget

In This Chapter

▶ Calculating your monthly spending and income

▶ Dealing with deficits (and surpluses)

▶ Distinguishing between high- and low-priority financial obligations

▶ Making your budget work month to month

We know. You *hate* the idea of a household budget. However, a budget is a basic and important money-management tool for getting out — and staying out — of debt. So if you're serious about improving the state of your finances and avoiding future problems, you need to lose your antibudget bias.

A *budget* is nothing more than a written plan for how you intend to spend your money each month, how much you'll contribute to savings and retirement, and so on. A budget helps you live within your means. It doesn't have to be scary. When you're drowning in debt, a budget is your financial life raft.

In this chapter, we show you how to create a monthly household budget and monitor your compliance with it. If you can't afford to pay all your obligations in a certain month, we tell you which debts to pay and which to put off. We also warn you against using certain types of loans to generate extra cash.

Over time, if you stick to your budget and follow the rest of the advice in this book, your financial situation will improve. But even when your financial outlook is rosier, you should continue to manage your money by using a budget. Otherwise, you may get careless about your spending or begin using credit too much, and your debt may creep up to dangerous levels again.

Living on a budget also makes it easier for you to

✔ Build up your savings so you have money to fall back on if you're hit with a big unexpected expense, if you lose your job, or if you have to take a pay cut.

✔ Purchase big-ticket items with minimal use of credit.

✔ Help make your family's financial dreams come true: a new home, a great vacation, college educations for kids, a comfortable retirement.

Comparing Monthly Spending and Income

Creating a monthly budget for your household is not a complicated process, but it can be time consuming. Simply stated, you need to do this:

✔ Compare your current total monthly spending to your current total monthly income.

✔ Reduce your spending as necessary so that it's less than your income.

✔ Allocate your dollars appropriately so that you are able to pay all your living expenses and debts.

Back in Book I, Chapter 1's Table 1-1, in the section "Comparing Spending and Income," we ask you to compare your annual spending to annual income to start getting a fix on the state of your finances. If you haven't already completed that exercise, do so now; that information is essential to the budgeting process in this chapter. Don't worry, we'll wait here for you. Ready?

1. **Divide each of the annual dollar amounts in Table 1-1 by 12 to come up with monthly amounts.**

2. **Make photocopies of the spending and income worksheet in Table 3-1 (so you can use it multiple times).**

3. **Record each monthly amount in the appropriate worksheet space.**

4. **Review the dollar amounts and adjust them up or down as necessary so they're as accurate as possible.** For example, the cost of your auto insurance may be about to increase, your child's tuition may be increasing next month, or your income may be decreasing. Always assume the worst scenario so that you build in a potential cushion.

If your annual totals don't include living expenses and debts that you should be paying but aren't because you don't have enough money, add them to your annual totals before you divide by 12. For budget-building purposes, you *must* have an accurate picture of *all* your living expenses and debts.

5. **Subtract your total monthly spending from your total monthly income.** Record that amount on the worksheet; it can be a negative number.

Table 3-1	Monthly Spending and Income Worksheet
Monthly Income	
Your household take-home pay	$_____
Child support income	$_____
Alimony income	$_____
Other income (specify the source)	$_____
Other income (specify the source)	$_____
Other income (specify the source)	$_____
Total Monthly Income	$_____
Monthly Spending	
Fixed Spending	
Rent	$_____
Mortgage	$_____
Home equity loan	$_____
Condo or homeowners' association fee	$_____
Car payment	$_____
Other loans	$_____
Homeowner's insurance	$_____
Renter's insurance	$_____
Health insurance	$_____
Auto insurance	$_____
Life insurance	$_____
Other insurance	$_____
Childcare	$_____
Dues and fees	$_____
Cable/satellite service	$_____
Internet access	$_____
Child support obligation	$_____
Alimony obligation	$_____
Other fixed expenses (specify type)	$_____
Other fixed expenses (specify type)	$_____
Other fixed expenses (specify type)	$_____
Other fixed expenses (specify type)	$_____
Total Monthly Fixed Spending	$_____

(continued)

Table 3-1 *(continued)*

Variable Spending	
Groceries	$
Cigarettes	$
Alcohol	$
Utilities	$
Cell phone	$
Gas for car	$
Public transportation	$
Tolls and parking	$
Newspapers, books, and magazines	$
Allowances	$
After-school activities for kids	$
Baby-sitting	$
Entertainment	$
Restaurant meals	$
Personal care products	$
Clothing	$
Body care (haircuts, manicures, massages)	$
Laundry and dry cleaning	$
Out-of-pocket medical expenses	$
Lawn care	$
Home repair and maintenance	$
Other (specify type)	$
Other (specify type)	$
Other (specify type)	$
Other (specify type)	$
Total Monthly Variable Spending	$

Periodic Spending	
Insurance	$_____
Auto registration and inspection	$_____
Subscriptions	$_____
Charitable donations	$_____
Tuition	$_____
Dues and fees	$_____
Income taxes	$_____
Property taxes	$_____
Other (specify type)	$_____
Other (specify type)	$_____
Other (specify type)	$_____
Other (specify type)	$_____
Total Monthly Periodic Spending	$_____
Monthly Contributions	
Savings	$_____
Retirement	$_____
Other (specify type)	$_____
Other (specify type)	$_____
Other (specify type)	$_____
Other (specify type)	$_____
Total Contributions	$_____
Total Monthly Spending and Contributions	$_____
Total Monthly Income	$_____
(minus)	–
Total Monthly Spending and Contributions	$_____
(equals)	=
Your Bottom Line	$_____

Making budgeting a family affair

Developing a budget and making it work is something that you and your spouse or partner should do together. After all, you're both spending your family's money. It's a good idea to involve your kids in the process, too. Sit down as a family and talk about why your family needs to live on a budget and what budgeting involves. Show your kids the income and expense worksheets you fill out as you work your way through the budgeting process. Share your current income and spending figures with them, let them know how much less your family needs to spend each month, and ask your kids for budget-cutting ideas, including things they are willing to give up. Also discuss any budget cuts you plan to make that will directly affect them.

At the end of each month, sit down as a family and compare your budgeted spending to your actual spending. Celebrate if your family's spending is in line with its budget by doing something inexpensive together — maybe ice-cream cones for all or a picnic in the park. When your comparison shows that your family spent more than was budgeted, talk about why you went over budget and what all of you can do to ensure that it doesn't happen again. When your children feel like an important part of your family's financial team and understand that you value their input, they will be more apt to pull with you, not against you. They'll also be less apt to resent changes that may affect them.

Tackling a Budget Deficit

If the "Your Bottom Line" number on your worksheet (see Table 3-1) is negative, you've got a *budget deficit*. You may be making up the difference between your total monthly income and your total monthly spending by using credit cards, getting credit card advances, borrowing money, writing hot checks, paying bills late, or not paying bills at all. Stop doing those things! They're only driving you deeper into debt.

Cutting expenses

Deal with your budget shortfall instead by reducing your spending. Review your budget, looking for expenses you can trim or eliminate. Focus first on your discretionary spending because those are nonessential items. You'll find most of your discretionary spending items in the "Variable Spending" category on your worksheet; however, some of your fixed and periodic spending items may also be discretionary. For example, cable TV is not an essential expense. Likewise, you may be able to find a cheaper Internet provider (or go to the library when you need the Internet) and cancel some of your memberships.

If your deficit is small and most of it is due to waste and fluff, you may be able to move your budget into the black just by eliminating nonessentials. But maybe not. Instead, you may have to go through several rounds of budget-cutting and do some serious belt-tightening before your household's total monthly spending is less than its total monthly income. Use your worksheet to calculate the impact of each round of cuts on your budget's bottom line.

For many spending-reduction suggestions, check out our ideas in Book I, Chapter 4.

Reducing debt before saving

If you contribute to a savings and/or a retirement plan, stop doing that for now. Use that money to cover your living expenses and pay down your high-interest debts. Why? The money in your savings and retirement accounts earns only a small amount of interest each month — most likely far less than the interest rates on your debts. When you have debt, every month you pay more in interest than you can earn in interest on your savings, and you fall further behind.

When your financial situation improves, start contributing to savings and retirement again. But for now, you must put every penny you have toward your essential living expenses and toward paying down your high-interest debts.

Using other strategies

Moving your budget from red to black may require more than budget-cutting alone. The same is true if you can afford to pay only the minimum due on your high-interest debts. When you pay just the minimum each month, it takes months, if not years, to pay off those debts, and you pay hundreds or even thousands of dollars in interest — dollars that you could put to better use. What else can you do? Many parts of this book (especially in Book III) expand on lots of ideas and strategies, but for starters, you can try these suggestions:

✔ **Increasing your household income:** Get a second job, turn your hobby into a part-time business, or let your boss know that you would like to work more hours. If your spouse or partner is not working outside the home, discuss whether a paying job makes sense — at least, until your finances improve.

✔ **Negotiating with your creditors:** Some of them may be willing to lower your monthly payments or make other changes to help you afford to continue paying on your debts.

✔ **Consolidating your debts:** Debt consolidation involves borrowing money to pay off high-interest debt and lower the total amount you pay on your debts each month.

✔ **Getting help from a reputable nonprofit credit counseling agency:** Such agencies can help you develop your budget and may also suggest that you set up a debt-management plan.

✔ **Filing for bankruptcy:** Bankruptcy should always be your option of last resort. When may it become your best option?

- If you're about to lose an important asset

- If your monthly expenses are so much higher than your income that it will take years of sacrifice and bare-bones budgeting before your debts are manageable and you have a little extra money left over each month

Gauging your finances by using standard percentages

Financial experts agree that, in general, your basic living expenses and the total amount of debt you owe (secured and unsecured) should equal no more than a certain percentage of your net household income. (*Net household income* is your income after deductions for taxes and other expenses — it's your take-home pay.) When you're developing your budget, one way to pinpoint expenses to reduce is to compare your numbers to the following standard percentages. When you have a budget, you can also use the standard percentages to monitor the state of your finances over time.

If your percentages are a little higher than the ones on the following list, you don't necessarily need to worry because certain expenses may be higher in your part of the country. Housing, for example, varies greatly from place to place. Some financial books and Web sites also may use slightly different percentages than these; no one correct set of figures exists. These percentages are just approximate amounts for you to use as spending guidelines:

✔ **Monthly housing expense:** 25 percent of your net household income (35 percent if you take into account homeowner's insurance, property taxes, home maintenance, and repairs)

✔ **Consumer debt (credit cards, student loans, medical debts, and so on):** 10 percent of your net household income

✔ **Utilities:** 15 percent of your net household income

✔ **Transportation:** 15 percent of your net household income

✔ **Savings:** At least 10 percent of your net household income

✔ **Everything else (food, clothing, medical insurance, prescriptions, entertainment, and so on):** 25 percent of your net household income

After reviewing your financial information, a bankruptcy attorney can tell you whether you should file for bankruptcy and which type of bankruptcy you can file: a Chapter 13 reorganization, which gives you three to five years to pay your debts; or a Chapter 7 liquidation, which wipes out most of your debts. (To be eligible to file a Chapter 7, you must pass a federally required means test that takes into account your income and your expenses.)

If you decide to file bankruptcy, the attorney will inform you that within six months of doing so you must go to a court-approved credit counseling agency. The agency will make sure that you understand your alternatives to bankruptcy and that there is no way that you can avoid having to file. If the agency concludes that bankruptcy is your only option, it will give you a certificate that you must provide to the bankruptcy attorney. The certificate permits you to file for bankruptcy. Without it you cannot pursue bankruptcy. For detailed explanations of your bankruptcy options and the bankruptcy process, check out *Personal Bankruptcy Laws For Dummies,* by James P. Caher and John M. Caher (Wiley).

Paying the Important Stuff If You Can't Pay Everything

If you've cut your budget to the bare bones and you still can't afford to pay all your debts and cover all your living expenses, you have to decide what you will and won't pay. Here's how to prioritize:

- ✔ **Essential living expenses:** Your essential living expenses belong at the top of your "Bills to Pay" list, including putting bread on your table, keeping a roof over your head, keeping your utilities on, and gassing up your car if you need it to earn a living. However, make sure that you have reduced those expenses as much as you possibly can.

- ✔ **Secured debts:** Your secured debts also belong at the top of the list of things to pay. Keep reading if you aren't sure what a secured debt is.

- ✔ **Certain unsecured debts:** Some of your unsecured debts should take priority over others. We go into detail in the upcoming section "Knowing when to prioritize an unsecured debt."

Distinguishing between secured and unsecured debt

A *secured* debt is a debt that you collateralized with an asset that you own. (The asset is often referred to as your *collateral.*) When you collateralize a debt, the lender puts a lien on that asset, which gives the lender the legal right to take the asset if you fall behind on your payments. For example, if you have a mortgage loan, your lender has a lien on your home. If you have a car loan, the lender has a lien on your vehicle.

A lot of your debt, like credit card debt, is probably *unsecured,* which means that the creditors do not have liens on any of your assets. If you don't pay an unsecured debt, the creditor will try to get you to pay up. If you don't, the creditor may bring a debt collector on board to try to get your money. If you still don't pay, the creditor must sue you to get the court's permission to try to collect what you owe. The creditor can ask the court for permission to

- ✔ Seize one of your assets.
- ✔ Put a lien on an asset so you can't borrow against it or sell it without paying your debt.
- ✔ *Garnish* your wages (take a portion of them each pay period), assuming that wage garnishment is legal in your state.

Knowing when to prioritize an unsecured debt

Depending on your circumstances, you'll want to treat certain unsecured debts as top priorities, given the potential consequences of not paying them. These unsecured debts deserve priority treatment:

- ✔ **Child support, especially if it's court ordered.**
- ✔ **Federal income taxes.** Uncle Sam has almost unlimited powers to collect past-due tax debts.
- ✔ **State income taxes.** If you don't pay these taxes, your state can sue you, garnish your wages, or seize your property.
- ✔ **Property taxes and homeowner's insurance, if these expenses aren't included in your mortgage payments.** When you don't pay your property taxes, the taxing authority will eventually take your home. If your homeowner's insurance gets cancelled for nonpayment, your lender will

buy insurance for you, but the insurance will be very expensive, so the total amount of your monthly mortgage payments will increase.

✔ **Federal student loans.** The IRS can collect what you owe when you fall behind on your federally guaranteed student loans.

✔ **Your health insurance, if you're responsible for the payments.** Keeping up with your health insurance is especially important if you or a family member has an ongoing health problem. Without insurance, an expensive illness or accident could push you into bankruptcy.

✔ **Medical bills.** A growing number of healthcare providers, including hospitals, are getting very aggressive about collecting on their patients' past-due accounts, even suing patients in some instances. If you owe money to a healthcare provider, contact the provider to try to work out a plan for paying what you owe.

If one of your unsecured creditors turns over your debt to a debt collector, no matter how much the debt collector may hound and threaten you, do not give in to the collector's demands if paying the unsecured debt means you won't be able to pay your priority debts or living expenses. In Book III, Chapter 1, we tell you how to deal with debt collectors.

Examining a Budget Surplus

If your monthly spending and income comparison shows that you have money left over each month, don't break out the champagne just yet. You may have a surplus because you're not paying some of your bills or you're meeting some of your obligations by using credit cards. If this is the case, you must still reduce your spending so your income covers all your bills and living expenses each month.

A key aspect of getting out of debt is *not using your credit cards.* We certainly understand that sometimes you may have to use a credit card to pay for a financial emergency if you have no extra money in your budget and you have nothing in savings. But you should resolve to pay off the amount you charge as quickly as possible — the next month, if possible. And you should try not to charge anything more until you've wiped out the new credit card debt.

You may also have a surplus because you're paying only the minimum due on your outstanding credit card balances each month. You'll never get out of debt that way! If you have any surplus in your budget, use it to accelerate the rate at which you pay off the balances, starting with the highest-rate card.

Even if you can cover your monthly obligations without using credit cards and while paying more than the minimum due on your card balances, don't assume that you shouldn't reduce your spending. You must be concerned about how much you owe to your creditors, or you probably wouldn't be reading this book. Cut back where you can, and use that additional money to pay off your debts as fast as you can, starting with the debt that has the highest interest rate. After you've paid off that one, focus on paying off the debt with the next-highest rate of interest, and so on. When you've paid down your high interest debts, use your surplus to start building up your savings.

Finalizing and Sticking to Your Budget

When you've reduced your spending as much as you can and decided what you will and won't pay if you can't afford to pay everything, you can finalize your household budget. Make a fresh copy of the worksheet from Table 3-1. Label it "Monthly Household Budget" and record your revised monthly spending amounts, as well as your monthly income amounts. Now you have a written plan for what you're going to do with your money each month.

Review the budget with your family members, and post it in a visible location so everyone can see it — maybe on a bulletin board in your kitchen or family room or on the refrigerator.

Steeling your resolve

Now comes the hard part: living according to your budget. Having a budget is meaningless if you and your family aren't going to stick to it. Sticking to your budget won't be easy, but keep your eye on the prizes: less financial stress, fewer debts, less damage to your credit history, and (eventually) more money to spend the way you want.

As you go through each month, be mindful of every dollar you spend, every check you write, and every time you use your debit card or go to an ATM machine. Cut up your credit cards, or use them only in emergencies. Refer to your budget regularly to make sure you're staying on track. If you find that you have overspent in one area, try to compensate by reducing in another area.

If your kids ask for things that you haven't budgeted for, remind them why your family is trying to spend less. If they're older, maybe they can earn the money they need for what they want.

TIP

Carry a small notebook or some other small record-keeping device with you for writing down everything you purchase with cash, a debit card, or a credit card each day. Keep all your receipts as well. You'll need this information at the end of each month when it's time to evaluate how well you're doing.

Checking your progress each month

To live on a budget, each month you must compare your actual monthly spending to what you budgeted. Here's how:

1. **On your monthly budget, add a column to the right of each dollar amount that's labeled "Actual."**

2. **Compile all your spending records for the month (check registers, bank statements, receipts, the information in your spending notebook) and all your income records to figure out your actual expense and income numbers.**

3. **Record these amounts in the appropriate places in the "Actual" column of your budget for the month.**

4. **Calculate subtotals and grand totals for the month.**

If you spent more than you budgeted on something, or if your total spending exceeded what you budgeted, try to figure out why you spent more. Here are some possible explanations:

✔ **You overlooked a living expense or debt when you developed your budget.**

✔ **Your budget isn't realistic.** It's too bare bones, so it's impossible for you and your family to live on it.

✔ **Your family didn't try hard enough to live according to your budget.** Making a budget work takes a 100 percent commitment from everyone in your household.

✔ **You were hit with an unexpected expense that month.** For example, you were working late at the office, so your childcare expenses increased, or your car broke down and you had to spend money to fix it.

✔ **Some of your expenses increased for reasons beyond your control.** The cost of gas went up or your insurance premium increased, for example.

✔ **Your income dropped.** Maybe you had to take a cut in pay, your sales commissions were lower than usual, or a client didn't pay you.

Avoid these loans

If you don't have enough money to pay all your living expenses and debts, do *not* raise the money you need by getting one of the following types of loans. Although they may give you some temporary financial relief, in the end, they'll make things worse — maybe a lot worse. When it comes to improving your finances, easy answers and shortcuts just don't exist. You've just got to bear down and do it.

✔ **Advance fee loan:** Just as its name implies, to get this kind of loan, you must pay money up front to the lender — sometimes as much as several hundred dollars. Some advance fee lenders will take your money and run, but others will give you a very high-interest loan. Traditional lenders do not make advance fee loans.

✔ **Finance company loan:** Finance companies make relatively small high-interest loans. Some finance company loans are downright dangerous: The lender may be less than honest about all the fees associated with its loan, or it may mislead you into thinking that you're getting an unsecured loan when the loan actually is secured by one or more of your household goods, such as your furniture, entertainment center, and so on. (This detail is usually buried in the fine print of the loan agreement.) If you default on the loan, you risk losing the asset(s). Some finance companies encourage consumers to get a bigger loan than the consumers can afford so they'll end up in default.

✔ **Payday loan:** This is a very short-term high-interest loan made by check-cashing companies, some finance companies, and businesses that do nothing but make payday loans. To get this loan, you write a personal check to the lender for the amount of money you want to borrow plus the amount of the lender's fee — usually a percentage of the loan amount or a set amount for every $50 or $100 you borrow — and you agree to repay the loan on your next payday. The lender pays you the amount of the check minus its fee but does not cash your check.

On your next payday when you repay the loan, you get the check back. If you can't repay the loan on the next payday, the lender rolls over the loan until the following payday in exchange for your paying the lender another fee, which will probably be higher than the first fee. Over time, if you keep rolling over the loan and paying higher fees, the cost of the loan skyrockets and you have a harder time paying it off.

Some states have payday loan laws. Contact a consumer law attorney or your state attorney general's office to find out if your state has such a law and what your rights are.

✔ **Pawnshop loan:** This is a short-term loan (no more than three months, in most states) with a very high interest rate. With this kind of loan, you give the pawnshop an item that you own, such as a TV, DVD player, piece of jewelry, or computer. The pawnshop lends you a percentage of the item's value. At the end of the loan period, if you cannot afford to pay the loan plus interest, the pawnshop keeps your item and sells it.

✔ **Tax refund loan:** Also known as a *tax anticipation loan* or an *instant refund loan,* this kind of loan involves borrowing against your future IRS tax refund. Some tax preparers, as well as finance companies, car lenders, retailers, and check-cashing companies, make this kind of loan. Usually the loan will be for no more than $5,000, and it will last for no more than ten days. In addition to having to pay a very high rate of interest on the loan, you must pay the lender an up-front fee, and you must file your tax return electronically to the tune of about $40. So when you consider the loan's interest rate plus the fees involved, the effective rate of interest you pay to borrow against your own money may be in the triple digits. When the IRS issues your tax refund, it deposits the money directly into an account set up by

the lender, who takes its money and gives you the rest.

✔ **Car title loan:** If you own your car free and clear, some lenders will make you a loan for a small fraction of what your car is worth. Usually the loan will be for no more than 30 days and will have a very high rate of interest. To get the loan, you must give the lender the title to your vehicle and a set of car keys. The major danger with this kind of loan is that if you miss a loan payment, you risk losing your car. Depending on the loan agreement, one missed payment may be all it takes.

Depending on your conclusions, you may need to revise some of the numbers in your household budget. If you have to increase the amount of an expense, try to decrease another expense by the same amount. If you have to revise your budget to reflect a decrease in your household's monthly income, try to offset the decrease with budget cuts as well.

If your monthly comparison shows that some of your expenses were lower than what you budgeted, don't revise your budget right away. Wait a month or two to see if the changes are permanent. If they are, put the extra money toward your high-interest debts, focusing first on paying off the debt with the highest rate of interest. Do the same if your income increases permanently.

Your budget is a dynamic document that should change as your finances change, hopefully for the better. Gradually, if you stick to your budget, you'll start paying off your debts faster. Eventually, you'll also be able to add some extras to your budget (maybe some of the things you've had to give up for now) and start contributing to savings so you'll have a financial safety net. If you continue to be careful about your spending and minimize your use of credit, before you know it, your family will be in a position to make its financial dreams come true.

Chapter 4

Cutting Spending and Boosting Income

*W*hen your monthly expenses are greater than your income, you must rein in your spending and stop using your credit cards. The same is true if you're just barely getting by each month, if you're paying only the minimum due on your credit cards, or if you have little or nothing in savings.

Finding ways to increase your family's income may also be essential, especially if you've cut your budget to the bare bones and you're still sliding backward, just treading water, or paying for every unexpected expense with a credit card. You may also want to consider working at another job or working more hours at your current job.

This chapter gives you practical suggestions for reducing your spending *and* boosting your income. Although every idea in this chapter probably doesn't apply to you, the advice we offer here may help trigger other ideas that do make sense for your particular situation.

Finding Ways to Spend Less

In this section, we offer a treasure trove of ideas for spending less, organized by category of everyday expense: housing, utilities, food, transportation, healthcare, and so on. Some of the ideas are small and simple but yield big benefits over time, especially when done in combination with other money-saving suggestions.

Don't reject any cost-cutting ideas right off the bat, even if implementing them means major changes in your lifestyle and a lot of sacrifice. Be open to anything and everything; try to focus less on what you're giving up and more on where spending less will help get you in the end.

After you give up a few "essentials," you may discover that you don't even miss them. You may find that not having them actually improves your quality of life. For example, using public transportation to get to and from work gives you time to read, think, and maybe even relax. And cutting out some activities that have filled your kids' after-school hours and weekends may open up new opportunities for you and your kids to interact.

Looking for good deals

Before we tackle specific areas of your household budget, we have a couple tips for getting the most out of your money, no matter what you're buying.

First is a Web site that should be on your list of favorites: www.yokel.com. Whether you're in the market for a prom dress, a car, a DVD player, or a new refrigerator, you can locate the best deals in your area by going to this site.

Next is a piece of advice about advertising: Although you should always try to buy things when they're on sale, you shouldn't buy an item just because it's discounted. Instead, make purchases based on whether you truly need an item. If you scan the Sunday ad flyers in your newspaper looking for good deals, you're bound to be tempted to buy things you don't really need. Keep this in mind: That item that looks like such a good deal today may get marked down even more in a week or two.

If you can't resist a sale, you may have a spending problem. People with spending problems tend to buy for the sake of buying, even when they know they shouldn't. Spending makes them feel good at the time but lousy later. Even so, they spend again. If you think you may have a spending problem, don't be embarrassed. Get help from other overspenders by going to a Debtors Anonymous (DA) meeting in your area. To find a DA chapter in your area, go to www.debtorsanonymous.org or call 781-453-2743.

Spending less on your housing

Housing is probably the single biggest item in your budget, especially if you are a homeowner and take into account the cost of maintenance, repairs, insurance, and taxes. You can rein in your housing costs in many ways.

Renters

Following are some options to consider if you're renting:

- If you're close to the end of your lease, find a cheaper place to live. If you've got time left on your lease, read your lease agreement to find out how much it costs to break it so you can move out early.

- Move in with your parents or other relatives while you work on improving your finances.

- Stay where you are, but get a roommate, if your lease allows.

Homeowners

If you own your home, consider the following possibilities:

- Look into mortgage refinancing to lower your monthly payments. Be careful, however, about refinancing with a mortgage that may create problems for you down the road, like an interest-only mortgage or one with a big balloon payment at the end. If you're confused about whether a particular mortgage is good or bad for your finances, talk to a financial advisor, a nonprofit credit counseling agency, or a real estate attorney.

- Rent out an extra room in your home.

- Lease your home to someone else and move into cheaper digs. Make sure the rent you charge covers your mortgage payments plus the cost of your homeowner's insurance, property taxes, and routine maintenance and repairs.

- Sell your home. We know this may be a lot to ask, but if you're paying for more house than you can truly afford, getting out from under the debt is a good thing.

Lowering your utility bills

The cost of heating and cooling a home always seems to go up, up, up. Add in the cost of water, wastewater, and lights, and you may find yourself gasping when you open your utility bills each month. Consider these suggestions for bringing down these costs:

- Use your heat and air conditioning less by keeping your home cooler in the winter and warmer in the summer. Keep your thermostat set at 68 degrees in the winter and no less than 78 degrees in the summer.

- Lower the temperature on your water heater, but not to less than 120 degrees.

- ✔ Ask if your local utility company offers free energy audits. You can find out where your house is losing energy and what you can do to make your home more energy efficient. The utility may also offer rebate programs that can lower the cost of your energy improvements, or you may qualify for a low-interest/no-interest home energy loan to finance expensive improvements like installing a more energy-efficient heating and cooling system.

- ✔ Find out if your utility offers an energy-saving program. For example, some power companies will automatically shut off your household appliances during peak use hours each day.

- ✔ Replace your commode with one that uses less water. Also replace old showerheads with new low-flow heads.

- ✔ Make your home more energy efficient by caulking, using weather stripping, and adding insulation, all of which are relatively easy do-it-yourself projects.

- ✔ Use fans, not air conditioning, to cool your home.

- ✔ Hang up your clothes to dry. Not only is using a dryer expensive, but all that hot air makes your clothes wear out faster.

- ✔ If you have to replace your washing machine, get one that loads from the front instead of the top. You'll reduce your energy use by as much as 50 percent and save on water, too.

- ✔ Take showers, not baths, and limit the length of your showers.

- ✔ Replace old-fashioned light bulbs with the new ultraefficient fluorescent bulbs.

- ✔ Never run a dishwasher that is only half full.

- ✔ Fix leaky faucets.

Eating for less

One of the easiest expenses to reduce is the amount you spend on food. Reducing your grocery bill may mean eating more homemade foods and fewer prepackaged items, which has some added bonuses: You'll be eating healthier, and you'll probably shed a pound or two!

- ✔ Plan your meals for the coming week based on your budget, and go to the grocery store with a list of the items you need. Buy them and nothing more.

- ✔ Minimize your trips to the grocery store. The more trips you make, the more you're apt to spend. Also, never shop when you are hungry. You're more apt to load your cart with items you really don't need.

✔ When you make a meal, double the recipe and store the extra half in your freezer. When you have to work late one night or are feeling frazzled after a difficult day at the office, you'll be less tempted to purchase prepared food or carryout on your way home because you have a meal waiting that you can just pop into the microwave.

✔ Clip coupons and read the grocery store inserts in your local newspaper for good deals on items you plan to buy.

Coupon Web sites like www.couponcabin.com, www.couponcraze.com, and www.coolcoupons.com offer savings at specific stores and on popular national brands. Some offer free product samples, too.

✔ Shop at several different grocery stores. Some may offer better deals on certain items that you use.

✔ Purchase house brands.

✔ Minimize your use of prepared foods and convenience items. You pay a premium for them.

✔ If you drink regularly, drink less and buy less-expensive wine, beer, or hard liquor.

✔ Purchase groceries at warehouse stores, discount houses, and buying clubs. When practical, buy in bulk.

But don't buy perishable items in large quantities unless you're sure you'll use them before they spoil. Also, don't buy items in bulk or on sale that you're not sure your family will use; these deals are good ones only if you actually use what you buy!

✔ Pack lunches for yourself and your family.

✔ Make your own morning coffee instead of buying it on your way to work.

✔ Eliminate sodas and junk food from your diet.

✔ Reserve dining out for weekends or special occasions only.

✔ Celebrate a special occasion with a picnic instead of a restaurant meal.

✔ Pop your own popcorn for the movies. Old-fashioned homemade popcorn tastes a whole lot better than the prepopped stuff available at most movie theaters, and it's a lot cheaper, too.

✔ When your family goes on a day trip, pack your meal instead of eating at a restaurant.

✔ Grow your own vegetables and herbs. If you don't have a green thumb or if you lack the space for a garden, buy your fruits and veggies at your local farmers' market.

Just how much do your vices cost?

You may find a silver lining in your cash crunch if you're a regular smoker or drinker. Not having the money you need to pay your creditors and cover your basic living expenses may convince you that it's time to become a nonsmoker, or to give up that glass or two (or three) of wine you sip at the end of each day, or that six pack of beer you throw back each evening.

Let's assume, for example, that you and your spouse or partner enjoy a $15 bottle of wine with dinner each night. In a week's time, your nightly bottle of wine costs you $105. That's $420 a month and more than $5,000 a year!

Now that's a lot of money to spend on the fruit of the vine. Just think what you could do with that money instead.

Now let's look at how much you may be spending to smoke. Let's assume that you smoke half a pack of cigarettes every day and that you pay $5 for each pack. More than $900 of your money is going up in smoke each year, which doesn't even take into account how much extra you're paying for life insurance because of your unhealthy habit. If you give up the habit, you can reduce the cost of your premium by as much as 30 percent. You'll probably pay less for health insurance as well.

Paying less for transportation

After the cost of housing, the cost of getting from place to place may be your second-biggest monthly expense. You may already have found ways to trim your transportation budget since the cost of a tank of gas has been rising, but you could well find some new ideas here.

- ✔ Use public transportation, ride your bike, walk, or carpool to work, if possible. If you use public transportation or carpool, you may be able to read and enjoy the passing scenery. If you ride your bike or walk, you may even lose a few pounds.

- ✔ Shop around for the best deal on gas. Driving a little farther to fill up your tank for less may be worth the extra miles and time.

- ✔ If your vehicle is a gas guzzler or is expensive to maintain, consider selling it and purchasing a reliable, less-expensive used vehicle.

- ✔ Change your own oil, and do your own simple car repairs. Your local community college or an adult education program in your area may offer a class in basic car maintenance, or maybe a neighbor or friend can show you the basics. Also, the *Car Talk* guys on National Public Radio feature a humorous but down-to-earth do-it-yourself guide to car repair and maintenance at their show's Web site, www.cartalk.com/content/diy.

- ✔ Pump your own gas and wash your own car. Also, don't buy a higher grade of gas than your car really needs.

✔ Find a reliable mechanic who won't charge you an arm and a leg every time you bring your vehicle to the repair shop. Ask people you know, especially people who drive cars similar to yours, for the names of good mechanics. A *shade tree* mechanic — someone who maintains and repairs cars in his backyard — may provide affordable, high-quality service. Avoid having your car repaired by a dealer or at a chain car repair shop.

The experts on the *Car Talk* radio show also maintain a "humongous database of over 16,000 great mechanics, recommended by — and for — the *Car Talk* community." Access their Mechanics File by going to www.cartalk.com/content/mechx.

✔ Ask your teenagers to pay for their own gasoline and auto insurance or to help contribute to the cost.

Having fun for less

Reducing your budget doesn't mean that you and your family have to eliminate fun from your lives. It means cutting out the frills and taking time to find affordable ways to have a good time. Think back to when you were just married and money was tight or to when you were a kid. What did you do for fun then? Do any of these cheap fun suggestions sound familiar?

✔ Use your public library instead of buying books and DVDs, or swap these items with your friends.

✔ Go to www.zunafish.com and exchange your used books, CDs, DVDs, and videogames with others online for a buck a trade. As the Web site says, "Trade the stuff you're done with for the stuff you want!"

✔ Commune with nature. Go for a hike, ride your bike, have a picnic in the park, go fishing, enjoy the babble of a swift running creek, and take time to enjoy the sunset.

✔ Have fun the old-fashioned way: Put together jigsaw puzzles, play card and board games, do crossword puzzles, play charades, create a scrapbook, or put all your photos into albums.

✔ Use your community pool.

✔ Take advantage of free events in your community.

✔ Entertain with potluck meals.

✔ Invite friends over for a backyard barbeque, and have everyone bring something to throw on the grill.

✔ Curl up with a good book.

- ✔ Use two-for-one coupons or share an entrée with your dinner companion when you want to dine out.

- ✔ Trade baby-sitting services with friends or relatives who also have young children, to make going out occasionally more affordable.

Looking good for less

When you're rolling in dough, you can afford to spend a bundle on salons, spas, personal trainers, and so on. But those are all luxuries you can't afford right now. Here are suggestions for keeping yourself and your family looking good for less:

- ✔ Do your own manicures and pedicures, or get together with a girlfriend and do them for each other.

- ✔ Cut and color your own hair, get it cut and colored less frequently, or look in your Yellow Pages or on the Web for a beauty school in your area. Most beauty schools offer free or low-cost cuts and coloring so students can hone their skills while being supervised by professionals.

- ✔ Cut your family members' hair.

- ✔ Get a massage at a massage school in your area. Find one in your local Yellow Pages, or go to `www.naturalhealers.com`.

- ✔ Eliminate expensive cosmetics, creams, and lotions. Although the packaging may not be as attractive as what you find on the high-priced stuff, drug store cosmetics, creams, and lotions usually do the job.

- ✔ Minimize your use of dry cleaning, and wash and iron your own shirts, blouses, and pants. If you hate ironing, watch TV or listen to music while you work out those wrinkles.

- ✔ If you belong to a health club and your membership is about to expire, find a less-expensive alternative or — if you rarely go — cancel your membership. Your local YMCA or community center may be an option.

- ✔ Speaking of health, give up your nightly wine or beer. Not only do they cost you money (see the sidebar "Just how much do your vices cost?"), but they also increase the number of calories you consume each day and jeopardize your health if you're a problem drinker.

Dressing for less

With a little planning and ingenuity, you and the rest of your family members can look like fashion plates without paying top dollar. The key is to plan ahead, eliminate impulse buying, and maybe rethink where you shop. Consider these suggestions for how to look like a million dollars on the cheap:

- ✔ Shop only when you truly need clothes, not for fun or out of boredom.

- ✔ At the end of each season, take inventory of the clothing items you need to replace because they're worn out or because your kids have outgrown them. Then take advantage of end-of-season sales.

- ✔ Check out thrift shops, nearly-new stores, and yard sales. You'll likely find some great deals.

- ✔ Buy on sale whenever possible, and shop at discount stores like T.J. Maxx, Target, Marshall's, and Kohl's.

- ✔ If you have young children, make their clothes last longer by buying them a little big. Then roll up the sleeves and pants bottoms, and shorten the hems on skirts and dresses.

- ✔ Swap clothes with friends or family members.

- ✔ If you've got the time and the skills, make some of your own clothes.

Reducing your phone costs

Over the past decade or so, the amount of money you spend to stay in touch has probably increased. Cell phones are ubiquitous, and phone companies offer a plethora of extras that are nice but unnecessary. Therefore, reducing the amount you spend on your phone service each month may not be much of a challenge, and those reductions should have little or no real impact on your lifestyle. You can implement some of these suggestions for staying in touch for less:

- ✔ Shop around for the best deal on phone service. If you're in the market for a cell phone and service plan, Web sites like www.letstalk.com and www.myrateplan.com can help you home in on your best options.

- ✔ Cancel your landline and go with Internet-based phone service through your cable company or a company like Vonage, SunRocket, or Skype. Typically, you pay a flat fee of about $25 for unlimited domestic calls. However, most of these companies require that you have high-speed Internet access, and you may need to purchase a headset; before you ditch your landline, put pencil to paper to be sure you'll save money.

- ✔ Make sure your calling plan matches the way you use your phone. For example, if you make a lot of in-state calls, your calling plan should have a low intrastate rate; if you frequently call out of state, be sure your plan offers low interstate rates. Some plans allow unlimited long-distance calling on weekends, in the evenings, or 24/7.

✔ Consider a family plan for your cell phone service if multiple people in your household have wireless phones. Also ask your teens to pay for the cost of having a cell phone.

✔ Get rid of your landline if you have a cell phone with an unlimited calling plan.

✔ Review the extras you're paying for, like voicemail, call waiting, caller ID, call forwarding, and so on. Do you *really* need them?

✔ Minimize or eliminate your use of directory assistance.

Saving on prescription drugs

If the cost of prescription drugs is taking a big bite out of your budget, don't do without — follow this advice for reducing what you pay for your pills:

✔ Ask your doctor for free samples whenever she prescribes a prescription drug for you or someone in your family.

✔ Ask your doctor if a generic or less-expensive alternative to a drug is available. Many newer drugs are more expensive than their older equivalents, but they're not necessarily better.

✔ Buy 90-day supplies of drugs when you order, to save on the dispensing fee that many pharmacies charge each time they fill a prescription.

✔ Talk with your doctor about prescribing a higher dose of the pill you normally take, and use a pill splitter to split it in half. You pay for fewer refills this way. However, your doctor should have the final say on whether this is a good option for your particular medication.

✔ Shop around before you get a prescription filled. You may be surprised by the range in prices from drugstore to drugstore.

✔ Purchase prescription drugs from an online pharmacy — one licensed by the National Association of Boards of Pharmacy through its VIPPS program. (The VIPPS seal of approval will be prominently displayed on the site.) Go to www.nabp.net for a list of the online pharmacies it has licensed. Reputable online pharmacies include www.costco.com, www.drugstore.com, and www.familymeds.com.

✔ If you take medications regularly, buy in bulk from a mail-order pharmacy.

✔ Find out if you qualify for a drug-assistance program. Some programs are income based, but others, like Merck's, offer prescription drug discounts to consumers who are uninsured, regardless of their incomes. Partnership for Prescription Assistance at www.pparx.org offers an online databank of drug-assistance programs.

Drug discount cards tend to be bad deals, in part because they have so many restrictions. For example, you may not be able to use your card to buy generic drugs or buy drugs online, or you may be able to use it only at certain pharmacies.

Inching down your insurance costs

Maintaining your insurance coverage is essential even when you need to cut back. Without it, a serious illness, a car accident, or flood or wind damage to your home could be financially devastating and push you into bankruptcy.

Shop around for the best deal on your insurance. An insurance broker can help, or you can explore your options by using a Web site like www.insure.com. For example, you may be able to get less-expensive coverage by switching to another provider, by raising your *deductibles* (the amount of money you have to pay out of pocket before your insurance company starts to pay) on your current policies, or by getting rid of any insurance bells and whistles you don't need.

Also make sure you're getting all the insurance discounts you're entitled to. For example, you may be entitled to a discount if you don't commute to work in your car, if you take a class to refresh your driving skills and knowledge, if you purchase your home and auto insurance from the same company, if you're over 65, if you install certain safety features in your home, and so on.

Homeowner's insurance

Following are specific tips for reducing your home insurance costs:

- ✔ When you insure your home, don't count the value of the land your home sits on. Insure the structure only.

- ✔ Find out if you'll save money by installing deadbolt locks and smoke detectors. If your home already has a security system, make sure it's reflected in your policy.

- ✔ If someone in your family was a smoker but has kicked the habit, find out if your insurance company will lower your premium costs. Households with smokers often pay a premium for insurance because burning cigarettes are a leading cause of house fires.

Auto insurance

Consider the following ways you may trim your auto insurance bill:

- ✔ If your vehicle is old and not worth very much, drop your collision coverage, especially if you're spending more on the coverage than your car is worth. Another option is to increase the deductible amounts for your collision and comprehensive coverage.

✔ Be sure that you're getting all the discounts you may be entitled to, such as discounts for

- A car with antilock brakes, automatic seat belts, and airbags.

- A particular profession. Statistics show that people in certain types of professions — engineers and teachers, for example — tend to have fewer accidents.

- Military service. Some insurance companies give you a break on the cost of your insurance if you're in the military or used to be.

✔ If you have to purchase a new car, buy one like your granny might drive. High-profile/high-performance cars cost more to insure.

✔ Find out if your association membership entitles you to a discount on your auto insurance.

Health insurance

Health insurance costs continue to skyrocket, and finding ways to reduce them can seriously help your household budget. Here are some suggestions:

✔ Talk with your employer's health plan administrator, or with your insurance broker or agent if you're not part of a group plan, about what you can do to lower your monthly health insurance costs. Possibilities may include increasing your annual deductible, switching insurance companies, or changing plans. Keep the following in mind:

- If you're willing to sacrifice the freedom to go to whatever doctor, pharmacy, or hospital you want, you can save money. Sign up with a plan that limits your choices; the more flexible, the more costly.

- If someone in your family has a preexisting medical condition, don't change plans or insurers before you know how coverage for that condition may be affected. Some plans or providers may refuse to cover the condition at all or may not cover it for a period of time — six months to a year, for example.

- Be aware that the insurance plan with the lowest premium cost is not a good deal if it doesn't offer the coverage and benefits you need. In the long run, paying a little extra to have the appropriate coverage may mean lower out-of-pocket expenses for doctors, hospitals, and prescription drugs.

✔ If your income is low and you have few, if any, assets of value, find out if you qualify for Medicaid, the federal/state health insurance program that is state administered. To check on your eligibility, go to www.familiesusa.org, click on "Consumer Assistance Program Locator," and choose your state. You'll get a link to your state's Medicaid office.

✔ If you don't qualify for Medicaid, you may be able to get health coverage for your children through the federal State Children's Health Insurance Program (SCHIP). Go to www.insurekidsnow.gov for information about the program in your state.

Blogs that can help you make every penny count

Blogs can be a great way to find out what other people in your same financial straits are doing to cut back and live on a budget. They can also provide you with moral support and encouragement. Here are a few blogs we think are worth a visit:

- The Budgeting Babe (`www.budgeting babe.blogspot.com`). This blog claims that it's dedicated to "all of the young working women who want to spend like Carrie in a Jimmy Choo store, but have a budget close to Roseanne . . ."

- Everybody Loves Your Money, (`www.everybodylovesyourmoney.com`). The author of this blog grew up in a family where money was tight.

- The Frugal Duchess (`www.sharonhr.blogspot.com`). A *Miami Herald* personal finance columnist who claims that she has "fine tastes and a small budget" writes this blog.

- *Stop Buying Crap* (`www.stopbuying crap.com`). The goal of this blog is to help people stop wasting money.

Bringing in More Bucks

If slashing your spending doesn't free up all the money you need to meet your financial obligations *and* accelerate the rate at which you pay off your debts, look for ways to increase your household's monthly income. Maybe to improve your financial outlook, you need to work extra hours at your current job (if you're paid by the hour), take a second job, or work as a freelancer. This section discusses the in and outs of each of these income boosters.

If your spouse or partner is a stay-at-home parent and is considering getting a paying job, take into account the costs of working outside the home, such as childcare and transportation, so you can be sure that the change makes financial sense. The online calculator at `www.fincalc.com/bud_06.asp?id=6` makes that analysis easy.

If making more money will be an uphill battle because demand for your skills is declining or because the industry you work in is depressed, consider getting trained for a new career by attending your local community college or a reputable trade school. Before you leap into anything, however, find out where the experts expect future job opportunities to be. Start your research by looking through the *Occupational Outlook Handbook* and the *Career Guide to Industries,* two publications available at the Web site of the U.S. Department of Labor's Bureau of Labor Statistics, `www.bls.gov`.

Earning more at your current job

Your current employer may be an immediate source of additional income. If you're paid by the hour, let your boss know that you want to work additional hours. If demand for your employer's product or service is growing or if your employer is opening a new office or store, you may be able to add another shift to your schedule, work longer each day, or work on weekends, especially if you have a good reputation as an employee.

Asking for a raise is another option, assuming that you can justify your request. For example, a raise may be in order if you haven't received one in a long time, if you have assumed new responsibilities without additional compensation, or if you recently completed an important project. Other possible reasons to ask for a raise include a stellar performance review and the fact that coworkers in your same position may be paid more than you.

Another way to earn more money at your current place of employment is to apply for a promotion. Let your boss know that you want to be considered for a higher-paying job in your same department. If you're qualified to work in other departments, schedule a time to meet with the managers of those departments to let them know that you're interested in working for them.

Looking for a new job

Getting a better-paying job with a new employer is another obvious way to boost your income. In this section, we share tips for starting a job search.

Doing your homework

Prepare for your job hunt by whipping your résumé into shape, writing a short but snappy cover letter, and honing your interview skills. If you need help doing any of these things, you'll find a wealth of free information on the Web. Here are a few sites to check out:

- ✔ **The Center for Communication Practices at Rensselaer Polytechnic Institute:** This site (www.wecc.rpi.edu) offers a clear, step-by-step process for creating a winning résumé. Click on "E-handouts" and look for "Resumes."

- ✔ **The Career Advice section of Monster.com:** At www.monster.com, you can find résumé assistance, help in figuring out how much salary to ask for, and a self-assessment center for evaluating your skills and abilities. You also get career-specific advice based on whether you want to change careers, are looking for a job, or are 50 years old or over. You can even go through a virtual interview to prepare for the kinds of questions you'll likely be asked in a job interview.

- **Career Builder:** This Web site helps you build an online résumé from scratch or improve the one you already have. Then you can post it at the site for employers who are looking for someone like you. To access the site's résumé-building help, go to www.careerbuilder.com and click on "Post Resumes" at the top of the home page. Then click on "Build Your Resume."

- ***The Wall Street Journal's* Career Journal:** The site http://online.wsj.com/careers features useful articles and tips on how to use the Internet to find a job, pointers on crafting effective résumés and cover letters, job-search strategies, interviewing tips, strategies for negotiating your salary, and more.

Finding out about new job opportunities

When your résumé and cover letter are up to date and you're ready to turn a practice interview into a real one, how do you find potential employers?

- **Let your friends know you're in the market for a better-paying job.** They can keep an eye out for opportunities at their workplaces.

- **Visit job search Web sites.** Scope out a variety of job sites to find ones that best meet your needs and are easiest to use. We've listed some possibilities:

  - National online job Web sites like CareerBuilder (www.careerbuilder.com), Job-Hunt.org (www.job-hunt.org), Monster.com (www.monster.com), and America's Job Bank (www.ajb.dni.us). Some of these sites send you email alerts to let you know about new job listings that match your criteria.

  - Niche online job sites that focus on a narrowly defined type of job or on jobs within a specific industry. For example, www.dice.com focuses on high-tech jobs; www.bankingboard.com zeroes in on jobs in the mortgage banking, title, escrow, and real estate fields; and www.allretailjobs.com focuses on — you guessed it — all types of positions in the retail world.

  - Your state's employment office. Most of these sites include a job bank of openings with local and national private-sector employers, nonprofits, state government, and sometimes local governments.

  - The Web sites of your local and county government. These sites may feature job banks with a focus on government job openings in your specific locale.

Book I

Taking Charge of Your Finances

- • The Web sites of any professional or trade organizations you belong to. Many of these organizations list job openings of specific interest to their members.

- • www.craigslist.org. Craigslist features traditional and offbeat job listings for many larger cities.

Visit QuintCareers (www.quintcareers.com/top_50_sites.html) for descriptions and links to 50 great job sites. You can also search for jobs by industry type — from jobs in the airline industry and law enforcement to jobs in academia, fashion, retail, finance, and advertising — at www.quintcareers.com/indres.html.

✔ **Read the employment listings in your local newspapers.**

✔ **Attend job fairs.** Job fairs are a great way to meet employers in your area that are hiring. You may even have the opportunity to do some initial interviews at the job fairs or set up interviews for a later date. You can find out about job fairs through your local media; by visiting www.careerfairs.com, www.careerbuilder.com, or other Web sites dedicated to job fairs; and by searching the Internet.

✔ **Network.** Many great jobs are never advertised online or in newspapers. Instead, they are filled via word of mouth, through networking. Networking involves letting anyone and everyone know that you're looking for a job, including your former bosses, professional associates, friends, relatives, neighbors, elected officials you may know, and even people you just happen to meet. Any of these individuals may know about a job opening that would be perfect for you.

You can also network by attending networking events. For example, your local Chamber of Commerce may sponsor breakfasts, luncheons, or happy hours that are organized to help professionals network. Other good networking opportunities include meetings of your alumni association, meetings of clubs and associations you may belong to, community events, cocktail parties and dinner parties, and conferences — just about anywhere that you'll be with other people.

When you're networking, be prepared to explain in concise terms exactly what type of job you're looking for and your skills and experience. You may have only a minute to make a first impression.

Carry business cards with you at all times to take full advantage of every networking opportunity that comes your way. And whenever you meet people who could be helpful in your job search, get their business cards so you can follow up. You may even want to carry copies of your résumé with you whenever you leave your home so you can pass them out when appropriate. For more information about all aspects of networking, go to http://online.wsj.com/careers.

✔ **Find a headhunter.** Schedule an appointment with an employment agency in your area or with an executive-recruitment firm (also known as a *headhunter*) if you're looking for a mid- to upper-level management position.

Employment agencies and executive-recruitment firms are paid a fee for linking up employers and employees. Typically, employers pay the fees of executive-search firms, but you may have to pay the fee if an employment agency finds you a job. Be clear about who will pay before you sign an agreement with a business that says it will try to help you find employment. If you'll be responsible for the fee, make sure you understand the amount and the conditions of the fee you'll owe.

Getting (and surviving) a second job

Thinking about making more money by working at another job, otherwise known as *moonlighting?* Join the crowd. According to the U.S. Department of Labor, about 7.2 million Americans hold down more than one job. See the job-hunting resources we suggest in the previous section.

Moonlighting can be a great way to make some extra bucks, as long as your second job doesn't interfere with your ability to be effective at your primary job. You also need to make sure you come out ahead financially after taking into account any additional expenses you may incur by working two jobs: transportation, childcare, food costs, and so on.

If you signed a contract with your current employer, read it before you take a second job. The contract may prohibit you from working for specific types of employers or from moonlighting at all.

If you feel like your life is already a juggling act, a second job will make keeping all your balls in the air even more of a challenge. However, you can take steps to alleviate some of the stress that working multiple jobs may create:

✔ Ask your spouse or partner and older children to assume more day-to-day chores if you're the one who is responsible for most of them.

✔ Create a schedule of when things need to be done and post it on your family's bulletin board or refrigerator.

✔ Accept the fact that, for now, some things at home will fall through the cracks, and everything may not get done according to your standards.

✔ Make casseroles, soups, and other nutritious one-pot meals that you can freeze and that will feed your family for several days.

✔ Try to find a second job you enjoy — maybe relating to a hobby or special interest. You won't resent the extra work if what you do is fun.

✔ Avoid taking a second job that involves a lot of pressure and stress, especially if you're already under a lot of pressure and stress at your main job. You'll quickly burn out, and this may create health problems.

✔ Look for a second job that is relatively close to either your home or your main job so you're not spending a lot of time commuting.

✔ Grab naps when you can!

Considering freelancing

Depending on what type of skills you have, you may be able to boost your income by doing part-time freelance work. When you're a freelancer, you are self-employed and offer your services to other businesses. For example, you may be a freelance copywriter, graphic designer, software designer, or CPA.

Working for yourself may sound appealing and can be quite profitable, but if you need an immediate infusion of cash, it's probably not your best bet. Usually, before you can expect to see any money from freelancing, you have to

✔ Prepare information explaining your services.

✔ Decide how and how much you will charge for your services (by the hour, by the project, or on a monthly retainer basis, for example).

✔ Let potential clients know about your services and then hope that some of them will contract with you.

✔ After you are hired, invoice your clients and cross your fingers that they'll pay you quickly.

Obviously, being a successful freelancer, especially when you're holding down a regular job, takes organization, self-discipline, the ability to manage numerous tasks simultaneously, and a little bit of luck. However, if freelancing appeals to you, you can use these avenues to find out more about the process and about potential freelancing opportunities:

✔ Talk to people you know who are already freelancing.

✔ Let your former employers know you would like some freelance work.

✔ Visit www.quintcareers.com/freelancing_career.html.

✔ Read *Freelancing For Dummies,* by Susan M. Drake (Wiley). You can find a *For Dummies* book for everything, can't you?

✔ Register at www.guru.com so that businesses looking for someone who offers your type of service know how to find you.

The skinny on business scams

Beware of business "opportunity" scams that you may find out about on the Internet, in your local newspaper, through the mail, and so on. Typically, the promoters of these scams promise you'll earn big bucks after you pay them for equipment, software, supplies, training materials, and/or business leads. Typically, the value of what they sell you is negligible and far less than the fee you pay. Two common work-at-home scams are envelope stuffing and medical billing.

If a business opportunity sounds interesting, ask the promoter to send you printed information about its offer. Among other things, the information should

✔ Indicate the promoter's name, address, and phone number.

✔ Explain the business opportunity in detail — what you will get for your money and what assistance the promoter will give you.

✔ State the opportunity's total cost, as well as how and how often you'll be paid, who will pay you, and all terms and conditions for getting paid.

Ask for the names and phone numbers of people who have pursued the business opportunity, and contact them to find out if it lived up to their expectations. If the business promoter offers instead to provide you with a list of testimonials

from happy business owners, don't accept it. The testimonials may be made up. Don't work with a business opportunity promoter who has no information to send you or no references you can contact.

Also ask to see a copy of the contract you will have to sign if you agree to work with the promoter. The contact information should match the company's printed information and whatever you may have been told via an email or over the phone.

Federal law requires promoters who charge more than $500 for a business opportunity to also tell you how much you can earn from the opportunity and the number and the percentage of individuals who have earned at least that much recently.

Never pay any money to one of these companies without checking first with your local Better Business Bureau and with the Better Business Bureau where the company is located, as well as with your state attorney general's office and with the Federal Trade Commission. They can tell you if they've received complaints from consumers who feel that a business opportunity promoter ripped them off. Contact these same organizations if you get ripped off by a business opportunity scam, and talk to a consumer law attorney if you lost a substantial amount of money as a result.

When you freelance, your clients won't deduct taxes from the money they pay you. Therefore, you owe those taxes to Uncle Sam on April 15. If you're making a considerable amount from freelancing, it's a good idea to pay your taxes quarterly. Otherwise, you may end up in hot water with the IRS if your tax return shows that you owe more taxes than you can afford to pay when April 15 comes around. Meet with your CPA to figure out the best way to handle your taxes as a freelancer.

Chapter 5

Fixing Up Your Credit Report

● ●

In This Chapter

▶ Grasping the importance of your credit report

▶ Identifying what a credit report is

▶ Uncovering the details in your credit report

▶ Knowing how negative information gets in your credit report

▶ Translating your FICO and Vantage credit scores

▶ Examining two specialized credit-reporting agencies

● ●

*M*any people used to put their credit reports in the same category as IQ results, SAT scores, school report cards, job reviews, and cholesterol readings — in other words, information that's important only when a particular situation arises. As soon as the situation goes away, so does the need to monitor it. Sort of like a diet. Once your belt stops cutting off your circulation, you can stop counting your calories. Right? Wrong! The same applies to watching your credit report and keeping track of your score periodically.

Today, with tightening credit, a larger-than-usual need to refinance a home by a larger-than-usual percentage of the population, and credit card debt at very high levels, your credit report and score have moved to center stage. And that doesn't begin to touch on the other problems that a low score or negative credit file can exacerbate. Insurance rates are rising and homeowner's insurance is getting not only expensive but, in some places near the water, also hard to find. The information in your credit report and score can make an important difference here as well. In this chapter, we explain why you need to be on frequent and intimate terms with your credit report.

Understanding Why a Credit Report Is Important

Your credit report doesn't come into play just when you want to borrow money. A bad credit report may affect what you pay for insurance, whether you can rent the apartment of your choice, or whether you'll be hired for certain jobs. A particularly finance-conscious romantic prospect may even nix you for a bad credit history!

Your credit score can cost you thousands of dollars and deny you opportunities you never even knew you missed. Clearly, what you don't know *can* hurt you. Consider two hypothetical life situations to illustrate this point:

- Say you signed up for a dating service. Now, what if all the information available to your prospective dates is given to them by people you've dated in the past? What if the quality of the dates you get in the future is directly tied to what all the people you've dumped (or been dumped by) say about you? Starting to sweat a little?

- Say you're applying for a job. Your salary, your job title, and the size of your office will be tied directly to what's on your résumé. But what if your past employers wrote your résumé — and mixed up your personnel file with the file of someone else who was fired for sexual harassment? Can you imagine walking into that job interview without any idea of what your former boss reported or whether it was correct?

Meeting your life partner, landing a great job — these situations are ones in which you have a great deal of personal interest in a successful outcome. Kind of like getting a good mortgage rate so you can afford or keep that dream home.

We're not saying that you're guaranteed to *like* the outcome of your date or job interview — but at least you know it's based on information you're privy to. The same is true with your credit report. You can't rewrite your own credit history, but you *can* be knowledgeable about what a credit report is and how much weight it carries as you try to negotiate your way through the financial universe. You *can* be savvy about situations that could cost you thousands of dollars more or deny you opportunities. And you *can* catch inaccuracies on your report (a common situation) and correct them.

You have no excuse for not knowing what's in your credit report. Getting a current copy of your credit report from each of the three credit bureaus (Equifax, Experian, and TransUnion) is easy. And don't even think about saying that you can't afford it, because you can now request your credit report from each credit bureau once a year for *free*.

So what's in your report? Is the information correct — or even yours? And if not, what can you do to fix it? Settle in for some facts that will open your eyes and save you money, time, and frustration.

What Is a Credit Report, Anyway?

In its most basic sense, your credit report is your financial life history of borrowing money. Credit-reporting bureaus or agencies gather, manage, maintain, and share this information. Trust us, you don't have to lift a finger to create it or disseminate it. As many as 20 credit-reporting bureaus exist; most are specialty reporting agencies. The following three are the biggies:

- ✔ **Equifax** (www.equifax.com; 800-685-1111)
- ✔ **Experian** (www.experian.com; 888-397-3742)
- ✔ **TransUnion** (www.transunion.com; 800-888-4213)

This section details the items in your credit report and who uses this information.

What your credit report says about you

As a snapshot of your financial life, your credit report may also indirectly predict your potential behaviors in other areas of your life. The fact that you have a history of making credit card payments late may tell a prospective landlord that you're likely to be late with your rent, too. A history of defaulted loans may suggest to a potential boss that you aren't someone who follows through with commitments. If you have a foreclosure in your file, it may tell someone that you may take on more than you can handle or are just one unlucky duck. If you've declared bankruptcy because your finances are out of control, perhaps you're out of control in other ways, too.

This snapshot, which brings into focus the details of your spending and borrowing and even suggests your personal life patterns, also paints a *bigger* picture of two important factors — characteristics that are critical to employers, landlords, lenders, and others. We cover these two critical characteristics in the following sections.

Do you do what you promise?

Your credit history is an indicator of whether you're someone who follows through with commitments — a characteristic important to most people, whether they're looking for a reliable worker, a responsible nanny, a dependable renter, or a faithful mate. Needless to say, a person or company who is considering lending you a sizable sum of money will want to know the same.

Based largely on your history of following through with your financial promises, you're assigned a credit score. People with higher scores generally get the best terms, including lower interest rates and reduced minimum down payments. People with lower credit scores may not get credit in today's economy, unless they pay higher interest rates and possibly additional fees or insurance. Even then, they may not qualify for anything, under tight approval guidelines.

Do you do it on time?

When it comes to your credit score, following through with your promises is only half of the game. The other half is doing it on time. In the lending business, the more overdue the payment is, the more likely it will not be paid at all — or paid in full. This fact is why, as you get further behind in your payments, lenders become more anxious about collecting the amount you owe. In fact, if you're sufficiently delinquent, the lender may want you to pay back the entire amount at once instead of as originally scheduled. (When it comes to money, your creditors' faith in you is only 30 to 90 days long. Car dealers, notoriously short on faith, see the end of the world happening in credit terms in a payment that's late by as little as two weeks.) So the longer you take to do what you promised, the more it costs you and the more damage you do to your credit score.

Uncovering your credit report's details

Many people believe that your credit report contains the intimate personal details of your life, ferreted out from interviews with your neighbors, your ex, and your business associates. Not true! You can rest assured that your credit report doesn't reveal whether you tend to drink too much at office parties, whether you sport a tattoo, or whether you had an eye-lift or indulged in a wild fling on your last vacation to Mexico.

The information in your credit report is specific, purely factual, and limited in scope. What it lacks in scope, however, it makes up for in sheer volume of material and the length of time it covers. If students cut a class, chances are no one will notice, but if they fail to pay a bill on time, a multibillion-dollar industry will notice, record it, and tell everyone who asks about them for the next seven years.

Consider the short take on what's in your credit report:

- **Personal identification information,** such as your name, Social Security number, date of birth, addresses (present and past), and most recent employment history.

Be consistent with your information, especially how you spell your name and address. Name, address, and date of birth are the most common sources used to identify which file is yours. Social Security number is fourth.

- **Public-record information** on tax liens, judgments, bankruptcies, child-support orders, and other official information.

- **Collection activity** for accounts that have been sent to collection agencies for handling.

- **Information about each credit account,** open or closed (also known as *trade lines*), such as whom you owe, the type of account (such as a mortgage or installment account), whether the account is *joint* (shared with another person) or just in your name, how much you owe, your monthly payment, how you've paid (on time or late), and your credit limits.

- **A list of the companies that have requested your credit file for the purpose of granting you credit:** Requests are known as *inquiries* and are one of two types:

    - *Soft inquiries* are made for promotional purposes (for instance, when a credit card issuer wants to send you a hot offer). These inquiries don't appear on the version of your credit report that lenders see. They are on the consumer's copy that you get.

    - *Hard inquiries* are made in response to a request from you for more or new credit. These inquiries *do* appear on the lender's copy of your credit report.

- **An optional message from you, up to 100 words in length, that explains any extenuating circumstances for any negative listings on your report.**

- **An optional credit score:** Your credit score is not really part of your credit report; it's an add-on that you have to ask for. Your score probably is different for each credit report because of data differences. (We cover the importance of your credit score later in this chapter.)

Credit reports are easy to read, although there's still room for improvement. Each of the three major credit-reporting agencies reports credit information in its own unique format. The credit-reporting agencies compete with each other for business, so they have to differentiate their products.

Among the list of items *not* included in your credit report are your lifestyle choices, religion, national origin, political affiliation, sexual preferences, friends, and relatives. Additionally, the three major credit-reporting agencies do not collect or transmit data on your medical history, checking or savings accounts, brokerage accounts, or similar financial records.

Book I

Taking Charge of Your Finances

You can see sample credit reports from Equifax, TransUnion, and Experian online at the sites listed here. You may have to hunt a bit for them on the sites, but they are there, along with endless offers to buy your report and credit monitoring:

- ✔ **Equifax:** www.equifax.com
- ✔ **TransUnion:** www.transunion.com
- ✔ **Experian:** www.experian.com

Who uses the info in your credit report?

Every day, businesses rely on the information in your credit report to help them decide whether to lend you money and at what price (otherwise known as the *interest rate* and *loan terms*). But because the information in your credit report can be sliced and diced many ways, your report becomes an important tool that serves different purposes for different people:

- ✔ For a lender, your credit report is a tool to determine how likely and able you are to repay a loan, and it's an indicator of how much interest and what fees to charge you based on the risk profile you represent — if you qualify for a loan or refinance at all.
- ✔ For an insurance company, your credit report is a tool to predict how likely you are to have an accident or have your house burn down.
- ✔ For an employer, your credit report is a tool to predict whether you'll be a reliable and trustworthy employee.
- ✔ For a landlord, your credit report is a tool to determine whether you're likely to pay the rent on time or at all.
- ✔ For you, your credit report is a tool to help you understand how you've handled your finances in the past and how you're likely to handle them in the future.

Many different types of people can look at this information and make an increasing number of significant decisions that can affect your life. For this reason, double-checking this information is essential. Establishing a positive credit history as soon as possible can help with jobs, insurance, and more.

Understanding How Bad Stuff Gets in Your Credit Report

Whether you're new to the world of credit or you're an experienced borrower, you need to keep a few key concepts in mind as you look over your credit report. Like the person who can't see the forest because there are too many trees in the way, when you get your hands on your credit report, you may be blinded by the amount of information. In the following sections, we help you focus on what matters and let go of what doesn't.

Nobody's perfect: Don't expect a straight-A report card

You aren't perfect. (We hate to have to be the ones to tell you this, but if you aren't married, someone has to!) The same goes for your credit report — and lack of perfection isn't a big deal, as long as your credit report shows more smooth patches than bumps. No matter how early you mail off that bill payment, it can still arrive late or get lost, which means you can expect to find some negative information on your credit report from time to time. The good news is that you can still be eligible for plenty of loans at competitive rates and terms without having a flawless credit report or qualifying for credit sainthood.

But how many bad marks are okay? How long do they stay? And how will lenders who view your report interpret them? For example, say you're a well-heeled, easy-going gal and you loan your boyfriend $5,000 for a very worthy cause. He promises to pay you back monthly over two years. But after four months without a payment, two things likely will happen: He'll no longer be your sweetie, and you'll have mentally written off any chance of collecting the debt. Plus, if you're smart, you'll think twice before lending money to a friend again. You may even mention the negative experience to your friends, especially if they were thinking of floating him a loan.

If you were to run into your ex-boyfriend sometime down the road, you'd probably mention the $5,000 — after all, you want your money back, and he still owes you. Whether you'd ask him to join you for dinner is another matter and may depend on his showing you some good-faith gesture.

In business, as in love, trust and faithful performance are keys to success. A creditor can tell your future and current creditors any repayment information that is correct and accurate through your credit report, in the same way that you can warn your friends about your ex-boyfriend. That information or warning may be modified at any time, as long as the new information is correct and accurate.

Just how much does a mistake cost you when it comes to your credit report? Well, it depends on your history. Along with the credit report and all the information that it contains, lenders can buy a *credit score* based on the information in the report. That score comes from a mathematical equation that evaluates much of the information on your credit report at that particular credit bureau. By comparing this information to the patterns in zillions of past credit reports, the score tells the lender your level of future credit risk. (Check out the section "Fleshing out credit score components," later in this chapter, for more information on credit scores.)

So people with a lot of information in their credit files will find that a lot of good credit experiences lessen the effect of a single negative item. Score one for the old folks with long credit histories! If you're a young person or a new immigrant with only a few trade lines and a few months of credit history (sometimes called a *thin file*), a negative event has a much larger effect in relation to the information available. Many young people think the world is stacked against them. In this case, it's true — but to be fair, it's also stacked against anyone with a limited credit history, regardless of your age or what country you come from.

Checking for errors: Creditors aren't perfect, either

Other people make mistakes, too — even banks and credit card payment processors. Considering that about 4.5 billion pieces of data are added to credit reports every month, it shouldn't be a big surprise that incorrect information may show up on your credit report. And we won't even get into the unrelated problem of errors caused as a result of identify theft. A number of conflicting studies have been done on what percentage of reports contain errors and, of those errors, how many were serious enough to affect either the terms under which credit was granted or whether credit was granted at all. So you may or may not have errors on your report. And they may or may not be serious. But unless you're feeling really lucky, we strongly suggest that you find out what's in your report.

Still, credit-reporting agencies have a vested interest in the accuracy of the information they report. They sell it, and their profits are on the line if their information is consistently inaccurate. If credit-reporting agencies consistently provide error-riddled data, companies that grant credit won't be as eager to pay money to get or use a bureau's credit reports.

Getting a copy of your credit report gives you a chance to check for these errors and — better yet — get them corrected! You can have inaccurate information removed by one of two methods: contacting the credit bureau or contacting the creditor.

Contacting the credit bureau

If you notice incorrect information on your credit report, contact the credit bureau that reported the inaccurate information. Each of the three major bureaus allows you to dispute information in your credit report on its Web site, or you can call the bureau's toll-free number (see "What Is a Credit Report, Anyway?" earlier in this chapter). If you make your dispute online, you need to have a copy of your credit report available; the report includes information that allows the bureau to confirm your identity without a signature. If you opt to call the toll-free number, you're unlikely to get a live person on the other end — this stuff is heavily automated — but you'll be told what information and documentation you need so that you can submit a written request. After you properly notify the credit bureau, you can count on action.

The Fair Credit Reporting Act (FCRA) requires credit-reporting agencies to investigate any disputed listings. The credit bureau must verify the item in question with the creditor *at no cost* to you, the consumer. The law requires that the creditor respond and verify the entry within 30 days, or the information must be removed from your credit report. The credit-reporting agency must notify you of the outcome. If information in the report has been changed or deleted, you also get a *free* copy of the revised report.

Contacting the creditor

The Fair and Accurate Credit Transactions Act (commonly referred to as the FACT Act or FACTA) covers another way to remove inaccurate information from your credit report. Under the provisions of the FACT Act, passed in 2003 and rolled out in pieces through 2005, you can deal directly with the creditor that reported the negative information in the first place. Contact information is shown on your latest billing statement from that creditor.

We strongly suggest that you do everything in writing, return-receipt requested. After you dispute the information, the reporting creditor must look into the matter and cannot continue to report the negative information while it's investigating your dispute.

For new delinquencies, the FACT Act requires that you be notified if negative information is reported to a credit bureau. That said, you may have to look closely to even see this new notice. Anyone who extends credit to you must send you a one-time notice either before or not later than 30 days after negative information — including late payments, missed payments, partial payments, or any other form of default — is furnished to a credit bureau. This stipulation also applies to collection agencies, as long as they report to a credit bureau. The notice may look something like this:

- ✓ **Before negative information is reported:** "We may report information about your account to credit bureaus. Late payments, missed payments, or other defaults on your account may be reflected in your credit report."

- ✓ **After negative information is reported:** "We have told a credit bureau about a late payment, missed payment, or other default on your account. This information may be reflected in your credit report."

The notice is not a substitute for your own close monitoring of your credit reports, bank accounts, and credit card statements.

Looking at the accurate information

Most of the information in your credit report likely is accurate. A popular misconception is that data stays on your credit report for seven years and then drops off. What really happens is that negative data stays on your credit report for seven years, although a few items remain longer, such as a Chapter 7 bankruptcy, which stays on your report for ten years. Even though the negative information is included for a long time, as the months and years roll by, it becomes less important to your credit profile. The fact that you were late in paying your credit card bill one time three years ago doesn't concern most creditors. Positive information, however — the good stuff everyone likes to see — stays on your report for a much longer time. Some positive data may be on your report for 10, 20, or even 30 years, depending on whether you keep your account open and depending on each bureau's policy.

Unscrupulous lenders may use negative information as a reason to put you into a higher-cost loan (and a more-profitable loan, for them), even though you qualify for a less-expensive one. This is just one example of a situation in which understanding your credit score can save you money. The scenario can go something like this: You're looking for a loan for a big-ticket item. Instead of going from bank to bank and wasting days of precious free time or risking being turned down after filling out long applications and explaining about the $5,000 your ex-boyfriend owes you, you go to a trusted financial advisor who knows how these things work. She pulls your credit report and shops for a loan for you. Your answer is that this is "a great deal considering your credit score." Translated, this answer means you're being charged a rate higher than the market rate because of your imperfect credit score. If you don't know what your score is and what rate that score entitles you to in the marketplace, you may be taken advantage of. So read on and get the skinny on credit scores, which have a big effect on your interest rates and terms.

Deciphering Your Credit Score

With billions of pieces of data floating around, it's little wonder that the people who use this data to make decisions turned to computers to help make sense of it all. Starting back in the 1950s, some companies, including one called Fair Isaac Corporation, began to model credit data in hopes of predicting payment behavior. (A *model* uses a series of formulas based on some basic assumptions to simulate and understand future behavior or to make predictions. Weather forecasters use models to predict your weather for tomorrow. Usually, the credit guys are more accurate because they're predicting the likelihood of something bad happening in the next year or so.) Until recently, the three major credit bureaus offered different scoring models that Fair Isaac, the developers of the *FICO score,* created for them. Each one called the score by a proprietary name. Now they also use an identical credit-scoring model called the VantageScore. Your credit score is a three-digit number that rules a good portion of your financial life, for better or worse.

You may have no credit score if you don't have enough of a credit history. Understanding what factors into your credit score is an important step in ensuring that yours is the best it can be. This section takes a closer look at the two main types of credit scores — FICO and VantageScore — and helps you understand what makes them up.

Fleshing out credit score components

For a score to be calculated, you need to have at least one account open and reporting for a period of time. In this category, the Vantage people have the current edge. They require that you have only one account open for at least 3 months, and that account must have been updated in the last 12 months. FICO requires you to have an account open (and updated) for at least six months. Although having no credit history makes it difficult for you to get credit initially, you'll find it a lot easier to build credit for the first time than to repair a bad credit history (which is like being down two runs in a ballgame and trying to catch up). In this section, we give you the skinny on both main types of scores.

The most widely used of these credit scores is the FICO score. Until recently, the proprietary formula for FICO scores was a well-guarded secret. Creditors were concerned that if you knew the formula, you may be tempted to manipulate the information to distort the outcome in your favor. Well, that may or may not be the case, but if creditors are looking for good behavior on your part, it only makes sense to tell you what constitutes good behavior. In 2001, Fair Isaac agreed with us, with a little help from some regulators, and disclosed the factors and weightings used to determine your credit score.

FICO scores range from 300 to 850. The higher the number, the better the credit rating. FICO takes into account more than 20 factors when building your score; the importance of each depends on the other factors, the volume of data, and the length of your history. Your FICO score consists of five components:

- ✔ **Paying on time (35 percent):** Payment history is considered the most significant factor when determining whether an individual is a good credit risk. This category includes the number and severity of any late payments, the amount past due, and whether the accounts were repaid as agreed. The more problems, the lower the score.

- ✔ **Amount and type of debt (30 percent):** The amount owed is the next-most-important factor in your credit score. This factor includes the total amount you owe, the amount you owe by account type (such as revolving, installment, or mortgage), the number of accounts on which you're carrying a balance, and the proportion of the credit lines used. For example, in the case of installment credit, *proportion of balance* refers to the amount remaining on the loan in relation to the original amount of the loan. For revolving debt, such as a credit card, this amount is what you currently owe in relation to your credit limit. You want a low balance amount owed in relation to your amount of credit available. Having credit cards with no balances ups your limits and your score.

- ✔ **The length of time you've been using credit (15 percent):** The number of years you've been using credit and the type of accounts you have also influence your score. Accounts that have been open for at least two years help to increase your score.

✔ **The variety of accounts (10 percent):** The mix of credit accounts is a part of each of the other factors. Riskier types of credit mean lower scores. For example, if most of your debt is in the form of revolving credit or finance-company loans, your score will be lower than if your debt is from student loans and mortgage loans. Also, the lender gives more weight to your performance on its type of loan. So a credit card issuer looks at your experience with other cards more closely, and a mortgagee pays closer attention to how you pay mortgages or secured loans. An ideal mix of accounts has many types of different credit used.

✔ **The number and types of accounts you've opened recently, generally in the last six months or so (10 percent):** The number of new credit applications you've filled out, any increases in credit lines that you requested (unsolicited ones don't count), and the types and number of new credit accounts you have affect your credit score. The reasoning is that if you're applying for several accounts at the same time and you're approved for them, you may not be able to afford your new debt load.

What constitutes a VantageScore?

A relatively new and up-and-coming entrant to the scoring field is the VantageScore. Vantage needs 3 months of history and an update in the last 12 months for a score. VantageScore's range is from 501 to 990. Your VantageScore is made up of six components:

✔ **Payment history (32 percent):** Again, payment history is the most significant factor when determining whether an individual is a good credit risk. Your history includes satisfactory, delinquent, and derogatory items.

✔ **Utilization (23 percent):** This factor refers to the percentage of your available credit that you have used or that you owe on accounts. Using a large proportion of your overall available credit has a negative effect.

✔ **Balances (15 percent):** This area includes the amount of recently reported current and delinquent balances. Balances that have increased recently can be an indication of risk and can lower your score.

✔ **Depth of credit (13 percent):** The length of history and types of credit used are included. A long history with mixed types of credit is best.

✔ **Recent credit (10 percent):** The number of recently opened credit accounts and all new inquiries are considered. New accounts initially lower your score because companies initially aren't sure why you want more credit. However, after you use the accounts and pay on time, they can help raise your score by adding positive information.

✔ **Available credit (7 percent):** This factor refers to the amount of available credit for all of your accounts. Using a low percentage of the total amount of credit available to you is a good.

If you're trying to build a credit history for the first time, you're an immigrant, or you're in the FBI's Witness Protection Program and you're looking for your first unsecured credit card in your new name, look for a lender that uses a VantageScore to grant credit after you have established a credit record. Examples of ways to start a credit history include using a secured card or using a passbook loan.

If you're too thin: The Expansion score

It used to be that if you didn't have much information in your credit file, known as a *thin file* in the business, you were in a pickle. Lenders had a more difficult time assessing your risk because they couldn't get a score for you. Well, thank heavens for Yankee ingenuity, because just as soon as a problem shows up, so does a solution.

FICO calls it an *Expansion score.* Essentially, it's a credit-risk score based upon nontraditional consumer credit data (in other words, it's not based on data from the three major national credit bureaus). The purpose of this new score is to predict the credit risk of consumers who don't have a traditional FICO score. The use of FICO Expansion scores gives millions of new consumers who don't have extensive credit histories an opportunity to access credit. This category includes the following people:

- ✔ Young people just entering the credit market
- ✔ New arrivals and immigrants to the United States
- ✔ People who previously had mostly joint credit and are now widowed or divorced
- ✔ People who've used cash instead of credit most or all of the time

Examining Specialized Credit Bureaus

The world of credit reports has the "big three" credit-reporting bureaus: Equifax, Experian, and TransUnion. But specialty credit-reporting bureaus, which are covered by the FCRA and the FACT Act, also exist. In fact, to allow for the large number and to allow for even more to come under the law, the Federal Trade Commission doesn't specifically name them as it does the big three — the list would be too long and would change frequently. Specialized credit bureaus report data about you in areas such as gambling, checking, medical, and insurance experience.

Exploring all these specialized bureaus would require a book of its own, but we do want to give you a sampling of what's out there. In the following sections, we fill you in on two types that are worth knowing about.

Getting to know national check registries

One of my favorite stories as a kid was the original 1932 *Tarzan, The Ape Man,* in which Tarzan goes to the elephant graveyard. The legend was that when elephants knew they were going to die, they all went to this big, secret graveyard to do it — and it was full of ivory! Well, where do checks go when they bounce? To the bounced-check graveyard, of course, and it must be full of rubber!

There are several repositories of information that cover your checking account activity. Two of the biggest are owned respectively by mega players First Data Corporation and Fidelity National Information Services. Both are major international information processors serving hundreds of thousands of retailers and financial institutions worldwide. They contain only *negative* information about your history — only bad news is reported to them. Each of these repositories has a database of information that its members, banks, retailers, and other subscribers use to help make decisions regarding the acceptance of checks or the opening of accounts. This information helps members reduce their financial losses from returned checks, improve customer service, and safeguard against identity theft and fraud. Here is contact information for two of them:

 ✔ **Chex Systems** (www.consumerdebit.com/consumerinfo/us/en/chexsystems/report/index.htm; 800-428-9623)
 ✔ **TeleCheck** (www.telecheck.com; 800-835-3243)

Maybe working with all that negative information has rubbed off on these companies, because they aren't as easy to deal with as the other relatively consumer-friendly credit bureaus. They're regulated under the FACT Act, so thanks to Uncle Sam you can get a free copy of your consumer report and dispute errors as you can with the other credit bureaus.

You can look at a sample report from ChexSystems online. Go to www.consumerdebit.com and, under Consumer Assistance, click Sample Consumer Report. Then, next to ChexSystems report, click View Sample.

Gambling with Central Credit Services

When you want credit, usually you want it now. Well, at least one credit grantor couldn't agree with you more! Every minute you go without credit can cost them money. Who are these guys? Why, they're none other than your friendly neighborhood casino or bingo parlor. And — what are the odds? — there's a credit-reporting agency just to serve their needs!

Getting credit casino style

The gaming industry is thrilled with Central Credit Services (CCS). And why not? In its own words, "Services from CCS help put more cash on the floor." Personally, we like cash in our pocket instead of on the floor.

Need a credit line of $10,000, $50,000, or maybe $1 million or more? Have a credit score of 300? Want the money fast, in cash, with no hassles, fees, or interest? How about 45 days, interest-free, to repay whatever you draw from the line of credit, with no strings attached? Oh, we almost forgot. How about dinner and a suite at the best hotel in town because you were such a good customer and borrowed a lot of money?

Sound like a lender's nightmare? Welcome to the world of Global Cash Access, the parent company of Central Credit Services and owner of the largest gaming-patron credit bureau database in the world. Every day thousands of gaming patrons make just such requests from casinos all over the United States and around the world. Instant financial reports on new and seasoned gamblers have to be available quickly, or the patron (the best patrons are sometimes affectionately call *whales*) will migrate to another casino.

Gamblers live in a culture of their own. It's no wonder they have a unique credit-granting system. Central Credit is the big Kahuna of what is called the gaming-patron credit database industry.

Making bets with markers

When a gambler needs cash at a casino, either he can go to an ATM and pay through the nose for a cash advance or he can stroll into the casino credit department and ask for a *marker.* The super-sophisticated modern gaming systems give you a card with a unique number — similar to what you get with your garden-variety ATM card — and the card ties into your file that contains your name, picture, birthdate, Social Security number, and *casino rating* (how much you bet, how long you play, and whether you win or lose) for that day and for your previous trips to the casino. Use this card at an automated cashier's window, and be sure to smile for the camera, because it may use face-matching technology to be sure you are who you're supposed to be.

A marker entitles you to interest-free chips or cash with very generous repayment provisions. Gamblers think only a chump would use an ATM or her own money when the free stuff is available and comes with oodles of customer service, freebies, and, yes, even that most elusive of commodities . . . respect! *Capisce?*

How does Central Credit Services do it? A worldwide network of casinos accumulates each patron's marker experience and makes it available in much the same way that creditors report your experience to the three credit-reporting bureaus. If you're late paying a marker, have too many markers outstanding at the same time, or have a derogatory notation (for example, you punched a dealer in the nose), it all gets tracked in the Central Credit database. This data, accumulated worldwide from casinos and gaming establishments, along with information from consumer credit bureaus and bank-reporting agencies, is entered into your patron record.

The stakes are high for both you and the casino. We're not talking about the lender losing out on a monthly 1 percent interest income ($500 on a $50,000 cash advance). We're talking about the whole $50,000 as potential income to the casino if you lose it all. These stakes are big numbers with big risks and big rewards. About 80 percent of a casino's profit comes from 20 percent of its customers. And these customers don't use credit cards — they use markers. So speed and accuracy in making underwriting decisions are critical to successfully doing business with some very particular people, whether you're in Vegas, the Bahamas, or Monte Carlo. In fact, the competition for business is so stiff and so profitable that to minimize the risk of a patron going next door to gamble, the goal is to offer the patron preapproved credit during the check-in process at the front desk. Now, that's what we call a welcome gift amenity!

You can contact Central Credit Services at its headquarters in — where else? — Las Vegas: 3525 East Post Road, Suite 120, Las Vegas, NV 89120; phone 702-855-3000 or 702-262-5000.

Book II

Managing Home and Personal Finances

"...and don't tell me I'm not being frugal enough. I hired a man last week to do nothing but clip coupons!"

In this book . . .

A man's home is his castle, and your castle, no matter how humble, is where you spend most of your time and money. They don't call them "kitchen table issues" for nothing. Earning money and spending it is something you can do casually and sloppily, paying the price one way or another for your negligence. Or it's something you can begin taking seriously. You'll likely be shocked at the amount you waste, as well as the amount you could be retaining rather than frittering away. That's where this book comes in: helping you find out how to better handle the everyday ins and outs of your money.

Here are the contents of Book II at a glance.

Chapter 1

Running a Money-Smart Household

So you've decided to become a frugal utility user and cut back a bit on your electricity, phone, and water use. Does that mean nothing but cold showers, dark rooms, and hot, miserable summers from here on out? No more warm, cozy winter nights? No more long-distance phone calls? No more evenings at home watching favorite movies? Hardly! Instead of living a Spartan life of shivers and shadows, pick a few ideas in this chapter to try.

Every little bit helps, and if you combine a number of these ideas, you just may see a substantial downward shift in your utility bills and fees for other monthly services, like cable and garbage pickup.

The first half of this chapter tackles cutting utility and service bills. The second half gives advice about saving on big-ticket items.

Reaching Out to Touch Someone

Do you have any "phone friends"? You know, those people who live too far away to see regularly in person, so your relationship stays alive through the wonders of the phone lines? Even though calling long distance can get expensive over time, it's still often much cheaper than the gas and time you would use to visit people. Email and traditional letter writing also help fill in some of the gaps created by long-distance relationships.

Saving on phone bills

Check your statement from the phone company and make sure you're not paying for extra services you never use or don't really need. If you have an answering machine, you probably don't need voicemail from the phone company. If you have a voicemail service but no answering machine, consider buying one. Purchasing your own machine is often considerably less expensive over a period of time than paying the monthly fees for the voicemail service.

Here are some other ways to save on your monthly phone bill:

- ✔ Check to see whether your phone company offers a flat rate or a measured service plan that can save you money based on how often you call or on the times and days you usually use the phone.

- ✔ Put off making long-distance calls until evenings and weekends, when rates are usually lower. If you make a lot of long-distance calls, check around for calling plans that suit the amount of calls you make.

- ✔ Try not to use operator assistance for placing long-distance calls unless absolutely necessary.

Using one of those access numbers you see advertised ("Call this number and your first 20 minutes are only 99 cents!") can save a lot of pennies if you're careful. Just talk until your 20 minutes are up, and if you're not done, the other party can call you back on the same plan.

Many companies charge the entire 99 cents even if you only reach an answering machine and hang up right away. Try calling first on your regular long-distance plan to see if the person you're calling is available (so you're charged for only 1 minute, not 20). Then hang up and call back immediately on the 99-cent plan.

Another way to reduce your phone bill if you call friends and family out of state regularly may be to get a cell phone. Some cell phone plans offer huge amounts of free long-distance calls.

Using email to stay in touch

As long as you don't have per-minute service charges connected with your email or Internet service, sending an email is free. And what's a better price than that? Some people have a home computer but don't want or need complete Internet access. If you're one of these people, you can get email-only services, often for free. Ask at your local computer store or talk to your friendly neighborhood computer geek for local ideas for free email-only services.

If money is really tight, sending an email greeting card from an online card company is much better than sending no greeting at all. (For a large collection of free email greeting cards and messages, go to www.bluemountain.com.)

Another way to save on the cost of a stamp or a long-distance call is to use online video-conferencing and instant-messaging services. You can also set up meeting times with family and friends in online chatrooms or message boards to exchange greetings.

Rediscovering the joys of letter writing

Letter writing seems to have become a relic of the past, as archaic as dinosaurs or Model Ts. But nothing can match the thrill of finding a hand-addressed envelope from a good friend or favorite family member in your mailbox. Sending cards and letters doesn't have to be much more expensive than the price of a first-class stamp if you watch for specials on stationery while you're shopping. You can often find beautiful note cards and stationery at garage sales and thrift stores for pennies. Dropping an inexpensive card or letter in the mail is still much cheaper than making an extended long-distance phone call or paying for Internet access.

If you don't have a long period of time to write a detailed letter to a friend, try carrying around a pad of stationery when you're out and about. Instead of being a source of frustration, a 15-minute wait in the doctor's reception area can be the start of a great letter. You can also use that time spent sitting in the van waiting for Junior to get out of school to keep in touch with far-flung family members.

Saving on Climate Control

The weather outside may be frightful, but your utility bills don't have to be. Whether it's warming the house in winter or cooling it in summer, you can put to use the helpful tips on temperature control in this section.

Dressing for the weather

Your first reaction to uncomfortable temperatures may be to run for the thermostat. An easier and more energy-efficient way to deal with the extremes of heat and cold is to dress appropriately. Wear light-colored, lightweight, breathable natural fabrics in summer. Spend your day in a T-shirt, shorts, and sandals. In the wintertime, wear woolen clothes or dress in layers, perhaps by adding a fleece vest. By trapping air between the layers, you're actually using your own body heat to keep warm. You'll also be amazed by what a difference a second warm pair of socks can make on a cold day.

Keeping your cool when the weather's not

If you can keep excess heat from entering your house in the first place, you've already won half the battle of trying to reduce your cooling bill. The primary source of heat inside a home during the hot summer months is sunlight absorbed through the roof, the walls, and the windows. Indoor appliances, especially in the kitchen and laundry room, give off heat, too.

Insulating yourself against the heat

If you want to drop your cooling — and heating — bills dramatically, add insulation to your home. First, insulate your attic floor. Then, when time and money allow, add insulation to your basement, exterior walls, floors, and crawl spaces (in that order). Insulation on the attic floor helps reduce the amount of heat absorbed through the roof and then through the ceiling of the house. Adequate ventilation under the eaves allows cooler air to enter and circulate. Install an exhaust fan in one of the attic windows (if you have them) to cut down on heat buildup under the roof. Even if you don't have a permanent exhaust fan installed in the upstairs window, you can set up a temporary box fan with the air flow pointed outward, to pull the hot air out of the house.

Shading your house from the sun

One of the coolest options of all is shade. Trees on the south side of the house are always a good investment, but if you're not planning to live in your home for a long period of time, you may not personally reap the shady benefits from planting a leafy friend. If your house isn't shaded by trees, install awnings over any windows that are exposed to direct sun during the day. Many awnings are removable and adjustable.

Filtering the sunshine: Covering your windows

Windows are a major source of unwanted heat during summer. Some easy ways to reduce the heat coming in through your windows include the following:

- Close the drapes during the hours of direct sunlight.

- Add reflective window tint to southern windows.

- Use bamboo window shades. By hanging old-fashioned bamboo shades on the outside of heat-producing windows, you create a bit of shade and a pocket of insulating air between the heat and the house. Bamboo shades are fairly inexpensive and are made to last in the elements for years. Look for them at garage sales. Shutters work well, too.

✔ Keep window coverings closed in unused rooms. If some bedrooms sit vacant all day, keep the curtains shut.

✔ Add reflective window curtain liners. Usually these liners have the reflective coating on only one side, so be sure to have the reflective side facing outward during the summer to keep the heat out of your house. Then during the winter, reverse them to reflect warmth back into the room.

Making efficient use of air conditioning and fans

An air conditioner can be the most expensive appliance in your home. Save a bit on the cost by implementing some of the following ideas:

✔ Turn up the thermostat a bit. If you normally have it set to 72 degrees during the summer, switch to 78 degrees. When it's 95 degrees in the shade outside, 78 degrees still feels comfortable and not too warm.

✔ Use fans to circulate air. Moving air feels several degrees cooler than still air. An overhead ceiling fan works well for cooling the whole room, but even a small box fan or oscillating fan keeps the air moving.

✔ At the end of the day, when the temperature outside cools down, turn off the air conditioning, open the windows, and place an outward-facing fan in a window to vent the hot air from the house. A vent fan in an upstairs window works best. Opening a downstairs window at the same time allows a full cross-breeze to develop throughout your home. The fan cools your house in a fraction of the time it takes to only open the windows and let the hot air sit in the house. Open the windows only if humidity is low, however. Otherwise, the air conditioner will have to work much harder to cool the humid air when you turn it back on.

Reducing the creation of inside heat

The first line of attack in reducing your cooling bills is to keep the heat *outside* your home, but reducing the heat you create inside your home is also important:

✔ Use your outdoor grill more often, to keep from heating up the kitchen.

✔ Use small appliances instead of the stove and oven for cooking. The microwave, slow cooker, electric skillet, and toaster oven give off less heat and are more energy efficient than the range.

✔ Dry clothes in the dryer on the no-heat setting. Add a clean, dry towel to the dryer load to help absorb extra moisture from your clothes.

✔ Hang your washed clothing on a clothesline in the backyard or on the porch. You can find retractable clotheslines that fit in almost any small space. Or simply put your clothes on hangers and hang them over the shower curtain rod or on a line in the laundry room.

✔ Use the no-heat drying cycle on the dishwasher. Don't open the door after the rinse cycle; you'll just add steam and more heat to the house.

✔ Take short showers to avoid a buildup of steam. Use the exhaust fans in the bathroom during the summer.

✔ Darker colors absorb more heat, so if the outside walls of your house are dark, consider painting the house a lighter color. Light-colored curtains reflect more heat back out of your house, too.

Warming the house

It never seems to fail: Opposites attract. Some people love the brisk air and like to see their breath in the house. "It's so invigorating!" Meanwhile, their partners sit huddled with four blankets and a down parka near a roaring fire. "Brrrr . . . turn up the heat!" Well, you can both be happy and still save money on your heating bills by following the hints in this section.

Staying warm without turning up the heat

The simplest way to save money on heating is to turn down your furnace a couple degrees. During the winter months, if you usually keep your thermostat set at 72 degrees, turn it down to 70. If you're used to 70-degree temperatures, turn the thermostat down to 68. Lower the temperature of your thermostat even further at night for when you're sleeping. Toss on an extra blanket if you're still a bit chilled. To keep your furnace running efficiently, have it inspected regularly and change the filters monthly during heavy use.

Consider these other ways to stay warm without running up your heating bill:

✔ If you heat with a wood-burning stove or fireplace insert, make friends with a builder. Builders often pay people to haul away the scraps of lumber around construction sites — they can be a great source for free firewood if you don't mind a bit of work to collect it yourself.

✔ Close off the vents and doors in rooms that aren't in use for long periods of time.

✔ A ceiling fan set to push air down into the room keeps the warm air circulating to the lower regions of the house.

✔ Add some steam to the air of your house. Higher humidity keeps the air warmer. Let steamy air from the bathroom escape into the rest of the house after a shower. Boil water on the stovetop. Keep a kettle or pan full of water on top of your wood-burning stove or radiator.

Insulating against drafts

New houses are often built with energy-efficient features such as thermal-paned windows, well-insulated walls, and energy-efficient water heaters and furnaces. If you aren't in the process of having a new house built with all the energy-efficient bells and whistles, consider using some of the following ideas to increase the benefits of your home's current heating system.

Book II

Managing Home and Personal Finances

- ✔ Add a layer of air between your windows and the great outdoors (the air insulates much better than the window glass alone). If you have storm windows, use them. You can also buy special sheets of plastic to stretch across the inside of your window frames.

- ✔ Use heavy curtains in the winter, or buy reflective curtain liners.

- ✔ After dark, hang blankets or quilts in front of the windows for added insulation. Install a decorative towel bar or curtain rod over your existing window treatment and simply fold a blanket or quilt over it.

- ✔ Open your curtains during daylight hours, especially on southern windows, for a bit of passive solar heating.

- ✔ Use weatherstripping or caulk around doorways and window frames. We've heard an estimate that, when all the various cracks and spots that lose heat in the average house are added together, they would equal a 2- or 3-foot square hole in the outside wall of your house.

- ✔ Use a draft stopper at the bottom of outside doors. You can make one yourself, buy one inexpensively, or even just roll up a bathroom towel and place it along the bottom of the door.

- ✔ Fill electric switch plates on outside walls with plastic foam, or purchase plastic insulation that's already cut to size and made for this purpose.

- ✔ Close the flue on your fireplace when you're not using it. Leaving a fireplace flue open is like having a vacuum hose hooked to your living room, sucking all the warm air right up the chimney.

Cozying up

Even if you're trying to save money on heating costs, you don't need to sit and shiver when the weather cools. Consider these simple ideas for staying cozy and warm this winter.

- ✔ Use a hot water bottle in bed. You can even use a 2-liter bottle filled with warm (never hot!) water; just tape the lid shut to prevent leaks.

- ✔ Use cotton flannel sheets during the winter.

✔ Keep a blanket or two as throws on the couch for snuggling when it's cold. Instead of running to the thermostat, grab a blanket.

✔ Happiness is a warm friend. Snuggle up on the couch and read a good book with your kids, your spouse, the dog, or a warm kitten. Sharing body heat really does keep you warmer.

Cutting Back on Electricity and Gas Use

Saving money on electricity and gas utilities can be as easy as making a few minor adjustments in your day-to-day life. Every penny and dime saved adds up to a considerable amount of money day after day. When combined, the following tips can help cut your electricity and gas use considerably:

✔ Wash clothes in cold water. The majority of electricity used for washing clothes is used to heat the water. Save hot-water washes for white towels, socks, and undergarments.

✔ Wash only full loads in the washing machine and dishwasher.

✔ Nuke it. Heating a cup of water in the microwave uses less energy than using the stovetop. When you're boiling water on the stove, always keep the pot covered because water boils much faster. Or use a teakettle. Don't boil more water than you actually need.

✔ Keep indoor lights off during the daytime. Position your desk near a window for adequate lighting.

✔ Turn off your computer, printer, scanner, monitor, and any other office equipment at night. Even when they're turned off, a lot of devices use electricity. Plug devices into power strips that you can flip off easily.

✔ Find out whether your local energy provider has off-peak hours when electricity use is less expensive. If so, do your laundry and run the dishwasher accordingly.

✔ Many power companies allow users to pro-rate their bills, paying a flat rate every month of the year instead of racking up really high energy bills in the heat of the summer and dead of winter. If the total energy use is higher or lower than the amount paid over the course of the year, the extra amount is charged or refunded accordingly the next year.

✔ Put a timer on your water heater so it runs for only four hours each day during peak times (for morning showers, evening dishes, and bath times).

✔ Use a programmable thermostat that you can set for different temperatures at different hours. This strategy costs a bit upfront, but you can
quickly recoup any money spent by not overheating the house all day
while the family is at work and school, or at night while everyone is
sleeping.

✔ If you have a heated waterbed, keep the bed made when you're not in it.
The blankets and bedspread help to insulate it.

Improving your appliance efficiency

Older refrigerators, freezers, and air conditioners are often inefficient and
sometimes run constantly, needlessly draining electricity and money. Buying
a newer appliance is often more economical than using an old one over a long
period of time. But if you're planning to move soon and won't be taking the
appliance with you, replacing it probably isn't worthwhile financially.

If you're in the market for a new major appliance, check the energy ratings.
Purchasing a slightly more-expensive but energy-efficient refrigerator or
washing machine can save you hundreds of dollars in energy bills over its
life.

Refrigerators and freezers work better if they're full. Fill the empty spaces
with clean milk jugs filled with water. Not only will your freezer run more
efficiently, but the ice-filled jugs will keep your freezer cold during a power
outage. You can also use the water for drinking in an emergency situation.

Consider these other ways to use your appliances efficiently:

✔ Clean the coils of the fridge regularly so the cooling mechanism can run
more efficiently.

✔ Whenever you open the refrigerator or freezer, always close it again as
quickly as possible.

✔ Gas stovetops heat up instantly, so they don't have to run as long.

✔ Use a water-heater insulation blanket and keep the water heater's temperature set at 120 degrees.

✔ Keep your dryer lint-free. A full lint trap doesn't allow the moist air to
escape properly, which slows the drying cycle.

✔ Have your air conditioner inspected and serviced every spring.

✔ If you have a window unit air conditioner, run a fan in the room at the
same time. The moving air makes the room feel cooler so that you don't
have to set the air conditioner thermostat so low.

Shedding some light on the subject

After appliances and heating, indoor and outdoor lighting is one of the biggest electricity users in an average home. By cutting down on the number of light bulbs turned on at any one time, you save substantially on your electric bills.

You can implement these easy tips for lighting-related savings:

- ✔ If you have outdoor lighting for safety reasons, install motion detectors on the lights. Limit outside lighting to the minimum required for safety.

- ✔ Replace frequently used light bulbs with fluorescent bulbs. They're a bit more expensive to buy, but they often last up to ten times longer.

- ✔ Use sunlight for indoor lighting as much as possible.

Trash Talk: Controlling Garbage Costs

Probably the best way to save money on garbage pickup and trips to the landfill is to limit the amount of garbage brought into the home. Remember the three Rs of the antitrash mantra: reduce, reuse, recycle. You can reduce the frequency of your garbage pickup, or at least the size of the container, if you reduce the amount of garbage created in your home.

Reducing what you throw away

Simple decisions such as using cloth grocery bags instead of disposable paper or plastic bags, or choosing items based on whether you can recycle the packaging can make a world of difference in your home garbage situation.

Avoiding trash by "precycling"

One method of cutting back on garbage production is referred to as "precycling." Precyclers choose which items to buy based on packaging. For example, someone who has a precycler mindset doesn't buy cereal that's packaged in a plastic bag inside a cardboard box. They skip that extra layer of potential garbage and go for the cereal that comes only in a plastic bag. The cereal in just the plastic bags is often less expensive, too.

Recycling items like paper, cardboard, plastic soda bottles, milk jugs, aluminum cans, and glass jars, and composting kitchen and garden scraps can reduce your garbage to a fraction of what it was before. Even a simple act like purchasing reusable lunchboxes cuts down on the need to throw away paper bags. And reuse plastic containers to store your food instead of using and throwing away single-use plastic wrap and foil. Avoid obviously disposable items such as paper plates, plastic utensils, plastic coffee cups, and plastic diapers. Look for the rechargeable (batteries, for example) and the refillable (such as printer cartridges).

Recycling to save money and reduce waste

Recycling not only saves money, but it has the added benefit of saving the environment. Buying items that are already recycled — and can be recycled again — helps the environment even more.

Having a compost pile in the backyard is one of the best ways to recycle assorted vegetable scraps. Just save all your trimmings and discards from salads and veggies, toss them on the old compost heap, and use the home-made compost to grow more fresh salads and veggies.

Reusing household items in creative ways

You can give many everyday trash items a new lease on life by creatively reusing the items in the home or office. Here are few easy examples:

- Use the backs of old envelopes for writing your shopping lists. You can even slip coupons right into the envelope before you leave the house.

- Cut cereal boxes to size to use for photo mailers.

- Cut off the fronts of old holiday cards and make them into holiday post-cards. You save on postage and on the price of new cards.

- Instead of grabbing a paper towel next time you spill something or need to dust, keep a supply of scraps of old T-shirts and other clothes. If someone else can still use an article of clothing, donate it to charity; if it has stains or holes, it's a prime candidate for a household rag.

- If you get plastic grocery bags at the supermarket, don't just throw them away. You can reuse plastic grocery bags in a multitude of simple ways:

  - Pack your lunch.

  - Use them as garbage bags for the trash can.

  - Wrap dirty cloth diapers in a plastic bag when you're out and about.

- Put dirty laundry in bags when traveling.

- Store shoes in bags to keep them separate from clothes in suitcases and travel bags.

- Wrap smelly garbage and bloody meat wrappers in plastic bags before putting in the trash.

Reducing Television and Cable Expenses

Getting rid of cable television can save substantially on your yearly household expenses. If you figure that your cable costs you $25 per month on the low end, you're paying a bare minimum of $300 per year, and if you add premium channels, you can spend more than $80 per month.

If cable television is absolutely essential to your life, the best way to save money is to stick with the bare-bones basic package. This package usually includes the major networks, public broadcasting, assorted educational channels, and a handful of others. It usually doesn't include many of the children's cartoon channels, however. Basic analog cable seems to run $10 to $15 per month throughout the United States, compared to more than $50 per month for expanded cable. You save at least a couple hundred dollars per year. With a fraction of that amount, you can rent all the movies you really want to see — or, better yet, borrow them from your library.

Cutting Down on Water Use

Conserving water does save money, so consider a few easy, less-extreme ideas for cutting back on water use around the house:

- ✔ Take short showers and shallow baths. Set a timer for three minutes and get in, get soaped, and get back out before it dings at you.

- ✔ Turn off the water while brushing your teeth or shaving.

- ✔ Rinse fresh vegetables in a sink or pan of standing water instead of under running water from the faucet.

- ✔ Reduce the amount of water used per flush by placing a tall plastic bottle filled (and sealed!) with sand or rocks in the back of the toilet tank. By displacing some of the water in the tank, you use less water each flush.

- ✔ Run the washing machine and dishwasher only with full loads. If you do wash dishes by hand, don't let the rinse water run while you're scrubbing the dishes. Either save all your soapy dishes to be rinsed at once, or use a dishpan of clear water for dipping and rinsing.

✔ Install low-flow showerheads.

✔ Keep a bottle or pitcher of water in the refrigerator to keep it cold. You waste gallons of water running the tap until the water gets cold. To chill tap water quickly, add ice to your glass before you fill it with tap water. Just don't let the faucet run needlessly.

✔ Fix leaky faucets and running toilets as soon as they occur. These problems can waste gallons of water each day.

✔ Sweep the driveway and walkways instead of spraying them clean with the water hose.

✔ Water lawns and gardens in the evening or early morning to minimize evaporation.

✔ Avoid using the garbage disposal. Disposals use a lot of water each time they're turned on, so try to recycle or compost your kitchen waste instead. When you do use the garbage disposal, run cold water only.

✔ Use the water-saving settings on your washing machine, if applicable.

✔ Don't use the toilet as a wastebasket. If you pick up a wad of stray hair or a bit of paper from the floor or carpet, put it in the trash.

Book II

Managing Home and Personal Finances

Keeping a Ceiling on Housing Budgets

Housing and transportation are two of life's biggest budget-busters. But you can find simple ways to keep your car from taking you to the cleaners and to keep your rent or mortgage payments from eating you out of house and home. You can also save money on appliances, other big budget-busters.

Saving money on rent

Renting has several advantages over owning a home:

✔ Renting give you the freedom to move, if needed.

✔ Renting doesn't saddle you with unexpected repair bills and general upkeep expenses.

✔ Rent in many apartment complexes also includes free use of an on-site gym, pool, and sauna, saving the cost of a membership at the local gym.

✔ Renting doesn't require yearly property taxes.

✔ Rent of an apartment or condominium often includes the cost of some utilities, so you don't have additional cable, water, or garbage bills to pay. The included utilities are also set at a flat rate.

✔ Renting an apartment usually doesn't involve any yard or grounds maintenance costs (unless you're renting a house).

✔ Renting may entitle you to a discount if you don't receive something you've paid for. For example, if your air conditioner doesn't work for a week, or you have to eat out a couple of days while a defective stove is replaced, the property manager may reimburse you for some of the rent you've paid that month.

✔ Renting requires a small upfront investment, compared to a house down payment. If you don't have enough money put together for the first and last month's rent and the usual damage deposit, check around. Some apartment complexes offer the first month free for new renters or don't require a deposit if you move in by a certain date.

One way to save money on rent, and maybe even qualify for free rent, is to become a property manager for an apartment complex. A property manager shows vacant apartments to prospective renters and oversees the general maintenance of the property. Many times managers take care of the on-site office work, as well. Look in the classified ads for apartment manager listings.

Saving money on home ownership

Often rental costs are nearly as much as — if not more than — the cost of monthly mortgage payments. The cost of the mortgage may actually be lower than you think when you take into account the tax deductions you receive when you itemize your tax return. For more information on buying a home, read *Home Buying For Dummies,* by Eric Tyson and Ray Brown (Wiley).

Keep in mind the risk of *house poverty* — when your house and the related expenses (mortgage payments, taxes, insurance, home and yard maintenance, and so on) swallow all your expendable income. You may have a nice house but not much of anything else to show for your hard-earned money.

If you make the big decision to buy a house, be sure to buy within your means. You want balance in your life, not just a bigger house. An occasional vacation, money for education, a fun evening out with your spouse or friends, furniture, a retirement account — these considerations can end up by the wayside if you buy more house than you can reasonably afford. Be careful when you're house hunting. Real-estate agents and lenders often try to convince you to buy as much house as possible, but they obviously have a vested interest in seeing you spend more of your money. The more money you spend on a house, the more money ends up in their pockets.

Don't assume that just because you don't have much money set aside for a down payment, you aren't eligible to buy a home. Ask a real estate agent about home-buying programs available in your area that allow a smaller down payment. These programs are more common for first-time home buyers. Several options also exist for low-income buyers, so don't let a lower income scare you away from looking into buying options. Ask conventional lenders whether they offer mortgages with low down payments combined with programs like Fannie Mae or Freddie Mac, or other governmental or nonprofit agencies.

A new, traditionally built home is sometimes out of reach for the frugal person who wants to become a homeowner. But if you're willing to investigate options like older fixer-upper houses or alternative homes (such as mobiles and prefabricated homes), you may find that home ownership is a real possibility after all.

Few home buyers are really in the market for fixer-uppers, or houses that need work. Most people want to move right in and enjoy the benefits of their new house without immediately needing to dive in with repairs and elbow grease. But if you want to own your own house and you're willing to do a little work, a fixer-upper can be just the ticket you've been looking for. The competition for these homes is low, giving you time to assess whether the amount of work needed is worth the overall savings.

The ideal fixer-upper requires minimum work, has been on the market for some time, and is being sold at a substantial savings. You can often find fixer-uppers that have been on the market for six months to a year and are being sold for 20 to 30 percent off the market price. Sometimes just a fresh coat of paint, some new windows, or aluminum siding can make a forlorn home dynamite. An older home with avocado green appliances, gold carpets, chipped paint, and out-of-date flooring can be a real eyesore, but if you look beyond the surface, you may find that cosmetic problems can be easy and cheap to fix.

Major renovations like a new roof or foundation repairs are expensive and don't usually give a good return on the monetary investment when you resell. If you're thinking of eventually reselling the fixer-upper for a profit, the most profitable repairs are the simple ones — like adding new wall-to-wall carpeting, painting the house inside and out, replacing kitchen cabinet doors, landscaping, adding new lighting fixtures, and installing up-to-date appliances (new refrigerator, range, dishwasher, and built-in microwave oven).

Always have a fixer-upper carefully inspected before you sign on the dotted line.

Book II

Managing Home and Personal Finances

Fixing up a house to finance a dream

We spoke with a woman who put together the money to buy her family's dream home by buying and fixing up two small houses that needed a great deal of love, care, and elbow grease (*sweat equity*). Four years after buying the two small houses, she sold them for a sizeable profit and had the down payment for her family's dream home on 5 acres of land — a home they never plan to leave. There are definite risks to this strategy, however, particularly in a market where both prices and sales are declining. If you're interested in fixing up and selling an older home, consider selling the house yourself, saving thousands of dollars in commission fees for a real estate agent. If you don't know how to sell your home, take a class. Spending $200 on a "for-sale-by-owner" seminar is a lot cheaper than paying $12,000 (or more!) in commission to an agent.

Another option for low-cost home ownership is to look into manufactured housing. Prefabs (modular homes that are put together on your building site) and mobile homes aren't necessarily the big metal boxes of days gone by. Many people think they have to live in a crowded mobile home park if they own a mobile home, but many areas allow you to install a mobile home on private property, and prefabs usually have the same building codes and requirements as any site-built home. The combined monthly payments for the property and a mobile home or prefab are usually significantly less than the payments on traditionally built houses. The resale value and appreciation benefits may not be as great with mobile homes, but if you're just looking for a roof over your head and not a future investment, consider a mobile home. Also, if you've always dreamed of owning acreage, buying a mobile home and putting it down on several acres can be just the answer for affording your dream come true. Check with your local city hall about zoning laws for mobile homes. The resale and appreciation on modular homes is the same as for site-built homes.

 You can also buy a used mobile home — still in good condition — for a fraction of what you'd pay for other living arrangements. You definitely want to look into this option if money is tight. Used mobile homes can be found in the classified ads or through mobile home dealers that sell new and used mobile homes.

Interest rates fluctuate over time, so you may find yourself paying a much higher interest rate than the current market rate. Look into refinancing your home loan at the lower rate, potentially knocking down your monthly payment considerably. Talk to your bank or lender for details.

Taking care of others' property

Property owners are increasingly hiring caretakers to watch over their land and property for them. Often the caretaker lives on the property rent free in exchange. Many national and state parks, nature preserves, national forests, and campgrounds employ caretakers. This type of job may be perfect for you if you have a recreational vehicle and like to use it. For example, you can live in an RV while working as a caretaker at a state campground or park. Keep in mind that although some of these positions are actually paid jobs that offer health insurance, regular wages, and other benefits, many are staffed by volunteers.

Some farmers need help working their fields. In exchange for your work, you receive a place to live and a portion of the profits. During the off season, many resorts and seasonal parks need caretakers. That beautiful mountain lake resort you love is empty during the rainy season and needs someone to keep an eye on it. It's still beautiful, and you'd have the place all to yourself.

Are you qualified to be a caretaker? It depends. Some individual landowners needing caretakers look for candidates with carpentry and groundkeeping skills. Some owners just want someone to stay on their property and give it a "lived in" appearance instead of letting it sit vacant for a long period of time. *The Caretaker Gazette* offers information on caretaking opportunities; visit www.caretaker.org.

Book II

Managing Home and Personal Finances

Cutting Transportation Costs

For most of us in the 21st century, transportation has progressed a long way from the horse and buggy, which is good . . . most of the time. But when a car payment can be higher than a mortgage and the cost of gasoline can outpace your commuting budgets, you may want to think twice about the sanctity of the family car. Do you have other options? More frugal alternatives? Ways to afford more car for less money? Yep. Read on!

Finding a deal on a set of wheels

Unless you live in the city on an excellent bus line, you'll need a vehicle at some point in your life. But paying $400 a month on a car payment isn't necessary if you follow some of the simple ideas in this section. For detailed help in buying a car, whether new or used, be sure to read *Buying a Car For Dummies,* by Deanna Sclar (Wiley).

Paying up front or lowering monthly payments

Many people think monthly car payments are a fact of life, like bad hair days and taxes. But the alternative, owning a car outright with no payments at all, can reduce a family's monthly expenses by several hundred dollars.

Most people today choose to take out a loan for a car, but you can save on your car loan by purchasing an older vehicle or one with fewer extras. You can carve as much as $100 a month off your monthly car payment simply by making a combination of frugal choices such as buying a new car with crank windows instead of power windows, choosing vinyl seats rather than leather, and forgoing a fancy built-in radio. Most of those choices need to be specially ordered, however. You're not going to find a bare-bones model of new cars on the lot. By choosing less-expensive options, basically, you're paying yourself $100 a month to roll down the windows and shift gears. That breaks down to about $3.35 a day — enough to treat your family to a DVD rental, a round of colas, a new puzzle, or a rented video game.

Finding a deal on a new-to-you set of wheels

An obvious alternative to buying a new car is to buy a used car. Doing so can save you quite a bit of money.

The moment you drive a brand-spanking-new vehicle off the car lot, it becomes a used car and begins to depreciate rapidly and drastically. Why not pay thousands of dollars *less* for a used car instead of top dollar for a soon-to-be-used car?

Also, consider carefully the type of car you're buying. You can buy a wide range of car models for the same price, but the insurance rates for those cars can vary significantly. Cars with higher safety ratings insure for less. But if you want the snazzy red sports car, be prepared to pay through the nose to insure it! See later in this chapter for additional ways to save on car insurance.

If you're thinking of buying a used car, check back issues of *Consumer Reports*'s annual auto report at the library. You can also search online for used cars in the price range and locality you need. You can get a general feel for what's available in your price range. For a good place to start, check out www.autotrader.com. Get the word out to friends, neighbors, and coworkers when you're in need of another car.

If you buy a car from an individual or even a dealer, pay the $30 or so to have a mechanic check it out before you sign the papers. A friend of ours learned this lesson the hard way. She bought a great-looking Cadillac a couple years ago for $2,500 and had an $800 repair bill within two weeks. But the car still wasn't fixed, so she decided to cut her losses and trade it in at a dealership. The car needed a new engine; the dealer gave her $1,200 for it. So a month after purchasing her "great deal," she found herself recovering from a financial bloodbath that she could have avoided if she'd simply taken it to a mechanic before she bought it.

Another good idea when you're considering a used car is to view the car's history report online. (You can get a report for $10–$20 at `www.carfax.com`.) You can tell whether the car has ever been in an accident, how many owners it has had, and whether it has been a rental or fleet car.

Other excellent resources for used cars include the following:

- **Rental car companies:** They have to clear out their entire inventory regularly, and even though the cars are used (sometimes heavily used), rental cars often get a higher level of continuous maintenance through-out their lives than most cars owned by private individuals. Call and find out when your local rental car businesses are holding sales of their out-of-service fleets.

- **Auctions:** Check various local classified advertisement listings for auctions. Many cars at auctions either have been repossessed, have been confiscated by the police, or are trade-ins from car dealerships.

- **Dealer repossession sales:** These sales provide reasonably good cars at less-than-market prices.

Saving on car insurance

Shop around. Rates are always higher for young, unmarried drivers compared to rates for people over age 25, but the rates from one carrier to another can vary widely. Call around and give each insurance company you talk to the same details: the amount of coverage you want, the deductible you're willing to pay, your age (or the age of the driver, if you're giving this information for your kids), the type of car, and the average amount of driving you do. Many states require comprehensive insurance on mortgaged vehicles, but switching to only liability insurance after the car is paid off can save you hundred of dollars each year.

Using public transportation

If you live in the country, chances are good that public transportation isn't great. But most people in moderate-sized communities and large cities have access to several transportation options other than their own private vehicle.

The wheels on the bus go 'round and 'round

A monthly bus pass easily pays for itself if you live and work near a local route. Buses usually offer low rates, discounts for multiple rides, and convenient locations near business and office centers. Commuting on the bus can be a relaxing way to catch up on reading or just sit back and watch the scenery go by without worrying about driving.

Bus passes for teens also provide some much-desired independence for the teens and cut down on Mom and Dad's Taxi Service.

Catching a ride on the subway or commuter train

Larger cities like Chicago and New York have additional public transportation options, like the subway or commuter train. Both of these alternatives offer the same benefits of bus systems. You've probably heard scary stories about subway systems, but most of them are quite safe if you use common sense. Riding a New York subway alone at two o'clock in the morning may not be the wisest course of action, but most commuters aren't riding the subway home at that time of night anyway.

Biking and walking

Many people are willing to pay high prices for a workout at the health club, but few consider simply biking or walking to work or school. You can also save on parking fees if you usually pay to park your car near your office.

An inexpensive saddlebag for bicycles can probably hold anything you need to transport back and forth. You can find auctions for new and used bicycle saddlebags at www.ebay.com. Search for "bicycle saddlebags" or "panniers." If you're walking to work or school, invest in a comfortable backpack. Keep a change of shoes in the pack so you don't walk in your dress shoes to work. If your work attire isn't conducive to biking or walking, bring a change of clothes and use the company washroom to freshen up before work.

Finding bargains on airfare and rental cars

Although extremely frugal people probably cringe at the expense of traveling by plane, air travel is often a fact of life. If you own your own business and have frequent travel obligations or you need to travel across the country to visit a sick relative, finding bargain transportation options is important. To get the best deals on airfare, keep these helpful hints in mind:

- ✔ Plan ahead. Reserve your flight as soon as you set your travel plans.

- ✔ Check online search engines such as www.expedia.com, www.orbitz.com, and www.travelocity.com for cheap flights. Be sure to compare the search prices to what the airlines are offering directly.

✔ Purchase electronic tickets (e-tickets) instead of paper tickets. If you lose a paper ticket, you're out of luck and have to buy a new one. With e-tickets, the airline can print you a new ticket.

✔ Consider bidding for tickets online. You can save a lot of money on major airlines. Check out `www.priceline.com`.

✔ When searching for price quotes, be sure to vary the details of your trip: time, day, airline, and airport. Sometimes altering your destination slightly by landing in a neighboring city, flying at night instead of the morning, or returning on Sunday can reduce airfares considerably. If your travel plans are flexible, watch for price wars between airlines.

Consider using a travel agent if your trip will include airfare and accommodations. Travel agents are experts at ferreting out the best package deals.

The rates for renting a car vary and depend on factors like the size and make of car (ask which model is cheapest), how long you need the car, how far you're driving, and whether you need to buy additional insurance. Be sure to find out whether it's cheaper to pick up your car at the airport or at some other location at your destination. You may save money by taking an airport shuttle to your hotel and picking up a rental car there. You don't know unless you ask. Also, when you call to reserve your rental, ask if they have any special promotional rates. Sometimes car rental agencies have lower rates on weekends or a special rate if you rent the car for a full week instead of just for a few days.

Check to see how much the car rental agency charges you per gallon if you bring the car back without filling up the tank. You usually save more than a few cents if you top off the tank at a local gas station before you return the car. Avoid the "buy a full tank upfront and bring it back empty option" most rental car companies offer these days. It's almost never a good deal. If you leave even one or two gallons in the tank, that usually offsets the discounted price they're selling you the gas for.

If you're a member of a frequent-flier program, you may get some special car rental discounts. You also may be eligible for discounts if you're a senior citizen or a member of AARP or AAA. Be sure to ask. If you're buying a package deal that includes airfare and accommodations, ask if a car rental can be included (and be sure to find out how much it will add). Some travel packages include unlimited car rental for free or for a greatly reduced price.

You can often find discounted car rental prices online at `www.orbitz.com`.

Opting to travel by train or bus

Before you commit to long-distance air travel, compare the cost of airfare to the cost of a bus or train ticket. Sometimes (but not always) you can find great deals on bus and train fare if you have extra time to spend reaching your destination. If you don't have far to travel, taking the bus can be a really good idea. But comparison-shop; don't assume that the bus is always cheaper. The same goes for train travel. A friend of ours decided to take a train from Seattle to Southern California, thinking that a train trip would be less expensive than flying. She was surprised to discover that flying was considerably less expensive.

Purchasing Appliances

Take your time making a decision about any major appliances you need to purchase. Even if your stove has broken down completely or the washing machine is beyond repair, don't make snap decisions. You can cook for a few days in the slow cooker or microwave, and you can always go to the all-night laundrette down the street if you're facing a dirty clothes emergency. Taking your time to shop around and look for good-quality secondhand appliances can save a lot of money if you're patient and don't make a hasty decision.

Keeping energy efficiency in mind

If you're in the market for an appliance (whether you buy it new or used), consider buying one that's more economical to use. For example, in many parts of the United States, the cost of electricity has far outpaced the cost of natural gas. Consider switching to a gas clothes dryer.

Some utilities give rebates to customers who purchase energy-efficient models of major appliances. Check whether any programs exist in your area before you buy. The rebate may mean the difference between buying just a standard washer and being able to afford a top-of-the-line energy-efficient model.

Used appliances are often not very energy efficient. Sometimes the increased cost per month on your utility bill from an older appliance can be more than the monthly payments on a new, more-efficient model. Check around to see if you can find the details about the energy efficiency of an older appliance you're considering buying. Often you can find a label on the appliance itself or information on the manufacturer's Web site. Figure out the energy efficiency of an appliance at www.eren.doe.gov/consumerinfo/refbriefs/ec7.html.

Shopping for scratch-and-dent and secondhand

You can find slightly used appliances for a fraction of the cost of new appliances by shopping the following locations:

- ✔ **Outlet, clearance, or warehouse stores:** Slightly damaged appliances (external scratches or small dents) are sometimes sold for a substantial discount compared to new, undamaged items. Call around to large stores and ask what they do with their scratch-and-dent merchandise.

- ✔ **Furniture rental stores:** You can find good deals on returns from furniture rental stores. The appliances are used, but usually haven't been used long.

- ✔ **Used appliance stores:** You can find reconditioned appliances that often come with warranties.

- ✔ **Auctions:** You can get really rock-bottom prices on good appliances at auctions. But remember, go early because the good items go quickly.

- ✔ **Family or neighbors:** Ask around. Get the word out that you're in need of a washer/dryer or freezer. Someone you talk to may have neighbors or family members who are updating their kitchen or moving out of state.

Thinking twice about renting-to-own

Ever see those rent-to-own ads on TV for complete furniture suites or big-screen television sets? Renting-to-own usually appeals to people who have a limited budget but are in need of some basics, like a living room couch or a washer and dryer. If you're renting to own an appliance, the store usually includes all repair work as part of the rental agreement.

The credit checks for rent-to-own businesses are usually minimal or nonexistent. If you stop making payments for some reason, the dealer simply takes back the appliance or piece of furniture.

By the time you've rented your rent-to-own appliance to the point of outright ownership, you've probably paid two to five times the retail price of your appliance. If you're short on upfront cash or need to build a credit rating, renting-to-own may be a good idea. But please note the word *may*.

Chapter 2

Home Ownership and Choosing the Right Mortgage

For many, the American Dream isn't complete until we have purchased our own home. Though the definition of a *home* can vary considerably — from a studio condominium apartment in a big city, to a neat-and-tidy single-story rambler in the suburbs, to a rustic log cabin nestled by a lake or high up in the mountains — owning a home is a key life goal for most people, and most of us will eventually own one during the course of our lives.

However, despite the recent bursting of the housing bubble and resulting crisis in homeownership (more on that in a coming sidebar), buying a home takes no small amount of financial wherewithal. Few of us can look at the price of a home, pull out our checkbook, and write a check for full payment of that amount. For the vast majority, buying a home means getting a mortgage loan.

In this chapter, we consider some mortgage basics and help you assess your financial situation so you will know what kind of home you can and can't afford. We consider the pros and cons of fixed- and adjustable-rate mortgages and help you figure out what mortgage is the best for you.

Mortgage Basics

Buying a home generally means getting a *mortgage* loan — that is, a loan specifically used to purchase real estate, such as a home or property or both. Indeed, your ability to obtain a mortgage will likely determine whether you will be able to buy the home of your dreams. And as many homeowners have seen in recent years, if you get on the wrong side of a mortgage — through changing economic conditions, because of inattentiveness to the kind of loan you obtained and its legal terms and conditions, or simply because of plain bad luck, such as the market value of the home falling below the amount of the mortgage — your dream can quickly and easily turn into the kind of nightmare that leads to many sleepless nights.

You must consider three key parts of any mortgage:

✔ **Size:** The amount of money borrowed to buy the property. For example, if you *fully financed* a $250,000 home, the mortgage size would be $250,000.

✔ **Term:** The length of the loan, usually expressed in years. A 30-year term is most common for mortgage loans, although 15-year loans are also commonly available. Generally, the longer the loan term, the lower your monthly payment, but the more interest you will end up paying the lender over the life of the loan.

✔ **Interest rate:** The price you pay for the money you borrow. In the United States, federal law requires lenders to provide buyers with the *annual percentage rate* (APR), which is the effective interest rate over the life of the loan taking into account upfront fees and other associated costs. With a *fixed-rate* loan, the interest rate remains the same for the duration of the loan. In the case of an *adjustable-rate* loan, the interest rate changes during the course of the loan term based on a specific formula spelled out in the loan agreement.

You have one more consideration when looking for a mortgage: Smaller mortgage loans are sometimes less expensive than larger mortgage loans. A *jumbo* mortgage is a loan that exceeds the Federal National Mortgage Association (FNMA, often written and pronounced *Fannie Mae*) single-family limit — which, as of January 1, 2008, is $417,000. The interest rate on jumbo loans is usually higher than the interest rate on *conforming* loans (that is, loans that are within FNMA's limit). Why? The federal government doesn't stand behind jumbo loans. Note that the FNMA limits on family mortgages in Alaska, Hawaii, Guam, and the U.S. Virgin Islands are 50 percent higher than the limits for the rest of the country.

Okay, you've got one *more* consideration when shopping for a mortgage loan. Although most people go to a bank or *mortgage loan broker* (a loan salesperson who can often obtain loans from many different sources, including banks and private investors), those sources may not be your only options. In some cases, you may be able to *assume* the home seller's mortgage — that is, simply take over the payments. In addition, some home sellers — particularly home sellers who are desperate to sell their homes — may be willing to offer *seller financing,* in which they act as the mortgage lender. Instead of making monthly payments to a bank, you would make the payments to the home seller. When economic times are bad, these alternative approaches to buying a home become more common.

Buying a home is likely to be the largest financial transaction you will make in your entire life. It is also the longest-term transaction, with the standard mortgage running for 30 years. Be sure you know what you're getting into before you sign on the dotted line. You want to be able to maintain your loan — and your dream of homeownership — no matter what happens out there in the cold, cruel world.

Assessing Your Financial Situation

Before you go out and buy that home you've been dreaming about, stop and assess your financial situation. Every individual, couple, and family has a unique financial situation. Some of us are better able to afford the many expenses — both immediate and ongoing — that obtaining a mortgage loan and paying for it over time necessitate.

The recent bursting of the housing bubble has caused most mortgage lenders to significantly tighten their lending standards. People who would have easily qualified for a loan a few years ago may have trouble obtaining the same loan today, even though their personal financial circumstances have not changed. Don't take it personally — these lenders are just trying to be sure that you really, really, *really* can afford your dream home and that you will avoid a messy foreclosure process (and possible bankruptcy for you).

Typical loan expenses

Many first-time home buyers are shocked at all the expenses involved in purchasing a house. When all these different expenses begin to hit, it's easy to feel like you're being nickeled and dimed to death. And, in a way, you are.

Down payment

The first major expense you'll encounter is the *down payment.* The down payment is some amount of money that you pay your lender to reduce the amount of your loan (thus reducing your monthly payment) and to demonstrate to the lender that you have a serious financial stake in the transaction. Some mortgage loans may not require a down payment, but most do — perhaps 5 or 10 percent or more of the price of the home. In the case of a $250,000 home, this amount could come to about $12,500 to $25,000 — or more.

The larger your down payment, the smaller your loan. If you make a 20-percent down payment on a $250,000 home ($50,000), you need only a $200,000 loan. If you make a 10-percent down payment on the same property ($25,000), you need a $225,000 loan.

The ratio of the total amount of the mortgage you apply for to the appraised value of your home (determined in advance by an independent appraiser or by a look at recent sales records) is known as the *loan-to-value ratio,* commonly abbreviated as LTV. In the 10-percent down payment example above, the LTV is 90 percent ($225,000 divided by $250,000), assuming that the appraised value of the home is the same as the sale price of $250,000. In the 20-percent down payment example, the LTV is 80 percent.

The Federal National Mortgage Association backs only loans that have an LTV of 80 percent or less. If the LTV exceeds 80 percent, the loan requires *private mortgage insurance* (PMI), which protects the lender in case you default on your home loan.

Closing costs

The down payment and PMI are hardly the end of it. You will encounter plenty of other expenses (commonly called *closing costs* because they are charged during the loan-closing process) as you work your way through the actual home-buying process. Consider these common closing costs:

- ✓ **Points:** These are fees (1 *point* is 1 percent of the loan amount) paid either to generate cash at loan closing to pay loan officers and origination departments, or to reduce the interest rate by compensating upfront for the interest the banks pay to their investors. Points are also sometimes called *loan origination fees.* See the sidebar later in this chapter for more information on points.

- ✓ **Credit report:** Your lender will want to check on your creditworthiness, to see if you are a good credit risk. Credit reports are widely available for less than $30.

- ✓ **Appraisal fee:** Your lender will likely require that the property you want to buy be *appraised,* in which a licensed and trained professional (coincidentally, known as an *appraiser*) assesses its true market value. This fee may vary from $250 to $1,000 or so, depending on the value of the house.

✔ **Title insurance:** This insurance policy protects you in case someone comes forward with a claim against your property after you have already bought it. Normally, it also pays for a thorough review of your property-to-be, to ensure that there are no hidden legal claims to it that might be an unwelcome future surprise.

✔ **Survey fee:** Your lender may require that a surveyor determine the precise boundaries of your property. Figure on $200 to $400 to cover this expense.

✔ **Recording and transfer fees:** Your local government probably charges a nominal fee to record your real estate transaction and transfer the deed into your name. Fees average about $50 to $150 for most jurisdictions.

✔ **Application fee:** Some lenders require payment of a fee to defray their costs for processing your loan application. Loan brokers are not allowed to charge an application fee, and banks rarely charge it except to cover the cost of an appraisal or credit report.

✔ **Flood determination:** This fee (usually no more than $30) is paid to determine whether your property is in a flood zone. If it is in a flood zone, you might want to think twice about wading into the transaction (or at least be sure to get flood insurance!).

✔ **Flood certification:** If your house is determined to be clear of a flood zone, this piece of paper certifies it.

✔ **Courier fee:** Someone has to get paid to run all your loan paperwork all over town at the last minute. Guess who that is? The courier.

✔ **Closing fee:** Your loan *closes* at the exact moment your real estate transaction is executed. The entity handling this transaction may be a title or escrow company, or an attorney. Fees generally average about $1.50 per $1,000 in loan value — probably more if you use a highly specialized real estate attorney to handle the closing.

Book II

Managing Home and Personal Finances

Your lender is required to disclose the costs you will pay for your mortgage to you by way of a *Good Faith Estimate and Truth in Lending Statement,* which details the interest rate paid for life of the loan (APR). By law, this statement must be provided to the borrower within three days of a loan application submission. Furthermore, whoever is handling the closing of your purchase must provide you with a copy of the *HUD-1 Settlement Statement,* a federal government–mandated form that details all the different costs that are charged as part of the transaction. Be sure to request these forms before your real estate closing. If you don't understand something — or if a cost seems out of line or inappropriate — have your lender, real estate agent, or closing party explain it to you in detail.

Determining whether you can afford to buy a home

We aren't going to pretend to tell you what you can and can't afford when it comes to buying the home of your dreams. We are, however, asking you to take a careful look at your personal financial situation before you sign on the dotted line. As you have seen, all sorts of expenses are involved in buying a home, and you might be surprised at your total bill when all is said and done.

After you have purchased your home — and when you have your closing expenses behind you — you'll be on the hook for a monthly house payment. This payment usually consists of three parts:

- ✔ **Mortgage payment:** Included is a payment toward the loan principal and interest.

- ✔ **Property taxes:** Many borrowers roll their annual property tax payments into their monthly mortgage payment, thus spreading the expense over an entire year instead of paying it all at once annually.

- ✔ **Insurance:** All lenders require borrowers to obtain *hazard insurance,* which pays for the loss of your home if it were damaged or destroyed in a fire or other covered situation. You may also be required to pay for private mortgage insurance, which protects the lender in case you default on your mortgage.

If you are paying all three of these parts with your monthly payment, you are paying what is known, perhaps appropriately, as *PITI,* which stands for *principal, interest, taxes,* and *insurance.*

In the United States, a generally accepted affordability guideline can help you figure out whether you can really afford to buy that home of your dreams. According to the powers that be, you can afford to buy a particular home if your monthly housing expense does not exceed 30 percent of your gross monthly household income.

Consider an example. Let's say you and your spouse both work and are taking home a total of $6,500 each month. You've got your eyes on a house that will require a monthly payment (including principal, interest, taxes, and insurance) of $2,500 each month. To determine whether you can afford this amount, divide your prospective monthly house payment of $2,500 by your monthly take-home pay of $6,500. You get a result of 38 percent, indicating that the house may be more than you can afford.

American dream . . . or nightmare?

It's no secret that, over the past few years, many Americans have seen their dream of owning a home turn into a nightmare. Indeed, the statistics are sobering. Foreclosure filings increased 60 percent in February 2008 compared with February 2007, to a total of 223,651 for the month. Of these foreclosures, 46,508 were bank repossessions, which doubled from the same month a year before. The states at the top of the list of foreclosures were some of the same states that saw the most dramatic run-ups in price during the height of the *housing bubble* (the too-quickly inflating price of homes, much of which was driven by speculators who hoped to make a quick buck by "flipping" their properties for a sizable profit soon after purchasing them): California, Florida, and Nevada. Foreclosure activity from February 2007 to February 2008 increased 131 percent in California, 69 percent in Florida, and 68 percent in Nevada.

How exactly did this state of affairs come about?

Well, the current (2007–2008) housing crash — with house prices plunging nationwide, creating a backlog of unsold homes — is the result of the perfect storm of a number of different events. The causes of the storm included a panic to buy property — any property — to make a quick profit as housing prices flew through the roof, the ready availability of money to people who wanted to borrow it, and lax lending standards that allowed almost anyone to qualify for

a mortgage loan, no matter how bad their credit (leading to the *subprime mortgage* mess).

So is an end in sight? The good news is that housing prices are cyclical. Yes, prices are currently decreasing, but they will at some point reach bottom and begin to climb again. The bad news is that no one knows for sure where the bottom is. According to the Federal Reserve, America's housing stock is worth about $21 trillion. Some economists are predicting a nationwide average housing price decline of about 20 percent through mid-2009 before prices begin to edge up again. A decrease of this magnitude would slice $4 trillion off the value of America's housing stock, making many homes worth less than their mortgages. As a result, some homeowners will be faced with a decision: Try to maintain their monthly payments (which may be increasing for people with adjustable-rate mortgages, as their home values decrease) or simply walk away — deliberately defaulting on their mortgage and allowing the bank to repossess.

Unfortunately, for many facing this decision, the choices aren't easy ones. Before doing something drastic, be sure to explore your options with your mortgage holder. You may find that you can work out a lower interest rate, a conversion to a fixed-rate loan, a payment holiday, or even a reduction in your principal or overall loan amount. You won't know until you ask.

Book II

Managing Home and Personal Finances

A number of factors may cause you to push the limits of housing affordability, including these:

> ✔ **Income changes:** If you expect to experience an increase in household income sometime in the foreseeable future, you might decide to buy a home that exceeds the 30-percent affordability figure. Of course, if that expected raise or bonus doesn't come through, you'll be stuck in an

unaffordable house with a monthly payment that might become increasingly hard to make — especially if your mortgage is an adjustable-rate one (see later in this chapter for more).

✔ **Location:** Although the 30-percent figure might be relatively easy to achieve in more-affordable areas of the United States — such as the Midwest and the South — you will have a very hard time finding an affordable home in most large cities such as Los Angeles, Seattle, Chicago, New York City, and Boston. Unfortunately, many people have been forced to buy unaffordable homes because they live in high-cost housing areas. If you live in a high-cost area, you may have little choice.

✔ **Equity growth:** When times are good and housing prices are rising fast, the promise of building large amounts of *equity* (the difference between what your home is worth and what you owe for it) may be one reason to push the 30-percent affordability guideline. When times are bad, however, house prices can decline — sometimes dramatically — and you may find that you actually owe more for your home than it is worth (sometimes called *being upside-down*). Many home buyers are currently learning this lesson firsthand and are hurting because of it.

No one knows what the future will bring. You may be tempted to buy a home that costs more than you can afford, but any number of situations can turn your dream home into a nightmare. Many people are only a paycheck or two away from bankruptcy. It's better to err on the side of buying a home that is just a bit too small, or one that's a bit too old, or one that doesn't have a pool or fancy kitchen than to buy a home that could put your finances in danger of collapse.

Is a Fixed-Rate Mortgage in Your Future?

Years ago, only one kind of mortgage was commonly available to prospective home buyers: a *fixed-rate mortgage.* With a fixed-rate mortgage, the interest rate you pay remains constant for the duration of the loan. So if you have a 30-year mortgage loan for $300,000 — with an interest rate of 7 percent — you'll pay the same 7-percent rate with your last payment as you did with your first.

Is a fixed-rate mortgage in your future? Time to take a closer look and see.

Understanding common fixed-rate mortgage loans

In many ways, fixed-rate mortgages are boring. They're plain (not a lot of complex terms and conditions), predictable (the rate never changes), and sturdy (they're built to hold up for the long haul). Of course, these very features also make fixed-rate loans attractive to so many potential home buyers.

Two major kinds of fixed-rate mortgages are available today:

- ✔ **30-year:** This fixed-rate mortgage is *amortized* (that is, the total cost of the loan — principal and interest — is spread out) over a 30-year period of time.

- ✔ **15-year:** This fixed-rate mortgage is amortized over a 15-year period of time — exactly half the time of a 30-year loan. Because of the significantly shorter loan term, a monthly payment for a 15-year fixed-rate mortgage is generally higher than for a comparable 30-year fixed-rate loan, although you actually pay far less interest over the life of a 15-year loan than you do with a 30-year loan. Additionally, the interest rate lenders offer is often lower than for a 30-year fixed-rate loan.

Other fixed-rate mortgages are available — you may find 10-, 20-, and even 40-year loans if you look really hard — but they are relatively uncommon. For most people, the good-old-fashioned but reliable 30-year fixed-rate mortgage is just right for the job.

Book II

Managing Home and Personal Finances

The good news about fixed-rate mortgages

Fixed-rate loans offer a number of advantages over other mortgage loan alternatives. These plusses are a few of the most notable:

- ✔ Because a fixed-rate loan doesn't change over the entire loan term, you always know exactly what your monthly house payment will be — yesterday, today, and tomorrow. Your long-term financial planning is thus much more accurate.

- ✔ You are protected against inflation because, as prices rise on other things you may buy during the coming years, your house payment remains the same. In other words, your home becomes more affordable over time (assuming your income increases).

- ✔ Because your payment is fixed and predictable, your financial risk is less than for nonfixed-rate loans, which may change at virtually a moment's notice.

The bad news about fixed-rate mortgages

If the news about fixed-rate mortgages was all good, no other options would be available. But, of course, plenty of other options abound. Here's a bit of the bad news about fixed-rate mortgages:

- ✔ The interest rate on a new fixed-rate loan is usually higher than the interest rate on an adjustable-rate loan. If the interest rate on your fixed-rate loan is high, you may pay more money over the life of the loan than for an adjustable-rate loan.

✔ Because the interest rate for a fixed-rate loan is usually higher than for alternative loan vehicles, it may be harder to qualify for a fixed-rate loan based on your income and other financial considerations.

✔ If market rates fall below the rate you are paying with your fixed-rate loan, you will be paying more for your home than someone entering into a comparable loan agreement.

Paying points

As mentioned earlier, *points* are simply upfront fees paid — most often by the home buyer — for one of two reasons:

✔ To generate cash at the closing to pay loan officers, mortgage brokers, and origination departments

✔ To reduce the interest rate by compensating up front for the interest the banks pay to their investors

Though you might not want to pay yet another cost as you go through the home-buying process, sometimes you need to make your deal work to give you a long-term financial advantage. For example, by paying a couple of points on your loan, you may be able to qualify for a lower rate, potentially saving you many thousands of dollars over the life of the loan. But you have to do the math.

In general, the shorter amount of time you plan to own the house, the fewer points you should be willing to pay in order to buy down the interest rate. In other words, short-term ownership in general favors paying a higher interest rate and fewer points as opposed to a lower interest rate and more points.

So exactly how much is a point worth? Depends on the size of your loan. A point is always worth 1 percent of the loan amount. If your loan is for $100,000, then a point (1 percent of the loan amount) is worth $1,000. If your loan is for $400,000, then a point is worth $4,000.

Points are usually whole numbers and eighth fractions, as in "one and two-eighths points." Because few of us express ourselves in eighths, it may be useful to refer to the following chart for quick conversion when you're in discussions with loan officers:

✔ $1/8 = .125$

✔ $1/4 = .250$

✔ $3/8 = .375$

✔ $1/2 = .500$

✔ $5/8 = .625$

✔ $3/4 = .750$

✔ $7/8 = .875$

✔ $1 = 1.000$

Keep in mind that — like most anything else in your purchase transaction — points are negotiable. However, make sure you negotiate up front, before the mortgage broker has invested his or her time in securing the best loan for you. Points are generally tax deductible for your primary and secondary residence, as long as the loan amount is less than $1 million. Be sure to check with your accountant to see what loan expenses are deductible in your particular situation.

Even if you find yourself in a bad fixed-rate mortgage — meaning you are paying an interest rate that is significantly higher than the current prevailing rate for a comparable loan — you've always got the option of refinancing your loan. Thus, you can take out a new mortgage loan that pays off your old loan and restarts the mortgage clock — this time with a better interest rate and probably a lower monthly payment.

Adjusting to an Adjustable-Rate Loan

During the early 1980s, interest rates for home mortgages went through the roof. At the time, fixed-rate mortgages of 13, 14, and 15 percent weren't just common — they were the norm. Many prospective home buyers simply didn't have enough income to qualify for fixed-rate loans at these rates, despite the fact that home prices were considerably less than they are today. As you learned in high school physics, nature abhors a vacuum. In response to this need for affordable mortgage loans, the industry invented the *adjustable-rate* mortgage (ARM) loan. Also known as a *variable-rate* loan, adjustable-rate mortgages start out at a relatively low rate — sometimes several points or more below a comparable fixed-rate loan — and then adjust up or down on a periodic basis.

If everything sounds a bit complicated, that's because it is. The next sections take a closer look at adjustable-rate loans.

Book II

Managing Home and Personal Finances

Understanding common adjustable-rate mortgage loans

A number of different adjustable-rate mortgage loans are available to prospective home buyers. The terms and conditions vary from loan to loan, but you can keep a few basics in mind as you shop around. Be sure to pay close attention — the devil in the details of adjustable-rate mortgages often trips people up.

- ✔ **Initial interest rate:** Every adjustable-rate loan has to start somewhere, and this somewhere is the initial interest rate — the rate you pay until your first loan rate adjustment. This rate, which may be *discounted* as an inducement to get you to sign on the dotted line, could last anywhere from one month to ten years.

- ✔ **Adjustment period:** After your initial interest rate expires, your ARM will adjust on a regular schedule called the *adjustment period.* At the end of the adjustment period, the rate is reset and the monthly loan payment is recalculated. The adjustment period may last anywhere from one month to five years.

✔ **Index rate:** Adjustable-rate mortgage interest rate changes are usually linked to changes in a specific index rate. The most common indexes include the rates on one-year constant-maturity Treasury (CMT) securities, the Cost of Funds Index (COFI), and the London Interbank Offered Rate (LIBOR). In some cases, lenders use their own cost of funds as an index.

✔ **Margin:** Most lenders add a few extra percentage points to the index rate to determine the actual interest rate that will be used when the ARM adjusts. The index rate plus the margin is called the *fully indexed rate* — the rate you pay. For example, if the index rate is 4 percent and the margin is 2.5 percent, the fully indexed rate is 6.5 percent.

✔ **Interest rate caps:** What keeps your ARM from completely going nuts and your interest rate from blasting into the stratosphere? *Interest rate caps* do the trick. A *periodic adjustment cap* is a limit on the maximum interest rate increase that can be charged at the end of each adjustment period, perhaps half a percentage point. A *lifetime cap* is the maximum interest rate that can be charged over the life of the loan, such as 12 percent.

As we mentioned earlier, many different kinds of adjustable-rate mortgage loans are available. Here are a few of the most common:

✔ **Hybrid ARM:** This kind of mortgage is a mix of a fixed-rate and adjustable-rate loan. Generally, a hybrid ARM starts with an introductory interest rate that is fixed for a period of time — commonly three, five, seven, or even ten years — and then converts to an adjustable loan after the introductory period expires. In the case of a 3/1 hybrid ARM, the introductory interest rate is fixed for three years and, after the three-year period expires, adjusts annually. In the case of a 5/1 hybrid ARM, the introductory rate is fixed for five years, after which the loan adjusts annually.

✔ **Interest-only ARM:** This mortgage loan is like a hybrid ARM, except that you only pay interest and not principal. Although this ARM makes qualifying much easier for many individuals, if the interest rate increases, the monthly payment can also increase, causing these same individuals to have problems coming up with the additional money necessary to keep their mortgages well fed and happy. Not only that, but because you're not paying any money toward the principal, you'll be stuck owing the entire loan amount when the mortgage term ends.

✔ **Payment-option ARM:** This unique adjustable-rate mortgage allows you to decide each month what kind of payment you want to make. The choices commonly include these:

- Making an interest-only payment.

- Making a standard payment of principal and interest.

- Making a minimum payment, much like the minimum payment on a credit card, that keeps your account current but that does not reduce your principal and interest owed. In fact, making only the minimum payment often causes *negative amortization,* a situation in which the amount you owe on your loan actually increases over time rather than decreases.

The good news about adjustable-rate mortgages

Despite the black eye that adjustable-rate mortgages have received lately, they offer advantages to people who select them:

✔ Because the initial interest rate on an adjustable-rate loan is often significantly less than for a comparable fixed-rate loan, a home buyer may save a significant amount of money — particularly in the first years of the loan.

✔ Adjustable-rate loans are often easier for home buyers to qualify for than fixed-rate loans.

✔ A lot of different adjustable-rate mortgage programs are available — you'll surely find the right one for you.

✔ Adjustable-rate loans can be good if you plan to keep your property for only a few years before you sell it.

✔ When interest rates are declining, an adjustable-rate loan gives you a distinct advantage over borrowers who are stuck in higher-interest fixed-rate mortgages.

The bad news about adjustable-rate mortgages

In case you haven't read a newspaper lately, most of the bad news about home loans involves adjustable-rate loans with increasing interest rates that are difficult for homeowners to keep up with. Yes, Virginia, there's no small amount of bad news about adjustable-rate mortgages. Here's some of the worst:

✔ Although adjustable-rate mortgages generally start at a lower interest rate than fixed-rate mortgages, this situation may not last forever. Many

Book II

Managing Home and Personal Finances

such loans experience their first (usually upward) adjustment just a year after loan inception, with subsequent adjustments on a quarterly or semiannual basis.

✔ Most adjustable-rate mortgages have a maximum interest rate cap, but the maximum rate is often far above what home buyers with fixed-rate mortgages will experience.

✔ In a worst-case scenario, if you make only the minimum payment your loan may *negatively amortize* — that is, your loan principal can grow instead of shrink as you make payments. Long story short, you can end up with a loan in a larger amount than you originally signed up for — definitely bad news.

✔ This kind of loan is unpredictable, making long-term financial planning difficult, if not impossible.

Deciding What Loan Is Best for You

Ultimately, you need to wade through all the different mortgage loan options available and decide which is best for you. The material in this chapter should help you make a decision, but you need to take a close look at your unique financial situation and take that into account. If you're unsure which way to go, don't hesitate to consult your real estate agent, CPA, mortgage loan broker, or real estate attorney.

 One of the best ways to help make the right decision for you is to compare the different costs of each kind of loan. Consider the following example that shows the impact of a number of common mortgage loans for a $200,000 home with a 10-percent ($20,000) down payment:

Traditional fixed-rate mortgage

30-year term; 6.7-percent interest rate

Loan balance after five years: $168,882

Equity after five years: $31,118 ($20,000 down payment plus $11,118 principal paid on mortgage)

Traditional 5/1 ARM

30-year term; 6.4 percent for first 5 years

Loan balance after five years: $168,305

Equity after five years: $31,695 ($20,000 down payment plus $11,695 paid on mortgage)

5/1 interest-only ARM

30-year term; 5 years of interest-only payments, and then 25 years of principal and interest payments; 6.4-percent interest rate for first 5 years

Loan balance after five years: $180,000

Equity after five years: $20,000 ($20,000 down payment)

Book II

Managing Home and Personal Finances

Payment-option ARM (Example 1)

30-year term; 5 years of minimum payments, and then recast for remaining term; starting interest rate of 1.6 percent for 1 month, then 6.4 percent; assume no rate increases

Loan balance after five years: $195,562

Equity after five years: $4,438 ($20,000 down payment minus $15,562 negative equity)

Payment-option ARM (Example 2)

30-year term; 5 years of minimum payments allowed, and then recast for remaining term; starting interest rate of 1.6 percent, and then 6.4 percent; 7.5-percent annual payment cap; assume rate increases 2 percent per year up to 12.4 percent. This loan will reach the 125-percent balance limit in month 49 and will be recast as an amortizing loan at the beginning of year 5.

Loan balance after five years: $223,432

Equity after five years: –$22,432 ($20,000 down payment minus $42,432 in negative equity)

As you can see, the good-old boring but reliable traditional fixed-rate mortgage is virtually tied with the 5/1 ARM in offering both the smallest loan balance after five years and the greatest growth in equity. What we don't know from this example, however, is what happens after five years. If interest rates climb, the fixed-rate loan was the better choice. If interest rates fall, the adjustable-rate loan was the better choice.

The payment-option ARMs do worst in this scenario, with the final example showing how such a loan can leave you owing more after five years than when you started. Combined with falling housing prices, this situation can be a recipe for financial disaster — one well worth avoiding.

Chapter 3

Avoiding Foreclosure

· ·

· ·

*H*omeownership is very much a part of the American dream. Granted, some people do prefer to rent or live with others, but if you're one of those people who have made the commitment to purchase a home, you probably consider anything else less than ideal. You worked hard to save for a down payment, and you take pride in knowing you're a homeowner.

Unfortunately, life throws some curveballs. If the purchase of a home is one of life's successes, then the loss of a home can be one of life's failures. When you default on most types of credit, all you end up with is a late fee or a small credit report ding. However, in the case of a mortgage, a seemingly small mistake or miscalculation compounded by inaction caused by embarrassment, indecision, or misinformation can result in a huge negative on your credit report and score, as well as cost you your home and tens of thousands of dollars.

A mortgage default is reported like most other negative items on your credit report for the usual seven-year period. Future loan underwriters and credit grantors view it as a more serious event because of the size of the obligation and the possible serious consequences to the lender if a mortgage fails. When lenders look at your credit report, they give special emphasis to how you have performed on similar types of loans. So a car lender pays special attention to car payments, and a mortgage lender looks hard at your mortgage history. If you're one of those people who think owning a home is the only way to live, be sure to pay special attention to your home loan payment record and this chapter.

Given the recent meltdown of the subprime mortgage industry and the general tightening of credit it has produced, this chapter is a critical one for any homeowner who is under financial stress. Money, self-esteem, and the very roof over your family's head are at stake, as is your good credit when a possible foreclosure is looming. This chapter gives you the advice you need to prevent foreclosure from becoming a reality, if possible, or to make the best of a bad situation if it's unavoidable. Options to save a delinquent mortgage have changed greatly in the last year or so and continue to offer more help to borrowers in trouble. However, you still need to seek help — and get it early. Fortunately, help *is* available, and this chapter guides you through the process of getting it.

Understanding That Mortgages Are a Different Credit Animal

Mortgages are quite different from other consumer loans, partly because of their huge size — a *lot* of money is on the line — and partly because they're backed by what historically has been the gold standard in collateral: your home. Furthermore, mortgages not only are underwritten differently from other types of credit, but they also have a different collection process, generally called the *foreclosure process*. When you *default* on a mortgage, the lender forecloses, or terminates the mortgage, and your house is consequently taken away from you.

From a credit score and credit reporting standpoint, mortgage defaults are among the most serious negatives out there (see Book I, Chapter 5 for more on credit reports and scores). Because of that, they can trigger *universal default clauses* in your credit cards, which means your low card rate can go up to 30 percent and make your already difficult life even more expensive. We tell you more about this topic later.

Obviously, foreclosures put a serious hit on your credit score and history. To help you minimize this hit, this section gives you an overview on how mortgages differ from typical credit, and how mortgages and your credit go hand in hand. Here you can find valuable information to help you understand when a late mortgage payment can quickly cause you problems and what you can do to get help.

Seeing a foreclosure coming

To get a firm grasp on everything related to mortgages and your credit, you first must understand what leads up to mortgage foreclosures. What exactly makes them tick? To start, some basic terminology can help you keep everything in focus. The following people and processes related to mortgages can have an impact on your credit:

- **Mortgage broker/banker/lender:** The person you worked with to fill out the mortgage paperwork and get your loan closed. This person typically, but not always, sells your loan to an investor.
- **Investor:** The owner of the loan and the one who makes the rules.
- **Insurer:** The one who insures the lender/investor in case the loan becomes delinquent.

- ✔ **Mortgage servicer:** The one who is responsible for handling customer service, processing payments, and working with delinquent customers. This person is the one you talk to and the one who knows what can be done and what exceptions can be made.

- ✔ **Loss mitigation:** The process of working with a customer to find a permanent solution to resolve delinquency. Also known as *homeownership preservation.*

- ✔ **Foreclosure:** Legal action to force the sale of a home.

So how exactly does a servicer foreclose? The key words to be aware of in the process are *quickly* and *quietly. Unless you speak up, it can all be over in as little as 120 days, depending on your state's laws.*

Book II

Managing Home and Personal Finances

A lender has a lot of money on the line with your mortgage, and the longer you're delinquent, the greater the risk is that the lender will lose money on a defaulted loan. Thus, the mortgage lender has a much lower tolerance for your delinquency than, say, a credit-card issuer. Here's an example: As long as you're less than 180 days past due on a credit card, it's not the end of the world. Generally, you can just pay the minimum due along with a late fee and go on your way. If it's really your lucky day, you may get the lender to waive the late fee and not report the delinquency. For a mortgage, though, once you're just 60 days late, you're well on your way to the edge of a cliff, and you may not even be aware of it.

The key number to avoid in a mortgage delinquency is 90 days late, not 180.

After 90 days, unless you get some help or work out an arrangement, the servicer will generally require that the entire arrearage be paid at once and may not accept partial payments. A 90-day mortgage delinquency on a credit report is very serious. To make matters worse, many people don't understand when the 90 days is up. It's not as simple as you may think, so we cover it in detail in the next section.

Many mortgages are packaged into large securities and sold to investors. Because the actual lender is often far removed from your community and your home, lenders use a *servicer* to collect your payments and work out any problems. The servicers don't have their own money at risk, so they don't get too excited about the prospect of a delinquency. Unlike the credit-card guys, who have little recourse in a default except to intimidate you into paying, mortgagees speak softly and may not even be heard over all the noise that your other creditors are likely to be creating in a financially stressful situation. Mortgagees won't call you at work or at night, and they won't yell or threaten you over the phone. On the contrary, the tone of their messages, often letters, is concerned, low key, and polite — and then you lose your home. But if you know where to get help, what to ask for, and what to avoid, this situation can change for the better. Needless to say, it pays to know the rules and what to ask and listen for.

Counting to 90

A major difference between mortgages and credit cards (or other types of consumer loans) is the amount of time you're allowed to be late. What's the "magic number"? After you're 90 days late on a mortgage, unless you take action, the servicer requires you to pay the entire overdue balance at once. If you fail to do so, the servicer proceeds to foreclosure.

Until then, you may be able to make partial payments on your own. If you're 30 or 60 days late and you make a partial payment, the servicer usually credits your account with the payment. However, if you cross the 90-day mark and then send in overdue payments from a month or two ago instead of the entire amount due, the servicer may send back the money, and the clock keeps ticking.

Furthermore, you may not be aware of the fact that when you're late on your first payment, *your grace period disappears.* (A *grace period* is a period of time specified in your mortgage loan agreement during which a default will not occur even though the payment is past due.) The grace period applies only to loans that are up to date, or current. The following example illustrates how this scenario works:

Imagine that your loan papers state your due date as March 1. Assuming that you have a typical two-week grace period, your payment actually has to be in by March 15. If you don't submit your payment by March 15, you miss that window of opportunity and lose your grace period. Your April payment is now due April 1. April 15 is no longer an option. In other words, you have no more grace period in April. If you pay April's payment on or before April 1, you get your grace period back for May and thereafter, as long as your payments stay on time.

If you lose your grace period, the company that services your loan starts counting the number of days you are late from the first of the month, not the 15th. So if you don't send in a payment on March 15, April 1, or May 1, then on May 2, you need to catch up all the payments for March 1, April 1, and May 1, plus any fees and penalties (which can be hundreds of dollars or more), all at once. This total is a huge amount for someone in financial difficulties. If you don't, then on May 2, the formal foreclosure process can start, and you may incur fees for collection costs, attorneys, title searches, filings, and more. When the foreclosure process begins — and it's up to the investor when it actually kicks in — the loan servicer can then can ask for the entire balance of the loan (a loan "acceleration"), not just the late part, to stop the foreclosure.

As Table 3-1 shows, a foreclosure in a *nonjudicial state* (one in which the foreclosure process does not go though the courts until the very end) can happen very quickly. Consider an example: After 30 days, you get a late notice; at 60 days late, you receive a demand letter; at 90 days, you receive an acceleration notice; and by 120 days, the foreclosure and sale/auction can be scheduled.

Table 3-1 illustrates the Department of Housing and Urban Development (HUD) time guidelines for lenders by state. These numbers are estimates; a foreclosure may take less time than allotted by HUD under these guidelines.

Table 3-1   HUD's Time Guidelines

State	Days[1] from Foreclosure Initiation to Sale	Foreclosure Method	State	Days[1] from Foreclosure Initiation to Sale	Foreclosure Method
Alabama	85	Nonjudicial	Nebraska	155	Nonjudicial
Alaska	140	Nonjudicial	Nevada	155	Nonjudicial
Arizona	125	Nonjudicial	New Hampshire	110	Nonjudicial
Arkansas	130	Nonjudicial	New Jersey	300	Judicial
California	135	Nonjudicial	New Mexico	250	Judicial
Colorado	130	Nonjudicial	New York	280	Judicial
Connecticut	220	Judicial	North Carolina	120	Nonjudicial
Delaware	250	Judicial	North Dakota	190	Judicial
Florida	170	Judicial	Ohio	265	Judicial
Georgia	80	Nonjudicial	Oklahoma	250	Judicial
Guam	250	Nonjudicial	Oregon	180	Nonjudicial
Hawaii	140	Nonjudicial	Pennsylvania	300	Judicial
Idaho	190	Nonjudicial	Puerto Rico	375	Judicial
Illinois	275	Judicial	Rhode Island	85	Nonjudicial
Indiana	265	Judicial	South Carolina	215	Judicial

(continued)

Book II

Managing Home and Personal Finances

Table 3-1 (continued)

State	Days[1] from Foreclosure Initiation to Sale	Foreclosure Method	State	Days[1] from Foreclosure Initiation to Sale	Foreclosure Method
Iowa[2]	315	Judicial	South Dakota	205	Judicial
Kansas	180	Judicial	Tennessee	90	Nonjudicial
Kentucky	265	Judicial	Texas	90	Nonjudicial
Louisiana	220	Judicial	Utah	165	Nonjudicial
Maine	355	Judicial	Vermont	360	Judicial
Maryland	85	Judicial	Virgin Islands	325	Judicial
Massachusetts	135	Judicial	Virginia	60	Nonjudicial
Michigan	75	Nonjudicial	Washington	160	Nonjudicial
Minnesota	110	Nonjudicial	West Virginia	145	Nonjudicial
Mississippi	130	Nonjudicial	Wisconsin	310	Judicial
Missouri	85	Nonjudicial	Wyoming	100	Nonjudicial
Montana	205	Nonjudicial			

1 State foreclosure time frames are in calendar days and occur after a default has resulted in a foreclosure notice.

2 State time frame represents the standard elapsed time for a judicial foreclosure without redemption. A longer time frame may be allowed if a borrower files a written demand to delay the sale.

Knowing where to turn for help

If you're having trouble making your mortgage payment on time, time is of the essence. Getting your mortgage issue resolved fast is critical. Remember, the mortgage company doesn't want your house; it just wants to keep your loan *performing* — that is, up to date or current. Following are a few ideas on where to turn for help (along with some tips on where *not* to turn). The essential point is to not wait, but take action. You can work directly with your servicer, but your loan servicer may offer you only what he or she thinks is the easiest solution, not the one you need, because your loan servicer doesn't know your situation in detail. We strongly recommend that you use a third-party intermediary approved by HUD. They come cheap, know what to ask for, and can help guide you through what can seem an insurmountable problem.

Your mortgage-servicing company

When you can't pay your mortgage on time, you can directly contact your mortgage company. Look at it as though you're trying to solve two problems — yours and theirs. Ask to speak with the loss-mitigation department, also referred to as the workout department or the homeownership retention department. This area is able to do more for the consumer and deals with complex issues better than the standard collection department, which usually offers only to make catch-up payment arrangements. You can find the contact information for your servicer in your loan documents, on your monthly statement, or in correspondence you receive from the company. When you call, get names and extension numbers so you can try to keep a single point of contact and continuity. Doing so may not be possible, but knowing whom you talked to, when you talked, and what you agreed to is important.

Take good notes!

To keep the call simple, we suggest you do some homework before you call: Know what will be necessary and for how long to remedy your situation. Write out what happened, what changed, what you need, and how to contact you or your counselor, if you're working with one. These notes will help keep you from rambling and get you to the solutions faster. Then ask for what you need — and also ask what other options may be available beyond the one offered to you.

Other available help

A number of housing counseling agencies are also available to help you work out a solution. We strongly recommend that you use one of these agencies to help you work out a deal with the servicers. These agencies work with people in similar situations every day, so they know what to ask for and will take the time to understand what you really need. Although the contact information may change over time and new players are continually offering this service, you can look for resources through HUD's Web site at www.hud.gov, or contact Neighborworks' Project HOPE at 888-995-HOPE or www.nw.org. We suggest that you call before you email or visit an office for quickest service. You may also contact the National Foundation for Credit Counseling at www.housinghelpnow.org or 866-557-2227. Many credit counselors are also HUD-certified housing counselors.

Not-so-helpful "help"

As you look for answers and help, keep in mind that not everyone out there has the same objectives that you do. Some are trying to help only themselves. Proceed with caution and consider the following tips as you evaluate any prospective source of help:

- Don't panic.
- Find out whether you're dealing with a nonprofit organization.
- Don't make payments to anyone other than your servicer or his or her designee.
- Be wary of any organization other than your servicer that contacts you to help.
- Never sign a contract under pressure.
- Never sign away ownership of your property.
- Don't sign anything with blank lines or spaces.
- If English isn't your first language, and a translator isn't provided, use your own translator.
- Get a second opinion from a person or an organization you know and trust.

If you're having trouble paying your mortgage, a predatory lender or foreclosure scam artist may try to get you to take out a high-risk second mortgage on your property. If these marauders come a-calling, run the other way — fast! These lenders are dangerous because they charge high fees you can ill afford to pay, and they distract you from real solutions by wasting critical time that you could otherwise spend solving your problem.

If you receive an offer saying you've been preapproved for a loan, it means you've been preapproved only for the offer, not the actual loan. Don't waste too much time chasing preapproved offers.

Other red flags to watch for include the following:

- **Phantom help:** This company wants to "help" charge you high fees for work you can do yourself, charge you for legal representation that never materializes, or offer you a loan even though you don't have the income to repay it.
- **Bailout:** Various schemes may try to get you to surrender your title to the house, thinking you'll be able to remain as a renter and buy back the house.

✔ **Equity stripping:** A buyer purchases your home for the amount of the arrearage and flips the home for a quick profit, pocketing the equity in your home that otherwise would have been yours.

Alternatives to Going Down with the Ship

If you're having trouble making your mortgage payments, you're not alone. You also may have some options to avoid the expense and upset of going though a foreclosure. Even if you can't or don't want to keep your house, you can lessen the damage to yourself, your family, and your credit by taking positive action. You can take control of your situation and turn this ship around before it sinks.

Before you take any action, assess your situation as dispassionately as you can. If stress and anxiety make that impossible, we suggest you get a third-party professional such as a nonprofit HUD agency (see "Other available help," earlier in this chapter) or an attorney to help you do so. Your situation may not be as bad as you think, or it may be worse. What's important is to know for sure where you stand. For instance:

✔ Will the problem that has caused your mortgage delinquency be corrected soon? Is it just a short-term event?

✔ If it's a longer-term event, how much extra time will you need to get back on track financially?

✔ Is the event long-term enough to reconsider whether you can stand the stress until it's resolved and stay in your home?

✔ Is your situation serious enough that you want to get out of your home-ownership obligation?

To help you find the answers to these questions, you need what's called loss mitigation counseling help. *Loss mitigation counseling* is help to develop a solution that will allow you to catch up on your payments, modify your loan terms, or otherwise rectify your situation so you can afford to keep your home or lessen the damage caused by a foreclosure.

The following section gives you some loss-mitigation alternatives to foreclosing to protect your credit history.

Starting with short-term solutions

Perhaps you believe that you have a plan to resolve your problem and, as a result, catch up or at least resume payments in three to six months. If that's the case, consider the following suggestions:

✔ **Find a good credit counseling agency.** This suggestion has nothing to do with credit counseling; it focuses on getting you an objective assessment of your overall financial picture and whether you can realistically afford your mortgage payments. The counselor can help you build a revised budget that may free up cash for your mortgage, and an expert opinion can help to prioritize your debts and expenses. Many agencies are also HUD-certified and can work with your servicer to get a solution that works for your situation.

✔ **Ask about mortgage-repayment plans.** These plans entail the servicer setting up a structured payment plan (sometimes called a *special forbearance plan*) that will get the mortgage back on track in three to six months. Sometimes this deal can be a verbal agreement with your existing lender. If it is, we suggest that you document the terms in a letter and send it to the lender so you're both clear on the terms of what you're doing. Typically during a repayment plan period, full monthly mortgage payments are made along with a portion of the past-due payments until the mortgage loan is back to "current payment" status. The sooner you get a plan in place the less damage you'll incur on your credit report.

✔ **Check the HUD Web site at `www.hud.gov` for resources and help.** Don't forget to talk to your lender about your need for assistance — and do it soon. Some servicers have programs only for borrowers who are not yet delinquent and other programs for borrowers who already are. For the greatest number of options, get started as soon as you know you have a problem making mortgage payments as agreed, and be sure to ask for all the options they have for you.

Considering solutions for long-term problems

For problems that will take longer than three to six months to remedy, you can ask for mortgage loan forbearance or loan modifications.

A *forbearance* temporarily modifies or eliminates payments that are made up at the end of the forbearance period. A forbearance is useful if you have a sale pending or you expect a windfall, but you can't afford the payments at present. It also prevents your credit from being damaged by a string of late payments.

A *loan modification* changes the terms of the original mortgage permanently in a way that addresses your specific needs. The modification may change one or more terms of the original mortgage agreement, such as adding delinquent payments and other costs to the loan balance, changing interest rates, or recalculating the loan. If this process seems intimidating, use a HUD agency to deal with the servicer and offer solutions on your behalf. Clear communication is key here.

These modifications need to be in writing, and both the servicer and the borrower must approve them because they're long-term and large in scope. You can expect goodwill to go only so far, so don't be surprised if the servicer asks for a fee of around 1 percent to cover the costs of processing a loan modification. After all, servicers always have an appetite for some immediate income for their banks or companies.

If you were delinquent on your loan before the modification, expect your credit history to show the prior delinquency. Mortgagees are very reluctant to change your credit history, but a modification and efforts to bring the mortgage current should show up on your credit report.

If you are also carrying credit-card debt, being late on your mortgage or having a loan modification on your credit report may set you up for a hike in your interest rates under *universal default rules.* Review the default provisions of the credit cards that you use to carry a balance and consider closing those accounts that have universal default provisions before they raise your rates. After the accounts are closed, your rates should stay the same during your repayment period. The small damage to your credit score from closing accounts will be a bargain compared to what can happen if you can't handle interest rates that may go to 30 percent or more. If you've had the cards for more than ten years, consider keeping them open if you can transfer the balances to cards without the universal default provision; these long-history cards count for more on your score than ones you've had for a shorter period of time.

Looking at longer-than-long-term solutions

Some problems take longer to resolve than anyone wants them to, and some can be resolved only by taking a step or two backward before making any progress. Even when you can't solve your problem or just can't stand it anymore, you still want to stay in control of the process. Doing so can lessen damage and expenses and keep your dignity — and maybe your sanity — intact.

Following are some of the many options available. And don't forget that you may have newer options as well. Be sure to check out the resources mentioned in the section "Other available help," earlier in this chapter.

- ✔ **Sell your home:** You may be able to sell your home in a short sale if you have no equity left, or in a pre-foreclosure sale if the value of the house still exceeds the remainder of the mortgage.

  - **Short sale:** In a *short sale,* you ask your lender for permission to sell your home for less than the mortgage value, and the lender uses a real estate agent to sell the home. The lender may allow a sale for an amount lower than the total debt. A short sale is generally cheaper for the bank and less stressful for the homeowner than a foreclosure. Because this solution is good for the investor, you can negotiate a bit. Ask that the loan deficiency be reported to the credit bureau as a zero balance instead of a charge-off.

Congress has passed a law called the Mortgage Forgiveness Debt Relief Act that affects how a principal residence foreclosure is handled for tax purposes. It exempts up to $2 million of forgiven mortgage debt, subject to certain conditions, from federal taxes. Normally, you would have to pay income tax on that amount. We suggest that you check to see whether you have state taxes due, because they aren't covered in this federal law.

- **Pre-foreclosure sale:** A *pre-foreclosure sale* arrangement allows you to defer mortgage payments that you can't afford while you sell your house. This solution also keeps late payments off your credit report.

✔ **Deed-in-lieu of property sale or foreclosure:** This option is becoming more popular. It requires listing your home with a real estate agent. If the home can't be sold, you sign over the home's title to the lender and move out. Usually, to qualify for this option, you can't have a second mortgage, an equity loan, or another lien on the property.

Handling a foreclosure if one has started

Even if you've gone down the delinquency path and are in the legal process of being foreclosed upon, you may still be able to talk to the servicer to try to work things out or buy yourself more time to come up with a solution or make a more dignified exit from the home. But once again, time is not your friend here, so don't wait!

✔ **Get a HUD-approved counselor involved and review loss-mitigation options with your servicer.** Most want to help. (Check out "Alternatives to Going Down with the Ship," earlier in this chapter.)

✔ **Contact and keep contacting the servicer's loss-mitigation staff until you get a solution you can live with.** If they don't offer workable suggestions, ask to speak to managers and vice presidents or higher. Now is no time to stand on protocol or accept "I'm sorry" for an answer.

✔ **See an attorney.** Ask for options. Review all the mortgage documents to be sure they were properly drawn and executed. The technical phase used here is "Truth in Lending Compliance." Ask about bankruptcy options and timing so you know all options available to you.

If none of these options works, you will go through the full foreclosure process. In short, the house will go to auction and be sold. The new owner will give you appropriate notice to leave the house, per your state statute. A notice may be placed on your front door detailing the terms.

Dealing with Deficiencies

When all is said and done, you may still owe some money. If your home sells for less than the amount still owed on the mortgage and fees, you may have what is called a _deficiency balance._ For example, say a borrower borrows $500,000 from a lender to purchase a home, but the borrower falls behind in payments and the bank forecloses. The home is ultimately sold for $400,000. The $100,000 that the lender lost on the deal is called a _deficiency._ Current practice is to forgive this amount. At one time this wasn't always the case, and the situation may change again in the future. The most important point is to realize that your problems may not be over when you leave the home. You may need to deal with the IRS if you don't qualify for mortgage debt forgiveness under their rules.

The following are some potential (and we stress _potential_) deficiencies you may face and what you can do to deal with them:

- **The lender asks for a note.** Doing so is not a current practice, but be aware of it for the future. This _note_ isn't the kind your mother wrote to school. This note is a promise to pay an unsecured amount to cover the mortgage deficiency after the sale. As with any loan, it has terms, interest rates, and payments due on certain dates. Many of these terms can be discussed before the sale takes place and may be modified to fit your situation. Use a lawyer if anyone suggests this solution to you.

- **The lender sends a demand letter.** As in asking for a note, this practice is not a current one. A lender may send a demand for payment of any deficiency following the sale of a home. Lenders use a _demand letter_ if they don't want to give you an unsecured loan for the balance due. In essence, the problem is all yours, and you need to work out a way to pay the balance. Here again, if this scenario ever happens to you, get an attorney to advise you.

- **The lender forgives the debt.** This is a current practice, but it can always change. The lender chooses to forgive the debt instead of pursue it. This practice is nice as far as it goes, but be prepared for the IRS to count the forgiven portion of the debt as income through the issue of a 1099 form. Forms 1099 A and C, which are normally used to document unreported income, are used to report forgiven debt. The amount of the forgiven debt becomes taxable income in most cases, unless you're covered by the Mortgage Forgiveness Debt Relief Act. If you're among the IRS's unforgiven and you get a 1099, and it is for a lot of money, we suggest that you see an attorney ASAP for legal options. Remember, the mortgage debt forgiveness law is federal and may not forgive state tax obligations.

- **The state you live in makes mortgages nonrecourse.** If you live in certain states, you may get a break relating to personal mortgage deficiencies.

Some states have passed laws saying that you are not responsible for any mortgage deficiencies. Some effectively make the mortgage a non-recourse loan. (*Nonrecourse* means the lender has no recourse to collecting money due other than the security on the loan.) You may not be personally liable. This protection may not apply to refinancing. See an attorney to find out whether it applies to you.

Subject to additions or deletions, the list of states that have passed some antideficiency protection legislation offering at least some protection for borrowers includes Alaska, Arizona, California, Minnesota, Montana, North Dakota, Oregon, Texas, and Washington.

✔ **The IRS wants more taxes.** Even though a loan may be uncollectable or forgiven, it is not beyond the reach of the IRS. You see, the lender gets to take a loss on its taxes for the bad loan. Not wanting to miss a tax opportunity, the IRS considers the lender's loss to be your gain. So you may owe taxes on the deficiency amount if you don't qualify for relief under the Mortgage Forgiveness Debt Relief Act. This law is scheduled to run only until 2010. This amount can be a very big number indeed.

A foreclosed borrower faced with a sizeable 1099 still has hope. If you file IRS Form 982, "Reduction of Tax Attributes Due to Discharge of Indebtedness," and you are insolvent at the time of the forgiven debt, the IRS may forgive the liability. Again, see your attorney for the details.

Chapter 4

Keeping a Lid on Medical Costs

- -

In This Chapter

▶ Finding ways to cut costs on medical expenses

▶ Saving on health insurance

▶ Taking action to attack medical-related financial troubles

- -

*W*e don't have to tell you that healthcare costs are skyrocketing and can eat up a very large chunk of your finances. This chapter helps you chip away at the different pieces of your medical costs one at a time. Here you'll find ways to save at the doctor's office and pharmacy, methods of finding good deals on health insurance, and ideas for dealing with medical-related debt.

Saving on Medical Expenses

Unexpected medical and pharmacy bills can take a huge bite out of the family budget. Even though you can't possibly plan for all emergencies and contingencies, you can cut back on regular medical-related expenses.

Keeping a close eye on bills

Remember to keep careful track of all your medical expenses and look over every itemized bill in detail. We know of a surgeon who accidentally billed a patient twice for the main surgical procedure, adding $800 to the total bill. When the patient pointed out the error, the doctor's office happily corrected it. Be sure to follow up on corrections like that. Sometimes the paperwork gets lost in the shuffle, and you need to remind the office more than once to take the charges off your bill.

Keep calm when you're haggling with doctors or hospitals over disputed amounts. They'll often negotiate and lower the amount due, especially if patients are assertive yet courteous. Keep written documentation of every phone call, letter, and bill related to the disputed charges. Be organized, confident, and polite.

If you belong to an HMO or PPO, make sure that every doctor and specialist working on you is part of your medical plan. Don't assume that just because you're in a plan-approved hospital, you're being treated by a plan-approved doctor, anesthesiologist, or nurse. A friend told us she once fought a $400 bill for more than a year: The emergency room was plan approved, but the doctor on call that night was not. It took a while, but eventually they wrote off the $400.

Looking into payment plans

If you're facing after-insurance charges that you can't pay for all at once, call the billing office of the doctor or hospital and see whether you can make some sort of payment arrangement. You may be surprised by just how much help you receive. We called the hospital about a surgical charge we couldn't afford to pay, and somehow in the conversation we discovered that we were eligible for a couple low-income food programs. The billing department wrote off the entire hospital bill! So don't be afraid to say you're having difficulty meeting your financial obligations. Doctors and hospitals are often quite willing to accept payment arrangements or make allowances for lower-income patients.

Coordinating insurance benefits

If you and your spouse both have medical or dental insurance coverage, be sure to coordinate benefits between your insurance companies for any medical services. Usually you have a primary insurance carrier that needs to be billed first; if you or your children are also covered under your spouse's insurance, be sure the secondary insurance company is billed after the first insurance has paid its portion. When insurance plans can coordinate benefits like this, you often don't have to pay much of anything out of pocket.

Finding less-expensive prescriptions

Pharmacy expenses are one of the most difficult medical bills to budget for in many families. Even with insurance coverage, out-of-pocket expenses can add up substantially over the course of an extended illness or during several rounds of drugs. Consider these simple ways to reduce pharmacy costs:

- ✔ If you can buy a larger amount of medication at once, you may save a bit of money. Each time you have a prescription filled, the pharmacy adds administrative charges. By ordering a full month's supply at once, you can save several service fees for filling the prescription.

- ✔ Pharmacies really do vary in their price for different medications. Before you fill your prescription, call several pharmacies and ask how much your particular prescription costs to fill.

- ✔ Don't forget to ask your doctor to prescribe the least-expensive or generic version of your medication.

- ✔ If you don't have prescription coverage, ask your doctor if equally effective over-the-counter medications are available.

Discovering What Makes a Great Health Insurance Plan

Facing serious, life-threatening illness is traumatic. We know, we've been there. Everything else you're worrying about in life suddenly becomes totally unimportant. The only thing that could make it worse is fear about your health insurance coverage. Fear that the escalating bills will exhaust your coverage limit. Fear that the specialist you want to see for treating your illness isn't approved by your insurance company. Fear that holes in the coverage will leave you personally responsible for some huge bills that could wipe out all your savings — even put you in serious debt. That's why a solid health insurance plan is so important.

An excellent health insurance plan must include five key ingredients:

- ✔ A coverage limit high enough that it won't likely ever be exhausted, even for the most catastrophic medical expenses

- ✔ An annual dollar limit on your out-of-pocket responsibility that you can live with

- ✔ No dollar limits on types of expenses, such as dollar limits on daily room charges or dollar limits for types of surgical procedures

- ✔ Freedom to see specialists without a referral

- ✔ Worldwide coverage

Do most plans meet all five criteria? Nope. We estimate that less than half of the individual and group health plans sold in the United States include all five elements that a great health insurance plan must include.

Your plan should include all five of the crucial ingredients because you want a plan that won't, even in the worst cases, cause you major financial hardship. And a plan that lets you choose the most-skilled care provider, especially in serious or life-threatening situations — such as treating your 6-year-old's leukemia, surgically removing your spouse's brain tumor, or the several skin-grafting operations needed after you've been badly burned.

Deciding Between Individual and Group

Sometimes you have a choice between individually owned coverage and group coverage through an employer when it comes to deciding where to insure your dependent children. This brief comparison of the advantages and disadvantages of both types of plans will help you make a good choice.

Pricing

Group policies are usually less expensive. Plus, the employer generally pays part of the bill. The employer typically has the employee's portion of the costs directly deducted from payroll using pretax dollars.

Underwriting

Group coverage wins again. When most people apply for group coverage, they're guaranteed acceptance, no matter how poor their health. They could have diabetes, heart disease, or even terminal cancer — the only eligibility requirement is that they be employed. Depending on the length of previous coverage, sometimes a waiting period of up to a year is enforced for preexisting conditions, especially if the applicant had no insurance at the time he or she was hired.

Individual coverage, on the other hand, is strictly underwritten. (*Underwriting* is the process of reviewing an application to determine whether the applicant is acceptable for coverage.) Medical questions are part of the application, and the insurance company often checks your past medical records. The company can do one of four things with your application: It can flat-out turn you down, issue you a policy with no restrictions at preferred rates, issue you a policy with an extra charge for your condition, or completely exclude coverage for a condition.

Benefit levels

Group coverage has the edge here, too, in most states. Many state legislatures have passed laws mandating benefits that must be included in health insurance plans. However, most of those laws apply only to group coverage (and, unfortunately, often exempt the largest employers, who partially self-insure their group claims). The benefits in a group policy that are required by law can be significant. Consider just a few examples from Minnesota:

- Maternity expenses are fully covered and treated as any other medical bill.

- Only one spouse needs to be insured to have automatic coverage on newborns.

- Mental health expenses (for prescriptions or therapy) are fully covered and treated as any other illness.

- Copayments and deductibles are waived for children younger than 12 (so financially strapped parents don't delay getting young children care).

- Annual mammograms are fully covered.

- Chiropractic care is fully covered.

Book II

Managing Home and Personal Finances

Renewability

Individual policies come out on top with regard to renewability. Most are guaranteed-renewable contracts that you can continue to hold up to age 65, regardless of your health.

Avoid buying individual policies that don't offer a renewability guarantee.

Insurance companies offering group policies, on the other hand, can cancel a group policy anytime they feel like it. Your employer probably can replace it with another group plan, but coverage may be less, rates may be higher, and, in some cases, your existing health issues may not be immediately covered.

Another risk of group coverage is that your employer may discontinue it. Perhaps the company you work for has some financial setbacks. Or perhaps employee claims have been so large that rates have skyrocketed 40 percent to 50 percent and are no longer affordable. Imagine if your employer stopped offering insurance and your child had leukemia. You would probably have to change jobs to get health insurance for your child.

Coverage flexibility

Another win for individual policies. With group coverage, you get what the employer offers. You can't cut costs by raising your deductible. You can't choose freedom-of-choice if your employer offers only managed care.

Nothing beats the flexibility of individual plans. You can choose whether to include preventive coverage. If you're childless, you can strip out the expensive maternity coverage. You can choose all different levels of deductibles. And you can raise your deductible to help offset future rate increases. Best of all, you can choose a plan offering access to the doctors and specialists that you want.

Saving Money on Individual Coverage

You can control costs for individual coverage in two main ways:

- ✔ **Direct:** You reduce coverage, and the insurance company gives you a direct premium credit.
- ✔ **Indirect:** You select a higher deductible when your health and self-care are exceptional, but the insurance company has no means to lower your premiums.

Saving directly

The best way to save money on an individual policy without cutting back on coverage is to become ten years younger. Because that's not possible at the time of this writing, the next-best way to save money on your health insurance premium is to not smoke and not use tobacco. Unlike group policies, almost all individual policies differentiate smokers from nonsmokers — significantly — because the claims costs for smokers are much higher. Blue Cross of Minnesota, for example, cuts 30 percent to 40 percent off its standard rates if you haven't used tobacco for three years.

You can also save by cutting out unneeded coverage (such as maternity coverage, if you're not expecting to need it), cutting back doctor choice (in other words, accepting managed care), or raising deductibles. The difference in cost, for example, between a $300 deductible and a $1,000 deductible with Blue Cross locally is a whopping 45 percent! As the size of your family or age increases, that 45 percent can save you a fortune — especially when you consider that you're assuming only $700 more risk per person each year. If you're paying $4,000 a year for just yourself, 45 percent would save you $1,800 in premiums! You're risking a "maybe" $700 for a "for sure" $1,800. Who wouldn't do that? Even if the savings were only 20 percent, that's still a $900 savings for a $700 risk.

The impact of higher deductibles on pricing

Table 4-1 illustrates what an insurance company rate card typically looks like for different deductibles and different ages. Notice that, as you increase the deductible, the amount of annual savings gets proportionally less. For example, a 25-year-old saves $1,650 a year to raise deductibles from $300 to $1,000, saves $550 to go from $1,000 to 2,000, and saves only another $450 to go from $2,000 to $5,000.

Table 4-1	ABC Health Insurance Company Annual Insurance Rate Card				
Deductible	**Age**				
	25	35	45	55	Children
$300	$3,800	$4,400	$6,000	$10,000	$3,400
$500	$3,000	$3,400	$4,600	$7,600	$2,600
$1,000	$2,150	$2,450	$3,400	$5,550	$1,600
$2,000	$1,600	$1,850	$2,550	$4,200	$1,450
$5,000	$1,150	$1,300	$1,800	$2,900	$1,000

Book II

Managing Home and Personal Finances

Computing your ideal insurance deductible

At this point, you have explored the marketplace in your area and determined which insurer(s) you are considering. You have ordered or downloaded their rates for various deductibles. You find the rate table that applies to you (smoker or non-smoker, needing or not maternity coverage, and so on). It should look something like Table 1-1 (except the rates on a typical rate display are usually monthly).

Next, using your favorite spreadsheet or a piece of paper, compare the difference in premium (annualized) to the difference in risk you would be taking. For example, the 25-year-old single person mentioned earlier saves $1,650 for taking a $700 risk (the difference between a $300 deductible and $1,000 deductible). Choosing the $1,000 deductible is obviously a no-brainer! Next, he saves $550 for taking another $1,000 risk (the deductible difference between $1,000 and $2,000; depending on his overall health, he may or may not want to take that extra risk). Finally, he saves $450 for taking a $3,000 risk (the difference between the $5,000 deductible and the $2,000 deductible). For most people, the payoff is way too small for the extra risk. This computation works the same for families except you have to do it for each person in the family. If you have more than three people in your family, check to see if the insurance company limits the number of deductibles that can be assessed in a year to three. Many do. See the sidebar on health savings accounts for some great tax breaks available to all citizens.

When deciding between two deductibles, choose the lower one, if in doubt. You can raise your deductible later anytime you want to. But to lower it, the whole family must qualify medically — not likely if you've just incurred some big medical bills.

Most medical plans, once the deductible is met in a calendar year, pay 80 percent, subject usually to a cap on your maximum out-of-pocket expenses in any calendar year. You need to be mindful of whatever that maximum is per person. However, it does not need to be part of your deductible decision because that 80-percent coverage is going to be about the same regardless of which deductible you choose.

Health Savings Accounts

A Health Savings Account (HSA) operates like an individual retirement account (IRA) coordinated with a high-deductible major medical health insurance plan.

✔ As with an IRA, contributions are income tax deductible. Also, like IRAs, Health Savings Accounts can be set up almost anywhere you can set up an IRA.

✔ Earnings on the account are tax sheltered.

✔ The maximum contribution per year is set annually by the government (for 2009, $3,000 for individuals and $5,950 for families). For each person age 55 and older, an additional "catch-up" contribution is allowed ($1,000 in 2009). To discover what the current allowable amounts are, Google *Health Savings Account* and choose the US Treasury Web site option.

✔ For the Health Savings Account contributions to be tax deductible, you must also have an IRS-approved High Deductible Health Plan (HDHP). The plan must include options for a minimum deductible and a maximum deductible set by the government each year. There must be a cumulative family deductible amount for policies insuring two or more people in the family. There is no coverage under the policy until the entire family reaches the family deductible in a calendar year. (Be careful when choosing your family deductible!) There must be an option for 80-percent coverage as well as 100-percent coverage once the deductible is satisfied. We always recommend that clients choose the 100-percent option. Once they have satisfied the high deductible in a calendar year, they have the peace of mind knowing that all covered expenses will be 100 percent paid for the rest of the year.

✔ From the account, you can pay your deductibles and most other medical and dental expenses that your health plan doesn't cover (laser eye surgery, glasses, contact lenses, all dental work). Because the HSA money has never been taxed, you're paying those bills with pretax dollars — a huge advantage.

✔ If you've stayed reasonably healthy, you can leave unused funds on deposit and either use them in future years or save them as supplemental retirement dollars. If you don't use them for medical bills, withdrawals are taxed much like traditional IRAs when you do retire.

You can set up an HSA account wherever you can establish an IRA — banks, savings and loans, investment houses, insurance companies, and so on. Because of the need to write checks to pay doctors and buy prescription drugs, I have found a bank works best because you can have an account with both checks and a debit card.

Here are a couple of tips to make your life a lot easier when using an HSA to pay deductible expenses and other expenses. First, do not pay any medical bill or pharmacy charge until your insurance company has reduced the cost to their negotiated discount pricing! Second, fund the account early in the year so you have plenty of cash available if medical bills are sizable in the first quarter of the year. Third, keep all your receipts for all services you have paid through your HSA (medical bills, pharmaceutical bills, dental bills, and so forth in a medical folder in case you ever get audited. See a complete list of IRS currently approved medical and dental expenses at www.irs.gov; choose publication #502.

If you have to buy individual health insurance, an HSA is a wonderful benefit to set up for yourself.

Book II

Managing Home and Personal Finances

Saving indirectly with self-care

Insurance companies that offer individual health plans give substantial price discounts to nonsmokers. And they don't insure people who are high-risk medically. Everyone else, from the superfit and superhealthy to the average or below-average health risk, pays the same rate and shares losses.

If you're healthy and practice good self-care (through exercise, diet, stress management, rest, and personal safety), how can you get credit if insurance companies don't offer any such credits for that? Answer: higher deductibles.

Remember, pricing for each level of deductible is based on average risk. If you're much fitter and healthier than average, you're paying more than your share, no matter what level of coverage you buy. But the more you self-insure through higher deductibles, the more you'll save. Being above average in terms of health, your chances of having to spend that higher deductible are much less — and a $2,000 deductible could save you 50 percent off your insurance costs.

Out of $5 million of lifetime health coverage, half the premium pays the first $2,000 of annual claims. The other 50 percent pays the other $4,998,000. Discover what deductible makes good economic sense and go for it, especially if you're in good health. (See the sidebar on Health Savings Accounts for even bigger savings using pretax dollars to pay your deductible.)

Coping with Health Insurance Problems

Sometimes you face tough decisions regarding health insurance. Examples include the following:

✔ You or a family member can't get health insurance because of existing medical problems.

✔ You've fallen on hard times and can't afford health insurance.

✔ Your son or daughter has reached the age at which he or she no longer qualifies for dependent coverage under your insurance.

✔ Your college student has coverage available through school.

✔ You or a family member needs temporary coverage.

✔ Your coverage under your spouse's group coverage is being terminated because of a divorce.

✔ Your and your children's group coverage ends because of a spouse's death.

✔ You're between jobs and without insurance.

✔ You're traveling outside the country and are offered travel insurance.

✔ The school offers school accident insurance for your children.

Read on to see how we recommend that you manage each of those problems.

Insuring the uninsurable

If you or a family member for whom you are responsible has a health condition for which you can't get insurance (you've been rejected for individual coverage), we suggest that you broaden your way of looking at the problem. Some people can get health insurance for a medically uninsurable condition if they're willing to make some life changes.

You may have read horror stories about families suffering financial ruin because of one member's medical expenses — often a child's. One story, in particular, involved a family who lost its insurance due to a job change. The new job didn't offer group insurance, and the son was uninsurable. He had an ongoing condition that required years of treatment and thousands of dollars of expenses. According to the story, this family sat helplessly while its life savings dwindled to nothing. We believe financial ruin could have been prevented if the family had considered some other choices. If you're willing to take one or more of the following actions, you can prevent a financial catastrophe from happening to you on account of an uninsurable family member.

✔ If your employer doesn't offer group coverage, talk to your employer about starting to offer a group plan. Enlist the support of other coworkers. The Health Insurance Portability and Accountability Act of 1996 (HIPAA) requires insurance companies to accept all members of a group, regardless of health. The worst-case scenario is that the company may not cover the condition in the first 12 months.

✔ Change employers. Get a job with a company that offers group medical coverage to its employees and their families.

✔ If you're in a state that has a major medical insurance plan for uninsurable people, sign up immediately. Call your state insurance department to find out.

✔ Move to a state that offers catastrophic individual major medical coverage for uninsurable citizens. Minnesota has such a plan, and so do many other states.

You may balk at the idea of doing something as seemingly drastic as changing jobs or moving to a different state to get health insurance for yourself or a sick family member. But those are far better alternatives than ruin.

Book II

Managing Home and Personal Finances

Staying insured through hard times

If you're in a financial crisis — temporary or permanent — and you just don't have enough money available for health insurance, you can still protect yourself somewhat by managing your medical risks in advance. If you don't develop a game plan for handling medical costs before you're faced with them, you may end up being personally responsible for the entire cost of any emergency care that you need. Look into various assistance programs for people in your circumstances that provide medical care either at no cost or at a nominal cost. In Minneapolis, for example, Lutheran Social Services and Catholic Charities offer such programs. In exchange for a very small amount of money per month, all family members receive the medical care they need. Participants are limited to designated medical facilities, but they get medical care now without facing a huge debt later.

If you or a family member is in economic distress, research what's available in your community and know where you'll go for care if and when you need it. A medical emergency isn't the right time to figure out what your options are.

Insuring your kids when your policy no longer covers them

Depending on your particular insurance policy terms, your children are covered under your family plan only to a certain age — usually 19 (22 or 25 for full-time students). Insurance policies are very inconsistent when it comes to the age at which they no longer cover children.

Managing the in-again, out-again school problem

If you have a son or daughter who can't seem to decide about going to college (she's in for a semester, out for a semester, back in for a semester, and so on), we recommend that you do the following if you're covered by a group policy and are usually eligible to continue coverage on your group policy under federal COBRA law (Consolidated Omnibus Budget Reduction Act — aren't you glad you asked?). The guaranteed coverage period for most job changes is 18 months, but it's up to 36 months for students coming off a parent's policy.

✔ When the student drops out, notify your employer to exercise the 36-month COBRA continuation option. This way, your child stays insured under your group insurance. The only difference is that you will foot 100 percent of her premium costs (if you weren't already) while she's out of school.

✔ When she returns to school (and is taking the required number of credits), cancel COBRA and add her back onto your coverage as a dependent.

✔ Each time she drops out and then returns, follow these same guidelines until she reaches the maximum age for students to be covered under your policy — usually 22 or 25.

✔ If she's still in school when she reaches the maximum age for students to be insured on your policy, or if she's without insurance for any other reason, exercise her COBRA option until she can arrange coverage on her own personal health policy.

If she's not eligible for COBRA (in other words, if you have an individual policy or your employer has too few employees to qualify for COBRA), set her up with her own individual policy the first time she drops out of school. The policy will stay in force during the revolving-door period.

Whether you have group or individual coverage, when your son or daughter reaches age 18, check with your insurance company or agent and find out exactly what your insurance company's rules are for maintaining coverage for your child. Also find out how many credits your children must carry per school term to stay eligible. Will they be eligible in the summer if they haven't registered yet for the fall semester? What if they drop out for a while? Get clear on all this beforehand. Claim time is not the time to find out that a child isn't insured.

Evaluating insurance available through college

Should you buy the optional student health insurance available from your child's college? If the insurance is provided automatically as part of tuition costs, should you remove your son or daughter from the family health policy and rely exclusively on the school coverage? Before deciding, take a good look at the college's student insurance policy. You may well discover that the policy has

- ✔ Excellent preventive care — coverage for physicals, eye exams, and so on — at the student health center on campus
- ✔ Excellent coverage for other doctor care, if the care is provided at the student health center
- ✔ Hospitalization coverage at the university's hospital, but usually only for a limited time (such as 30 days)
- ✔ Poor medical coverage away from school — both hospital and doctor
- ✔ Poor coverage for substantial medical bills
- ✔ Often no coverage during the summers

Book II

Managing Home and Personal Finances

Keep your student insured on the family health plan. But if you can't afford it, consider buying a high-deductible individual plan supplemented with the student health coverage. The coverage is usually pretty inexpensive. Also, many family health plans don't cover expenses incurred at your student's college health center. The student health insurance plans available from colleges always cover these expenses. If college students can just drop by the campus health center, they're a lot more likely to get the care they need than if they have to trek to the hospital or doctor that your plan covers. As a result, the student health plan can help keep your student healthier.

Never drop your college student from your family health insurance plan, even if you buy the student health insurance offered by the college. You'll need your family plan for any serious claims.

Understanding temporary health insurance

Many states allow health insurance companies to offer the public *short-term* or *temporary* health coverage to meet short-term needs. These were created, for example, for someone between jobs or a college student who isn't covered by student health insurance during the summer. Coverage is usually available in increments of 30, 60, 90, 120, and sometimes 180 days. Coverage is usually quite good in many respects. Typically, temporary policies have a coverage limit of $1 million or more. They usually include freedom-of-choice and a maximum amount on out-of-pocket expenses. The biggest advantage of a temporary policy is that you can qualify with almost no medical questions. Coverage can be immediate, if needed.

But temporary coverage has at least six disadvantages:

- Preexisting conditions aren't covered. If you've ever been treated for a condition in the past, you won't be covered if it flares up again.

- The insurance is usually not renewable.

- When the coverage period you've chosen ends, so does the coverage — often even if you're lying seriously ill in the hospital.

- Claim payments are often delayed.

- Maternity expenses usually aren't covered.

- Coverage outside the country is often excluded.

Because of these major limitations, you generally want to avoid buying temporary insurance unless you have no other option. If you're between jobs, continue your group coverage from your previous employer under COBRA, if you can. For summer coverage, keep college students continuously insured under your family plan.

In one situation, temporary coverage makes sense: when you're applying for individual coverage and you currently have no insurance. You complete an application and pay a premium to apply for individual coverage. If the insurance company approves you, it generally issues your policy retroactively, if you desire, effective on the date you applied. If you were hospitalized or incurred other medical bills while your application was pending, they're covered.

But suppose the company declined your application and returned your money because of your past health or medical problems? You would be uninsured for any bills accumulated since you applied, even if the medical conditions were new.

Even after you apply for individual coverage and pay the initial premium, you're not necessarily covered. Only if the company later approves you — a process that normally takes 30 to 60 days — will you have been covered since the date of your application. That's a long time to risk being uninsured.

Use short-term coverage this way to protect yourself when you have no insurance and while your application for long-term coverage is being considered:

1. Buy a 60-day short-term policy to be assured of insurance coverage for any new medical condition or injury that occurs while your long-term application is being considered.

2. Apply simultaneously for long-term coverage, requesting an effective date, if approved, for 60 days from now, to coincide perfectly with the expiration of your short-term policy.

Then if the company rejects your long-term policy application, you at least had coverage for new conditions while your application was being reviewed. Without the short-term coverage, the new medical problems would be uninsured.

Continuing coverage following a divorce

About half the marriages in the United States end in divorce, so the problem of continuing health insurance after a divorce is significant.

Getting spousal coverage

If both spouses are employed full-time and have their own group health insurance coverage available, getting health insurance isn't a problem. If one of the spouses is covered under the other's policy, that spouse simply needs to apply for coverage at his or her own place of work within 30 days of being dropped from the other policy, to avoid having to qualify medically. If the spouse who's being dropped doesn't have group coverage available at work, that spouse can, of course, obtain an individual policy through an agent.

Insuring the children after a divorce

If both parents are employed and each has coverage at work, the best thing to do normally is to continue the children's coverage through the parent whose coverage is best for the children. But what if one parent is required in the divorce decree to pay for the children's coverage and the children are currently not on that parent's policy? Say Sue and Tom divorce. The court orders Tom to pay the children's health insurance costs to age 19. But Sue has them insured under her plan. Their options are as follows:

- ✔ Sue can continue having them on her plan with Tom reimbursing her — but getting that reimbursement sometimes can be a source of conflict.

- ✔ Tom can move them to his plan, usually without the children having to qualify medically if the move is done within 30 days of the divorce. But transferring coverage is a problem if Sue doesn't like Tom's policy or his plan won't cover the children's doctors.

- ✔ Sue can set up an individual policy covering just the children, with the bills sent to Tom (assuming that the children can qualify medically).

We like the option of setting up an individual policy, especially if Tom has the premiums paid electronically from his checking account and Sue's mailing address is on the policy. This way, the premiums are always paid on time, so the chance of a canceled policy and a resulting uninsured claim is reduced. By having Sue's mailing address listed on the policy, Sue gets copies of the policies and changes and any late premium notices if the electronic payment isn't made for whatever reason.

Book II

Managing Home and Personal Finances

The ideal divorce decree

If you're involved in a divorce and if the court deems you responsible for paying the children's health insurance costs, and you prefer to set them up on an individual plan, the divorce decree should do more than state which parent is responsible for the premiums. It should specify the type of coverage plan, the deductibles and copayments (and who's responsible for paying them), whether there must be freedom-of-choice for doctors and hospitals, and that the premium payments must be paid automatically and electronically from the responsible parent's checking account. If you follow this advice, you'll eliminate 90 percent of the conflict surrounding your children's health insurance.

An individual plan gives the parents more flexibility to determine the coverage they want on the children. And the coverage won't end if Tom or Sue's job ends, which is safer for the children and much less stressful for their parents.

Deciding on a conversion policy

Most state laws require that people coming off a group policy be offered the right to convert their group coverage to a personally owned policy that they can keep indefinitely, regardless of their health.

Requiring that conversion policies be offered is a good concept in theory, but the policies are seldom practical. Most states don't set limits on how much the company can charge, nor do they prohibit the company from watering down the coverage. As a result, most conversion policies are half the coverage of the previous group coverage at about twice the price. (Why? Because losses are so high. Usually, only those in poor health exercise the option.)

If your state law requires the group insurance carrier to offer you a conversion policy with essentially the same broad coverage you had under the group without an increase in price, definitely consider it. Otherwise, avoid conversion policies unless you have absolutely no other health insurance option (in other words, you can't qualify medically for a personal policy and your state doesn't have a health insurance pool for those who can't get insurance).

Consider HIPAA instead

HIPAA — The Health Insurance Portability and Accountability Act — gives everyone leaving a job the right to continue health insurance as established by state guidelines whenever their COBRA period ends, or if not eligible for

COBRA immediately. The purpose of HIPAA is to prevent "job lock" — being trapped in a job you hate because of family member health history problems. Now, if you quit a job, you're guaranteed a quality individual health policy regardless of health of the family members!

Evaluating options for survivors of a premature death

People have died and left their entire family uninsured because the family was covered through the deceased person's group insurance plan. Luckily, the family has a couple options:

✔ If the surviving spouse is employed and has group coverage available, she can add herself and her kids to her group plan without proof of good health if she applies within 30 days of losing the other group coverage.

✔ If she chooses not to work outside the home indefinitely or is self-employed, we recommend the following:

- Continue coverage through COBRA, if available, but only temporarily.

- Buy an individual policy if she and the kids are healthy enough to qualify — a policy that won't end in three years, as COBRA does. If you're in this situation, buy the policy *now*. Your health may change and disqualify you later.

- Family members who don't qualify need to either go to a state pool for uninsurables or use COBRA for the three years and then exercise a HIPAA option for an individual policy, if that option is available.

Hip HIPAA hooray!

Before HIPAA

Bill, a bright 43-year-old engineer, is stuck in a dead-end job doing work he hates. He knows about some much better-paying jobs he would be perfect for, but he can't take them. He's stuck. Why? Because he has an 8-year-old son with an enlarged heart condition that has already required two surgeries with at least two more scheduled in the next five years. If Bill takes a new job, his son will either be turned down for coverage or the heart condition will be excluded. So Bill's hands are tied. He can't make the job change he would love to make.

After HIPAA

Bill can take the best job he can find without any insurance concerns. Since he's had continuous coverage for more than the past 12 months, HIPAA guarantees that he can't be turned down, nor can there be a preexisting condition applied for his son's heart. Bill is a happy camper.

But suppose Bill wanted a break. He takes a six-month sabbatical between the old job and the new. How can he keep all the protection of HIPAA? Simple. He just has to elect to continue his prior group coverage, under COBRA, during the sabbatical.

Evaluating options when becoming self-employed

If you're leaving your job to become self-employed, don't continue your COBRA option for the entire 18 months before you apply for individual coverage. A lot of people make this mistake. The problem with this strategy is that it risks future insurability. Your health may go bad, and when the 18 months are over, you'll be stuck with less-than-desirable choices.

A three-point plan reduces the risk of coming up short on COBRA:

✔ Continue your group coverage under COBRA, if you are eligible, when you leave your job, to have uninterrupted coverage.

✔ Stay with COBRA while you test the self-employment waters. If you don't like self-employment, just continue COBRA until you're back working for another company and are covered by its group plan.

✔ The moment you decide to stay self-employed, apply for a good individual health plan, but keep COBRA while your application is being evaluated. If you're approved, drop COBRA. If you're declined, keep COBRA until you've located replacement insurance through HIPAA.

Evaluating school accident insurance

Most elementary and secondary schools send information home with students about insurance for injuries that occur on school grounds or at school events. This insurance is most commonly offered to student-athletes. Do this:

✔ Assuming that you don't have to worry about any exclusions and that the insurance is reasonably priced, buy it if you have a high deductible on your health insurance plan.

✔ If you have minimal deductibles or copayments, don't buy it. It just duplicates coverage you already have.

Evaluating dread disease insurance

We all have fears of some kind. We universally fear cancer. Those of us close to other serious diseases probably fear those as well. Some parts of the insurance industry have responded to our fears with policies that cover only those things we fear. We're totally against what we call Las Vegas insurance — policies that pay only on the first Tuesday after a full moon, like travel accident insurance, travel life insurance, accidental death insurance, rush-hour auto liability insurance, and so on. Most of the time, these either are wasteful policies because they duplicate other coverage or, if you're really tempted to buy them, are a warning to you that you may be underinsured in certain areas. Buying travel life insurance, for example, sends a red flag that you feel your current life insurance is inadequate. Skip the travel insurance and use the money you save toward increasing your life insurance coverage.

If a person has a high-limit (like $2 million), quality major medical policy that covers cancer, buying another $1 million just for cancer coverage is throwing money out the window. However, if a person has a poor medical policy (such as one with a $250,000 lifetime limit), then buying an extra million dollars of coverage is a good idea — but not just for cancer.

If you're considering buying a dread disease insurance policy (a policy that covers only specific illnesses) because your health insurance isn't very good, don't. Save your money and use it instead to get a top health insurance policy or an excess major medical supplement to the policy you have that covers all illnesses and injuries — not just the ones you fear.

Book II

Managing Home and Personal Finances

Evaluating travel insurance

We address two types of medically related travel insurance here. One pays medical bills you incur through travel, within a certain date range and up to a dollar limit (such as $5,000). The other covers the costs of airlifting you from a remote area, in a medically equipped aircraft, to a top hospital. The former usually duplicates your health insurance; the latter fills an important gap.

Travel medical insurance

Travel medical insurance is Las Vegas insurance. In other words, you're gambling that you'll get sick while you travel. Not a smart gamble — it violates almost all the rules for buying insurance. It often unnecessarily duplicates your health insurance. The only time the insurance may be of value is if you have a very large deductible on your health plan and you're buying travel medical insurance to cover the deductible while traveling.

Be very careful if you do buy travel medical insurance. Read the policy carefully. Many are *very* restricted; you may as well throw money down a rat hole.

If you're traveling abroad, call your health insurance company before you leave to discover its preferred method of handling claims incurred abroad. Can you call a 24-hour toll-free phone number? Does the policy have any coverage restrictions abroad?

Medical evacuation insurance

If you travel much, especially if you travel abroad, and you get seriously ill, the hospital or treatment facility you end up in may be terrific — or it may not be state-of-the-art in terms of doctors, equipment, or both.

Medical evacuation insurance does not duplicate any other insurance you have. A good policy covers the cost (about $50,000) to bring an intensive-care jet to wherever you are in the world, fully staffed and medically equipped, and to fly you to your preferred treatment facility. Coverage is available from travel agents, tours, and credit-card companies on a per-trip basis, and from travel assistance companies who sell the coverage to those who travel frequently.

The benefits of medical evacuation insurance

Connie, a childhood friend and current client, vacationed annually with her mother in Mexico. During their last vacation, her mother collapsed on the bathroom floor. She was rushed to the closest hospital. Doctors told Connie that her mother would die if they didn't perform heart bypass surgery. Connie wasn't comfortable with the level of care available but reluctantly okayed the surgery — she had no other option. Her mother died. Connie had the task of bringing her mother's body home — a horrible experience.

If Connie's mother had had medical evacuation insurance, Connie may have been able to fly her home at no cost, where she could have received the best care. Her odds of survival would have gone up. But even if her mother had died in Mexico before she could have been flown to a U.S. hospital, a good medical evacuation service would have flown to Mexico and brought the body home for burial.

If you buy medical evacuation insurance, try to obtain a policy that

- ✔ Pays for you to be transported to your home hospital or another hospital of your choice (not just the nearest hospital)

- ✔ Has no dollar limits on costs (the cost to evacuate you from China may be $100,000)

- ✔ Transports you at your option, regardless of medical necessity

- ✔ Covers you within your home country — not just abroad

- ✔ Provides a full medical staff

The best company we've encountered is Med Jet Assistance (800-9MEDJET; www.medjetassistance.com). It meets all the criteria just listed. The policy is underwritten by Lloyds of London, and it's reasonably priced: around $300 for an entire year.

If the coverage and the company are good, we think medical evacuation insurance is a good idea, especially if you travel a lot or have a health condition (like a heart problem) that places you more at risk for being in a medical emergency abroad.

Be sure the policy you buy does not exclude your preexisting conditions!

Taking Decisive Action

If you've got high medical bills and you're worried about how to pay them, first try to reduce the amount of the bills as much as possible:

- ✔ **Be sure the bills are accurate.** When you find errors, get them corrected and get your bills adjusted.

  Don't assume that medical billing errors don't matter if you have health insurance. They do. These errors can mean higher copays and out-of-pocket costs and maybe even higher premiums when renewed.

- ✔ **Make your insurance company pay for everything it should.** If your bills are the result of an accident that someone else caused, get that person's insurance company to pay as many of the bills as possible.

- ✔ **Pursue all medical discounts you may be eligible for.**

- ✔ **Take advantage of medical bill-paying assistance if you're eligible.** You may qualify for help if you have a low income or no health insurance.

In the sections that follow, we detail each of these options.

Reviewing bills with a fine-tooth comb

Too many people put doctors and hospitals on pedestals. They assume that medical bills are always accurate or are afraid to speak up when they find errors. Get over it! Medical professionals are human beings just like you and me, which means that they sometimes make billing mistakes.

Usually, the mistakes are innocent — information gets keyed in wrong, for example. But even innocent errors can be costly. And some billing errors are deliberate. For example, a doctor may use one code to describe the treatment he provided to you but use a different code to charge more for his services. Or a doctor may purposefully charge you for a procedure you never received, or bill for more hours of operating time than were actually required.

Studies show that the incidence of hospital billing fraud is rising. Protect yourself by reviewing every medical bill you receive line by line. Look for overcharges, double billings, and charges for care and services you didn't get.

If you have health insurance, be sure your medical provider doesn't bill you for charges you're not responsible for. For example, your medical provider may bill you for the difference between the total amount of your bill and the amount the insurance paid on the bill, even though you're responsible only for making a small copayment. If this happens, fight it; contact the provider's billing office first and get the insurance company involved if necessary.

You may be thinking, "Review my medical bills? Easy for you to say, but have you ever tried to decipher one of those things?" You're right. Most medical bills are full of codes, numbers, and abbreviations that mean nothing to you. If you can't make heads or tails of your bill, call the medical provider's billing

Book II

Managing Home and Personal Finances

office. Ask questions, and don't be afraid to ask more questions if you don't understand an explanation or if something doesn't seem right. Politely but firmly let the person you speak with know that you're not going to pay your bill until you understand exactly what you're being charged for. The bigger the bill, the more important that you conduct a thorough audit.

For help figuring out your medical bills, order the medical billing workbook by Medical Billing Advocates of America (www.billadvocates.com).

Making your plan pay what it should

If your health plan refuses to pay one of your medical claims or doesn't pay as much as you think it should, read your policy to see if you can find a reason for the company's decision. You may get a good explanation. But if not, contact your plan's customer service office and ask for one.

If you're not satisfied with what you find out, get help resolving your claim issue from your insurance agent or broker, or from your employer's plan administrator if you receive health coverage through your job. If these people can't help you, send a letter to the insurance company after calling to get the name and title of the person to whom you should write. Be as specific as possible in your letter about why you think your claim should be paid or why you think more of the claim should be paid.

If your letter doesn't get results, your next avenue of recourse is to appeal your plan's decision. Your policy or plan booklet probably spells out the appeals process. At the same time, you may want to file a complaint against the insurance company with your state's insurance department. (It may be called an insurance *commission.*) The department may have a complaint-resolution process for resolving problems between consumers and their health plans.

If you let your insurance company know in writing that you have filed a formal complaint against it with the insurance department in your state, the insurer may decide to rethink how it handled your claim. Insurance companies don't want problems with state insurance departments.

Finally, if the amount of money at issue is substantial, you may want to hire a consumer law attorney to help you collect on a claim. A letter from the attorney may be all it takes to convince the insurance company to reverse its decision. Or you may have to file a lawsuit to get results. If the attorney feels that you have a strong case, she will probably agree to represent you on a *contingent fee basis:* You won't pay the attorney an upfront fee, but if you win and the court awards you money as a result, your attorney takes a percentage. Exactly how much your attorney takes and all the other terms of your financial arrangement should be put in writing.

Taking advantage of hospital discounts

Pursue all rate reductions you may be entitled to when you or someone else in your family is hospitalized. For example:

✔ If your income is very low and you own few, if any, assets of value, you may qualify for the hospital's charity program. To be eligible, you may have to prove that you applied for and were denied Medicaid coverage. Medicaid is a federal/state program for people with limited incomes. Individual states administer the program and set their own eligibility rules, although the federal government sets broad eligibility guidelines. For more information about the Medicaid program and about your state's particular eligibility rules, go to www.cms.hhs.gov/home/medicaid.asp.

✔ Some states require hospitals to offer discounts to any uninsured patient, regardless of the patient's income. However, hospitals may offer this discount only if you ask for it, so speak up if you don't have health insurance. Then make sure the discount is reflected on your hospital bill.

✔ If your state doesn't require hospitals to offer discounts to uninsured patients and you have no insurance, ask the hospital to charge you the same prices it charges insurance companies. Insurance companies are billed for services at a much lower rate — as much as 60 percent lower — than what uninsured patients are charged. If the first person you talk to in the hospital's billing office says "no," ask to speak to the manager.

Remind the hospital that charging you the same rates it charges insurance companies makes it easier for you to pay your hospital bill and less likely that you'll have to file for bankruptcy. If you file for bankruptcy, the hospital will receive little or nothing on the bill.

If you don't ask for a discount before you're billed by a hospital, ask for it later and request an adjusted bill.

Reducing your medical debt

Depending on your income and the total value of your assets, you may have other options for reducing the amount you owe to medical providers:

✔ If your medical bills are the result of an auto accident that wasn't your fault, make sure that the insurance company of the other driver pays as much as possible on the bills.

✔ Contact churches and social-service organizations in your area to find out whether any of them can help you with your medical bills.

✔ Apply for Medicaid. In most states, after you are enrolled in the program, Medicaid not only helps you pay future medical bills, but also pays bills that are as old as three months, assuming they're for Medicaid-covered services. For information about your state's Medicaid program, go to www.cms.hhs.gov/medicaid/stateplans.

Some hospitals let you whittle down your debt by doing volunteer work. If this option interests you, speak to a hospital financial counselor.

Chapter 5

Using the Internet to Help Manage Your Finances

Different people have different definitions of wealth. For some, being wealthy means having a Cadillac with a chauffeur (remember *Driving Miss Daisy?*). For others, it means taking world cruises or retiring comfortably.

Today thousands of "middle-class millionaires" reside in the United States. These folks didn't inherit millions, didn't become wealthy overnight, and didn't hit the lottery. They became rich incrementally, by facing their financial issues one at a time and using effective strategies to take control of their personal finances.

At the end of the day, we define *wealth* as building enough net worth to comfortably achieve your goals.

The Internet is ideal for everyone who wants to maximize personal wealth by making every dollar count. This chapter shows you how to use the Internet to get more from what you already have and how to reach your personal financial goals without drastically pinching pennies or giving up luxuries.

Becoming wealthy doesn't center on some secret strategy; all it takes is planning and discipline. The key is organizing and maximizing your assets. Wealth is created when your *inflows* (the amount of cash you receive) are greater than your *outflows* (the amount of cash you spend) over time. As you invest your excess cash in savings, securities, real estate, and related investments, your net worth grows (that's the idea, anyway).

The greater your net worth, the wealthier you are. *Net worth* is defined as the total of all assets minus the total liabilities of an individual or company. Assets can include property, vehicles, or investments whereas liabilities are debts such as mortgages and credit-card bills. That is, Assets – Liabilities = Net Worth. The bigger the difference between your assets and liabilities the greater your personal wealth.

When you spend every dime you make, regardless of how much you make, you can never be wealthy. You need to save and invest, which means developing a plan to do so and sticking to it (see Book IV for much more on saving and investing). At the end of the road, you'll likely find financial independence.

Giving Yourself an Online Financial Makeover

The Internet can help you set your financial goals, and establishing financial objectives is a great way to start planning for the future. Long-term goals may include owning a home, buying a car, saving money for your children's educations, and so on. Short-term goals cover the things you want to do today, next week, or within the next few months.

A personal financial plan can help you accumulate wealth and create a clear financial path for you and your family. Keep in mind that your financial plan needs to be flexible so you can accommodate life's little changes. Moreover, your personal financial plan needs to be

- ✔ **Realistic:** Make sure your goals are achievable.

- ✔ **Appropriate:** Make sure your goals are consistent with your personal lifestyle.

- ✔ **Time-specific:** Establishing milestones and deadlines along the way helps you reach your long-term goals.

Don't forget to include your personal values and to use your financial plan as a standard upon which you base your decisions. After you create a budget and a financial plan (see Book I's Chapter 3 for more), you'll have a better idea of how much money you need to reach your financial goals.

Table 5-1 gives you an online financial makeover that's designed to help you locate extra money for your short-term or long-term financial goals. You'll soon discover that by using online resources and looking at your entire personal financial picture, you can make the most of your long-term finances by reorganizing the money you have today.

Table 5-1	Online Financial Makeover
Category	*Financial Makeover Questions and Online Resources*
Getting started	Are your savings and investments performing as well as they should? Get the latest information about savings and investment returns. Imoney.com (www.imoney.com), Wall Street Journal (www.wsj.com), and MarketWatch (www.marketwatch.com).
Getting a handle on borrowing	Are you paying just the minimum monthly payment on your debts? Myfico.com (www.myfico.com), Creditinfocenter.com (www.creditinfocenter.com), and MyVesta (www.myvesta.org).
Taking advantage of lower interest rates	Can you negotiate a lower interest rate? You can often get your credit card interest rate lowered with just one phone call. Bankrate (www.bankrate.com) and Fiscal Agents (www.fiscalagents.com/learningcentre/credittips.shtml).
Determining your financial health	Do you know where you're spending your money? BYG Publishing (www.pygpub.com/fnance/cashflowcalc.htm).
Managing your money	Are you tracking income and expenses by banking and paying bills online? MsMoney.com (www.msmoney.com) and Spending Profile (www.spendingprofile.com).
Protecting your assets	Are you prepared for an emergency? MS Money (http://moneycentral.msn.com/content/banking/p43410.asp) and SmartPros (finance.pro2net.com/x32994.xml).
Protecting your future	Do you have enough insurance? InsWeb (www.insweb.com), Ensurance.com (www.ensure.com), and Progressive (www.progressive.com).
Planning for retirement	Do you know how much to expect in Social Security benefits? Social Security Administration (www.ssa.gov/planners/calculators.htm).
Rebuilding your nest egg	Do you know how much you'll need to live on when you retire? Yahoo! Finance (http://finance.yahoo.com/how-to-guide/retirement/18303) and MainStreet.com (http://mainstreet.com/beginning-your-retirement).

(continued)

Table 5-1 *(continued)*

Category	Financial Makeover Questions and Online Resources
Investing in your future	Does your employer match your contribution to your retirement fund? How do you plan to invest the money? 401k. com (`http://401k.fidelity.com/public/ content/401k/Tools/ContributionCalc`) and Kathleen Sindell's Online Investment Program (`www. kathleensindell.com/twelve_point_investing_ program.htm`). Or purchase *Investing Online For Dummies*, 6th Edition, by Matt Krantz (Wiley).

Using the Internet to Budget

The difference between doing financial planning and setting your budget is that financial planning involves defining your financial goals and objectives, determining the best strategy to achieve those goals and objectives, and measuring your progress. Budgeting, on the other hand, starts with establishing the spending targets that help you stay within your means of paying your bills.

On average, most Americans spend about 10 percent more than they have, and in most cases, they overspend because they have only a vague idea of where their money goes. Often the notion of living on a budget seems like punishment for hard work, yet the better way to think about a budget is as a spending plan — nothing more, nothing less.

Creating a budget using a pencil and paper usually takes one to three hours, but if you've already started organizing information about your income and spending and make use of a *canned online budget* (a predetermined online budget based on your annual income), you can probably reduce the time required to build a budget to just several minutes.

Unless you're in debt trouble, base your budget on organization, not penny-pinching. Getting organized can show you how to save money without giving up the things you love. Your spending plan easily and instantly tells how much money you have to spend at any given time, and this valuable information enables you to profit from opportunities and react in a positive way to emergencies.

Yahoo! Finance offers three online budget calculators that get you pointed in the right direction by helping you answer these important questions:

- **How much am I spending?**

  (`http://finance.yahoo.com/calculator/banking-budgeting/bud-02`)

- **How much should I set aside for emergencies?**

  (`http://finance.yahoo.com/calculator/banking-budgeting/bud-03`)

- **What's it worth to reduce my spending?**

  (`http://finance.yahoo.com/calculator/banking-budgeting/bud-11`)

Book II

Managing Home and Personal Finances

The Internet and personal-finance software programs have taken much of the drudgery (and pain) out of setting up a budget. In general, follow these steps to setting up a budget (see Book I's Chapter 3 for another method — you can also use the budget you create in that chapter to get you started here):

1. **List your income and expenses.**

   Everyone needs to start somewhere. List your income and expenses to determine how well you're doing. I list several online net cash flow calculators later in this section so you can gain a quick view of your starting point.

2. **Determine the time frame of your budget.**

   Decide on the time period for your budget. If you're paid every two weeks, a two-week budget may work for you. If you pay bills monthly, a monthly budget may be more to your liking. Most people find an annual or semiannual budget (based on real estate taxes and fees for annual insurance premiums) difficult to work with. No hard-and-fast rules dictate which time period is best.

3. **Choose a simple tracking technique.**

   You may want to track your expenses in a notebook or use a personal finance software program like *Quicken* (`www.quicken.com`) or *MS Money* (`www.microsoft.com/money/`). Tracking your expenses online at `www.quicken.com` and downloading them to a spreadsheet application program may be easier for you. Choose the tracking method that is the most comfortable for you to use.

4. **Determine general categories.**

   You may want to start with categories such as housing, car, and food, and then add subcategories like house payment and home improvements, car payment and auto insurance, and groceries and dining out. You can always add categories you need or delete ones you don't use.

5. **Establish income and spending amounts.**

Tally your income and deduct your expenses to find out whether you've been overspending, and then compare your spending habits to the averages for others with a similar net income at `www.msfinancialsavvy.com/calculators/cash_flow.php`. In what areas are you overspending or underspending?

6. **Monitor your inflows and outflows.**

Closely track your expenses to prevent *spending leakages* (unaccounted dollars spent). If your cash purchases represent more than 5 percent of your budget, start collecting receipts so you can recall what you purchased and can realign your budget accordingly.

7. **Reevaluate and review your budget often.**

Budgets aren't chiseled in stone, but as long as they're working, more power to you. However, you'll always run into a reason to make an adjustment. Your reasons for budgeting may change over time: new car, kids' education, retirement.

You may find these two online budget worksheets helpful:

- ✔ **About.com's Budget Worksheet** (`www.financialplan.about.com/library/blbudget.htm`) uses preselected categories for budgeted amounts, actual amounts, and the differences. About.com also provides a budget worksheet for college students that's set up the same way.

- ✔ **Fidelity Investments** (`http://personal.fidelity.com/planning/investment/content/budgetwork.html`) provides an annual personal budget. For your convenience, the Fidelity budget worksheet is printable. Deduct your outflows (your core and everyday expenses) from your inflows (your regular income). The difference is your personal *net cash flow.* Whenever the number is positive (everyone hopes it is), you have money to save or invest. Your savings can help you reach important financial goals, such as a down payment on a house, paying off debt, and enjoying a financially comfortable retirement.

Inflows – Outflows = Net Cash Flow

Whenever the difference between your income and expenses is a negative number, you're going into debt. Overall, a negative number indicates that you need to increase your income and/or analyze your expenses to see how you can reduce them.

Consider these useful online net cash flow calculators:

✔ **Raymond James Financial, Inc.** (www.raymondjames.com/calc_budget.htm) offers an online worksheet that tracks your income and expenses. After your totals are calculated, print the form and compare your income and expenses with your budget to make sure you're not overspending.

✔ **Kiplinger** (www.kiplinger.com/tools/budget) has an online worksheet that can assist you in getting on top of your monthly living costs by projecting expenditures in various categories, and then comparing those projections to what you actually spend. You can save your worksheet on your own computer or simply bookmark the page to use over successive months.

✔ **Tomorrow's Money** (www.tomorrowsmoney.org/section.cfm/389) offers an online calculator to assist you in determining your typical monthly and annual expenses. By subtracting those expenses from your income, you see where you can begin creating additional savings and how much you have to invest for your future. All you need is your checkbook, your most recent bank statement, and a pay stub to get started.

Book II

Managing Home and Personal Finances

Finding Online Resources to Track Your Income and Expenses

The best way to start your spending plan (or budget) is to track all your income and expenses — everything — from now, backing up to six months ago. This record provides you with the latest information about what you're earning and spending. Don't forget: Keep your tracking method simple. Selecting a tracking method that's too complex makes your work too difficult, and you'll likely abandon your effort. Bear in mind that your spending plan is a communications tool. Difficult-to-explain spending plans won't win the support of others in your family.

The most difficult part of budgeting comes at the beginning, when you must take a good, honest look at where you're spending your money. Sharing this information and having discussions about it with a spouse can be painful. Take heart in the fact that you're not alone. Many people have their own foibles about spending money.

If you don't yet have online access to your brokerage, bank, and credit card statements, check your statements or their Web sites (often given on the statements) to find out how to get started. As you begin accessing your accounts online, you may notice that you have to visit several Web sites to gather all the personal finance information you need. Some people like having their accounts scattered throughout cyberspace because they think doing so discourages hackers and impedes identity thieves. However, many people find having to deal with a plethora of passwords annoying. The solution is an account-aggregation service. You can try any of the many free personal finance-aggregation services available on the Internet. Aggregation services are essentially Web sites that consolidate all your online financial information so that it's easier to access. Two varieties are available — bank and nonbank-aggregation services.

On the other hand, if you're not ready to move your accounts online, write everything in a notebook. Keep in mind that you have to start making categories for your income and expenses. Categorize any amounts of more than $25. Regardless of which method you use, make sure you can customize it to suit your unique needs and requirements. Your spending plan can start as a canned online calculator or software program, but you need to be able to quickly and easily customize it to reflect your individual needs, goals, and objectives.

Almost any type of financial transaction can be completed with online banking. In the past clients could complete basic transactions such as transferring money from one account to another and pay bills online. Today, banks are offering online tools that let you transfer funds between institutions, pay bills faster, and analyze your spending. Many of these online tools were reserved for customers of private banks, such as the JPMorgan Private Bank. Now you don't have to be a high-net-worth depositor to view your bank accounts and nonbank accounts together on one page; link nonbank checking accounts to your bank account; and, in the case of ING Direct, even transfer money from their bank to other banks, such as Washington Mutual (WaMu).

The best part of these increased banking services is that they are generally offered free of charge. By getting customers to spend more time on their Web sites, banks are hoping they will increase customer loyalty and inspire customers to open more accounts. Here are two examples of financial institutions that provide this type of expanded service:

- ✔ **HSBC** (www.hsbc.com) provides online access to more than 3 million customers. Customers can use HSBC's *EasyView* service that allows you to bring your HSBC and non-HSBC accounts together on one Web page. With *EasyView* you never have to log in individually again. For those people who have a slow Internet connection or hate jumping from Web site to Web site, this can reduce financial stress and save time.

- ✔ **ING Direct** (www.ingdirect.com) has over 60 million customers worldwide. The bank does not have traditional checking accounts. For example, there are no paper checks. You can pay online with bill pay, use ATM services and a MasterCard debit card. However, ING will link non-ING checking accounts to your ING Electric Orange account. This way you can view all your spending in one spot.

 Some nonbank Web sites offer the same services that bank or credit union Web sites provide. For example, Yahoo! Finance Money Manager (`www.finance.yahoo.com/accountaccess`) lets you obtain and view your brokerage, banking, and credit card account balances all in one place. Yahoo! Money Manager also provides expense-management and net-worth features. This Yahoo! service is free and helps users quickly get an online snapshot of their current financial situation, enabling them to stay on top of their personal finances more easily and make more informed decisions.

Book II

Managing Home and Personal Finances

Using the Internet to Get Free Financial Advice

Knowing where you're headed financially can make a big difference in how you plan to use your finances. Everyone has different incomes, spending patterns, and financial priorities, so making the effort to visualize where the money is coming from and where it's going is a great first step in managing your finances. In general, financial planning includes the following:

1. **Determining your financial goals and objectives**: Many of us believe we are working for a variety of financial goals. However, we generally don't take the time to write down exactly what our goals are. Written goals have a greater probability of being achieved. This process helps "monetize" your objectives. For example: *In five years I want to retire with $1 million in investable assets.*

2. **Analyzing your current financial situation:** Take the time to locate all your financial documents (bank and brokerage statements, IRS returns, real estate tax statements, credit card and mortgage bills, and so on). Complete cash flow statement to determine exactly how much you can invest or save. Next complete a net worth statement. Now you have a starting point for creating your financial plan.

3. **Creating a financial strategy for achieving your goals:** At this point you know where you want to go (financially speaking) and where you are. How can get to your financial objective? Can you achieve your goal within your desired time period? Develop a strategy that is adaptable and flexible. Make certain that everyone in your family is working for the same goals.

4. **Implementing your financial plan:** Executing your plan can take from a few days to a few years. Most people get wealthy incrementally. If you are not an overnight millionaire, don't be discouraged.

5. **Monitoring and evaluating your financial plan:** Once you have implemented your financial plan, revisit it at least annually. Keep in mind that everything changes over time.

The Internet can provide expert advice for your personal financial plan at little or no cost. With a little effort, you can use free (or inexpensive) online resources to maximize your personal wealth. Several online Web sites offer free expert personal finance advice, including these sites:

- **CNN Money.com** (http://money.cnn.com/magazines/moneymag/money101) has a step-by-step guide for gaining control of your financial situation. Lesson 1 is setting priorities, Lesson 2 is making a budget, and Lesson 3 covers the basic of banking and saving. There are a total of 23 easy-to-understand lessons.

- **Kiplinger.com** (www.kiplinger.com) offers trusted personal financial advice, business forecasting, and investing advice in addition to a wide variety of financial-management tools.

- **SmartMoney.com** (www.smartmoney.com) provides expert but basic personal finance advice on a number of topics. The Web site includes calculators and worksheets for personal financial planning. Subscribers can save their worksheets (subscriptions are from $6 to $29 per month).

- **MSN Money** (www.moneycentral.msn.com) freely offers the expertise of a variety of columnists. Start by selecting a topic that's most interesting to you.

- **Yahoo! Finance** (www.finance.yahoo.com) is a large financial information portal loaded with good money-management advice and news. You'll discover practical personal finance advice, calculators, and investing tips.

Finding Out What You're Worth

Many individuals don't know their net worth, yet this calculation is important in your financial planning. Knowing your exact starting point enables you to determine how much you need to accumulate to achieve your financial goals. For most folks, increasing their net worth is the name of the game.

Before making plans for the future, you must know where you stand today. If you know only your bank balance, you're standing on shaky ground. To determine what you own, first add up all your assets. Next, subtract everything you owe. The difference is your *net worth*.

Figuring your net worth isn't only an important step in financial planning, but it also comes in handy for many other financial situations. For example, mortgage lenders require a net worth statement, college financial aid is based on net worth, and personal loans and lines of credit require net worth statements for approval. Additionally, wealthy individuals use net worth statements of $1 million or more to qualify for high-risk investments.

To determine your net worth, subtract your total liabilities from your total assets. If the number is positive, you're already on your way to accumulating wealth. All you need to do is get organized and start maximizing what you have. If the number is negative, you need a game plan to change that negative number into a positive one.

If you compute your net worth now and then again three months from now, you can tell whether your financial picture is improving or getting worse.

The free Web-based net worth calculators listed here do all the math for you. That is, they subtract your liabilities from your assets and tally up the difference.

- ✔ **Altamira** (www.altamira.com/altamira_en/education-guidance/calculators/net+worth+calculator.htm) has a net worth calculator designed to help users determine their current net worth and track changes in that value over time. Just input the relevant figures, and the calculator takes care of the rest.

- ✔ **CalculatorWeb** (www.calculatorweb.com/calculators/netwcalc.shtml) provides a variety of online calculators. Its net worth calculator is great for a quick snapshot of your financial position.

- ✔ **Understanding and Controlling Your Finances** (www.bygpub.com/finance/NetWorthCalc.htm) provides an online net worth calculator with detailed definitions of asset and liability categories that enable both experienced individuals and financial newbies to easily walk through the calculating process.

Book II

Managing
Home and
Personal
Finances

Book III
Dealing with Debt

"Coming out of bankruptcy, I can say I learned my lesson—don't spend what your relatives don't have."

In this book . . .

Almost everybody goes into debt at some point in their lives. Whether it's a credit card, a car loan, a mortgage, or even that 20 bucks you still owe your brother, it's likely you've borrowed moolah from someone. And that's not in itself a bad thing. Where it gets bad is when you can't pay it back according to the terms under which you borrowed it. Luckily, there is a lot you can do to get out of the red and into the black, and that's what this book is all about.

Here are the contents of Book III at a glance.

Chapter 1

Tackling What You Owe

Going into debt is as American as Mom's apple pie and fireworks on the Fourth of July. It's the American way! Unfortunately, if it's also *your* way, you may be so deep in debt that you live paycheck to paycheck, using credit cards and home equity loans to make ends meet and pay for unexpected expenses. Maybe you despair of ever being able to buy a home, having a comfortable retirement, or taking a vacation with your kids. (Are we hitting a nerve?) Your "American way" may have led you to give up on the American Dream.

Many creditors claim that consumers owe too much because they're irresponsible spenders, but recent studies tell a different story. For example, a 2006 study based on information from the Federal Reserve Board reveals that U.S. wages have been flat (after adjustments for inflation) since 2001, while the costs of such basics as housing, medical care, food, and other household essentials have increased. In other words, not all U.S. consumers are in debt because they're spendthrifts; instead, we've all taken a national pay cut.

Okay, so consumers at all but the highest income levels are being stretched to their limits — including you, which is undoubtedly why you are reading this chapter. But chances are, you haven't yet taken decisive action to improve your financial situation. Maybe you haven't even acknowledged the state of your finances, much less altered your lifestyle and become more careful about your spending. Even if you're well aware that you're in financial jeopardy, chances are you don't know what to do about your situation. You may be frozen by fear and confusion.

If you're trying to keep up with your financial obligations but you feel like poor Sisyphus, struggling to keep the boulder he's pushing uphill from rolling over him, you're in the right chapter. Starting here, we give you the information you need to take control of your debts and turn them around.

Taking Stock of Your Finances

You need a clear idea of the current state of your finances to figure out the best way to deal with your debts. Book I, Chapter 1 goes into more detail, but in a nutshell, here's the scoop:

- ✔ **Compare your monthly spending to your monthly income.** Prepare yourself for a shock. Most people underestimate the amount that they actually spend relative to what they earn. By doing this comparison, you may quickly realize that you're using credit to finance a lifestyle you can't afford, and you're spending your way to the poorhouse. If that's the case, you *must* reduce your spending to meet your financial obligations, and you may need to do a lot more than that, depending on the seriousness of your financial situation.

- ✔ **Order copies of your credit histories from the three national credit-reporting agencies: Equifax, Experian, and TransUnion.** (See Book I's Chapter 5 for contact details.) Your credit history is a warts-and-all portrait of how you manage your money — to whom you owe it, how much you owe, whether you pay your debts on time, whether you are over your credit limits, and so on. Being charged higher interest rates on credit cards and loans is a direct consequence of having a lot of negative information in your credit history.

- ✔ **Find out your FICO score.** Your FICO score, which is derived from your credit history information, is another measure of your financial health (also discussed in Book I, Chapter 5). These days, many creditors make decisions about you based on this score instead of on the actual information in your credit history.

We understand that things beyond your control — like bad luck and rising prices — may be partly to blame for your debt. We also know that, chances are you're at least partly responsible as well. For example, you may

- ✔ Pay too little attention to your finances. You forget to pay your bills on time; you don't pay attention to the balance in your checking account, so you bounce checks a lot; and/or you have a lot of credit accounts.

- ✔ Maintain high balances on your credit cards. As a consequence, you can afford to pay only the minimum due on the cards, you pay a lot in interest on your credit card debts, and all that debt has lowered your FICO score.

✔ Have little (or nothing) in savings, so you have to use credit to pay for every unexpected expense.

✔ Mismanage your finances because you don't know how to manage them correctly.

The National Foundation for Credit Counseling surveyed its member credit counseling agencies in early 2006 to determine the key reasons consumers were filing for bankruptcy. The survey showed that 41 percent of consumers blamed their bankruptcy on poor money-management skills, 34 percent attributed it to lost income, and 14 percent cited an increase in medical costs.

If compulsive spending is the cause of your financial problems, get help from an organization like Debtors Anonymous (www.debtorsanonymous.org) or from a mental health therapist. Compulsive spending is an addiction just like alcoholism, and you can't beat it on your own. You'll always have debt problems if you can't control your spending.

Using a Budget to Get Out of Debt

After you assess the seriousness of your financial situation, you need to prepare a plan for handling your debt, including keeping up with your creditor payments — or at least keeping up with payments to your most important creditors. One of the first things you should do is prepare a household budget (or *spending plan,* as some financial experts euphemistically call it).

Whether your annual household income is $20,000 or $100,000, living on a budget is probably the single most important thing you can do to get out of debt and to avoid debt problems down the road.

A *budget* is nothing more than a written plan for how you intend to spend your money each month. A budget helps you

✔ Make sure that your limited dollars go toward paying your most important debts and expenses first.

✔ Avoid spending more than you make.

✔ Pay off your debts as quickly as you can.

✔ Build up your savings.

✔ Achieve your financial goals.

In Book I, Chapter 3 we walk you through the budget-building process from start to finish. Reducing your spending and making more money often go hand in hand with creating a budget — we provide lots of practical suggestions for doing both in Book I, Chapter 4.

Book III

Dealing with Debt

Getting out of debt usually requires that you change your spending habits. Because those changes may affect everyone in your family, if you have children (especially preteens or teens), you and your spouse or partner should invite them to help you create your household budget. They can suggest expenses to cut and things they can do to improve your family's financial situation. If you involve them, your kids will be less apt to resent the effects of budget cuts on their lives. Also, you'll be giving your kids the education they need to become responsible money managers as adults.

Taking the Right Steps When You Have Too Much Debt

If you don't owe a *ton* of money to your creditors, living on a budget may be all it takes for you to whittle down your debts and hold on to your assets. If you owe a lot, though, living on a budget is only the first step in the get-out-of-debt process. You may also need to do some or all of the following:

- **Cut deals with your creditors.** Ask your creditors to help you keep up with your debts by lowering your monthly payments on a temporary or permanent basis, reducing the interest rate on your debts, or letting you make interest-only payments for a limited period of time. Before you approach any of your creditors, you've got homework to do. For example, you need to create a list of all your debts and the relevant information pertaining to each one. You should also review your budget to figure out how much you can afford to pay on your debts every month, starting with the ones that are the most important. Don't allow a creditor to pressure you into agreeing to pay more than you can afford.

Whenever you talk with a creditor, explain why you're calling and exactly what you're asking for. If the first person you speak with says *no* to your request, politely end the conversation and ask to speak with a manager or supervisor.

- **Borrow money to pay off debt.** When you get new debt to pay off existing debt, the process is called *consolidating debt.* We realize that going into debt to get out of debt may not sound sensible, but if it's done right, it can be a smart debt-management strategy. To do it right, however, all the following should apply when you consolidate:

  - The interest rate on the new debt is lower than the rates on the debts you pay off.

  - The monthly payment on the new debt is lower than the combined monthly total for all the debts you consolidate.

- The new debt has a fixed interest rate.

- You commit to not using credit again until you've paid off the new debt.

In Book III's Chapter 3, we explain the various ways to consolidate debt, including transferring credit card debt to a lower-rate card and getting a bank loan. We also discuss debt-consolidation offers that will do you more harm than good.

✔ **Get help from a credit counseling agency.** The advice and assistance of a credit counseling agency can be a godsend when you have a lot of debt and are struggling to take control of it (see Book III's Chapter 4 for more details). This kind of agency can especially help when you are confused about what to do or lack confidence about your ability to improve your finances on your own. A credit counseling agency can

- Help you set up a household budget.

- Evaluate a budget you have already created, to suggest changes that will help you get out of debt faster and avoid loss of assets.

- Negotiate lower payments with your creditors and put you into a debt-management plan.

- Improve your money-management skills.

Not all credit counseling agencies are on the up and up, so take time to choose a reputable one. First and foremost, that means working with a nonprofit, tax-exempt agency that charges you little or nothing for its services. In Book III, Chapter 4, we offer a complete rundown of all the criteria to consider when you are choosing a credit counseling agency. Also in that chapter, we warn you against mistaking a debt settlement firm for a credit counseling agency. If you're not careful, it can be an easy mistake to make because some debt settlement firms try to appear as though they are credit counseling agencies. However, the two have big differences between them. The goal of debt settlement firms is to profit off financially stressed consumers — not help them improve their finances. These firms charge a lot for their services, and many of them don't deliver on their promises. Consumers who work with debt settlement firms often end up in worse financial shape than they were before.

✔ **File for bankruptcy.** When you owe too much relative to your income, your best option sometimes is to file for bankruptcy, especially if you're concerned that one of your creditors is about to take an asset that you own and don't want to lose. You can file a *Chapter 7 liquidation bankruptcy,* which wipes out most but not all of your debts, or a *Chapter 13 reorganization bankruptcy,* which gives you three to five years to pay what you owe and may also reduce the amounts of some of your debts. Book III, Chapter 5 explains how bankruptcy can help you deal with various types of debts.

Handling Debt Collectors

Being contacted by debt collectors can be unnerving, especially if they try to pressure you into paying more than you think you can afford. Some will call you constantly, threaten you, and use other abusive tactics. Some debt collectors can be so difficult to deal with that you may promise them just about anything to make them leave you alone. Don't.

Realizing your rights

Debt collectors don't like taking *no* for an answer. Most of them are paid according to how much they collect, and they know from experience that pushiness pays off. They also know that most consumers are unaware of the federal Fair Debt Collection Practices Act (FDCPA), which gives consumers rights when debt collectors contact them and restricts what debt collectors can do to collect money. For example, the FDCPA says that you have the right to

- Ask a debt collector for written proof that you owe the debt he's trying to collect from you. The debt collector is obligated to comply with your request.

- Dispute a debt if you don't think that you owe it or if you disagree with the amount. You must put your dispute in writing and send it to the debt collector within 30 days of being contacted by the debt collector for the first time.

- Write a letter to a debt collector telling him not to contact you again about a particular debt. After the debt collector receives your letter, he cannot communicate with you again, except to let you know that he'll comply with your request or to inform you of a specific action he's about to take to collect the money you owe.

The FDCPA also says that a debt collector cannot

- Call you before 8 a.m. or after 9 p.m. unless you indicate that it's okay.

- Contact you at work if you tell the collector that your employer doesn't want you to be called there.

- Call you constantly during a single day or call you day after day. That's harassment!

- Use profane or insulting language when talking to you.

- Threaten you with consequences that are not legal or that the debt collector has no intention of acting on.

Many states have their own debt-collection laws. Sometimes those laws provide consumers with more protections from debt collectors than the federal law. Contact your state attorney general's office to find out if your state has such a law.

If a debt collector violates the law, get in contact with a consumer law attorney right away. The attorney will advise you of the actions you may want to take.

We're not suggesting that you should never deal with a debt collector. If you agree that you owe a debt, and if your finances allow, you may want to work out a plan with the debt collector for paying your debt over time, or the debt collector may agree to let you settle your debt for less than the full amount.

Understanding why debt collectors behave as they do

The adage "Know thy enemy" certainly applies to debt collectors. Understanding why debt collectors behave as they do helps take away some of their power and empowers you in return.

One of the main reasons debt collectors are so darn persistent (and can be quite aggressive at times) is money. Most of them are paid according to the amount of money they collect: The more they collect, the more they earn; if they collect nothing on your debt, they get nothing. Other debt collectors actually purchase your bad debt from the creditor you originally owed the money to. These collectors need to recoup the investment they've made by purchasing your past-due debt.

A second explanation for the behavior of debt collectors is that they know that most consumers don't have a clue about their legal rights related to debt collection. Debt collectors are more than willing to push the legal envelope because experience shows that a lot of consumers will pay at least a portion of what they owe if collectors harass them enough and scare them into submission.

There's a third reason for pushy collection practices as well: If the debt collector's phone calls and letters don't get you to pay your past-due debt, he has to invest additional time and money to take further action. This situation applies specifically to the collection of *unsecured* debts, like credit card debts or unpaid medical bills. When you acquire an unsecured debt, you don't have to give the creditor a *lien* on one of the assets you own (which would give the creditor an automatic right to take the asset if you didn't pay your debt). That means that if you can't or don't pay a past-due unsecured debt, the debt

Book III

Dealing with Debt

collector has to sue you for the money, which costs him time and money. Then if the debt collector wins the lawsuit, he has to try to collect the money you owe by doing one of the following:

- ✔ Seizing one of your assets (assuming that you have an asset the debt collector can take)
- ✔ Having your wages garnished (if your state allows wage garnishment)
- ✔ Placing a lien on one of your assets so you can't sell it or borrow against it without paying the debt first

All three options cost the debt collector more time and money. If your debt is small, the debt collector may decide it's just not worth the effort to sue you; his time is better spent going after other consumers with debts that he thinks will pay off better. The same is true if you are *judgment proof,* meaning that you don't have any assets the debt collector can take or put a lien on, you are unemployed, or your state doesn't permit wage garnishment.

Some debts, called *high-stakes debts,* deserve special attention because the consequences of falling behind on them are especially serious. For example, depending on the type of debt, you may risk losing an important asset, being evicted, or having your income tax refunds taken (or intercepted).

Talk with a consumer law attorney as soon as you become concerned about your ability to keep up with payments on a high-stakes debt. The attorney can help you figure out a way to avoid a default. If you're already in arrears and being threatened with a foreclosure, repossession, lawsuit, or some other serious legal action, run — don't walk — to the attorney's office.

Getting a Financial Education

What would you do if you had no debt? Would you buy a new house? Take a great vacation? Boost your retirement savings? Hopefully, you'll eventually have to answer that question for yourself because your debt will disappear and you'll have money to put toward your financial goals. Getting from here to there won't be easy, but you can do it. If you're having trouble getting yourself psyched up for the challenge, take a look at Book I's Chapter 2.

To make sure you succeed, we encourage you not only to deal with your debt head-on, but also to become the smartest money manager you can be. After all, when you get to the other side of your debt problems, you never want to return.

The difference between good debt and bad debt

Considering that you have serious problems with debt, you may be surprised to hear this: We eventually want you to use credit cards and get loans again. Why on earth would we steer you back into debt when getting out of it is such hard work? Because owing money to creditors is not necessarily a bad thing.

Whether debt is good or bad depends on why you took on the debt in the first place and how you manage it — whether you make your payments on time, for example. It also depends on how much debt you have relative to your income, because too much debt, even if you're able to keep up with your payments, harms your credit history and brings down your credit score.

Why debt can be a good thing

Going into debt can be a good thing, in many circumstances. For example, you could go to your grave trying to save up enough money to purchase a home with cash, so a mortgage is a wonderful thing — especially if the value of your home grows over time. Also, a home equity loan is a good financial tool when you use it to improve or maintain your home (again, with the goal of increasing its value).

A car loan is another example of good debt because most of us need a vehicle to get to and from work, and most of us can't afford to purchase a car with cash. Debt is also good when it helps you build your wealth; for example, you borrow money to purchase your home or rental property. Some debt helps you save money in the long run, like getting a loan to make your home more energy efficient so you can reduce your energy bills.

When debt isn't so good

Debt is detrimental to your finances when you run up your credit card balances to live beyond your means or to purchase goods and services that don't have any lasting value for you or your family. For example, restaurant meals, happy hour drinks, clothing, jewelry, and body care services don't have any lasting value, but they sure can run up your credit card balances.

Debt is also a negative thing when you have so much that you can't afford to repay it (especially when your home is at risk), when the amount you owe lowers your credit score, or when you borrow money from shady operators (like finance companies or payday loan companies) that charge high interest rates.

Book III

Dealing with Debt

Distinguishing between types of credit

You may think that all credit is created equal. A lot of people think so, which is one of many reasons they run into debt problems. In this section, we brief you about various types of credit. They definitely aren't created equal, and you should get familiar with these terms so you can become a better credit consumer.

Here are the types of credit you should be familiar with:

- **Secured:** With this kind of credit, the creditor guarantees that it will be paid back by putting a *lien* on an asset you own. The lien entitles the creditor to take the asset if you don't live up to the terms of your credit agreement. Car loans, mortgages, and home equity loans are common types of secured credit.

- **Unsecured:** When your credit is unsecured, you simply give your word to the creditor that you will repay the money that you owe. Credit card, medical, and utilities bills are all examples of unsecured credit.

- **Revolving:** If your credit is revolving, the creditor has approved you for a set amount — your *credit limit* — and you can access the credit whenever you want and as often as you want. In return, you must pay the creditor at least a minimum amount on your account's outstanding balance each month. Credit cards and home equity lines of credit are examples of revolving credit.

- **Installment:** With installment credit, you borrow a certain amount of money for a set period of time and you repay the money by making a series of fixed or installment payments. Examples of installment credit include mortgages, car loans, and student loans.

Seeing yourself through a creditor's eyes

To be a savvy consumer, you also need to know the criteria that creditors use to evaluate you when you apply for new or additional credit. Although creditors may take other factors into account, the following are the three biggies:

- **Your character:** Does your credit history show that you've got a history of repaying your debts?

- **Your financial capacity:** Can you afford to repay the money you want to borrow?

✔ **Your collateral:** If you have a poor credit history, or if you are asking to borrow a lot of money, creditors want to know whether you have assets that you can use to secure your debt or guarantee payment on it.

These criteria not only determine whether a creditor will approve or deny credit, but they also impact how much credit you're given, what your interest rate is, and what other terms of credit apply.

Building a better credit history

Right now, when you're smothered by debt, you may not be able to think about improving your credit history — you've got too many other immediate concerns. But tuck this topic into the back of your mind because when you've had money troubles, rebuilding your credit history should be one of your first goals. Having a positive credit history is essential to getting new credit with attractive terms.

The credit-rebuilding process is quite simple: You get small amounts of new credit and repay the debt on time. For example, you get a MasterCard or Visa card, use it to purchase some goods or services you need, and pay off your card balance according to your agreement with the card issuer. You could also borrow a small amount of money from a bank and pay off the loan according to the terms of your agreement with the lender.

As you do these things, you add new positive information to your credit history. Meanwhile, the negative information in your credit history gradually begins to disappear because, with a few exceptions, most damaging credit record information can be reported for only seven years and six months. As time passes, your credit history will gradually contain more positive than negative information, assuming that you manage your finances responsibly.

Why is rebuilding your credit history so crucial? First, if you have a negative credit history, you won't qualify for a credit card with a low interest rate, you'll have trouble borrowing a significant amount of money from a bank, and your credit score will be lower than it would be if your credit history was full of positive information. Consider some other potential consequences of a negative credit history:

✔ Potential employers who review your credit record as part of the job application process may not hire you. You may also be denied a promotion with your current employer if it checks your credit report as part of the process.

Book III

Dealing with Debt

✔ Life insurance companies may penalize you by charging you a higher premium or not selling you as much insurance as you would like.

✔ Landlords may not want to rent to you.

✔ You may not be able to get a security clearance or certain types of professional licenses.

Avoid companies that promise to rebuild your credit or claim to be able to — *presto chango* — make the negatives in your credit history disappear. Not only are you wasting your money, but (depending on the tactics a credit repair firm uses) you also may violate federal law if you do what the firm tells you to do.

Chapter 2

Understanding How Credit Works

- -

In This Chapter

▶ Seeing yourself as lenders see you

▶ Understanding credit reports and credit scores

▶ Establishing credit for the first time

▶ Handling mortgage problems

▶ Living happily ever after

- -

*W*hatever did people do before there was credit? In the olden days, it was much more difficult for the average person to buy the goods and services that we take for granted today — like a car, a home, and a college education, to name a few. Imagine if first-time home buyers had to save $267,000 (the national average for the cost of a new home in 2008, according to the Federal Housing Finance Board) before taking ownership and stepping over the threshold. If that were the case, they'd likely be using walkers to enter their new abodes.

Credit is a powerful tool — powerful enough even to move mountains. Unfortunately, it can also bury you beneath one if you use it improperly. Credit doesn't come with an instruction manual or a warning label. The subject generally isn't well taught in schools or, for that matter, in the family. So where do you get an understanding of this genie in a bottle before you make your three wishes? You're holding the answer in your hands.

We firmly believe that if you know the rules of the credit game, you stand a much better chance of getting a good score. We all make mistakes, and this truism applies to credit use as much as anything else. What's important is knowing how to recover from your mistakes without compounding the damage.

We start with the basics so you can better understand the principles and concepts behind credit. Consider this chapter your jumping-off point to this book and to the world of credit. Our goal is to make your credit the best it can be and keep it that way — not just for the sake of having good credit, but so you can live the American dream of having a decent job, a place to call home, and whatever else you desire for yourself and the people you love.

Defining Credit: Spending Tomorrow's Money Today

Credit has its origins in the Latin word *credo*, which means "I believe." These considerations are the real underlying issues of credit: Do you do what you promise? Are you believable and trustworthy? Have you worked hard to build a good reputation? Little is more precious to a person than being trusted — and that's what credit is all about.

You (and Webster's) can also define credit as follows:

✔ Recognition given for some action or quality; a source of pride or honor; trustworthiness; credibility

✔ Permission for a customer to have goods or services that will be paid for at a later date

✔ The reputation of a person or firm for paying bills or other financial obligations

The concept of credit is simple: You receive something *now* in return for your promise to pay for it *later.* Credit doesn't increase your income. It allows you to conveniently spend money that you've already saved — or to spend the money today that you know you'll earn tomorrow.

Because businesses can make more money when you use credit, they encourage you to use it as often as possible. For creditors to make as much money as possible, they want you to spend as much as you can, as fast as you can. Helping you spend your future earnings today is their basic plan. This plan may make them very happy — but it may not do the same for you.

Consumers can avail themselves of many types of credit today, which is no surprise to you. We suspect you receive as many offers for various types of credit cards and lines of credit as we do. But despite the endless variations and terms that seem to exist, most credit can be classified as one of two major types:

✔ **Secured credit:** As the name implies, *security* is involved — that is, the lender has some protection if you default on the loan. Your secured loan is backed by property, not just your word. House mortgages and car loans fall into this category. Generally, the interest rates for secured credit are lower and the *term* (the length of time before you have to pay it all off) may be longer because the risk of loss is lessened by the lender's ability to take whatever you put up for security.

✔ **Unsecured credit:** This type of credit is usually more expensive, is shorter term, and is considered a higher risk by the lender. Because it is backed by your promise to repay it — but not by an asset — lenders are more vulnerable if you default. Credit cards fall into this category.

Chances are, you've always looked at credit from your own perspective, the viewpoint of the *borrower*. From where you're standing, you may be the customer who should be catered to. Consumer spending is two-thirds of the U.S. economy, and much of that is generated using lines of credit or credit cards. Whether you use credit as a convenience or because you need to spread out your payments, you keep the economy humming and people employed. Right? From the lender's perspective, however, you represent a risk. Yes, your business is sought after, but the lender takes a chance by giving you something now for a promise to pay later. If you fail to keep your promise, the lender loses.

The degree of doubt between the lender making money and losing money dictates the terms of the credit. But how does a lender gauge the likelihood of your paying on time and as promised? The lender needs to know three pieces of information about you to gauge the risk you represent:

✔ **Your character:** Do you do what you promise? Are you reliable and honest?

✔ **Your capacity:** How much debt can you handle, given your income and other obligations?

✔ **Your collateral:** What cash or property could you use to repay the debt if your income dries up?

Book III

Dealing with Debt

But where can this information be had — especially if the lender doesn't know your sterling attributes firsthand? The answer: your credit report and, increasingly, your credit score. That's why, before you open that line of credit that allows you to buy the new dining room set on a 90-day-same-as-cash special, you have to fill out and sign some paperwork and wait a few minutes for your credit to be checked out.

Sometimes, however, an unscrupulous creditor may try to take advantage of you and charge you more than the market price for the credit you want. Why? Because they like to make money. So how do *you* know if you're being overcharged? The same way the lenders decide whether to offer you credit and what to charge you for it: by knowing what's in your credit report and your credit score.

Meeting the Cast of Characters in the Credit Story

Before we delve into the saga of credit and all its complicated plot twists, allow us to introduce the characters. In most lending transactions, three players have lead roles: the buyer (that's you), the lender, and the credit reporter.

The buyer: I want that now!

The cycle of credit begins with the buyer — a person who wants something (that's you!). A house, a car, a plasma TV . . . it doesn't matter what you want — the definitive factor is that paying for it up front is either inconvenient or impossible. Maybe you just don't have the cash with you and you want the item now, or perhaps the item is on sale. Or maybe you haven't even earned the money to pay for the purchase, but you know you will and you don't want to pass up an opportunity.

"Hmm," you calculate as you gaze longingly at the coveted find. "I really want to get this now. If I wait until I have the money, it may be sold or the price may have gone up, so it only makes sense to buy it now." Or, if you're generous (or making excuses), you may say, "My sweetie would love this — and me — if I bought this. Who cares that I don't have the money right now? I will someday. I just know it."

Enter creditors, stage right.

The creditors: Heroes to the rescue

The creditor spots your desire a mile away, and it stirs the compassionate capitalist within him. "Hey," says the person with the power to extend you credit, "no need for you to do without. We have financing. We just need to take down a little information, do a quick credit check, and you can walk out the door with this thing you're lusting for."

If businesses can't sell you something or lend you money, they can't make a profit. So, believe it or not, they really do want to loan you money. But there's that risk factor: They need to find out how risky a proposition you may be. To get the lowdown on your credit risk, they call the credit bureau.

Knowledge is power: Knowing your rights

When it comes to credit, you have rights — a lot of them. Two big laws address your rights pertaining to credit:

✔ **Fair Credit Reporting Act (FCRA):** The Fair Credit Reporting Act ensures fairness in lending. It has been updated by the Fair and Accurate Credit Transactions Act (FACTA, or the FACT Act), which addresses credit report accuracy and entitles you to free access to your credit report and rights to dispute inaccuracies. It also addresses the problem of identity theft and gives you leverage to deal with this crime if it happens to you.

✔ **Fair Debt Collections Practices Act (FDCPA):** None of us is perfect. This law spells out our rights if we fall behind on payments and a code of conduct for anyone collecting a debt.

Enter credit bureau, stage left.

The credit bureaus: In a supporting role

The merchant most likely contacts one of three major credit-reporting bureaus — Equifax, Experian, or TransUnion (see Book I, Chapter 5 for more on these organizations) — to get the credit lowdown on you. The credit bureaus make the current lending system work by providing fast, reliable, and inexpensive information about you to lenders and others.

The information in your credit report is reported by lenders doing business with one or more bureaus and put into what is the equivalent of your electronic credit history file folder. This file of data is called your *credit report* (Book I, Chapter 5 is devoted to credit reports).

Over the years, as more information has built up in credit reports and faster decision-making has been found to result in more sales, lenders have increasingly looked for shortcuts in the underwriting process that still offer protection from bad lending decisions. Thus emerged the *credit score,* a shorthand version of all the information in your credit report. The credit score predicts the likelihood of your defaulting on a loan. The lower the score, the more likely you are to default. The higher the score, the better the odds of an on-time payback. By far, the most-used score today is the FICO score. FICO scores range from 300 to 850.

Book III

Dealing with Debt

Understanding the Consequences of Bad Credit

Aside from the obvious increase in borrowing costs and maybe a hassle getting a credit card, what are the very real costs of bad credit? The extra interest you have to pay is only the tip of the iceberg. The real cost of bad credit is in having reduced opportunities, dealing with family stress, and having to associate with lenders who, more often than not, see you as a mark to be taken for a ride and dumped before you do it to them. And, believe us, they're better at it than you are. In this section, we fill you in on some of the unpleasant consequences of bad credit.

Paying fees

From your perspective as the borrower in trouble, extra fees make no sense. You're having a short-term problem making ends meet, so what do your creditors do to help you? They add some fat fees onto your balance. Thank you very much.

How do these fees help you? They don't. The fees help the *creditor* in two ways:

- ✔ They focus your attention on *that creditor's* bill instead of someone else's.
- ✔ The creditor gets compensated for the extra risk you've just become.

As bad as the fees can be on your credit cards, they can be even worse on your secured loans. If you fall three months behind in your house payment, you can be hit with huge fees, to the tune of thousands of dollars.

Secured lenders tend to be low-key. Don't let that calm voice or polite, non-threatening letter lull you into complacency. They're low-key because they don't *have* to shout — they'll very quietly take your home or other collateral, unlike the credit card guys, who can be heard from across the street. Pay attention to the quiet guy, and take action early.

Late fees, overlimit fees, legal fees, repo fees, penalty fees, deficiency payments, and default rates — when the fees show up, it's time to get serious. Call the creditor and ask to have the fees waived. Explain your plan to get current (make any past-due payments) and let them know that you need their help, not their fees. Book I, Chapter 3 of this book helps you put together a budget so you know exactly how much you can afford. If you have difficulty developing a budget, your creditors may accept a debt-management plan, which you work out with the help of a credit counseling agency. Take action early enough in the game, while you and your account are still considered valuable assets, and you're more likely to have success getting the fees removed.

Being charged higher interest rates

Consider two home buyers, one with a credit score of 760, the other with a credit score of 659. The happy new homeowner with the lower score won't be so happy to learn that, because of that lower score, he'll pay more than $90,000 more in interest over the life of the loan. Why? Because the mortgage company offers an interest rate of 5.3 percent to the individual with the 760 score, and an interest rate of 6.6 percent to the borrower with the 659 score.

The concept works basically the same in any lending situation. What impact would these scores have on a new car loan? A 36-month interest rate is more than *50 percent higher* for the person with the 659 score versus the 760 score!

Your credit score is based on your credit actions yesterday, last year, and maybe even ten years ago. If you miss a payment or two, that low-interest-rate credit card on which you're carrying a high balance can take your breath away. Watch the rate climb to the mid- to upper-20s or even 30-something — *percent,* that is! After all, you made a mistake and may stop paying altogether. So the lender is going to make money on interest while it can.

You think that getting your interest rate hiked for a minor infraction is unfair? That's not the end of it. Under the policy of *universal default,* if you have an issue with one lender, all your other lenders can hike their rates as well — yes, even though you're still paying the others on time and as agreed! In fact, some companies even use a deteriorated credit score as reason to escalate your rates to the penalty level. Even though you're paying that loan on time, a change in your credit score (perhaps from too many account inquiries or carrying higher balances) gives the creditor that has a universal default policy full rein to hike up your interest rates. This scenario is all the more reason to pay all bills on time and keep track of your credit report and credit score on a regular basis.

Book III

Dealing with Debt

Losing employment opportunities

Prospective lenders aren't the only ones who judge you based on your credit report and credit score. Potential employers check out your credit report, too. Why is that, you ask? Businesses reason that the way you handle your finances is a reflection of your behavior in other areas of your life. If you're late paying your bills, you may be late for work. If you default on your car loan, you may not follow through with an important assignment.

Even if your credit woes can be explained, bad credit is a distraction, from the employer's perspective, and it detracts from worker productivity. Recent research shows that employees with credit problems are significantly less productive on the job than employees without.

Increasingly, credit checks are a standard part of the hiring — and even promotion — process at companies large and small throughout the United States. And from the employer's perspective, it's easier to hire someone with good credit than to bother to find out what's going on with someone whose credit is bad.

Facing increased insurance premiums

The brain trusts at the insurance companies (known as *actuaries*) love their numbers. They sniff out a trend, sometimes even before it happens, and slap a charge on it faster than a cat can catch a mouse. The fact that a strong correlation exists between bad credit and reported claims hasn't escaped the attention of these people. The upshot: Bad credit will cost you a bundle in insurance-premium increases and may result in your being denied insurance.

Some states have gotten very excited about safe drivers and homeowners getting premium increases with no claims being reported. About 50 percent of states have restricted the use of credit-based insurance scores (and, to a lesser extent, credit reports) in setting insurance prices. To find out whether (and to what extent) scores and credit reports are used in your state, contact your local state insurance department. The states are still battling with this issue and it's difficult to say whether current laws will be overturned or upheld, or whether more will be added.

We're not talking about your garden-variety credit score here. Fair Isaac has developed an Insurance Score. This score is calculated by taking information from your credit report, but the formula differs from the one used to figure your typical credit score. Insurance scores range from 500 to 997, with 626 to 775 being average. The Federal Trade Commission recently weighed in on the topic when a study it conducted found that these scores are effective predictors of the claims that consumers will file.

Getting a divorce

Would your better half dump you because of bad credit? Maybe not, but one thing is sure: Half of all marriages end in divorce, and the biggest cause of fighting in marriages is due to financial issues — such as bad credit.

Spouses want to be proud of their mates. And with credit playing a bigger role in so many aspects of modern American life, living with bad credit has to be a real blow to your image and self-esteem. We advise couples who are serious about pursuing a life together to talk about their attitudes on money and credit use. Sweeping this topic under the rug is too easy. Having a credit card refused for payment (often in front of others), worrying about which card still has available credit, or getting collection calls in the sanctuary of your home can be part of the credit nightmare you face as a couple. If you can't seem to find the words to talk about this sensitive topic or agree on a solution, get some professional advice before it becomes too late.

Consider this advice on bad credit and marriage:

- ✔ Get a credit report before you marry.
- ✔ Discuss money and credit, and agree on goals.
- ✔ Find out whether your honey is a spender or a saver.
- ✔ Fix your credit before it fixes you (as in "My cat is going to get fixed").

Dealing with a Thin Credit File

Book III

Dealing with Debt

Are you new to credit? Is your credit history file a tad thin? (No, your credit history hasn't been on a diet.) A *thin file* means that you don't have enough information in your credit file on which to base a credit score or make an underwriting decision. Typically, people who have just graduated from school, who are recently divorced or widowed, or who are new to the country have a thin file. The good news is, this group of newbies is so large and potentially profitable in today's comparatively saturated credit market that they've been given their own name — the *underbanked.* Basically, the underbanked are individuals who don't have access to the basics of the banking system, such as checking and savings accounts and credit services.

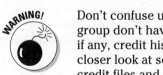

Don't confuse underbanked with *subprime.* The folks in the underbanked group don't have blemished credit histories. They simply don't have much, if any, credit history. A better term may be *preprime.* This section takes a closer look at some of the subgroups among the underbanked who have thin credit files and discusses some important points.

When you're new to the country

Individuals who are new to the United States may bring old attitudes about banks with them. Well, not only does the Statue of Liberty welcome you, but so do many banks and lenders. Furthermore, many immigrants have to overcome misconceptions and understand that, in this country, banks are safe and insured for deposits, currency doesn't become worthless overnight, and the government is unlikely to nationalize the banks.

Social classes don't carry much weight in American banking. Anyone who walks into a bank or credit union gets treated with respect, regardless of what they do for a living. In fact, in many states with large-enough concentrations of immigrants, banking services are being offered in different languages and in informal community settings, not just traditional banking offices.

Credit is essential to making a full and comfortable life in the United States. Lending, employment, insurance, and more are tied into establishing a positive credit history. The American Dream, if you will, is intimately related to the credit system. So where do you start? Here are some points to consider:

- You don't need a Social Security number to open a bank account if you are a foreign national. A consular ID or taxpayer identification number is sufficient for many banks.

- Credit bureaus don't require a Social Security number to establish a credit history for you. Name, address, and date of birth all come before the Social Security number when it comes to linking credit histories with individuals.

- Credit doesn't consider race, national origin, gender, or any of those discriminatory categories.

- Building a relationship with a mainstream lender can help you avoid overpaying for credit products.

After one of life's many transitions

People who have just graduated or gone through a divorce also often have thin credit files. If you fall into this category, you're probably looking for ways to build your credit history. To begin your journey, we suggest you set some long-term and interim goals as your destinations. Financial goals, like traveling goals, make sense, if only to keep you from wandering aimlessly. A car, a better apartment, a home, or a vacation are all good goals and reasons to save your money and use credit wisely.

You can also do the following to help you begin to build credit:

- **Establish credit easily using a secured credit card.** You make a deposit into an insured bank account and are given a credit card with a limit up to the amount of your deposit. Your deposit guarantees payment and allows you to have positive credit reported in your name. Soon you'll qualify for an unsecured card and larger credit lines.

✔ **Open a passbook loan.** With a passbook loan, you make a deposit into a savings account and take out a small loan using the account as security. You don't use a credit card — you just get a lump-sum payment. But you can build a credit history when you make your payments on time, over time. Plus, the secured nature of the loan keeps costs very low. Credit unions, in particular, like these little starter loans.

Identity Theft: The Crime That Turns Good Credit Bad

Companies and schools seem to be losing the war on hackers and laptop thieves who are reported to be compromising databases with alarming frequency. Identity theft can devastate your credit and your ability to get loans, employment, insurance, and some security clearances and licenses without your ever having done anything to deserve it. An identity theft can also put you on the defensive, burdening you with the responsibility of proving that you are not the person collectors are after.

Protecting your identity from theft

To avoid the havoc wreaked by identity theft, your best bet is to avoid being a victim of identity theft altogether. Consider these tips:

✔ **Protect your financial information at home.** Don't leave credit card numbers and statements, Social Security information, bank account information, and other financial data unprotected. Most identity theft is low-tech (that is, paper-based). And most is carried out by people you know: friends, relatives, acquaintances, coworkers, and people you invite into your home for a variety of reasons.

Shred statements before putting them in the trash and lock away your sensitive information. Using your computer more (as long as you use it properly, password-protect information, and use a firewall on your home network) is an even better way to avoid theft.

✔ **Watch the mail.** Most people think that no one is watching their unprotected mailboxes. And most are right, but that leaves the rest of you with sensitive account numbers and documents containing your Social Security number sitting all day in an unlocked mailbox outside your home or apartment. By comparison, electronic bill-paying is much safer.

Taking action if you're victimized

If you're a victim of identity theft, you may first discover that fact through a collection call on an account you never opened, or unusual activity on a credit card or credit report. When you suspect your identity has been compromised, respond immediately. Here are some tips:

- ✓ **Write down everything.** This process may not be quick or simple, but it is critical.

- ✓ **Call any creditors affected and close your accounts.** Don't forget ATM and debit cards — you have higher limits of liability for these cards than you do credit cards, so they're particularly important.

- ✓ **Freeze your credit report.** (You can unfreeze it later.) Each bureau has a slightly different process, but in general you request by certified mail that a security freeze be placed on your credit file. Your request should include: Your name, address, date of birth, Social Security number, proof of current address such as a current utility bill, and any payment of applicable fees. Details can be found at each bureau's Web site.

- ✓ **Call the police and make a report.** Some creditors and collectors require a report to take action. Be sure to get a copy of the report.

Chapter 3

Consolidating Your Debts

*D*ebt consolidation is another option for managing your debts when you owe too much to your creditors. It involves using new debt to pay off existing debt. When done right, it can help you get out of debt faster and pay less in interest on your debts. Although debt consolidation is not *the answer* to your money problems, in many situations, it can help when you use it together with other debt-management strategies in this book. However, if your finances are in really bad shape, consolidating your debts probably won't help much, if at all.

In this chapter, we explain when debt consolidation is and isn't a good debt-management strategy. We also review the various ways you can consolidate your debts, explain how each option works, and review their advantages and disadvantages. We then warn you against dangerous debt-consolidation offers that harm, not help, your finances.

Knowing When Debt Consolidation Makes Sense

When you consolidate debt, you use credit to pay off multiple debts, exchanging multiple monthly payments to creditors for a single payment. When done right, debt consolidation can help you accelerate the rate at which you get out of debt, lower the amount of interest you have to pay to your creditors, and improve your credit rating. However, to achieve these potential debt-consolidation benefits, the following criteria need to apply:

- ✔ **The interest rate on the new debt is lower than the rates on the debts you consolidate.** For example, say you have debt on credit cards with interest rates of 22 percent, 20 percent, and 18 percent. If you transfer the debt to a credit card with a rate of 15 percent, or you get a bank loan at a rate of 10 percent and use it to pay off the credit card debt, you improve your situation.

- ✔ **You lower the total amount of money you have to pay on your debts each month.**

- ✔ **You don't trade fixed-rate debt for variable-rate debt.** The risk you take with a variable rate is that although the rate starts out low, it could move up. In the worst-case scenario, the rate could increase so much that you end up paying more each month on your debt.

- ✔ **You pay off the new debt as quickly as you can.** Ideally, you apply all the money you save by consolidating (and more, if possible) to pay off the new debt.

- ✔ **You commit to not taking on any additional debt until you pay off the debt you consolidated.**

Paying less on your debts isn't the only benefit of debt consolidation. Another advantage is that by juggling fewer payment due dates, you should be able to pay your bills on time more easily. On-time payments translate into fewer late fees and less damage to your credit history.

However, too many consumers consolidate their debts and then get deep in debt all over again because they are not good money managers, because they have spending problems, or because they feel less pressure after they've consolidated and get careless about their finances. For these consumers, debt consolidation becomes a dangerous no-win habit.

Considering Your Options

You can consolidate your debts in several ways:

- ✔ Transferring high-interest credit card debt to a credit card with a lower interest rate
- ✔ Getting a bank loan
- ✔ Borrowing against your whole life insurance policy
- ✔ Borrowing from your retirement account

Deciding whether debt consolidation is right for you and which option is best can be confusing. If you need help figuring out what to do, talk to your CPA or financial advisor, or get affordable advice from a reputable nonprofit credit counseling organization (see Book III, Chapter 4). The more debt you're thinking about consolidating, the more important it is to seek objective advice from a qualified financial professional. Otherwise, you may make an expensive mistake.

Transferring balances

Transferring high-interest credit card debt to a lower-interest credit card — the lower, the better — is an easy way to consolidate debt. You can make the transfer by using a lower-rate card that you already have, or you can use the Web to shop for a new card with a more attractive balance transfer option. Sites to shop at include www.cardtrak.com, www.cardweb.com, and www.cardratings.com.

Before you transfer balances, read all the information provided by the card issuer that explains the terms and conditions of the transfer — the stuff in tiny print. After you review it, you may conclude that the offer isn't as good as it appeared at first glance. For example, you may find that the transfer offer comes with a lot of expensive fees and penalties, and that the interest rate on the transferred debt can skyrocket if you're just one day late with a payment.

Also, higher interest rates (not the balance transfer interest rate) apply to any new purchases you make with the card, as well as to any cash advances you get from it. If the credit card offer does not spell out what the higher rates are, contact the card issuer to find out.

When a credit card company mails you a preapproved balance transfer offer, the interest rate on the offer may not apply to you. That's because most offers entitle the credit card company to increase the interest rate after reviewing your credit history.

To be sure that a balance transfer offer will really save you money, ask the following questions:

 ✔ **What's the interest rate on the offer, and how long will the rate last?** Many credit card companies try to entice you with a low-rate balance transfer offer, but the offered interest rate may expire after a couple months, and then it may increase considerably. In fact, you could find yourself paying a higher rate of interest on the transferred debt than you were paying before. If you can't afford to pay off the new debt while the low-rate offer is in effect, don't make the transfer unless the higher rate will still be lower than the rates you are currently paying.

Some people try to avoid higher rates on transferred credit card debt by regularly moving the debt from one card to another. Doing so damages your credit history and hurts your credit scores.

✔ **What must I do to keep the interest rate low?** Know the rules! Usually, a low rate will escalate if you don't make your card payments on time. However, if the card you use to consolidate debt includes a *universal default clause,* the credit card company can raise your interest rate at any time if it reviews your credit history and notices that you were late with a payment to another creditor, took on a lot of new debt, bounced a check, and so on.

The method you use to transfer credit card debt — going to the bank to get a cash advance through your credit card, writing a convenience check, or handling the transfer by phone or at the Web site of the credit card company — can affect the interest rate you end up paying on the new debt, as well as the fees you're charged as a result of the transfer. Typically, getting a cash advance at your bank is the most costly option. Before you transfer credit card debt, be sure you know the interest rate and fees associated with each transfer option, and choose the one that costs the least.

If you decide to use one of the convenience checks you receive from a credit card company, be aware that some of those checks may have lower interest rates than others, and the interest rates associated with some of the checks may last longer than with others. The credit card company should spell out the terms associated with each check in the information it mails with the checks. If you're confused, call the credit card company.

✔ **When will interest begin to accrue on the debt I transfer?** Usually, the answer is "right away."

✔ **How much is the balance transfer fee?** Fees vary, but typically they are a percentage of the amount you transfer, although some credit card companies may cap the amount of the fee at $50 to $75. Some credit card companies charge a flat balance-transfer fee.

✔ **What method will the credit card company use to compute my monthly payments?** Credit card companies use one of several types of balance-computation methods to determine the amount you must pay each month; some methods cost you more than others.

Look for a card that uses the *adjusted balance* or the *average daily balance (excluding new purchases)* method to figure out your minimum monthly payments. Avoid credit cards that use the *two-cycle average daily balance* method, if you can.

Also note whether the card has a 20-, 25- or 30-day *grace period* — the number of days between statements. You pay the most to use a card with a 20-day grace period.

If you plan to make purchases with the credit card after you've paid off the transferred card balances, also pay attention to the interest rate that applies to new purchases. Also, if you use the card to make purchases, the bank that issued you the card will probably apply your payments to the lowest interest rate balance first. So every time you make a purchase, you're potentially converting lower-rate debt to higher-rate debt.

Getting a bank loan

Borrowing money from a bank (or a savings and loan or credit union) is another way to consolidate debt. However, if your finances aren't in great shape, you may have a hard time qualifying for a loan with an attractive interest rate.

You can use different types of loans to consolidate debt: debt consolidation loans, loans against the equity in your home, and loans to refinance your mortgage.

When you're in the market for any type of loan, it pays to shop around. Some lenders offer better terms on their loans, and some loan officers may be more willing than others to work with you. However, if you have a good long-standing relationship with a bank, contact it first.

Taking out a debt consolidation loan

As the name implies, a debt consolidation loan has the specific purpose of helping you pay off debt. Depending on the state of your finances and how much money you want to borrow, you may qualify for an *unsecured* debt consolidation loan — one that doesn't require a lien on your assets.

If you qualify for only a *secured* debt consolidation loan, you have to let the bank put a lien on one of your assets. That means that if you can't keep up with your loan payments, you risk losing the asset. It also means that if you have no assets to put up as collateral, getting a debt consolidation loan is out of the question.

If a lender tells you that the only way you can qualify for a debt consolidation loan is to have a friend or family member cosign the note, think twice before you do that. As cosigner, your friend or family member will be as obligated as you are to repay the debt. If you can't keep up with your payments, the lender will expect your cosigner to finish paying off the note, and your relationship with the cosigner may be ruined as a result. Plus, making the payments could be a real financial hardship for your cosigner, and if she falls behind on them, her credit history could be damaged.

Borrowing against your home equity

If you're a homeowner and are current on your mortgage payments, some lenders may suggest that you consolidate your debts by borrowing against your home's equity. *Equity* is the difference between your home's current value and the amount of money you still owe on it. Most lenders will loan you up to 80 percent of the equity in your home.

Some lenders let you borrow more than the value of your equity in some cases. Never do that! If you borrow more than the value of your equity and then you need or want to move, you won't be able to sell your home because you owe more on it than it is worth.

Consolidating debt by using a home equity loan can be attractive for a couple reasons:

- ✔ It's a relatively easy way to pay off debt, and the loan's interest rate is lower than in some other debt-consolidation options.
- ✔ Assuming that you're not borrowing more than $100,000, the interest you pay on the loan is tax deductible.

However (and this is a really big *however*), your home secures the loan, which means that if you can't make the loan payments, *you can lose your home.* If your finances are already going down the tubes, borrowing against the equity in your home is risky business and just doesn't make sense. And even if you're able to meet your financial obligations right now, if you owe a lot to your creditors and you have little or nothing in savings, a job loss, an expensive illness, or some other financial setback could make you fall behind on your home equity loan.

Also, be aware that if you sell your home and you still owe money on your mortgage and on your home equity loan, you have to pay back both loans for the sale to be complete. In other words, if your home doesn't sell for enough to pay off everything you owe on your home, you have to come up with enough money to pay the difference. If the housing market in your area is cooling off, and especially if you paid top dollar for your home, consolidating debt by tapping your home's equity is probably not a good move.

If you do decide that a home equity loan makes sense for you, keep the following in mind:

- ✔ Borrow as little as possible, not necessarily the total amount that the lender says you can borrow.
- ✔ Pay off the debt as quickly as you can. Lenders typically offer very relaxed home equity loan-repayment terms, and why not? The longer it takes you to repay your home equity debt, the more money the lender earns in interest.

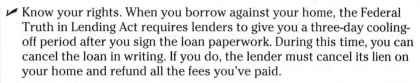

✔ Know your rights. When you borrow against your home, the Federal Truth in Lending Act requires lenders to give you a three-day cooling-off period after you sign the loan paperwork. During this time, you can cancel the loan in writing. If you do, the lender must cancel its lien on your home and refund all the fees you've paid.

✔ Beware of predatory home equity lenders who encourage you to lie on your loan application so you can borrow more money than you actually qualify for. These lenders gamble that you'll default on the loan and they'll end up with your home. The same is true of unscrupulous home equity lenders who *overappraise* your home (give it a greater value than it's really worth) in order to lend you more money than you can afford to repay.

Also steer clear of lenders who want you to sign loan agreements before all the terms of the loan are spelled out in black and white, and avoid loans with prepayment penalties.

You can tap the equity in your home in one of two ways: by getting a home equity loan or by using a home equity line of credit. Here's a quick overview of how each option works:

✔ **Home equity loan:** The loan has a fixed or variable interest rate, and you repay it by making regular monthly payments for a set amount of money over a specific period of time. If you apply for a variable-rate loan, be sure you understand what will trigger rate increases and the likely amount of each increase. If you're not careful, the initial rate can increase so much that you may begin having problems making your loan payments.

✔ **Home equity line of credit (HELOC):** A *HELOC* functions a lot like a variable-rate credit card. You're approved to borrow up to a certain amount of money — your credit limit — and you can tap the credit whenever you want, usually by writing a check. Typically, a lender will loan you up to 80 percent of the value of the equity you have in your home. The lender also reviews your credit history and/or credit score and takes a look at your overall financial condition.

Although you have to repay a home equity loan by making fixed monthly payments that include both interest and principal, with a HELOC, you usually have the option of making interest-only payments each month or paying interest and principal on the debt. If you opt to make interest-only payments, the amount of the payments depends on the applicable interest rate and on how much of your total credit limit you are using. For example, if you have a $10,000 HELOC but you've borrowed only $5,000 of that money, the amount of interest is calculated on the $5,000.

Shopping for a home equity loan or line of credit

When you're in the market for a home equity loan or a home equity line of credit, you're not obligated to apply only to the lender who holds your home mortgage. You can apply to any lender who does home equity lending. So shop around for the best deal by using the following terms of credit to compare your options:

✔ **Annual percentage rate (APR):** This is the cost of your borrowing expressed as a yearly rate. It includes all fees and other costs that you must pay to obtain the credit.

✔ **Monthly periodic rate:** Also referred to as a *finance charge,* this is the rate of interest you'll be charged each month on your outstanding debt. The higher the rate, the more the debt will cost you.

✔ **Fees:** The more fees and the higher the fees you have to pay, the more it will cost you to borrow against your home equity. Fees are usually negotiable, but if you're not in a strong financial position, you won't have much bargaining power. Many home equity loans come with the fees built in. This means that you end up borrowing more money but getting less cash and paying more in interest.

✔ **The amount of your monthly payments:** If you start to fall behind on your payments because they're more than you can afford, your interest rate may increase. If you fall too far behind, you may lose your home.

✔ **How long you have to repay the borrowed money:** The longer you take to repay it, the more interest you pay and the greater your risk that something will happen in your life that will make it impossible for you to repay your debt.

✔ **Whether you have to make a balloon payment:** A *balloon payment* is a lump-sum payment that you may owe at the end of a loan or when a home equity line of credit expires. If you can't afford to make the payment, you risk foreclosure, even if you've made all your monthly payments on time.

The problem with making interest-only payments is that the longer the principal is unpaid, the more your HELOC costs you, especially if the interest rate starts to rise. Also, if your HELOC expires after a certain number of years and there is no provision for renewing it, the lender will probably want you to pay the total amount you still owe in a lump sum, also known as a *balloon payment.* If you can't afford to pay it, you may lose your home.

Federal law requires lenders to cap the interest rate they charge on a HELOC. Before you sign any HELOC-related paperwork, get clear on the cap that applies. Also find out if you can convert the HELOC to a fixed interest rate and what terms and conditions apply if you do.

Refinancing your mortgage and getting cash out

If you're still paying on your mortgage, refinancing the loan at a lower rate and borrowing extra money to pay off other debts may be another debt consolidation option to consider. (The new mortgage pays off your existing mortgage.) However, refinancing is a bad idea if

> ✓ **You've been paying on the mortgage for more than ten years, assuming it's a 30-year note.** During the first ten years of a loan, your payments mostly go toward the interest on your loan and only a relatively small amount of each of your payments is applied to your loan principal. However, after ten years of making payments, you begin whittling down the balance on your loan principal at a faster rate. This means that with each payment you are closer to having your mortgage paid off and to owning your home outright. If you refinance your loan however, you start all over again with a brand-new mortgage, which means that you'll be paying mostly interest on the loan for a long time to come. Even so, if the new loan has a shorter term than your previous loan, paying mostly interest at first may not be an issue.

> ✓ **You can't afford the payments on the new loan.** If you fall behind, eventually your mortgage lender will initiate a foreclosure.

It may make sense to consolidate debt by going from a 30-year note to a 15-year note, assuming that you can afford the higher monthly payments. (You pay less interest on a 15-year mortgage, so going from a 30-year to a 15-year loan won't mean doubling your monthly payments.) Run the numbers with your loan officer.

You're playing with fire if you use a mortgage refinance to consolidate debt by trading a traditional mortgage for an interest-only mortgage. Sure, your monthly payments may be lower initially, but after five years (or whenever the interest-only period ends), they will increase substantially, maybe far beyond what you can afford.

Borrowing against your life insurance policy

If you have a whole life insurance policy, you can consolidate your debts by borrowing against the policy's cash value. If you have this kind of policy, you pay a set amount of money each month or year, and you earn interest on the policy's cash value.

This option has two advantages:

> ✓ You don't have to complete an application, and there's no credit check.

> ✓ After you borrow the money, you won't have to repay it according to a set schedule. In fact, you won't have to repay it at all.

But there's a catch, of course. After you die, the insurance company deducts the loan's outstanding balance from the policy proceeds. As a result, your beneficiary may end up with less than he or she was expecting, which can create a financial hardship for that person. For example, your surviving spouse or partner may need the money to help pay bills after your death, or your child may need the policy money to attend college.

Before you borrow against your life insurance, read your policy so you understand all the loan terms and conditions. Also be clear about any fees you may have to pay because they will affect the loan's total cost. If you're unsure about anything, talk with your insurance agent or broker.

Borrowing from your 401(k) retirement plan

If you're employed, you may be enrolled in a 401(k) retirement plan sponsored by your employer. If your employer is a nonprofit, you may have a 403(b) retirement plan, which works like a 401(k). The money you deposit in your retirement plan is *tax-deferred* income. In other words, whatever you deposit in the account each year isn't recognized as income until you begin withdrawing it during your retirement years. Your employer may match a certain percentage of your deposits.

Most employers that offer 401(k) plans allow their employees to borrow the funds that are in their retirement accounts, up to $50,000 or 50 percent of the value of the account, whichever is less. If the value is less than $20,000, your plan may allow you to borrow as much as $10,000 even if that represents your plan's total value. No matter how much you borrow, you have five years to repay the money, and you're charged interest on the unpaid balance.

Borrowing against your 401(k) plan may seem like an attractive way to consolidate debt — after all, you're just borrowing your own money! You have no loan application to complete and no credit check. However, unless you're absolutely sure that you can and will repay the loan within the required amount of time, taking money out of your retirement account to pay off debt is a *really* bad idea. Here's why:

✔ If you don't repay every penny within five years (and assuming that you're younger than 59½ when you borrow the money), you have to pay a 10-percent penalty on the unpaid balance. On top of that, the IRS treats whatever money you don't repay as an early withdrawal from your retirement account, which means that you're taxed on it as though it's earned income. As a result, on April 15, you can end up owing Uncle Sam a whole lot more in taxes than you anticipated, and you may not have enough money to pay them.

You may promise yourself that you'll repay your retirement account loan, but with no lender (or debt collector) pressuring you into paying what you owe, are you disciplined enough to do that? If you're like a lot of consumers, you'll keep promising yourself that you'll pay back the loan, but you'll never get around to it. Or if you begin having trouble paying for essentials, those expenses will take priority, and you may have no money left to put toward repaying your retirement account loan.

✔ Every dollar you borrow represents one less dollar you'll have for your retirement if you don't repay the loan. Using your retirement account like a piggy bank could make your so-called *golden years* not so golden.

✔ While the loan is unpaid, your retirement account earns less tax-deferred interest. Therefore, the account will have less money when you retire.

✔ If your employer matches the contributions you make to your retirement plan, those contributions may end while you're repaying the loan. This also means less money for your retirement.

✔ Your employer may charge you a steep loan application fee — a couple hundred dollars or more. The fee increases the total cost of the loan.

✔ If you leave your job before you've paid off the loan — regardless of whether you leave because you found a better job, you were fired or laid off, or your employer went belly up — your employer will probably require that you repay the full amount of your outstanding loan balance within a very short period of time, somewhere between 30 and 90 days. If you can't come up with the bucks, the IRS will treat the unpaid money as an early withdrawal for tax purposes, and you'll also have to pay the 10-percent early withdrawal penalty.

Use the online calculator at www.bankrate.com/brm/calc/401kl.asp to figure out whether borrowing from your 401(k) is a good idea.

If you're younger than 59½, you may qualify for an early hardship withdrawal from your 401(k), even if your plan doesn't permit you to borrow from it. A withdrawal differs from a loan because you take the money out of your account without the option of repaying it. Therefore, you are permanently reducing the amount of money you'll have for your retirement. To be eligible for a hardship withdrawal, you must prove to your employer that you have "an immediate and heavy financial need" and that you've exhausted all other financial avenues for handling the need. Although your employer determines what constitutes "an immediate and heavy financial need," avoiding an eviction or foreclosure or paying steep medical bills almost certainly qualifies. You have to pay federal taxes on the money you take out for the year in which you get the money, and you also have to pay a 10-percent early withdrawal penalty. There's no free lunch in life, is there?

Book III

Dealing with Debt

Avoiding Dangerous Debt-Consolidation Possibilities

When your debts are creating a lot of stress, your judgment may get clouded. You may start grasping at straws and do something really stupid that you would never do if you were thinking clearly — like fall for one of the many debt-consolidation offers out there that are outrageously expensive, and maybe even scams. Here are some of the worst offenders to avoid:

- **Debt-counseling firms that promise to lend you money to help pay off your debts:** If you get a loan from one of these outfits, it will not only have a high interest rate, but you may have to secure the loan with your home. Watch out! In Book III's Chapter 4, we tell you how to find a reputable nonprofit counseling agency that can help you deal with your debts. That chapter also explains how to avoid agencies that pretend to be nonprofits.

- **Finance company loans:** These companies often use advertising to make their debt consolidation loans sound like the answer to your prayers. They are not. Finance company loans typically have high rates of interest and exorbitant fees. As if that's not bad enough, working with a finance company will further damage your credit history.

- **Lenders who promise you a substantial loan (probably more than you can afford to repay), no questions asked, in exchange for your paying them a substantial upfront fee:** No reputable lender will make such a promise. Not only will these disreputable lenders charge you a high percentage rate on the borrowed money, but they will also put a lien on your home or on another asset you don't want to lose.

- **Companies that promise to negotiate a debt consolidation loan for you and to use the proceeds to pay off your creditors:** In turn, they tell you to begin sending them money each month to repay the loan. The problem with many of these companies is that they never get you a loan or pay off your creditors. You send the company money every month while your credit history is being damaged even more, and you're being charged interest and late fees on your unpaid debts.

Chapter 4

Negotiating with Creditors and Getting Help

*I*f slashing your spending, making more money, and living on a strict budget are not enough to resolve your financial problems, it's time to bite the bullet and contact your creditors. You want to find out if they will negotiate new, more affordable debt payment plans so you can get caught up with whatever is past due and continue paying on your debts. You may resist the idea of negotiating, but getting some relief from your debts can mean no more futile struggles to keep up with what you owe, an end to threatening letters and calls from annoying debt collectors, and less damage to your credit history.

We can't guarantee that 100 percent of your creditors will agree to sit down at the bargaining table with you. But if you contact them soon enough — as soon as you realize it's going to be a struggle to keep up with your debts, or as soon as you begin to fall behind on your payments — we bet that most will agree to work with you. They may not give you everything you ask for, but just a few concessions from your creditors can make a big difference to the state of your finances and, ultimately, can help keep you out of bankruptcy court.

In this first part of the chapter, we tell you about the preparation you should do before you contact any of your creditors, and we fill you in on how to contact them and who to speak with. We also explain what you should and should not say during your negotiations and highlight the importance of putting in writing the details of any agreement you may reach with a creditor. In the second half, we let you know what to do if you find yourself needing help from a credit counseling company.

Getting Ready to Negotiate

Upfront planning and organizing is essential to the success of any negotiation, whether you're trying to negotiate world peace or convince one of your creditors to let you pay less each month or have a lower interest rate.

Your upfront planning and organizing should include

- ✔ Creating a detailed list of your debts.
- ✔ Deciding which debts to negotiate first and what you want to ask from each of your creditors.
- ✔ Reviewing your budget (or creating one if you don't have one yet — see Book I, Chapter 3).
- ✔ Pulling together your financial information.

In this section, we walk you through each of these steps. If you don't do the necessary planning and organizing, you won't have any idea what you really need from each creditor and what you can offer in return. You'll be shooting in the dark, and the results could be disastrous for your finances.

If you don't feel comfortable about doing your own negotiating, you may want to ask your attorney or CPA to handle it for you, if you have a long-established relationship with that person. Assuming you have that kind of relationship, the CPA or attorney may agree to help you out for very little money. Another option is to get negotiating help from a nonprofit credit counseling agency in your area (see later in this chapter). You can also ask a friend or relative for help, especially if you know someone who is good at making deals.

Listing all your debts

Create a list of all your debts, separating the ones that are high priority from the ones that are low priority. For each debt on your list, record the following information:

- ✔ The name of the creditor
- ✔ The amount you are supposed to pay every month
- ✔ The interest rate on the debt
- ✔ The debt's outstanding balance

Also, note whether you are current or behind on your payments. If you are behind, record the number of months you are in arrears and the total amount that is past due.

You should also note whether a debt is secured or unsecured. For each secured debt, write down the asset that secures it. For example, your car secures your auto loan, and your house secures your mortgage and any home equity loans you may have. (In Book I, Chapter 3 we explain the differences between secured and unsecured debts.)

When you list your unsecured debts, like your credit card debts and past-due medical bills, list them according to their interest rates. Put the debt with the highest rate at the very top of the list, followed by the one with the next highest rate, and so on.

Leave space next to each debt on your list for recording the new payment amount you would like each creditor to agree to, or for recording any other changes you want from a creditor, such as a lower interest rate or the ability to make interest-only payments for a period of time. You will record this information after you have reviewed your budget.

Zeroing in on certain debts first

All debts are not created equal. Some debts are more important than others because the consequences of falling behind on those obligations are a lot more severe. For example, if you don't keep up with your secured debts, the creditors may take back their *collateral:* the assets you used to guarantee payment. You could also lose assets if you don't pay the taxes you owe to the IRS. Therefore, when you are preparing to negotiate with your creditors, negotiate these debts first:

Book III

Dealing with Debt

✔ Your mortgage

✔ Your past-due rent

✔ Your car loan

✔ Your utility bills

✔ Your court-ordered child support obligation

✔ Your past-due federal taxes

✔ Your federal student loans

During your negotiations, don't be so eager to reach an agreement with one of your creditors that you offer to pay more than you really can afford. Also, don't agree to a temporary change in how you pay a debt if you really need the change to be permanent. If you can't live up to the agreement as a result, most creditors probably won't negotiate with you again.

When you negotiate your lower priority debts, which will probably all be unsecured debts (such as credit card debt and medical bills), start by negotiating the one with the highest rate of interest — because the debt is costing you the most each month.

Reviewing your budget

After you create your list of debts, it's time to review your household budget. You need to figure out exactly what you need from each creditor in order to be able to pay off any past-due amounts and keep up with future payments. For example, you may want a creditor to agree to

- ✔ Lower the amount of your monthly payments on a permanent or temporary basis.
- ✔ Lower your interest rates.
- ✔ Let you make interest-only payments for a while.
- ✔ Waive or lower certain fees.
- ✔ Let you pay the amount that is past due by adding that total to the end of your loan rather than paying a portion of the past-due amount each month.

If you are at least 120 days past due on a debt, you may want to ask the creditor to let you settle the debt for less than the full amount you owe on it. The creditor may be willing to do that if it's convinced that settling is its best shot at getting at least some of what you owe. For example, the creditor may know that suing you for the full amount of your debt would be a waste of time because you are *judgment proof:* You have no assets that the creditor can take, and your state prohibits wage garnishment.

There can be federal tax ramifications to settling a debt for less than the original amount. Please don't start tearing out your hair, but the amount the creditor writes off is actually treated as income to you and may increase the amount you owe to the IRS when your taxes are due. For example, if you owe $10,000 to a creditor and the creditor agrees to let you settle the debt for $6,000, it sends the IRS a 1099 form reporting the $4,000 difference as your income. However, you may not be affected if you are insolvent by IRS 1099 standards. A CPA can tell you if the IRS considers you to be insolvent.

When one of your creditors agrees to let you settle a debt for less, ask the creditor to report the debt as current and to remove all negative information related to the debt from your credit report. The creditor may or may not comply with your requests, but you won't know unless you ask.

Pulling together your financial information

Some creditors may want to review your financial information before they agree to negotiate with you or agree to the changes you request. Prepare for that possibility by gathering together the following information and putting everything in one place for easy access:

- ✔ Your household budget
- ✔ The list of all your debts
- ✔ A list of your assets and their approximate values
- ✔ Copies of your loan agreements

Sharing information about your assets with your creditors can be dangerous. If one of them decides to sue you to collect on your debt, you've made it easy for that creditor to figure out which asset(s) to go after. However, if you are anxious to strike deals with your creditors so you can continue paying off your debts, you are between a rock and a hard place; you may have no option but to share the information with them. Another risk you take by sharing information about your assets is that a creditor may demand that you sell one of your assets and give it the sale proceeds. However, you don't have to take that step unless you want to and unless doing so is in your best financial interest.

Book III

Dealing with Debt

After you have pulled together your financial information, review your list of assets to determine whether you can use any of them as collateral. (Ordinarily, you must own the assets free and clear in order to use them as collateral.) Perhaps you own a boat, motorcycle, or RV, for example. As a condition of agreeing to lower your monthly payments or to let you make interest-only payments for a couple months, one of your secured creditors may require that you increase your collateral. If you do not have any assets that you can use as collateral, the creditors may decide it is too risky to work with you and take back the collateral you've already used to secure your debts with them.

A creditor may make having a cosigner a condition of any new agreement. We suggest that you determine ahead of time whether a friend or relative would be willing to cosign for you. As a cosigner, your friend or relative will be as responsible for living up to the agreement as you are, which means that if you default on the agreement, the creditor can look to your cosigner for payment. To be fair, before you ask someone to cosign for you, be sure that you can live up to the terms of the agreement. Also, make your friend or relative aware of the risks of cosigning before she signs any paperwork related to the agreement.

Negotiating basics

When they sit down at the bargaining table, savvy negotiators employ some basic rules to increase their chances of leaving with a deal that makes them happy. So take a cue from them by keeping the following in mind when you negotiate with your creditors:

✔ **Never put all your cards on the table.** When you tell a creditor how much you can afford to pay on a debt each month, the number of months that you want to make interest-only payments, and so on, always hold a little back. By not letting the creditor know right away what your bottom-line offer is, you give yourself some room to negotiate. If you are lucky, the creditor will accept your initial offer. But if the creditor responds with a counteroffer — maybe he wants you to pay a little more each month than you've suggested, or he offers to lower your interest rate two percentage points when you had asked for a four-point reduction — you can either respond with another offer or accept the creditor's offer and still be better off financially than you are now.

✔ **Know your bottom line.** Know the minimum that you need to get out of your negotiations and the most that you can afford to give to a creditor. Never agree to more than that.

✔ **Understand that you have to give a little to get a little.** A negotiation is successful when both parties leave the bargaining table with something. For example, in exchange for a creditor agreeing to lower your monthly payments, you may have to give the creditor a lien on another one of your assets. However, your goal is to give as little as possible in exchange for getting as much as possible.

✔ **Recognize who has the edge in your negotiations.** Whoever has the edge will have a stronger bargaining position, and the other person will have to give a little extra in order to have any chance of leaving the bargaining table with something. Your creditors will almost always be in a stronger position than you. That's certainly true for your secured creditors because if you can't strike a deal with them, they know they can always take your collateral back.

✔ **Never be demanding and never get angry or confrontational.** If you do, the creditor may simply cut off the negotiations. When you feel like you are about to lose your cool, end the conversation and resume it after you've had an opportunity to clear your head and calm down.

Getting Down to Business: Contacting Creditors

After you've completed all your upfront planning and organizing, you're ready to begin contacting your creditors. How you contact them — in person or by phone — and whom you talk to depends on the type of creditor. For example, if the creditor is local (and not part of a national chain), an in-person meeting is appropriate, and you probably want to meet with the owner, credit manager, or office manager. However, if you want to negotiate your MasterCard or Visa bill, your mortgage, or the debt you owe to a national retail chain, for example, you start negotiating by calling the company's customer service number.

If a creditor asks you to put your negotiating request in writing, send the details of your request via certified mail and request a return receipt. That way, you have confirmation that your letter was received, and you will know when to follow up.

Whenever you speak with someone, maintain a record of who you spoke to (name and title), the date of your conversation, what you asked for, how the creditor responded, and the specifics of any agreement you reached. You should also file away all correspondence related to your negotiations that you send or receive.

When you contact a creditor for the first time, explain that you are having financial problems and provide a general explanation of why the problems have occurred. For example:

- ✔ You lost your job.
- ✔ Your child is ill, and you have been saddled with a lot of unreimbursed medical expenses.
- ✔ Your former spouse is not paying you the child support you're entitled to.
- ✔ You took on too much credit card debt.

Give the creditor confidence that you'll be able to live up to any agreement you may reach with one another by explaining what you are doing (or have already done) to improve your financial situation and to minimize the likelihood that you'll develop money problems in the future. For example:

- ✔ You are living on a strict budget.
- ✔ You have enrolled in a money-management class.
- ✔ You are working at a second job.
- ✔ Your spouse has taken a job outside the home.

Tell the creditor that you want to continue paying on your debt, but in order to do so you need the creditor to agree to some changes. Be specific about exactly what you want the creditor to agree to. For example, you would like to pay $200 less each month on your debt or to make interest-only payments for three months.

If you get nowhere with the first person you speak with, end your conversation and try negotiating with someone higher up, like a supervisor or a manager. That person is likely to have more decision-making authority and to be in a position to agree to your request. In fact, when you call a creditor for the first time, you may want to ask the person you speak with if he has the authority to negotiate with you. If that person does not, ask who does.

Book III

Dealing with Debt

Some of your creditors may refuse to negotiate directly with you and may indicate that you should contact a credit counseling agency and let it do the negotiating for you. Later in this chapter, we tell you how credit counseling agencies work.

If the person you are negotiating with tries to pressure you into paying more than you can afford, stick to your guns.

Making the Agreement Official: Putting It in Writing

Whenever you and a creditor reach an agreement, ask for the agreement to be put in writing. If the creditor refuses, prepare the agreement yourself, date and sign it, and then send a copy to the creditor. The agreement should include

- ✔ Its duration.
- ✔ All deadlines.
- ✔ All payment amounts.
- ✔ Applicable interest rates.
- ✔ The amount of any fees you have agreed to and under what circumstance you must pay each fee.
- ✔ Everything the creditor has agreed to do or not do. For example, the creditor may agree to waive certain fees, forgive a past-due amount, or not report to the credit bureaus that your account is delinquent.
- ✔ When you and the creditor will be considered in default of the agreement and the consequences of the default.

If a problem develops with your agreement after it is official — if your creditor violates some aspect of the agreement or accuses you of doing the same thing — and you do not have the terms of the agreement in writing, resolving your differences may be difficult. Each of you is apt to have different memories of the agreement details. As a result, you may both have to hire attorneys to help you work out your disagreement, and you may end up in court where a judge will decide what to do.

Before you sign any agreement that you may reach with a creditor, especially if it involves a lot of money or an asset that you do not want to lose, ask a consumer law attorney to review it. You want to be sure that you are adequately protected and that the agreement does not have the potential to create future problems for you.

Don't hire an attorney until you have found out how much he will charge to do the review, which should not take more than one hour of his time. Most attorneys charge between $100 and $500 per hour for their services, depending on where they practice law and the size of the law firms they work for: Attorneys in metropolitan areas on the East and West coasts tend to charge more than attorneys in rural areas or in the Midwest. Attorneys who work for large firms tend to charge more per hour than attorneys with smaller firms.

If you cannot afford to hire an attorney, you may be able to get help from the Legal Aid Society in your area, which is essentially a law firm for poor people. Also, if there is a law school in your area, it may run a legal clinic, and an attorney or law school student with the clinic can review your agreement for free. Another option is to contact your local or state bar association to find out if it can refer you to a consumer law attorney who does a lot of pro bono work for financially strapped consumers.

After you have a final agreement with a creditor, revise your budget accordingly. When you are ready to contact another creditor, be sure that you prepare for your negotiations by working with the revised budget, not with your old one.

Knowing the Deal with Credit Counseling

Feeling overwhelmed by your debts and unsure how to take control of your finances, despite the advice you've read in this chapter and book so far? Have you tried without success to pursue the self-help options we discuss elsewhere? Take heart: There is a calm port in the storm called the *credit counseling agency.* Among other services, the agency can help you develop a budget and figure out a way to deal with your debts.

The benefits of credit counseling presume that you work with a reputable, nonprofit credit counseling agency that employs trained and certified credit counselors and that charges fairly for its services. Many credit counseling agencies talk a good game and have impressive Web sites, but they charge an arm and a leg for their services and deliver little in return. If you work with one of them, your finances could end up worse, not better. Yikes!

If you're in the market for credit counseling, read on. Here we give you the information you need to locate a reputable organization. We explain how good credit counseling agencies operate. And we provide you with a set of questions to ask before you agree to work with an agency. We also give you the lowdown on debt-management plans in case a credit counseling agency suggests that it set one up for you, and we tell you how to get the most benefit from such a plan.

We also illuminate the dangers of working with a *debt settlement firm* — a firm that agrees to settle your debts for less than what you owe on them. Some consumers confuse debt settlement for credit counseling; we explain how they differ. Finally, we tell you what to do if you are ripped off by a credit counseling agency or a debt settlement firm.

Finding a Reputable Credit Counseling Agency

A reputable credit counseling agency evaluates your finances and comes up with a plan for helping you get out of debt and avoid financial problems in the future. Among other things, the agency

- **Reviews your budget to make sure it is realistic and suggests improvements and/or additional cuts.** If you do not already have a budget, the agency helps you develop one.

- **Assesses the state of your finances.** After reviewing your financial information, the agency gives you a realistic picture of where you are right now financially: no better or worse off than a lot of consumers, on the brink of bankruptcy, or somewhere in between.

- **Figures out how you can keep up with your debts.** The agency may revise your budget in order to generate more *cash flow* (the amount of money you have to spend) each month so you can pay your debts off faster. Or it may recommend that you participate in a debt-management plan in order to lower your monthly debt payments to amounts you can afford. If your finances are in really bad shape, the agency may suggest that you meet with a consumer bankruptcy attorney.

  If the credit counseling agency advises you to pay off your debts through a debt-management plan, the agency will explain how the plan works and review its pluses and minuses. Also, the agency should give you a general idea of how much you'll have to pay on your debts each month if it sets up a debt-management plan for you.

  When a credit counseling agency sets up a debt-management plan for you, the plan will address your *unsecured* debts, like credit card debts, unpaid medical bills, and student loans. Most credit counseling agencies will not help you with your *secured* debts, such as your mortgage, home equity loan, and car loan.

- **Helps you set financial goals and provides you with financial education.** The financial education may include workshops and seminars on various aspects of money management, as well as brochures and workbooks.

Telling the good from the bad

Most credit counseling agencies are truly interested in helping consumers get a handle on their debts and develop a solid foundation for a financially sound future. However, some agencies are mostly out to make a buck (or lots of bucks) off consumers who are desperate for help and unaware of the differences between reputable and disreputable credit counseling agencies.

Sadly, consumers who work with a bad apple agency are apt to pay it a lot of money — money they could have used to pay their debts or their living expenses — and get little or nothing in return. In fact, many of these consumers end up worse off financially than they were before. For example, bad-apple credit counseling agencies may charge excessive fees, push consumers into debt-management plans when they don't need them (so the agencies can charge plan administration fees each month), and offer no financial education or goal-setting assistance.

That's the bad news. The good news is that it's relatively easy to find a good credit counseling agency, assuming that you know the questions to ask and the telltale signs that an agency may not be on the up and up.

If an agency's promises about what it can do for you sound too good to be true, they probably are. Watch out! No matter how much you may want to believe what it says, look for another credit counseling agency to work with.

Avoid credit counseling agencies that solicit your business by phone or email. Also, don't be impressed by agencies that spend money on glossy print ads and regular ads on TV or radio. Reputable organizations do not spend a lot of money on advertising and rely mostly on referrals and word of mouth.

Book III

Dealing with Debt

Locating agencies in your area

When you look for a credit counseling agency to work with, check out a couple so you can feel confident that you are going to get good help. Ask friends or relatives who have had a good past experience with credit counseling for a referral. Don't know anyone who's worked with this kind of agency? Here are two other excellent resources for finding a good one:

- ✔ **The National Foundation for Credit Counseling:** www.nfcc.org or 800-388-2227

- ✔ **The Association of Independent Consumer Credit Counseling Agencies:** www.aiccca.org or 800-450-1794

The counselors who work for credit counseling agencies that are affiliated with these two organizations are trained and certified.

Another excellent source of reputable credit counseling agencies is the Web site of the United States Trustee. These days, people who want to file for bankruptcy have to obtain a *certificate to file* from a credit counseling agency. Only credit counseling agencies that have been certified by the federal Trustee's office can issue this type of certificate. We think it's safe to assume that the certified agencies are reputable. To find a certified credit counseling agency in your state, go to www.usdoj.gov/ust and click on "Credit Counseling & Debtor Education."

If you don't find credit counseling agencies in your area, or if you would have a difficult time going to a credit counseling agency's office during business hours, many good agencies offer online counseling that can be just as effective as meeting face to face with a credit counselor. However you choose to get the counseling, your method of selecting a credit counselor and your expectations should be the same.

Knowing what to ask and what to expect

After you have the names of some agencies, ask each the following set of questions by meeting with a representative from each agency, emailing them from their Web sites, or talking with them on the phone. Do not pay a credit counseling agency any money or sign any paperwork until you have received satisfactory answers to each of these questions:

✔ **Are you a federally approved, nonprofit, tax-exempt credit counseling agency?** Nonprofit agencies will charge you the least for their services and provide you with the most in return. Some credit counseling organizations are for-profit businesses even though their names make them sound like they are nonprofits.

Get proof that a credit counseling agency is truly a nonprofit by asking for a copy of its IRS *approval of nonprofit status* letter. The letter is a one-page document. Don't work with an agency that refuses to let you look at this letter or never provides it.

✔ **Do you have a license to offer credit counseling services in my state?** Although some states do not license credit counseling organizations, many do. You can find out if your state requires licensing by contacting your state attorney general's office. If your state does issue licenses, ask for the name of the licensing agency and then get in touch with it to confirm that the credit counseling agency has a valid license.

✔ **What services do you offer?** The upcoming section "Working with a Credit Counselor" describes the services the agency should offer.

✔ **How do you charge for your services?** Reputable credit counseling agencies charge little or nothing for most of their services. However, if you participate in a debt-management plan, you will be charged a small monthly administrative fee — probably $40 per month tops. Less-reputable agencies charge substantial upfront fees — as much as several hundred dollars — as well as steep monthly fees if they put you in a debt-management plan.

Some credit counseling agencies that are not on the up and up don't charge large fees but charge a lot of small fees instead. Over time, all those small fees really add up. Ask the credit counseling agency for a comprehensive list of fees. If it refuses to provide a list or tells you it does not have one, steer clear!

Some states regulate the amount of money a credit counseling agency can charge to set up a debt-management plan and to administer it. Contact your state attorney general's office to find out if it regulates these fees.

Watch out for credit counseling agencies that encourage you to give them voluntary contributions. The *contributions* are nothing more than fees to make the agencies more money at your expense.

✔ **Will I be assigned a specific credit counselor to work with?** You should expect to work with one credit counselor.

✔ **How do you pay your credit counselors?** Reputable agencies pay their counselors a salary or pay them by the hour. Avoid agencies where the credit counselors make money by selling services to consumers. The counselors are nothing more than commissioned salespeople who have a financial incentive to get you to buy as many services as possible whether you need them or not.

✔ **Can I see a copy of the contract I must sign if I work with you?** Don't work with an agency that does not use a contract or that won't share a copy with you. The contract should clearly state exactly what services the agency will be providing to you, a timeline for those services, and any fees or expenses you must pay. It should also provide information about any guarantees the credit counseling agency is making to you, as well as the name of the credit counselor you'll be working with and the counselor's contact information.

✔ **How will you keep my personal and financial information private and secure?** With identity theft on the rise, you must feel confident that the agency has a strong policy in place to protect your information from strangers.

After you find an agency you'd like to work with, check it out with your local Better Business Bureau and with your state attorney general's office. If either organization indicates that numerous consumers have filed complaints against the agency, reconsider your decision.

Book III

Dealing with Debt

You should also check with the Federal Trade Commission (FTC) at www.ftc.gov or by calling 877-382-4857. The FTC is aggressively cracking down on businesses that pretend to be nonprofit credit counseling agencies.

Working with a Credit Counselor

After you have chosen a credit counseling agency, your assigned credit counselor will spend time becoming familiar with you and your finances. If you meet face to face with the counselor, you should expect your initial meeting to last about an hour, and you should expect to have a couple follow-up meetings. If you get your counseling online, you will exchange information and get your questions answered via email.

Sharing your financial situation

At your first meeting (or soon after), be prepared to provide your counselor with such information as

- Your household budget, if you have one.
- A list of your debts, including whether they are secured or unsecured.
- The amount of money due on each debt every month.
- The interest rate for each debt.
- Which debts you are behind on.
- The assets you own and their approximate *market values* (meaning how much you could sell them for).
- Copies of your most recent tax returns or pay stubs reflecting your monthly take-home pay.

The counselor uses all this information to prepare a get-out-of-debt plan customized just for you. Not only will the plan provide you with a road map for getting out of debt; it should also help you work toward your financial goals like buying a home, saving for your retirement, helping your children pay for their college educations, and so on.

As part of your plan, the credit counselor may suggest that you enroll in one or more of the agency's money-management seminars and workshops so you can gain the information and tools you need to avoid debt problems in the future and achieve your financial goals. The seminars and workshops may focus on topics like smart budgeting, managing debt, financial goal-setting, and so on. Also, the counselor may give you free money-management materials to read.

Whittling down your debt with a debt-management plan

If your counselor is unable to figure out a way for you to pay off your debts by reducing your expenses and maybe making more money, the counselor may recommend that you participate in a debt-management plan. When you participate in such a plan, the counselor tries to negotiate smaller monthly payments with your creditors.

Getting creditors to buy in

The counselor determines exactly how much you can afford to pay to your unsecured creditors each month in order to eliminate each debt over a three- to five-year period. Then the counselor contacts the creditors to find out if they will agree to let you pay the amounts you can afford. In some instances, the counselor may also ask the creditors for other concessions, such as lowering your interest rates and reducing or waiving any fees you may owe to them.

If your unsecured creditors believe that giving you what you need is their best shot at getting the money you owe, and if they believe you are likely to file for bankruptcy otherwise (which means they may not get a penny from you), they will probably agree to the plan the credit counselor has proposed. However, most large creditors will have a minimum amount that they expect you to pay on your debts each month; unless you commit to paying it, they won't agree to participate in your plan. If some of your creditors refuse to work with you, you have to continue paying them according to the original agreements with them.

Many creditors are willing to offer special concessions to consumers who pay off their debts through a debt-management plan. In return, they expect that consumers will not incur additional debt while they are in their plans.

Working the plan

After the credit counselor has prepared your final debt-management plan, ask for a copy. Do not sign it until you have read it carefully, understand everything in it, and are sure that you can live up to it. Note any restrictions in the plan. For example, it may prohibit you from taking on additional credit with your current creditors or applying for new credit while it is in effect. If you violate any aspect of your plan, you risk having it cancelled.

When your plan is official, you pay your credit counselor every month the amount of money you have agreed to pay on your debts, as well as the required monthly fee. In turn, the counselor pays your creditors.

Make sure your debt-management plan says that your credit counselor will send you regular monthly updates on the status of your debt-management plan, including confirmation that each of your creditors was paid according to the terms of the plan.

Book III

Dealing with Debt

Beware of credit counseling agencies that spend little or no time evaluating your finances before advising you to enroll in a debt-management plan or that ask you to begin paying on a debt-management plan before your creditors have agreed to work with you.

Also, be aware that some creditors who agree to be part of your plan may report you as slow paying or as paying through a debt-management plan, which will damage your credit history a little. However, statistics show that successfully completing a debt-management plan actually increases your *FICO score* — the numeric representation of your creditworthiness that is derived from the information in your credit history. (For more on FICO scores, see Book I, Chapter 1.)

Actively managing your plan

Even when you are careful about choosing a credit counseling agency to work with, if you participate in a debt-management plan, problems can develop that may undermine the plan benefits. Follow these tips to minimize the potential for problems:

✔ After your counselor tells you which of your unsecured creditors have agreed to participate in your debt-management plan, contact them to confirm their participation before you send the counselor any money.

However, taking this step before paying any money may not always be possible. Due to cost constraints, a nonprofit credit counseling agency may not contact your creditors to find out if they will participate in your debt-management plan until you have given the agency an initial month's payment on the plan. The agency wants to be sure that you are serious about paying your debts before it spends time negotiating the plan details with your creditors.

✔ If your counselor tells you that one of your creditors won't agree to participate in your plan until you send the counselor an upfront payment, contact the creditor to confirm that what the counselor says is true.

✔ Make sure that the schedule your counselor sets up for paying your debts provides enough time for your creditors to receive what they are owed each month before the payment due dates. Otherwise, you risk racking up late fees and penalties.

✔ Every month, just after the date that your counselor is due to make a payment, confirm with the counselor that the payment was made on time.

✔ Whenever you receive a monthly statement of your account from one of the creditors participating in your debt-management plan, review it carefully to make sure your account was credited appropriately. Also, make sure that each creditor made whatever concessions it agreed to make, such as lowering your interest rate, waiving certain fees, or allowing you to make reduced payments or interest-only payments for a while.

Avoiding Debt Settlement Firms

Some people confuse debt settlement firms, also known as *debt negotiation firms,* with credit counseling agencies. Don't make this mistake. Although a debt settlement firm may try to confuse you by choosing a name that sounds like a nonprofit credit counseling agency, debt settlement companies are in business to make money. The services they offer are very different from those of a legitimate credit counseling agency. Also, if you work with a debt settlement firm, you risk harming your finances and damaging your credit history and your FICO score.

Being wary of false promises

Debt settlement firms claim that they can settle your unsecured debts for less than the full amount you owe on them. In other words, after you pay the settlement amounts, your creditors will consider the debts to be paid in full. For example, if you owe $10,000 in credit card debt, a debt settlement firm may tell you that it can get the creditor to agree to let you pay the debt off for $6,000.

You can try to settle your own debts, for free (see first half of this chapter). You don't need a debt settlement firm to do it for you.

(But keep in mind, as we mentioned, that if a creditor agrees to forgive part of your debt, the IRS will probably treat that forgiven amount as income to you, and you will be taxed on it. If you receive an IRS 1099 form related to a debt that you settled, talk to a CPA. If the CPA can prove that you were insolvent at the time that the amount of the debt was forgiven, you won't be taxed on that amount. You're *insolvent* if you don't have enough money to pay your debts and living expenses and you don't have any assets you can sell to pay off the debts.)

Some debt settlement firms also promise that after they settle your debts, they can get all the negative information related to those debts removed from your credit history. Not true! Only the creditors that reported the negative information can remove it.

If you agree to work with a debt settlement firm, you may be told to stop paying your unsecured creditors and to begin sending that money to the firm itself. The problem is that a debt settlement firm may be all talk and no action. It may not be able to settle your debts for less. In fact, it may not even try. Furthermore, if it does intend to try to settle your debts, it may take months for the firm to accumulate enough money from the payments you are sending to be able to propose settlements to your creditors. Meanwhile, your debts are going unpaid, your credit history is being damaged further, and the total amount you owe to your creditors is increasing because late fees and interest are accumulating.

Book III

Dealing with Debt

If you question a debt settlement firm about the consequences of not paying your debts, you may hear that your unsecured creditors won't sue you for their money. That is flat-out wrong.

Preventing worse financial problems

Debt settlement firms charge much more money than legitimate credit counseling agencies. If you work with a debt settlement firm, you may have to pay one or more substantial upfront fees, as well as additional fees that may be based on the number of unsecured credit accounts you have, the amount of debt you owe, or the amount of debt that the firm gets your creditors to forgive. In the end, the cost of working with a debt management firm may be more than the amount of money you save from settling your debts.

Be careful if a debt settlement firm offers to loan you money, maybe more than you can really afford to pay. Not only is the loan likely to have a very high interest rate and other unattractive terms of credit, but if you are not careful, you may sign paperwork giving the firm the right to put a lien on an asset you own. The firm is hoping that you'll fall behind on your loan payments so it can take the asset from you.

Getting Relief If You Get Ripped Off

If you get taken by a disreputable credit counseling organization or by a debt settlement firm, contact a consumer law attorney right away. The attorney will advise you of your rights. He may recommend sending a letter on his law firm stationery to the credit counseling organization or debt settlement firm threatening legal action unless the firm makes amends to you (such as by giving you your money back). The credit counseling organization or debt settlement firm may agree to the attorney's demands in order to avoid a lawsuit. If it does not respond or refuses to do what the letter asks, you can decide if you want to go forward with a lawsuit.

Assuming that you have a strong case, the attorney will probably represent you on a *contingent fee* basis. This means that you won't have to pay the attorney any money to represent you. Instead, the attorney gambles that you will win your lawsuit, and the attorney will take his fee from the money that the court awards you as a result. If you lose your lawsuit, you do not have to pay the attorney a fee. However, depending on your agreement with one another, win or lose, you may have to pay the attorney's court costs and any other fees and expenses related to your case.

Regardless of whether you sue the credit counseling organization or debt settlement firm, you should file a complaint against it with your state attorney general's office, your local Better Business Bureau, and the Federal Trade Commission (FTC). Although none of these organizations can help you get your money back or undo any damage done to your credit history and your FICO score, other consumers who may be thinking about working with the same credit counseling agency or debt settlement firm may think twice after reading your complaint. Also, if your state attorney general's office or the FTC receives a lot of complaints about the credit counseling agency or debt settlement firm, it may take legal action against it. For example, it may file a class action lawsuit on behalf of everyone who was ripped off.

Book III

Dealing with Debt

Chapter 5

Considering Bankruptcy

· ·

· ·

Maybe you were socked with an unexpected and uninsured medical expense, and you didn't have the savings to cover the bills. Perhaps you lost your job and can no longer juggle your car and mortgage payments. Maybe you dipped into personal assets in a desperate (and futile) bid to salvage your business. Perchance your husband split and left you holding a big bag of joint debts. Or you bought into the easy-credit, instant-gratification, shop-till-you-drop mentality encouraged by lenders and retailers and found yourself mired in financial quicksand. In any case, things got out of hand and now you're up to your ears in debt.

Finance companies are warning that if you don't pay up, and soon, they'll take your home and car. Credit card firms are threatening to haul you into court. Debt collectors are pursuing you relentlessly. Your finances are a disaster. Your personal and professional relationships are strained. You're losing sleep, and you're becoming a perfect candidate for ulcers. Welcome to the club. Millions of Americans are in the same leaky boat.

Thankfully, you have a perfectly legitimate way to stop foreclosures and repossessions, put an end to lawsuits, protect your paycheck from garnishments, get those menacing debt collectors off your back, and regain control of your life: bankruptcy.

Bankruptcy is shrouded in myth and prejudice. If you're like many folks, the first step on the road to financial recovery is overcoming your feelings of inadequacy, shame, guilt, and fear of the unknown.

In this chapter, we encourage you to put aside myth and prejudice, and look calmly at the advantages and disadvantages of bankruptcy. Only then can you make a rational decision about whether bankruptcy is the best choice for you and your loved ones.

Viewing Bankruptcy in a Historical Context

In the United States, the concept of bankruptcy is unique. Here, bankruptcy is viewed legally and perceptually as a means to an end, not *as* the end of a debtor's financial life. The Founding Fathers provided for bankruptcy right there in the Constitution. A series of laws passed (and sometimes repealed) by Congress during the 1800s shaped the American view of bankruptcy as not only a remedy for creditors, but also a way to give honest yet unfortunate debtors financial rebirth. The Bankruptcy Act of 1898 established that debtors had a basic right to financial relief without creditor consent or court permission. American bankruptcy laws have come to be recognized as far more compassionate and much less punitive to debtors than the laws of other countries.

Like much of American law, the country's bankruptcy statutes reflect the constant tension between the competing interests of debtors and creditors. Think of it as a perpetual tug of war, with each side striving mightily but never pulling its opponent all the way over the line. To this day, the balance of influence between creditors and debtors is in an ever-present state of flux. Sometimes debtors have the upper hand. Other times, creditors get the edge. At the moment, thanks to a law that took effect in October 2005, creditors are holding the trump card.

The constant, however, is that Americans have always been (and remain) entitled to a fresh start. The obstacles that you must clear to obtain this fresh start are not constant; they're always changing.

Modern-day bankruptcy is rooted in the Bankruptcy Code of 1978, a federal law that was produced after more than ten years of careful study by judges and scholars. More recently, creditors and their lobbyists essentially rewrote what was a pretty well-reasoned and fair law in their own image. The result was the Bankruptcy Abuse Prevention and Consumer Protection Act of 2005 — often known as the Bankruptcy Abuse Reform Fiasco, or BARF. In our opinion, it's not good for consumers. It's not good for the economy. It flies in the face of the risk/reward principles at the core of capitalism. And, in the long run, it's probably not even good for the credit industry, which wrote it.

So how did a one-sided, ill-considered bucket of BARF happen to pass both houses of Congress and presidential scrutiny?

Some think the eight-year lobbying campaign by the credit card industry and the $100 million spent on campaign contributions may have had something to do with it. Some speculate that lawmakers simply didn't pay a whole lot of attention to the fine print in an incredibly complex amendment that's about the size of a metropolitan telephone book.

Bankruptcy's roots

The word *bankruptcy* evolved from the Italian phrase *banca ratta,* which means "broken bench or table." In medieval times, when a merchant failed to pay his debts, creditors ceremoniously broke the bench or table from which he conducted his business. The forgiveness of debts, on the other hand, has biblical roots.

Consider the Old Testament: "At the end of every seven years, you are to cancel the debts of those who owe you money. This is how it is done. Everyone who has lent money to his neighbor is to cancel the debt: he must not try to collect the money: the Lord himself has declared the debt canceled." (Deuteronomy 15: 1–2).

Debt forgiveness also is a prominent New Testament theme. In Matthew 18:21–27, Jesus relates the story of a servant who was indebted to his master. The master ordered the servant and his entire family into slavery, but upon reconsideration, he forgave the debt. Jesus used the parable to explain the virtue of debt forgiveness. (On the other hand, the apostle Paul admonishes debt in Romans 13:8, "Render therefore to all their dues . . . owe no man any thing." So maybe we can't afford to get too pious here.)

In any case, throughout history, creditors have not exactly displayed an attitude of Judeo-Christian charity toward debtors. And neither have governments.

The early Romans hacked up and divided the bodies of people who didn't pay their debts. In early England, people who were in over their heads financially were tossed in dungeons. The initial bankruptcy law, passed in 1542 during the reign of Henry VIII (the guy who kept beheading his wives), viewed debtors as quasi-criminals but, for the first time, provided remedies other than imprisonment or mutilation.

Apparently, creditors finally realized that killing, maiming, or imprisoning debtors only ensured that they'd never get their money and that, even if the debtor survived, he'd never be able to support himself and his family or become a productive member of society.

During the more enlightened reign of Queen Elizabeth I, a comprehensive bankruptcy law was passed that remained in effect for more than a century. The aim of the 1570 bankruptcy law was most certainly *not* to grant relief to debtors. Instead, it was designed to help creditors. It applied only to merchants (ordinary debtors still were imprisoned) and essentially laid out procedures by which a bankruptcy commissioner could seize the debtor's assets, sell them, and divide the proceeds among creditors. Debtors who did not cooperate had one of their ears lopped off.

The very idea of a bankruptcy law aiding debtors or forgiving debts remained somewhat unimaginable until 1705, when Parliament enacted the first law that enabled a person to wipe out unpaid financial obligations. However, the terms were rather harsh: Consent of the creditor was required, and anyone who fraudulently sought bankruptcy relief faced the death penalty.

Before the United States won its independence, the various colonies handled bankruptcy their own respective ways, and little uniformity existed from colony to colony — except for the fact that settlers generally maintained the British tradition of jailing debtors (which extended to the father of one of the British Empire's greatest literary stars, Charles Dickens.). In fact, Robert Morris, known as the "financier of the American revolution" and a signer of the Declaration of Independence, spent three years in debtors' prison (and six years in the United States Senate). Supreme Court Justice James Wilson fled Pennsylvania to avoid a similar fate.

Book III

Dealing with Debt

Debunking Bankruptcy Myths

Bankruptcy is an economic decision, not a morality play, and you needn't be deceived into viewing it as anything else. The following sections look at some of the usual myths that are cast about by the credit industry.

"People who go bankrupt are sleazy deadbeats"

People file for bankruptcy because they're in debt. The more debt there is, the more bankruptcies there are. Well, duh! It really is that simple.

The credit industry stereotypes folks who file bankruptcy as worthless deadbeats taking advantage of a loophole-ridden legal system to dump their moral obligations on the backs of the rest of us. This stereotype is false, discriminatory, and manifestly unfair. Sure, bankruptcies have increased dramatically along with consumer debt, although the number of bankruptcies per $100 million on consumer debt has remained remarkably constant. From the 1970s to the 1980s, filings virtually doubled. The pace continued to increase in the 1990s, with bankruptcy filings setting new records year after year, even with a seemingly robust economy and near full employment. In fact, by the mid-1990s, bankruptcy filings, on a per capita basis, were running some eight times ahead of filings of the Great Depression. About 1 out of every 75 households in America has a member who has filed bankruptcy.

As soon as BARF went into effect on October 17, 2005, the number of bankruptcies plummeted, yet the financial health of the middle class continued to deteriorate. This is explained by the following facts:

- ✔ Record numbers of people rushed to file bankruptcy before BARF went into effect.
- ✔ BARF made it more tedious and time-consuming to file bankruptcy.
- ✔ Because of the additional work involved, the fees attorneys charge for bankruptcy have doubled.
- ✔ Bill collectors have been lying to folks, telling them that they're not eligible to file under the new bankruptcy law.

But the days of declining bankruptcies are over, and the number of folks filing has been steadily increasing since BARF, and will continue to increase, especially as homeowners try to avoid foreclosure.

And who are these people filing for bankruptcy? Chances are, they're your neighbors, regardless of what neighborhood you live in. Bankruptcy is an equal-opportunity phenomenon that strikes in every socioeconomic bracket.

The fastest-growing group of bankruptcy filers are older Americans. More than half of people 65 and older who are forced into bankruptcy are forced because of medical debts. Also, more families with children, single mothers, and single fathers are being driven into bankruptcy; the presence of children in a household triples the odds that the head of the household will end up in bankruptcy.

In any case, the image of the sleazy, deadbeat bankruptcy filer is a phantom and a scapegoat for irresponsible lending. The bankruptcy filer can be more accurately described as an ordinary, honest, hardworking, middle-class consumer who fell for aggressive and sophisticated credit marketing techniques, lost control, and unwittingly surrendered his financial soul to the devil that is debt.

"Bankruptcy is the easy way out for folks who can pay their bills"

Creditors have been making this claim since the 1800s, and it's as demonstrably wrong today as it was back then.

In recent years, the credit industry funded several *studies* — a handy euphemism for *propaganda,* the more accurate description — that supposedly support their argument that people are skipping to bankruptcy court to skip out of their obligations. Independent sources have debunked every one of these self-serving reports. Two financial arms of Congress, the General Accounting Office and the Congressional Budget Office, discredited several of these studies.

Bankruptcy isn't the cause of debt; it's the result. And it isn't the disease; it's the cure. Restricting access to bankruptcy court won't solve the problem of debt any more than closing the hospitals will cure a plague.

"Bankruptcy threatens the ethical foundations of our society"

Gee, you'd think that bankruptcy was the greatest threat to apple pie and motherhood since Elvis Presley and bell-bottom jeans!

Credit card companies furiously push plastic on virtually anyone willing to take it. At present, more than 1 billion credit cards are in circulation —about 10 for every household in the United States. Lenders mail out billions of credit card solicitations every year. Low- and moderate-income households, high school students, and the mentally disabled — or, in their vernacular, *emerging markets* — are popular targets of lenders.

Book III

Dealing with Debt

It's enough to make you BARF

A five-year study published in the medical policy journal *Health Affairs* in February 2005 found that between 1981 and 2001, medical-related bankruptcies increased by 2,200 percent — six times the increase in the number of all bankruptcies during the same period. And most of the medical filers were not the uninsured poor, but middle-class folks with health insurance. According to the study, lack of insurance doesn't wipe people out; copayments, deductibles, and uncovered services do.

According to the Administrative Office of the United States Courts, consumers between the ages of 18 and 25 are one of the largest-growing segments (next to senior citizens) of bankruptcy filers — students and other young people who lack the maturity and resources to handle debt.

Anyone with a brain can figure out that extending credit to folks with no income, no assets, and no track record is kind of dumb (not to mention morally questionable). But creditors are more than willing to ignore the dangers of tomorrow so that they can reap exorbitant interest rates today. They're counting on — literally banking on — your ignorance of the situation. They encourage robbing Peter to pay Paul by using credit card advances to pay off credit card bills. They convince many middle-class consumers to bleed all the equity out of their homes through aggressively marketed home-equity loans — with much of it going to finance consumable products (mall junk) instead of the homestead of the American Dream. That hundreds of solid, middle-class folks find themselves in bankruptcy court isn't surprising.

But why, in the face of increasing credit card losses, does the credit industry continue to dispense credit with utterly reckless abandon? The answer is simple: Because it's profitable . . . extremely profitable — or least it used to be.

During the decade prior to BARF, bankruptcy filings increased 17 percent, while credit card profits have soared 163 percent!

But, as mortgage lenders are coming to learn, the chickens ultimately come home to roost after an irresponsible lending orgy. It remains to be seen how long it will take for credit card lenders to wake to the fact that they will likely suffer catastrophic losses even greater than those that now plague the mortgage lending industry.

"Honest folks pay a 'tax' to support people who are bankrupt"

Claiming that honest taxpayers are supporting people who are bankrupt is nothing short of an outright, bald-faced lie. The theory, trumpeted in press releases, is that hundreds of thousands of Americans routinely ignore their obligations, intentionally or recklessly drive up their debts, and then declare themselves insolvent, stiffing creditors and, ultimately, every God-fearing, bill-paying, hard-working, patriotic American.

Creditors note that they write off billions every year. Thus, the reasoning goes, if access to bankruptcy were restricted, the credit industry wouldn't suffer losses that it must pass along to consumers. So, they say, BARF is good for consumers.

They're not saying that they'll pass along any savings to their customers, though, and, historically, that has not been their practice. Besides, do you really believe that the credit industry paid politicians tens of millions of dollars to enact BARF in order to save you money? Not likely.

Understanding What You Can Gain Through Bankruptcy

Book III

Dealing with Debt

If you have no way to pay your bills, you certainly need to consider bankruptcy. If you have an income but cannot repay your debts in full within three years while maintaining a reasonable standard of living, bankruptcy may be a wise option.

Bankruptcy isn't the solution when your motive is anything other than reasonable relief from your debts. The U.S. Bankruptcy Code was established to assist *honest debtors,* not to provide a haven for chiselers and charlatans. If your aim is to jerk some creditor around, weasel out of debts you can easily pay, evade child support, or generally just stiff someone, bankruptcy is the wrong route. No one should use bankruptcy for vengeance or as a stopgap measure, or as a ploy or a bargaining chip. Don't file bankruptcy unless you're serious about following through.

Bankruptcy can

- ✓ Halt almost every kind of lawsuit.
- ✓ Prevent garnishment of any wages you earn after filing.

- Stop most evictions if bankruptcy is filed before a state court enters a judgment for possession.

- Avert repossessions.

- Stop foreclosures.

- Prevent your driver's license from being yanked for unpaid fines or judgments. (The stay doesn't prevent revocation or suspension of your driver's license for failing to pay court-ordered support.)

- Bring IRS seizures to a skidding stop.

Bankruptcy generally *doesn't* prevent

- Criminal prosecutions.

- Proceedings against someone who cosigned your loan, unless you file a Chapter 13 repayment plan and propose paying the loan in full.

- Contempt of court hearings.

- Actions to collect back child support or alimony, unless you file Chapter 13 and propose to pay off that obligation during the life of your plan.

- Governmental regulatory proceedings.

In recent years, some self-proclaimed "mortgage consultants" and "foreclosure service" outfits have made a business out of essentially tricking their clients into filing bankruptcy. These con artists exploit the bankruptcy laws to delay foreclosure, collect rents from the property during the delay, and then head for the hills. In the end, unsuspecting clients usually lose their homes and wind up with a bankruptcy on their records without realizing they'd even filed for bankruptcy. Bottom line: Discuss your options with an experienced bankruptcy attorney, not some fly-by-night flimflam operation.

Stopping creditors in their tracks

The moment that you file a bankruptcy petition, a legal shield called the *automatic stay* kicks in, prohibiting creditors from contacting you, suing you, repossessing your property, or garnishing your wages.

After you file, a creditor can ask for permission to proceed with a repossession or foreclosure. But the creditor must obtain permission in advance, and the bankruptcy court judge may well turn down the creditor, if you propose a reasonable plan for paying that particular debt. (The following sections cover filing bankruptcy to eliminate some bills and pay others.)

Whenever a creditor is foolish enough to ignore the automatic stay, he'll have a federal judge on his back and may get zapped with a fine and an order to pay your attorney fees.

American bankruptcy

Our forefathers had radical ideas when it came to bankruptcy.

The founders foresaw the possibility that honest people might suffer severe economic misfortune or make poor choices (Thomas Jefferson, certainly one of the most productive and accomplished individuals in the history of the world, was perpetually on the brink of bankruptcy during his later years). They had the wisdom to provide for bankruptcy in the U.S. Constitution.

After the Constitutional Convention of 1787, the framers of the Constitution added a bankruptcy clause empowering Congress to pass uniform bankruptcy laws to prevent some states from establishing debtors' havens. In 1800 — 11 years after the ratification of the Constitution — Congress passed (by a single vote) a national bankruptcy law that enabled debtors to wipe out unpaid debts. But the provision was repealed three years later because of creditor complaints. Consequently, states began passing their own bankruptcy laws, a practice that the U.S. Supreme Court struck down.

By 1833, the federal government abolished debtors' prisons. Honest debtors would no longer be incarcerated. But bankruptcy was still viewed as a remedy for creditors, not debtors.

The tide began to shift when Congress, spurred by the powerful oratory of Daniel Webster, passed the Bankruptcy Act of 1841, a seminal event that established clearly that bankruptcy law was for debtors *and* for creditors. For the first time in history, the advocates for debtors had prevailed over the interests of creditors.

The victory was short-lived, however. Only three years later, creditors successfully had the law withdrawn. A similar choreography occurred just after the Civil War: Congress passed the Bankruptcy Act of 1867, which again enabled debtors to wipe out their debts. Eleven years later, creditors got it repealed. The threshold problem was this: Debt elimination was viewed as a privilege, dependent on creditor consent or court permission, not a fundamental right.

In the late 1890s, a revolutionary and uniquely American idea emerged: Bankruptcy relief had to be available to an honest person without consent or permission from others. This concept, which has come to be known as the *unconditional discharge,* was carved into the Bankruptcy Act of 1898.

Regardless of the long history and legal tradition underlying the unconditional discharge, creditors never cease trying to turn back the clock to the days when your bankruptcy relief required their permission.

Whenever the political climate appears favorable, creditors predictably scamper to Congress, whine about their losses, and claim that the "crisis" of "out-of-control" bankruptcies threatens to undermine the whole of Western civilization.

And therein lie the roots of BARF!

(See David A. Skeel, Jr., *Debt's Dominion: A History of Bankruptcy Law in America*, Princeton University Press, 2001.)

Book III

Dealing with Debt

Wiping out most of your debts

Bankruptcy wipes out or *discharges* most debts. Credit cards, medical bills, phone charges, loans, and judgments all are usually *dischargeable*. However, some obligations generally are not eliminated in bankruptcy. These *nondischargeable* debts include the following:

- ✔ Student loans
- ✔ Alimony and child support
- ✔ Damages for a personal injury you caused while driving illegally under the influence of drugs or alcohol
- ✔ Debts from fraud
- ✔ Financial obligations imposed as part of a criminal conviction
- ✔ Taxes arising during the past three years

Catching up on back mortgage and car payments

Sometimes even dischargeable debts continue to haunt you when they're tied to one of your essential possessions. For example, you can wipe out loans secured by your home or car, but the creditor can still foreclose on your house or repossess your vehicle if you don't pay.

In a Chapter 13 bankruptcy (one in which you pay what you can toward your debts and the remainder is forgiven), you can propose a partial-repayment plan to avoid foreclosure and make up back mortgage payments over a five-year span. You can prevent repossession of your car by catching up on back payments of the life of the plan. In some situations, you have to pay only what the vehicle is worth instead of the whole loan balance.

Filing bankruptcy to pay some debts over time

Although some debts are not dischargeable, filing a Chapter 13 reorganization enables you to pay debts such as support obligations or back taxes over a five-year period and protects you from being hassled while you're paying down the balances. You can also gradually catch up on missed mortgage payments. In the meantime, most of your other debts are eliminated while you just pay for current expenses and keep current on future house and car payments.

Noncitizens of the U.S.A.

You don't even have to be an American citizen to qualify for a fresh start. Neither citizenship nor even formal resident-alien status is required. As long as you have property or a business in the United States, you're eligible for bankruptcy relief. But courts disagree on just what "property in the United States" constitutes, and some have rejected attempts by foreigners to create eligibility by simply obtaining a U.S. mailbox or establishing a nominal bank account. Others take a more liberal view.

For example, Ernestine didn't live, work, or do any business in the United States, but she had a few hundred bucks in a bank account. The court said Ernestine was eligible to file bankruptcy in the United States — and expressed bewilderment as to why American credit card companies would offer massive amounts of credit to a foreigner with no job and $522 to her name.

Using bankruptcy to pay all your debts

Sometimes filing bankruptcy actually provides a way of paying all your debts instead of escaping them.

If the value of your property is sufficient to pay all your debts if only you had enough time to sell your assets, you can use bankruptcy to hold aggressive lenders at bay until your property is sold for the benefit of all your creditors — and possibly producing a surplus for you.

Say, for example, that you own investment property worth $150,000, on which you have a mortgage of $100,000, and that you have other debts totaling $25,000.

If you can sell the property, you can pay off the mortgage and other debts and still have something left over for yourself. But if the mortgageholder forecloses, neither you nor your creditors will likely receive a cent. Although the property *is* put up for public auction in a foreclosure, bidders rarely show up, and the only bidder typically is the mortgageholder, which merely bids the amount that's owed on the mortgage. In other words, the mortgage company ends up owning the property without paying any cash. Filing bankruptcy interrupts the foreclosure so that the property can be sold for everyone's benefit.

Book III

Dealing with Debt

Knowing What You Can Lose in Bankruptcy

Although bankruptcy may be that miracle cure you sought for your financial woes, you may encounter some unpleasant side effects. Consider the disadvantages of filing bankruptcy:

- **You can lose assets.** Depending on how much your home is worth and where you live, it is possible, but unlikely, that you'll lose it by filing bankruptcy. In most bankruptcies, debtors don't have to give up any of their belongings, but . . .

- **Bankruptcy is a matter of public record.** As more records are stored on computers and accessible on the Internet, searching that data becomes easier for anyone who's interested. In other words, if your nosy neighbor wants to know whether you filed bankruptcy, how much you owe, and who you owe it to, the information may be just a few mouse clicks away.

- **Bankruptcy affects your credit rating.** Bankruptcy may have a negative effect on your credit rating, but that fact may well fall into the "So what?" category for you. Even with a bankruptcy on your record, your odds of obtaining credit are very good. With a little work and perseverance, you can reestablish credit almost immediately. Some credit card companies actually target folks right after bankruptcy because they know that these people are free of all their existing debts and probably won't be eligible to file another bankruptcy any time soon. For a few years after bankruptcy, you may have to pay higher interest rates on new credit, but this result will ease over time, even if your credit report still shows a bankruptcy. So don't pay too much attention to the horror stories bill collectors tell you about the disastrous effect bankruptcy has your credit.

- **Friends and relatives can be forced to give back money or property.** If you repaid loans to friends or relatives or gave them anything within the past year, they can be forced to repay a trustee the money they received, if you don't know what to watch out for. You can usually avoid these kinds of problems by carefully timing your bankruptcy filing.

- **Bankruptcy can strain relations with loved ones, especially parents who were raised in a different era.**

- **A stigma may still be attached to filing bankruptcy.** This drawback is especially true in small communities, but it is much less likely to be a problem in cities, where newspapers rarely bother printing the names of nonbusiness bankruptcies.

- **Bankruptcy may cause more problems than it solves when you've transferred assets to keep them away from creditors.**

✔ **You can suffer some discrimination.** Although governmental agencies and employers aren't supposed to discriminate against you for filing bankruptcy, they may still do so in a roundabout way. Prospective employers may also refuse to hire you.

Considering Alternatives to Bankruptcy

Bankruptcy isn't for everyone, and sometimes better solutions are available. If it appears that the negatives outweigh the positives, another route may be your best choice. Depending on your situation, one of these options may be the best alternative:

✔ Selling assets to pay debts in full

✔ Negotiating with creditors to reduce your debts to a manageable level

✔ Restructuring your home mortgage

✔ Taking out a home-equity loan

✔ Doing nothing if you have nothing, expect to acquire nothing, and don't care about your present or future credit rating

In any event, weigh your decision on a simple, rational scale. Ask yourself whether the benefits outweigh the drawbacks. Many people, ravaged by guilt and shame, think they need to fully exhaust every alternative before considering bankruptcy, including the following:

✔ Making payments that never reduce the principal balance owed

✔ Taking out second mortgages to pay credit card debts

✔ Borrowing against pensions

✔ Withdrawing funds from retirement accounts

✔ Obtaining loans from friends and relatives

✔ Taking second jobs

Think seriously about the strain your financial distress places on your health, marriage, and family. Granted, bankruptcy is a very serious step that you shouldn't take lightly, but that doesn't mean you have to wait until you've lost everything. Think of it in these terms: If you have some blocked arteries, it just may be smarter to have bypass surgery *before* you have a heart attack. The same is true of bankruptcy. Think of bankruptcy as preventive medicine.

Book III

Dealing with Debt

Introducing the Different Types of Personal Bankruptcy

Consumer bankruptcies are covered mainly under two parts of the U.S. Bankruptcy Code:

- ✔ **Chapter 7 liquidation** enables you to eliminate most of your debts but may require you to forfeit some of your assets for distribution to creditors.

- ✔ **Chapter 13 reorganization** enables you to pay off all or a portion of your debts during a three- to five-year time span but doesn't require you to forfeit any of your belongings or assets to pay *unsecured debts* (debts that are not secured by property, such as your car or another valuable asset).

Likewise, other special kinds of bankruptcy exist. Chapter 11 bankruptcy is available to individuals but primarily applies to large business reorganizations. Chapter 12 bankruptcy, which is similar to Chapter 13 bankruptcy, addresses the unique problems family farmers and family fishermen face. As a practical matter, almost all consumer cases are covered under Chapter 7 or Chapter 13 of the code.

Liquidations (Chapter 7)

Chapter 7, commonly referred to as *straight bankruptcy,* is often what people mean or think of when they use or hear the term generically.

In its simplest form, Chapter 7 wipes out most of your debts; in return, you may have to surrender some of your property. Chapter 7 doesn't include a repayment plan. Your debts are simply eliminated forever. If you buy a lottery ticket the day after filing and hit the jackpot, yippee for you and tough beans for your creditors! You obviously can *voluntarily* pay back your creditors if you suddenly strike it rich, but, legally, you don't owe a dime after your debt is discharged. Most property you receive after filing Chapter 7 doesn't become part of your bankruptcy, but a few exceptions exist. Income tax refunds for prebankruptcy tax years go to pay your debts, as do divorce property awards, inheritances, and life insurance that you become entitled to receive within 180 days of bankruptcy.

Theoretically, a debtor's assets can be seized and sold for the benefit of creditors. All nonexempt assets owned on the petition date are fair game. They can be sold, with the proceeds distributed to your creditors. But in practice, 96 percent of consumer bankruptcies are *no-asset cases,* meaning that no property is taken away from the debtor because it's all exempt or worth so little that it's not worth the trouble.

To qualify for Chapter 7, if you earn more than the median income for your state, you must pass a new *means test,* in which you show that you don't have enough income to pay a significant portion of your debts. Although the test is ungodly complicated, when all is said and done, just about everyone can pass. The toughest part is just assembling the information you have to provide.

Consumer reorganizations (Chapter 13)

Chapter 13 involves a repayment plan in which you pay all or part of your debts during a three- to five-year period. In a Chapter 13 bankruptcy, you propose a debt-repayment plan that requires court approval and thereafter keeps creditors at bay as long as you keep making payments. This plan can be a great relief when you're able to establish and live within the confines of a budget.

A budget plan that demands frugality to the point of misery is doomed to fail ("Frugality is misery in disguise," observed Pubilius Syrus some 2,000 years ago). One that is reasonable has a good chance of succeeding. The operative word, however, is *reasonable.*

Every Chapter 13 plan must pass two tests:

- The *best-interest test,* which mandates that unsecured creditors be paid at least as much as they would receive if you filed a Chapter 7 instead of a Chapter 13.

- The *best-efforts test,* which requires that you pay all your disposable income (the amount left over after paying reasonable living expenses) to the trustee for at least the first 36 months of your plan. If your monthly income is more than the median for your state, allowable expenses will be based on Internal Revenue Collection Financial Standards, and the plan must run for five years. Otherwise, the amount of your payment will be based on your actual expenses, as long as they are reasonable.

When you're done, you're done. Most creditors have gotten all they're going to get. Life goes on.

Weighing the Consequences of Not Filing Bankruptcy

In the same way that filing bankruptcy can have negative consequences, *not* filing can also have negative consequences. If you're eligible for bankruptcy but opt against filing, creditors have a number of options they can pursue, depending on whether a particular debt is secured by your property.

Claims secured by your car

If your car secures a debt, the creditor can repossess the vehicle and sell it to cover the loan. The proceeds of a repossession sale usually aren't enough to pay the debt, so you'll lose the car and still have to pay the balance that you owe on it — the worst of both worlds.

Although the law requires a creditor to sell a car in a "commercially reasonable" manner, that doesn't necessarily mean that the creditor will receive nearly as much as you can by selling it yourself. Before allowing repossession, you may want to try selling the vehicle. Your chances of getting more money for the car are greater than the finance company's. If you and your lawyer agree that it's best to get rid of the car because you just can't afford it, you can voluntarily surrender it to the lender instead of waiting for them to repossess it. Despite what people may tell you, your credit report will not look that much better, but at least you'll avoid the hassle of finding your car gone when you come out of the supermarket, or the embarrassment of a tow truck showing up at your house.

Claims secured by your home

Mortgage companies can't simply boot you out of your home and onto your derrière if you miss a few payments. They must first go through a foreclosure procedure to extinguish your ownership rights. Although not all foreclosures involve court proceedings, all do take time — at least three months, in most cases, and frequently much longer. You can continue to live on the property until the foreclosure is completed.

Student loans

Government agencies can *garnish* (siphon off) up to 10 percent of your disposable income without going to court. A garnishment is almost like a withholding tax — the money is gone from your paycheck before you ever see it. You also need to be aware that Congress canceled state statutes of limitations on student loans. In other words, you can't just wait it out. You must deal with student loans. They won't disappear on their own.

Support obligations

Although debtors' prisons are officially a thing of the past, a divorce court can still send you to jail for neglecting your support obligations, and some states have programs to revoke professional licenses — such as licenses for practical nurses or accountants or cosmetologists — of people who haven't kept up with their support.

Fines and restitution

If you've been ordered to pay a fine or make restitution in connection with a criminal proceeding and don't pay, accommodations at the local jail may await you. Don't tempt the judge; some of them don't need much tempting to have you hauled off in handcuffs.

Taxes

The IRS has truly scary powers to seize your bank account, your pension, real property, or even the shirt off your back. State taxing authorities also have similar special powers. In addition, your town or city, your student loan creditors, or your ex-spouse or kids may be able to grab your tax refund whenever you owe alimony or support.

Lawsuits

Creditors with other types of claims can't do much without first suing you and obtaining a judgment. To do this, they must serve you with legal documents and give you a chance to dispute the debt in court. If you don't respond, a default judgment can be entered against you. That means the ruling goes against you even though you never presented your case.

Book III

Dealing with Debt

Using the Statute of Limitations

Most debts — student loans being the most notable exception — eventually evaporate simply through the passage of time. In most cases, the *statute of limitations* (the time period within which an action must be commenced) is six years or less. But whenever a judgment has been entered against you, it can be as long as 20 years.

Sometimes the statute of limitations (usually ten years) can make federal taxes disappear.

Relying on the statute of limitations is a tricky proposition. If a creditor does sue to collect before the statute expires, the debt technically does not go out of existence, but merely becomes uncollectible. If someone sues you on a debt barred by the statute of limitations, they can still win and get a judgment unless you raise the statute of limitations as a defense to the suit. And there are reports of scavengers who pay pennies for debts barred by the statute of limitations and then try to collect them.

Also, it's frequently tough to figure out when the statute of limitations clock began ticking. Sometimes just making partial payments or acknowledging a debt can start the time running all over again. And you sure don't want that to happen.

Book IV

Saving and Investing

The 5th Wave   By Rich Tennant

"That reminds me – I have to figure out how to save for retirement _and_ send these two to college."

In this book . . .

Where does it all go, and why can't you seem to save as much of your income as you'd like to? Well, if you're like most people, the answer to that question is complex and many-splendored. You have to unlearn bad habits and discover new ways of holding onto what's rightfully yours. And you have to stash your money in smart places where it works for you earning interest. Here is where you'll find lots of juicy tips on just how to do that.

Here are the contents of Book IV at a glance.

Chapter 1

Becoming a Saver

In This Chapter

▶ Budgeting your money, not pinching your pennies

▶ Seeing savings as a reward, not a punishment

▶ Freeing yourself from debt

▶ Starting to save at any age

*W*hy aren't you saving enough money? As much as you realize that you need to save money, you're probably not doing it — or, at least, not as much as you could be. You're sure you have the will, the desire, and the need — you just seem to lack the cash.

This chapter dissects your life and your spending habits (just a little bit). It shows you that adding more money to this equation isn't the only way you can ever increase the amount of cash you save. Although finding additional money is always nice, you can use a variety of methods to carve some savings out of what you already have.

You can call it a budget, a financial plan, or microeconomics, but whatever name you give it, the most important part of the family economic dynamic isn't *how much* money you have, but rather how you *spend* the money you have. If you focus attention on budgeting, you can gain control over your family's finances and find that extra money you need to start saving for college. (Book I, Chapter 3 has more on budgets.)

The mechanics of your family's budget are fairly straightforward. You bring in a certain amount of money, through work, entitlement programs such as Social Security or other pensions, or investments. From that money, or income, you need to pay for the basic needs of your family — housing and utility costs, food, clothing, transportation, insurance, and so on — and for the frills your family has come to expect: cable television, vacations, and fancy gifts at birthdays and holidays.

Although that sounds simple enough, you may find that your family's needs and expectations slightly exceed your income. You may also want to save a significant piece of your income each month, but when the end of the month comes, you find that you're a bit short. If you find yourself in either situation (thinking that saving money for college, for example, is impossible), check out the following tips on how to dig for the dollars you need in your monthly budget to start saving.

Eliminating Most of the Fat

The first step in gaining control over your family's finances is not to cut off the cable television or the Internet connection or take the family dog to the pound. Instead, take a step back and look at the big picture. You need to know not only how much money you have coming in, but also how much is going out and where that money is headed.

Making lists of where you are now

Before you can start making changes to your family's finances, you need to understand what you have right now, at this moment. For a very detailed method of doing this, see Book I, Chapter 3. If you want to rough it out for now, read on. Sit down and make a list of your monthly income and, if your income tends to be seasonal, your yearly income (and then divide that by 12). List all your income, from every source. Don't declare this account or that resource as off-limits. Put every income item on the table (no, the IRS isn't looking over your shoulder).

Make another list that includes payments that you absolutely, positively need to make, including the following:

- Rent or mortgage (plus necessary repairs)
- Food
- Utilities (*not* including cable)
- Insurance (life, disability, medical, homeowners/renters, and car)
- Car and other transportation costs
- Student loan payments
- Taxes
- Charitable contributions
- Annual clothing costs for your family

Again, if amounts change seasonally, add up a year's worth of bills and expenses and then divide by 12.

Catalog so-called discretionary items — entertainment costs, travel, cable or satellite television, Internet access, gym memberships, private school tuitions, and so on. Depending on your family, this list can be quite extensive.

Finally, take a good look at how much you pay each month on outstanding consumer debt (plus the total amount you owe). Make sure you add your credit card payments to your lists of expenditures, as well as any bank fees that you may pay on your checking account.

Try to be as accurate and honest as possible when preparing these lists. It's one thing to lie to your accountant, but lying to yourself doesn't help here.

After you have all your lists prepared, you'll be able to see where your money goes and how much of it you actually fritter away.

Carving away the truly wasteful

With your income and current spending patterns laid out in front of you, you probably won't have any trouble spotting the expenditure items that are really, really wasteful. Right at the top of the list are bank and finance charges. You may consider these charges to be minimal, but adding up those minimal costs can be another story. Check out the following examples of potential fees you could face, depending on how you manage your money:

- **Minimum balance penalty:** Some banks assess fees if your checking account carries a balance below the minimum for the month. For example, if your checking account balance drops below $750 in any month (even it's $749), your bank might hit you with a fee of $7 per month.

- **Insufficient funds penalty:** We don't know of any bank that doesn't slap a fee of at least $20, if not more, on bounced checks.

- **Credit card interest:** Carrying a balance on your credit card can cost you between 10 and 20 percent (or more) per year for the loan of that money — *in interest alone.*

- **Over-limit fees:** Most credit card companies charge a fee if you go over your credit limit. As with bounced checks, we don't know of any credit card that charges less than $20 a month for going over the credit limit.

- **Late-payment fees:** If your payment check doesn't arrive on time, it'll probably cost you at least $20 for the month. (Late payments also decrease creditworthiness and increase the cost of later loans to you.)

Table 1-1 paints a picture of how these fees can add up for a typical family.

Book IV

Saving and Investing

Table 1-1	Truly Wasteful Spending			
What You're Paying	**Monthly Amount (Good Credit History)**	**Annual Amount**	**Monthly Amount (Slightly Flawed Credit History)**	**Annual Amount**
Bank finance charges	$7	$84	$12	$144
Credit card interest	$25 ($3,000 debt at 10% a year)	$300	$62.50 ($5,000 debt at 15% a year)	$750
Late mortgage payment	$25 (5% of $500 payment)	$300	$50 (5% of $1,000 payment)	$600
Over-the-limit credit card fee	$29	$348	$35	$420

Bank and finance charges aren't the only wastes of your money. Consider these:

✔ Paying health club dues to a club you haven't attended for more than a year.

✔ Continuing a newspaper subscription that you just haven't gotten around to canceling.

✔ Hitting the coffee shop for a cup o' joe in the morning because you don't get up early enough to make your own.

✔ Going out for dinner or lunch instead of eating at home.

You can curb wasteful spending if you take the time to assess your spending. We're not necessarily advocating that you punish your family by getting rid of a health club membership, but we are advocating that you rid yourself of expenses that you don't need or put to use. Add up what you waste each month. Start making payments on time, maintaining the minimum balance in your checking account, brewing coffee at home, and canceling memberships or subscriptions that you don't use.

Lowering Your Debt

If you've crossed off all the wasteful spending, or if you had no wasteful spending to begin with, you can still lower your total expenses each month. Check out what's left of your expenses and see whether you can take advantage of additional ways to save.

The biggest piece of most budgets is the amount folks pay to their mortgage company, their car finance company, and their credit card companies. Many people are surprised to find that they pay more than they need to in many of these areas. Check out the following ways to reduce your monthly debt:

- ✔ **Consider refinancing your house.** Look at your current housing, car, and credit card payments. You may be able to consolidate all these loans into one mortgage and leave your mortgage closing with one monthly payment that's significantly less than the total of all debt payments you had been making. Although this isn't true in every case and depends on interest rate fluctuations and the current value of your house, it's certainly worth an afternoon or evening of your time to investigate.

- ✔ **Consolidate your student loans.** If you're currently paying off student loans and you haven't yet consolidated them, now may be the time. Depending on the amount you owe and current interest rates, you may be able to significantly lower your monthly payment.

- ✔ **Liquidate your assets.** Another way to lower debt payments is to liquidate assets that you have and pay down your debt. For example, if you have shares of stock that aren't increasing in value, selling the stock and paying off your credit cards may be worthwhile.

- ✔ **Lower your credit card interest rate.** If you can't retire your credit card debt entirely, negotiate with your credit card companies for lower rates. You'll need a history of timely payments; one late payment will muddy the water considerably — two or more, and they'll probably just laugh. If your current company won't negotiate, go shopping. Many banks are eager for your business, often with introductory rates as low as 0% for three, six, or nine months. Transfer your high-interest balance and pay it off before the introductory rate expires.

- ✔ **Trade down when you trade in.** Take a close look at your car and the size of your car payments. When getting a new vehicle, consider something less than a Mercedes, even if the dealer says you can afford it. He's trying to put his own kids through college, but your responsibility extends only as far as your own family — not his.

- ✔ **Consider debt consolidation.** If you're *really* burdened by debt and can't find *any* reasonable way out (robbing a bank isn't reasonable), making an appointment with a reputable credit counselor isn't the worst idea. Counselors can often negotiate deals with your creditors that you won't be able to get on your own, and through their services you may be able to eliminate hundreds of dollars from monthly credit card and other loan bills. If you're so deeply in debt that you need to consult with one of these services, you're probably also missing payments, making late payments, and otherwise messing up your credit rating. In the long run, your creditors will likely be relieved to see you gaining some control over your finances. (Book III, Chapters 3 and 4 talk a lot more about debt consolidation and counseling.)

Trimming Other Costs

Clearly, you need electricity, water, telephone service (landline, cell phone, or VoIP), heat, and so on. And usually these costs are not negotiable — the utility companies have cultivated a world of monopolies, and, in most cases, no bargains are to be found as far as price per unit goes. However, you may be able to reduce costs within your own household, and these are well worth exploring.

- ✔ **Ask for a lower rate.** Telephone and heating oil companies are highly competitive. Don't hesitate to shop around, and ask your current company to meet, or beat, a competitor's lower price.

- ✔ **Pay for only what you use.** Don't pay for more cable and/or satellite service than you need or can use. Cut back to a place that still provides the programming you want but doesn't give you a whole lot of extras that you rarely use.

- ✔ **Practice energy conservation.** Upgrade your house with energy- and water-efficient appliances and improvements. Many of these have small upfront costs (energy-efficient light bulbs and low-flow toilets, for example) but pay off in huge savings over their lifetimes.

- ✔ **Comparison-shop for insurance.** Seek out the most competitive price for all your insurance needs — life, disability, homeowners/renters, car, and medical (if you pay for your own). Many folks can trade a costly whole-life policy for a much less expensive term-life policy. Your life insurance coverage can remain the same for a fraction of the cost.

- ✔ **Trim the grocery bill.** You can slash your grocery bill by using coupons and store affinity cards and by shopping on sale. Also don't forget that house brands are almost always less expensive than the national brands, and for many items, the quality is the same. Just because you've always used a certain brand doesn't mean you have to continue to use it.

You'll be most successful in your trimming program if you don't slash costs willy-nilly. If you're content with how you're living right now, cutting out the funds to do the things you love will only create a savings ogre that sucks the joy out of your life in exchange for money in the bank.

Changing Your Perspective and Watching Your Savings Grow

Saving for any purpose, whether for college, retirement, a new home, or that dream vacation, isn't a punishment, nor does it need to be a deferral of pleasure. Some people (and we all know someone like this) squeeze every penny until it squeals and never seem to have any fun. Who can forget Ebenezer

Scrooge? He began to live only after he stopped clutching his money quite so tightly. And the miser is, of course, the epitome of the saver.

Well, Scrooge is a fictional character, and plenty of savers out there still know how to have a good time. And maybe they even have a better time because, at the end of the evening, they know they have the money to pay the bill.

Saving money can and should be neither painful nor pleasurable; it should just *be*. Hopefully you can view putting cash into your savings plans and accounts in the same way as you view paying your other bills.

Paying yourself first

You've probably heard this advice more than once but never put it into practice: Pay yourself first. As you look at your income, you should carve a portion of that income out and earmark it for savings.

That money needs to be physically separated from the rest of your income (so you're not tempted to dip into it, even a little, for that extra something you've been wanting to buy). Only after you've subtracted it and put it elsewhere should you figure out how much money you have available for all your other expenses, which need to fit into this smaller amount. After putting aside your savings amount, if you can't pay the rest of your monthly bills, you need to change something — find a cheaper mortgage, eat out less frequently, or buy fewer books (not counting this one). The choice is yours. The only item that isn't on the negotiating table is your savings amount.

Systematically saving

You can successfully save if you put the same amount of money into some sort of savings account every week or month (depending on when your income is paid to you). Even if the periodic amounts may seem small to you, Table 1-2 illustrates how those savings can add up to considerable nest eggs at the end of 1, 5, 10, or 20 years.

Book IV

Saving and Investing

Table 1-2 Systematic Savings at 5% Interest, Compounded Weekly				
Amount Per Week	*1 Year of Savings*	*5 Years of Savings*	*10 Years of Savings*	*20 Years of Savings*
$10	$532.96	$2,952.26	$6,742.58	$17,865.55
$25	$1,332.39	$7,380.65	$16,856.46	$44,641.38
$50	$2,664.78	$14,761.30	$33,712.91	$89,282.76
$100	$5,329.57	$29,522.60	$67,425.83	$178,565.52

Earmarking certain pieces of income for savings

Beyond their normal income, paid at regular intervals, most people also have periodic injections of additional cash. This extra money may come in the form of overtime wages, significant salary increases, holiday bonuses, gifts and/or inheritances, or even income tax refunds. Many people also use additional withholdings on their pay as a way to save money.

If you've been doing your job and dissecting your budget, you've probably already figured out how to live comfortably on what you earn on a regular basis. Hopefully, you're also now saving systematically and regularly.

So what should you do when a little extra money comes your way? Of course, to us, the answer is obvious. *Save, save, save.* You've figured out how to live nicely without it, and you won't miss it, so put it in a safe place and forget about it!

Ah, but vacations, jewelry, or kitchen remodels are dancing through your head. Obviously, if your household budget hasn't included money for some glaring need (perhaps your roof is leaking) and you've just been waiting for some extra cash to pay for that project, you can divert at least some of that money for that purpose. But if you've managed to pare your spending to a point at which you're managing beautifully with what you have, take a big chunk of that extra money and sock it into your savings plans. What's out of sight is also out of mind, and these additional funds may be just the ticket to beef up a somewhat anemic college savings or retirement account.

Educating yourself about investing

The world of investing can be a scary place, and the days when stockbrokers did your buying and selling have mostly gone the way of eight-track cassettes. Investing is now a do-it-yourself operation that can present many pitfalls for the unwary. Before you even think about sticking your big toe in the investing pool, make sure you have a handle on the following.

Know what you're buying

Your success with any investment rests squarely on your understanding of what you're buying. Know what you're paying for, whether it's an individual stock or bond, a mutual fund, or even a certificate of deposit. You wouldn't purchase an orange without first making sure it wasn't rotten; don't assume that every security the so-called experts are touting is as solid as Fort Knox. Do your own research and make your own decisions (and be sure to read the next chapter).

Understand and be able to live with risk

When you move beyond bank savings accounts, certificates of deposit, and mutual fund money market accounts, you enter the world of ever-increasing risk. Whether you invest in individual securities or in mutual funds (which are nothing more than pools of individual securities), the price of those securities can rise or fall. That's risk.

Risk is inherent in the investment world. Whether you buy small pieces of companies (stocks, or equities) or lend companies and/or governments money (bonds, or debt instruments), your money is only as secure as the company or companies you've tied it to. Investments also depend on the general economic conditions both in the United States and around the world.

In other words, if you can't even contemplate that your savings may be worth less next week or next year than they are today, you may want to reconsider plunging your money into a junk bond fund. (*Junk bonds* are loans to companies that Wall Street has serious doubts about, so they're considered risky.) Instead, you may want to consider a mutual fund that purchases nothing but U.S. Treasury bonds and notes (very, very safe).

If you own an investment that's keeping you awake at night, there's no crime in selling it, whether at a profit or a loss. Even if you don't sell a security at its absolute height, you need never apologize for making a profit. Likewise, if your investment is leaking value, remember that this isn't a sinking ship and you're not the captain. Jump overboard and live to invest another day.

Balance risk and expectations against future monetary needs

Not every great investment is a great investment for you. If you want to gamble on which company will be the next Microsoft or IBM, you need the luxury of time to allow that company to develop and grow. You may need to be patient; many startup companies struggle initially, and the big payoffs, if they do develop, come about over time.

If you'll need to make that next tuition payment within the next five years, you may want to temper your level of risk by keeping a larger portion of your savings in cash and cash equivalents such as money market funds or certificates of deposit. We're not saying you can't invest your teenager's college savings funds in Wonder Widget, Inc., but you may want to invest only a small portion of those savings in it and keep most of your money invested in less-risky ventures.

Identify the cost

Just because you invest directly with a mutual fund company or through an Internet brokerage doesn't mean that you can avoid paying anything for the privilege of investing your money. Face it, people aren't in this business for their health; they're in it to make money. And they make a lot of it. And as far as purchasing individual securities goes, the cost of each transaction usually shows up right there on your confirmation slip.

Still, identifying exactly what a mutual fund costs you may be difficult because the management costs may be buried deep inside the prospectus. Search for these costs. A company may charge its fee based on a percentage of the value of the assets within a fund, or it may charge a percentage of income collected. Know how the fees in your accounts are calculated, and then factor that into total return for that fund.

Choose mutual funds carefully. Excessive fees can eat into your savings as easily as market declines.

Read the fine print about total returns

Every mutual fund company offers literature about how well its fund has performed against other similar funds and about the percentage of increase (or decrease, but those numbers tend to be in much smaller print) the fund has realized over time. The literature probably also touts the expertise of the fund manager, who chooses what to buy and what to sell within the fund.

Unless your fund's manager is an expert crystal-ball reader, these numbers are of historic value only. Mutual funds tend to follow the trends of the overall stock and bond markets, and their fortunes rise and fall in concert with the markets. Past performance isn't an indicator of how the fund will do for you, and the bygone wizardry of a fund manager may never be repeated.

Taking advantage of giveaways

You get something for nothing very few times in life, and money-back offers from credit cards and from retailers may or may not qualify as one of those times for you. Still, if you can take advantage of an offer without spending any additional money to do so, well, you would be foolish not to.

Credit card offers

Many credit cards are now offering a rebate equaling 1 percent of your total purchases toward a Section 529 plan (see Book IV, Chapter 4) for yourself or your child. This plan may be in addition to, or instead of, other incentives that credit cards often offer, such as air miles, travel insurance, rental car insurance, and double warranties. Others may give you a percentage of every purchase as cash back, or may even deposit the difference into a savings account for you, in cents, between the amount of each and every charge you make and the next higher dollar. So, if you charge $47.37 for a tank of gasoline, the credit card company will then add $0.63 to your savings account.

If you don't handle credit cards well, these offers may be ones you should avoid. The interest or other fees the credit card company will charge you will more than swallow up any incentive the credit card company is offering.

Good debt and bad debt

The good news: Some types of debt are good, are factored into your monthly budget, and shouldn't hinder you from saving. The bad news: Some types of debt are bad, should be paid off as quickly as possible, and prevent you from saving.

Clearly, you're not planning to pay off your entire mortgage before you start saving for college, at least if you intend for your children to begin college before their hair turns gray. And you probably feel the same about your car payment, which is factored into your budget as a transportation cost, and any student loans that you still have outstanding.

Even after you finish paying off the loan amounts for your house, your vehicle, and your education, those items should still have value to you. And from a creditworthiness standpoint, most credit-rating companies expect you to have some form of this debt, so the fact that you have these sorts of loans actually makes you more attractive as a potential borrower than having no loans at all (provided that you make your payments on time). This is *good debt:* debt that you plan for, budget for, and manage appropriately.

On the other hand, your credit cards (if you carry unpaid balances from month to month), your rent-to-own accounts, your layaway accounts, and all your so-called consumer debts are considered *bad debt* that you should reduce or completely eliminate, if possible.

Consumer debt is money that you have borrowed to purchase either something that is a consumable (like groceries) or something that has a very limited life (last year's clothes, perhaps, that your teenager won't wear because they're no longer fashionable). Basically, after you buy things in these categories, they cease to have any monetary value.

Now, we're not saying that you shouldn't buy food or clothing, or even a new television set. You do need to eat, after all, and watching television is still a relatively cheap form of entertainment. What you shouldn't be doing, though, is *borrowing* money to satisfy these needs. And that is exactly what you do when you carry balances on your credit cards. You're not only paying interest on last night's dinner, but you also may still be paying for last year's holiday gifts and your wedding dress from ten years ago.

However you dig yourself out from under your debt, you need to also break yourself of the credit card habit. Stop thinking that, just because you still have credit available, you can feel free to indulge yourself in anything that crosses your path. If you can't use your cards responsibly and pay them off in full every month, it's time to make a plastic salad. Sliced and diced credit cards in a glass bowl can make an attractive focal point in a room, and they also serve as a powerful reminder of spending habits run amok.

On the other hand, if you use a credit card anyway, you may want to investigate changing card companies to avail yourself of a particularly attractive offer. Doing so won't put your child through school, or allow you to retire any earlier; however, every dollar that someone else puts into your savings plan is one less dollar you need to find.

Upromise and BabyMint

In a unique twist on the credit card theme, Upromise and BabyMint have devised a scheme by which they sign up retailers, manufacturers, restaurants, and various sorts of service providers who gift a percentage of your spending into a general account maintained by Upromise or BabyMint. You can then invest the funds in these accounts in a Section 529 plan. For example, a major gasoline company may offer you 1 cent per gallon, an office supply store may give 2 percent of your total purchases, and the return on a new car or home could be in the hundreds.

Granted, these are all small amounts by themselves, but just as your small weekly deposits of savings add up over time, so do these. Depending on how many of the associated stores and products you use and how much you spend, your savings here could be substantial. You can find out all the details on the companies' Web sites at www.upromise.com and www.babymint.com.

Saving While in Debt

Being in debt doesn't preclude you from saving money. Sure, it makes doing so more difficult, but the following strategies can make saving while paying down debt more manageable.

✔ **Understanding the difference between needs and wants:** *Needs* fulfill a necessary function ably, but *wants* add other elements, at a price. For instance, you need a new television. The television you *need* is the one tucked away on the bottom shelf: 27 inches, color, with a remote. But the one you *want* is on center display: It's high-def, has picture-in-picture and surround sound — and who cares how many inches it is, it's nearly as big as your wall. However, the TV you *want* costs much more than the one you actually *need.* Buying the one you need can make you just as happy, fulfill the need for a television, and ensure that you don't break the bank or borrow money for it (like using your credit card) and have to pay it off in installments.

As you slice away at your consumer debt and, hopefully, finally retire it, nurture the habit of looking at every potential purchase and expenditure from a need-versus-want perspective. Although denying yourself everything that you want may, in the end, be self-defeating and make you miserable (you're not a monk, after all, and you never took a vow of poverty), constant self-indulgence will prove equally disastrous.

✔ **Learning to defer gratification until you can afford it:** No matter how badly you want that new gadget (whether the stripped-down or the deluxe version), don't buy it until you've saved enough to pay for it.

Most folks see a television as a necessity, but doing without for a period of time won't kill you, and you may actually use the extra time you have to rediscover old hobbies, visit with friends, or otherwise pleasurably spend time. When the time comes to plop down your hard-saved cash on the store counter, you'll likely be more pleased with the less-expensive TV than you would be with the bells-and-whistles model that you paid for with your charged-to-the-max piece of plastic.

✔ **Using credit as a tool, not a weapon:** Consumer credit is not, by definition, a bad thing; used properly, it can be a valuable tool. Paying for purchases using credit cards negates the need to carry large amounts of cash, allows you to pass unmolested through the checkout line at the grocery store, and, at the end of the month or the year, gives you an easy way to track your spending habits. If you use it improperly, though, it becomes a weapon that destroys your finances and demolishes good intentions. Be responsible: If you can't pay your credit bill in full every month, destroy your cards and use cash instead. Budgeting cash enables you to insert a line-item for savings.

Chapter 2

Investing in Stocks, Bonds, and Mutual Funds

*H*ow would you like to make money while you sleep or generate enough extra cash to do the things you need and want to do in the near term, such as buy a home, send your kids to college, or take a long vacation in some distant land? Or maybe you want to create a financial nest egg that will allow you to retire with enough money to enjoy your golden years without worrying where the next paycheck will come from?

Whatever your short- and long-term financial goals, investing in stocks, bonds, and mutual funds can help you achieve them. When it comes to building wealth and financial independence, investing is one of the best ways to achieve your goals. However, you can invest in a right way or a wrong way. If you invest in the right way, you may be set for life, enjoying the sense of well-being that comes with being financially independent. If you invest in the wrong way, you may find yourself in enough financial trouble to keep you up late at night, wondering where your next dollar will come from.

The good news is, if you're willing to play by some fairly simple investing rules, you can minimize your personal financial risk while maximizing your potential to achieve your long-term goals. In this chapter, we take a close look at the most common investing instruments: stocks, bonds, and mutual funds. We consider the pros and cons in deciding whether to manage your own investments or farm out the job to an investment professional. We also describe five of the most common investing mistakes and give you advice on how to avoid them.

Stock: Owning a Piece of the Rock

Have you ever wanted to own your own business? Maybe a computer software manufacturer such as Microsoft, a grocery store such as Safeway, or a fast-food chain such as McDonald's? Now, what if you could own your own business without showing up for work — ever? Well, you *can* own any one of these businesses — or, at least, a piece of them — without ever setting foot in the front door. How? By buying their stock.

Stock is a proportional share of ownership in a company, in the form of a piece of paper (a *stock certificate*) that grants you your ownership rights. Shares of stock are bought and sold in specialized marketplaces known as stock exchanges. The biggest and best known include the New York Stock Exchange and the NASDAQ in the United States, and the London, Hong Kong, Bombay, and Tokyo stock exchanges elsewhere in the world.

In this section, we take a closer look at what stock is, the different kinds of stock, and some basic stock-investing strategies.

Understanding stock

When you buy a share of stock in a company, you're actually buying part ownership in it — that is, a portion of its assets and its profit. One share of stock doesn't represent a very large portion of ownership for the typical large corporation, which may have hundreds of millions of shares outstanding. At the time of this writing, for example, General Motors has issued more than 566 million shares of stock. The more shares of stock you accumulate in a company, the more of the company you own. Someone who owns stock in a company is known as a *shareholder*.

The idea of stock is not a new one; stock ownership has actually been around for centuries. According to historians, stock first appeared in ancient Roman times, when shares of ownership were sold in public businesses known as *publicani*. After the fall of the Roman Empire, stock disappeared until after the Middle Ages, when the Dutch East India Company, the world's first multinational corporation, began issuing shares of stock in 1606 as a way of pooling capital to finance the building of ships that were used in the trade of spices and other goods.

Generally, you can make money in stocks in two different ways: through *appreciation,* the increase of a stock's price over time, and *dividends,* a portion of a company's profit, paid out to eligible shareholders on a per-share basis.

Conducting business in stock exchanges

For shares of stock to have value, a mechanism must exist for readily buying and selling them. When a company issues its stock to the public, buyers and sellers all around the world can buy and sell that stock. *Stockbrokers* conduct the actual buying and selling transactions for their clients and take a small commission with each transaction.

However, it would be grossly inefficient if individuals had to directly seek out other individuals who just happened to have the stock they wanted to buy — and for sellers to have to do the same thing. Stock exchanges, designed to provide a place where consumers can easily buy and sell stock, efficiently conduct millions of stock transactions each day. Two major categories of stock exchanges exist in the United States:

✔ **Listed exchanges:** In a listed exchange, such as the New York Stock Exchange (NYSE) (founded in 1792 as the result of a meeting of 24 large merchants), brokerage firms provide specialists responsible for all buy and sell transactions for a particular stock. The NYSE is perhaps the most famous stock market in the world.

✔ **Over-the-counter market:** In this kind of stock exchange, brokerages act as "market makers" for specific stocks, buying and inventorying their shares for consumers who may want to buy them. In the United States, the three largest over-the-counter markets are the Nasdaq, the Nasdaq Small Cap, and the OTC Bulletin Board.

Generally, when you want to buy or sell a share of stock, you do so through a broker (full service, discount, or online), who conducts the transaction on your behalf via one of these exchanges.

Brushing up: a quick stock glossary

The basic idea of stock — a share in the ownership of a company — is a simple one, but this simple idea gets more complicated when you start to dig into the different kinds of stock and the many different ways to manipulate it for financial gain. As you explore the wonderful world of stock, you're bound to read or hear all sorts of terms bandied about. Take a look at some of the most common:

✔ **Common stock:** The most basic form of stock, which conveys a fractional ownership in the company that issued it, including a share of its assets and profits. Common stock usually gives shareholders the right to vote on important matters to the corporation, such as membership on the board of directors, with one vote for each individual share of stock owned.

Book IV

Saving and Investing

✔ **Preferred stock:** Stock that gives its owners priority in the payment of dividends or in the event of liquidation (sale and dismantling) of the company.

✔ **Penny stock:** Generally, a stock that sells for less (often far less) than $1 a share. Many investors buy penny stocks hoping that their value will increase dramatically someday.

✔ **Share price:** The price to buy one share of stock, most commonly expressed in the United States in terms of U.S. dollars and cents. The share price for any given stock often fluctuates from day to day — and even hour to hour or minute to minute — based on general economic conditions and expectations, as well as industry and company news or events.

✔ **Price-to-earnings (P/E) ratio:** The current market price of a particular share of stock divided by its earnings (profit) per share over the previous 12 months. Investors often use this ratio to determine and compare the relative value of different company stocks. In the United States, the average P/E ratio for stocks from 1900 to 2005 is 14.

✔ **Yield:** The annual rate of return of a stock, generally expressed as a percentage.

✔ **Dividend:** A payment that a corporation makes to its shareholders out of its profits for a given period of time.

✔ **Split:** When a company increases the number of shares of stock outstanding without changing the proportionate of individual shareholders. For example, in a two-for-one split, 100 shares of stock with a current price of $10 per share and a total value of $1,000 become 200 shares of stock at a price per share of $5 — still worth $1,000. A *reverse split* works in the opposite direction, by decreasing the number of shares of stock and increasing the price per share.

✔ **Initial public offering (IPO):** The initial offering of a company's stock to the public, such as when Google offered its stock for sale to the public for the first time on August 19, 2004, raising more than $1.5 billion for the company in the process.

✔ **Market capitalization:** The value of a company on the stock market — *market cap,* for short. This figure is determined by multiplying the total number of shares of company stock issued by the share price. For example, a company with 1 million shares of stock outstanding, with a share price of $10, has a total market capitalization of $10 million.

✔ **Option:** The right to purchase or sell a specific number of shares for an agreed-upon price during a specified time period. The right to purchase the stock is known as a *call option.* The right to sell the stock is known as a *put option.*

✔ **Future:** An agreement that obligates someone to sell a fixed quantity of stock at a specific price on a particular future date — for example, 100 shares of Microsoft stock at a price of $35 on September 30, 2012. Note that if the actual market price of Microsoft stock is lower than $35 on the date of the future transaction, the buyer loses money on the deal. If the actual market price is higher than $35, the buyer makes money on the deal.

✔ **Blue chip:** A particularly high-quality stock, usually issued by a large company with a long history of stable earnings and profitability. Although the idea of which companies constitute blue-chip stocks changes over time, currently, companies such as Apple, Nike, Wal-Mart, Procter & Gamble, and Coca-Cola would make most investing observers' list of such stocks.

✔ **Dow Jones Industrial Average (DJIA):** The most commonly used indicator of overall American stock market health and vitality. The average is derived from a price-weighted average of 30 blue-chip stocks chosen by the editors of the *Wall Street Journal.*

✔ **Bull market:** A prolonged increase in the overall market value of stocks, usually 20 percent or more.

✔ **Bear market:** A prolonged decline in the overall market value of stocks, usually 20 percent or more.

This list includes just the basic definitions of key stock terms — you'll uncover many more specialized ones if you dig deeper. For additional definitions, take a look at the InvestorWords Web site (www.investorwords.com).

Picking a stock-investment strategy

Over time, stock investors have developed a variety of novel strategies for deciding when to buy and sell stock. Some are highly analytical, taking into account all sorts of numbers, facts, and figures, and some aren't so much. Read over some of these most popular and long-lasting stock investment strategies:

✔ **Technical analysis:** Investors use stock market data, such as charts of price and volume, to predict future market trends (particularly short-term trends) of selected stocks.

✔ **Fundamental analysis:** Investors use company financial and operations data, such as sales, earnings, debt, management, and competition, to predict future market trends of selected stocks.

✔ **Buy and hold:** This strategy advocates buying and holding stocks for very long periods of time (10 to 20 years or more), regardless of short-term market fluctuations, on the assumption that the stock price will continue to increase over the long term along with the overall growth in the economy.

✔ **Growth investing:** Within a particular industry — say, automotive — some companies perform better than others, and some industries do better than others, too. In this strategy, you pick out the companies that are performing better than their peers and invest in them, hoping that they will continue to outperform the market into the future.

✔ **Value investing:** The opposite of growth investing, value investing involves seeking out company stock that is undervalued compared to its peers, with the hope that the stock is poised to increase in value after company management addresses whatever fundamental issues are holding down the value of the stock.

✔ **Dollar cost averaging:** This strategy involves buying a specific dollar amount of stock each investment period — say, $1,000 each month — regardless of the stock price. When stock prices are up, you purchase fewer shares; when stock prices are down, you purchase more shares.

✔ **Market timing:** Investors use price, volume, and economic data to try to predict the overall future direction of the stock market. *Day traders* do this when they buy stock, but their time frame usually is only a day, whereas most market timers have a much longer time horizon.

✔ **Buy what you know:** This strategy involves investing in companies that you have personal experience with. For example, maybe you notice that as overall economic conditions worsen, your local Wal-Mart store is substantially busier and it's harder to get a parking spot. This personal experience may indicate to you that Wal-Mart's business prospects will continue to improve in the future, leading you to buy 100 shares of Wal-Mart stock.

✔ **Dogs of the Dow:** In this strategy, at the end of each year, you look at the list of the 30 stocks that make up the Dow Jones Industrial Average and buy shares of the 10 that have the highest yields. You hold on to these stocks for the entire year and then repeat the process at the end of year, selling the stocks that fall off the top-ten list and buying the ones that are added.

Plenty of other stock-investing strategies exist — see which ones work best for you. If you're not happy with one approach, try another until you find one you like.

Buying Bonds for Fixed Income

When you buy stock in a company, you are actually buying a real stake in its ownership — that is, you have a claim on its assets and its profits. Companies generally sell stock to raise the capital they need to expand their operations and grow. Although organizations also use bonds to raise capital, they work differently than stock.

In this section, we take a closer look at bonds — what they are, how they work, and some basic bond-investing strategies.

Understanding bonds

A *bond* is essentially a loan to the organization that issues it, whether that organization is a corporation or a government agency. Whereas stocks tend to be relatively volatile and unpredictable investments — stock price can vary widely, depending on overall economic conditions or company financial results, and sometimes for no particular reason at all — bonds are generally stable, with predictable payouts even years into the future.

When buying bonds, keep these key considerations in mind:

- **Par value:** The amount of money that is returned to the bondholder when the bond matures, also commonly known as *principal* or *face value.* Most bonds available in the United States have a par value of $1,000.

- **Price:** The actual cost of a bond to a buyer in the open market. The price paid may be above, below, or at par value depending on market forces.

- **Maturity date:** The date on which the issuer promises to return the par value of the bond. Depending on the terms of the bond, the par value can be returned to the bondholders early, known as a *call.*

- **Coupon rate:** The interest rate paid to the bondholders as a percentage of par value. For example, a bond with a par value of $1,000 with a 12 percent coupon rate pays its bondholders $120 a year until the bond reaches maturity or is called. Payments can be made monthly, quarterly, semiannually, or annually, depending on the specific bond terms.

- **Yield:** The coupon rate divided by the price of the bond, which may vary considerably from its par value.

Bonds are generally sold in two different markets, the primary market and the secondary market.

- **Primary market:** When a company or government organization first issues a bond, buyers (usually brokers) purchase it directly from the issuer. This market is the primary market. The issuer generally fixes the price.

- **Secondary market:** When buyers in the primary market later sell bonds to investors, this market is the secondary market. Prices for bonds in the secondary market can vary significantly from their initial price in the primary market because of a variety of different factors, such as expectations for future interest rates and economic conditions, as well as the amount of time remaining before the bond matures.

Book IV

Saving and Investing

Calculating yields on different bonds enables you to compare them and make decisions on which bonds are the better investment. Consider the following example:

For a bond with a par value of $1,000, a current price of $800, and a coupon rate of 12 percent, the yield is calculated as follows:

Yield = $120 ÷ 800 = 0.15 = 15 percent

The higher the yield, the better. In the secondary market, expect to pay more for bonds that have higher yields.

Sorting out different kinds of bonds

All sorts of bonds exist, issued by all sorts of organizations for a variety of purposes. These bonds are the most common kinds you'll likely encounter as you explore bonds as an investment vehicle:

- **Corporate bonds:** Companies issue these bonds through the pubic securities markets in much the same way that they sell stock. To attract investors, corporate bonds often have higher coupon rates than government bonds, which are generally considered to be safer investments.

- **Municipal bonds:** State, local, or city governments issue these bonds to raise funds for capital-improvement projects such as new roads, school improvements, or water pipes. Interest paid to municipal bondholders is often exempt from federal, state, and local income taxes. This fact, combined with the relative security of the government institutions that issue the bonds, makes municipal bonds attractive investments, particularly for investors in high tax brackets.

- **Treasury bonds:** The federal government issues these long-term bonds, with maturities of more than 10 years. Also known as T-bonds, these bonds are backed by the full faith and credit of the United States government and they are considered to be one of the safest investments available anywhere.

- **Agency bonds:** U.S. government agencies such as the Federal National Mortgage Association (Fannie Mae) and the Federal Home Loan Mortgage Corporation (Freddie Mac) issue these bonds. Agency bonds are not considered to be as safe as Treasury bonds because, although they are backed by the U.S. government, they are not guaranteed by it.

- **Zero-coupon bonds:** These bonds pay no coupons or interest, although they do pay bondholders the full amount of the par value upon maturity. They are attractive to investors because they are generally sold at a significant discount from their par value, giving investors an opportunity to make a significant return on their investment.

✔ **Junk bonds:** These bonds are particularly risky bonds issued by companies with low credit ratings (BB or below). Junk bonds often have high yields, attracting investors who can tolerate their inherent risk.

Interpreting bond ratings

Any investment can be risky, and bonds are no exception. Some bonds, such as government-issued bonds, are much safer than others, such as junk bonds. So how do you know the quality of a particular bond? A variety of independent third-party organizations rate bonds to indicate their relative safety. Some of the most well-known bond-rating services include Standard & Poor's (www.standardandpoors.com) and Moody's (www.moodys.com).

Take a look at the Standard & Poor's bond ratings:

✔ **AAA:** An obligation rated AAA has the highest rating assigned by Standard & Poor's. The organization issuing the bond is highly likely to meet its financial commitment, and the bond is extremely safe.

✔ **AA:** An obligation rated AA differs from the highest-rated obligations only to a small degree. The organization's capacity to meet its financial commitment is very strong, and the bond is very safe.

✔ **A:** An obligation rated A is somewhat more susceptible to the adverse effects of changes in circumstances and economic conditions than obligations in higher-rated categories. However, the organization's capacity to meet its financial commitment is still strong as is the safety of the bond.

✔ **BBB:** An obligation rated BBB exhibits adequate protection parameters. However, adverse economic conditions or changing circumstances are more likely to weaken the organization's ability to meet its financial commitment. These bonds are not as safe as the A-rated bonds, but may still be safe enough for many investors.

✔ **BB, B, CCC, CC, and C:** Obligations rated BB, B, CCC, CC, and C are regarded as having significant speculative characteristics. BB indicates the least degree of speculation, and indicates C the highest degree of speculation. Although such obligations likely have some quality and protective characteristics, they may be outweighed by large uncertainties or major exposures to adverse conditions.

✔ **BB:** An obligation rated BB is less vulnerable to nonpayment than other speculative issues. However, it faces major ongoing uncertainties or exposure to adverse business, financial, or economic conditions that may weaken the organization's ability to meet its financial commitment. These bonds are not very safe investments.

Book IV

Saving and Investing

- **B:** An obligation rated B is more vulnerable to nonpayment than an obligation rated BB, but the organization currently has the capacity to meet its financial commitment. Adverse business, financial, or economic conditions will likely impair the organization's capacity or willingness to meet its financial commitment. These bonds are speculative, especially in uncertain economic times.

- **CCC:** An obligation rated CCC is currently vulnerable to nonpayment and is dependent upon favorable business, financial, and economic conditions for the obligor to meet its financial commitment. In the event of adverse business, financial, or economic conditions, the obligor will not likely be able to meet its financial commitment. These bonds are not safe investments.

- **CC:** An obligation rated CC is currently highly vulnerable to nonpayment. These bonds are particularly risky.

- **C:** A subordinated debt or preferred stock obligation rated C is currently highly vulnerable to nonpayment. The C rating may be used if a bankruptcy petition has been filed or a similar action has been taken but payments on this obligation are being continued. These are extremely risky bonds.

- **D:** An obligation rated D is in payment default. The D rating category is used when payments on an obligation are not made on the date due, even if the applicable grace period has not expired, unless Standard & Poor's believes that such payments will be made during the grace period. The D rating also is assigned if a bankruptcy petition has been filed or a similar action has been taken and payments on an obligation are jeopardized. Extremely risky investments.

- **Plus (+) or minus (–):** The ratings from AA to CCC may be modified by the addition of a plus (+) or minus (–) sign to show relative standing within the major rating categories.

- **NR:** These letters indicates that no rating has been requested, that insufficient information exists on which to base a rating, or that Standard & Poor's does not rate a particular obligation as a matter of policy.

Mutual Funds: The Power of Many

Individuals stocks can be quite volatile and can vary considerably in price, depending on a variety of both internal and external factors for the companies that issued them. Although bonds are not as volatile, their prices can also move up and down, depending on prevailing interest rates and economic expectations.

What if you could create a basket of stocks and/or bonds that would generally rise over the long term, with the losses of some of the securities more than balanced out by the gains of the other securities? Well, you may be able to do just that by investing in mutual funds. In this section, we explore mutual funds and take a look at some basic mutual fund investment strategies.

Understanding mutual funds

A *mutual fund* is nothing more than a pool of stocks and/or bonds that a mutual fund manager buys and sells. The mutual fund manager researches the securities and makes all buy and sell decisions. When you buy a share of a mutual fund, you buy a proportional stake in the pool's assets. As such, you have no input in or control over the buying and selling decisions that the mutual fund manager makes. Mutual fund managers generally charge a yearly fee as compensation for their efforts.

Keep an eye on mutual fund sales fees and commissions; they can be a significant drain on your investment returns. Consider some of the ways managers may charge mutual fund fees:

- **Front-end load:** The sales fee is paid when shares of the mutual fund are purchased.

- **Back-end load:** The sales fee is paid when shares of the mutual fund are sold.

- **Level load:** The sales fee is paid once a year, as a fixed percentage of a mutual fund's average net assets.

- **No load:** No sales fee is required when shares of the mutual fund are bought or sold.

Defining different kinds of mutual funds

Mutual funds come in many different kinds. These funds are some of the most common:

- **Stock funds:** Consist of company-issued common stock.

- **Bond funds:** Consist of bonds.

- **Balanced funds:** Hold both stocks and bonds, in an attempt to balance the long-term fixed-income aspect of bonds with the potential for price appreciation that stocks offer.

✔ **Sector funds:** Pool securities in specific industries, such as technology, financial, or energy.

✔ **International/global funds:** Invest in companies outside the United States.

✔ **Index funds:** Duplicate the mix of stocks in specific stock indexes, such as the Standard & Poor's 500 or the Dow Jones Industrial Average. As these indexes increase or decrease in value, so do these mutual funds.

Selecting the best mutual funds

Personal finance expert Eric Tyson has done extensive research on mutual funds to determine which ones are worth your while and which ones you should avoid like the plague. In his book *Investing For Dummies, 4th Edition,* (Wiley) Tyson names the following mutual funds as the best ones for your investment dollar.

U.S. stock funds

✔ American Century Income & Growth

✔ Dodge & Cox Stock

✔ Fidelity Disciplined Equity, Equity-Income, and Fidelity Low Priced Stock

✔ Masters' Select Equity, Smaller Companies, and Value

✔ Neuberger & Berman Focus

✔ T. Rowe Price Spectrum Growth

✔ Vanguard Total Stock Market Index, Primecap, Tax-Managed Capital Appreciation, and Tax-Managed Small Capitalization

International stock funds

✔ Artisan International

✔ Fidelity Diversified International

✔ Harbor International

✔ Masters' Select International Equity

✔ Oakmark International and Global

✔ TIAA-CREF International Equity

✔ Tweedy Browne Global Value

✔ Vanguard International Growth, Tax-Managed International, and Total International Stock Index

Bond funds

- ✔ Vanguard Short-Term Tax-Exempt
- ✔ Vanguard Limited-Term Tax-Exempt
- ✔ Dodge & Cox Income
- ✔ Harbor Bond
- ✔ USAA GNMA
- ✔ Vanguard GNMA, High Yield Corporate, and Total Bond Market Index
- ✔ Fidelity Spartan Intermediate Term Municipal Income
- ✔ USAA Tax-Exempt Intermediate Term
- ✔ Vanguard Intermediate-Term Tax-Exempt
- ✔ Fidelity Spartan CA Muni Income
- ✔ Vanguard CA Long-Term Tax-Exempt
- ✔ Fidelity Spartan CT Muni Income

Balanced funds

- ✔ Dodge & Cox Balanced
- ✔ Fidelity Asset Manager, Freedom Funds, and Fidelity Puritan
- ✔ TIAA-CREF Managed Allocation
- ✔ T. Rowe Price Balanced
- ✔ Vanguard LifeStrategy Funds, Wellesley Income, and Wellington

Doing It Your Way Versus Using a Broker

When you invest in stocks, bonds, mutual funds, and other securities (investment instruments issued by companies or government organizations), you can choose to do the research and buying and selling yourself, you can choose to leave these tasks to a stockbroker, or you can do something in between.

Whether you decide to take on these tasks yourself or leave them to a pro depends on your personal level of interest in the investing process, your level of investing expertise, and the amount of spare time you have to undertake these tasks. In this section, we explore some of pros and cons of each approach, including using online brokers.

Book IV

Saving and Investing

The very best discount brokers

In his book *Investing For Dummies, 4th Edition*, personal finance expert Eric Tyson lists his favorite discount brokers. This list includes the following:

Broker	Phone Number	Web Site
T. Rowe Price	800-638-5660	www.troweprice.com
Vanguard	800-992-8327	www.vanguard.com
TD Ameritrade	800-454-9272	www.tdameritrade.com

Full-service brokers

Full-service brokers are the most expensive approach to buying and selling stocks. When you engage the services of a full-service broker, you have an actual living, breathing person assigned to your account. This investment professional guides your investments by doing all the research on different investing options, advising you in your decisions, and structuring an investment portfolio to best help you achieve your short- and long-term investing and life goals. This portfolio will likely contain a variety of financial products, including stocks, bonds, mutual funds, and perhaps even insurance.

Of course, all this service comes with a price — a full-service broker charges a commission every time he or she buys or sells one of the items in a client's portfolio. Buy 100 shares of IBM? Your broker charges some commission. Sell 1,000 shares of Home Depot? Your broker charges some more commission. The downside of this approach to compensating your broker is that he or she isn't rewarded for increasing the value of your portfolio; your broker is rewarded for keeping stocks, bonds, and other financial instruments moving in and out of it.

If you decide to engage the services of a full-service broker, consider a few tips:

- Ask your friends, family, and business associates for a referral. It makes much more sense to find a good broker based on the recommendations of someone you trust than to figure it out after much trial and error.

- Find a broker whose personality and investing philosophy are compatible with your own.

- Work hard to build communication and trust with your broker. If your broker violates that trust, don't hesitate to take your business elsewhere.

- Keep an eye out for "churning," in which a broker buys and sells items in your portfolio for no apparent reason other than to generate sales commissions.

Discount brokers

Over the past couple of decades, a revolution in stockbrokers has arisen — a *discount* revolution. On May 1, 1975, the U.S. Securities and Exchange Commission (SEC) deregulated the brokerage industry, allowing firms to charge whatever fees they desired. This action enabled the birth of discount brokers.

Discount brokers offer their customers a lower-priced alternative for buying and selling stocks. This approach leaves most of the research to customers, along with the decisions of what stocks, bonds, and other financial instruments to include in an investment portfolio. In exchange for this transfer of duties, investors pay far lower commissions than they would to full-service brokers. If you have the time and the inclination to do this research yourself, you can save a lot of money by using a discount broker to buy and sell your securities.

Online brokers

Online brokers cut out people altogether, enabling you to execute your own buy and sell orders through their Web sites. Online brokers work with extremely low overhead, cutting their costs to the bone and passing on the savings to their customers. If you need a broker simply to execute buy and sell transactions, you'll most likely want to do so online. Trading online is the ultimate in doing it your way — you do all the research and make all the investing decisions, including which securities to buy and sell, when, and for how much. See Book IV, Chapter 5 for a lot more about trading online.

The very best online brokers

Broker	Phone Number	Web Site
E*TRADE	800-387-2331	www.etrade.com
Muriel Siebert	800-872-0711	www.siebertnet.com
Scottrade	800-619-7283	www.scottrade.com
T. Rowe Price	800-638-5660	www.troweprice.com
Vanguard	800-992-8327	www.vanguard.com
TD Ameritrade	800-454-9272	www.tdameritrade.com

Book IV

Saving and Investing

Five Common Investing Mistakes

Some people seem to think that investing in the stock market or other securities markets is all a matter of luck — buy the right stock at the right time, and you're sure to get rich. Although you certainly can get lucky in the stock market — people do from time to time — chances are you'll do far better over the long run by actively participating in the investing process and not just leaving your future hopes to chance. If you take time to understand your investing goals and then develop your own personal investing plan and guidelines, you can minimize the downside risk while maximizing the upside potential to do well.

But make no mistake about it — you can lose when you invest your money, and you can lose *big*. In this section, we explore five of the most common investing mistakes you can make. Avoid these mistakes, and you'll be well on the way to becoming a successful investor and achieving the investing goals you've set for yourself.

Investing before you're ready

How long could you survive if you were fired or laid off from your job? How long would your savings last if you were injured and forced to spend several months in the hospital? How many mortgage or rent payments, expensive tanks full of gasoline for your SUV, or shopping carts of groceries for your family would you be able to afford before your account balance hit zero? If your answer to these questions — and questions like them — is "not many," you may not be ready to invest yet.

Believe it or not, just because you've got some money in the bank or a wallet full of cash doesn't mean that you should start buying stock or bonds or finding other ways to invest your hard-earned funds. You should first have a well-funded savings or money market account — with enough cash available to help get you through rough financial times or emergencies — before you begin investing. In addition, you should have your credit card and other unsecured debts paid down to a reasonable level. Until then, you're not ready, for two main reasons.

First, if you someday find yourself in a real financial pickle, the money you have put aside for this rainy day (or the money that is otherwise tied up in liquid assets) will support you and your family until you get your feet back on the ground. Although you can sell stock fairly quickly if you need to, you may have to sell it at a loss. Most people should have at least six months of living expenses socked away, in case of emergency. If you're concerned that your job is on thin ice and you have no ready alternatives, save even more — up to a year's worth of living expenses.

Second, if you're carrying a heavy load of debt, you'll probably be making a better financial move by first paying down this debt and cutting the amount of interest you're paying out each month.

So before you start investing your money in stocks, bonds, mutual funds, and other investments, make sure you've got your financial act together. Investing before you're ready can stretch your financial resources way too thin and can land you in serious financial trouble before you know what happened to you.

Investing without goals

To be effective, every investor needs goals — that is, an idea of what future outcomes he or she wants and expects to achieve. If you don't have goals, how will you know when you've succeeded? Goals give you direction and let you know when you've achieved success in the investing approaches you have selected. The goals you select make a huge difference in your optimal investing strategies. Here we list the common goals for most investors — remember, no right or wrong goals exist. Your goals simply are the ones that you decide are most important for you to achieve.

- Accumulating enough money to retire comfortably — when and where you want
- Building a strong, diversified investment portfolio that can weather the ups and downs of the markets and continue to grow over the long run
- Saving enough money to put kids through college
- Building up a substantial down payment on a dream house — or to pay for a vacation home on the beach in Hawaii
- Buying a new car or truck or big-screen television

Believing those "hot" tips

Consider a typical scenario. You're standing at the water cooler at work, chatting with a colleague and minding your business. Suddenly she whispers in your ear, "Guess what I heard? Acme Widgets stock is about to go through the roof. If you buy now, you'll make a killing in the market!" People in the investing business call this a *hot tip*. But you can't always believe what you read — or what a friend, acquaintance, or family member tells you, no matter how well intentioned someone is.

Most hot tips are actually not so hot — in fact, they're often big money losers. One reason for this fact is that people sometimes hype the value of not-so-great stocks and other investments by starting a whispering campaign about how the stock is about to jump in price. And if you act fast, you can get in before the stock takes off. Of course, instead of taking off as promised, the stock price most often sinks like a rock — usually shortly after you buy it.

Instead of relying on hot tips for your investing decisions, it's far better to do some research on your own to determine whether a particular investment will help you achieve your goals. Consider the industry — for example, if gasoline prices are going through the roof, automobile stocks may not be the best investment in the near term. Consider the company: Does it have a history of steady growth, or is it subject to wild swings in revenues and earnings? Consider the investment itself: Has it performed well over a long period of time, or is it in the doghouse more often than not?

Not diversifying your portfolio

Life is unpredictable. Just when you think that you've got it all figured out — and that the status quo will remain just that far into the future — life throws you a curve ball, and everything you thought was stable and predictable turns upside down. Stock, bond, and other securities markets act in much the same way, as do the individual financial instruments that make them up. Just when you think you've got your retirement funded, as a result of the several tens of thousands of shares of stock you bought in Acme Widgets over the past couple of decades, the company declares bankruptcy and those thousands of shares of stock that you bought become worthless overnight.

When putting together your investing plan, it's particularly important to select a variety of different investment vehicles — from stocks in different industries, to bonds, to mutual funds — so that losses in any one financial instrument are balanced by gains in your other financial instruments. The more diversified your portfolio, the lower the risk of your overall investment strategy; the less diversified your portfolio, the higher the risk.

If you want to stick with buying stocks, consider putting together a portfolio of at least 15 different stocks in at least 5 different industries. If your portfolio includes stocks, bonds, and mutual funds, five investments in each of these areas is a reasonable minimum or starting place.

Selling too soon (or too late)

"Shoulda, coulda, woulda" are three words that no investor wants to hear come out of his or her lips. The road of investing is littered with the bodies of men and women who sold their assets too soon and lost out on a significant increase in price that was just around the corner or who waited too long to sell their assets and rode the price all the way down to the basement.

Wachovia's six investment rules

The Wachovia Securities Financial Network (www.wachovia.com) suggests that you consider the following six rules to become a more effective and successful investor:

✔ **Know your objective.** Every investor needs goals and objectives — they are the road map to help you design an investment program that will get you where you want to go in life. Whether it's helping to fund your child's college education, to enable you to retire while you're young enough to enjoy it, or to buy a new home or car or other expensive item, being clear about your goals and knowing your objectives — and how much time you've got until you reach it — is half the battle in achieving them.

✔ **Set up a regular investment plan.** It's not enough to invest every once in awhile when you think you've got enough money to spare. To increase the probability of reaching your goals and objectives, you need to invest regularly — and early. The more money you invest — and the sooner you start doing it — the greater your overall returns will be as the power of compounding goes to work. In compounding, the value of an investment increases exponentially over time as the financial returns from the investment are added back into the original investment.

✔ **Create a diversified portfolio.** Investing your money can indeed be a risky proposition. When it comes to investing, you have no guarantees that you will achieve the financial returns you seek and expect — or any return at all. However, when you diversify your investments by putting your assets into a variety of investments, you can reduce the risk of one or two investments going bad. Imagine, for example, that you buy three different stocks — one in the technology sector, one in automotive, and one in agribusiness. The price of your automobile stock may be down because of a run-up in gasoline prices, but your agribusiness stock may be up because

of the increasing use of ethanol in automobiles. Your technology stock may be neutral, showing neither a gain nor a loss. Diversification doesn't eliminate all risk in investing, but it can often cushion the blow when a particular investment goes bad.

✔ **Rebalance periodically.** Investments are reflections of the companies and financial instruments they represent. As such, they are in a state of constant change and flux as global economic circumstances change and as the fortunes of companies that issued them rise and fall. In addition, your own investment — and life — goals and strategies will undoubtedly change over time. Because of these reasons and more, you should periodically rebalance your investments — that is, move them from one type of investment to another. You may decide that you want higher income growth, for example, which may mean moving your assets out of slow-growing blue-chip stocks and into riskier technology or international stocks.

✔ **Think long term.** An investing strategy takes time to produce substantial results. You may occasionally get lucky and pick an investment that produces a substantial short-term return, and some investments may lose large amounts of value seemingly overnight. But understand that markets can often be volatile and that being patient will pay off in the long term. Indeed, when prices are down, you often have the perfect opportunity to buy more of a particular stock, not to sell it off at a big loss.

✔ **Rely on a professional.** If you have the time, interest, and expertise, you may can take on many of the day-to-day tasks of researching, monitoring, and even buying and selling your own investments. However, keeping up with fast-changing business and financial markets takes a lot of time. Consider using a professional investment advisor to help you navigate the markets and keep an eye out for new opportunities — and dangers.

Book IV

Saving and Investing

Refuse to follow the herd. If people are bailing out of stocks, you probably want to hold on to the stocks that you have while you buy up as much stock as you can at the newly lowered prices. If people are buying up stocks, pushing prices into the stratosphere, you may want to sell. Above all, don't let the actions of others cause you to panic. Stop, take a deep breath, access your situation, and then act accordingly.

Chapter 3

Saving for Retirement

· ·

· ·

Spontaneity can be a lot of fun. But it's the last thing you want when you're planning for retirement. Saving for retirement involves delayed gratification, planning, and discipline, but today's sound-bite society may find this news hard to swallow. Luckily, tools like a 401(k) can help make the process less painful because a lot of the saving is automatic after you set up the plan.

If you're young, you may wonder whether it's too soon to plan for something 30 or 40 years away. The truth is that the earlier you start, the better: Your savings will have more time to build up through *compounding* (as the earnings on money in your account continue to earn even more money). Starting to save early gives you more freedom later to decide what you want to do.

On the other hand, if you're already in your 40s or older, you may wonder whether it's too late for you to plan. The bottom line is that it's never too late. But you may need to scale back some of your goals or increase the amount you save each year. This chapter aims to help you set and meet retirement goals and develop a detailed plan for achieving them. It walks you through the steps of deciding on a target date to retire, calculating how much income you'll need in retirement, developing a savings plan to achieve that amount of income, and tracking your progress as you save over the years.

Setting a Target Date for Retirement

The first step in planning for retirement is deciding *when* you want to retire. This can be trickier than it sounds. Attitudes about what retirement means and when it should happen have been changing over the last decade or two.

Retirement used to be clear-cut — you worked until you were 65 (or maybe 62), and then you were forced to retire with a gold watch and a pension. Social Security checks started arriving in the mail soon after your 65th birthday. Nowadays, things are different. No standard retirement age applies to everyone and every type of account. Consider the following:

- ✔ If you were born in 1960 or later, you can take full Social Security benefits when you turn 67, not 65.

- ✔ You're *allowed* to withdraw money from your 401(k) without penalty at age $59^{1}/_{2}$ (or age 55, if you leave your employer).

- ✔ You're *required* to start withdrawing money from your 401(k) when you're $70^{1}/_{2}$ — unless, that is, you're still working for the company sponsoring the 401(k). Then you can wait until you retire to take out your money, unless you own more than 5 percent of the business.

Whew! With all those different ages, how can you know when to retire?

You need to estimate when you'll have to start withdrawing the money in your retirement accounts, and whether that money will be supporting you entirely or whether you'll have other sources of income.

Choosing an age now can help you plan how much you need to save and how much time you have in which to save it (your *time horizon,* in financial planning lingo). The advantage of estimating a retirement age now is that you can see whether that goal is reasonable. If it's not, you may have to rethink it. The key is to remain flexible.

In choosing a target date for retirement, consider the following:

- ✔ When you can access your various sources of retirement income
- ✔ What you'll do when you retire
- ✔ Whether living to the age of 100 runs in your family

Determining when you can access retirement income

When you retire and no longer earn a paycheck, you'll need to get income from somewhere. If you plan well, you'll have that income available from several sources.

Social Security

The first source of income you'll have during retirement is *Social Security*, the federal government's social insurance program that pays monthly benefit payments to retirees. Every worker who earns enough credits (by working) is eligible for Social Security benefits in retirement.

Many people mistakenly think that they'll start receiving Social Security checks when they turn 65. In fact, for anyone born after 1937, the age to receive full Social Security benefits (called the *normal retirement age*) is at least a couple months *past* their 65th birthday. If you were born in 1960 or later, as mentioned, you won't be eligible for full Social Security benefits until your 67th birthday.

You *can* choose to receive reduced benefits at age 62 (even if you were born in 1960 or later). If you retire at age 62, your benefits are reduced to 80 percent of the full benefit if 65 is your normal retirement age, and 70 percent of the full benefit if 67 is your normal retirement age. Keep in mind that you'll always receive the reduced benefits if you retire at age 62; they won't increase when you reach your normal retirement age.

Table 3-1 shows the full retirement age for different birth years after 1937.

Table 3-1   Social Security Full Retirement Age and Reduction in Benefits for Early Retirement

Year of Birth (If you were born on Jan. 1, refer to the previous year)	Full Retirement Age	Total Reduction in Benefits If You Retire at 62 (in %)
1937 or earlier	65	20.00
1938	65 and 2 months	20.83
1939	65 and 4 months	21.67
1940	65 and 6 months	22.50
1941	65 and 8 months	23.33

(continued)

Table 3-1 *(continued)*

Year of Birth (If you were born on Jan. 1, refer to the previous year)	Full Retirement Age	Total Reduction in Benefits If You Retire at 62 (in %)
1942	65 and 10 months	24.17
1943–1954	66	25.00
1955	66 and 2 months	25.83
1956	66 and 4 months	26.67
1957	66 and 6 months	27.50
1958	66 and 8 months	28.33
1959	66 and 10 months	29.17
1960 and later	67	30.00

Source: Social Security Administration (www.ssa.gov).

In sum, you can't expect to receive any retirement benefits from Social Security before age 62, and you can increase the amount you receive if you wait until 65, 66, or 67 (whatever your "normal retirement age" is), or even 70.

Some years ago, the Social Security Administration (SSA) began mailing annual statements to workers who are over 25 years old. These statements estimate how much money they'd receive monthly at age 62, at full retirement age, and at age 70, based on their income to date. If you threw yours away or can't find it, you can contact the SSA for a new one at www.ssa.gov/mystatement/. Or if you prefer not to send personal information over the Internet, you can download a form that you mail in to request the statement. You can also request the form by telephone, at 800-772-1213, or by appearing in person at your local Social Security office.

You can factor the estimated benefit amount into your planned retirement income, but remember that Social Security was never meant to be your only source of retirement income. What's more, the future of Social Security is somewhat uncertain. Although Social Security benefits may not disappear completely during the next 20 to 30 years, they may be reduced.

Other sources

Now, what about your other sources of income during retirement? The following list highlights possible retirement resources above and beyond Social Security:

Social insecurity?

Social Security is known as a "pay-as-you-go" system. When you pay Social Security taxes out of your paycheck, the taxes don't go into an "account" in your name. The taxes go to pay the benefits of today's retired folks. In the same way, today's toddlers and teenagers will be supporting you one day — hopefully. But when the 76-million-strong Baby Boom generation starts turning 65 in 2011 (and doesn't stop until 2029), their needs will place a tremendous strain on the system. In 1945, an estimated 41.9 workers were paying for every retiree. Nowadays, the ratio has dropped to an estimated 3.3 workers for every retiree. By about 2030, the ratio is expected to drop to *two workers for every retiree.* Clearly, something will have to give.

The Social Security program is projected to begin running a deficit around 2017. In 2002, the U.S. government estimated that the trust fund will run out of money completely in 2041 if nothing were done to shore it up.

✔ **401(k):** As long as you're working for the employer that sponsors the plan, you generally can't take money out of a 401(k) before you're 59$^1/_2$. If your plan does permit you to withdraw money, you have to pay taxes and an extra early withdrawal penalty on the money you take out. If you leave your job at age 55 or older, you can withdraw the money without any penalty tax, but you still have to pay income tax. You can also roll it over into an IRA.

✔ **Other tax-favored retirement accounts:** Accounts similar to a 401(k), such as a 403(b) or IRA, have rules similar to those of 401(k)s. Generally, you can't count on having easy access to your money before age 59$^1/_2$, or possibly age 55. The rules are different for 457 "deferred-comp" plans. In some circumstances, you may be able to get at your retirement account money before age 55 without paying an early-withdrawal penalty.

✔ **Traditional defined-benefit pension plan:** If your employer offers one of these plans, your human resources or benefits representative may be able to tell you what your expected payment will be if you qualify to receive benefits.

✔ **Life insurance:** Some people buy a type of life insurance policy that allows them to build up a cash account (a *cash value* policy) instead of buying term life insurance, which is worth nothing after you stop making payments. If you have a cash value policy (such as whole life or variable life), it should have a cash account that you can tap at retirement.

✔ **Regular taxable savings:** A taxable account is any kind of account (such as a bank account, mutual fund account, or stock brokerage account) that doesn't have special tax advantages.

✔ **Part-time work:** No matter when you retire, you may want to take a part-time job that will keep you active and give you extra income.

Book IV

Saving and Investing

> ✔ **Inherited wealth:** You shouldn't count on any inheritance until you actually receive it. But if you do inherit a substantial amount of money, integrate at least part of it into your overall financial plan, to give yourself a higher retirement income.

If you plan to retire before age 65, don't forget to factor in the cost of medical insurance. The availability and cost of medical care is a major issue if you plan to retire before you and your spouse are eligible for Medicare, the government-sponsored medical program for those age 65 and older.

You can take the first step toward figuring out the age when you can feasibly retire by writing down your sources of income and when you can access them.

Figuring out what to do when you retire

Assume that your retirement begins tomorrow. What will your life be like? Retirement calculators don't ask this necessary question. Most important, what will you do six months after the novelty of retirement wears off, when you're tired of golfing, shopping, traveling, or being a couch potato? Many people find it difficult to go straight from full-time work to full retirement, particularly when they haven't developed outside interests.

According to an Employee Benefit Research Institute Retirement Confidence Survey, 24 percent of retirees said they had worked at least sporadically since retiring. Of those, more than half said the reason they continued to work was that they enjoyed working and want to stay involved. About 25 percent said they worked to keep health insurance or other benefits, while 22 percent said they wanted money to buy extras.

Having an idea of what you'll do in retirement is important so that you can avoid these common mistakes:

> ✔ Retiring too early, realizing that your money isn't going to last, and being forced to go back to work. In the meantime, you've lost out on contributing more to your 401(k) — and possible employer contributions as well.

> ✔ Retiring, becoming totally bored within six months, and begging for your old job back.

Keeping the family gene pool in mind

When you think about the age at which you want to retire and how long you'll need to finance your retirement, keep your genes in mind. If you have a history of longevity in your family, plan financially to live until 100. (If you're the cautious type, you may want to do this anyway, even if you don't think you'll live that long.)

Calculating the Size of Your Nest Egg

After you decide when to retire, your next step is to consider how you'll feel when you're retired and no longer have a paycheck. You'll probably need close to 100 percent of your income (in the year before you retire) to maintain your standard of living. How much savings will it take to provide this level of income? The answer is "a lot."

We recommend trying to save ten times the income that you expect to earn in the year before you retire. This formula is a good starting point if you plan to retire at your Social Security normal retirement age (65, 66, or 67). If you retire earlier, you'll need to save more. If you have a company pension or other sources of income, or if you retire later, you may be able to get away with saving less.

If you're retiring in the near future

Assume that you're retiring at the end of this year and that your salary is $50,000. According to the benchmark, you should save $500,000 to hit the "ten times" goal.

Sound like a lot of money? It is, but it would provide approximately an average of $30,000 a year of *inflation-adjusted income* (see the nearby sidebar "What goes up — or inflation-adjusted income") over 25 years, assuming that

- The rate of inflation is 3 percent.
- Only a small cushion will remain at the end of 25 years.
- You invest half your nest egg in stocks and half in bonds during this period.

A yearly income of $30,000 may not sound like much, but remember that your taxes will be lower when you retire, and you won't need to save income for retirement anymore. And your expenses will likely be less than when you were working. Your income likely will also be supplemented by your taxable savings and Social Security, as well as any of the other sources listed earlier in the chapter, giving you an adequate level of retirement income.

Book IV

Saving and Investing

What goes up — or inflation-adjusted income

What is inflation-adjusted income? *Inflation* is the rate at which prices increase over time. When you plan for the future, you have to plan for prices to go up; otherwise, your money will run out too soon. *Inflation-adjusted income* essentially refers to the *purchasing power* of your money — what your bucks can buy. For example, if over the next 25 years you want to be able to buy what will cost $30,000 today, you'll need more than $30,000.

You can't know for sure what the inflation rate will be. We use an assumption of 3 percent, which is on the low side from a historical perspective but, we believe, realistic for long-range planning.

The following table shows how much income is needed to keep the buying power of $10,000 over the years. (Using $10,000 makes it easy to adjust to whatever income you think will be right for your situation.) For example, you can calculate that you'll need $60,984 in the 25th year of your retirement to buy what $30,000 will buy in the first year ($20,328 × 3).

Year After Retirement	Annual Income Needed	Year After Retirement	Annual Income Needed
1	$10,000	15	$15,126
2	$10,300	16	$15,580
3	$10,609	17	$16,047
4	$10,927	18	$16,528
5	$11,255	19	$17,024
6	$11,593	20	$17,535
7	$11,941	21	$18,061
8	$12,299	22	$18,603
9	$12,668	23	$19,161
10	$13,048	24	$19,736
11	$13,439	25	$20,328
12	$13,842		
13	$14,258		
14	$14,685		

If your retirement is further off

We can hear you calling, "Hey, a little help here. . . . I'm not retiring tomorrow, so how do I know how much I'll be earning the year before I retire?" Not to worry. Table 3-2 is here to help.

Table 3-2	Earnings Adjustment Table				
Number of Years Till Retirement		**Assumed Annual Income Growth**			
	3%	3.5%	4%	4.5%	5%
1	1.03	1.035	1.04	1.045	1.05
2	1.06	1.07	1.08	1.09	1.10
3	1.09	1.11	1.12	1.14	1.16
4	1.12	1.15	1.17	1.19	1.22
5	1.16	1.19	1.22	1.25	1.28
6	1.19	1.23	1.27	1.30	1.34
7	1.23	1.27	1.32	1.36	1.41
8	1.27	1.32	1.37	1.42	1.48
9	1.31	1.36	1.42	1.49	1.55
10	1.34	1.41	1.48	1.55	1.63
11	1.38	1.46	1.54	1.62	1.71
12	1.42	1.51	1.60	1.70	1.80
13	1.46	1.56	1.67	1.77	1.89
14	1.51	1.62	1.73	1.85	1.98
15	1.56	1.68	1.80	1.93	2.08
16	1.60	1.74	1.87	2.02	2.18
17	1.65	1.80	1.95	2.11	2.29
18	1.70	1.86	2.02	2.21	2.41
19	1.75	1.93	2.10	2.31	2.53
20	1.80	1.99	2.19	2.41	2.65
21	1.86	2.06	2.28	2.52	2.79
22	1.91	2.13	2.37	2.63	2.93
23	1.97	2.21	2.46	2.75	3.08
24	2.03	2.29	2.56	2.87	3.23
25	2.09	2.37	2.66	3.00	3.39
26	2.15	2.45	2.77	3.14	3.56
27	2.22	2.53	2.88	3.28	3.74
28	2.28	2.62	3.00	3.43	3.92
29	2.35	2.72	3.12	3.58	4.12
30	2.42	2.81	3.24	3.74	4.33

Book IV

Saving and Investing

Assume that you're 41 and you want to retire when you're 62. You need to project your current income to what you think you'll be earning 20 years from now — at age 61, the year before you retire.

Decide on an average rate that you expect your income to increase — say, 3 percent. Go down the Number of Years column in Table 3-2 to 20, and over to the 3% column, where you see the factor of 1.80. Multiply your current income — say, $50,000 — by 1.8, and you'll see that your expected income at retirement is $90,000. Using the ten-times rule, your desired nest egg becomes $900,000 (10 × $90,000). This is an easy way to get a rough idea of how big a retirement account to build, regardless of your current age or income.

Using a retirement calculator

Another way to develop a workable retirement plan is to use one of the many retirement calculators and other tools available on the Internet or through the financial organization that handles your 401(k) money. Remember that each calculator uses different methods and assumptions, so different calculators can produce widely varying results. Check the assumptions each calculator uses to see if they make sense for your situation.

Here's where you'll find a few of the better general calculators we've seen:

✔ www.cnnmoney.com (click Calculators)

✔ www.asec.org (click Resources, then Retirement, then Tools, Calculators, and then Games)

✔ www.psca.org (click Resources and Training, and then Retirement Calculator)

✔ www.smartmoney.com/retirement (use the Retirement Worksheets)

The major benefit of using a retirement calculator is that it gives you an investment reality check. Will the amount that you're saving and the investment mix enable you to accumulate what you need? A good retirement calculator answers this question and also helps you decide how to close any savings gaps. Generally, you can close a gap by increasing your contributions, adjusting your investments to achieve a higher long-term return, or using a combination of the two.

Some independent companies such as mPower, Financial Engines, and Morningstar are excellent sources of retirement-planning information and calculations. They go further than simple calculators and actually give you specific advice on how to invest money in your 401(k) plan and other retirement accounts.

In the meantime, here's where you can find mPower, Financial Engines, and Morningstar on the Internet.

- ✔ **mPower:** www.mpower.com
- ✔ **Financial Engines:** www.financialengines.com
- ✔ **Morningstar:** www.morningstar.com

Developing a Retirement Savings Plan

When you recover from the shock of how much you'll need in your retirement account, your first thought will probably be, "How on earth do I accumulate ten times my annual income — and then some — by the time I retire?"

The key is to start as early as you can. The earlier you start saving, the longer your money has to benefit from compounding, even if you start by putting away only small amounts.

Cutting down on your expenses

We realize that many workers barely earn enough to pay for basic necessities and can't eke out anything extra for a 401(k) plan contribution. But it's important to try. Or you may be in your 40s and want to save more to catch up, but you can't figure out where to find the money. You may be surprised by some of the places you can save money (this book is full of ideas on this). Often a few minor spending adjustments can free up money for savings.

Like most everything, it all boils down to making choices. Table 3-3 lists suggestions for cutting your spending. None of the expenses listed is a necessity — and cutting out one or two, or reducing the cost of a few, can help begin your savings program.

Book IV

Saving and Investing

Table 3-3	Ten Tips for Saving Money
Expense	*How to Save*
$1 each day or week for a lottery ticket	If you buy one ticket daily, cut back to one a week. If you buy one a week, cut back to one a month.
$25 a year for a subscription to a magazine you never read	If you have three or four, you're approaching $100. Cancel them.

(continued)

Table 3-3 *(continued)*

Expense	How to Save
$25 for a carton of cigarettes	Cut down the number you smoke or, better yet, quit. Not only will you save money, but your life insurance premiums should go down — not to mention other health-related costs.
$25 for a movie and popcorn for two at a cinema	Pay $3 to rent a video or, better yet, see what your local library offers for free. Pop some popcorn yourself — it'll probably taste better, anyway.
$5 a day for an alcoholic beverage	Instead of going out every night with your friends, do it just on weekends.
$3 a day for various other beverages of choice (bottled water, soda, coffee, and so on)	Drink what's provided at your office, or buy in bulk and bring it to work.
$5–$10 a day for lunch	Pack a lunch three times a week.
A $500 monthly car payment versus a $350 payment	Do you *really* need an SUV with leather seats and GPS?
A $250,000 home versus a $150,000 home	This depends on where you live. In California, add $400,000 to each price.
A $500 vacation versus a $2,000 vacation	Visit attractions close to home, to avoid plane fares. Go to places people would go if they were visiting you.

You're probably wondering whether all this nickel-and-diming is really worth it. We're not suggesting that you give up *everything* on the list — only that you look at what you spend to see if you can cut some costs without feeling too much pain. Giving up a few nonessential items today is far better than struggling *without necessities* during your retirement years.

We've never met a 401(k) participant who claims to have saved too much. And we've never heard participants say that wished they'd spent more money earlier. Instead, many older participants say they wish they'd started saving sooner.

This may be difficult to believe, but the important thing about money is *not* how much you earn. It's how you manage what you have. Spenders will always spend what they have or more, regardless of how much they earn. A spender who gets a substantial increase in income will adjust his spending habits to the new level within a very short period of time.

If you have a tendency to spend, you should automatically put a portion of any pay increase into a 401(k) or similar forced savings vehicle before you get used to having it in your hot little hands. Otherwise, you may never break your spending cycle.

Considering sample plans

After you begin to save, keep checking to make sure you're on track. Certain benchmarks can generally help you gauge where you should be.

The following savings goals are designed for 25-year-olds just starting their savings programs. If you're over age 25, these benchmarks can still tell you if you're on target with your retirement planning. If you're significantly behind these benchmarks, you're certainly not alone.

Remember that these are ideals; they're not here to make anyone feel defeated. Instead, the intention is to motivate you to sit down and develop a workable plan for catching up. This may mean that you have to work longer than you'd like or substantially increase your savings rate. If you feel depressed looking at these, just be glad you're starting now. If you'd waited, imagine how much more catching up you would have to do!

   ✔ **Savings goal by age 35: one times your pre-retirement income.** Your goal should be to accumulate the amount of your annual income by age 35. Table 3-4 shows what you need to do to accomplish this goal.

Table 3-4	How to Accumulate Your Pre-Retirement Income by Age 35				
Age	Your Pay	Your Contribution	Employer's Contribution	Total Return	Year-End Value
25	$25,000	$1,000	$500	$68	$1,568
26	$26,000	$1,300	$650	$229	$3,747
27	$27,040	$1,622	$811	$446	$6,626
28	$28,122	$1,687	$844	$710	$9,867
29	$29,246	$1,755	$878	$1,006	$13,506
30	$30,416	$1,825	$912	$1,339	$17,582
31	$31,633	$1,898	$949	$1,710	$22,139
32	$32,898	$1,974	$987	$2,126	$27,226
33	$34,214	$2,053	$1,026	$2,588	$32,893
34	$35,583	$2,135	$1,067	$3,104	$39,199

Book IV

Saving and Investing

The numbers in Table 3-4 are based on the following assumptions:

- Annual pay increases of 4 percent
- Employee contributions of 4 percent of pay the first year, 5 percent the second year, and 6 percent in subsequent years
- Employer-matching contribution of 50 cents on the dollar, limited to the first 6 percent of pay that the employee contributes
- An average investment return of 9 percent

The 50-percent employer-matching contribution is a big help. You have to adjust your contributions if you're in a plan that has a lower employer contribution or none at all.

✔ **Savings goal by age 45: three times your pre-retirement income.** Assume that in the next 10 years, you increase your contribution rate to 10 percent. You continue to receive a 50 percent match (equivalent to contribution of 3 percent of your pay from your employer), your annual pay continues to increase by 4 percent per year, and your investment return is 9 percent per year. Table 3-5 shows the results.

Table 3-5   How to Accumulate 3 Times Your Pre-Retirement Income by Age 45

Age	Your Pay	Your Investment	Employer's Contribution	Total Return	Year-End Value
35	$37,006	$3,700	$1,110	$3,744	$47,753
36	$38,487	$3,849	$1,154	$4,523	$57,279
37	$40,026	$4,003	$1,201	$5,389	$67,872
38	$41,627	$4,163	$1,249	$6,351	$79,635
39	$43,292	$4,329	$1,299	$7,420	$92,683
40	$45,024	$4,502	$1,350	$8,604	$107,139
41	$46,825	$4,683	$1,405	$9,917	$123,144
42	$48,698	$4,870	$1,461	$11,368	$140,843
43	$50,646	$5,065	$1,519	$12,973	$160,400
44	$52,672	$5,267	$1,580	$14,744	$181,991

By age 45, you'd be ahead of schedule, with an accumulation of more than $3^1/_2$ times your annual pay.

✔ **Savings goal by age 55: seven times your pre-retirement income.** Assume that everything stays the same for the next ten years — except that you increase your contribution rate from 10 percent to 15 percent at age 50, your annual salary increases by 4 percent per year, and your investment return continues at 9 percent until age 50. The return then drops to 8 percent from age 50 to 55 because you sell some of your more risky stock investments in favor of investments that provide a more stable but lower return. Table 3-6 shows the result.

Table 3-6   How to Accumulate 7 Times Your Pre-Retirement Income by Age 55

Age	Your Pay	Your Investment	Employer's Contribution	Total Return	Year End Value
45	$54,778	$5,478	$1,643	$16,699	$205,811
46	$56,970	$5,697	$1,709	$18,856	$232,073
47	$59,248	$5,925	$1,777	$21,233	$261,008
48	$61,618	$6,162	$1,848	$23,851	$292,869
49	$64,083	$6,408	$1,922	$26,733	$327,932
50	$66,646	$9,997	$1,999	$26,714	$366,642
51	$69,312	$10,397	$2,079	$29,828	$408,946
52	$72,085	$10,813	$2,162	$33,235	$455,156
53	$74,968	$11,245	$2,249	$36,952	$505,602
54	$77,967	$11,695	$2,339	$41,571	$561,207

At this point, you will have accumulated 7.2 times your annual pay. As you near retirement, your goal is within reach.

✔ **Savings goal by age 60: ten times your pre-retirement income.** Assume that your contribution rate remains at 15 percent, your employer's contribution rate remains at 3 percent of your salary, and your pay continues to increase by 4 percent per year. Your investment return remains at 8 percent. Table 3-7 gives you the numbers.

Table 3-7   How to Accumulate 10 Times Your Pre-Retirement Income by Age 60

Age	Your Pay	Your Investment	Employer's Contribution	Total Return	Year-End Value
55	$81,085	$12,163	$2,432	$45,480	$621,282
56	$84,329	$12,649	$2,529	$50,311	$686,711
57	$87,702	$13,155	$2,631	$55,573	$758,130
58	$91,210	$13,682	$2,736	$61,307	$835,855
59	$94,858	$14,229	$2,845	$67,551	$920,480
60	$98,652	$14,798	$2,960	$74,348	$1,012,586

Book IV

Saving and Investing

> At this point, you should be in a good position to consider various alternatives — including retiring, working fewer hours at your current job, or shifting to another income-producing activity that interests you.

These projections are based on assumptions that may differ considerably from your actual experience. Use all these figures as guidelines to help you understand the important features of investing for retirement.

Sticking with your retirement savings plan for the long haul

The purpose of the previous sample plans is to show you how a specific plan gives you a tangible way to measure your progress each year. Knowing some assumptions in the previous savings goal examples is helpful here:

✔ Money is saved for retirement every year. You should even add to your retirement savings during periods when you're not eligible to contribute to a 401(k).

✔ All the money is left in the plan until retirement. None of the money is withdrawn for other purposes.

✔ The assumed return requires at least 60 to 70 percent in stock investments (mutual funds or a diversified mix of individual stocks) up to age 55. After age 55, the stock holdings drop to 50 to 60 percent.

Your retirement nest egg comes from your own contributions and your employer's contributions, and the investment return that's earned on these contributions. Table 3-8 shows this final breakdown among the three sources, using the example of savings progress at age 60 from the previous section.

Table 3-8	Account Breakdown by Source
Source	*Amount*
Employee contributions	$226,173
Employer contributions	$57,812
Investment return	$728,601
Total	$1,012,586

You've probably heard about the magic of *compounded growth,* a term used to explain how money can grow over time. This magic is significant only over long periods of time — 20 to 30 years or longer. This is why starting to save at an early age and sticking with your program is so important. If you wait ten years before you start, you substantially reduce your investment return. You can make up the difference only with a much larger savings rate or by working and saving longer.

Chapter 4

Saving for College

∙ ∙

In This Chapter

▶ Figuring out what and how to save

▶ Considering Section 529 plans

▶ Taking a look at Coverdell Education Savings Accounts

▶ Evaluating other savings options

▶ Considering costs of different types of schools

∙ ∙

You may have just found out you're pregnant — or the college catalogs are beginning to accumulate on your dining room table. Or perhaps your family is somewhere in the middle, with your children out of diapers but not yet into calculus. Wherever your family falls in the age spectrum, one thing is certain: Either in your immediate family or in your extended one, some people will want to continue their educations beyond that once-adequate but now insufficient stopping point of a high school graduation.

And therein lies a problem: Although your child can receive a primary and secondary education without incurring any added expense in your budget (unless you take into consideration all those fund-raisers and extracurricular activities), post-secondary education of any type isn't free. You must pay for the privilege of having your child attend college or university. If you've already explored the costs of a post-secondary education, you know that the numbers being discussed are large; if you haven't yet experienced the pleasure, rest assured that the amounts in question will likely take your breath away.

In solving any problem, you need to remain calm and focused on the task at hand. This chapter helps you do just that — by making you methodically look at your lack of college savings, helping you leave your misconceptions about saving at the door, and showing you ways to actually begin saving. When you convince yourself that you're able to save something and actually begin to put away some money, you've won a major victory; everything that follows will be easier. Just keep in mind that saving now will create opportunities and open doors for your children in the future.

Saving for college is a very large topic — much too big for one chapter. Here you get an overview of what to expect. See *529 & Other College Savings Plans For Dummies,* by Margaret A. Munro (Wiley), for the full scoop on your options.

Doing the Numbers

Until now, crunching the numbers and figuring out what you think college will cost was usually where you could expect to begin and end your exploration of how to pay for future educational costs. But after you resolve to start saving and you create a plan to save for the projected costs, it's time to take this exercise a bit more seriously.

Figuring up the costs

Depending on the size of your family and your expectations, adding up the cost of a college education can be a fairly straightforward calculation, or it may become quite involved.

Be realistic, both about the capabilities and ambitions of your future student and your ability to pay.

Your straight-A daughter may have to scale back her MIT dreams if your budget, including amounts that you can add from your current earnings, goes only as far as your local state college (although not necessarily — she may want to apply for scholarship aid).

Likewise, saving for an Ivy League education is pointless if your child has plans to open his own auto repair shop. And clearly, the more children you're sending to college, the thinner your resources may be stretched per child.

No matter how late you begin to save for future college costs, the entire weight of the enterprise doesn't necessarily need to rest solely on your shoulders, nor do you need to begin to save for college from nothing.

Saving efficiently

Too many people equate saving for the future with current deprivation. For most people, living expenses currently equal, or even exceed, income, and they may not have money left in the family budget for saving. Clearly, if you fit into this category, you won't be able to save unless you make some changes in your life (see the first two parts of this book for a lot more).

Exploring Section 529 Plans

Saving money is a good thing, or so the federal government would have you believe. Uncle Sam is prepared to back up that philosophy with a variety of savings programs that contain built-in tax incentives, some of which you may already be using, such as a 401(k) or IRA. One of the newer types of incentive savings plan is the *Qualified Tuition Program,* or *Section 529* plan, which is designed solely for the purpose of saving for college or any other type of qualified post-secondary education. As with almost everything else the government cooks up, though, Section 529 plans aren't simple to navigate.

Following the rules

Section 529 of the Internal Revenue Code is long, complex, and not for the faint of heart. Yet savings accounts that fall under its regulations can be a fantastic way to save for future educational expenses. To make this plan work, you have to understand the requirements; setting up one of these accounts is pointless if you don't cross your *t*'s and dot your *i*'s just like the IRS wants. Remember, the IRS doesn't have a category of "close, but no cigar." Either your account will qualify under the regulations for tax exemptions, or it won't. And if it doesn't, the consequences may be costly.

Check out www.irs.gov/publications/p970/ch08.html on the IRS Web site for all the current details on 529 plans.

Making your money work for you

Creating a successful savings plan involves more than following the rules, although compliance is a big part. *You're* a big factor in determining whether your savings program flies or falls. Your understanding of the various ways your savings may earn money and of the different investment options available to you is important in creating the substantial amount of savings you'll need to see your children through college.

Book IV

Saving and Investing

Choosing the best options

Even when you understand the rules, manage to regularly save major portions of your income, and discover how to manipulate the investment choices to your best advantage, events in your life may require you to make sudden changes in your Section 529 plan savings accounts. Life happens, whether you're prepared or not, and often the last thing you want to think about when it does is the effect on your investments.

Checking Out Coverdell Accounts

If the world of tax-exempt savings accounts were an ice cream parlor, Coverdell Education Savings Accounts (ESAs) would be a new and improved flavor — still not everyone's favorite, but just what you may want on a particular day. And, not surprisingly, when shopping for a way to save money for college, many people prefer Coverdell accounts, whether for their wider range of investment options, the account owner's increased level of control over the account, or the fact that certain expenses qualify for tax exemption under Coverdell rules that aren't under Section 529 requirements.

Understanding the rules and regulations

Code Section 530, covering Coverdell ESAs, follows hot on the heels of Code Section 529 (those government sorts are sticklers for going in numerical order). In it you find all the rules, regulations, and other assorted gobbledy-gook that govern these sorts of accounts.

Check out www.irs.gov/publications/p970/ch07.html for everything you ever wanted to know about Coverdell accounts.

Getting the most from a Coverdell account

You've probably discovered by now that successful savings involves far more than sticking your money in a passbook savings account at your local bank. And although your investment options are seriously limited with a Section 529 plan, you have far more latitude in investment decisions when you open a Coverdell ESA.

But Wait! There's More!

People went to college long before an Internal Revenue Code existed, and parents and grandparents saved for college costs even when tax deferrals and/or tax exemptions weren't around. You can save money in a lot of other ways, some of them even specifically for college. Even though they may not be as tax advantageous as Section 529 plans and Coverdell ESAs, they may make perfect sense in your overall savings plan. And if you're not able to save enough to cover the full cost, all is still not lost: Various scholarships, grants, and loan programs are available to cover any shortfall you may have between what you've saved and the cost of your child's education.

Rediscovering U.S. savings bonds

Whether you're able to save only small amounts, are uncertain about your potential student's future plans, or love the safety and security found only in U.S. savings bonds, you may find them to be an attractive way to save for future college expenses and still take advantage of some tax exemptions on the interest earned on your bonds. (See *529 & Other College Savings Plans For Dummies,* by Margaret A. Munro [Wiley], for more details.)

Saving for college the old-fashioned way

It may seem strange to even think this thought, but the trade-off for taking advantage of the income tax breaks available through Section 529 plans and Coverdell ESAs is that you're guaranteeing that you will use that money to pay for qualified educational expenses. If only all of life were so certain and so sure.

You may be hesitating over how much to save in these plans, or whether to save at all, because of your great uncertainty over your child's future plans. When you save in traditional investment and savings accounts, you eliminate that uncertainty because you're not tied to using your savings in any one way. Of course, in exchange for that freedom to spend your savings as you will, you lose any opportunity to defer or exempt tax on your earnings. But if your world is an uncertain place, you may find that's a small price to pay.

Putting your faith in a trust fund

For most people, the phrase *trust fund* brings to mind visions of great wealth and privilege; in other words, it has nothing to do with you. That picture couldn't be further from the truth. If you're able to save money in any form, you're a potential candidate to create and fund a trust.

Book IV

Saving and Investing

Saving in your retirement accounts

Using retirement funds to pay for college probably isn't the best way to put away money for college. In certain limited circumstances, however (such as when parents are older or you face completely unplanned educational expenses), it may make some sense to access funds from a retirement account to pay qualified educational expenses.

Accessing your home equity

If you (or you and the bank) own your own home, you may be sitting on a larger nest egg than you ever considered. A combination of rising home values and shrinking mortgage loan balances has created a large pool of equity for many people that may be made available to fund educational expenses. However, recent housing market jitters and credit crises may have made this avenue less attractive.

Identifying sources of free money

Not every potential student is an academic genius or a future first-round NFL draft pick, but you don't necessarily need to conclude that your child won't qualify for scholarships and grants. Your local high school guidance counselor or library should be able to point you in the right direction. Many states now offer full scholarships to academically qualifying students at their state universities and colleges, and some private universities and colleges are capping tuition costs for low- and middle-income families.

Borrowing to fill in the gaps

You're probably reading this section because you don't want to have to resort to borrowing money to pay for your children's college costs. But if you do, it's not the end of the world. Many types of financial aid are available at low interest rates.

Maximizing Your Savings, Minimizing Your Tax

At its heart, this book is about successfully saving and investing money for future college costs, on one hand, and paying little or no tax, on the other. And if that were the beginning and end of the matter, you'd be looking at a fairly straightforward task, one in which, if you followed all the rules, you'd achieve the desired result at the end of the game.

Unfortunately, you don't live your life in a vacuum, and many forces impact your ability to save adequately, to achieve reasonable investment returns on your savings, and to limit the amount of income tax you'll pay on those investment returns. You're operating on a field that is rarely level and that shifts and shimmies through no fault of your own. As a result, you need to be aware of how large and small changes, whether they're a result of government policy, market forces, or changes in your family's projected college cost needs, will affect your savings programs. And you need to be prepared to move with those changes — to adjust your savings programs to account for these other factors.

At the end of the day, your success will depend not only on how often you make deposits into your college savings plans or how large the deposits are, but also on how well that money works for you. Your goal is not to achieve a large balance in one or more college savings accounts. Your goal is to watch your children begin their adult lives with good educations, marketable skills, and no college debt.

Checking Out the Cost of College

Whether or not you went to college (and regardless of who paid for your education, if you did), the joy of planning and saving for that event for your children, your grandchildren, or even yourself and your spouse has to be tempered somewhat by the uncertainty of the financial costs involved. That uncertainty is the exact amount of the eventual bill because, clearly, cost is going up, up, up, and never down. How can you possibly know how much to save if you can't figure out how much college will cost?

This section breaks down all the costs of education into their component pieces and compares different types of education. If you know that your prospective student plans to attend a prestigious medical school at the end of the rainbow, you need to plan accordingly. If, however, your budding student has a fascination with all things dead and tries to embalm the family pet before burial, you may be looking at a funeral services school, which certainly costs much less than medical school. The point is that you need to be realistic about your expectations and about the talents and desires of the prospective student before you jump into your savings program. You want to save enough, but saving far more than you need for college is pointless.

Because tuition is usually the largest cost for college, many people make the mistake of saving _only_ for tuition. But other costs, such as housing, books, and supplies, can account for a large chunk of college expenses — a large enough chunk that you should include those costs in your savings plan.

Although this section covers the major costs of college, they aren't the only costs you may encounter when sending your child to college. We don't suggest that you start saving for a beer fund, but be prepared to pay for parking permits, transportation, health insurance, movie tickets, and jeans.

Book IV

Saving and Investing

Tackling tuition

Tuition refers to probably the largest cost for college: the fees for actual instruction. For the academic year 2007-2008, in some instances, the tuition costs for a state university exceeded $10,000 for an in-state student and more than $21,000 for an out-of state student — and many private four-year universities charged more than $31,000 for tuition alone!

If you're planning for a baby about to be born, who won't matriculate until 2026, and if tuition continues to increase at a rate of approximately 5 percent each year (which is what has been happening lately in the private universities), that annual tuition fee could increase to a whopping $24,066 for an in-state student at a public university, $50,539 for an out-of-state student at a public university, or $74,605 for a student at a private university — or more than $103,000, $217,000, or $321,000, respectively, for four years. If your baby thinks carrying a briefcase is cool or asks for the professional doctor kit by age 2, tack on several extra years for graduate or professional school.

These numbers may seem insurmountable, especially if you're entering the savings game fairly late; however, some relief may be available. Only a small percentage of students and families actually pay the top-dollar price. Not all universities charge in that price range; many offer huge amounts of outright grants and other forms of financial aid (other than loans, although loans are available to all), and scholarships and grants from other sources may be available. Be sure to look into these possibilities at any school you are considering.

If you're fairly certain that your child will attend a public college, you may want to begin investigating whether your state offers a Section 529 prepaid tuition plan to help you pay for those upcoming tuition bills. Even if you aren't able to save for tuition costs in one of these plans, saving money in any Section 529 plan or Coverdell Education Savings Account will allow your college savings to grow faster than conventional savings accounts.

Accounting for housing

You may come from a family that assumes that everyone going on to higher learning will receive their post-secondary education at the local campuses, and you fully expect that, when your student reaches that point, he or she will be living at home. If so, you can probably skip this part, although you should be stashing away some money for good, reliable transportation, whether that means a car or bus or subway fare.

On the other hand, if you suspect that your student won't be satisfied going to the local schools (or if your area doesn't really have many post-secondary offerings), you need to add the cost of housing into your savings plan — either college-owned housing or local rental real estate.

College-owned housing

Most colleges provide some sort of room and board options in the form of on-campus or university-owned housing, and they gladly tack those fees on to the tuition bill. Because most university-owned housing is mandatory for all noncommuting students for at least the first year or two, these costs must factor into your savings plan. For 2007-2008, college-owned housing costs (including a meal plan) averaged $7,400 for public colleges and universities, and almost $8,600 for private. Differences in costs depend on a few factors, such as the following:

- **Location:** Generally, city schools have higher housing costs.
- **Size:** Generally, larger colleges tend to have higher housing costs than smaller colleges.
- **Number of students in a room:** If your child insists on having a room to herself, expect to pay a premium for that privilege. Generally, the more students crammed into a single room translates into less money you'll have to pay for your student.

You can use tax-free distributions from your Section 529 and/or Coverdell plans for room and board charges paid directly to an *eligible* school (the school can tell you whether it's eligible).

Local rental properties

Although colleges and universities try to expand their student populations, many fail to increase their own housing to meet the increased number of students. This on-campus housing shortage pushes more students into the local housing market. In areas where rental units are being added, an on-campus shortage isn't a problem; the rental units increase at a rate equal (hopefully) to the number of students seeking housing. However, many older cities have very limited rental housing, and the increased number of students seeking it has forced prices up sharply. So if you plan to rent an apartment or house for your student, costs become more variable, making it more difficult for you to predict how much you may need to save for your student's housing needs.

If you live close to the college your child attends, the easiest way to check local rental costs is to read the classified ads and haunt the rental board in the college's housing office. If you're living farther away from the action, use the Internet. Many newspapers, both big and small, have Web sites that almost always include the classified ads. Also check out the classifieds at Craig's List, www.craigslist.org.

The cost of a rental may not include utilities (heat in the northern states and air conditioning in the southern states can be very expensive), and it certainly doesn't include food. You need to add the cost of any utilities not included, plus money for either food or a meal ticket at the university, to accurately compare your costs to the university's room and board plan.

Check the amount of room and board that the college considers to be a "qualified education expense." (You can often find this information buried on its Web site, or you can phone one of the college's financial aid officers.) You can use tax-free distributions from your Section 529 and Coverdell plans to pay rent to a nonuniversity landlord; however, if you spend more than the college's estimated amount of room and board on a nonuniversity landlord, you may want to pay the excess some other way. Distributions taken from your Section 529 and Coverdell plans in excess of "qualified expenses" are subject to tax and a 10 percent penalty.

Factoring in books and supplies

Okay, so maybe you know you've enough saved for tuition and room and board, but the need for money doesn't stop after you unload the SUV on the first day of orientation. When your student is at school, he needs to buy books and other supplies, and he won't know which books and supplies he needs until after the first few days of school.

The costs for books and supplies are substantial. Figure on putting aside at least an additional $1,000 per year for books, plus $500 to $1,000 for other supplies, such as lab coats, protective glasses, notebooks, or even pens and pencils. In comparison to the tuition and room and board fees, this amount may not seem huge, but it's still substantial. Over the course of four years, that bill can be anywhere from $6,000 to $8,000. A laptop computer? Add another $750.

Unlike tuition costs, which are set by the university, and housing and food costs, which are set either by the university or by the conditions in the local economy, you *can* somewhat control how much your student spends on books and supplies. Your student can purchase most books used and then resell them when he's finished with them. Supplies, such as notebooks, don't need to have the university or college crest on them to function properly, and using the computer lab sure is cheaper than buying a computer.

Provided that the books and supplies your student purchases are required by the college, you can pay for these supplies using tax-free or tax-deferred distributions from either a 529 plan or a Coverdell account.

Ignore this category at your peril. Saving enough money to send your student to the school of her choice is pointless if you then leave her in the lurch, without the tools to completely access the education being offered.

Looking into the Costs of Various Types of Schools

No matter where your student decides to attend college, you have to pay the tuition and the books and supplies, and then you have to come up with some solution to the housing question. But because you may need a crystal ball to figure out where your child plans to attend college, the next piece of the puzzle isn't quite as straightforward: estimating the tuition and fees you need to save for. However, when you have an idea of what type of school your student plans to attend, or if your student either is not yet born or just recently populating the planet, or if you have decided on what type of school you *hope* your student attends, you can begin some significant planning for the future.

To make that planning a little easier — short of resorting to tarot cards — consider some real numbers for each type of school your child may attend.

Exploring career and vocational training schools

Smaller, more specialized schools, such as career and vocational training schools, train students in very specific areas for very specific careers, such as funeral services, dental hygiene, piano tuning, or even bartending. The cost of these programs (which may exist entirely independently of or be attached to community colleges or even four-year colleges) tends to be much smaller than the cost of your typical college.

Taking community college and continuing education classes

Almost every city of any size has at least one community college, an institution of higher education that gives college-level learning without the college-level price. In addition, many large universities have a division of continuing education that provides much the same function as a community college, including the low cost.

Don't assume that because you can't afford an Ivy League college through the normal channels, you also can't afford to take courses in the continuing education division. Tuition at Harvard University in 2007-2008 was $31,456; per-course fees at the Harvard Extension are $800 for most courses.

You can use funds from all your college savings plans to pay either community college or continuing education tuitions, provided that the school you attend is an eligible institution. However, to pay for housing using savings from these plans, you must be at least a half-time student. Be aware of this stipulation, and be vigilant; a mistake here will cost you not only income tax on the distribution, but also a 10-percent penalty.

Going for a four-year public education

Each state has its own public university/college system. Because the universities are larger than the colleges and offer much more programming, they tend to be considerably more expensive than the colleges. If your student has a very clear idea of where she's going in life, it will be most cost effective to find that program at a state college instead of a state university, especially one that's in your state.

Unlike public elementary and secondary schools, public universities and colleges aren't funded totally by tax dollars (in fact, they may actually be funded very little by tax dollars). However, state-run colleges and universities are one of the best bargains around, especially for in-state students. Any state subsidy, no matter how small, is better than no state subsidy for keeping costs down, as reflected in the size of tuition bills.

Getting your education in private

Public education may be the cornerstone on which our country is built. However, a vast network of private schools is available at every level, for students who can afford to pay. And because no college education is free (unless you look at the U.S. military academies, where the payment is in kind), all schools that don't rely on public subsidies are referred to as *private*. Private universities can be various types of institutions, from Ivy League schools to hundreds of private four-year institutions throughout the country.

Each of these colleges and universities offers a unique educational opportunity, as well as a unique price tag. Overall, prices are high and climb higher every year, and no relief is in sight. The college sets tuition and room and board fees; no public oversight comes into play. Furthermore, college presidents and trustees retain their jobs on the basis of how well their institutions are doing financially — if it takes tuition hikes to keep it that way, that's just too bad.

Checking out in-state versus out-of-state tuition

What makes a university or college public is the fact that, to a greater or lesser extent, funding for it comes from a public source: taxes. Although not every state provides huge amounts of assistance to its state schools, every state provides some amount of subsidy. And because any state subsidy comes from the state's taxpayers, students who live in the state are given not only preference in admissions, but also preferential tuition cost. This special treatment reflects that they — and their families — are already contributing through their tax dollars.

Even for out-of-state students, tuition at state colleges and universities often provides great value. The vast size of the state systems, their centralized administrations, and the typically lower salaries they offer their employees keep overall costs down. The top tuition price for an out-of-state student, while significantly higher than for an in-state one, is still substantially less than at many private four-year colleges and universities.

Tuition is the only variable between the cost to in-state students and the cost to out-of-state students. All other expenses, including room and board, books and supplies, and so on, are the same for both.

Historically, state university systems have controlled the rate of increase in tuition and other fees more than private colleges, especially for in-state students. The annual budget is open to the public for comment, and political futures can rise and fall on the fate of a budget that increases too fast. Sometimes, though, state budget shortfalls can put pressure on state legislatures to increase fees at a more draconian rate, with the hope that keeping other state services intact (and maybe not raising taxes) will keep the political fallout to a minimum. When states do increase tuition and other fees by a large amount, out-of-state students typically feel the effects more than in-state students. Remember, in-state students — and their parents — are voters, and voters unhappy with the rate of tuition increases can effect some powerful changes.

If your savings are a bit lacking when the time comes to start forking over tuition payments, the smartest way to look for a private school may be to shop by endowment (the amount of money that the school has invested, with the income available for building projects, professors' salaries, and tuition grants) instead of by tuition ticket price. Schools with large endowments usually devote a large percentage of the earnings from the fund to outright grants, awarded on the basis of need.

Book IV

Saving and Investing

Chapter 5

Working with an Online Broker

During the peak of the market back in March 2000, online brokerages had 12 million to 15 million accounts, and online investors accounted for about a third of all trading on the New York Stock Exchange and NASDAQ systems. A June 2006 report by Tiburon Strategic Advisors (www.tiburon advisors.com) listed 50 online brokerages. The "Big Five" of the industry currently are Charles Schwab & Company, Fidelity Investments, TD Ameritrade, E*TRADE, and Scottrade. Fidelity has 11.90 million accounts (35 percent of the complete population of online brokerage accounts), Schwab has 7.14 million accounts (21 percent), TD Ameritrade has 6.12 million accounts (18 percent), E*TRADE has 4.42 million accounts (13 percent of the total), and Scottrade has 1.36 million accounts (4 percent of the total). The other online brokerages have 3.06 million accounts (9 percent).

Tiburon in its study indicated that clients of the Big Five online brokerages are fairly active. For example, the total trades per year, per account for Scottrade customers was 20.8 trades, TD Ameritrade clients made 12.0 trades per year, Schwab customers made 11.8 trades, E*TRADE account-holders made 10.8 trades, and Fidelity Investment account-holders made 6.9 trades per year. The number of trades per year for other firms was 28 trades. However, Scottrade customers are the most active traders of the Big Five. In other words, Scottrade account-holders are almost twice as active as its nearest Big Five competitor.

Mintel's survey, *Online Trading in the United States 2007*, discovered that about one out of every six (or 17 percent) of respondents have used an online brokerage company in the past 12 months. Today, according to the Pew Internet and American Life Project, about one out of every ten Internet users has bought or sold stocks online.

However, you may be intimidated by the thought of do-it-yourself investing because you're new to the Internet, new to investing, or both. Actually, the Internet is a great place to learn the basics!

In this chapter, we show you how to select the online broker that's best for you. We explain what to look for when selecting a broker and we compare the industry leaders. You find out where to look online for brokerage ratings and how to open your own brokerage account. Finally, we explain how to use online simulations to practice online trading and we show you how to make your first trade. We conclude this chapter by discussing how to know when to hold and when to fold.

Sorting Them Out: Selecting an Online Broker

These days, securities brokers come in a wide variety of shapes and sizes. You must decide for yourself how much assistance you need in selecting your investments and how much you're willing to pay for it. Because of the rabid competition among brokers, you can count on better customer service today than what was available five years ago. Discount and online brokerages have increased their customer service and added more servers so that customer trades are executed rapidly. Full-service brokers are increasing the capabilities of their Web sites and charging less for their services. Consider a few guidelines when selecting the broker for you:

- **Full-service brokers:** Full-service brokers usually charge higher commissions and fees than discount brokers, but they also offer services that aren't available through discount brokers. Full-service brokerages offer expert advice and good ideas that are especially helpful and needed when the stock market is gyrating. Other services include ways of establishing personal financial profiles, estate planning, and tax advice.

- **Discount and online brokers:** If you know what you want, why not use a discount or online broker to purchase securities as inexpensively as you can? Full-service discount brokerages like Charles Schwab (the first discount brokerage) and TD Ameritrade have added a lot of advisory and account-management services. The research available to account-holders is staggering, but each firm currently charges hefty commissions for infrequent trades and a maintenance fee whenever your account balance falls below a certain minimum. In contrast, discount brokerage E*TRADE still offers trades with low commissions and few frills. However, you can't visit a branch office to talk to someone or make a quick deposit.

One of the drawbacks of discount and online brokers is server downtime when markets are experiencing high-volume trading. This problem can be compounded by checks being lost in the mail, orders going unfilled, and other types of financial horrors.

✔ **Buying mutual funds:** Mutual fund buyers have the choice of purchasing a fund through a broker or purchasing a fund directly from the fund company. Many brokerages offer only a limited number of funds and may charge you a brokerage commission. However, if you buy a fund that your brokerage owns and manages, the firm usually waives the trading commission.

What to look for in brokers

Some discount brokerages simply aren't suited to the needs of certain types of online investors. As a general rule, online investors who use discount brokerages aren't seeking advice. They just want low-cost trades and excellent customer service. Individuals who are new to investing or online investing may want more of the bells and whistles of traditional brokerages. For example, premium discount (full-service) online brokerages may be a better match for infrequent traders, affluent investors, and individuals who want access to in-depth research resources and tools. You may want to consider these elements when evaluating an online brokerage (later in this chapter you'll find a short review of the online brokerage mentioned in this section):

✔ **Trade executions:** You may want to investigate online brokerages for the ability to handle Internet, wireless, and phone trade executions. Some firms offer five-, two-, and one-second guaranteed trade executions. Kiplinger (www.kiplinger.com) evaluated which firms were shopping for the best spreads for your order (you quickly get the best price). Top marks went to TD Ameritrade (www.tdameritrade.com) and TradeKing (www.tradeking.com).

✔ **Analytical and research tools:** When offered by your online broker include but are not limited to real-time quotes, reports on insider trading, economic forecasts, company profiles, breaking news, and earnings forecasts. Automatic broker emailed end-of-the-day prices, online calculators; retirement resources, stock research, charts, and graphs may also be included. Kiplinger ranked the quantity and quality of stock research offered by online brokerages and found that Fidelity Investments (www.fidelity.com) and Charles Schwab & Company (www.schwab.com) were among the best.

Book IV

Saving and Investing

✔ **Breadth of securities traded:** Ascertain which types of investments the broker enables you to trade — for example, stocks (foreign and domestic), options, bonds (corporate and agency), exchange-traded funds (ETFs), Treasury securities, zero-coupon bonds, certificates of deposit, precious metals, mutual funds, and unit investment trusts, IRAs, Roth IRAs, and education savings plans (Coverdell ESAs, Custodial accounts, and 529 Plans). E*TRADE and TD Ameritrade offer an extensive array of investment products.

✔ **Banking and account services:** The ability to use your account for checks, ATM withdrawals, or debit card purchases is often an important element in selecting an online brokerage. You may also want information about your cash balances, order status, and portfolio value. In addition to a historical view of your trades and an easy-to-understand statement for your taxes. Kiplinger believes an online broker should allow you to make quick work of your income taxes. They highly rank Fidelity and OptionsXpress (www.optionsxpress.com) for their annual tax-basis summaries.

✔ **Customer service and security:** Many online brokerages offer branch offices or the ability to talk to an actual person on the telephone. Online help includes email support, live chat, virtual tours, demos, and tutorials. Often you'll find a frequently asked questions page (FAQ), user forums, and service details. Keep in mind that the brokerage you select must be insured by the Securities Investor Protection Corporation (SIPC). The SIPC insures securities and cash in a brokerage account for up to $500,000 (with no more than $100,000 in cash). You should determine if the Web site is secured and if fraud protection is offered. In regards to responsiveness and broker knowledge Kiplinger highly rates OptionsXpress, TradeKing (www.tradeking.com), and FirstTrade (www.firstrade.com).

✔ **Mutual fund investing:** Some online brokerages have zero fees for trading mutual funds, offer rebates for 12(b)-1 fees, and have a "supermarket" of mutual funds to choose from. Fidelity offers 15,186 mutual funds, and Schwab offers 13,021 mutual funds. E*TRADE offers a rebate on 12(b)-1 fees. *Note:* 12(b)-1 fees are an annual marketing or distribution fee on a mutual fund. The 12b-1 fee is considered an operational expense.

✔ **For novice investors:** Elements that novice investors should look for in an online brokerage include $0 cost or nearly $0 cost to open an account, no minimum investment requirements, and no minimum account balance needed. No extra account fees and an automatic investment program. A good place to get started is ShareBuilder (www.sharebuilder.com).

✔ **For advanced investors:** Elements that advanced investors need are very different from the requirements of novice investors. If you are becoming an advanced investor, look for low margin rates and costs as low as $0.05 per trade and the brokerage's ability to buy and sell options, Canadian or foreign stocks, and bonds. Special trading platforms are useful, as are Level I and Level II quotes and speedy trade executions. Level II quotes enable investors to identify the market maker offering the lowest bid-ask spread. If you are in the market for a new online brokerage with an advanced investor platform, Charles Schwab & Company (www.schwab.com) and E*TRADE (www.etrade.com) are good places to start your investigation.

Considering costs

Many brokerages advertise terrific deals for new accounts. However, you may get tapped for extra fees if you don't read the fine print. Consider a few examples:

- ✔ **Higher fees for limit orders:** *Market orders* (which direct your broker to buy or sell shares at the best price currently available) may be cheaper than *limit orders* (which direct the broker to buy or sell shares only at a specified maximum or minimum price). The lower market-order fee may be the commission fee the brokerage advertises.

- ✔ **Higher fees for different kinds of securities:** Some brokerages charge higher fees for trading over-the-counter (OTC) stocks than they do for trading listed stocks. *Listed stocks* are traded on all the major exchanges. Stocks that aren't listed are referred to as *OTC stocks*. OTC stocks often are traded on the NASDAQ or American Stock Exchange.

- ✔ **Higher fees for trading a certain number of shares at one time:** Some brokerages charge additional fees for trading more than 1,000 shares at one time. You may also discover additional fees for trading fewer than 100 shares, an amount that's called *an odd lot*.

- ✔ **Higher fees for closing your account or for withdrawing funds from your account:** Some brokerages don't charge for transferring some or all of the funds from your IRA account but do charge for withdrawing or transferring funds from your trading account. Several brokerages charge more than $100 per account.

Comparing industry leaders

Table 5-1 provides a quick overview of several top-rated online brokerages. Ameritrade and TD Waterhouse are considered discount brokerages. As a general rule, the discount brokerages are geared toward investors who have a few to tens of thousands of dollars to invest. Discount brokerages usually offer lower fees, less customer service, and fewer banking amenities than their premium discount brokerage brethren. Charles Schwab and Fidelity Investments are considered *full-service discount brokerages.* Full-service discount brokerages often are customer-service-oriented online businesses that target investors with several thousands of dollars to invest.

Table 5-1   Comparison of Top-Ranked Online Brokerages

Account Minimum Information	TD Ameritrade	E*TRADE	Charles Schwab & Company	Fidelity Investments
Minimum to Open	$2,000	n/a	$1,000	$2,500
Minimum Acct Balance	$2,000	$1,000	$1,000	$2,500
Rate of Interest on Cash	1.65%	1.0%	0.96%	3.58%
Commission Structure: Online Trades				
Market Order	$9.99	$6.99-$12.99	$9.95-$12.95	$8.00-$19.95
Limit Order	$9.99	$6.99-$12.99	$9.95-$12.95	$8.00-$19.95
Options	$9.99 + $0.75 per contract	$6.99-$12.99 + $0.75 per contract	$9.95-$12.95 + $0.75 per contract	$8.00-$19.95 + $0.75 per contract
Margin Rate	BR+ -1,50% -1.25%	BR + 3%	BR+ .5%-2.0%	6.0 - 11.05%
Other Attributes				
Free Trades for Opening an Account	45 days of free trades	100 free trades for opening a qualifying account	Open & fund an account for 50 free trades	No free trades
Web Site Design	Frequent traders	Frequent traders	Buy & hold investors	Buy & hold investors
Retail Centers	100+	15+	270+	100+
Compatible with Quicken/MS Money	Yes	Yes	Yes	Yes
ATM and checking	Yes	Yes	Yes	Yes
Tax Information	Yes	Yes	Yes	Yes
Dividend reinvestment	Yes	Yes	Yes	Yes

Here are more details about the online brokerages in Table 5-1:

- **TD Ameritrade** (www.tdameritrade.com) is the most utilitarian of the brokerage Web sites in Table 5-1. You'll discover real-time trades with 5-second trade execution guarantees and extended trading hours. TD Ameritrade is geared for active traders because it offers time and sales data, complex charting, and streaming news. You'll find a voice-response phone trading system, streaming Level II quotes, and complex options trading. The Market Motion Detector helps map market trends. You can also set trade triggers to take immediate advantage of market opportunities. To lower costs, trade confirmations and statements are presented online. You can track your online history for a year and a half, so don't be concerned about having to immediately print your monthly statement. TD Ameritrade has teamed with GainsKeeper to offer a tax-accounting tool that automatically tracks your online trading capital gains and losses. GainsKeeper is available to everyone; the gain/loss tracking feature can help you keep track of all of your online trading capital gains and losses throughout the year.

- **E*TRADE** (www.etrade.com) offers online global trading in six currencies, and you can customize the trading platform. E*TRADE offers a 2-second trade execution guarantee or one commission-free trade on all S&P 500 stocks and exchange traded funds (ETFs.) Investors receive streaming, real-time quotes, research, advanced screening tools, investment income estimator, and portfolio analyzer. E*TRADE Market Maker is a Web-based trading platform that allows investors to research, track, and trade from one page. Investors can receive streaming quotes, easy order entry, and integrated account information in addition to a watchlist feature, news, charts and independent analyst research. For advanced traders there is the Power E*TRADE Pro platform. This is E*TRADE's no-fee, software-based trading platform. Power E*TRADE Pro is fully customizable, with advanced charting package and technical studies, NASDAQ Total View quotes, complex options trading, custom screeners, Dow Jones news, and one-click trading access. E*TRADE provides Level II quotes for an extra $9.99 per month. For $29.99 per month, you can receive streaming news.

- **Charles Schwab & Company** (www.schwab.com) offers Schwab One accounts that are divided into two tiers based on the number of trades per quarter and account balances. Schwab offers online trading, investing tools, technical and fundamental research, scanning capabilities, and pre-prepared queries for finding trading opportunities. For advanced investors, Schwab provides StreetSmart.com, a Web-based trading platform with real-time streaming quotes, news, interactive technical charts, linked trading tools, and an interface you can customize. For the more sophisticated investor there is StreetSmart Pro, a Web-based, advanced customizable trading platform with Level II quotes, strategy testing, interactive technical charts, screening, conditional orders, alerts, and streaming data you can personalize to your specific needs. CyberTrader is a software platform for the very active, advanced trader. CyberTrader supplies Level II data, direct access to trading technology that sends orders to the Exchange, ECN, or more than 450 market makers. Per-share commissions are also available.

Note: Just because a stock is listed on the New York Stock Exchange (NYSE), the NASDAQ, or another exchange doesn't mean every share is bought and sold there. Stocks and mutual funds are often traded directly through Electronic Computer Networks (ECNs).

✔ **Fidelity Investments** (www.fidelity.com): The steady, slow-moving Fidelity of the past is long gone. Today Fidelity offers wireless trading and has beefed up its retirement-planning tools and zeroed in on the needs of active traders. Fidelity accounts are tiered according to the number of trades and account balance. Investors receive real-time stock quotes, portfolio performance figures, and tax status. There is a 1-second trade execution guarantee on qualifying trades, or they are commission-free. For active investors, Fidelity offers Active Trader Pro, a Web-based trading platform that features multi-trade order entry, trailing stop losses, and conditional orders. Active Trader Pro offers one-click trading, skip order previews, and directed trading from multiple market centers. For the more sophisticated investor there is streaming market data, Level II quotes, and interactive advanced charting, in addition to watchlists, real-time margin balances, and cost basis tracking for tax purposes. Fidelity's Wealth-Lab Pro is a Windows-based software application geared for investors who want to design and back-test customized trading strategies. Option Trader Pro provides streaming pricing, directed trading, and analytics.

Checking online brokerage ratings

Some companies provide speedy trades, whereas others are ranked for their customer service and commission costs. To gain an idea of which companies stand out from the crowd and meet your individual requirements, see the following online brokerage-ranking services.

✔ **J.D. Power** (www.jdpower.com/finance/ratings/online-investment-firm-ratings) states that online investors' priorities are shifting when dealing with online brokerage firms. Lower commission costs, customer service, and the integrity of the firm now are the focus, according to the J.D. Power and Associates 2007 Online Trading Investor Satisfaction Study. Visit the Web site for the top-to-bottom rankings study and check out www.jdpower.com/corporate/news/releases/pressrelease.aspx?ID=2007252 for the press release.

✔ **Kiplinger.com** (www.kiplinger.com/magazine/archives/2006/07/ brokers.html) is a trusted personal finance advice and forecast Web site that provides rankings of online brokerages. In addition, it has an online slide show you can view to evaluate brokers at a glance. However, what makes this Web site so great is its Web-based tool for determining which online broker is best for you.

✔ **Smart Money** (www.smartmoney.com/brokers/index.cfm?story= june2008-broker-survey) offers its May 2008 evaluation of online brokerages. This survey is important to investors who know what they are looking for in a brokerage (and what they want to avoid in an online brokerage).

Opening Your Online Brokerage Account

If you're uncertain about what information a brokerage firm needs or the requirements for opening a trading account, try the online simulation at InvestingOnline.org (investingonline.org). This interactive tutorial clearly explains what you need to know when you complete an online application form to open an account with an online brokerage.

Brokerage firms are responsible for executing your trades, maintaining your account records, providing updates and information about markets and mutual funds, and supplying other related services. The brokerage you select must be insured by the Securities Investor Protection Corporation (SIPC). The SIPC insures securities and cash in a brokerage account for up to $500,000 (with no more than $100,000 in cash).

Nothing is stopping you from having more than one online brokerage or trading account. For example, you may have an account with a mutual fund company. Another account may be for short-term to midterm positions at a brokerage known for low trading fees. Finally, you may have a brokerage account for your long-term investments, such as your child's college fund or your IRA. Varying your trading styles with each account or brokerage can help you smooth out your returns in a bumpy market. Keep in mind that you can open a trading account with a brokerage firm by completing an application via telephone, through the U.S. mail, or online. Follow these steps when you're opening an account online:

1. **Provide personal contact information.**

   Because of the Patriot Act, when you open your account, you'll be asked for more personal information than in the past. Brokerages ask for your name, address, date of birth, and other information that enables them to identify you. The brokerages also may ask to see your driver's license or other identifying documents. (Often you can fax these documents to brokerages.)

Book IV

Saving and Investing

2. **Determine the type of account you want to open.**

   Both online and offline brokerages offer several types of accounts. The type of account you open depends on how you want to use your trading account and on whether you're putting retirement dollars or other tax-advantaged funds into the account. Examples of brokerage accounts include taxable, tax-deferred, or individual accounts, or accounts for you and another person.

3. **Determine whether you want a cash or margin account.**

   A *cash-only account* means that you can place only trades that you can cover with money in your account. A *margin account* includes a line of credit from your brokerage (for which you pay interest on outstanding balances) to fund your trades. Trading on margin isn't recommended for beginning investors.

4. **Fund your new account.**

   Many brokerages require a minimum initial deposit. To fund your account, you can make an automatic transfer from your bank account or send a check to the brokerage. You can also open the account by transferring existing securities from another brokerage, bank, or mutual fund company, or by presenting existing stock or bond certificates.

5. **Take the last steps.**

   If you're funding your trading account from your bank account, make sure you have sufficient funds in the account. After the brokerage receives the minimum required initial deposit, you receive your account number and password by U.S. mail or electronically. This information enables you to log in to your trading account. You're now good to go for your first trade.

Ready, Set, Go! Making Your First Online Trade

Before you trade your first dime, you may want to try out your trading strategies using an investing game. The following are a couple of the Internet's more interesting trading simulations and games.

✔ **Fantasy Stock Market** (www.fantasystockmarket.com) enables you to discover the basics by investing $100,000 in fantasy money. The Fantasy Stock Market game ranks the top-performing players every month and lists the most actively traded stocks. The seven-day trial is free. Subscriptions are $19.95 per year.

✔ **Virtual Stock Exchange** (`http://vse.marketwatch.com/Game/Homepage.aspx`) is absolutely free. With your free registration, you receive $1,000,000 in virtual money that you can trade on any stock exchange. You can create public or private games with a cash balance you set. Choose from thousands of available games and test your strategy with a personal portfolio, in addition to leveraging news and research sources from MarketWatch.

Using the right buying technique to increase profits

Smart online investors are informed investors. To get a real-time quote, check with your online brokerage. Each brokerage quotes securities in a different format. To find a stock, bond, or mutual fund, you need to know the ticker symbol. Your brokerage should provide a feature to look up a symbol. If you don't want to use your brokerage, financial news services, such as Bloomberg.com (`www.bloomberg.com`), Yahoo! Finance (`http://finance.yahoo.com`), and CNN Money (`http://money.cnn.com/markets/xstream`), offer online ticker symbol look-ups.

Online investors must specify the type of order to execute for their own stock orders. Knowing how to designate the terms of your order can increase the chances that your order will be executed at the price you want. When you look at your online brokerage's order form, you'll notice several ways to buy or sell securities. In the past, a full-service broker decided which type of order was best. Today you select the method that you think is best. We list the four most frequently used ways to specify a trade here:

✔ **Market orders:** With a market order, you buy or sell a security at the then-current market rate. A market order doesn't expire at the end of the trading day. For example, if you place an order after the market closes, it's usually filled immediately after trading opens the next day.

✔ **Limit orders:** You set a maximum and a minimum amount for buying and selling an investment. Limit orders can be *good till canceled* (GTC), which means that the order stays in place until you cancel it or the security hits your maximum or minimum price requirements. Limit orders can also be day orders — your limit order expires at the end of the day.

✔ **Stop orders:** When a security reaches the price set by the investor, the order becomes active. When the order is activated, the order is executed; however, the investor isn't guaranteed the execution price.

✔ **Stop-limit orders:** When a security reaches the investor's predetermined price, the order is activated. The order can be executed only at the set price or better, so the order may not be completed.

When placing your trade, you need to know how to make a few decisions in advance. You must know how many shares you're buying or selling, the ticker symbol for the security you want to trade, your target price for buying or selling the security, the type of order you want to place, and when you want your order to expire. After you've placed your order, you receive confirmation on your screen. If you don't receive a confirmation message, telephone your brokerage immediately.

Many brokerages have online trading demos that allow you to practice trading. Even if you don't have a brokerage account, you still can try your hand at online trading by using the interactive simulation at Investing Online (www.investingonline.org/isc/index.html).

Sometimes you may experience the ever-so-common operator error when placing a trade, and your trade isn't completed. At other times, the servers at your brokerage may be offline or down because of a high volume of trades. Contacting your brokerage always is the best way to get to the bottom of problems. Whatever you do, don't enter your order again without first talking to your broker. If both orders are executed, you get double your order — and you may not be able to afford it!

A few caveats before you trade

Online investing has revolutionized the securities industry in several important ways. Not only can individuals readily use the Internet to access sophisticated research materials and financial data that previously were available only to financial institutions, but you also can use this newfound information to independently evaluate a security's performance. Online investors now can place trades without the assistance of a registered securities representative by entering an order with an online brokerage. Undeniably, online investing is an excellent opportunity and tool, but it has these limitations:

- ✔ Clicking a mouse is easy, but making a sound investment decision requires using a thoroughly researched analytical investment strategy. After all, if you find a great investment method, you want to implement it again and again. However, an easy investment isn't necessarily a sound investment. "Investigate before you invest" should be the slogan of all online investors.

- ✔ Making a trade with a click isn't the same as executing a trade. The technology is not instantaneous. Your order must travel through several market layers and may encounter delays before actually being executed.

- ✔ Frequent trading doesn't necessarily equal successful trading. Trading again and again may work for some people, but for most traders, long-term investing in sound securities is the best way to realize profits.

✔ Trading fees may be more complicated and expensive than you expect. Read the fine print so you know the exact cost of the trades you expect to make. Additionally, you may want to find out, among other pertinent information, whether the online brokerage charges a fee for maintaining or closing your account.

Knowing When to Hold and When to Fold

Keeping your portfolio in balance may require you to replace or swap some of your investments for others. You can use online portfolio trackers to determine which investments to prune. Most online brokerages include portfolio tracking; however, what your brokerage offers may not meet your specific needs. Here are a few examples of what you can find online:

✔ **GainsKeeper** (www.gainskeeper.com) provides accurate cost basis, capital gains tax lot data, and trade-decision tools that can maximize your after-tax returns. With GainsKeeper, you can import your portfolio information from your broker, MS Money, Quicken, or Excel files. You also can export results to Excel files, Turbo Tax, Tax Cut, and other tax software programs. Expect to pay $69 to track 150 stocks, $179 to track 1,000 stocks, and $499 to track 5,000 stocks.

✔ **Morningstar.com** (www.morningstar.com) has a premium membership that includes access to the one page, print-perfect Morningstar Analyses which are available for mutual funds and are free for Premium members. The Morningstar Portfolio X-Ray allows you to check for economic sector, investment style, world region exposure, expenses, asset allocations, and key financial performance statistics totaling nine additional screens more than those available with the free membership. Access to the Premium Fund/Stock Screener can assist you in narrowing your stock and fund choices quickly and in a more detailed process than the Basic selectors on the free site. Premium membership allows access to detailed reports and Morningstar Analyses. (Analysts' reports cover 3,800 stocks and mutual funds.) Daily Portfolio Alerts are succinct email reports that alert you to significant changes in your holdings and help you gauge when to buy and sell. You receive unbiased News and Views, which include updated financial and market news, Morningstar analysts' takes on stocks, funds, strategies, and events. The 14-day trial is free. Premium membership service is $16.95 per month, $159 per year, $269 for 2 years, or $369 for 3 years.

✔ **Reuters** (www.reuters.com/finance) requires your free registration to take advantage of its portfolio tracker. The Reuters portfolio tracker is easy to use and allows you to set up multiple portfolios with on-demand research for domestic and international stocks, U.S. funds, and cash. You can edit your portfolios by adding or deleting companies and changing investment amounts or shares. You can view your portfolios by performance (how the portfolio is doing), fundamentals (how investments compare with others), valuation (whether any gains or losses have occurred), and daily action (whether a trade is needed). Help icons provide additional information about portfolio functionality.

✔ **Risk Grades** (www.riskgrades.com) is based on a complicated scientific formula for calculating the risk of your investments. With your free registration, you receive five portfolios, graphing features, risk-versus-return analysis, risk alerts, "what-if" analysis, and historical event simulations. Using these tools, you can determine which investments are beyond your risk-tolerance level.

Book V
Protecting Your Money and Assets

The 5th Wave   By Rich Tennant

"My portfolio is gonna take a hit for this."

In this book . . .

*E*ven if you're the most dedicated, miserly saver in the world, that world is still full of risk and pitfalls. It seems like there are people and institutions out there who do little but wait for openings through which they can reach out for your money. Fortunately, a number of strategies and instruments are available by which you can minimize your financial risks and keep the wolves at bay. This book is where we talk about those in detail.

Here are the contents of Book V at a glance.

Chapter 1

Combating Identity Theft

*W*hen someone steals your identity, he pretends to be you. Not in a way in which he would have to convince people who know you that he is you, but in a much easier way: by using your numbers with strangers. Thieves use the myriad numbers that are associated with your name to become you. Whether they steal your mail, hack into your computer, break into your home, or sift receipts and personal information from your trash can, identity thieves gain access to valuable data that allows them to tap into your existing accounts and lines of credit or to open new accounts.

With your data in hand, these thieves can take vacations, buy cars, rent apartments, order designer furniture, pay for a week at the Ritz, get a job, max out all the credit card accounts they have access to, and profit financially because the businesses they're dealing with believe they're *you.* This activity, of course, hits your credit report. But if the thief is lucky — and you aren't — you may not discover that your evil twin is living it up and wrecking your credit rating for months or maybe longer, sometimes much longer. You may apply for a line of credit and discover you're rejected. Or you may get a flurry of aggressive calls from collection agencies that are sure you're the one responsible for unpaid bills.

Of course, you get to defend yourself and prove otherwise, but the process can be expensive and may take a long, long time to resolve. And while you're doing it, you may be subjected to unwarranted harassment, be passed by for that new job you've applied for, be turned down for a credit card or car loan, or miss out on all kinds of other opportunities because your credit report includes negative information put there by someone else pretending to be you.

In this chapter, we let you know how you can protect yourself, your identity, and your credit from these crooks. And we help you deal with ending the situation as quickly as possible if you've already been hit.

Protecting Yourself from Identity Thieves

Although you may think your identity is most likely to be stolen by someone you don't know, many times the culprits are people victims willingly let into their lives — friends, relatives, or coworkers. So you can significantly reduce your chances of falling victim to identity theft just by making yourself more secure in your home: In short, don't leave financial documents and confidential information where they can be easily seen.

In response to the billions of dollars lost to identity theft, Congress amended the Fair Credit Reporting Act (FCRA) with the Fair and Accurate Credit Transactions Act (the FACT Act or FACTA) to help reduce the threat of identity theft and help victims by giving them new rights.

Leaving bank statements or checks on the table today is like putting them out in the middle of the street. Anything you don't want in the middle of the street is something you should take care to keep out of sight in your home. This simple image will help you stay focused. Do you want your bank statement in the middle of the street? No? Then put it out of sight.

In the following sections, we walk you through some simple steps you can take to reduce the chances of having your identity stolen.

Taking advantage of online transactions

One of the easiest ways to protect yourself is to handle bill paying, information transfers, and financial transactions electronically. Having bills and statements delivered to your password-protected computer is much better than having them delivered to your mailbox outside your home — or, as we like to say, dropped off in the middle of your street. The more information you send and receive electronically, the lower the chances of identity theft.

Using a computer has other benefits as well: When you get your information online, as in the case of your bank statement, you can check up on it anytime you want. No need to wait for the end of the month. In fact, we recommend that you do a quick once-over every week or have periodic or dollar-level alerts emailed to you. For example, you can have transactions greater than $1,000 generate an email automatically — that way, you can spot a problem early.

Take precautions when conducting business via the Internet. You still may be at risk for identity theft. As long as you use only secure Web sites and ensure you're protected by a firewall, you're much better protected than you are with snail mail. (See the next section for info on determining whether a Web site is secure, and the section "Keeping computer data safe" for a few words on firewalls.)

Avoiding phishing scams

Phishing occurs when a stranger pretending to be someone you trust (for example, a representative of your bank or credit card company) emails you and asks you to confirm critical information about your account. For example, they want you to reply with your password, Social Security number, or other personal information. Phishing can also be perpetrated via a spyware program that you download to your computer without realizing you've done so, by clicking on a link or opening a file; the program then records any personal information you've stored on your computer and sends that information to others.

Phishing scams are increasing in number, and they're also becoming more sophisticated. Bottom line: Be extremely careful when giving out your personal information over the Internet. As with phone solicitation, don't give out your personal information unless you've initiated the transaction.

Use these do's and don'ts to help keep you and your personal information safe:

✔ **Do be suspicious of any email with urgent, exciting, or upsetting requests for personal financial information.** The sender is using your emotions to stimulate an immediate, illogical response to the request.

✔ **Don't give out personal or financial information unless you're certain of the source and you confirm that the link is secure.** You can tell you're on a secure Web site if you see a little padlock or key icon in the corner of your Web browser. Also, the address of the site will begin with `https://` instead of `http://`. Note that your emails are almost *never* secure, which means you should never email your credit card number, Social Security number, or other personal information to anyone — even if you're sure you're sending this info to someone you can trust — because your emails can be seen and intercepted on the Internet.

Exceptions apply when you're communicating with a coworker using an internal network at work, or you and the person you're emailing both have special security software in your email programs. These exceptions are pretty uncommon, so to be safe, we recommend never giving out private information via email, no matter what kind of network you're on.

✔ **Don't ever respond to emails that aren't personalized or that have your name misspelled.** If the message has your name wrong or doesn't have your name at all, don't reply.

✔ **Don't ever click on links in email messages to find out what the great offer is.** If you click on the link, you may end up downloading spyware onto your computer, and your security may be compromised.

✔ **If you suspect that you're being phished, do forward the email to the Federal Trade Commission at** `spam@uce.gov` **and file a complaint at the Internet Fraud Complaint Center (IFCC) by going to** `www.ic3.gov`. The IFCC is a partnership between the FBI and the National White Collar Crime Center (NW3C). The IFCC Web site not only lets you report suspected Internet fraud, but also provides disturbing statistics about this growing crime.

Keeping computer data safe

Safeguard your computer so it doesn't end up in the middle of the street, metaphorically speaking. Here are some computer safety rules to consider:

✔ **Don't leave your laptop out where it can be picked up.** Whether at home, in a hotel, or at work, when you're not in the same room as your laptop, put it away and out of sight. Would you leave a $100 bill laying out? The same consideration applies here.

✔ **Don't walk away from your computer and leave files with personal information open — particularly if you're online.**

✔ **Come up with a username and personal identification number (PIN) or password that isn't obvious and set your computer so that this information is required to turn your computer on.** You can also use a screensaver that has a password so that if you walk away from your desk for a certain period of time and the screensaver comes on, you need to enter a password to get back to your desktop.

Including at least one number, capital letter, or special character in your password is good (for example, Steve@1). Don't use birthdates or Social Security numbers — they're too easy for hackers to guess.

✔ **Don't keep a list of your passwords near the computer.** That's the computer equivalent of leaving your house key in your front door lock.

✔ **Install a firewall.** If you use a wireless network, make sure you set up a firewall with all the security you can handle. (You can get firewalls for your home computer at most office-supply stores like OfficeMax and Staples.)

✔ **Use antivirus and spyware protection to keep key loggers off your computer.** *Key loggers* are programs that send out any information that you type to the crook, including your credit card numbers, usernames, passwords, Social Security number, and so on.

✔ **Be sure to thoroughly delete all personal information on your computer if you decide to get rid of your computer and really put it in the middle of the street.** Your best bet is to completely reformat your hard drive, which wipes it out and gets rid of everything. (Check with your computer manufacturer to find out how to reformat your hard drive.)

Identifying vulnerable spots for theft

Although people seem to be spending more time than ever on their computers, most of us still spend more time in the *real* world than in cyberspace. Not surprisingly, so do the identity thieves. Most cases of identity theft that involve a known source of information occurred in the most mundane situations. A major study in 2006 found phishing or computer hacking made up only 2 percent of the known cases.

The top five known sources of identity theft are as follows:

- ✔ Friends, relatives, and acquaintances
- ✔ Purchases or other transactions
- ✔ Lost or stolen wallets and checkbooks
- ✔ Companies that maintain personal information
- ✔ Stolen snail mail

Keeping passwords private

Social engineering is using social situations to get information about otherwise secure data out of the unwitting. To make sure you're not being socially engineered, follow these suggestions:

- ✔ **Don't give anyone your password.** If tech support or the guy in the next cube over wants to be helpful, you can enter your password for him.
- ✔ **If you have to give out your password, be sure you trust the source —** and then change your password immediately.
- ✔ **Don't share your clever password with coworkers or friends.**
- ✔ **Don't use your kid's or pet's name or birthday for your password.**

Avoid giving out confidential information to friends, acquaintances — even your kids. They may not be identity thieves, but they sure are great, naive sources of information.

Safeguarding your mail

Although tampering with the U.S. mail is a federal crime, your mailbox is one of the most common targets of identity thieves. The culprit removes some statements from your mailbox and, before you miss them, begins the process of changing addresses and opening new accounts. He can also easily convert that check you sent off for the heating bill into ready cash. Acid-washing the original recipient off the check and replacing the name isn't difficult for enterprising thieves.

Protecting active-duty military personnel

The last thing the United States wants its active-duty servicepersons to worry about when they're safeguarding you and me is who's safeguarding *them* from identity thieves. We can tell you from experience that servicepersons are as fine and trusting and *naive* a group of young idealists as we have ever met. They're often targeted for scams. Fortunately, just in time for what seems to be an increasingly active period of military deployments in the world, the FACT Act has created another new alert. The *active-duty alert* allows active-duty military personnel to place a notation on their credit report as a way to alert potential creditors to possible fraud.

While on duty outside the country, military personnel — as well as their families at home in the United States — may lack the time or means to monitor their credit activity. (Calling TransUnion about an error isn't exactly a high priority when you're being shot at.) It seems only fair that, while soldiers are protecting their country, their country should protect them from credit problems.

If you're in the military and away from your usual base or deployed, you can place an active-duty alert on your credit report. An active-duty alert stays on your credit report for at least one year. This alert helps minimize the risk of identity theft by requiring that a business take "reasonable" care to verify your identity before issuing you credit. However, if you're in some distant land trying to keep the peace, that may not be feasible. So to keep the creeps away from your credit, you can appoint a personal representative to place or remove an alert.

Before you leave your base or home for active duty, be sure to appoint a personal representative and provide contact information to the credit bureau. If you don't, a creditor only has to "utilize reasonable policies and procedures to form a reasonable belief" before granting credit to someone who claims to be you. This process is way too *reasonable* for our comfort level. Be sure to appoint someone you trust!

An active-duty alert on a credit report requires a creditor to take extra steps to verify your identity not only before granting new credit, but also when issuing an additional credit card on an existing account or raising your limits. When you put an active-duty alert on your credit report, you receive a copy of your credit report and, as a bonus, your name is removed from preapproved-offer lists for credit cards, insurance, and loans. You can place additional alerts if your deployment lasts longer than a year.

To place or remove an active-duty alert, call any one of the three major credit-reporting bureaus. Whichever one you call will require you to provide appropriate proof of identity, which may include your Social Security number, name, address, and other personal information.

You have to contact only one of the three companies to place an alert — the companies are required to contact the other two. (If you call all three, they'll be calling each other and getting confused — and they're easily confused.)

If your contact information changes before your alert expires, update it or have your representative do so.

We suggest the following tips to help you reduce your exposure to mail fraud:

- ✔ **Convert as much of your financial business to online transactions as possible.** Doing so helps you avoid delivering information to the waiting hands of the criminal scouting your unattended mailbox.

✔ **Explore alternatives to your unlocked, end-of-the-driveway mailbox.** Consider using a post office box or a locked mailbox that will accept mail (not unlike the old slot in the door).

✔ **Don't mail checks or financial information from your home mailbox.** Use your local post office mailbox or bring your mail to work with you. (Don't forget the stamps, or the boss may cancel your work identity.)

✔ **Ask your bank to hold new check orders and pick them up at the bank.**

✔ **If you're away for a day or more, have someone pick up your mail, or, better, have the post office hold it until you return.** Don't let it sit in your mailbox overnight.

Maintaining financial data in your home

When you gain control of the mail flow in and out of your home, you can feel more comfortable knowing that you've closed off some key avenues for potential identity theft. Yet inside your sanctuary, that pile of documents must be protected and secured. Your information is still accessible to house thieves, not to mention others who may gain access to your inner sanctum through other means. You can protect yourself in your home in the following ways.

Storing your confidential documents and information

Keep all financial, confidential, and legal documents and information in a secure place — a strong box or a metal filing cabinet. Not only will your valuable data be safe from prying eyes and sticky fingers, but you'll also benefit from having all critical information in one place, in case you need to access it quickly.

Sometimes a simple act can save the day. Making and securely storing a photocopy of the contents of your wallet and account numbers is one of them. If you haven't already done so, empty the contents of your wallet or purse and photocopy everything, front and back. Write the contact phone numbers next to each item and file the paper in a locked cabinet. Voilà! You're now better prepared to deal with an identity crisis.

Shredding the evidence

Your mailbox is not the only source of private information for identity theft. Your garbage can is also rife with potential (not to mention with banana peels and expired yogurt). A determined thief won't mind sifting through your detritus if it means snagging a credit card number from those coffee-ground-covered receipts. For thieves, a fishing expedition in the backyards and trash cans of suburbia promises a good catch.

Purchase a good home crosscut shredder and shred all old financial mail that contains account numbers, including savings, checking, and credit card statements. Don't overlook all those preapproved offers for credit you receive. Get a shredder that has a large capacity because the shredded paper takes up a lot of space, and it fills up fast. Also be sure the shredder is easy to empty — the shredded, confetti-like material tries to fly all over the place.

Freezing your credit information

The option of freezing credit to keep it from identity thieves has become available to everyone. The concept is simple: You can freeze or lock up your credit information so that anyone who is looking to extend credit has to ask you to *thaw out* (unlock) your file. Freezing your credit information seriously hampers an identity thief from opening credit in your name without your knowledge because few lenders will extend credit without a credit report in hand.

The main consideration surrounding to-freeze-or-not-to-freeze is whether you value access to instant credit more than you fear your personal information being compromised. Only you know the answer to that question.

But the strategy is not foolproof. Thieves can still pirate, use, and abuse existing accounts by simply swiping your mail, changing your address from Peoria to Las Vegas, and getting replacement cards issued. So a freeze may help protect your *information,* but it may not protect your *money.* Given the low personal level of liability on credit cards, however, your monetary losses would probably not be significant.

If your information is stolen and the thief opens new lines of credit in your name, you can get all sorts of grief from collectors who are trained not to listen to excuses. "But I *swear,* I was never *in* Las Vegas and I never authorized that purchase of a $5,000 lap dance." They've heard it all before. So the bottom line of freezes is as follows:

- ✔ All the bureaus allow you to freeze your credit files, regardless of the laws in your state.
- ✔ Freezing doesn't prevent abuse of existing accounts.
- ✔ Thawing an account takes a few days and may keep impulse or sale purchases from happening — which can be good or bad, depending on how you look at it.

A fraud alert is similar to a minifreeze, in that it requires only verification of identity. When you place a fraud alert on your file, it remains on your credit report for a specific amount of time after a theft has occurred.

Shielding your credit card number from identity thieves

One of the easiest ways you can guard your identity is to ensure thieves don't have access to your credit card numbers. Luckily for you, the FACT Act has made this task a tad easier for you. Electronically generated receipts for credit and debit card transactions may not include the card's expiration date or more than the last five digits of the card number. If you receive a receipt that has your full account number on it, bring it to the attention of the business and insist that they get with the program — now!

Another FACT Act section allows consumers who request a copy of their credit file to also request that the first five digits of their Social Security number (or similar identification number) not be included in the file.

Spotting Identify Theft When It Happens

If your identity is stolen, you may not receive any obvious indication that you've been victimized —no broken window or missing masterpiece serves as a clue. The evidence, unfortunately, may not make itself known until your credit has been sorely compromised and you're fighting on multiple fronts to restore your good name.

That said, by being vigilant, you can spot signs of identity theft. This crime is one that you'll probably be the first to notice, and vigilance on your part can make all the difference between a minor inconvenience and a major identity crime. The following sections identify some key signs to watch out for.

Instituting an early-warning alert

The FACT Act requires that creditors give you what may be called an *early-warning notice*. This notice can serve as your first sign that something is amiss with an account and give you the opportunity to halt devastating abuse of your credit in its early stages.

Anyone who extends credit to you must send you a one-time notice no later than 30 days after negative information — including late payments, missed payments, partial payments, or any other form of default — is furnished to a credit bureau. This stipulation also applies to collection agencies, as long as they report to a credit bureau. The FACT Act doesn't dictate how *big* of a notice you get. You may have to look closely to even see it, so be sure you do your part by closely monitoring your credit reports, bank accounts, and credit card statements.

Predicting identity theft

The FACT Act demands that financial institutions establish procedures to attempt to spot identity theft *before* it occurs. Predicting an identity theft before it happens may seem as far-flung as calling in a psychic on a murder case. But like our trusty weather forecasters who look to the skies for clues to tomorrow's weather, financial prognosticators are writing programs to look for specific activity in your financial records that may indicate a problem. In fact, several credit card companies are now touting their own programs to fight identity theft.

Certain events — such as a change of address, a request for a replacement credit card, or efforts to reactivate a dormant credit card account — may signal a potential fraud. That said, you can do only so much to protect yourself from identity theft, so even with prevention programs in place, in most cases, you won't know about a problem until after the fact.

This notice means something bad is in your account history, and if it's reported to the credit bureau, it will be negative. Whether it's reported or not, it's lurking out there. Before negative information is reported, the early-warning notice may look something like this:

> *We may report information about your account to credit bureaus. Late payments, missed payments, or other defaults on your account may be reflected in your credit report.*

After negative information has been reported, the early-warning notice may look like this:

> *We have told a credit bureau about a late payment, missed payment, or other default on your account. This information may be reflected in your credit report.*

The wording makes it sound as though the bad information may not show up. It will — and probably already has.

Receiving a collections call

The call, likely an unpleasant and adversarial one, will be one demanding a payment on an overdue account, one the collector is certain you owe. What should you do? The FACT Act, designed to address identity-theft issues, states that you need to tell the collector very clearly that you did not make the purchase and you believe that your identity may have been stolen.

When you tell the collector you think your identity may have been stolen, the collection agency is required by law to inform the creditor. You're also entitled to get a copy of all the information the collection agency or creditor has about this debt, including applications, statements, and the like, as though this account or bill were really yours.

The best part is that, under the FACT Act, as soon as you notify the creditor or collector that the debt is the work of an identity thief, the debt cannot be sold or placed for collection.

Discovering unrecognized credit card charges

To find charges on your statement that you didn't make, you have to actually read your statement in detail. Many people just look at the amount due and make a payment. Instead, take a minute to review your charges — you just may be surprised.

Don't rely on your memory as you review your statement. 'Keep all your credit card receipts in a file — and pull them out when reviewing your monthly statement. Keep it all in a convenient place, at least until you receive, verify, and pay your statement.

If you see any unauthorized charges on your statement, call the customer-service number and get the details. You may have to dispute the charge, but that's no big deal. Also, the representative may see some indication of identity theft and recognize it as fraud right away. Make the call.

Being denied credit or account access

Rejection is always painful — but it's especially painful when you're rejected because of something you're not responsible for. If you get rejections for credit, you may want to ask why — but your best bet is to order a copy of your credit report and look for evidence of identity theft (accounts you never opened and activity you don't recognize).

Another sign of identity theft is receiving a notice that you've been rejected for credit you never asked for. Take this notice seriously. Someone who shouldn't be may be applying for credit in your name. Also, you may try to access an ATM and get a denial message. If so, contact your bank immediately to determine whether it's the result of identity theft.

Missing account statements

Your monthly statement is really late. Hmm . . . now that you think of it, you didn't receive a statement last month, either. Yes, not getting statements may be one of your birthday wishes, but the real reason you're not hearing from your creditors could be more sinister. It could mean an identity thief has changed your address in order to use your bank accounts, hoping you won't notice for a few months.

Create a system by which you remind yourself when statements are due and bills must be paid. This way, you're more likely to stay on top of your payment schedule and be alerted when something is amiss. As you may imagine, if you pay bills and get statements via computer instead of snail mail, you make it harder on the thieves (and easier on yourself).

When Identity Theft Happens to You

If you discover you're a victim of identity theft, you need to act quickly and comprehensively. Don't rely on others to resolve this mess. You have the biggest interest in getting this situation stopped, fixed, and behind you, and you need to assume all responsibility for doing so.

If your identity has been stolen or you believe it has (you don't need a smoking gun, videotapes, or a confession to act), do everything in the following sections right away. Most of these places are open for business 24 hours a day, so a late-night call won't wake anyone.

Who you gonna call? Contacting everyone who needs to know

You may read different advice on whom to call *first* if you discover you're a victim of identity theft. Some sources recommend calling the police, others suggest you call your creditors or the credit bureaus. Our advice is to begin in one of two places, depending on your circumstances:

- ✔ If your existing accounts have been compromised, call your creditors first.
- ✔ If you're hearing about accounts you've never had, call the credit bureaus first.

Either way, don't wait long between the two calls.

Before you pick up the phone, get a notebook and a pen; you'll need to start writing down everything that happens from now on. You want names, badge numbers, phone numbers, names of supervisors, and so on. Documentation is critical because this situation may go on for a long time and require a lot of calling and writing to resolve. Don't trust your memory or count on anyone to call you back when he says he will. Be responsible and get the facts.

Canceling your credit cards

If your credit or debit cards have been compromised, call the card companies, ask for the fraud department, and cancel the cards immediately. You can find the phone number on your monthly statements or in your terms-and-conditions brochure. Your card may also have a customer-service number you can call.

A small comfort: Your liability on stolen credit card accounts is relatively low — $50 maximum. Even so, you need to contact all your creditors as quickly as possible so that the thief doesn't continue to rack up charges in your name, creating a bigger loss for the credit card company.

For ATM and debit cards, your maximum liability is $50 if you report the loss within 48 hours of noticing it, but $500 or even *unlimited* (including any overdraft protection) if you delay too long.

Contacting credit bureaus

Calling one of the bureaus results in a 90-day fraud alert being placed on all three of your credit files within 24 hours. A *fraud alert* can make it more difficult for someone to get credit in your name because it tells creditors to follow certain procedures to protect you. (Refer to the section "Sending out a fraud alert," later in this chapter, for more about this action.)

Consider putting a freeze on your accounts until you know how severe the damage is. You can always thaw your accounts later, and a freeze shuts off access to your information much more completely than a fraud alert does.

You can also add a *victim's statement* to your credit report. The victim's statement informs anyone getting your report that your file has a problem and it may not be relied upon to be completely accurate. Most creditors take strong notice of this fact and won't issue new credit in your name.

Adding a victim's statement to your report may motivate creditors to close existing accounts that weren't affected until they can determine you're safe again — which may keep you from using your accounts for a while.

After you've notified the credit bureau of your situation, you'll receive a credit report from each of the bureaus. Be sure to keep a copy of all reports (store them with those copious notes you're taking).

Contacting the Federal Trade Commission

The Federal Trade Commission (FTC) has an entire department that handles identity-theft issues. The folks in the identity-theft clearinghouse don't follow up on specific instances, but they play an important role in looking for patterns and accumulating statistics that help everyone concerned with stopping identity thefts.

Call the FTC's ID Theft Hotline at 877-438-4338. From a purely self-serving perspective, contacting the FTC bolsters your claims regarding unauthorized credit card charges or accounts thieves open in your name. Go to `https://www.ftccomplaintassistant.gov` to fill out the Identity Theft Affidavit form. You can use a copy of this form when disputing accounts or charges with creditors, as well as when filing a police report.

Contacting the police

Would your local sheriff flip on his flashing lights and tear around town to find the thief? Probably not. But the FACT Act requires that you be official on your end, just as the government is required to be on its end. You have a crime on your hands, so you do need to call the police and report it.

The police report is also a way for others in the process to get a straight, consistent story from a third party about what happened and when. You'll have less difficulty convincing that collector you aren't kidding about the Las Vegas lap-dance bill if you can refer him to your local police or send an official police report to bolster your story. Be sure to get a copy of the report as soon as it's available — or at least get the police-report number for reference.

Here's how the police-reporting process works:

1. **Contact your police station when you discover an account and/or activity on your credit report that isn't yours, and you suspect someone is using your identity.**

   You don't need legally acceptable proof or a smoking gun — it's your identity, and your suspicion is enough to file a police report.

2. **File the report, giving all the facts and circumstances.**

   No standard form or procedure exists; each police department has its own.

3. **Make sure you get the police-report number, with the date, time, police department, location, and name of the person taking the report.**

   You're likely to have to provide this info if you deal with insurance claims or work with credit card companies and other lenders to clear your account.

4. **Be persistent if the police seem reluctant to take your statement, but be polite.**

Some police departments may not recognize identity theft as a crime they're responsible for handling. They may question their jurisdiction or not want to take the time to take a report. Remind them that, without a police report, credit bureaus may not block fraudulent items on your report, and law enforcement may be inadvertently helping a crook.

Furnish as much documentation as you can to prove your case — debt-collection letters, credit reports, your notarized Identity Theft Affidavit (see preceding section), and so on. The police report will also help cover you against liability in case someone assumes your identity and is arrested for criminal activity using your name and personal data.

Notifying the post office

Many identity-theft cases are the result of unauthorized and illegal access to your information via the U.S. mail. Messing with the mail is a federal crime. If you're a victim of identity theft and think your mail played a role, the post office recommends that you contact the nearest U.S. Postal Service Inspection Office and report your concerns. If you know for sure it happened via the mail, call to report a crime. Find the office closest to you by contacting your local post office, or go online to `http://usps.com/postal inspectors/ifvictim.htm`.

Taking advantage of the FACT Act

The FACT Act has numerous provisions for businesses, credit reporters, and you. An entire book could easily be written on the topic, but in essence, the FACT Act was designed to address issues surrounding incomplete or inaccurate credit reporting, not to mention identity theft. The following list highlights the consumer-oriented provisions of the act that we think are most informative or useful:

- ✔ **You can receive at least one free credit report each year from each of the three bureaus.** Under certain circumstances, you can get more than one. Specialty reporting agencies, such as insurance and landlord reporting services, must also give you a free report if you ask (see Book I, Chapter 5).

- ✔ **You have the right to dispute the information in your file directly with the party furnishing the data, instead of having to go through a third party.** The credit reporting agencies have up to 45 days to respond.

- ✔ **You can sue creditors and the bureaus for violations of the FACT Act for two years after discovery or five years after the violation took place.** Your case is especially strong if they continue to sell, transfer, or place your account for collection after you've communicated that it's because of identity theft and placed a block on the trade line.

✔ Creditors and collectors cannot continue to report information based on an account that you've reported as fraudulent or that you've shown to be inaccurate or incomplete.

✔ You must be notified about any adverse credit actions, such as being offered less-than-favorable credit terms or having a creditor send a negative item to your credit report.

✔ Businesses must cooperate with you to help clear your name in the case of identity theft. They must provide copies of records about goods or services they provided to the thief. The business may require a police report and may take up to 30 days to comply.

✔ You can opt out of information sharing between affiliates. If you don't want Citibank to tell Smith Barney (its brokerage affiliate) that you're a big spender (and should be called to invest some of that money), it won't.

✔ You may place a 90-day fraud alert, a 7-year extended fraud alert, and a 1-year military active-duty alert on your file.

✔ You may have fraudulent trade lines on your credit report blocked if you've reported the crime to a police department or law-enforcement agency.

✔ You may request that your Social Security number be *truncated* (shortened) on your credit report and communications in case it falls into the wrong hands. And credit report users can't just throw your used reports into a trash bin. They have to dispose of the report in an approved manner.

✔ Businesses must truncate your credit card number on credit card receipts. In other words, your restaurant receipt shouldn't show your entire credit card number — just the last five digits.

Sending out a fraud alert

Contacting the credit bureaus is one of your first steps when you discover an identity theft. When you contact them, you have the opportunity to place a fraud alert and a victim's statement in your file. These two items indicate to anyone looking at your report that the request for credit they've received recently may not actually be from you. Generally, the creditor contacts you before approving the credit request.

If your ex-brother-in-law is pretending to be you and he's at a car dealership waiting to drive away with a new Rolls Royce, the fraud alert and victim's statement work well. The dealership has to verify who he is. The fraud alert does create a bit of an extra step or delay if you're simply trying to legitimately open a new credit card to take advantage of a 10 percent discount on items you're purchasing today at the local department store — but this delay may be one you're willing to live with because of the protection it provides.

A fraud alert is placed on your account for 90 days. Any new activity, including your own, is researched and reported to you. So if you open new credit lines during this time, you may notice a slower-than-normal process. Although this delay may be inconvenient, this safeguard is in place to protect you.

If you aren't sure whether your identity has been stolen, but the information necessary to steal it has been compromised, consider an *extended alert* on your credit report. An extended alert lasts seven years. Why use an extended alert? Say you lose your wallet. A thief may not use your information right away — he may save your information for future use. The extended alert covers a long enough time period to prevent the information from being used to open an account, say, next year. It works sort of like that weed killer you use to keep the little creepers from sprouting in the first place. Though it may be a nuisance, an extended alert serves to warn you of any suspicious activity — even after you've forgotten about the original event that triggered you to establish the alert in the first place.

A small silver lining: After you put the alert on your file, you're entitled to *two* free copies of your credit report at any time during the next 12 months from all three agencies, not just the annual report now available to all consumers.

Blocking that line

"Block that line" may sound like a football cheer, but it can be a powerful tool. Be sure to request that the bureaus block any lines of credit that you believe are fraudulent. This block prevents those items from being sold, transferred, or placed for collection. In addition, ask the credit bureaus to remove any inquiries on your record as a result of those fraudulent lines.

Finally, ask the credit bureaus to notify anyone who may have received reports over the last six months with the erroneous information and inquiries on them. Doing so helps alert creditors and other interested parties to the situation — and saves your reputation.

Accessing Credit after Identity Theft

If you're a victim of identity theft, you're likely to experience emotions common to any victim: You feel traumatized, battered, fearful, and angry. You're likely to avoid any experience with credit and borrowing in the future.

We encourage you to strive to overcome these feelings. After all, credit — though it certainly can be abused and exploited — also brings great benefits to responsible individuals, allowing them to achieve personal and financial goals they otherwise wouldn't realize. We suggest that you adopt a strong offense and move forward with your personal goals. Whether you're planning to buy a house or you're simply buying back-to-school supplies at their lowest prices, don't be afraid to use credit to your advantage. You can take steps to get your credit going again, without putting yourself at renewed risk to identity thieves.

Closing and reopening your accounts

Whether your personal accounts were broken into, stolen, or just sniffed at, change all your PINs, passwords, user IDs, and account numbers. You'll probably have to close accounts and reopen them. Doing so may be a hassle, perhaps — but if you've been a victim of identity theft, you already know the real meaning of *hassle*.

Consider this list of which accounts to close and reopen:

- ✔ **Bank accounts:** When your information is compromised, you never know if or when trouble will pop up. Changing the account numbers results in a dead end for a thief.

- ✔ **Credit card accounts:** When you contact the card companies, you'll be asked for proper identification. (This inquiry is good — you *want* them to be suspicious and thorough!) They're used to closing accounts and reopening new ones quickly and painlessly. Reopen only the accounts you use. If you haven't used a card in two years, you should wonder why it's taking up space in your wallet.

  Be careful, however, about closing your older accounts. These accounts tend to help your credit score.

- ✔ **Other accounts:** Contact your Internet service provider and utility companies to alert them to your circumstances. Get new account numbers in every situation. If your long-distance calling card has been stolen or you discover fraudulent charges on your phone bill, close your old account and open a new one.

Changing your PINs and passwords

When you change those accounts at the bank, change your personal identification numbers (PINs), too. And when you access money at ATMs or in public places, make sure no one can see you enter the number. Getting close to the machine may block the sightline of a camera with a telephoto lens or someone using binoculars across the street. (Yes, thieves really *do* go that far.)

Switch to a *passphrase* instead of a password. A passphrase uses a short series of words like "ElvisIs#1" instead of a single password. Passphrases tend to be longer and harder to crack. Include some numbers and special characters in them, if you can.

Book V

Protecting Your Money and Assets

Changing your Social Security number and driver's license

If you can't seem to shake the damage done by the identity theft (because either new theft occurrences keep popping up or collectors keep landing on you like blue-bottle flies), you may need to take more serious action. Contact the Social Security Administration to inquire about getting a new Social Security number.

Getting a new Social Security number is a huge pain to everyone, including you. Imagine all the places you've used your old number. Prepare to change all your records yourself — no one handles this change for you. For more information, visit the Social Security Web site at www.socialsecurity.gov or call 800-772-1213 (800-325-0778, TTY for the hearing impaired).

If you go this route, you won't be the first. Besides the storied federal witness protection program, Social Security numbers are changed for domestic-violence victims when warranted. But with all the emphasis on national security, changing your number isn't easy.

A few circumstances can prevent you from changing your Social Security number. You *cannot* get a new Social Security number if any of these conditions apply to you:

✔ You've filed for bankruptcy.

✔ You intend to avoid the law or your legal responsibility.

✔ Your Social Security card is lost or stolen, but no evidence indicates that someone is using your number.

Be sure to document everything. This dog can have a very long tail. You may need to dig up some documentation a year or two after you thought all the dust had settled. Good records, with everything in writing and names and dates, will be a godsend.

While you're at it, grab a good paperback book, go down to the Department of Motor Vehicles, and get your driver's license number changed — especially if someone is using yours as an ID.

Chapter 2

Online Banking

In This Chapter

▶ Discovering two types of online banks

▶ Deciding what types of banking accounts you need

▶ Locating the online bank that matches your individual requirements

▶ Opening an online banking account

*O*ne of the main attractions of online banking is the 24/7 convenience. Online banks also make user interfaces friendlier and easier to navigate. And transactions take place faster as Internet users convert to cable modem or DSL access. In this chapter, we help you get started in online banking by showing you the differences between online banks and explaining the benefits and limitations of traditional banks. We help you define what type of banking services you already have, and we review the types of banking services that are available so you can decide what you need. Finally, we make it easier for you to assess which bank is the right fit for your user profile and we explain how to open an online checking account.

Online and Traditional Banks

Online banks are divided into two categories: online (Web only, or virtual) banks and traditional banks with online services.

▸ **Online banks:** Virtual banks don't have any physical branch offices, so no tellers are available to answer your questions. As far as customers are concerned, virtual banks exist only on the Internet and are governed by the same rules and regulations as traditional banks. As a general rule, the virtual bank passes on the money it saves on overhead, reduced bank personnel costs, and branch office facilities to customers in the form of higher yields on interest-bearing savings accounts, checking accounts, certificates of deposit (CDs), and money market funds.

✔ **Traditional banks with online services:** A regular bank that has a Web site, maintains branch offices, and offers online services is called a *click-and-brick* bank. Today most national and regional banks and many smaller banks offer online banking. These online banking services frequently have names that make the service seem more familiar to the customer, such as *PC banking, home banking, Internet banking,* or *electronic banking.* Click-and-brick banks offer a variety of services. Generally, national banks offer fully functional online banking either for free or for a small fee. Smaller banks may offer limited online access, such as read-only access to your account.

Advantages of online banking

Most online banks make opening an online account easy. Customers can always access their accounts 24/7/365. If you're traveling in the U.S. or overseas, you still can log on to your account to take care of a banking problem from virtually anywhere.

Online banks generally process and confirm transactions faster than traditional banks. Online banks enable customers to complete routine transactions (account transfers, balance inquiries, bill payments, and stop-payment orders) online whenever and wherever they want to. Companies like Wells Fargo (www.wellsfargo.com) permit customers to scan checks at their desks, key in the dollar amounts via its CEO Portal, and electronically send the deposit to the bank. They then view their deposit activity through the portal in real time.

Customers can usually download account information to personal software programs, such as Microsoft Money or Intuit Quicken, for easy bookkeeping. Fees are often comparable to traditional banks and, in some cases, are lower.

Online bank access

The three ways to access an online banking account, in order of increasing popularity, are as follows:

✔ **Personal-finance software packages:** The leading personal-finance software packages are MS Money and Intuit Quicken. Account information downloads in seconds for both programs. Quick downloads enable you to track, verify, and categorize the income and expenses for your brokerage, checking, credit card, and other accounts. At some banks, this specialized type of connection service is free. At others, you pay a fee of around $6 per month.

- ✔ **Your bank's mobile banking network:** Some banks allow access to your accounts from your mobile device. For Internet-enabled devices, including Apple iPhones or Apple iPod touch phones, you simply log in. You can view account balances and transactions, make one-time transfers between eligible accounts, make one-time bill payments, and pay e-bills.

- ✔ **Your bank's Web site:** When you travel, accessing your bank's Web site often is the best way to keep tabs on your accounts. Frequently, you can check on account balances and transactions, view check images online, pay bills, set up recurring bill payments, transfer money between accounts, send funds to any U.S. bank account, reorder checks online, and view and print transactions from the past 90 days.

Accounting for Your Accounts

Banks offer a wide variety of accounts, but you generally can boil them down into the five types we describe in the sections that follow. The Federal Deposit Insurance Corporation (FDIC) usually insures each type of account for up to $100,000. Most banks offer all five kinds, so you can select one or more at the same location or elsewhere. Review each overview of the accounts listed below to determine what types you have.

Savings account

Savings accounts are designed to encourage individuals to save by paying them interest on the funds they maintain in the account. Generally, the amount of interest paid for a savings account is more than for an interest-bearing checking account but less than for a money market deposit account (MMDA) or CD. Banks often charge a fee whenever a savings account balance falls below a specified minimum.

For example, at SunTrust (`www.suntrust.com`) if your savings account balance falls below $400 you are charged a fee of $10. You often can view savings account information on your bank's Web site. If you use software like MS Money or Quicken, you also can download your savings account information to the program. Additionally, if you want to transfer funds from your savings account to another account at the same bank, you can use your personal financial software or the bank's Web site to do so. Keep in mind that a transfer or other similar transaction usually is completed by the beginning of the next business day.

Basic checking account

Basic checking accounts have a limited set of features. The average minimum initial deposit for opening a basic checking account is about $50. With this account, you can write checks, download information, and receive monthly statements. However, these bare-bones accounts don't pay interest on account balances and may restrict the number of checks you can write per month or charge fees when you write more than a certain number of checks per month.

Keep that balance up! The convenience of using a basic checking account can cost upward of $200 a year in banking fees when you fail to maintain the minimum balance in your account.

Interest-bearing checking account

With an *interest-bearing checking account,* you earn interest on your account balance, can write an unlimited number of checks, *and* have access to the convenience of using a debit card. The amount required to open an interest-bearing checking account often is $100, and the bank usually sets a minimum balance (frequently $1,500 or more) for maintaining the account without a service charge. If you fall below that amount, you'll be dinged with the fee.

The amount of interest that you earn in an interest-bearing checking account frequently isn't as much as you'd otherwise earn by investing the minimum balance in equally insured financial products. Although the account's debit card looks like a credit card, it actually is connected to your bank account. In other words, no credit is involved in debit card transactions. Remember: Inflation usually outpaces what banks pay in their interest-bearing accounts.

MMDA or MMA

In a *money market deposit account* (MMDA) or *money market account* (MMA), your balance is invested in short-term Treasury bills, commercial debt, or certificates of deposit. Interest rates, in general, are higher for MMDAs than they are for interest-bearing checking accounts, but the balance in an MMDA usually has to be higher than that of an interest-bearing checking account before it begins earning interest. In addition, you're usually limited in terms of the number of transfers and checks you can make and write each month, and you're charged a service fee whenever your account balance falls below a specified amount.

CD

Certificates of deposit (CDs) actually are geared to specific dates. Basically, you have to agree to keep all your CD-invested money in the account for a set period of time, which can range from three months to six years. The longer the time period, the higher the interest rate you earn. Heavy penalties are leveled for early withdrawals, so longer-term CDs are not a terrific place for parking your emergency funds.

Choosing an Online Bank That's Right for You

Before you even think about opening an account, you need to determine what your *user profile* is and what types of accounts and services you need to be able to take control of your personal finances. Different features of online banks appeal to different user profiles. For example, experienced Internet users may be more concerned about online costs and resources than savers, who rarely visit the Web site. Confidence and the highest interest rate possible are issues of concern to savers. The ease of navigation may be more important to an online all-in-one-stop shopper than it is to a borrower. A borrower may be more concerned than the saver about low interest rates and customer service.

Identifying your user profile

Every person has an individual profile that can help determine what type of online banking and bank is best. Your user profile can be classified as follows:

- ✔ **Experienced Internet user:** You have more than two years of online experience and regularly surf the Internet and use email.

- ✔ **All-in-one-stop shopper:** You have more than five years of experience on the Internet, regularly pay bills online, track your investments online, and don't want to travel from one Web site to another to complete your financial housekeeping.

- ✔ **Saver:** You're interested in protecting your savings and looking for the online bank offering the highest interest rates and the lowest fees.

- ✔ **Borrower:** You seek low interest rates on your loan, the ability to track your loan payments online, and the ability to talk to someone if something goes wrong.

Comparing a bank's attributes to your user profile can help determine exactly which bank best fits your user profile. These attributes can affect your decision making:

- **Overall cost:** How much does the bank charge for usual services? Does it have additional handling fees or a required minimum balance? What are the interest rates?

- **Customer service:** Can you make a service request or inquiry or get advice online? Can you personalize your data or reuse your data for future transactions? Does the online bank have a customer loyalty program?

- **Online resources:** Does your online bank offer a menu of services and financial products? Can you complete transactions (applying for your mortgage online is one example) for each service or product online?

- **Confidence:** How reliable is your online bank's Web site? Will your bank protect your privacy? Does your online bank provide security guarantees?

- **Ease of navigation:** How simple is opening an account? Do customers have an easy pathway to the Web site? Can you access your data easily?

Seeing how the banks stack up

As a means of assessing how the several leading online banks compare with each other, we've prepared the following reviews:

- **Bank of America** (www.bankofamerica.com) provides a fairly easy-to-navigate Web site. Bank of America offers a wide variety of financial products. For example, there are 5 different types of checking accounts and over 400 different credit cards. Products include checking accounts, savings accounts, CDs, money market accounts, mortgages, home equity loans, investment products, and student banking options, in addition to the "keep the change" savings program. Online bill pay, ATMs, and maintenance of student checking accounts are free. The monthly maintenance fee for the MyAccess checking accounts is $5.95 (free if direct deposit).

- **Chase** (www.chase.com) supplies a good Web site for existing customers. All you have to do is enter your personal information and Chase account numbers. New customers sign up for the type of account they want (for example, there are six types of checking accounts). Then click on the Open an Account link. After you become a Chase account-holder you can easily enroll in other banking services. Chase offers online bill pay, the ability to view check images online, personalized account alerts, overnight check service, transfers between Chase accounts, same-day transfers to any U.S. bank account, the ability to reorder checks and deposit slips online, and to view and print transactions from the past

90 days. There is no monthly fee for certain Chase checking accounts. Chase Basic Checking, Chase Balance Checking, Chase Checking with Interest, and Chase Budget Checking have a $4 monthly fee. Online bill pay is free. The Chase Free Checking requires a $25 deposit to open the account but the minimum required balance is $0. The Chase Free Checking account has a $6 monthly maintenance fee if you do not use direct deposit. Chase has more than 780,000 ATMs around the world.

✔ **Citibank** (www.citibank.com), at this time, has one of the most functional yet simple Web sites around. Citibank offers online checking and savings accounts, online bill pay, email and wireless alerts, online bank statements and check images, and online account transfers. Citibank's online bill pay services are more sophisticated than your normal bank. With Citibank you can pay a person or company that doesn't normally receive electronic payments. Citibank will cut a physical check and mail the check for you. Online banking and bill paying are free. There is a $3/month maintenance fee for EZ checking (there is no fee for this service with direct deposit). Citibank offers rewards-based checking. All you need to do is get 16,000 ThankYou Points, redeemable for $150 in Gift Cards: Just open a Citibank account, enroll in the ThankYou Network, and do qualifying activities. With an enrolled Citibank checking account you have more ways to get monthly reward points for your checking relationship. Citibank will even triple your points for the first year for your debit card purchases and for everyday banking activities linked to your checking..

✔ **WaMu** (www.wamu.com), formerly known as Washington Mutual, has a well-designed Web site. WaMu offers free checking with free checks for life, instant credit card approval, $1 minimum opening deposit when opening a checking and savings account together, online CDs, online bill pay, mobile banking, and a high rate of return on savings deposits. Additionally, you'll receive a $.03 reward for each debit card purchase transaction up to $250 per year with your WaMu Free Checking Account. There is a $4 service charge for savings accounts that fall below the $300 minimum. There is no charge for worldwide ATM withdrawals. WaMu offers free checking and online bill pay. There is a $20/month fee for platinum checking and a $12 fee for money market accounts.

✔ **HSBC** (www.hsbc.com) supplies a Web site that has relatively few links. This makes it seem less overwhelming than other banking sites. However, you need to be an HSBC customer to appreciate all the site has to offer. HSBC provides a view of your account balances, transactions and purchases online, online bill pay, and views of e-statements. You can view of your HSBC and non-HSBC accounts with its EasyView service and make transfers between HSBC accounts. HSBC does not charge for online banking and bill pay services. Free checking accounts and student checking accounts do not have monthly maintenance fees (and no minimum balance is required).

If your favorite bank isn't listed above, don't despair; check out InvestorGuide at www.investorguide.com/links-dir-banklist.html.

Don't forget the fees when you shop

The following checklist outlines the fees you need to evaluate so you can determine exactly what you need from an online bank account:

- ✔ **"Foreign" ATM fees:** ATM fees include the amount of money other banks charge you for using their ATM machines to access your bank. Frequently, account-holders must pay fees to their own bank and the other bank for using an ATM that's "foreign" to their home banks.

- ✔ **Call-center charges:** The fee that you're charged when you contact customer service is referred to as a *call-center charge.* As part of being competitive, most banks don't charge for this service; however, some banks may offer this service for free during a trial period and then start charging you a fee after a predetermined period of time. So watch out.

- ✔ **Canceled check fee:** Gone are the days of seeing copies of your checks and deposit slips for free — to say nothing of actually getting them returned in the mail.

- ✔ **Fee for printing checks and deposit slips:** This fee is the amount your bank charges you when you have checks, deposit slips, or other paperwork printed.

- ✔ **Low-balance penalties:** If your account sinks below a minimum balance, the bank charges a penalty fee. For example, if your balance goes below the minimum for just one day, you may lose more than a month's worth of earned interest.

- ✔ **Money order fees:** Banks make you pay for money orders. Bear in mind that Internet-only banks may not offer money orders at any price.

- ✔ **Monthly maintenance fees:** These fees are what your bank charges you for physically maintaining your account or accounts. Some online banks have the option of increasing monthly maintenance fees at any time.

- ✔ **Other bank fees:** Banks find other ways to get money out of you. Miscellaneous other bank fees can include bank analysis fees when you want a particular transaction to be investigated.

- ✔ **Overdraft charges:** Who doesn't know about these fees? An overdraft charge is the amount of money your bank charges for covering one of your checks when you don't have enough money in your account to do so. Overdraft charges vary from one bank to another, and your bank has the option of increasing its overdraft charges.

Exercising your online banking rights

Whenever you have a dispute about a transaction, contact your bank immediately. You have 60 days from the date of your bank statement to notify your bank of an error. You can notify your online bank in person, by telephone, or in writing. This kind of problem needs to be resolved within ten business days of your notification. To be on the safe side, keep a paper trail of all your transactions and payments. To find out how you can pursue a dispute with your bank, become an educated consumer at the FDIC Consumer Protection Web site at `www.fdic.gov/consumers/`.

✔ **Per-check charges:** With some basic checking accounts, you're required to pay a fee for each check you write. You also may be charged a fee for each check you write over a certain number of checks you're allowed to write from your interest-bearing checking account.

✔ **Returned-check/NSF fees:** NSF fees are the money the bank orders you to pay when it's forced to reverse a transaction and return a check to you via U.S. mail for insufficient funds. Remember, you owe not only the NSF fee, but also the amount of the check.

✔ **Traveler's check fees:** This amount is what your bank charges for issuing you traveler's checks. Keep in mind that your Internet-only bank may not offer traveler's checks.

Beware of boozing and banking. According to BBC News (`http://news.bbc.co.uk`), on Sunday mornings the help desks of many banks are overwhelmed with calls from customers who made transactions they regret. These transactions often occur after midnight and are fueled by alcohol consumption. Customers sometimes sign up for online services, buy products they really didn't want, or occasionally make transactions they can't remember.

Laughing all the way to your online bank

You don't have to go beyond your keyboard to find special deals for Web-based banks. The following list includes a few good deals that are geared just for Internet shoppers; you'll also find the APY and minimum deposit required to open an account. Don't forget to go to the bank's Web site to check for any additional deals or changes, and, of course, remember to read the small print. (Keep in mind that as time changes these rates will also change.)

- ✔ **Bank of the Internet USA** (www.bankoftheinternet.com) offers an interest-bearing e-checking account that bears 3.4 percent interest. The minimum deposit needed to open an account is $500. A minimum balance of $5,000 is required, and there is a $7.50 monthly service fee. Bank of the Internet USA offers a money market account (MMA) with a return of 3.6 percent. It costs $100 to open an account. No minimum deposit is required, and there are no monthly services fees. This MMA account has check-writing privileges. Bank of the Internet USA also offers a savings account with a 2.0 percent return. It costs $100 to open the account, and there are no minimum deposit requirements or monthly maintenance fees.

- ✔ **Zions First National Bank** (www.zionsbank.com) offers an online checking account that bears 1.01 percent interest. You'll need $2,500 to open an account. There is no minimum required deposit and no monthly maintenance fee. The return on the Zions's MMA is 3.39 percent. No minimum balance is required, and there are no monthly service fees. There are check-writing privileges for this account.

- ✔ **Everbank** (www.everbank.com) supplies a checking account bearing 2.25 percent interest. It takes $1,500 to open an account. No minimum deposit or monthly service fees. The return on a MMA account is 4.65 percent, and 3.45 percent after the introductory rate period. It costs $1,500 to open a MMA account and $1,500 must remain in the account to avoid fees. There are check-writing privileges for this account.

- ✔ **E*TRADE Bank** (http://us.etrade.com/banking) provides an interest-bearing checking account with a rate of 3.0 percent. It only takes $100 to open an account. To avoid fees you need to maintain a minimum deposit of $5,000. Monthly service charges are $15. The return on an MMA account is 1.75 percent. It costs $1 to open an account. There are no minimum deposit requirements and no monthly service fee. There are no check writing privileges for this MMA account. The return on a savings accounts is 3.30 percent. It takes $1 to open an account. There are no minimum deposit requirements or monthly service fees.

- ✔ **ING Direct** (http://home.ingdirect.com) provides a checking account bearing 1.75 percent interest. There are no minimum deposit requirements or monthly service fees. ING Direct offers a savings account with a return of 2.26 percent. It costs $1 to open an account. No monthly minimum deposit is required and there are no monthly service fees. There are no check-writing privileges for this savings account.

- ✔ **Charles Schwab Bank** (www.schwabbank.com) supplies an interest-bearing checking account of 2.01 percent. It costs $1 to open an account. No minimum deposit requirements or maintenance fees.

- ✔ **UnivestDirect** (www.univestdirect.com) offers an interest-bearing checking account of 1.75 percent. $100 to open an account and no deposit minimums or monthly service fees. It offers a savings account with a return of 2.96 percent. It costs $1 to open a savings account. No minimum deposit is required, and there are no monthly service fees.

Remote banking and your cell phone

In the United States, online bank users have been slow to adopt remote banking. However, banks are beginning to use wireless banking to build customer loyalty and lower service costs. The economics of customers using wireless devices can't be ignored and are likely to force banks into offering wireless customer service, alerts, and other related services. Remote banking is a wireless delivery channel that can extend the reach and enhance the convenience of Internet banking. Remote banking occurs when customers access their account balances, holdings, and other status via a Web-enabled cell phone, personal digital assistant (PDA), or Blackberry. The following are a few banks that offer remote, wireless banking and alerts:

✔ **Citibank** (www.citibank.com) offers email and wireless alerts. It's a free service that delivers information about your deposit accounts and linked Citibank credit card accounts to your text or Web-enabled mobile device, email address, or both. You can set up alerts for your Citibank account balances, deposits, bill payments, checks, maturing CDs, and linked Citibank credit cards.

✔ **Wachovia** (www.wachovia.com) provides remote wireless banking services that let you bank from your cell phone. There are two ways to access your accounts from your mobile device. The first is a mobile browser (an Internet-enabled mobile device) that does not require any mobile banking enrollment. The second is a mobile banking application used through a supported mobile device. Both methods allow you to view account balances and transactions, make one-time transfers between eligible accounts, make one-time bill payments, and pay e-bills.

✔ **WaMu** (www.wamu.com) offers mobile text messaging with which you can review account balances and transaction histories and look for WaMu branches and ATMs on the go. You'll need a mobile phone that can send and receive text messages, enrollment in WaMu Online banking, and an eligible checking or savings account. WaMu Mobile Banking does not charge for the service. However, you may encounter some additional mobile phone carrier service fees.

Opening Your Online Bank Account

Many online banks require you to be 18 years or older and have a U.S. address, a Social Security number, a driver's license or state ID, and a second form of identification, such as a U.S. passport, military ID, or major bank or credit card. Some banks may ask for the address of your employer and may even check your credit history.

Using PayPal

According to the Federal Deposit Insurance Corporation (FDIC), PayPal (www.paypal.com) isn't a bank or savings association. PayPal is designed to only transfer money. The transfer is immediate and guaranteed. PayPal's security is the SSL, the same as used by banks. PayPal doesn't transfer funds unless the buyer has a credit line or the required amount needed to complete the transaction in his or her bank account.

PayPal is a peer-to-peer payment service that secures transactions when paying for goods and services via email. Basic PayPal accounts are free for consumers, with no hidden expenses or monthly fees. At this time, PayPal has about 100 million registered users in more than 55 countries. Transactions can be in six currencies: the euro, U.S., Canadian, and Australian dollars, the Bristish pound, and the yen. With PayPal, you can send money to anyone in the United States with an email address. You can also use PayPal on a Web-enabled cell phone.

When you enroll for a PayPal account, you need to add a funding source for your payments. For immediate payments, you need a credit card or debit card. You can also use PayPal Buyer Credit (click at the bottom of the home page for the online application) if you've already been approved. To pay for a purchase, click the Send Money tab and then enter the recipient's email address and the amount of your payment. Remember, you can fund your PayPal account using your PayPal balance, your U.S. checking account (which usually takes two or three days), or a credit card.

PayPal may become like a fifth credit card. Fearful of credit card fraud and identity theft, many online shoppers prefer using PayPal in place of credit cards to complete their online transactions. Consequently, PayPal plugs into e-commerce sites so that online shoppers can pay for purchases using Visa, MasterCard, American Express, Discover credit cards — and PayPal.

Go to the Web site of the bank of your choice. (You may want to check out the online banks listed earlier in this chapter.) Complete the online application form. For example, you may want to start with just a basic checking account, or you may want to open several different types of accounts (like an account for your college fund or a special vacation). After you complete the account application, you'll receive a new customer package usually within five business days (although some online banks can complete this process within the same day).

If your bank is in a different state, reread the fine print about fees and charges. Because of state banking regulations, the fee structure may be different than you expected. One easy way to get started is to open an online checking account with your current bank. Note that even if the branch office is just in the next block, you'll have to wait for the user identification number and password instructions to be sent to you via the U.S. mail.

If you encounter a problem downloading bank information to your personal finance program, you may be batted back and forth between your online bank and your software vendor. Don't let these organizations wear you down! If you're persistent, at some point everything will work out, and you won't ever have to worry about getting timely, accurate information again.

Chapter 3

Homeowner's Insurance

· ·

In This Chapter

▶ Understanding the six coverages universal to all homeowner's insurance policies

▶ Discovering how to choose limits for your home and its contents

▶ Finding out what you need to know before buying a homeowner's policy

▶ Using loss-reduction tips to lower risk and reduce premiums

· ·

*W*e consider homeowner's insurance policies to be outstanding values. They offer tremendous amounts of coverage for very few dollars. We also consider them to be the most dangerous personal policies you can buy because they contain the largest number of exclusions and limitations.

Therefore, it's critical when buying homeowner's insurance to identify what you're exposed to that falls outside the basic box of coverages. Then you can develop a strategy for avoiding, reducing, retaining, or transferring (via insurance) those exposures before you experience a serious uninsured loss.

When do most people find out they have inadequate insurance? At claim time, when the loss isn't covered!

Most people make the mistake of shopping for their insurance on price alone. They usually end up with a cheaper price for the wrong coverage.

To buy homeowner's insurance right, you must first understand something about the basic policy. In this chapter, we introduce you to the fundamentals of homeowner's insurance.

Introducing the Six Parts of a Homeowner's Policy

All homeowner's policies have six major coverage parts (except renter's policies, which have four). Table 3-1 presents these parts.

Table 3-1	The Six Major Coverage Parts of a Typical Homeowner's Policy
Type of Coverage	*What It Covers*
Coverage A	Damage to or destruction of your residence
Coverage B	Damage to or destruction of detached structures
Coverage C	Damage to, destruction of, or theft of personal property anywhere in the world
Coverage D	The added living costs you incur as a result of a loss covered by A, B, or C (lodging, meals, and utilities)
Coverage E	Personal liability (nonautomobile) for injuries and property damage at home and anywhere else worldwide
Coverage F	Medical payments to guests injured on your premises, regardless of any fault

Coverages A and B don't apply to renters. You find out about each of the six coverages, including some of the pitfalls to be careful of, in the rest of this chapter.

Insuring your residence (Coverage A)

If you arrange the coverage on your residence properly, the insurance company fully repairs or replaces your home if it is damaged or destroyed by a covered cause-of-loss — fire, tornado, or whatever your policy happens to cover. Be aware of two possible claims penalties for insuring your home for less than its full replacement cost.

The first penalty occurs if you are underinsured for a *total loss* — for the complete destruction of your home. Say the home you bought and insured for $275,000 burns to the ground. The cost to rebuild that house in today's market may be $350,000. Because you insured the house for $275,000, you suffer an out-of-pocket loss of $75,000.

The second penalty for underinsurance occurs when your home is partially damaged. Say you purchase a beautiful two-story, turn-of-the-century home. You insure it for the $250,000 you paid for it (the purchase price of $300,000 minus the $50,000 lot value). If you built this home new today, it could cost you $500,000. Assume that you have a kitchen fire with extensive smoke and water damage, and that the total cost to repair your home is $150,000. Your insurance company pays you $100,000. You're out $50,000!

Why? The vast majority of homeowner's policies pay the full cost to replace partial damage to your home only if you insure your home for at least 80 percent or more of the cost to rebuild new. If you insure your home for less than 80 percent of the home's full replacement cost, your claim settlement is depreciated. On older homes, that may reduce your claim settlement by 35 percent or more. In the earlier example, the cost to completely rebuild your 100-year-old home isn't the $250,000 you insured your home for, but $500,000. Because $250,000 is far less than 80 percent of $500,000, your settlement will be depreciated.

Translated into English from insurance-ese, the policy essentially says that if you insure your home for its depreciated market value (in this case, $250,000), the insurance company settles with you on a depreciated basis at claim time. The $50,000 penalty in the example represents the amount of depreciation deducted from the repair costs.

On the other hand, if you insure your home for its cost to build new (or at least 80 percent of that value, according to the formula in the policy), the insurance company settles your claim for the full replacement cost of the damage — up to your policy limit.

In short, if you insure for depreciated values, at claim time the insurance company deducts depreciation from repair costs. If you insure for the cost to rebuild, the insurance company pays the full repair costs at claim time.

Always insure for 100 percent of the estimated new replacement cost. Paying the extra premium is far easier than facing thousands of dollars in losses out-of-pocket at claim time from either not having enough insurance to rebuild if your home is destroyed or having your repair costs substantially depreciated on partial losses. And add a home replacement guarantee, if it's available — more on this addition later.

Insuring detached structures (Coverage B)

Virtually all homeowner's policies extend 10 percent of Coverage A — the residence coverage — to detached structures. In other words, if your home is insured for $200,000, you've got up to $20,000 worth of coverage for any detached structure. This feature is yours for no added charge. Example structures include garages, pole barns, and in-ground swimming pools. Always check your particular policy. This chapter is written with the average or typical policy in mind, but your policy may differ.

Excusing the exclusions

Why do homeowner's policies have so many property exclusions and limitations? One reason is fairness. Remember, insurance is just a mechanism by which people facing similar risks pool resources (pay premiums) into a large pot (the insurance company). Compensation for damages from fires, thefts, lawsuits, and so on is paid from that pot. Insurance companies don't pay claims, really. We do with our premiums. The insurer is simply a middleman. The company collects money from those of us who don't have losses and redistributes it to those who do.

People who share losses must be similar in the risks they face. That way, people with greater risks than the norm aren't being subsidized by people with normal residential risks. For example, people with vast amounts of jewelry have considerably more jewelry claims than the usual homeowner. If jewelry coverage were unrestricted in the policy, the rates for non–jewelry owners would go up every time the jewelry owner lost or had another piece stolen.

Contrary to public perception, then, these exclusions and limitations are not in the policy to be nasty. They exist primarily to make sure that the premiums are fair to all payers. For an additional charge, you can insure most of what is limited or excluded in the basic policy.

This coverage has two pitfalls, including the possibility of underinsurance if the structure can't be replaced for the 10 percent automatic coverage. The second pitfall is that, with most insurance companies, any structure used even partially for business is excluded. Here's an example from our own files that illustrates both pitfalls: Bob and Bobbie have a home insured for $150,000. They have a four-car, detached garage with an upstairs loft. If they built this garage new today, it would cost them $35,000. They have automatic coverage from the policy that covers their house in the amount of $15,000 (10 percent of $150,000). To be properly insured, they must buy an additional $20,000 of detached structure coverage, to bring their total coverage to $35,000.

Make sure your detached structure limit equals the total replacement value of all detached structures on your premises.

Continuing with our story, Bob is self-employed. He owns and manages several rental properties. Besides storing vehicles, his detached garage houses business equipment, like lawn mowers, snow blowers, and so on. In addition, his business office is located upstairs in the loft portion of the detached garage. Now, assume a tornado comes through and destroys his $35,000 garage. Because he bought the extra $20,000 coverage, he does have $35,000 of insurance. His adjuster shows up with a $35,000 check the next day, right? Wrong. Because Bob stored business equipment in that garage, the insurance company could deny his entire claim.

It certainly doesn't seem fair, but coverage works this way. The equipment had nothing to do with causing the destruction of the garage. Yet all the insurance company has to prove to deny the claim is that the garage was even partially used for business purposes. There's no requirement that the business in the garage must have had anything to do with the loss.

If you have a detached structure on your home premises that you even remotely use for business other than for storing business vehicles, and if your homeowner's policy excludes coverage if even partially used for business, you *must find out if your policy has this business use exclusion.* If so, you must request an endorsement to your homeowner's policy that permits that business use.

Before a serious loss happens, read your policy to know what is limited or excluded so that you can properly modify the policy to cover what is otherwise not covered.

Insuring your belongings (Coverage C)

Even renters need the next four coverages, starting with coverage on belongings. You can value personal belongings for insurance purposes in two ways — as used belongings, referred to in the policy as *actual cash value,* or as new, referred to as *replacement cost.*

Buy the replacement cost option! It's generally only about 10 percent more expensive, but you receive on average 30 to 40 percent more at claim time. If the total cost of replacing your belongings after a major loss was $100,000, with replacement value coverage, you would receive $100,000 minus your deductible. With actual cash value coverage, you would probably receive from $60,000 to $70,000, after deducting depreciation. Believe me, at claim time, you'll be glad you bought the better coverage.

The replacement value coverage stipulates that you actually replace the damaged or stolen property. Until you do replace it, the insurance company pays you only the depreciated or used value.

For residence owners, the basic homeowner's policy comes standard with personal property coverage of 50 to 75 percent of your Coverage A building limit. The exact percentage varies, depending on the insurance company. If you have a lot of high-end personal property, the automatic coverage the homeowner's policy provides may not be enough. Later in this chapter, we show you some tools to help estimate what your belongings are worth.

Continuing with the Bob and Bobbie example, in addition to the usual personal belongings, Bob owns $30,000 of mechanic's tools. (He's a former auto mechanic.) He maintains only his own vehicles with the tools, so they're not excluded under business-use provisions. Bob and Bobbie insure their home for $150,000, with a home replacement guarantee and replacement cost contents coverage. Their automatic contents limit is 70 percent of the $150,000, or $105,000. They feel they need the entire $105,000 to replace their normal household property. So to customize their policy to their unique needs, they purchase an additional $30,000 coverage for the tools, or a total of $135,000.

Be sure you evaluate the contents-coverage limit on your policy and customize it to your needs. Don't just take what comes automatically with your policy; it may not be enough.

Insuring additional living expenses (Coverage D)

Your house is blown away by a tornado. Your kitchen sink is in the next county. You check into a motel and call your insurance agent. You will need a place to live until you rebuild. You'll need to eat your meals out. You'll need a daily massage to soothe your shattered nerves. But you won't have much in the way of utility bills. And you won't be buying any groceries. Some of your living expenses will go way up. Others will shrink. The difference between the two expenses — the *additional living expense* — is covered by Coverage D, additional living expense coverage.

This helpful coverage pays the additional — not the total — expenses you have to incur for lodging, meals, utilities, and so on as a result of a covered loss, such as a fire, smoke, or windstorm, that causes you to vacate your home. It usually pays these costs up to the policy limit, if any, or for 12 months, whichever is exhausted first. With some insurers, the benefit is unlimited (always a plus). With others, the benefit is a percentage of the Coverage A building limit. Though higher limits are available, the odds of exhausting the base benefit are quite slim, so almost no one buys more. After all, can't Aunt Matilda put you up for a few weeks in her basement?

Insuring your personal liability (Coverage E)

The cost of coverage for your personal liability for injuries and property damage you cause represents a small part of your total homeowner's bill, but, in our opinion, it is just about the most important coverage in the policy. Why? Because it covers lawsuits — and the cost of defending against lawsuits. And it's so comprehensive, covering most of your nonvehicle personal liability worldwide. Consider some examples of claims Coverage E would cover:

- ✔ Your 6-year-old spills red punch on the neighbor's white carpet, which requires a $3,000 carpet replacement.

- ✔ You get sued by a neighbor who, in spite of your repeated warnings, has allowed his child to climb your fence and harass your German shepherd. The child gets mauled, and you get sued.

✔ Your riding lawn mower kicks up a rock into a neighbor and injures her.

✔ A child is hurt while you are baby-sitting her.

✔ In a baseball game, your teenage son throws errantly to home plate and hits another player in the face, causing a loss of vision. That player grows older, still suffers from a loss of vision, and sues five years later for $100,000.

✔ You hit someone in the face while playing racquetball.

✔ You are snowboarding and collide accidentally with a skier who sues for injuries.

✔ Playing golf, your errant tee shot hits a bystander in the head (happens all the time).

The bottom line? It's great coverage! Most homeowner's policies usually include the first $100,000 of personal liability coverage at no extra charge.

The two biggest mistakes people make with this personal liability coverage are not buying *more* than the $100,000 free coverage and not setting their liability limit to match their other liability policy limits (on cars, a cabin, or boats). To illustrate the latter, we often see people buy $100,000 homeowner's liability coverage, $300,000 automobile liability coverage, and $50,000 boat liability coverage. You don't know where the lawsuit may come from, so you want the same pool of money protecting you, no matter where it does come from. You wouldn't want different liability limits for different policies any more than you'd want different liability limits for different days of the week.

How much liability coverage should you buy? Here are some considerations:

✔ **Your suability factor:** The size of your bank account, your income, your future income, and your asset prospects (in other words, inheritances) affect how suable you are. In short, this factor represents how likely it is that an attorney for the person you injure will come after you personally if you don't have enough insurance.

✔ **Your comfort zone:** How high do you need the limits to go for your own peace of mind? Don't risk more than you can afford to lose.

✔ **Your sense of moral responsibility:** Many people with a modest income and few assets buy high liability limits, to be sure anyone they may hurt gets provided for.

✔ **The insurance cost of higher limits is minimal:** Additional liability insurance is truly one of the best values in the insurance business. An extra $200,000 costs only about $15 a year. And an extra $400,000 costs only about $25 a year. Never risk a lot for a little. Accepting the $100,000 basic limit and not having an extra $200,000 to $400,000 of lawsuit coverage, when the cost is $15 to $25 a year, clearly violates this principle. If you need to scrimp, do it where the potential pain is much less, such as an extra $250 added to your deductible. Your life won't be ruined if you have a higher homeowner's property damage deductible, but it may be if you owe hundreds of thousands of dollars when you lose a personal liability lawsuit that exceeds the limits of your coverage.

Another consideration in setting your liability limit is the economic value of the injury you cause. How much would you sue for if you were the one injured? Imagine yourself with a serious back injury caused by someone else. Imagine that you're at their house and you fall through a floorboard that they forgot to nail back into place. You're hospitalized for a while and undergo a couple surgeries. Then you need several years of medical care and rehabilitation. You are off work two or more years. Table 3-2 illustrates the economic value of your injury.

Table 3-2	Economic Value of an Injury
Type of Expense	*Expense*
Total medical bills	$125,000
Lost wages	$100,000
Years of pain and suffering	$250,000
Total	$475,000

Assume this is the judge's ruling: "I hereby award you the amount of your own homeowner's liability limit!" Now pull out your policy. Look at your liability limit. Could you live with that? Could you live with it if your injury resulted in your paralysis?

So how much liability coverage should you buy? Choose a liability limit that considers your current and future assets and income, feels emotionally comfortable, satisfies your sense of moral responsibility to others, and matches what you would expect if you were the one suing.

Don't dismiss the last point as trivial. A strong correlation exists between the amount you would sue for, based on your own financial position and expectations, and the amount someone else may sue you for, also based on your financial position. The bottom line? In our opinion, anyone with less than $500,000 liability coverage is underinsured. Most of us should have limits of $1 million or more.

Whatever limit you decide on, be sure to adjust your auto, boat, and personal liability limits to match.

Insuring guests' medical bills (Coverage F)

Coverage F is the sixth and final (and least important) homeowner's coverage part. This part does not act as health insurance for you or your family. Instead, it's what we call *good neighbor* coverage. If a guest gets hurt on your premises, even if the injury is caused by the person's own carelessness, this coverage pays her medical bills up to the coverage limit, usually $1,000.

You can increase the limit for an extra premium, but we say save your money. Most guests have health insurance already. If they are seriously hurt and sue, your liability coverage responds. Just be aware that you have this coverage if you have an injured guest. Like we said, it's good neighbor coverage.

Choosing the Right Homeowner's Property Coverages

Coverages A, B, C, and D of homeowner's policies cover property damage to your dwelling, detached structures and their contents, and any increase in living expenses related to property damage. Homeowner's policies are similar here. They differ in the kinds of losses they cover. All homeowner's policies cover damage from fire or a windstorm, for example. But only some policies cover water damage from cracked plumbing or toilet overflows. And no policy automatically covers damage from a flood or an earthquake, although you can purchase both coverages. To make a good decision when choosing the homeowner's policy best suited to your needs, you must understand your choices for which causes-of-loss are covered and which are not.

Understanding the causes-of-loss options

When you have a homeowner's claim for damage to your property, the first question is, "Was the cause of the damage covered by the policy?" If "yes," your claim is paid. If "no," your claim is denied. Most insurance companies offer three choices for the types of losses covered — the Basic Form, the Broad Form, and the Special Form.

- **Basic Form causes-of-loss:** Offers very limited coverage. Limited to a handful of covered causes-of-loss, including fire, wind, vandalism, and very limited theft. Rarely sold or purchased anymore.

✔ **Broad Form causes-of-loss:** Covers about 15 causes-of-loss, including the vast majority of the kinds of loss that damage a home or contents. If the cause of your loss is on the list, you're probably covered. If it isn't on the list, you're probably not covered.

✔ **Special Form causes-of-loss:** The best. Covers any accidental cause-of-loss unless that cause-of-loss is specifically excluded. (Damages from floods, groundwater, sewer backup, earthquakes, and a few other causes-of-loss aren't covered.)

Do not buy the Basic Form coverage. The coverage is way too restrictive. We like any of the choices that include the Broad Form coverage because most of your losses are covered. Our favorite is the Special Form because it puts you in the driver's seat. No matter how bizarre the cause, from Martian invasions to some kind of damage from new cybertechnology, your loss is covered.

Consider some example losses that the Broad Form list does not cover but that the Special Form does:

✔ Massive interior water damage from roof leaks to a townhouse. $30,000 paid.

✔ Interior damage to ceilings and walls caused by melting ice and snow that backed up under the shingles. Claims have averaged $4,000 to $10,000.

✔ Scorched counters or floors from hot pans dropped onto them. Claims to replace counters and floors run $5,000 or more.

✔ Paint spills on furniture. Average claim runs $2,000.

✔ Spills of any liquids on oriental rugs. Claims to replace the rug range from $600 to $20,000.

Probably the most unusual example we've heard of involved someone who took a month-long winter vacation in Florida. To keep the pipes from freezing back home in the cold North, they set their thermostat at 50 degrees. Shortly after they left home, the thermostat malfunctioned and never shut off. The combination of 90-degree heat and winter dryness warped all the floorboards in the house, requiring the entire flooring to be torn up and replaced. Most of the floor coverings — tile, carpet, and so on — which had to be removed to get at the floor, also had to be replaced. If that happened today, the claim cost could easily be in excess of $75,000.

Neither "thermostat malfunction" nor "excessive heat" is on the list of covered losses on the Broad Form. But the Special Form covered the loss in full because "thermostat malfunction" is not on the list of exclusions. The annual extra insurance cost for the Special Form over the Broad Form? Probably $75 a year. We'd say the homeowner with the faulty thermostat got his money's worth!

Introducing the six most common homeowner's policies

If you looked at a typical menu of homeowner's policies available from most insurance companies, you would see six entrees, from light fare to a full-course meal. One is designed specifically for renters, one specifically for townhouse or condominium owners, and the rest for owners of private residences.

Table 3-3 shows the six homeowner's forms most commonly used in the industry, the type of buyer they are designed for, and the causes-of-loss covered under each (Basic, Broad, or Special).

Table 3-3	The Six Homeowner's Policy Forms		
Type of Buyer	*Form #*	*Building Coverage*	*Contents Coverage*
Homeowner	1	Basic	Basic
Homeowner	2	Broad	Broad
Homeowner	3	Special	Broad*
Renter	4	N/A	Broad*
Homeowner	5	Special	Special
Townhouse or condo owner	6	Broad*	Broad*

*The Special Form is available as an option at additional cost.

To choose the best homeowner's form for you, first determine what type of buyer you are — homeowner, renter, or townhouse/condominium owner. Second, determine the causes-of-loss you want covered — Basic, Broad, or Special — for the building and again for the contents.

For example, if you rent, you would choose Homeowner's Form 4. It comes automatically with Broad Form coverage. You can buy the Special Form for an extra charge. If you're a homeowner and you want Special Form coverage on your structures but are comfortable with Broad Form coverage on your belongings, you would choose Homeowner's Form 3.

Which form do most insurers sell and 90 percent of homeowners buy? Form 3, covering buildings with the Special Form and contents with the Broad Form. The logic behind this decision is that the structure is the biggest property risk and is totally exposed to the elements, whereas most contents are more protected by being inside. It's a reasonable argument. We think Form 3 is a reasonable choice for most people.

If you have expensive personal belongings, fine arts, or expensive rugs, paintings, or antiques, or if you simply like having the best, Special Form contents coverage is the best choice for you. It's only about 10 percent more expensive than Broad Form coverage.

Here's how to get Special Form coverage for both your home and its contents:

- ✔ **If you own a home,** you have two choices: Buy a Homeowner's Form 5, if available, or buy a Form 3 and add a Special Perils contents endorsement.

- ✔ **If you own a townhouse or condo,** add a Special Perils endorsement to Coverage A (building coverage) and add a Special Perils contents endorsement.

- ✔ **If you rent,** add a Special Perils contents endorsement.

Establishing Property Coverage Limits

Insuring your home and contents properly to get the very best payout at claim time means insuring both for their full replacement cost. You have a pretty good idea of the market value of your home. But where do you find the replacement value? And how in the world do you compute the cost new of all your furniture, clothing, appliances, and other belongings without taking six months off from work and consuming a drawer full of pain relievers for all the headaches you will have?

You can use some tools to help you establish the approximate replacement cost of your building and contents.

Determining the replacement cost of your home

Most insurance companies and/or their agents estimate the replacement cost of your home by using a computer program designed for that purpose. But how can you be sure their estimate is accurate?

Insuring your home for its replacement cost is important to avoid serious penalties at claim time. But not spending more than you need to by overinsuring your home is important, too.

Perhaps the most accurate way to estimate your home's replacement cost is to spend $200 to $500 (or more) and have a professional appraisal done. But that strategy is tough on the budget. And it violates the KISS rule — to keep it simple, silly.

You have four alternatives to a professional appraisal that are quicker and far less costly and that still yield a pretty accurate replacement cost estimate. We recommend you use at least one to double-check your insurance company's estimate.

Double-check the agent's worksheet

Have the agent send you her worksheet. Make sure all the features and square footage are correct. Many times the information is not correct because of the difficulty of the computation process.

Use your home mortgage appraisal

If you've financed or refinanced your home recently, you paid for an appraisal. You're entitled to a copy. If you don't have a copy already, call your mortgage company and have it send you one. True, the appraisal is for market value, not cost new. But in almost all appraisals, the appraiser also lists the replacement cost. These numbers are typically conservative, so be sure your building insurance equals or exceeds the mortgage appraisal's replacement cost estimate.

For example, if the insurance agent calculates the cost, new, of your home at $278,000 and your bank appraisal estimated it at $262,000, you can be comfortable with the agent's number. But if your bank appraisal estimated the cost, new, at $175,000, we'd make an issue out of that big difference. If you send the agent your bank appraisal, we'll bet you can get her to adjust her number downward. Even if the agent has all the correct features and square footage, she still can err. Why? Because in the agent's replacement-cost computer program, one major criteria is judgment based — the quality of construction. A huge gap between your bank appraisal and the agent's estimate could mean that the agent misjudged the class or quality of construction of your home.

For what it's worth, we use our clients' bank appraisals constantly to check numbers and judgment. You're human and so is your agent.

Deduct the lot value from the market value

If your home is newer and you have a good idea of its current value, subtract from that amount the value of the lot and detached structures. You can get those values from your bank appraisal or from a good real estate agent.

Assume that the home was built four years ago at $245,000. Now, four years later, the cost new is somewhat larger. If the agent's replacement cost is $258,000, new, that seems reasonable. But if the agent's calculation is $205,000, it would have to be in error, since the cost to rebuild the home will never be less than the cost spent to build it four years ago.

If the agent's calculation is $378,000, and considering your four-year-old value of $245,000, the agent must have made an error. If you don't contest it, that $100,000-plus error will cost you $400 a year too much — $4,000 if you keep your home for ten years!

Use a builder

A builder who knows your neighborhood (or your builder, if you had your home built) can give you a rebuilding estimate on the basis of cost per square foot. Multiplying that cost per square foot by the number of square feet gives you an estimated cost to rebuild.

None of these four methods is precise, but any of them will give you some leverage in negotiations with the insurer. We've found that the larger and/or more customized your home is, especially if it's an older home, the more likely it is that the insurance company's estimate is wrong. Determining the replacement cost of your home is a difficult process but is definitely worth your time.

Guaranteeing you'll have enough insurance to rebuild

You've done your homework. You've double-checked your agent's replacement cost estimate and made appropriate coverage corrections. Suddenly, your home burns to the ground. You've insured your home for $258,000, but after the fire, the true cost to haul all the debris and rebuild is $292,000. You tried your best to buy the right coverage, but your out-of-pocket loss is $34,000! ($292,000 minus $258,000.) Good news! This problem has a great solution — an optional home-replacement guarantee usually called "Extended Replacement Cost" coverage.

There are usually three requirements you must comply with for the guarantee to be honored at claim time:

- You initially insure your home for 100 percent of its estimated replacement cost as determined by your agent or insurance company (with your input, of course).

✔ You agree to an inflation rider that annually adjusts your coverage limit by the construction cost index for new homes in your area and you pay the premium increase each year.

✔ You notify your insurer anytime you spend $5,000 or more in structural improvements and agree to the change in coverage and higher premium that results.

Be careful. Many people forget about the third requirement, which voids their guarantee. However, spending $5,000 or more is reportable only if it makes your home more expensive to rebuild new. Examples of expenditures that do not void your guarantee are replacing worn out items like roofs or heating and cooling equipment. Or cosmetic changes to your home that increase your enjoyment and probably increase the market value, but don't affect the replacement cost at all such as replacing kitchen cabinets or stripping off wallpaper and repainting walls with contemporary colors.

As a result of the lessons of Hurricane Andrew, many insurers have capped their home-replacement guarantee (usually 125 percent of your building coverage). Unlimited coverage is still available, though. We like the unlimited coverage option, especially if you have an older home for which the exact replacement cost is difficult to determine.

Not all homeowner's insurance companies offer this guarantee on older homes. We recommend you consider only insurance companies that do offer it.

When insuring your home, always double-check the insurance agent's replacement cost estimate so you don't overinsure your home and thus pay too much for your insurance. And always buy the optional home-replacement guarantee — without a cap, if possible.

Estimating the cost to replace belongings

The most accurate way to determine the cost of replacing all your belongings, of course, is to take a full inventory of *everything* that you own. No one does that. But three methods get you close enough, whether you own or rent.

The 200 percent method

We like this method and use it a lot because you can do it in 30 minutes or less (remember the KISS principle).

1. **Total the estimated new cost for all the major items in your home — furniture, stereo, TVs, appliances, computers, and so on.**

2. **Double the total.** Doing so ensures not only that you have enough coverage to replace all the major items you own, but also that you have an equal amount available for all the smaller items — clothing, dishes, linens, athletic equipment, seasonal and stored items, and so on.

3. **Add to that the values of any exceptional property or collections, artwork, tools, home workshops, and so on.**

Keep it fast and simple. Use your best guess on values. No catalogs or phone calls to stores, or it won't get done.

Remember Bob and Bobbie from earlier in the chapter? When they used this method to estimate the value of their belongings, they came up with a total of $43,000 for their major items (stereo, TV, furniture, and appliances.) Doubled, that came to $86,000. Then they added Bob's auto-mechanic tools, with a replacement cost of $35,000, for a total of $121,000. That's how much they have their possessions insured for.

The square-footage method

A leading property-appraisal firm furnishes the insurance industry with guides they developed by actually going to people's homes and apartments and physically adding up the replacement values of people's personal property and then relating those results to either the number of rooms or the total square feet. If your agent has this guide, he can help you estimate the average value of the belongings for a home or apartment your size. You can use your judgment to increase or decrease that average value.

The percent of building-value method (for homeowners only)

Oddly, the vast majority of homeowner's insurance buyers accept the amount of contents coverage that comes with their homeowner's policy (usually 70 percent of the building-coverage value). Why? Partly because it's easy, and partly because most people have no idea of the significant value of property they have accumulated over the years.

If you accept the percent of building-value method as a means of determining the amount of content coverage you have, make one modification. Inflate your contents limit by the value of any exceptional property: fine arts, collectibles, antiques, tools, and so on.

Don't accept as gospel the estimates of others when they value your property, and don't automatically accept the stock coverage that comes with your policy.

Choosing your deductible

The usual deductible that comes with a homeowner's policy is $250 per claim. Most insurers allow you to increase the deductible to $500, $1,000, or more, in exchange for a lower premium. When deciding how big a deductible to carry, use three criteria:

- ✔ How much can you comfortably afford, financially, out of cash reserves?

- ✔ How much can you emotionally afford? (If parting with that much of a deductible would bring on tears, it's too high.)

- ✔ How much premium credit are you receiving for taking the extra risk?

The average home property claim typically occurs once every seven to ten years. Pick the deductible that has a seven- or eight-year *payback period.* You determine that by dividing the extra risk of a higher deductible by the annual savings. If you can recoup, in premium savings, the added risk in eight years or less, pick the higher deductible. Remember, the payback period is the result of dividing the difference in deductibles by the difference in premiums.

Documenting Your Claim

Suppose your house burns to the ground, along with every shred of your belongings. Or suppose you come home to an empty house after that cheap "moving company" steals most of your furniture. What do you do?

"No problem," you say. "I read *Insurance For Dummies* and I bought all the right coverages: the replacement cost on building and contents, the home replacement guarantee, the special causes-of-loss form. I'm set."

The insurance adjuster comes to your door, and the first thing she does is compliment you on the brilliant design of your insurance coverage: "My, you have a wonderful insurance plan! How did you learn how to plug all those gaps in our insurance policy?" You grin and share your *For Dummies* secret. (She quickly calls her supervisor and urges the insurance company to buy up the remaining supply of books so that this scenario can't happen again.)

Her day is ruined. For once, she's cornered and has to pay the entire claim without penalty. Then a smile comes over her face as she remembers her secret weapon: Hidden in the fine print of the policy is the requirement that you have to prove what you lost, and that any property you forget to claim she won't have to pay you for. "You don't happen to have records of everything that you own, do you?" she asks. How would you respond? Don't feel bad. Few people have adequate documentation of their loss at the time of a major claim.

Loss-reduction tips

You can take some steps to reduce risk, reduce the chances of having a claim at all, and reduce the severity of any claim you do have. You can save on your insurance premiums by putting some of these tips into effect.

✔ Install an Underwriters Laboratories (UL)-approved smoke detector on each floor. Replace the batteries yearly (doing it on your birthday is an easy way to remember).

✔ Install a UL-approved dry-chemical fire extinguisher in the kitchen for grease fires. Check it periodically to make sure it's fully charged.

✔ Install deadbolt locks on all access doors.

✔ Install a motion detector alarm.

✔ Install a central burglar-and-fire alarm (the premium savings are huge for this one — 10 to 20 percent).

✔ Have your fireplace, flues, and chimney cleaned regularly to prevent chimney fires (and all the horrible interior smoke damage that results).

✔ If you want a wood stove, buy a UL-approved one and have it professionally installed.

Don't leave it unattended. Have it professionally cleaned annually.

✔ Change your locks immediately if your purse or keys are ever stolen.

✔ Install a sump pump system to prevent damage from groundwater, which is excluded by virtually every homeowner's policy. (Be sure to buy optional sump pump failure coverage.)

✔ Keep trees trimmed so they are safely away from the house.

✔ Keep walkways clear and safe.

✔ If you have a swimming pool, have an approved fence. Take out the diving board (where most injuries occur). Add a locking pool cover to prevent unauthorized use.

✔ Buy your kids membership to a health club that offers a supervised trampoline instead of buying a trampoline yourself, to avoid all the potential liability for injuries to the neighbor kids.

✔ Install a carbon monoxide detector.

Consider these easy ways of documenting your home and its contents. Keep these records off-premises so they aren't lost in a fire.

✔ Take photos of the exterior of the house and any detached structures.

✔ Take photos of any special structural features in the interior, like stone fireplaces, built-in buffets, custom woodwork, and so on.

✔ Have a photographic inventory of all your personal property. Take pictures of every cupboard and closet with the drawers open. Don't forget storage areas, the basement, and property in garages and other structures. (Photos can be video or digital. Either method is simple, cheap, and easy to update.)

✔ Keep your home blueprints, if you have any. They are wonderful for making sure you get exactly the house you had. (It wouldn't hurt to put a copy of your home appraisal with the blueprints.)

Without documentation, even great coverage won't get you an easy — or full — claim settlement.

Having photos, blueprints, and other documentation won't help at all if they burn up in the fire. So be sure to keep them off-premises.

Chapter 4

Auto Insurance Basics

. . . .

In This Chapter

▶ Reducing the risks of automobile ownership

▶ Determining the amount of lawsuit protection you need

▶ Protecting yourself from those who don't have enough insurance

▶ Deciding what deductible is right for you

. . . .

Americans have a love affair with cars — and we own more cars per capita than people anywhere else in the world. A good place to begin examining insurance risks, then, is to look at those associated with the ownership, maintenance, and use of our beloved *PTU* (personal transportation unit). Unless you walk around with a loaded gun in your pocket, an automobile represents the most dangerous device you own. In one split second, you can experience lawsuits, death, long-term disability, major medical expenses, and major property damage. Pretty scary stuff!

You can see why setting up a solid car insurance program is so important: Good insurance will keep you from suffering heavy financial losses following a serious car accident. We show you how to create a solid car insurance program in this chapter.

Managing Your Lawsuit Risks

Your personal automobile represents the single largest possible source of catastrophic lawsuits and legal judgments against you for major injuries, death, and property damage. Because of that, you need to be especially diligent in the strategies you adopt to manage this risk.

Reviewing noninsurance strategies

Before we show you how to best choose necessary insurance coverages, consider some proven noninsurance strategies that lower your risks — and often lower your insurance costs as well.

- ✔ Obey traffic laws, including the speed limit — laws designed to reduce both the frequency and severity of automobile accidents.

- ✔ Perform regular safety maintenance of your vehicle (brakes, tires, steering, lights).

- ✔ Purchase a safer vehicle that is highly rated for low damageability and passenger safety. (Go to the Insurance Institute for Highway Safety Web site www.iihs.org.)

- ✔ Pay extra for added safety features like additional air bags or antilock brakes.

- ✔ Always wear your seat belt and insist that your passengers do, too.

- ✔ Buy the highest-rated child safety seats and always use them.

- ✔ Take behind-the-wheel defensive-driving classes.

- ✔ Require your teenager to have at least 30 hours of practice behind the wheel on his permit under all sorts of driving conditions before you allow him to get a driver's license. No one can ever develop the skills needed to be a safe driver in just a few hours of mandatory driver's education.

- ✔ Allow your teenager to drive based on your determination of his or her ability to responsibly operate a car — *regardless* of when your state says your teenager can drive. A teen who behaves immaturely and irresponsibly out of a vehicle usually behaves in similar fashion inside a vehicle.

These examples are just a few ways to reduce your personal automobile risks.

Buying liability insurance

People who buy liability insurance that provides for their defense and pays legal judgments on their behalf frequently make two mistakes:

- ✔ They buy far too little coverage, not realizing the substantial amount of money involved in a death or an injury suit — in both the cost of a judgment and the costs to defend the case.

- ✔ They buy inconsistent limits ($100,000 on their car, $300,000 on their home, $50,000 on their boat, and so on), even though they are protecting the same income and monetary assets, not realizing the danger of inconsistent coverage.

In the preceding example, suppose you injure someone seriously with your car. You have only $100,000 of coverage, yet had the same injury occurred at home, you would have $300,000 of coverage. See how illogical that is? Your only hope for enough coverage in this scenario is to drag the victim's bleeding, unconscious body home, throw him down the stairs, and hope he doesn't remember the car accident!

"How much is enough liability insurance?" you may be asking. It depends on who the victim is. It also depends on how suable you are. I call this your *suability factor*. See the section titled "Knowing your suability factor," later in this chapter.

Understanding why who you hit matters

You're on your way to work. You're running behind schedule. You decide to run a yellow light. But just before you reach the intersection, it turns red. You slam on your brakes, but it's too late. You broadside another vehicle, right in the driver's door, seriously injuring the driver. The driver is taken to emergency care, undergoes surgery, and spends a month in the hospital. Following his release, the driver spends two years in rehabilitation, in and out of physical therapy, and misses two years of work. Table 4-1 shows hypothetical claim values for four different situations.

Table 4-1	Your Potential Liability			
Occupation	**Medical Bills**	**Lost Wages**	**Pain/ Suffering**	**Total Claim**
Teacher	$100,000	$60,000	$300,000	$460,000
Banker	$100,000	$120,000	$400,000	$620,000
Doctor	$100,000	$300,000	$500,000	$900,000
Baseball player	$100,000	$12 million	$10 million	$22.1 million

Pretty eye-opening, isn't it? Can you imagine what the numbers would be if the driver were killed or had a permanent disability with a lifetime loss of income? We're not trying to scare you, but we are trying to show you how vastly underinsured you may be for lawsuits. The most common liability limit we see when we review a prospective client's insurance is $100,000! That number is ridiculously low.

We're not suggesting that everyone rush out and buy $22 million or more in liability insurance. More than $5 million to $10 million is generally not even available. We *are* suggesting that you reevaluate your coverage limit based on a combination of this new awareness, the cost and availability of higher insurance limits, and how suable you are. See the next section, "Knowing your suability factor," to help you determine how suable you are. We suggest that you help pay for the increased insurance costs for higher liability limits by shifting premium dollars away from less-important coverages or by selecting higher deductibles on coverage for damage to your own vehicle.

Knowing your suability factor

We define *suability factor* (SF) as the probability of an injured party suing you for large sums — often for more than the amount of insurance you're carrying. For that to happen, you must be worth something, either currently or in the future. Why? Because if there's nothing to go after, no pot of gold at the end of the rainbow, many attorneys won't take the case and help an injured party sue you. Your SF is influenced by several elements. Table 4-2 shows four of those elements.

Table 4-2	Your Suability Factor
SF Elements	*Examples of People with a High Suability Factor*
Current income	Athlete, doctor, investment banker, lawyer, executive
Current assets	Successful retiree with high net worth
Future income	Medical intern, law student, MBA student
Future assets	Anyone with a potential inheritance

People with high current incomes or assets usually are aware of their suability. But people with little current income or few assets often overlook their future income or asset potential and the effect it has on their current suability.

The bottom line is that if you have one or more of these four elements contributing to a high SF, you are more apt to be sued for amounts greater than your insurance coverage, and you need higher liability limits on all your insurance policies. An added advantage of higher liability limits is that the closer your liability limit comes to the economic value of the injury you cause, the greater the likelihood that the injured party will settle for your insurance policy limit and not pursue you — personally — beyond that. Another variable in choosing a liability limit for many people is their sense of moral responsibility. For example, a person who is not very suable may buy a higher liability limit than they would otherwise need, to make sure that any fellow human being they injure is provided for financially. If you are one of these people, my hat goes off to you in admiration.

You may be wondering how much it costs to raise your liability coverage — well, it costs very little. We invite you to call your agent and find out for yourself. You'll be amazed! (Don't forget to raise all your liability limits on your other personal policies to the same limit as your car insurance.) Table 4-3 shows an example of fairly typical costs involved in raising liability coverage from $100,000 for two cars, a home, a cabin, and a boat. The numbers may vary, depending on the insurance company and the circumstances of the insured.

Table 4-3	Cost of Raising Liability Limits from $100,000
New Liability Limit	**Additional Annual Premium**
$300,000	$70
$500,000	$120
$1.5 million	$270
$2.5 million	$350
Each additional $1 million	$75

Note that coverage beyond $500,000 is sold in $1-million increments under a catastrophic excess policy commonly referred to as an *umbrella* policy.

When you look at what you're spending for the first $100,000 of coverage, you see that you can tremendously increase your catastrophic lawsuit coverage (not to mention your peace of mind) for just a small additional amount. Additional liability coverage is the best value in the insurance business.

Avoiding the danger of split liability limits

Insurance companies sell most liability coverage for homes, boats, recreational vehicles, and other personal policies as a single limit (such as $300,000) that applies to all injuries and property damage you cause in a single accident, no matter how many persons are injured or how much property is damaged. In other words, if you're in an accident, you have one pool of money to pay for all your liability. Liability coverage for car accidents is also available as a single limit, but just as commonly, it's sold with *split limits*.

With split limits automobile liability coverage, you select three limits. You select one *limit* — the maximum your policy pays — for injuries you cause to a single person. You select another limit for all injuries you cause in a single accident involving two or more people. And you select a third limit for all damage to property you cause in a single accident.

See Table 4-4 for examples of three of the most typical combinations of split limits.

Table 4-4	Typical Split Limits Policies Sold		
	Example 1	**Example 2**	**Example 3**
Injury limit per person	$50,000	$100,000	$250,000
Injury limit per accident	$100,000	$300,000	$500,000
Property damage limit per accident	$25,000	$50,000	$100,000

If you buy a single liability limit of $300,000 on your home, cabin, and boat policies, you should get the same $300,000 limit on your car insurance. If you request that limit from an agent selling only split limits, instead of a single limit of $300,000, the agent may suggest these split limits as an alternative:

- ✔ $100,000 per person for injuries you cause

- ✔ $300,000 per accident for injuries (two or more people injured)

- ✔ $50,000 per accident for all property damage you cause

The danger of buying split limits coverage is a false sense of security from the injury limit *per accident.* The limit you are actually most likely to exhaust in a car accident is the injury limit *per person.*

Suppose you buy the limits shown in the second column in Table 4-4. Your policy limits you to $100,000 per person and $300,000 per accident for injuries you cause. Here are some hypothetical injury claims, what a jury may award, and what your policy pays with those split limits.

- ✔ You rear-end a car ahead of you with only one occupant, resulting in injuries to the driver's neck and back. Jury award: $250,000. You have a $300,000 limit per accident for injuries, so you're fine, right? Well, your limit per person that you injure is $100,000, so you're out $150,000.

- ✔ You rear-end the same car, but with two occupants. Both have neck and back injuries, one more serious than the other. Jury awards: $200,000 to one, $50,000 to the other. You guessed it. The policy pays the full $50,000 for the person with less-serious injuries, but only $100,000 for the person with more-serious injuries. You're out $100,000 ($200,000 minus the $100,000 per person limit).

None of the scenarios involves catastrophic lawsuits, permanent serious injuries, or death. They are, in short, relatively ordinary. But look at what you would owe with split limits coverage!

In both accident examples, the total amount of jury awards is within the $300,000 per accident limit. But because the policy also has a per-person limit, the judgment costs you astronomical sums of money that you would not have owed if you had a $300,000 single limit coverage.

Don't forget about legal fees. Legal fees in an accident defense case can run $50,000, $100,000, or more. When you've used up your liability limit per accident, those legal costs come from your pocket. Every time you are sued for more than your policy limits, you receive a friendly letter from your insurance company (certified mail, of course) that tells you after your policy limits have been reached, you are on your own.

So how can you avoid the per-person pitfall of split limits coverage? Because the vast majority of car accidents involve cars occupied by only one person, we recommend one of three strategies:

- ✔ Select a per-person limit high enough to meet your lawsuit coverage needs for one person's injuries. In the two accident examples just given, for example, $250,000 to $500,000 of liability coverage per person would have saved you hundreds of thousands of dollars out of pocket for as little as $100 a year in additional insurance costs, if you're insuring two cars.

- ✔ Buy *single limit coverage* — one pool of money large enough to cover all injuries and property damage without a limit on the amount paid to any one person. This amount includes property damage, and any amount spent to pay for property damage reduces the amount left to pay for injuries, so be sure to buy a little extra coverage. Consider $300,000 to $500,000 as the least amount of coverage.

- ✔ Buy a second layer of liability insurance, called an *umbrella* policy, of $1 million or more.

Insuring Your Personal Injuries

Injuries, often quite serious ones, happen in car accidents far more than in any other type of accident — plane, train, industrial, and so on. If you are injured in a car accident, you usually have more than one source from which to collect your medical bills and lost wages. One source may be your own health and disability insurance. Another source may be the personal liability coverage of the other driver, if the accident was his fault and if he has any insurance. But the process of collecting from the other driver can take months or even years. A third source is your car insurance.

You have two types of coverage in a personal auto policy for your injuries in a car accident:

- ✔ Coverage for compensatory damages (what your injuries would be worth in a court, including compensation for pain and suffering) for your injuries caused by uninsured or underinsured motorists

- ✔ Coverage for your medical bills (and lost wages in some states) regardless of fault

We address them separately because we have different recommendations for each.

Understanding how uninsured and underinsured motorist coverage works

When you're injured in a car accident caused by the other driver, you can legally sue the other driver in most states to collect the fair value of your injury. If that driver has auto liability coverage, his policy pays you on his behalf, up to the liability policy limit he purchased. The economic value of your injury equals your out-of-pocket expenses plus compensation for your pain and suffering. But what if the other driver has no insurance? Or what if the insurance limit he has is less than the value of your injury? You can get a legal judgment against him and try to collect from him personally. But that can be an expensive, long, drawn-out process. Plus if he's not worth very much and has a limited income, you may not collect very much.

Fortunately, your own car insurance policy can solve the problem if you buy *uninsured motorist* and *underinsured motorist* coverage:

- ✔ **Uninsured motorist:** An at-fault driver who has no auto liability insurance at all or is not identifiable because he fled the scene (hit and run).
- ✔ **Underinsured motorist:** An at-fault driver who has less auto liability coverage than the economic value of your injury.

We see these two coverages as a form of *reverse liability,* in that you collect some or all of the economic value of your injuries caused by another driver from your own insurance company, almost as if they were the other driver's insurer. In short, uninsured and underinsured motorists coverages make up the gap between the other driver's liability coverage and the amount of liability coverage he would have needed to pay your claim in full.

How do the two coverages work? Say you're injured in a car accident by another driver who runs a stop sign. The economic value of your injury is $450,000. Further, assume that you bought $500,000 of both uninsured and underinsured motorist coverage under your own auto policy. For an underinsured motorist, first, you collect for your injury from the other driver's insurance in the amount of the other driver's liability limit — say, $100,000. Then you collect the balance of $350,000 from your own insurance company under your *under*insured motorist coverage. Had the other driver been without *any* insurance, you would have collected all $450,000 under your *un*insured motorist coverage.

Debunking some common myths

People often ask why they should have to pay extra premiums because other drivers either buy inadequate insurance coverage or have no insurance. It's not fair, true. However, if you buy the higher liability limits recommended in this chapter, the vast majority of other drivers are underinsured compared to your fine coverage. And because the process of collecting from the other driver any amounts over the other driver's insurance limits is laborious and expensive, the combination of uninsured and underinsured motorist coverage is the most effective way to make sure you have adequate funds available to properly compensate you for your injury — an injury you did not cause.

Book V

Protecting Your Money and Assets

You may object to the idea that the other driver (the underinsured) benefits from your good uninsured and underinsured motorist coverage by avoiding action against him for damages.

Even though it may seem like the other driver gets away without having to carry insurance, that's simply not true. The other driver is still held accountable. These two coverages just assure you that a pool of money is available to you, easily accessible and provided by your own insurance company. However, after you have been paid, you transfer your rights to sue the other party to your insurance company. The insurance company then has the right to pursue the other party's assets and income until it's fully reimbursed. By buying these two coverages, you are compensated much more easily and quickly, and you avoid the hassle and expense of chasing down the other driver for payment. You also avoid the risk that the other party may not have the resources to compensate you adequately for the damages caused in the accident.

You may think that by carrying uninsured and underinsured coverage, you're duplicating coverage that you have elsewhere, such as in your personal health and disability insurance — or even the medical coverage of a car insurance policy. To some degree, this assumption is true. If you are injured by another driver, you *can* collect for your medical bills and lost wages from some of the other policies you personally own. However, none of your other coverages compensates you for the economic value of your pain and suffering the other driver caused. You've got only three sources for that compensation:

- ✔ The other driver's automobile liability insurance
- ✔ The other driver's personal assets and income
- ✔ Your own uninsured and underinsured motorist coverage

Therefore, if you want to make certain that you have adequate coverage to compensate you for your potential pain and suffering, the *only* sure way is to buy these two coverages. Of course, this statement begs the question, "How much coverage should I buy?"

Our recommendation is to buy as much protection for your own injuries (as caused by another) as you buy to cover the injuries you yourself cause to someone else. In other words, buy the same uninsured and underinsured motorist coverage limits as you buy liability insurance limits, to the extent those coverages are available in your state. Why? Because you are worth every bit as much as a complete stranger whom you may injure. Cover yourself accordingly.

Preventing some dangerous mistakes

One of the most common mistakes people make when buying insurance is in the areas of uninsured and underinsured motorist coverage. They either buy one coverage without the other, buy lower limits than their auto liability limits, or buy inconsistent limits (a higher limit for one coverage than the other). The following list gives each of these pitfalls and what you're saying, in effect, if you make the mistake.

- **Buying uninsured and not underinsured coverage:** "I'm willing to bet that the other driver will have zero insurance. If I am injured by a driver with less insurance than he needs to pay for my injuries and no suable assets, I'm willing to not be compensated fully."

- **Buying less uninsured and underinsured coverage than you buy in liability coverage for injuries you cause to others:** "I sincerely believe my injuries and suffering are worth less than the injuries and suffering of someone I may hit."

- **Buying inconsistent uninsured and underinsured limits (for example, $300,000 uninsured and $50,000 underinsured):** "I'm willing to accept less compensation when injured by an underinsured driver than when I'm injured by an uninsured driver."

Clearly none of these assumptions makes any logical sense. It bears repeating: Buy uninsured and underinsured motorist coverage limits in equal amounts, and equal to the liability limits you buy.

Saving money on medical coverage

We've stressed the importance of buying high protection limits for injuries you cause, as well as for injuries caused to you. Both strategies increase your insurance costs. In this section and the next, "Dealing with Damage to Your Vehicle," we show you strategies that lower your costs and help you afford better coverage for the big stuff, like higher liability coverage. Coverage for your medical bills (and sometimes lost wages and *replacement services* — help around the home you have to hire) is generally offered by car insurance companies. Depending on your state's laws, this medical coverage generally comes in two flavors:

- **Medical payments** (Med Pay) coverage (plain vanilla)
- **Personal injury protection** (PIP) coverage (banana fudge supreme)

Both coverages are similar, in the sense that they pay your medical bills suffered in a car accident, regardless of fault, up to the limit you purchased. Personal injury protection has the added advantage (at a considerably greater cost) of also reimbursing you for some of your lost wages or replacement services. Some states even allow you (for an additional premium) to add together the medical coverage limits per car (called *stacking*) to cover a single injury. ($5,000 coverage per car × 3 cars on the policy = $15,000 total medical coverage for a single injury.)

Keep in mind three points when buying either coverage: First, check the law in your particular state. State laws on Med Pay or PIP coverages vary dramatically. Second, buy only as much medical-related coverage as the law requires. Medical and disability costs should be covered under other policies you have or definitely should have; therefore, having additional car insurance coverage is redundant. Third, buying additional coverage for your medical bills and/or lost wages from car accidents only is betting that those particular kinds of expenses will happen just from an auto accident.

Not buying more than minimum coverage limits for either Med Pay or PIP is an area in which you can save money on your insurance. To fully transfer the risks of medical payments and personal injury — not just those arising from car accidents, but also those from any illness or injury — you need major medical insurance and long-term disability insurance. Both types cover financial losses no matter how the losses are caused, rendering special insurance to cover the damages caused only by car accidents superfluous.

If you do not already have major medical and long-term disability coverage in your insurance portfolio, we urge you to consider adding both immediately.

Dealing with Damage to Your Vehicle

In this section, we discuss how to manage the risks of damage to your vehicle —fire, theft, collision, vandalism, glass breakage, and so on. Consider just a few examples of how to use noninsurance strategies to reduce risks:

- ✔ Carry an onboard fire extinguisher, to reduce the risk of a serious fire.

- ✔ Always lock your car and install a burglar alarm to reduce the theft risk.

- ✔ Park in a locked garage at home and always park in well-lit, nonisolated areas when away from home, to reduce both theft and vandalism risks.

- ✔ Drive a safe distance behind the vehicle ahead of you to reduce the risks of both glass breakage and collision. You can use the retaining strategy by either choosing higher deductibles or not buying damage insurance and paying all claims out of your own pocket.

Deductible psychology

Make sure you can emotionally afford a high deductible before you change your policy. A number of people choose higher deductibles but, when the loss occurs, shed tears when they actually have to part with the money. One well-to-do client could easily replace her new Jaguar out of petty cash but opts for the lowest deductibles the insurance company offers. She knows herself well enough to be aware that parting with *any* money at claim time would be emotionally traumatic.

Insurance for vehicle damage is usually offered in two parts:

- ✔ **Collision** coverage, covering damage from colliding with another object (for example, a vehicle, post, or curb), regardless of fault

- ✔ **Comprehensive** (also known as *other than collision*) coverage, covering most other kinds of accidental damage to the vehicle, such as fire, theft, vandalism, glass breakage, a run-in with a deer, wind, or hail

Both of these coverages are subject to a front-end copayment on your part, called a *deductible*. When buying either or both of these coverages, assume as much risk as you can afford, financially and emotionally, through electing higher deductibles — or possibly not purchasing these coverages. Keep in mind these points here:

- ✔ Make sure that the insurance company gives you enough of a price discount for taking the additional risk. We offer some guidelines for choosing the most cost-effective deductibles, as well as for determining the point at which dropping these coverages on an older car makes sense, later in this chapter.

- ✔ If you're on a tight budget but still need higher liability insurance limits to protect future assets or income (for example, if you're a student in medical school), it may make sense to carry higher deductibles even if the money to cover them isn't currently available. The savings often pays for most or all of the cost of the additional liability coverage you need.

  Incredibly, the savings for raising your collision coverage deductible by just $250 (from $250 to $500) is often enough to pay for an extra $200,000 of liability insurance. No matter how tight money is, coming up with another $250 to fix dents is far easier than coming up with $200,000 to cover lawsuits!

 If your driving record has deteriorated and your premiums are in danger of rising significantly with one more claim, we recommend very high deductibles, such as $1,000 or even $2,500. In all likelihood, you won't file a small claim — and risk higher rates — so why pay for something you're not going to use?

Choosing cost-effective deductibles

We estimate that the average client has a claim for damage to a vehicle every four or five years. Therefore, I advise clients to choose a higher deductible if the *extra risk* (the difference in deductibles) can be recouped via premium savings within a reasonable time (in other words, four to five years). The number of years it takes to recoup that added risk is called the *payback period.* The formula looks like this:

Payback period = the difference in deductibles ÷ the difference in annual premiums

If you're trying to figure out the most economical deductible, look at the hypothetical examples (Tables 4-5 through 4-8) to better understand how to determine the best deductible for you.

Table 4-5	A 3-Year-Old Lexus Coupe, Driven by a 47-Year-Old Female for Business	
	Collision	*Comprehensive*
Deductible	$250/$500/$1,000	$100/$250/$500
Extra risk (difference)	$250/$500	$150/$250
Annual premiums	$500/$400/$300	$250/$200/$150
Annual savings	$100/$100	$50/$50
Payback period (extra risk ÷ savings)	2.5 years/5 years	3 years/5 years

Here's an example of how to use a table:

Table 4-5 is an example of insurance costs for collision and comprehensive coverage for a 3-year-old Lexus driven by a 47-year-old female and used for business. Reading across from left to right, the first row, *Deductible,* shows the different deductible choices for both damage coverages. The second row, *Extra Risk,* shows the dollar amount of difference between each deductible (the extra dollar amount you will be at risk for if you choose a higher deductible). The third row, *Annual Premiums,* shows the annual insurance cost for each deductible. The fourth row, *Annual Savings,* shows the annual insurance cost savings if you choose the next-higher deductible. And the fifth row, *Payback Period,* represents the number of years it would take without a claim to save, through your reduced premiums, the amount of extra risk you would assume by opting for higher deductibles. The payback period is determined by dividing the extra deductible risk in row 2 by the annual insurance premium savings in row 4. If the payback period is less than four or five years, choosing the higher deductible makes good sense.

In Table 4-5, the extra risk from the second row to increase your collision coverage deductible from $250 to $500 is $250. The annual premium savings, from row 4, to make that change is $100. Dividing the $250 extra risk by the $100 annual savings gives you 2.5 years. Thus, if you go 2½ years without any claims, you save $250 on your insurance costs — the amount of the added risk you took by raising your deductible. Using the rule of choosing a higher deductible if the payback period is less than four or five years, it's clear that raising the deductible makes sense.

The payback period from the example in Table 4-5 — even for the highest deductibles — is only five years for collision and comprehensive coverages, making it logical to take the added risk for both coverages.

Table 4-6 shows a 5-year-old Honda that a 35-year-old male uses to commute to work. Although the premiums are less than they are for the more-expensive Lexus in Table 4-5, the extra risk of the higher deductibles can still be recaptured in five years and is still worth taking.

Table 4-6	A 5-Year-Old Honda Accord, Driven by a 35-Year-Old Male 10 Miles Each Way to Work	
	Collision	*Comprehensive*
Deductible	$250/$500/$1,000	$100/$250/$500
Extra risk (difference)	$250/$500	$150/$250
Annual premiums	$300/$200/$100	$150/$100/$50
Annual savings	$100/$100	$50/$50
Payback period (extra risk ÷ savings)	2.5 years/5 years	3 years/5 years

Table 4-7 shows an older Chevy driven by a 19-year-old with three recent speeding tickets whose rates are much higher because of both his age and his driving record.

Table 4-7	A 12-Year-Old Chevy Cavalier, Driven by a 19-Year-Old Male with Three Speeding Tickets	
	Collision	*Comprehensive*
Deductible	$250/$500/$1,000	$100/$250/$500
Extra risk (difference)	$250/$500	$150/$250
Annual premiums	$1,200/$1,000/$800	$600/$450/$300
Annual savings	$200/$200	$150/$150
Payback period (extra risk ÷ savings)	1.3 years/2.5 years	1 year/1.7 years

Clearly, with payback periods of 2.5 years or less for each deductible, this high-risk driver is better off with the highest deductibles possible. With three tickets, he won't be turning in small claims anyway because the insurance company may drop him. Would he be better off not carrying the coverages at all? See the section "Knowing when to drop collision and comprehensive coverage" for tips on making that call.

In Table 4-8, check out what happens to the insurance costs for this same Chevy if the 19-year-old sells the car to his 74-year-old granny who has never had a ticket in her life. The payback period for the highest deductibles far exceeds the four-to-five-year guideline. This driver would clearly be better off with low to midrange deductibles.

Table 4-8	The Same 12-Year-Old Chevy Cavalier, Driven by a 74-Year-Old Widow with a Clear Record	
	Collision	*Comprehensive*
Deductible	$250/$500/$1,000	$100/$250/$500
Extra risk (difference)	$250/$500	$150/$250
Annual premiums	$150/$100/$50	$75/$50/$30
Annual savings	$50/$50	$25/$20
Payback period (extra risk ÷ savings)	5 years/10 years	6 years/12.5 years

Knowing when to drop collision and comprehensive coverage

When deciding whether a vehicle's value has decreased enough to drop one or both of these vehicle damage coverages altogether, you apply the same four- to five-year payback guideline. The only difference is that the extra risk you're assuming is the full value of the vehicle (minus any salvage value collectible from a junkyard).

Assuming that an old Chevy has a junk value of $300 and would cost $2,500 to replace with an equivalent automobile, the net risk is $2,200 (the $2,500 value minus the $300 salvage value). Dividing the $2,200 risk by the collision and comprehensive premium gives you the payback period. Drop the coverage if the payback period is five years or less.

Evaluating Road Service and Car Rental Coverages

Other coverages most insurers offer are towing/road service coverage and loss of use/car rental coverage. We believe road-service coverage, though inexpensive, is better suited to automobile clubs like AAA, Amoco, and others. They are good at it, claims are paperless, and they offer a number of other vehicle services — all for a flat fee. On the other hand, the coverage under car insurance is usually not paperless — you must pay the claim first yourself (usually), then file a formal claim report, and wait two to three weeks for reimbursement. Coverage also is often limited to a dollar amount ($25, $50, $75, and so on). And a large number of these claims combined with other tickets and accidents can impair your relationship with your car insurance company. We've seen it happen several times.

Loss of use/car rental coverage is quite important. Everyone depends on a vehicle. If a collision or other covered loss deprives you of your car, you'll probably need a substitute. If your car is badly damaged or you have to wait out a parts delay, that car rental bill could be several hundred dollars out of your pocket. Loss of use covers the daily cost to rent a vehicle while yours is out of commission from a covered loss. Costs covered typically range from $10 to $50 per day for up to 30 days. We recommend buying at least a $30-per-day benefit.

There is another major benefit to loss-of-use coverage. Any delays by the claims adjuster in getting to your car, because she is either busy or slow, penalize the insurance company — not you — by increasing the cost of the claim. So it is to their advantage to see your car as quickly as possible. And the coverage saves you a lot of aggravation repair delays would otherwise cause you.

Chapter 5

Buying Life Insurance

. . . .

In This Chapter

▶ Determining how much life insurance you need

▶ Deciding between term and cash value insurance

▶ Buying life insurance smartly

▶ Debunking myths and avoiding mistakes

. . . .

*W*e buy life insurance because we love. We love spouses and children and others who depend on us financially. We love them enough to face the cold reality of death (after all, none of us gets out of here alive). We love them enough to acknowledge the possibility that we could die young, leaving loved ones suffering without our income. We love them enough to plunk down our hard-earned dollars for insurance that will make sure that if we do die early, our death will not burden them financially — house payments will be made, groceries will be on the table, and college dreams can be realized.

Assessing the Need

Life insurance isn't for everyone. Neither is car insurance. Both are excellent ideas and provide good coverage. But if no one would be hurt financially by your death, you wouldn't buy life insurance any more than you'd buy car insurance if you don't drive and don't own a car. Here's a look at some guidelines for who does and who doesn't need life insurance.

Who doesn't need life insurance

Two groups of people do *not* need life insurance:

▸ **Anyone who's financially well off enough that survivors can meet all their financial needs and obligations using existing financial resources, without the possibility of depleting those resources:** For example, if you're married with one teenage child, and you've managed to put away $1 million and pay off your house, you may not need life insurance. Existing resources can support your child through college and also give your spouse a cushion.

✓ **Anyone whose death won't cause a hardship to others:** For example, a married couple with no children who both earn a high enough income can easily support themselves if the other one dies. Another example is a single homeowner with a home mortgage and no dependents. If she has enough in savings to pay for final expenses and is okay with the mortgage company taking over the home if she dies, she doesn't need insurance.

Who does need life insurance

Two groups of people *do* need life insurance:

✓ **People with someone who depends on their income:** The classic example is a wage-earning parent: If he or she dies prematurely, the surviving family members will need the financial help that only life insurance offers. Other examples include an adult son paying the bills for his elderly mother's assisted-living apartment. Life insurance will make sure that she's taken care of. Likewise, a philanthropist with a favorite charity that relies on her generous annual gifts needs life insurance to keep those gifts coming indefinitely.

✓ **People who provide services that would need to be hired out in the event of their death:** The classic example is a stay-at-home mom. If she dies when her children are young, her spouse will suffer a financial loss. At the very least, he'll need money to pay for childcare. If he desires some sanity, he may want to hire household help as well. Over a ten-year span, childcare and occasional help around the house can cost $200,000 or more. Life insurance can make that outlay possible.

Also, as the surviving spouse, you may not want to work the same way if your stay-at-home spouse dies. You may want a different work schedule — fewer hours while your children are growing up. If you have more money, you can ask your employer for more flexible hours and less pay so that you can be the present parent. Life insurance can make that possible.

Another example of a person in the second group is an adult who takes care of his elderly father's home — cuts the lawn, paints, and does all the handyman chores. Hiring a service to do that if the son dies may cost $500 a month. The interest on $120,000 of life insurance can make sure that those services are provided to Dad as long as Dad stays in the house. And when Dad needs additional help, the $120,000 from the insurance policy can help pay his nursing home costs. As I said earlier, buying life insurance is an act of love.

Determining How Much Coverage You Need

If you die early, exactly how much money will your loved ones need? How much will it take to pay off debt? How much will it take to replace your income? Is providing funds to cover college costs for your children important, and, if so, how much money will that take? How do you account for inflation?

Looking at a hypothetical family

To give you a better feel for evaluating how much coverage you need, consider a hypothetical family: Flip and Jennifer and their three children — Michael, age 11; Molly, age 10; and Flip Jr., age 7. Flip is a 38-year-old systems engineer earning $70,000 a year. Jennifer, age 37, is a high school math teacher earning $50,000 a year.

If either one of them dies prematurely, Flip and Jennifer's goal is to have enough life insurance and other resources to enable the survivors to maintain the current status of living, to pay off all final expenses, and to pay for the cost of four years of college at the state university, which currently costs $30,000 per student ($7,500 a year). If their children want to attend a more-expensive school, they can either get a scholarship or pay the difference themselves.

Flip and Jennifer chose not to consider retirement because each of them has an excellent retirement plan at work.

Assessing liquid assets

Any stocks, bonds, or other liquid assets that Flip and Jennifer have can be used at death to meet financial obligations and reduce the amount of life insurance needed. Flip and Jennifer have $10,000 in cash, another $20,000 in liquid investments, $80,000 combined in 401(k) retirement accounts, and $75,000 in home equity.

We don't recommend using retirement money to cover today's needs, even in a situation as dire as the premature death of a spouse. The survivor will still need those funds at retirement. We also don't usually recommend using home equity, for two reasons. First, it's not very liquid; second, the surviving spouse will probably want to keep the house. If the couple have no life insurance, $30,000 is available for the survivors to live on — the current assets in cash and liquid investments. (We have many clients who prefer not to count the $30,000 and want to keep it instead for a family emergency fund — an excellent idea.) You never know what unexpected surprises lie ahead for your survivors, so err a little on the high side of what you think they will need.

Deducting "free" life insurance

Flip and Jennifer each have, through their jobs, employer-paid life insurance equal to one times their salary. That counts against any life insurance needs. They also buy supplemental group life insurance at work, which is not used for the calculation because, if you change jobs, it stays with the job. Plus, in most cases, you can buy it for less in the open market. Most often, personally acquired life insurance is both cheaper and better than supplemental group term insurance. Group insurance costs are greater than individual costs because the group often insures anyone, regardless of medical problems or smoking status.

Using the multiple of income method

Financial experts typically recommend that you have at least enough life insurance and liquid assets to equal five times your annual income, ignoring inflation, and seven to eight times your income factoring in inflation. If you have children, be safe and err on the side of too much. I recommend that you buy ten times your income. Why? Because term life insurance is cheap — especially for young families, when the need for life insurance is greatest.

When buying life insurance, aim high. For the people you love who survive you, too much is far better than too little.

Using the Web to estimate needs

The Internet offers several life insurance sites that help you estimate your life insurance needs. It is best to use a site that doesn't sell insurance, such as MSN Money. If you prefer to use such a tool rather than a multiple of income, have your most recent Social Security statement handy. You will be asked what the monthly survivor benefit will be.

When estimating those percentages for inflation and investment earnings, stay conservative. Don't use less than 4 percent for the assumed inflation rate — the percentage you expect the cost of living to rise each year. And use no more than 3 percent for the assumed interest rate — the percentage return you expect to earn on the life insurance proceeds being invested for your survivors' future needs.

Estimate your needs by using both the multiple of income method of this chapter and a credible, computerized estimate. Then compare the results and buy an insurance amount based on whichever method yields the higher recommended insurance amount.

Insuring homemakers

When you're estimating life insurance needs, overlooking or underestimating the economic value of a spouse who chooses to stay at home and care for the children is easy. After all, how *do* you determine the life insurance needs of a homemaker? You can't use the multiple of income method when the person doesn't have any income.

We have no ironclad rules for this decision. So much depends on the surviving spouse's preferences. How much cooking, cleaning, and laundry do you want to do when you get home from a hard day at work? Do you want to hire replacement care for your children in your own home, or do you prefer to haul them to a daycare provider? Do you want the freedom to work fewer hours and a more flexible schedule to be able to attend the special events in their lives?

When insuring a homemaker, buy enough insurance to give the surviving parent the option of paying for the nicest and least-stressful "replacement" — a full-time, in-home nanny. To determine the amount of life insurance needed to make that possible, check the prices of an in-home nanny service, including cooking, cleaning, and so on, plus driving the kids wherever they need to go. Then multiply that cost over the number of years needed and round up for inflation. Your losing a beloved spouse and your children losing a beloved parent is tough enough without adding extra financial or work-load stress to your lives.

And give the surviving spouse the economic freedom to choose if he wants to lighten his work schedule to be there more for the kids. One way to do that is to buy enough life insurance to both hire a nanny and pay off the mortgage and all other debt.

We don't recommend less than $250,000 to $500,000 coverage on a homemaker.

Speaking the Language

Before we look at the different types of life insurance and the best places to buy them, we need to cover a few definitions of insurance industry jargon. Some of the terms are used in the chapter, and some may be helpful when you buy your policy.

The *beneficiary* is the person or organization to whom the life insurance proceeds are payable at the death of the person insured. It could be a spouse, your children, a sibling, or a favorite charity. Every life insurance policy covering you — both policies you buy and policies at work — should name two beneficiaries: a primary beneficiary and a contingent beneficiary.

> ✔ A *primary beneficiary* is the person or organization to whom the life insurance proceeds are paid if that beneficiary is alive or in existence when you die.

✔ A *contingent beneficiary* is the person or organization to whom the life insurance proceeds are paid if the primary beneficiary is dead or no longer in existence. If no contingent beneficiary is named, the proceeds are paid to the estate of the primary beneficiary and are possibly subject to delays and additional taxes.

The *face amount* (also known as the *death benefit*) of a life insurance policy is the amount of money payable at the time of death. You can usually find the face amount on the first page of the policy (the *face* page).

The *owner* of a life insurance policy may or may not be the person whose life is insured. The owner is the person or organization who controls the policy, pays the bills, chooses the beneficiary, and so on. Consider these examples of when the owner is different from the person insured:

✔ A corporation owner insuring the life of a key scientist whose talents are vital to the company's survival

✔ A family trust owner insuring an aging parent to pay estate taxes due at death

✔ A parent insuring the life of a child to cover final expenses

Purchase options are options available with some policies that give the person insured the right to purchase additional coverage every few years, regardless of health. Coverage is guaranteed up to a certain amount per option. The options usually cease when the person is between ages 40 and 50.

For example, a couple, both 24, are engaged to be married and are planning to buy a home and have children in two to three years. They're both in good health. They don't want to spend a lot on life insurance that they don't need right now. They want to guarantee, while they're still healthy, that they can buy coverage later even if their health sours. They may buy starter policies for $50,000 coverage on each and add a purchase option that every three years gives them the right to buy an additional $50,000 of coverage, regardless of their health, their hobbies, or their increased size.

The *suicide clause* denies coverage for suicide during the first two years of the policy. After two years, suicide is fully covered.

Waiver of premium is an optional coverage that suspends your life insurance premium after you've been totally disabled for (usually) six months, until you are no longer disabled. It has two disadvantages: It's more expensive than personal disability coverage, and it won't normally pay if you can work part time. You may not need it if you have plenty of disability coverage and you've included your life insurance premium in your estimated coverage needs.

Understanding the Types of Life Insurance

After you've determined how much coverage you need, you need to decide where to buy it and which type of policy is best suited to your needs.

Really only two types of life insurance exist, although the two types come in many shapes, sizes, and colors. (We cover the variations of each type shortly.) The biggest difference between them is how long the coverage lasts.

- ✔ **Permanent life insurance** covers you for your entire life. Your death is certain. And when you die, it pays the death benefit.

- ✔ **Term life insurance** covers only a part of your lifetime. When that part or *term* ends, so does the coverage. It pays a death benefit only if you die within the designated term.

Here's a comparison of ideal use, pricing, and agent compensation for both types.

Ideal use

Permanent life insurance is ideally suited to permanent needs. Good examples are providing supplemental retirement dollars for a surviving spouse, covering estate taxes due upon your death, or paying final expenses — burial, legal costs, and so on. Term life insurance is ideally suited for covering life insurance needs that are not permanent. Good examples include covering a 20-year mortgage, college costs for children, or family income needs while the kids are growing up.

Pricing

Every life insurance policy has two core parts to its price: the *mortality cost* — determined by your odds of dying at that moment — and the *policy expense cost* — your share of insurance company expenses (rent, staff, and agent commissions). The mortality charge increases each year as you age and your risk of dying increases. The expense charge stays relatively constant.

Changing agent compensation

The current system of paying agents five to ten times more for the same death benefit to sell you permanent insurance instead of term insurance for the same coverage amount is flawed. Taking the time to help a client determine the proper amount of coverage and then shopping for the best deal, including completing and processing an application, is about a three- to five-hour proposition. Most term insurance commissions fall far short of paying for that effort. No one can succeed for long losing money on each sale.

One possible solution is to pay the agent well for either type of policy but to pay about the same dollar amount, regardless of which type of policy is sold. Then agents would have no incentive to recommend a permanent policy when term insurance is better.

The biggest single negative consequence to consumers of the current system is that young families with tight budgets who need the most protection they can afford are often sold permanent instead of term insurance and are almost always far underinsured. We guarantee that if a premature death leaves a young family struggling financially because the deceased was grossly underinsured with permanent insurance, the family won't care a lick about cash value.

Of the more than 300 young families we've had as clients over the years who had permanent life insurance in place when we met them, not a single one had nearly enough death protection to meet all the family's needs. We don't recall even one that was close to adequate. That's a tragedy.

Insurance companies should pay agents the same dollar amount of compensation for the same death benefit (that is, an agent would get paid the same $600 for selling a $250,000 ten-year level term policy or a $250,000 permanent policy). Doing so would take away all incentives to do anything other than what's best for the customer.

The impact of equalizing the commissions would be as follows:

✔ Term insurance costs would increase a little to cover the increased commissions.

✔ Permanent insurance costs would come down a little to reflect the reduced commissions.

✔ More term insurance would be sold because agents could finally afford to sell it and because they wouldn't be influenced anymore to sell permanent policies when term insurance is better.

✔ Young families would be much better protected — not only because term insurance costs less, but also because agents would get paid more only if they sold larger coverage amounts. The only negative to that system is that a family may have "too much" life insurance, and what a shame that would be. Instead of just getting by, the remaining parent and the kids would be able to live comfortably without fear of how they would make it. They could eat a little better, drive a little nicer car that wouldn't break down quite as often, and thank God every day for that agent who sold them a little more than they "needed." And for the parent who loved them enough to pay for it.

Most permanent life insurance policies have level premiums for life. How is that possible if the mortality charge increases each year? The insurance company averages the increasing mortality charges over your remaining expected life. In short, you overpay in the early years so that you can underpay in the later years. That overpayment in the early years is set aside in a reserve for you, called *cash value*. If you cancel a permanent policy, by law, you're entitled to the return of much of those overpayments — that cash value. The cash value is minimal in the first couple years because of heavy first-year costs — underwriting, medical exams, and agent commissions.

Term insurance costs, on the other hand, increase regularly as you age. Sometimes the increase is annual, and sometimes it's every five or ten years or more. Term insurance costs can be averaged over 10, 20, or even 30 years so the price is level for the entire term. However, term insurance does not have a cash value element. If you drop a term insurance policy in its early years, you receive no refund of any overpayment.

Agent commissions

Because term insurance has no cash value element, premiums in the first several years are considerably lower than permanent insurance premiums for the same death benefit. For example, a 30-year-old male nonsmoker may pay $200 the first year for $250,000 of term life insurance. He may pay $1,000 the first year for $250,000 of permanent life insurance. The agent selling the $200-per-year term life insurance policy typically makes $100 to $120 — often not enough to cover the costs of designing your plan and processing your application. The agent selling the $1,000-per-year permanent policy generally earns $700 to $1,000 or more — good compensation for three to five hours of work.

The practice of paying agents covering the same death benefit five to ten times more for selling a permanent policy than for selling a term policy leads to heavy pressure on agents to sell permanent insurance, especially if they would lose money by selling you a term policy. See the sidebar "Changing agent compensation" for more information.

Understanding the Variations of Permanent Life Insurance

All permanent policies have three components: mortality costs, expense charges, and cash value. Insurers offering permanent insurance compete in three ways: lowering mortality costs, lowering expense charges, and having better investment yield on the cash value.

Understanding life insurance dividends

Several life insurance companies that sell permanent life insurance policies offer what they call *dividends* to their policyholders.

Unlike dividends paid on common stock holdings, life insurance dividends are essentially a refund of premiums paid. In most cases, you've paid your premiums with after-tax dollars, so these premium refunds (the dividends) are tax-free to you.

How can some insurers pay dividends and others not? Companies that do pay dividends charge a little more on the front end — your premium. Then if they have a good year — their investments do well — they refund some or all of that overpayment to you in the form of a dividend. Note that dividends are not guaranteed, although they are very likely. If the insurance company has a worse-than-expected year, it can choose not to pay a dividend at all.

If you choose a permanent policy that pays dividends, you have four choices in how they are paid to you. You can leave them on deposit to earn interest, you can have them paid in cash and returned to you, you can apply them to reduce your premium, or you can buy *paid-up additions*. Paid-up additions are small increases in your life insurance coverage that are paid up for your lifetime. Your premiums don't increase, but when you die, your beneficiary gets your original death benefit, such as $100,000, plus the total of all paid-up additions paid for by the dividends, such as another $1,500 for a total of $101,500 paid to your beneficiary. For most people, using dividends to buy paid-up additions is the wisest of the four dividend options.

Permanent policies vary by whether they guarantee the following:

✔ Mortality and expense costs

✔ Yield on the cash value

Three types of permanent life insurance are on the market: whole life, universal life, and variable life. Every life insurance company offers hybrids of these three. See Table 5-1 for a quick overview of how they compare.

Table 5-1	Comparing Permanent Life Insurance Types		
	Whole Life	**Universal Life**	**Variable Life**
Mortality costs	Fixed	Variable	Fixed or variable
Expenses	Fixed	Variable	Fixed or variable
Cash value yield	Fixed	Variable	Variable
Investment risk to cash value	None	None	Yes

	Whole Life	*Universal Life*	*Variable Life*
Option to vary the premium	No	Yes	Usually
Option to change the death benefit amount	No	Yes	Usually
Option to vary or suspend premiums	No	Yes	Yes

Whole life

People who choose whole life insurance want a lifetime policy with zero risk. They want the insurance company to guarantee, for life, the monthly cost. If an epidemic breaks out, significantly killing off a large part of the population and raising mortality costs to the insurance company, this policy cost isn't affected at all. Conversely, if science reduces heart disease rates and cures cancer, lowering deaths and mortality costs, the insurance company reaps more profits because it continues to receive the higher, guaranteed mortality charges of the whole life policy.

The same is true for expense costs. If the insurance company's expenses rise because it buys a new building or pays agents higher commissions, it can't pass on those higher costs to the whole life customers. Similarly, if it improves efficiency and cuts costs, only the insurance company reaps the benefits.

Finally, a whole life policy pays a minimal but guaranteed rate of return — usually from $3^1/_2$ to $4^1/_2$ percent for life. So guaranteed, in fact, that the policy contains a page showing what the cash value will be for each year of the future. Today $4^1/_2$ percent guaranteed looks good. Twenty years ago, when interest rates were in the double digits, it looked horrible.

With a whole life policy, the insurance company takes all the risks. You take none. The insurance company bites the bullet when things sour and reaps extra profits when things improve. ***Note:*** If you buy a whole life policy that offers dividends, you share a little in good years and overpay in bad years. See the sidebar "Understanding life insurance dividends" for more information.

Universal life

In the 1980s, interest rates were rising to unexpectedly high levels, approaching 20 percent. Inflation was running rampant. Not only were the fixed rates of whole life insurance eliminating most new sales, but existing customers were dropping their old policies in droves as, one by one, insurance companies began to offer a more flexible policy called *universal life insurance,* offering flexible rather than fixed interest rates on the cash value. At that time, a 13 to 14 percent return was common. Universal life insurance later proved to be both good news and bad news for consumers.

The good news is that universal life insurance is a flexible product. Everything that's fixed and guaranteed in a whole life policy is flexible and not guaranteed. The risks of changes in mortality costs, expense costs, and interest rates are mostly passed on to the buyer. If costs decrease or interest rates rise, the customer reaps the benefit. If costs rise or interest rates plummet, primarily the customer takes the hit. The only risk the insurer takes is that the universal life policy has a ceiling on how high the mortality charges can go and a guaranteed minimum interest rate on the cash value — usually 4 to $4\frac{1}{2}$ percent.

What we like about a universal policy is its flexibility — not only its adaptability to changing market conditions, but also its flexibility with the death benefit. With whole life, if you want to raise your coverage, you have to take out an additional policy. With universal life, you can lower the death benefit at any time and keep the same policy. You also can raise the benefit anytime, if you can prove good health, without having to buy additional policies.

Another thing we like about a universal policy is the ability to vary premium payments: to lower them or even temporarily suspend them, such as during hard times, or to pay in additional amounts when the rate of return is attractive — especially considering that the earnings are tax sheltered (free of income tax until withdrawal). With universal life, you have the option at any time to dump large additional sums into the cash value account, subject to federal maximums.

Be careful not to dump in additional amounts if any penalties for withdrawal exist. If penalties are attached, usually it's best not to make the additional deposit.

Now the bad news. Universal life has one pitfall to be wary of, especially when interest rates are high. The sales illustration you receive estimates the amount of annual premium needed to be paid, assuming that the current (high) interest rate remains constant, to fund the policy for life. When interest rates are high, that estimated premium is low because higher interest earnings will defray some of the policy costs. But when interest rates drop significantly, as they have in recent years, the original estimated premium will be inadequate to fund the costs, and you'll be required to significantly increase your contribution or cancel the policy. What a nasty surprise.

If you want to be fairly safe from unexpected premium increases happening to you when you buy a universal life policy, choose a premium payment based on a very conservative interest rate. We recommend using the minimum guaranteed rate (that is, $4\frac{1}{2}$ percent). If you do, you should never have to pay higher premiums later.

Variable life

When attached to life insurance, the term *variable* means that customers have a half-dozen or more investment options with their cash value — including investing in the stock market. The good news with variable policies is that you have the potential to outperform what you would have earned under a nonvariable contract. The bad news, as with any stock market risk, is that you can lose part of your principal.

If you choose a variable policy, understand up front that if the cash value principal declines, you must make up the loss and pay increased premiums to fund the policy properly.

Cash value options when dropping permanent insurance

If you decide to cancel a permanent policy that has accumulated cash value, you have three options (called *nonforfeiture values*) for how to use that cash to your benefit:

- ✔ You can receive the cash value in cash.
- ✔ You can receive prepaid permanent insurance for life, for a reduced death benefit.
- ✔ You can receive term insurance for a certain length of time for the full death benefit.

Illustrating your choices

Assume the following scenario: You're a 43-year-old female. You own a $250,000 whole life policy that doesn't pay dividends. You've had the policy for ten years, for which you've paid $1,500 a year. You decide to drop the policy. Your cash value is $12,000. You can receive that sum in cash, but you have other options as well.

Given a $12,000 cash value and your age, your options may look like this:

- ✔ Prepaid permanent insurance of $35,000. You never pay another premium, and $35,000 is paid to your beneficiary whenever you die, now or 40 years from now.
- ✔ Extended term life insurance of $250,000 for 28 years and 6 months. Without ever paying another premium, you can continue your full $250,000 of protection until you're in your early 70s.

A fourth cash value option: Policy loans

A good way to access your cash value in a permanent insurance policy, especially when you need cash but want to continue the insurance, is to borrow against it with interest. "But it's my money," you protest. "Why can't I just pull it out? Why would I ever borrow it? And why would I have to pay interest for using my own money?"

Some permanent policies do allow you to access the cash by pulling it out. But in the first ten years or so, some surrender charges exist. If you've had the policy for a number of years, pulling out the cash value may cause some tax consequences. Borrowing from the funds has neither problem. A policy loan also has the psychological advantage of encouraging repayment, which is a good idea if you plan to keep the policy for life.

You do have to pay a modest interest charge — usually about 8 percent of the loan. But that is done only for two reasons: a) to cover the handling expenses and b) because while the money is in your hands, the insurance company still credits your policy with the policy guaranteed interest rate — usually $4\frac{1}{2}$ percent. So the true cost of the loan to you is only about 3 to 4 percent.

If you do take a policy loan, your death benefit is reduced by any unpaid balance. So if you have a $250,000 death benefit and have an outstanding policy loan for the $12,000 cash value at the time of your death, your beneficiary will receive $250,000 − $12,000 = $238,000. Whether to borrow your cash value or withdraw it outright is not an easy decision. Consult your agent for the pros and cons of both options before you decide.

Making the best choice

Continuing with the example, under what circumstances would you choose one option over the other? Here are a few pointers:

✔ Choose the $12,000 cash option when your need for life insurance has ended (that is, the kids are grown, the mortgage is paid, and you've become financially independent). Some people choose the cash option during hard times. If you're having financial difficulties but still need life insurance, here are two great options:

   • If you temporarily can't make the premium payments, the cash value can pay them until you're back on your feet.

   • If you simply need cash, you can borrow against the cash value via a policy loan at about a 3 to 4 percent net interest rate. (See the sidebar on policy loans in this chapter.)

✔ Choose the reduced, prepaid permanent insurance of $35,000 if your life insurance needs have diminished (the kids are grown, the mortgage is paid, and so on) but you still have life insurance needs, such as covering final expenses.

> ✔ Choose the extended term insurance option if you still need the full death benefit of $250,000 and either can't afford or don't want to pay any more premiums. Term insurance is a great option, especially if the need you're trying to cover with the insurance will end (for example, college costs and living expenses for your children) before the term insurance runs out.

Understanding the Variations of Term Life Insurance

Term life insurance contracts are differentiated based on the length of the coverage term, whether they can be renewed, the length of the price guarantee, and whether they can be converted to permanent insurance. Here we cover the three most common types of term life insurance.

Annual renewable term (ART)

Annual renewable term (ART) insurance is pay-as-you-go life insurance. Each year, you pay for your mortality costs for that 12-month period, plus expenses. On each 12-month anniversary, you're a year older, your mortality costs have increased slightly, and your premium increases slightly as well.

You can renew ART policies every year simply by paying the premium. The ability to renew could end, per the policy, in as few as ten years, but more typically it's guaranteed renewable until you're age 70 or even 100. Future prices are projected but normally not guaranteed for more than five or ten years. Premiums can increase; however, most policies do contain guaranteed maximum prices. If your health deteriorates, your future rates won't be affected, and normally you can *convert* (that is, exchange) the policy to a permanent policy anytime, without medical questions being asked.

Fixed-rate level term

Instead of annual price increases, as with annual renewal term insurance, level term policies allow you to lock in pricing for anywhere from 5 to 30 years in 5-year increments. The most common options are 10, 20, and 30 years.

The process of setting up new life insurance policies (administering medical exams, ordering doctor reports, and so on) is expensive. The insurance company can spread these expenses over a longer period by selling level term insurance policies because people keep the policies longer than they keep annual term policies. As a result, insurers compete harder and offer more competitive prices for level term policies than they do for annual renewable term products.

Most level term policies can be converted to permanent policies anytime, regardless of health (although some policies limit the conversion period to 15 years or so). Also, most can be renewed beyond the first term. Where level term policies differ most dramatically is in how that renewal happens and what happens to the price.

Never buy term life insurance that doesn't have an option to convert to permanent insurance, regardless of your health. You never know what the future may hold, so keep your options open.

Traditionally renewable level term

At the end of the first term, traditionally renewable level term policies renew for another period of the same length, without requiring you to requalify medically. The price changes on the renewal date, based on your age.

For example, assume that at age 30 you bought a 10-year traditional level term policy at preferred rates. On the renewal date 10 years later, you receive a bill offering to renew for another 10 years, only now at a preferred 40-year-old rate, without having to qualify medically and also at preferred rates.

Reentry renewable level term

Renewable level term insurance works exactly like traditional level term insurance in all respects except two. The premiums are about 40 percent less than traditional term insurance. And the renewal billing at the end of the original term is for your new attained age, but at sky-high rates that usually climb higher each year. Only if you're still healthy and can qualify medically (in other words, if you can reenter) can you reapply for the lowest preferred rates.

Because insurance companies aren't obligated to offer the lowest rates on renewal, reentry renewable level term policies are the lowest-priced term policies in the insurance market. The bad news is that their renewal price is the highest in the market if you're no longer in good health. This type of term life insurance is what we have recommended for years now for young families almost exclusively. So much more "bang for the buck."

If you decide to buy this type of product because of its great front-end price, give yourself a cushion. Buy it for a term of five to ten years longer than you think you'll need it to protect yourself (somewhat) from possible sky-high rates. And definitely don't use the product for a permanent need.

Mark's reentry story

Mark's $500,000, ten-year reentry term policy renews this month. Mark, who has exercised and eaten healthfully all his life, was diagnosed with cancer two years ago. Instead of the $2,000 renewal bill he would have qualified for if he were in good health, his renewal offer came in at $14,000 a year for the first year and increased about $1,000 a year thereafter.

Fortunately, Mark's policy includes a conversion option. The cost to convert to a permanent policy with cash value is only $8,500 a year. We say *only* because $8,500 is far less than $14,000, the premiums won't increase, and the permanent policy builds cash value. Mark pays $8,500 a year so that his daughter will get a $500,000 death benefit — given Mark's illness, that's a bargain. He couldn't find a new life insurance policy anywhere at any price. Even if he lives for ten more years, he'll pay $85,000 in premiums and his daughter's trust will receive $500,000. An easy decision!

Decreasing term

Decreasing term policies have coverage that reduces annually, but the premium stays level for the duration — usually 15 to 30 years. Two types of decreasing term policies exist:

- ✔ **Level decreasing term coverage** reduces coverage a flat amount each year (for example, a 25-year level decreasing term policy reduces 4 percent a year).

- ✔ **Mortgage decreasing term coverage** reduces to match a mortgage payoff. As with a mortgage, coverage reduces very slowly in the first few years and picks up steam in the later years. The rate of reduction is tied to the mortgage interest rate and the length of the mortgage. So if you buy a 10-year, 7 percent mortgage decreasing term policy, like the mortgage balance, coverage declines much faster than a 30-year, 9 percent mortgage decreasing term policy. The 10-year, 7 percent policy is also far less expensive than the 30-year, 9 percent policy.

The good news about either type of decreasing term policy is that the rates usually won't change for the duration of the term you choose. The bad news is that your life insurance coverage is reducing at a time when your living expenses are rising. Not a good idea. The other bad news is that your life insurance normally ends when the term ends — the policies aren't renewable. But in all likelihood, your need for life insurance hasn't ended. And the rates for this type of coverage aren't nearly as good as level reentry term rates for the same coverage period.

If you're thinking of buying a decreasing term policy, don't. Unless decreasing term life insurance coverage is court ordered (covering the mortgage of an ex-spouse and children) or mandatory as part of a loan, buy reentry level term instead of decreasing term. You get coverage that doesn't decrease and a much lower cost.

Insurance from your mortgage company

If you have a home mortgage, you probably receive offers in the mail for mortgage decreasing term insurance from the mortgage company. Buying the policy is tempting. You die; the mortgage gets paid. The price looks reasonable, and they can include the insurance premium with your house payment. What could be sweeter?

Buy it. Buy all that you can. But only if your health is bad, you're obese and a chain smoker, or you've been given six months to live. And only if coverage is automatic (no medical questions). In short, if you can't qualify for life insurance in the open market, buy all the mortgage decreasing term insurance you can get your hands on. If you're healthy, buy your insurance elsewhere. Here's why:

- ✔ Insurance from the mortgage company is almost always more expensive — often considerably more — than coverage you can buy privately.

- ✔ The coverage ends when you sell your home, whereas the same coverage purchased privately will not end. That point is important, especially if your health has soured.

- ✔ The beneficiary is the mortgage company, not your family. Never a good idea. Your spouse may not want to pay off the mortgage with the money, such as if she could earn 10 percent in a money market account and the mortgage rate is only 7 percent. (Not to mention the tax write-off of the mortgage interest!) Or something unexpected may have happened and she desperately needs the money for something more important.

 Be careful if the price from the mortgage company appears really attractive. A few years ago, an employee, Mary Jo, got an offer for mortgage insurance from her mortgage company. The rates were amazing, and she was thinking of buying it. The nice brochure gave several examples of dying: car accidents, plane crashes, falls from a roof, and so on. The brochure lacked only one piece of information — it failed to mention that it was *accident coverage only!* It included no coverage for death from natural causes — which is, even for young people, the cause of the vast majority of deaths.

Making Your Choice

Clearly, a potpourri of different types of life insurance are out there. How do you choose among them? Consider a few pointers:

✔ If you have a permanent need, buy permanent life insurance if you can afford it. If you need it but can't afford it, buy cheap reentry level term that's convertible to permanent, regardless of your health. A permanent need is a need that, no matter how old you are today, will require cash for your survivors when you die — paying estate taxes, supporting an adult child with Down's syndrome in a group home, continuing to support a favorite charity after your death, or providing supplemental lifetime income to a surviving spouse.

✔ If you have a nonpermanent need, buy term life insurance. Examples of nonpermanent needs include covering living expenses while the children are growing up, paying off a mortgage, and paying for the children's college education.

✔ Buy annual renewal term insurance if your need is pressing for only a year or two, but only if the price is less than that of a five-year reentry level term policy.

   Buy reentry level term if your need is great and your budget is small, such as if you're a parent with young children. However, make sure that you're clear on when the initial level term period ends. If you still need life insurance at that time, you may need to convert what you have into a much higher-priced permanent policy if you can't qualify medically for reentry. For that reason, we recommend that you buy reentry term insurance for a period of at least five to ten years longer than you think you'll need it. Also, because you want the company to be around when you convert, make sure that the quality of the insurance company is high. We suggest an A. M. Best rating of A or better. (A.M Best has been an independent rater of insurance companies for more than 100 years now. You can access its ratings at www.ambest.com.)

✔ For a small charge, some reentry term products offer a guarantee that, at the end of the first level term period, you can renew for another term at the low reentry rate, regardless of your health. Unless you're 100 percent sure that you won't need coverage beyond the first term, buy this option if it's available.

✔ Buy only guaranteed renewable and convertible term products. You never know what the future may hold.

✔ Buy traditional non-reentry level term coverage anytime you find its pricing reasonably close to reentry term costs, or if you're willing to pay extra for the peace of mind of keeping preferred rates without ever having to requalify.

- ✔ Unless the price is significantly lower, always buy privately owned term life insurance instead of group insurance through employers, associations, or creditors and banks. Coverage from the latter sources can end (such as coverage from your employer ending when you leave your job).

- ✔ Be very wary about buying decreasing term life insurance. Prices usually aren't that competitive, and coverage is normally not renewable. Plus, people's coverage needs rarely decrease.

Evaluating Life Insurance Sources

As you get inundated with life insurance solicitations, do you ever feel that the first thing astronauts will encounter when landing on Mars will be a coin-operated machine selling accidental space-death insurance? You'll find no shortage of places to buy life insurance out there.

After you have determined how much coverage you need and the type of policy — term or permanent — that best suits your needs, you can search out the best place to buy what you need.

Considering an agent

Permanent insurance is available almost exclusively from insurance agents. I recommend that you buy permanent insurance only from a top agent. Keep in mind that, because of its complexity and cash value element, permanent insurance requires added expertise in choosing among different products.

Buying term insurance is a completely different issue. Unlike almost any other kind of insurance, term insurance is close to a commodity. Term policies are the least-complex policies you can buy. The policy boils down to one sentence: "If you die, we pay." Unlike most other policies, term insurance policies don't have a lot of hidden exclusions, limitations, and other dangers, so buying it direct, without an agent, is less risky than buying any other policy direct.

However, using an agent doesn't cost that much more (if anything). We recommend using one, but separate the wheat from the chaff and pick only a skilled agent. Hiring the best won't cost you a dime more because all agents get paid about the same amount, determined by the premium you pay. A good agent can help you determine the right amount of coverage, determine the best type of term insurance product to use, set up the policy owner and beneficiary properly, and be an advocate for you if you're having problems with the insurance company. A top agent can also help you choose a financially solid company that will endure. Finally, if your application is rejected due to health, weight, or other problems, a good agent can help you search for a company that will insure you.

As for possible sources of agents, life insurance is available from career life insurance agents whose primary occupation is the sale of life insurance, from the agent who helps you with your auto and homeowner's insurance, and from many financial planners.

Career life insurance agents

The principal advantage of using a career life insurance agent is that life insurance is the agent's specialty. They tend to have a higher level of expertise, especially if they have more than five years in the business. Life insurance agents who have taken advanced classes and earned professional designations, such as the Chartered Life Underwriter (CLU), are especially good bets.

Be careful of inexperienced agents, especially if you have complex needs. Many don't last. The washout rate for life insurance agents is one of the highest of any profession — close to 90 percent in the first two years! Most new agents also have less expertise than experienced agents (unlike the rest of us, who were geniuses the first day on the job). In many states, a person can legally sell life insurance with just a week of schooling.

If you do work with a new agent and you have any concerns about what's being recommended to you, get a second opinion. If you decide to work with an agent, you may get a lot of pressure to buy permanent life insurance when you're asking for term life insurance. The dramatically higher commission that agents earn by selling permanent insurance compared to term insurance may be the reason. If the agent who's "helping" you insists that permanent insurance is your best option when your need isn't permanent, walking away from that agent may be your only option. But some real pros, who care about your welfare, may also believe that permanent insurance is the only way to go. After all, permanent insurance will always be there for you and your loved ones, as long as you pay the premiums.

We don't have a problem with buying permanent insurance, provided that you can afford the higher premiums for the coverage your survivors will need. What matters most isn't the type of policy you buy; it's that your survivors are well taken care of. The biggest problem we've seen, over and over, is that most young people who buy permanent instead of term end up underinsured.

Multiple policy agents

Many agents who sell auto and home insurance also have life insurance licenses. But less than half know much about life insurance or even actively sell it. And probably only 20 percent are quite knowledgeable about the subject.

If you like your current auto and homeowner's agent's skills in those areas but he is not an expert on life insurance, ask for a referral to a life insurance specialist. If your agent is good at his specialty, chances are excellent that the agent he refers you to will also be good. If your current agent is skilled with life insurance, working with him in that area, too, is to your advantage.

Having one agent for everything simplifies your life. And the washout rate on these multiple policy agents is very small.

If you prefer one agent to help you with all your insurance needs, include life insurance expertise on your agent-shopping list.

Financial planners

Two types of people licensed to sell life insurance fit the broad *financial planner* category. The first is money managers, who primarily dispense investment advice but also are licensed to sell life insurance. The second is career life agents, who also offer investments. The primary difference between the two is that the former more often recommend buying term life insurance with your investments separate, whereas the latter often recommend permanent life insurance with its cash value as a part of your investment portfolio.

If you're considering buying life insurance from a financial planner, a pretty safe bet is that planners who recommend term insurance for your nonpermanent needs are the better choice. Permanent insurance is not considered a good investment product. Buy permanent insurance if it's the best insurance for your needs, but don't buy it solely as an investment, for three reasons:

- Permanent life insurance is nonportable — if something better comes along, it's hard to move without a significant penalty.

- The mortality charges are usually higher than those charges for term insurance. To get a true reflection of the rate of return on the cash value of a permanent policy, you need to deduct the hidden costs of those extra mortality and expense charges. How? By shopping for the lowest term life policy, requesting that the agent disclose those same charges in the permanent, and then subtracting the difference between the two results from the cash value gain. What looks like a 6 percent rate of return on the cash value may, after deducting these hidden charges, may only be 4 percent.

- The heavy front-end cost of permanent insurance from the high sales commission significantly affects the cash value performances.

We're not advising you not to buy permanent life insurance. Just (as a rule) don't buy it as an investment.

Buying without an agent

If you're considering buying term life insurance direct from an 800 number or on the job, first check with your favorite agent to see if she can match the price. Most of the time, she can — in which case, use an agent. If your agent can't match the quote or come close, consider paying the agent a fee (perhaps $100) to review your plans and make sure that you're not shooting yourself in the foot. All the following sources of term life insurance allow you to buy without an agent:

- ✔ **The Internet:** Several sites are set up to comparison-shop term life insurance.

- ✔ **Creditors:** Banks, mortgage companies, and credit card companies regularly solicit their customers to buy *credit life insurance* from them to pay off any balance if the customer dies. Look at what they get! If you buy the insurance from your mortgage company, for example, it makes a nice up-front commission on the sale; later, if you die, it gets paid your outstanding balance. What a good deal (for them)!

But how good is the deal for you? Not very. Life insurance rates from creditors are usually much higher than rates on the open market. And the creditor — not your survivors — is the beneficiary. Unless your health makes you uninsurable through traditional life insurance sources, avoid obtaining insurance from your creditors.

A Christmas gift from a credit card company

We received an offer from my credit card company one December — apparently a Christmas present to its beloved cardholders. Here's what the form said: "Open Enrollment. My card balance paid in full if I die, up to $5,000; 5 percent of my card balance paid monthly if I'm disabled or unemployed more than 30 days. Cost: Only $0.59 per month per $100 of balance." If by chance we were crazy enough to turn down this offer, it requested refusal in writing. With a sentimental and grateful tear in my eye, we madly dashed to the phone to arrange for overnight express mail delivery when that dark inner Scrooge said, "Bah, humbug! How good a deal is 59 cents? Cheeseburgers, maybe. But credit card insurance?"

Let's see — 59 cents per $100 per month is $70 per year per $1,000 of card balance. Life insurance costs between $1 and $5 per $1,000 for most age groups. That leaves about $65 for the disability and unemployment insurance, which pays only 5 percent of the balance monthly. So that's worth another $5 to $10 a year per $1,000 of balance. Expenses would run another $5,

which leaves $45. What's left? "Profit," you say? Oh, ye of little faith!

You're overlooking one important item: "Open Enrollment," which means that you qualify *regardless of health!* So this offer is really one for the "near-dead." It's the card company's way of saying thanks to you on your way out. Yes, Virginia, there is a Santa Claus! Suppose you have six months to live. The creditor apparently wants you to get ten of these cards, buy card insurance on each, and run each up to the $5,000 limit with cruises, vacations, cars, and the like. That's $50,000 of fun for 59 cents per $100 per month, or about $300 per month. Six months later, you're gone. The debt is wiped clean. You've enjoyed $50,000 of fun for only $1,800! Can you think of a more generous offer? (And you were skeptical! Aren't you ashamed?)

You ask, "Wouldn't it have been easier to just say 'Don't buy credit card insurance unless you're uninsurable or near death' instead of telling this tongue-in-cheek tale?" Of course! But saying that isn't nearly as much fun.

✔ **Associations:** A lot of groups and associations offer term life insurance as a membership benefit. Sometimes the price is fantastic. Most of the time, the price is mediocre. The problem is that if you leave the association or the association stops offering the coverage, you lose your life insurance.

As a general rule, don't buy life insurance from an association; however, do buy as much as you can if you're uninsurable and the insurer asks no medical questions.

✔ **Group life:** First, let us say, "Take all the free life insurance your employer offers you." Second, if (and only if) your health is poor and you can't qualify for other types of life insurance, buy all the supplemental life insurance your employer offers on a nonmedical basis. (Sometimes that can be $50,000 or more.) Third, if you're healthy, don't buy any more than the free coverage paid for by your employer through work. Buy it privately. Why? Two reasons: You lose group insurance when you leave the job, and the rates are almost always higher than rates on the open market if you're in good health.

✔ **Direct mail and telemarketing phone solicitations:** Again, unless they offer guaranteed coverage and you're otherwise uninsurable, stay away from direct mail and 800 number sources. Most have a fly-by-night feel. Plus, they rarely offer prices that can compete with prices you can get in the market if you're healthy.

✔ **Slot machines:** We mean those coin-operated flight insurance dispensers at airports and similar dispensers of "fear insurance." Unless you know ahead of time that the plane is going down, don't buy this stuff. (Or better yet, don't take the flight!) But *do* listen to your fear. It's telling you that you feel inadequately insured. Act on that fear and raise your life insurance coverage to a high-enough level that you can comfortably walk by these machines (with a smile) the next time you fly.

Debunking Myths and Mistakes

All kinds of half-truths, myths, and common mistakes are associated with buying insurance. In this section, we show you the most common ones so that you can avoid falling into any traps.

Mistake: Trading cash value for death protection needs

Being underinsured with permanent life insurance may be the biggest single mistake that people make in buying life insurance. They get swayed by the lure of the investment portion or cash value of the policy but can't afford to have their cake and eat it, too. In other words, they can't afford to pay for all the death protection they need plus the investment, so they buy a cash value policy with less death protection than they need, in order to have some investment — something to show for it in the end when they don't (unlike the rest of us) die. However, when they do die, their family doesn't have enough money to live on, creating a serious financial problem.

The most important part of life insurance is the protection. Determine how much life insurance you need by using a credible method. Then buy as much of that protection as you can afford, using term insurance — even lower-cost reentry products, if necessary. If your budget has something left over, and you have solid coverage in every other major loss area — major medical bills, long-term disability, major lawsuits, and the destruction of your home — only then is it okay to look at permanent life products for part of your coverage. Never trade critical protection for less-important investment opportunities.

Myth: Supplemental group life is cheaper

Group insurance pools healthy and unhealthy people. Group insurance rates are, therefore, cheaper only if you're uninsurable or if the employer pays all or part of the premium.

Before buying optional coverage at work, compare the coverage with what the open market has to offer. Chances are, you will do as well or better on your own, plus you can keep the policy when you leave the job.

Mistake: Buying life insurance in pieces

Buying your life insurance in pieces is a lot more expensive than covering all your needs in one policy. Plus, buying in pieces leaves you vulnerable to a gap in your coverage. Examples of piecemeal buying are having mortgage insurance through your lending institution, credit card insurance through your credit card company, credit life insurance with your car loan, supplemental group life insurance at work, flight insurance at the airport, and so on. With some of these insurances, you don't have to qualify medically; therefore, if you're in poor health or near death, buy all you can. Otherwise, they're often three or four times the price of what you would pay if you're in good health.

Besides the higher prices, the concern I have about buying life insurance in pieces is that you take care of only part of the risk, leaving a lot of needs unprotected. Using the piecemeal approach, you could buy a little grocery life insurance so that when you die, your family's groceries will be paid for. (The supermarket could offer it at the checkout.) Or insurance on your utility bills. If you die or become disabled, your survivors wouldn't have to pay utilities for a year or two.

When buying life insurance, figure out how much insurance you need to do the whole job and buy *one* policy.

Mistake: Accidental death/travel coverage

Both accidental death and travel accident policies are varieties of Las Vegas insurance, transferring only the accidental portion of your risk. In other words, you have no coverage for death from natural causes. Buying these policies is an especially bad move if you buy them in lieu of the full life insurance you really need. Our belief about travel accidental death coverage is that anyone who buys it at the airport or from a travel agent is really saying, "I'm not comfortable with the amount of life insurance I have." The bottom line is that if you need insurance to cover a flight you're taking, you also need it for a drive down the street, potential heart attacks, and the like.

When buying life insurance, buy only coverage that pays for any death — natural or accidental.

Mistake: Covering only one income

Covering only one income in a marriage is a serious mistake. If your household has two incomes and you depend on both of them, don't just cover one income (unless you have a crystal ball). One income may be larger than the other, but if the person with the lesser income dies and the surviving spouse can't make it on his or her income alone, you have a problem.

When buying life insurance in a marriage, always insure both incomes unless the person with the larger income brings home enough pay to completely support himself or herself and the second income is just gravy.

Mistake: Ignoring a homemaker's value

If one spouse stays home with the children and takes care of the home (cleaning, doing the shopping, and so on), that person has a real economic value to the household because a lot of those services would have to be hired out in the event of death. Many couples overlook insuring the homemaker because no outside income is being brought in. Big mistake.

Buy life insurance on a homemaker. Estimate the amount of coverage you need by determining the cost to hire someone to perform the same tasks that the homemaker does. Multiply that by the number of years you need help, and then add in money for an emergency fund, college fund, and so on. (Also consider funds for longer vacations and shortened workdays for the surviving spouse.) We recommend at least $250,000 to $500,000.

Mistake: Covering children not parents

When Johnny or Susie is born, you try to be a responsible parent. You're deluged with a lot of solicitations about life insurance because of the birth announcement in the paper. You have hopes and dreams for your children, so you buy a nice cash value policy on your baby. It's understandable — you're proud. But the economic effect on the family of a child's death is minimal compared to the impact that one of the baby's parents dying would have.

When a child is born, seriously reevaluate and raise the amount of life insurance coverage that Mom and Dad have.

Mistake: Decreasing term insurance

Decreasing term life insurance generally gives you level premiums for a period of years, with the protection amount decreasing each year. This type of policy is often used with mortgage insurance so that it decreases as the mortgage decreases. At first glance, going with a decreasing policy to cover a decreasing mortgage seems to make sense. And if that's the only life insurance need that you have, perhaps that is a logical solution to the problem. But most people have many other life insurance needs. When some expenses are decreasing in your life, others are increasing, thanks to inflation.

Don't buy decreasing term insurance. Instead, buy the cheapest reentry level term insurance you find. The coverage won't decrease. The cost will be significantly less than the cost of decreasing term. If you need less coverage down the road, you can always decrease your reentry level term life insurance coverage simply by exchanging it for a lesser policy.

Mistake: Being unrealistic about how much life insurance you can afford

Young people often commit more money than they can actually afford to a large cash value life insurance policy and then two or three years later drop it and take a large financial loss — and perhaps even be exposed to the risk of a death without insurance. We recommend term insurance for young families. It provides the most coverage for the money. If you want a permanent policy later with more bells and whistles, you can always convert your term policy.

Mistake: Buying before you need it

Many single people have expensive cash value life insurance years before anyone in their life would suffer financially by their death. Remember that you wouldn't buy car insurance if you didn't own a car. Don't buy life insurance unless someone depends on you financially.

Myth: It's cheaper when you're young

Life insurance really is cheaper when you're young. So are dentures, but you don't buy them until you need them, either. This myth started because the *annual* cost of life insurance is cheaper *per year* when you're young because your chances of dying are lower. But the *total* cost that you pay over the life of the policy is not cheaper! How could it be? Suppose that you buy life insurance for $100 a year at age 25 and your friend waits until age 35 and has to pay $110 a year for the same coverage. Now you're both 35 and you pay $10 less per year — but how about the $1,000 that you paid for the ten years you didn't need it? Plus interest? Don't buy life insurance until you need it.

Chapter 6

Dealing with the Tax Man

. . . .

In This Chapter

▶ Filing federal and state taxes

▶ Figuring out deductions

▶ Avoiding mistakes and dealing with audits

▶ Paying penalties and interest

▶ Getting help

. . . .

*I*n this chapter, you find out what you need to know about filing and payment deadlines, ways to pay (and ways not to), how to pay only what you
should and not more, and how to sidestep some of the most common mistakes (the source of most audits). If you do have a problem with the IRS, you
can consult this chapter for how best to deal with them and what options
may be available to minimize penalties and interest. Finally, you get tips on
what to do if you find yourself in hot water with the IRS — what they can, and
can't, do to collect what they're owed.

Filing Federal Taxes

April 15 is drawing near, and you're in a panic. You owe income taxes to
Uncle Sam, but you don't have enough money in your bank account to pay.
What to do, what to do? Here's what *not* to do: Don't bury your head in the
sand! It'll cost you, big time!

At the very least, file your tax return on time, or file IRS Form 4868,
"Application for Automatic Extension to File," which gives you until October
15 to get your return to the IRS. You can download the extension request
form at www.irs.gov/pub/irs-pdf/f4868.pdf, order it by calling 800-
829-3767, or pick it up at your local IRS office.

An extension to file your tax return is *not* an extension to pay your taxes. Taxes are due on April 15, come hell or high water, and the IRS begins charging interest and penalties on your unpaid taxes on April 16 (as we explain in the next section). For this reason, paying some of your taxes on April 15 is better than paying nothing. The more you pay, the less your tax debt will grow because of interest and penalties.

If you don't have enough money in your bank account to pay all the taxes you owe by April 15, you may want to consider using one of the following options to get them paid. Each of these options can be costly, so try to avoid them unless all your other options are worse. Consulting a tax specialist, such as a CPA, enrolled agent (someone licensed by the U.S. Department of the Treasury as a tax specialist, commonly referred to as an EA), or other financial advisor about these options is also a good idea.

- ✔ **Pay with plastic.** You have to pay a fee of about 2.5 percent on the amount that you charge to the IRS. And, of course, if you don't pay the full amount of your tax debt when you receive your account statement, you pay interest to the credit card company.

  Don't assume that you can pay your taxes with a credit card, declare bankruptcy, and make the debt disappear. If you file for bankruptcy before you've paid off your tax-related credit card debt, the bankruptcy court treats the debt exactly the same way it would treat your taxes if they were still outstanding. In other words, if the taxes would be dischargeable in bankruptcy, you'll be able to use bankruptcy to get the credit card debt discharged. However, if the taxes cannot be discharged in bankruptcy, you cannot use bankruptcy to get rid of that portion of your credit card debt.

- ✔ **Use a credit card convenience check.** This option is relatively expensive because you probably have to pay a fee to the credit card company for the privilege of using the convenience check. Plus, if you can't pay off the amount of the check right away, interest accrues.

- ✔ **Borrow against your home equity.** The good news is that the interest you pay on the borrowed money is probably tax deductible. The bad news is that if you can't repay the borrowed money, you may lose your home.

A professional advisor may suggest that you're better served paying what you owe in installments to the IRS than paying installments to your credit card company. An advisor may even recommend that you try to settle your debt for less than the full amount through an Offer in Compromise. We discuss both of these payment options later in this chapter.

Filing State Taxes

Most states rely on some form of income tax to fund their expenditures. And, in most cases, those tax returns are reasonably easy to prepare because they *piggyback* on your federal return, using either the adjusted gross income you've calculated on your Form 1040, 1040A, or 1040EZ as a jumping-off point, or the federal taxable income. From either of those points, you may add some items of income not taxable for federal purposes, subtract others, and do some other math calculations to arrive at your state's taxable income.

Some states (Colorado, Illinois, Indiana, Massachusetts, Michigan, Pennsylvania, and Utah) apply a flat income tax rate; others use a graduated scale. State income tax rates are almost always lower than the corresponding federal taxes, but many states begin taxing amounts that are lower than the federal thresholds, or don't allow as much for deductions or exemptions. You may find that you owe state income taxes even though you don't owe anything to the IRS.

Of course, not every state follows the so-called *piggyback* model in income taxation. Massachusetts, for example, requires that you start at square one on Form 1. And New Hampshire and Tennessee tax only dividends and interest, not wages, rents, or capital gains. Still other states have no personal income tax: Alaska, Florida, Nevada, South Dakota, Texas, Washington, and Wyoming.

What may make preparing your state income tax returns a bit tricky is that certain items of income that are taxable on your federal return aren't taxable on your state return. These items primarily include interest earned from U.S. Treasury obligations (U.S. Treasury bonds, notes, and bills, as well as some Federal Home Loan Bank and Federal Farm Loan Bank obligations [which are bought and sold just like other government bonds], but not any federally backed mortgage obligations, such as GNMA or FNMA).

Other items that aren't taxable on your federal return are taxable on your state return, such as tax-exempt interest earned on municipal bonds from other states. So, if you live in Vermont and own a New York municipal bond, you won't pay income tax to the IRS on the interest, but you will pay tax to Vermont. Remember, though, municipal bonds from Puerto Rico, the U.S. Virgin Islands, American Samoa, and any other U.S. possession or territory are tax-exempt not only federally, but also in every state.

If you live in one state for the entire year and you only own real estate or business interests (including pieces of real estate or closely held businesses that may be owned by a partnership, tenancy-in-common, or even a Subchapter "S" Corporation) located in that state, you have to file an income tax return in only one state. But if you own a rental property in another state, participate in a business that operates across state lines, or live in one state and work in another, you have *nonresident source income* and must file a tax return in (and pay tax to, if you have enough income) a second state. Likewise, if you moved partway through the year from one state to another, you need to file state returns in each state where you lived and earned money. Don't worry that you'll end up overpaying your taxes. Every state gives credit for taxes paid to other states, so you end up paying tax in each state only on either your income while you were living there or the income derived from sources inside that state. If you're required to file multiple state returns, you may want to consult a qualified tax advisor; calculating which state is owed what tax can sometimes get pretty confusing.

Coming Up with Deductions

One of the most misunderstood areas of income taxation is the fact that the government allows you to deduct certain expenses from your income before calculating the taxes you owe. Most people find the greatest benefit in using the so-called *standard deduction,* which the IRS adjusts yearly for inflation. However, many taxpayers shortchange themselves by failing to itemize their deductions. Whether they find the task of compiling the information too daunting or feel that attaching a Schedule A to their Form 1040 presents a red audit flag to the IRS, it's hard to tell. But itemizing your deductions may reduce your tax burden substantially — as long as the expenses you're listing are legitimate and you can back them up with solid information, there's no reason you should neglect to take them.

Collecting and maintaining good records is essential if you're going to itemize, but it doesn't have to be difficult. Create a file or other sort of container at the beginning of each tax year. As you receive any receipts for deductible expenses, throw them in the file or box. At the end of the year, simply sort them into Schedule A categories. When you've finished preparing your return, keep those receipts clipped, stapled, or otherwise attached to the copy of the return you're keeping.

Among the deductions you can take, if you qualify, are the following:

- ✔ **Medical expenses** (above 7.5 percent of your adjusted gross income): This category includes not just doctors' and hospitals' fees and prescriptions; you can also deduct certain travel costs, certain education costs for learning-disabled children, wigs for chemotherapy patients, guide dog expenses, and even a clarinet lesson (to alleviate severe teeth malocclusion). The list is quite extensive; as long as you're not being reimbursed for these costs by your insurance company or paying for any of these costs using pretax dollars, you may include them in your calculations. Obtain and keep receipts every time you spend any money for medical purposes, to prove your deduction.

✔ **Home mortgage interest:** You can deduct only interest on your first and second residences, and you must actually live there. The bank or mortgage company that you make your monthly mortgage payments to will provide you with Form 1098, which is an annual statement of the interest you paid.

✔ **Certain state and local taxes:** These taxes include state and local income taxes, real estate taxes, and taxes on personal property, such as car excise taxes. Remember, for a payment to qualify as a tax, it must be based on an underlying value of property. So if you pay an excise tax to register your car based on the car's value, that tax is deductible. On the other hand, if you pay a set fee for those registration costs, that's a fee and isn't deductible. Keep copies of receipted tax bills; those receipts, together with your bank or credit card statements showing the payments you made, provide adequate proof of the deduction.

✔ **Charitable contributions:** You're entitled to take an income tax deduction when you give money or property to a charitable organization, or otherwise segregate it for charitable use by funding a charitable foundation or other type of charitable trust. You can't just give stuff away, though, and then expect the IRS to allow your deduction; you must keep very good records. You must have receipts from all organizations you've donated to for any single donation worth $250 or more. For donations worth $249 or less, a credit card receipt, canceled check, other bank notation, payroll stub showing a payroll deduction, or receipt from the organization qualifies as proof for the IRS.

✔ **Casualty losses:** When the unthinkable happens, and your house burns or is blown away by a hurricane or tornado, you're entitled to some tax relief. Unless your personal disaster is located in a federally declared disaster area, you can deduct on Schedule A any amounts of loss in excess of 10 percent of your adjusted gross income plus $100. Of course, when your former house is now a pile of rubble on a foundation, finding adequate proof of your deduction can be difficult. Be sure to take plenty of pictures of the aftermath, and search among family and friends (if you don't have pictures and other information already stashed in a secure location) for "before" pictures. Although the IRS likes as much backup as possible to support your deduction, it's generally not heartless; as long as you make a reasonable effort to re-create your cost in the property and the extent of your loss, the IRS will likely accept it.

✔ **Miscellaneous itemized deductions:** Most of these costs, such as tax-preparation fees, safe-deposit box rentals, union dues, and investment advice, are deductible, but you must subtract 2 percent of your adjusted gross income from the total for this category when calculating your deduction. Certain miscellaneous itemized deductions aren't subject to this 2 percent haircut: gambling losses (limited to the extent that you have gambling winnings, so be sure to save all those losing scratch tickets), deductions for estate taxes paid, and excess deductions you may be eligible to use when an estate terminates.

Choosing not to itemize when you would benefit from doing so only hurts you. If you're hesitating because you've never itemized or you think you'll become audit bait, think again. For the most part, as long as itemized deductions fall within reasonably generous ranges for your income level and location, they aren't scrutinized particularly closely. Even if the IRS does send you a letter requesting proof for a certain deduction you've claimed, don't worry. Remember, you needed that to claim the deduction in the first place.

Avoiding Tax Mistakes

Given the complexity of the tax code, you may think that the most common errors on tax returns are the result of misconstruing some esoteric tax law or regulation. You'd be wrong — writing down an incorrect number, or failing to include a number that should be there, is the single most common fault found on any income tax return, whether you've transposed numbers on your Social Security number, placed a state tax refund on the capital gains line, or made a transposition error (written *45* instead of *54,* for example).

Among the simplest ways to make sure your tax return is free of mistakes are the following:

- ✔ **File electronically.** The IRS computers spit out any return whose numbers don't add to or match the information in their files (including matching your name to your Social Security number), so you'll know that the numbers on your return aren't sending up any red flags if your return is accepted for electronic filing.

- ✔ **Use the peel-off label from the IRS.** If the information is correct on the label, and you're filing a paper return, don't reinvent the wheel. Use the label provided.

- ✔ **If you've changed your name because of marriage or divorce, notify the Social Security Administration.** File a new Form SS-5 with the Social Security Administration as soon as possible, and then be sure to notify your employer, as well as any banks or brokerages where you hold accounts.

- ✔ **Enter all Social Security numbers for yourself, your spouse, and any dependents, and enter only one filing status and the correct exemption amount on your return.**

  Staple one copy of Form W-2, "Wage and Tax Statement," to your return if any federal income taxes have been withheld from your income. If you had taxes withheld from any other sources, such as dividends and interest, unemployment compensation, or Social Security or other retirement benefits, attach a copy of the Form 1099 showing the withheld amount to the face of your return.

✔ **Do the math correctly.** Nothing is more embarrassing than having the IRS send you a notice telling you that you can't add and subtract.

✔ **Double-check your tax calculation.** Whether you're preparing a Schedule D computation (to calculate using maximum capital gains and qualified dividend rates) or relying on either the tax tables or the tax charts, do the math at least twice before you write down the final number.

✔ **Make sure that you're showing at least as much income on your return as people have reported to you.** Every little piece of paper that you receive in January that comes to you from banks, brokerages, your employer, the state, businesses in which you own an interest, Social Security, your pension and IRA trustees, the local casino, or even your next door neighbor, who paid you to mow the lawn weekly, is also reported to the IRS. The IRS is expecting to see those numbers on your income tax return. If they're not all there, you can expect a notice from the IRS, together with a bill for unpaid taxes on the missing amounts, usually between 6 and 12 months after the return was due. If some of those amounts don't really belong to you, show them on your return anyway, and then show the name and Social Security number of the person who's really responsible for paying the tax on it.

✔ **Don't forget to sign and date your return.** If you're filing a joint return, don't forget to have your spouse sign, too. A return that's correct in every respect will still be rejected if no valid signature and date appear on the bottom. And a rejected return is an unfiled return. Although you may have sent the return on time, by the time the IRS notifies you that you forgot to sign, it's probably well after April 15. Now, not only is your face red because you forgot to put your John Hancock on the bottom line, but you'll also have to pay penalties for late filing. Ouch!

Facing the Dreaded Audit

For many, being audited may be more frightening than being arrested. But *audit* doesn't have to be a dirty word, and if you are chosen, the process shouldn't be more painful than a root canal without anesthesia. In addition to the tips listed previously in "Avoiding Tax Mistakes," consider a few more items when trying to avoid that dreaded audit:

✔ **Declare all your income.** You're not allowed to pick and choose what income you think you should be taxed on. If it's income, it's taxable.

✔ **File your return on time (as extended, if necessary).** Even if you're not in a position to pay what you owe when you file your return, file the return anyway. Despite the fact that it's receiving millions of tax returns, the IRS will eventually catch on to the fact that yours isn't there and will chase you for it. Far better to be up front about your inability to pay than to pretend that the problem just doesn't exist.

✔ **Avoid displaying champagne tastes if your declared income supports only a beer budget.** IRS agents are people with eyes and will wonder if they see a tiny amount of income showing on your return while you're living in a mansion and driving a Mercedes. Although, conceivably, some people manage to balance legitimately small incomes with larger-than-life lifestyles, the life you lead tends to march hand in hand with the amount of money you earn from whatever sources. A vast discrepancy between the two only raises a lot of red flags.

Of course, people will do a lot to avoid having their return selected for audit, even if it means failing to take deductions to which they're entitled. Remember, paying more than you have to in tax is an expensive price to pay for limiting your exposure to the IRS. And, strange though it may seem, it doesn't necessarily make you audit-proof, either. Here we list some of the legitimate tax breaks and techniques that some people ignore, in an effort to avoid audit:

✔ **Filing for an extension of time to file:** Millions of people do file for permission to take more time to file their tax returns, and it doesn't make them any more likely to be audited than people who file by April 15 every year. Whether you don't receive all your information in time, your tax preparer decides to decamp to Fiji in early April, you're sick and can't seem to pull together everything you need in time, or your spouse is out of town on that fateful day and you can't get his or her signature, you can file for an automatic six-month extension of time on Form 4868, "Application for Automatic Extension of Time to File U.S. Individual Income Tax Return." Just remember that an extension of time to file isn't an extension of time to pay; make sure you pay what you think you owe by April 15, or be prepared to pay some additional money to the IRS in the form of penalties and interest.

✔ **Itemizing your deductions:** Many people support the mistaken belief that, because everyone is entitled to the standard deduction, a return that uses it won't ever be selected for audit. But at what cost? If you have more deductions, whether from medical, mortgage interest, taxes, charitable contributions, casualty losses, or miscellaneous than the standard deduction available to you, fill out Schedule A and deduct the full amount you're entitled to. Even if the IRS later asks you to back up your claims, don't worry. Just be sure to hang on to the receipts, bank records, or other proof of your claim.

✔ **Taking all the business expenses you're entitled to on Schedule C when you own your own small, unincorporated business.** The IRS does look at this area closely, but that doesn't mean you should limit the amounts you're legally able to deduct from your income. Take all the deductions to which you're entitled, and make sure you keep good records to buttress your claims, including the following:

- **Deducting depreciation:** Many people don't understand *depreciation,* or deducting the cost of a business asset, such as a computer, furniture, or fixtures, over the course of its useful economic life. But even if you don't actually deduct your depreciation on your income tax return, these assets still depreciate, and the IRS will deem that you deducted the allowable amounts, even if you didn't.

- **Failing to show a profit:** Businesses often don't make money, especially when they're first established or when the general economy hits hard times. And business losses are deductible on your income tax return. Just because your business has a loss in a particular year doesn't mean you'll be audited. Take advantage of that loss to reduce other taxes, or apply it to either a past or future year's income; both techniques are allowed. Just be aware that if you fail to show a profit in at least three out of five years, the IRS may decide that you're actually engaging in a hobby, not a business. You can challenge that determination, but you'd better be able to prove that you're running your business using best business practices and that you're generating losses as a result of factors beyond your control.

Of course, despite your best efforts to file accurate and complete tax returns on time, occasionally that angst-creating envelope lands in your mailbox, requesting more information or, even worse, outlining the additional amount the IRS thinks you should pay, based on the information it has collected about you.

Audits make everyone anxious, but take a deep breath and really read what the IRS letter has to say. Review the contents of the letter against the copy of the return that you've saved, and identify each of the items the IRS is questioning. Most of the time, the problem is a simple misunderstanding — income reported to you that you know was declared on someone else's return, or information that was reported twice to the IRS but that you know you received only once. Sometimes you failed to report some item of income, possibly because you moved and never received the Form 1099 or W-2 from the payor.

If the error is yours, pay the amount shown on the front of the notice and send it back within the requested time frame. That should solve the problem. On the other hand, if the IRS has goofed, write a letter outlining the issue and where you feel the IRS has erred. Back up your assertions with documentation — receipts, if that's what required, or a copy of the tax return where the missing income was actually reported. If the IRS continues to pursue the matter, take the next step and contact your taxpayer advocate, who can assist you. *Taxes For Dummies* (Wiley) tells you how. Every state has at least one taxpayer advocate.

Also be aware of a couple items to never, ever do when your return is being audited:

- ✔ **Never ignore IRS notices.** If you've received that first notice, the IRS definitely knows where you live — and they won't forget. Remember, the IRS isn't a toothless giant, and it hates to be ignored. Deal fairly with the agent assigned to your case, and you will get through the process reasonably intact.

- ✔ **Never offer more information than what's requested.** By telling an agent more than he or she is asking, you're opening up more areas of your return for review. Just keep to the topic at hand and make your answers as short as possible — answer the questions asked, but no more.

- ✔ **Follow through on any deals you make.** If you arrange a payment plan, be certain to make all your payments when they are due. Late payments will cancel a payment plan, and your total tax liability will become due and payable immediately.

If you're being audited and are representing yourself, you have the right to stop the audit at any time and get expert advice. You always have the right to have an expert be in the room with you, if you have a face-to-face audit (which is reasonably rare). You even have the right to have your representative, who must be a Certified Public Accountant, and attorney, or an enrolled agent, attend the audit on your behalf, without your being present.

What Can Happen If You Don't Pay on Time

If you don't pay the full amount of your income taxes on April 15, you can expect your tax bill to increase — and you can expect to hear from the IRS.

Tallying penalties and interest

On April 16, the IRS begins charging you penalties and interest on your unpaid taxes.

- ✔ **Penalties:** For every month or part of a month that you have an outstanding income tax debt, you're charged a penalty that equals 5 percent of what you owe (including accrued interest and penalties), with a maximum penalty of 25 percent. If 60 days pass and you've still not filed your tax return, the *minimum* penalty becomes $100 or the full amount of money that you still owe to the IRS — whichever is less.

 ✔ **Interest:** You're charged interest, compounded daily, on your outstanding tax debt (taxes plus accumulated interest and penalties). The interest rate is the federal short-term rate, which is set every three months, plus 3 percent.

The IRS may agree to reduce the amount of penalties you owe if you have a good reason for needing a reduction. For example, maybe your family has faced a serious illness or death, or maybe a fire, flood, or earthquake has destroyed your tax records. Unfortunately, owing too much to your other creditors or mismanaging your money does not warrant a reduction.

Unlike penalties, over which the IRS has a great deal of discretion, interest is statutory, which means that only an act of Congress can get you out from under that burden. Still, if you can prove to the IRS that it miscalculated the amount of interest it says you owe or made some other error affecting the amount of interest being charged, the IRS will likely reduce the amount of interest it says you owe so far.

Being pressured to pay

In addition to penalizing you financially for a past-due tax bill, the IRS starts asking you to pay up.

First, you receive a "Notice of Taxes Due and Demand for Payment," which is essentially an IRS bill for the taxes you owe plus interest and penalties. If you disagree with the amount stated on the bill, immediately contact the IRS office shown at the top of the notice. You may either call the phone number on the notice or send a letter, outlining why you disagree with the IRS calculations. It can sometimes help to walk into your local IRS office and speak directly with an agent on duty there.

If you ignore the first notice, you receive a second notice asking for payment. However, this notice comes with an IRS publication explaining that the IRS may put a federal tax lien on all your assets and/or *levy* (seize) some of them to collect your tax debt.

Next, an outside debt collector may get in touch to try to collect your tax debt or to obtain information that the IRS can use to collect what you owe, possibly by setting up an installment plan for you. (The collector gets 25 percent of any money he collects.) Outside debt collectors may not place any liens or levies on your property and also may not work with you to reduce what you owe; you must deal directly with the IRS for any abatements or other reductions in tax.

Figuring out how to pay

If you couldn't pay your taxes on April 15, you probably can't pay them in full after that date, either, especially because interest and penalties increase the debt. If that's the case, you probably have only three ways to take care of the debt and prevent the IRS from taking steps to collect the money from you:

- ✔ **Set up an installment payment plan.** Depending on how much you owe in income taxes and the overall state of your finances, an IRS payment plan may be the way to go. In the next section, we explain how installment plans work.

- ✔ **Make the IRS an Offer in Compromise (OIC).** Under certain circumstances, the IRS will let you settle your debt for less than the full amount you owe. However, getting the IRS to consider an OIC, much less accept it, can be an uphill battle. In the upcoming section "Using an Offer in Compromise to cut a deal with the IRS," we clue you in on how OICs work.

- ✔ **File for bankruptcy.** If your finances are in dire shape, and you owe a bundle to the IRS, filing for bankruptcy may be your best bet, especially if you file before the agency puts a federal tax lien on your assets. However, filing won't get rid of your tax debt — it will be waiting for you to pay it when you complete your bankruptcy — nor will it stop the collection efforts of the IRS. Read the section "Filing bankruptcy to deal with your tax debt," later in this chapter, for more details.

Paying your taxes in installments

When you can't afford to pay your income taxes in full, you may be able to pay them through an IRS installment plan, which requires you to make monthly payments. However, the IRS won't give you an installment plan if you haven't filed any of your tax returns for previous years.

The process for setting up an installment payment plan depends on how much you owe to the IRS: less than $10,000, more than $10,000 but less than $25,000, or more than $25,000. (The more money you owe to the IRS, the more paperwork you have to fill out.) But the first step, regardless of how much you owe, is to fill out IRS Form 9465, "Installment Agreement Request." To get this form, go to www.irs.gov/pub/irs-pdf/f9465.pdf, call 800-829-3767, or visit your local IRS office.

When you complete the form, you have to indicate the following:

- ✔ **How much you want to pay on your tax debt each month:** The faster you pay off your tax debt, the less you end up paying in interest and penalties. In the best-case scenario, you can afford to pay the debt before next year's taxes are due.

Book V

Protecting Your Money and Assets

However, don't agree to pay more than you really can afford. If you fall behind on your payments, the IRS will cancel your installment plan and may take steps to collect what you owe. See Book I, Chapter 3 for help creating a monthly budget so you know what a realistic payment is.

✔ **How each payment will be made:** The easiest and safest way to ensure that each payment will be made in full and on time is to have payments automatically debited from your bank account or to have your employer treat them as automatic payroll deductions. However, you can tell the IRS that you will make the payments yourself.

After you've filed your request for an installment plan, the IRS contacts you within 30 days to let you know whether your request has been approved or rejected. The agency may tell you that it needs more information before it can make a decision. If your plan is approved, you pay a $43 plan setup fee, which the IRS takes out of your first payment.

If the IRS okays your installment plan, it expects you to comply with two specific terms and conditions. You must do the following:

✔ **Make each installment payment in full and on time.** Here's an excellent reason to be realistic about how much you can afford to pay to the IRS each month.

✔ **Pay your income taxes and file your tax returns on time while your plan is in effect.** In lieu of filing a return, you may file an application for an extension to file, as long as you do so by April 15.

If you don't comply with these conditions, the IRS considers you in default, which means it may cancel the plan and try to collect the money you owe. In other words, you may find yourself facing the very consequences you hoped to avoid by setting up an installment plan in the first place.

Paying off less than $10,000

When you owe the IRS less than $10,000, the agency automatically greenlights your installment plan request, assuming that the following are true:

✔ The IRS is satisfied that you cannot pay what you owe in a lump sum.

✔ You (or you and your spouse, if you file jointly) filed each of your tax returns on time over the previous five years or filed extension requests on time.

✔ You paid any taxes due on time during the previous five years.

✔ The amount of your monthly payments is high enough to get your income tax debt (including all interest and penalties) paid in full within three years.

Paying off more than $10,000 but less than $25,000

If you owe this much, approval of your installment plan isn't automatic. However, the IRS will probably agree to an installment plan, assuming that your monthly payments are large enough to wipe out your income tax debt within five years.

If you can't afford to pay your tax debt within five years through an installment plan, you can ask the IRS to allow you to take longer. However, to get the agency's permission to do that, you have to fill out Form 433-A, "Collection Information Statement." We talk about this form in the next section.

Paying off more than $25,000

When you owe the IRS more than $25,000 in taxes and you want to pay that debt in installments, you must complete two forms: IRS Form 9465 and IRS Form 433-A, "Collection Information Statement." You may also have to provide the IRS other information about your finances.

The Collection Information Statement asks for a lot of detailed information about your finances. Among other information, you must provide details about your assets, monthly expenses, and sources of monthly income. Filling out the form is time-consuming.

When you fill out the Collection Information Statement, you tell the IRS exactly what it needs to know if it decides later to try to collect your tax debt, maybe because you default on your installment payment plan. Sure, the IRS can find out the information on its own, but that process takes time. So by completing the Collection Information Statement, you make it a whole lot easier for the IRS to collect from you. However, you have no choice if you need to pay your tax debt in installments.

The IRS uses the information on the Collection Information Statement to figure out how much you can afford to pay on your tax debt each month. To help it make this calculation, the IRS compares your total monthly income from all sources to your total monthly living expenses.

When the IRS adds up your expenses to get a monthly total, it includes only those expenses it considers to be *essential,* and its definition of *essential expenses* may be quite different from yours. For example, its total doesn't include the monthly cost of your cable television or your gym membership. Also, it doesn't include the monthly payments you may be making on your credit card debts or on other unsecured debts. In other words, the IRS may end up with a monthly expense total that vastly understates what it really costs you to live. (You may be able to get the IRS to change its mind about an expense that it considers nonessential if you can prove that the expense is essential to your ability to earn a living.)

Wait, it gets worse! When it comes to expenses that the IRS *does* consider to be essential, such as food and clothing, it may not recognize the total amount that you're spending every month. The IRS uses standard monthly guideline amounts to budget for essential expenses, which may be less than what you actually spend. For example, if you spend $400 per month on food but the agency's guidelines say you should be spending only $350, the IRS uses $350 when it calculates what you can afford to pay on your income tax debt each month.

In other words, the IRS may conclude that you can afford to pay more each month on your tax debt than you feel is realistic. Unless you can do some drastic budget-cutting, paying off your debt through an installment plan is wishful thinking. What are your options? Get the IRS to accept an Offer in Compromise, or file for bankruptcy. (We discuss each of these options in upcoming sections.) Or try to get the IRS to change its mind about what you can afford to pay each month. Doing so probably requires that you formally appeal the agency's decision. For an overview of how the appeals process works, read the sidebar "Appealing an IRS decision."

If your knees shake and your mouth gets dry when you think about negotiating with the IRS, ask someone else to do it for you. That someone else can be an attorney, a CPA, an enrolled agent, or someone who has power of attorney to conduct your financial affairs. Your representative completes IRS Form 2848, "Power of Attorney and Declaration of Representative," which you can download at www.irs.gov/pub/irs-pdf/f2848.pdf. If you want that person to also have access to confidential information and documents relating to your taxes and your finances — information that the IRS normally shares only with you — your representative also needs to complete IRS Form 8821, "Tax Information Authorization," which you can download at www.irs.gov/pub/irs-pdf/f8821.pdf. You can also obtain both forms by calling 800-829-3767 or by visiting a local IRS office.

Using an Offer in Compromise to cut a deal with the IRS

If your finances are in such dire shape that you cannot afford to pay the full amount of your income tax debt in installments or any other way, the IRS may agree to let you settle the debt for less — maybe for pennies on the dollar — through an Offer in Compromise (OIC). However, OICs are hard to get, and you aren't eligible for one unless all your tax returns for the previous five years have been filed and you're not already in bankruptcy.

Settling your debt for less with the IRS can be tricky business. Although you can try doing it yourself, you increase the odds of success by hiring a pro such as a CPA, an EA, or a tax attorney with experience negotiating OICs.

Beware of companies that advertise on the Internet offering to help you prepare your OIC (for a fee, of course). Many of them have little or no expertise with OICs and, therefore, offer little chance of getting the IRS to accept yours.

You initiate the OIC process by completing IRS Form 656, "Offer in Compromise," which is actually a package of forms and worksheets, including a Collection Information Statement for Individuals. You must also pay the IRS a $150 OIC application fee, although you can get the fee waived under certain conditions. Don't pay the application fee until you know whether you qualify for a waiver.

In addition, you must make a nonrefundable partial payment on your OIC when you submit your request. The amount of the payment depends on how much you are asking to settle your debt for and the terms of your offer, such as how long you want to take to pay it. Usually, the more time you want, the bigger your offer must be. For example, if you agree to pay your settlement amount in one lump sum, the IRS will probably agree to take less money from you than if you want to pay the settlement amount in installments over a year or more.

After you file all the appropriate IRS forms and pay the application fee and the nonrefundable partial payment on your OIC, the IRS agrees to formally consider your offer if it concludes that one of the following conditions applies to you:

- ✔ You will probably never be able to pay the full amount you owe to the IRS, and it will probably never collect the money from you — maybe because you have no assets of value and you make very little money relative to the amount of your tax debt.

- ✔ The amount of taxes that the IRS says you owe is incorrect. You probably have to make this case to the IRS; the agency won't likely make it for you.

- ✔ Your tax debt *shouldn't* be collected because of an economic hardship or some other special circumstances that you face.

If the IRS decides that one of these conditions applies to you, it evaluates your OIC by using the information on your Collection Information Statement. Meanwhile, the agency halts any actions it may already be taking to collect from you, which means no more calls from debt collectors, no more wage garnishment, and no asset seizures. (If the IRS rejects your OIC, its collection efforts can immediately resume.)

While the IRS is reviewing your OIC, the ten-year statute of limitations on collecting your tax debt is suspended. After the IRS makes its decision, the statute of limitations begins running again. If you're unhappy with the agency's decision regarding your OIC and you file an appeal, the statute of limitations is suspended again while your appeal is being considered. When you have the statute of limitations suspended, the period of time during which the IRS can try to collect from you gets pushed further into the future.

Getting the green light

If the IRS gives your OIC request the go-ahead, and if you agreed to pay the amount in a lump sum, you must make the payment within 90 days. If you agreed to a short-term deferred payment plan, you have up to 24 months to pay what you owe. And if you set up a longer-term plan, you have to pay the settlement amount in equal payments over the period that remains on the statute of limitations for collecting your tax debt.

When you pay the settlement amount in installments, regardless of the term of your payment plan, you must make each payment on time *and* you must file your tax returns on time and pay any taxes you owe on time while your plan is in effect. If you don't, you will be in default of your agreement with the IRS, and the agency may take action to collect what you still owe.

Being rejected

You're notified in writing if the IRS rejects your OIC. The notice you receive explains why your offer was rejected. Most OICs get rejected because the IRS thinks that the amount of the settlement offer is too small. In other words, the IRS believes it can reasonably expect to collect more from you, given the value of your real and personal assets and the amount of your future income.

If the IRS rejects your offer for this reason, it tells you what it considers to be an acceptable settlement amount, given your finances. If you don't understand the explanation or disagree with the agency's decision, call the number on the IRS notice.

You can submit a new offer to the IRS if it rejects your first one. If you are working with a CPA, EA, or attorney, she may call the IRS revenue officer (also called a *field officer*) assigned to your case to discuss what kind of offer the IRS would find acceptable. If you're handling your own OIC, you can make the same call.

You can also appeal the agency's decision about your OIC. The notice explains how to file an appeal. The sidebar "Appealing an IRS decision" summarizes the appeals process.

Filing bankruptcy to deal with your tax debt

Filing for bankruptcy is a good way to deal with your tax debt when your finances are in such bad shape that neither an installment plan nor an OIC is a real option. This move is also a smart one if you think that the IRS may be about to seize some of your assets or garnish your wages. Exactly how bankruptcy affects your tax debt is a complicated matter determined by a variety of criteria and considerations, including how long you've owed the taxes and whether the IRS has already put a federal tax lien on your assets.

If the IRS has not yet filed a tax lien, and assuming that your tax debt is more than three years old and that you filed your tax returns on time during those three years (or filed for an extension), you can do one of the following:

- File a Chapter 7 liquidation bankruptcy to get rid of your tax debt.

- File a Chapter 13 reorganization bankruptcy to reduce the total amount that you owe to the IRS and get three to five years to pay your remaining tax debt, including interest and penalties, in full.

If your income tax debt is less than three years old, you *cannot* use Chapter 7 to get rid of the debt. Instead, you must file Chapter 13, which gives you up to five years to pay the full amount of your income tax debt, including all penalties. If the IRS has already filed a tax lien, you must also pay interest on your outstanding tax debt.

If you file for bankruptcy after the IRS has filed a federal tax lien, your tax debt becomes a secured debt. As a result, you can't do the following:

- You can't use Chapter 7 to wipe out the debt. Instead, you have to pay the full amount when your bankruptcy is over. However, paying it should be easier because you won't owe as much to other creditors.

- You won't be able to reduce your tax debt through Chapter 13, and you have to pay the full amount of the debt while you are in bankruptcy (over a three- to five-year period). In addition, while you are in bankruptcy, the bankruptcy court charges you interest on your unpaid tax balance. The interest rate will be a local rate.

What the IRS can't take from you

To collect the taxes you owe, the IRS has the power to take just about any asset of yours that it can get its hands on. However, a few exceptions apply. These exempt assets are specific to the IRS. In other words, they are not the same as the assets that you can keep when you file for bankruptcy.

The IRS must keep its mitts off the following:

- Your fuel, food, furniture, and personal items, up to a certain amount

- The books and tools you need to earn a living, up to a certain amount

- Unemployment payments

- Worker's compensation payments

- Certain types of public assistance payments

- Service-related disability payments

- Certain annuity and pension benefits

- Court-ordered child support payments

So what's the lesson in all this? When you can't afford to pay your federal income taxes and you are thinking about bankruptcy, consult with a consumer bankruptcy attorney immediately — before the IRS puts a lien on your assets. For more information about federal income taxes and personal bankruptcy, get a copy of *Personal Bankruptcy Laws For Dummies,* by James P. Caher and John M. Caher (Wiley).

Coping with Interest and Penalties

The government charges interest and imposes heavy penalties when you don't pay your taxes on time. Sometimes interest and penalties add up to more than the tax itself.

Interest is treated differently than penalties in bankruptcy. In addition, different rules exist for interest and penalties that accrue before you file for bankruptcy (*prepetition*) and interest and penalties that arise after you file (*postpetition*).

Prepetition interest charged on unpaid taxes is, for the most part, treated the same as taxes in both a Chapter 7 and a Chapter 13 bankruptcy. When the tax is nondischargeable, so is the interest. Penalties, on the other hand, are discharged in a Chapter 7 bankruptcy if they are more than three years old. In a Chapter 13 bankruptcy, however, prepetition penalties are dischargeable regardless of when they arose.

Postpetition interest on nondischargeable taxes continues to accrue during and after a Chapter 7 case. Interest stops accruing in a Chapter 13 case when it's filed. Yet whenever a Chapter 13 bankruptcy is dismissed or converted to a Chapter 7, interest is added as if no Chapter 13 had been filed.

Consider this wrinkle: If you filed a joint return for taxes included in your Chapter 13 case, but your spouse didn't join you in filing Chapter 13 bankruptcy, the IRS still can come after her for interest that accrues while your Chapter 13 case is open.

Penalties on nondischargeable taxes aren't assessed while a Chapter 7 or a Chapter 13 case is open. Keep in mind that a Chapter 7 case is usually not open very long — typically just a few months — unlike a Chapter 13 case, which ordinarily lasts for at least three years.

Dealing with Liens and Levies for Past-Due Taxes

If you ignore your IRS tax debt, or if you and the IRS can't come to an agreement about an installment payment plan or an OIC, the agency may take steps to collect what you owe. Whether it does, how quickly it does, and exactly *what* it does depend in large part on the specific IRS revenue officer handling your case. Some revenue officers are aggressive (a little like pit bulls), but others are more likely to help you figure out a way to pay your tax debt so that you can avoid what comes next.

Besides the personality of the revenue officer, other factors help determine whether the IRS tries to collect your debt:

✔ **How much you owe:** The more you owe, the more likely that the IRS will try to collect its money.

✔ **The amount of your income:** The IRS may decide to garnish your wages to collect what you owe.

Law prohibits the IRS from collecting from you if you can prove that your income is less than your living expenses and that, therefore, your tax debt is uncollectible. However, the IRS determines your expenses according to its standard guidelines, which are very low. Proving that your tax debt is uncollectible may be a losing battle, but a tax attorney, a CPA, or an EA with experience dealing with the IRS may be able to make your case.

✔ **Whether you have any assets that the IRS can take:** If you do, the IRS puts a federal tax lien on all of them. The lien also applies to any assets that you may acquire in the future. The next section offers a quick lesson on federal tax liens.

When the liens are in place, the IRS may *levy,* or take, some of your assets. The levy may happen right away or not for some time. Find out how levies work in the upcoming section "Losing your assets because of a levy."

If you earn next to nothing and all your assets are exempt from the IRS, you're safe — for now, anyway. (The agency will probably let interest and penalties continue to accrue, so your tax debt will grow larger by the day.) Periodically, the IRS reviews your financial situation to see if it has improved. If it has, and assuming that the ten-year statute of limitations for tax debt has not expired, the IRS will collect as much as it can from you. The sidebar "What the IRS can't take from you," in this chapter, offers an overview of the assets that are safe from the clutches of the agency.

Knowing how tax liens work

Before the IRS can put a lien on your assets, it must send you a Notice and Demand for Payment. If you don't pay the full amount of your tax debt within ten days of the notice date, the IRS puts a federal tax lien on your assets, including assets that you have only an interest in. The lien also applies to any assets that you may acquire or have an interest in some time later. The lien may even get attached if you apply for an installment payment plan within the ten-day period.

The IRS files the tax lien in your county courthouse, making it part of the public record. Therefore, the lien shows up in your credit history and harms your credit score. You cannot sell, borrow against, or transfer any of the assets that the lien is attached to without paying off the tax lien.

You can get a lien released in only a few ways:

✔ Pay the full amount you owe to the IRS in a lump sum, including all penalties and interest.

✔ Pay your debt in full through an installment payment plan. Some IRS agents release a tax lien after your installment plan has been set up.

✔ Settle your debt for less through an Offer in Compromise.

✔ Wait for the ten-year statute of limitations on your tax debt to run out. However, the IRS likely will refile the lien before the ten years are up.

After you get the tax lien released, the IRS sends you a Release of Federal Tax Lien notice. It also files that notice with your county courthouse so the public records reflect the fact that the agency no longer has a lien on your assets.

When you receive the IRS notice, contact the three national credit bureaus in writing and ask them to remove the tax lien information from your credit files. Attach a copy of the IRS notice to your letter. A month or two later, check your credit histories to find out if the information has been removed. If you have problems getting the lien information removed, contact a consumer law attorney who has experience resolving problems with credit-reporting agencies.

The process of getting a lien removed may seem straightforward, but it's often not an easy matter to get the IRS to release a lien. After all, the agency's interest was in collecting what you owed; when you no longer owe the money, they sometimes lose interest in tying up all the loose ends. It's far better never to have the lien put on in the first place. If you receive notice that the IRS is about to place a lien on your property, call the IRS office where the notice was generated and speak to the agent in charge of your case immediately. Agents have the authority to place a hold on an account while a resolution is being negotiated, so negotiate in good faith. In the end, reaching a mutually satisfactory resolution without the IRS having to resort to strong-arm tactics is much better, and healthier, for you.

Appealing an IRS decision

You can appeal most IRS decisions related to your outstanding tax debt by using one of two processes: the Collection Appeals Program (CAP) or the Collection Due Process (CDP).

When you appeal a collection action that the IRS may be about to take, the IRS must suspend the action while your appeal is being considered. (Your appeal has no effect on the accrual of interest and penalties on your unpaid taxes.) If the agency rules against you, the IRS can resume whatever it was doing.

✔ **The Collection Appeals Program (CAP):** You can use this process to try to clear up a dispute related to a lien before or after it has been filed, a pending levy, the seizure of one of your assets, or the denial or termination of an installment payment plan. The good news is that the CAP is relatively fast. The bad news is that if you're unhappy with the outcome of your appeal, you can't take the IRS to court.

Consider how the process works: If you are notified of an IRS decision related to an issue covered by the CAP, contact an IRS collections staff person to let him know that you are disputing the agency's action. (The number to call should be on the notice you receive.) If you get no satisfaction, ask to speak to an IRS collections manager. This person should speak with you about your dispute within a day of your request. If you don't like what the manager tells you, either, ask to have your dispute forwarded to an appeals officer.

If an IRS revenue agent contacts you about an IRS decision — for example, she tells you how much the IRS has decided you owe — and you want to appeal the decision, ask to have a conference with a collections manager. If the meeting doesn't resolve your problem, file a request for an appeal with the IRS Office of Appeals right away by completing IRS Form 9423, "Collection Appeal Request." You can download the form at www.irs.gov/pub/irs-pdf/f9423.pdf or get it by calling 800-839-3676. The IRS must receive your request within two days of the meeting. Otherwise, it can resume its efforts to collect from you. If you file your request for an appeal on time, the appeals officer decision is legally binding on you and on the IRS.

✔ **The Collection Due Process (CDP):** You can pursue this kind of appeal if you receive a tax lien notice or a levy notice from the IRS. In most instances, you must file your appeal with the IRS Office of Appeals within 30 days of receiving the notice. Fill out IRS Form 12153, "Request for a Collection Due Process Hearing," which you can obtain at www.irs.gov/pub/irs-pdf/f12153.pdf. During the 30-day period and while your appeal is being considered, the IRS will put its collection actions on hold, as long as it doesn't think that its ability to collect from you may be in jeopardy. For example, it may not put things on hold if it believes that you are getting ready to transfer or hide an asset that it wants to take from you.

When the hearing is over, the IRS sends you a letter telling you what the Office of Appeals has decided. If you agree with the decision, you and the agency must abide by it. However, if you don't agree, you have 30 days from the date that the decision was issued to request a judicial review in federal tax court or in a U.S. District Court. If the court reviews your case and decides in favor of the IRS, it's the end of the road for you.

Losing your assets because of a levy

A *levy* is a powerful collection tool that the IRS can use to seize your real or personal assets. For example, it may levy the money in your bank accounts; your home and other real estate you own; your car, motorcycle, boat, or RV; and so on. It may also take any commissions you earn and any dividends and rental income you receive. It can take money out of your retirement account, seize the cash value of your life insurance policy, and garnish your wages.

(In some states, you can be fired just because the IRS is garnishing your wages. For example, if you are responsible for a lot of money, your employer may fire you out of concern that your financial problems may cause you to steal from the business.)

Usually, the IRS won't levy your assets unless you've ignored all its efforts to get you to pay what you owe, or your efforts to pay your debt through an installment plan or with an OIC have not worked out. The bigger your debt, the more likely that the IRS will try to seize some of your assets.

If you do nothing to stop the levy, the IRS eventually serves you with a Notice and Demand for Payment, a Final Notice of Intent to Levy, and a Notice of Your Right to a Hearing. These papers are served no less than 30 days before a levy is scheduled to occur. If you're not already working with a bankruptcy attorney or tax professional, get one pronto. The attorney may be able to stop the levy or at least put it on hold, to give you more time to figure out what to do. For example, you may decide to appeal the agency's levy plans. However, you have a limited amount of time to appeal, so don't dillydally. (The sidebar "Appealing an IRS decision" provides a broad explanation of how the appeals process works.)

For the best results, never handle your own appeal. Hire a CPA, an EA, or a tax attorney who understands the appeals process and the lingo to help you.

If the levy moves forward and the IRS takes one or more of your assets, you can appeal its action, assuming that you can make a case that the agency didn't follow all the legally required procedures related to a levy.

If the IRS levies your bank account, the bank cannot give your funds to the IRS for 21 days, which gives you time to figure out how to avoid the loss of your money. As soon as you find out that the IRS is going to levy your bank account, meet with a bankruptcy attorney because filing for bankruptcy will stop the levy. If you don't file, or you don't file in time, the bank sends the money in your account, up to the amount of your tax debt, to the IRS.

The IRS can levy any bank accounts that have your name on them, even if the funds are not for your own use. For example, if your name is on your mother's checking account so you can help manage her financial affairs, that account is in jeopardy as well.

If the IRS takes one of your assets

When the IRS seizes one of your assets, it uses newspaper advertising and fliers to let people know that the asset will be sold in a public auction. Then it must wait at least ten days to conduct the sale.

Before the sale, the IRS decides on a minimum bid amount for your property. Usually that amount equals about 80 percent of the forced sale value of your asset minus the amount of any liens other creditors may have on it. (For example, the IRS may have taken your car and your bank has a $5,000 lien against it, or the IRS may have seized your home and your mortgage company has a $100,000 lien on it.) If you think that the minimum bid amount set by the IRS is too low, you can file an appeal to ask the agency to either recompute the amount or use a private appraiser to make the calculation.

After your property is sold, the IRS uses the sale proceeds to reimburse itself for the costs it incurred taking and selling your property. Then it applies any money left over to your tax debt. If the sale doesn't generate enough to pay that debt in full, you have to pay the balance.

If your property sells for more than enough to reimburse the IRS for the expenses it incurred in taking and selling your property and to pay off your tax debt, you're entitled to ask for the IRS to give you whatever money is left. However, if your creditors have liens on your assets and they file claims with the IRS, the IRS will pay their claims with the leftover money before it pays you a dime.

How to get the asset back from the IRS

You may be able to get the asset back from the IRS before it's sold if one of the following is true:

- ✔ You pay the agency the full amount you owe.

- ✔ The agency decides that the cost of selling the asset will exceed what you owe.

- ✔ You can prove to the IRS that having the property back will help you pay your tax bill.

- ✔ The agency's Taxpayer Advocate Service (TAS) determines that returning the property to you is in your best interest and in the best interest of the government. For example, some of your real estate may have toxic chemicals on it, and the IRS decides that you should incur the cost of cleaning up the chemicals. The sidebar "You've got a friend at the IRS" explains what the TAS does and doesn't do.

You can also request that the IRS return the property to you — even after it has been sold — if you can prove that the IRS did not do the following:

- ✔ Provide you with all the legally required notices before taking your property, or give you the proper amount of time to respond to one of its notices.

✔ Follow established agency procedures. For example, before it took your asset, the IRS may not have confirmed exactly how much you owed to it, the IRS failed to make certain that you had equity in the asset it took, or the agency did not ensure that it couldn't collect from you in some other way.

✔ Abide by the terms of the installment payment plan you negotiated with the agency (if the agreement states that the IRS will not levy your property).

If the IRS sells some of your real estate, you can redeem or buy it from whoever purchases it within 180 days of the sale. However, you must be able to pay the same amount that the buyer paid for your property plus interest at an annual rate of 20 percent.

Getting Help

Unquestionably, tax problems can take on lives of their own and make your own life an anxious and miserable place. But unless you choose to walk this road alone, plenty of people are available to help you.

Good tax advice can save your bacon; bad advice can cost you big time. When hiring anyone to help you with your tax issues, be sure to obtain references. Often the best source for help is a referral from a friend or family member whose advice you trust. Remember, anyone can claim to be an expert in any field, but only actual knowledge makes it so. If you're not happy with the service you're receiving or feel that your "expert" is doing you more harm than good, don't hesitate to get a second opinion.

Among the professionals who deal with the IRS and the various state tax agencies on a daily basis are the following:

✔ **Attorneys:** Licensed by the bar associations in each state, attorneys can be experts in many areas, of which tax law is just one. Using an attorney for a straightforward tax problem may be overkill because their hourly rates can head into the stratosphere. If your tax problem is based more on interpretation of the law than implementation, though, a good tax attorney may become your best friend. You can find lists of attorneys through the state Bar Association, or you can search for one online at www.martindale.com.

✔ **Certified Public Accountants:** Also licensed in the state in which they practice, CPAs can handle all your accounting needs, not just your tax needs. CPAs usually charge either an hourly rate or a flat rate per tax return (depending on its complexity), and their rates will generally be a step below what you can expect to pay for a tax attorney of similar stature and experience. All CPAs in your state are registered with your state's Board of Accountancy.

✔ **Enrolled agents:** EAs are tax specialists licensed by the United States Department of the Treasury, not by any one state. They are often retired IRS agents or have taken a rigorous licensing exam, similar to both the CPA and state bar exams. These individuals specialize in tax only. As with CPAs, EAs typically charge either by the hour or by the return, and their fees are usually somewhat lower than rates of attorneys or CPAs. EAs don't have any one national database, but most belong to the National Association of Enrolled Agents (NAEA), which you can find at www.naea.org.

✔ **Unenrolled preparers:** Licensed by no state or federal authority, some of these individuals may be excellent; others may be hacks. Fees for unenrolled preparers are usually calculated on the basis of the complexity of the return, not on an hourly basis.

Communicating with the IRS

Because using the telephone is so easy, we've become an instant-gratification society when it comes to contacting people with our questions and receiving answers. When dealing with the IRS, though, you may want to put your hands in the air and step away from that phone. Recognize that, when you have a tax problem, you're interacting with one of the largest bureaucracies imaginable, one that's saddled with a very old computer system. You're bound to face glitches along the way, so keeping a paper trail of all your contacts with the IRS is key to arriving at a satisfactory conclusion.

Put all your communications to the IRS in writing, and make sure you keep copies of everything. The address to send your letter to is the one on the top of the notice you receive, not the service center where you filed your return.

When writing to the IRS, be respectful and keep your arguments as clear and simple as possible. Document independently everything you're stating in your letter. For example, if you're asserting that the reason you failed to file your income tax return on time was that you were ill, attach doctors' statements to that effect. If you were out of the country, enclose copies of your plane ticket stubs. If someone who needed to sign the tax return died, send a copy of the death certificate.

If the pertinent part of a supporting document is a date or some other snippet of information, you can assist the agent reading your letter by using a highlighting pen on the salient information. Mail only copies of documentation to the IRS and you keep the originals; more than one letter containing volumes of documentation has gone astray and had to be replaced.

Finally, be certain that you keep proof that you mailed what you said when you said you mailed it. Whether you use the U.S. Postal Service or a private delivery service, be sure to obtain, and keep, proof that you sent an item, using either Certified Mail or some other private delivery proof of mailing. And if you need to positively know that the IRS received what you sent, attach a Return Receipt; then keep that receipt with your copy of the letter and all supporting documentation.

Don't rely on phone calls when trying to sort out a problem with the IRS. You'll never get the same agent twice, and the agent who does answer the phone may have no idea about the discussions you had previously with other agents. What's more, if the proof of your position is sitting in front of you while you speak with the agent, that agent can't see it and doesn't know that it really exists.

You've got a friend at the IRS

The Taxpayer Advocate Service (TAS) is an independent agency within the IRS that is charged with protecting the rights of taxpayers. Its main office is in Washington, D.C., but it has at least one local office in every state. For contact information for the office nearest you, go to www.irs.gov/advocate and click on "Contact Your Advocate" and then "View Local Taxpayer Advocates By State." Or you can call 877-777-4778. The local offices report directly to the national TAS office, not to the IRS.

You can ask the TAS for help if you're unable to resolve an issue related to your tax debt, despite following the appropriate IRS rules and procedures, including rules that apply to the IRS appeals process. For example, you may believe that an IRS employee didn't follow IRS rules or didn't act in a timely manner and feel that you were harmed or will be harmed as a result. The TAS will not help you just because you disagree with an IRS decision.

You can also ask the TAS for help if you believe that you will suffer "a significant economic hardship" as a result of an action that the IRS is about to take or has taken — seizing one of your assets, for example, or garnishing your wages. Examples of "a significant economic hardship"

include not being able to pay for necessities such as food, shelter, and clothing; not being able to get to work; and possibly putting your job at risk. Medical emergencies usually qualify, too. The TAS may respond to a hardship by issuing a Taxpayer Assistance Order (TAO) to stop an IRS collection action.

After the TAS office in your area receives your request for help, a case advocate reviews it, listens to your point of view, and determines whether you have legitimate cause for complaint. If your problem falls within the purview of the TAS, someone is assigned to help you. While the office is trying to resolve your problem, the IRS must suspend certain kinds of collection actions. For example, it may not put a lien on your assets or levy of your assets until it knows the outcome of the TAS efforts.

File IRS Form 911, "Application for Taxpayer Assistance Order," to ask the TAS for help. You can download this form at www.irs.gov/pub/irs-pdf/f911.pdf or obtain a copy at your local IRS office. You can also call 800-829-3767 and ask to have a copy of the form mailed to you.

Book VI

Retiring Comfortably

The 5th Wave   By Rich Tennant

"The first thing we should do is get you two
into a good 401(k). Let me get out the
'Magic 8 Ball' and we'll run some options."

In this book . . .

Most people have vague, dreamy ideas of what
they want to do in retirement, whether it's travel,
pursuing a hobby full-time, or doing as little as possible.
All of those things require an income to live, and the sad
fact is, most people do not plan properly for retirement.
The good news is, it's not rocket science. By putting away
a portion of your income for your retirement as much as
possible during your working years, you can eventually
stop working and live without worry. Finding ways to do
that without causing too much pain is where this book
comes in.

Here are the contents of Book VI at a glance.

Chapter 1

401(k) and 403(b) Retirement Investing

*N*ot too long ago, many people asked, "What the heck is a 401(k)?" Today, however, *401(k)* is a household word. People discuss their 401(k) investments at social gatherings. These once-obscure plans are in the national media nearly every day.

401(k) plans have helped more than 40 million American workers save for retirement. Because Social Security alone won't provide adequate retirement income, and fewer companies offer a traditional pension plan, 401(k)s have become an essential part of the average worker's future plans.

Even young people, for whom retirement normally is low on the priority list, have jumped on the retirement savings bandwagon. They're the smart ones because, in some respects, *how long* you save is more important than *how much* you save.

Unfortunately, the stock market nosedive and corporate scandals in the early 2000s caused 401(k) plans to come under some fire. Many workers who made bad investment choices saw large drops in the value of their accounts. Some blamed the 401(k) itself, but that's like blaming the messenger who brings you bad news. If you take the time to understand and follow basic investing principles (see Book IV), your 401(k) can grow into a nest egg that can help you retire comfortably. The beauty of a 401(k) is that it makes saving easy and automatic, and you probably won't even miss the money that you save.

What a 401(k) Does for You

A 401(k) plan lets you put away some of your income *now* to use *later,* presumably when you're retired and not earning a paycheck. This procedure may not appeal to everyone; human nature being what it is, many people would rather spend their money now and worry about later when later comes. That's why the federal government approved tax breaks for 401(k) participants to enjoy now. Uncle Sam knows that your individual savings will be an essential part of your retirement and wants to give you an incentive to participate.

When you sign up for a 401(k) plan, you agree to let your employer deposit some of your paycheck into the plan as a *pretax contribution*, instead of paying it to you. Your employer may even throw in some extra money, known as a *matching contribution.* You don't pay federal income tax on any of this money until you withdraw it.

You also have the option to pay taxes before your contributions go into the plan, have the money grow without taxes, and then withdraw the entire amount without paying any taxes. These after-tax contributions are known as Roth contributions. They are similar to Roth IRA contributions, but they go into your 401(k). A number of rules must be satisfied in order to get the tax break when you withdraw your Roth contributions.

Of course, there's a catch. Some 401(k) plans may not allow you to withdraw money while you're still working. Even if yours does allow you to do so, if you're under $59^{1}/_{2}$ years old, withdrawals can be difficult and costly.

How much your 401(k) will be worth when you retire depends on a number of factors, such as what investments you choose, what return you get on those investments, whether your employer makes a contribution, and whether you withdraw money early. The next few sections take a look at the benefits of participating in a 401(k).

Lowers how much tax you pay

A 401(k) lets you pay less income tax in the following two ways:

- ✔ **Lower taxable income:** You don't have to pay federal income tax on your pretax contributions to your 401(k) plan until you withdraw it from the plan.
- ✔ **Tax deferral:** You don't pay tax on your 401(k) investment earnings each year — you do so only when you make withdrawals of pretax contributions or Roth contributions that don't qualify as tax-free distributions. The Roth contributions must be held in the plan for at least five years to qualify for a tax-free distribution.

The government provides these big tax breaks in an attempt to avoid having a country full of senior citizens who can't make ends meet. (Nice to know the government's on top of things, huh?)

The money that you contribute to a 401(k), other than Roth contributions, reduces your *gross income,* or *taxable income* (your pay before tax and any other deductions). When you have lower taxable income, you pay fewer of the following income or wage taxes:

- ✔ **Federal taxes:** These taxes increase as your income increases — for 2002, the rate for most workers is either 15 or 27 percent, and the top tax rate is 38.6 percent.

- ✔ **State taxes:** Many states impose their own income or wage taxes, ranging from less than 1 percent to as much as 12 percent in 2002, depending on the state.

- ✔ **Local/municipal government taxes:** Many local and municipal governments also have income or wage taxes.

Book VI

Retiring
Comfortably

In most states, you aren't required to pay state or local taxes on contributions to your 401(k). However, a few states may require you to list all or part of the money that you contribute to a 401(k) as taxable income on your state tax return. You still get the federal tax break, however. Check with your state and local tax authorities if you're not sure what the rules are where you live.

Taxes that you don't avoid, because everybody has to pay them on gross income (including 401(k) contributions), are Social Security/Medicare (FICA) and unemployment (FUTA).

Without a 401(k) plan, taxes eat away the money that you can save. Assume that your employer doesn't offer a 401(k) or other retirement plan and that your total tax rate is 37.65 percent (7.65 percent FICA/FUTA, 27 percent federal income tax, 2 percent state income tax, and 1 percent local wage taxes). After paying these taxes, it takes almost 16 percent of your gross income to have 10 percent left to invest for retirement. The following example shows how this savings works.

Assume that you earn $50,000 a year and your goal is to save 10 percent, or $5,000. You would have to earn $8,017 to have $5,000 left "after-tax."

Pretax earnings required	$8,017
Federal income tax	−$2,164
State/local wage tax	−$240
FICA/FUTA taxes	−$613
Amount left to save	$5,000

Now assume that your employer offers a 401(k) plan and that you can save the $5,000 in your 401(k) account. In this case, the only tax you have to pay at the time you make the contribution is FICA/FUTA. As a result, you need to earn only $5,414 to be able to contribute $5,000 to the 401(k) plan.

Pretax earnings required	$5,414
Federal income tax	–$0
State/local wage tax	–$0
FICA/FUTA taxes	–414
Amount left to save	$5,000

Without a 401(k) plan, it takes you $8,017 in pretax income to save $5,000 after taxes. When you can save pretax money in your 401(k), it takes only $5,414 to save the same $5,000. In other words, with a 401(k), it costs you less of your current earnings to save the same amount. Pretty good deal, don't you think?

Some plans allow you to make *after-tax* contributions. You don't get the initial tax break of lower taxable income, but you do benefit from deferring taxes on your investment earnings.

In addition to the income tax savings on your contributions, you save when it comes to paying tax on your investment earnings.

The gains in your 401(k) aren't taxed annually, as they would be in a regular *taxable* bank savings account, a personal mutual fund account, or a brokerage account (which you may use to buy and sell stocks and other investments). With a 401(k), you defer paying taxes on your investment earnings until you withdraw the money.

Tax-deferred compounding lets your money grow faster than it would in a taxable account.

Gets you something extra from your employer

Whoever said there's no such thing as a free lunch didn't know about *employer matching contributions* — money that your employer contributes to your 401(k) if you contribute to the plan. (Not all employers make this type of contribution, but many do.)

How 401(k) became a household "word"

The 401(k) is named after the section of the IRS "rulebook" (the Internal Revenue Code, or IRC) that governs how it works.

Section 401 applies to many different tax-qualified retirement plans — plans with special tax advantages for you and your employer. It begins with paragraph (a) and includes paragraph (k), which was added when Congress enacted the Tax Reform Act of 1978.

Paragraph (k) was one of those special-interest paragraphs added to the bill in the 11th hour. Its original objective was to cover a specific type

of Section 401 plan that banks sponsored for their own employees.

Only a couple years later did we realize that paragraph (k) offered additional possibilities. The result was the first 401(k) savings plan with employer matching contributions and employee pretax contributions made through payroll deductions. The practice wasn't universally accepted at first, but after the Treasury Department okayed it in 1981, it began to catch on.

And the rest, as they say, is history.

Book VI

Retiring Comfortably

The most common formula is for the employer to put in 50 cents for every dollar you contribute, up to 6 percent of your salary. Because 50 cents is half of $1, the most your employer will contribute is half of 6 percent, or 3 percent of your salary. You get this full 3 percent only if you contribute 6 percent of your salary.

The employer matching contribution can be the single most important feature of your 401(k) plan. The more you get from your employer, the less you have to save out of your own paycheck to achieve an adequate level of retirement income. In fact, if your employer offers a matching contribution, make sure that you contribute enough to your plan to get it all. If you don't, this money is lost to you.

You may have to stay with your company for a minimum length of time before the employer contributions *vest,* or belong to you. But if you can meet that requirement, the money's yours, along with any return it has earned in the meantime.

Saving Without Tears

A big benefit of signing up for your 401(k) plan is that you don't have to think about the fact that you're saving. "Out of sight, out of mind" is what happens to most people — they don't even miss the money because it's taken out of their paycheck before they have a chance to spend it.

This semiforced savings is one of the most valuable benefits of 401(k) plans. The payroll deduction has the power to convert spenders into savers. Most people are unable to save over a long period of time if they have to physically write the check or make the deposit each pay period. Saving becomes the last, not the first, priority. Many participants have said that the 401(k) has helped them save thousands of dollars that they otherwise would have spent carelessly.

It's a good idea to increase your 401(k) contributions if you get a raise or a bonus. In fact, do it right away so that you don't get used to spending the extra money.

Taking Your Savings with You When You Change Jobs

When you change jobs, you can take your 401(k) money with you — and keep the tax advantages — by putting it into your new employer's 401(k), 403(b), or 457 plan, or into an IRA (individual retirement account).

Transferring your money to a new employer's plan or an IRA is known as a *rollover* or *trustee-to-trustee transfer*.

Many employers require you to work for a minimum number of years before the employer contributions are yours to keep (known as *vesting*).

Because your 401(k) is "portable," you can build up a retirement nest egg even if you change jobs fairly frequently. This portability beats the traditional defined-benefit pension plan (in which you receive a set amount from your employer each month in retirement, if you qualify). With those plans, you can lose *all* retirement benefits if you don't work at the company for the minimum vesting period — this period can be at least five years, or even longer at some companies.

Letting the Pros Work for You

Have you ever wished that you could hire a professional money manager to handle your investments? A 401(k) lets you take a step in that direction by offering *mutual funds*.

Mutual funds are investments that let you pool your money with the money of hundreds or thousands of other investors. An investment expert called the *fund manager* decides how to invest all this money, trying to get the best return on your investment based on the fund's *investment objective*. Because the fund manager invests your money along with the money contributed by other investors in the fund, she has more money to invest and can spread it around to different companies or sectors of the economy. This *diversification* helps reduce the amount of risk that you take with your investments.

What do mutual funds mean for you? If you choose your fund carefully, you benefit from a professional money manager who's seeking the best return for the fund's investors, based on the fund's investment objectives.

In most cases, your employer is responsible for choosing the mutual funds (and any other investments) offered by your 401(k) plan. More than 8,000 mutual funds are registered in the United States. If your employer does a good job of narrowing the offering to a handful, it can save you a lot of time.

Instead of relying on choices made by their employer, however, some investors prefer to choose their own investments, such as individual stocks, mutual funds, or other investments that aren't included in their plans. Some 401(k) plans now offer a *brokerage window* that allows you to choose your own investments. But you generally pay an extra fee if you use this feature.

Book VI

Retiring Comfortably

Buying More When Prices Are Low

When you invest a specified amount at regular intervals, as you do with automatic 401(k) contributions from your paycheck, you are using an investment strategy called *dollar cost averaging*. (You didn't know you were that smart, did you?) This investment strategy may lower the average price that you pay for your investments. How? Because you're spending the same amount each time you invest, you end up buying more shares of your investments when prices are low and fewer shares when prices are high. By averaging high and low prices, you reduce the risk that you will buy more shares when prices are high.

Of course, if stock prices only go up for the entire time you invest, this strategy doesn't work. But if you contribute to a 401(k) over a long period of time, there will likely be periods when prices go down.

Improving Your Chances of an Ideal Retirement

Investing in a 401(k) gives you a chance at extra savings for your retirement years. The additional savings can mean the difference between merely surviving retirement and actually living it up.

Did you ever stop to think how much money you'll need in retirement to keep up your current lifestyle? Most financial planners suggest that you'll need at least 70 to 80 percent of your preretirement income. But many people may need closer to 100 percent, or more.

Some people think that their Social Security benefits alone will be enough to cover their retirement needs. But don't rely on Social Security to finance your retirement. Financial security during retirement requires income from a variety of sources. Social Security's current problems are serious, but the system was never intended to be the sole source of retirement income for Americans.

Try to estimate how big of a retirement account you'll need, and develop a savings plan to try to accumulate that amount. When you retire, you'll have to manage your nest egg so that you don't run out of money before you die.

Protecting Your Money

Investing money always involves some risks, but money in a 401(k) plan is protected in some ways that money in an ordinary savings account, brokerage account, or IRA isn't.

Meeting minimum standards

401(k) plans are governed by a federal law called *ERISA* — the Employee Retirement Income Security Act. Passed in 1974, ERISA sets minimum standards for retirement plans offered by private-sector companies. (Some nonprofits also follow ERISA rules, but local, state, and federal government retirement plans, as well as church plans, don't have to.)

ERISA requirements include the following:

- ✔ Providing information to you about plan features on a regular basis, including a *summary plan description* outlining the plan's main rules, when you enroll in the plan and periodically thereafter

- ✔ Defining how long you may be required to work before you can sign up for the plan or before employer contributions to the plan are yours to keep if you leave your job

- ✔ Detailing requirements for the *plan fiduciary,* essentially including anyone at your company or the plan provider who has control over the investment choices in the plan (Participants can sue a fiduciary who breaks the rules.)

This last point, *fiduciary responsibility,* is important to understand. Essentially, it means that anyone who has a decision-making role in your 401(k) plan's investments is legally bound to make those decisions in the best interests of the plan participants (you and your coworkers), *not* in the best interest of the company, the plan provider, or the fiduciary's cousin Joe. For example, the committee in charge of choosing a 401(k) provider can't choose Bank XYZ just because the company president's cousin runs the bank.

But fiduciary responsibility doesn't necessarily mean that you can sue your employer if your 401(k) doesn't do well. (Keep in mind that lawsuits are often costly and won't endear you to your employer.) If you lose most of your money because you make bad investment decisions or the stock market takes a nosedive, but your employer has followed ERISA rules, your employer is off the hook. Your employer may gain limited protection through something called *404(c)*. Without going into too much detail, Section 404(c) of ERISA requires your employer to provide you with specific information about your plan, including information about the investment options, and to allow you to make changes in your investments frequently enough to respond to ups and downs in the market. In return, *you* assume liability for your investment results.

Plan operation was a critical point in the case of Enron, the Houston-based energy trading company that declared bankruptcy in late 2001. Many employees suffered huge losses in their 401(k)s because they had invested heavily in Enron stock based on the rosy picture that senior management painted about the company's fortunes. When that rosy picture turned out to be a fake, employees hollered that they wouldn't have invested so much in Enron stock (one of their 401(k) investment options) if they had known the truth.

The Pension Protection Act also contains a provision that enables employers to obtain fiduciary relief. This provision is called a Qualified Default Investment Arrangement (QDIA). An employer may default participants who choose not to select their own investments into specific investments that qualify as a QDIA. Employers are protected from fiduciary liability if the QDIA satisfies the requirements set by the government.

Avoiding losses in bankruptcy

Many people wonder whether their 401(k) money is at risk if their employer goes belly-up. The answer is usually no, with a few caveats:

- ✔ If the money is in investments that are tied to your employer, such as company stock, and the employer goes bankrupt, you may lose your money. (This risk is a compelling argument for you to limit the amount of your 401(k) that you invest in a single stock.)

✔ In the case of fraud or wrongdoing by your employer or the trustee of the 401(k) account, your money may be at risk. (The trustee is personally liable to return your money, but that's no help if he has disappeared.) These situations are rare; what's more, your employer is required to buy a type of insurance — a *fidelity bond* — when it sets up the plan, which may enable you to recoup at least some of your money in the event of dishonesty. (Fidelity bonds generally cover 10 percent of the amount in the entire plan, or $500,000, whichever amount is smaller.)

✔ You may lose part of your money if your employer goes out of business or declares bankruptcy before depositing your contributions into the trust fund that receives the 401(k) money that is deducted from your paycheck.

Federal law says that if you declare personal bankruptcy, your creditors generally can't touch your 401(k). They may be able to get at your other savings, but your 401(k) should be protected. Exceptions include if you owe money to the IRS or if a court has ordered you to give the money to your ex-spouse as part of a divorce settlement. In both of those cases, your 401(k) money is vulnerable.

Watching Out for Potential Pitfalls

The tax advantages you get with a 401(k) have a flip side: rules about when you can take out your money out, whether you'll have to pay a penalty, and even what you can invest in. All of these rules are out of your control after you decide to contribute to a 401(k) plan. This section tells you what pitfalls to watch out for.

Withdrawing money while you're working is difficult

It can be difficult, if not downright impossible, to make a withdrawal from your 401(k) while you're working for the company that sponsors the plan.

Many employers permit you to borrow money from your 401(k), but not necessarily for any old reason. Many plans permit *hardship withdrawals,* which are withdrawals from your account to pay expenses when you're in financial difficulty. Your employer may permit withdrawals only for reasons approved by the IRS.

People often think that they're automatically allowed to withdraw money from a 401(k) for higher-education expenses or for buying a home, and that they won't owe an early withdrawal penalty on the amount. This assumption is false. Your plan *may* allow you to make a withdrawal for these reasons, but it doesn't *have* to.

When you leave your employer, either to retire or to change jobs, you generally have a window of opportunity to get your money. In most cases, you can receive payment of your account or transfer the money into an IRA or another employer's retirement plan. We highly recommend transferring the money to another plan or IRA, or leaving the money in the plan, to avoid a high tax bill (see the following section).

Book VI

Retiring
Comfortably

Taking money out before 59¹/₂ costs more

If you do manage to withdraw your pretax contributions or non-qualifiying Roth contributions for a hardship withdrawal before you turn $59^1/_2$ and the 5-year minimum holding period for Roth contributions, you'll be heavily taxed. Not only will you owe federal and perhaps state and local income tax on the amount withdrawn, but you'll also owe a 10 percent federal early withdrawal penalty on the entire amount. Some states may also impose additional early withdrawal penalties of a few percent. All of these penalties combined could mean that you pay more than 50 percent of your withdrawal in taxes and penalties, depending on your tax bracket.

Taking out a loan lets you avoid these penalties; however, other costs are involved.

Earning more may mean contributing less

If you earn enough to qualify as a highly compensated employee, your contributions to your 401(k) plan may be limited to only a few percent of your salary. Many 401(k) plans are required to pass *nondiscrimination tests* each year to make sure that highly paid employees as a group aren't contributing a lot more to the plan than their lower-paid colleagues. In requiring these tests, Congress is looking out for the little guy (and gal).

Being at the mercy of your plan

A well-administered, well-chosen, flexible 401(k) plan can be a wonderful benefit. A poorly administered plan with bad investment choices and little flexibility can be a nightmare. We've heard stories of companies that don't invest employee contributions on time or that take money from the plan, companies that don't let employees contribute the maximum permitted, and companies in which employees pay useless fees for a plan because the managers who set it up were incompetent, uninformed, or even criminals.

In most cases, the tax benefit of a 401(k) is a good enough reason to take advantage of the plan offered by your employer. However, if the investments the plan offer are truly bad, the fees charged are exorbitant, or administration of the plan is questionable, you may be better off investing your retirement money elsewhere until you have a better 401(k).

Telling the Employer's Point of View

For employers, setting up and running a retirement plan is no cakewalk. An employer has to select a plan, decide how to administer it, find a company to provide the investments, comply with paperwork and other regulations, possibly contribute money to employees' accounts, and so on. Small-business owners may find that 401(k)s don't meet their needs.

403(b): Different Name, Same Tax Breaks

If you're a public school employee, hospital worker, member of the clergy, or employee of a 501(c)(3) nonprofit organization, chances are good that you have a 403(b) plan for your retirement savings. Although these plans are often similar to 401(k)s, they're not exactly the same.

403(b) plans let you put off until tomorrow what the tax man would have you pay today. In other words, they offer the same tax advantages to you as 401(k) plans.

✔ Your contributions to a 403(b) are deducted from your salary before taxes, reducing your taxable income.

✔ Money grows tax deferred in the account — you don't pay income tax on your contributions, any employer contributions, or earnings in your account until you withdraw money from the account.

In addition, many rules and contribution limits are the same for both 403(b) and 401(k) plans. (This wasn't the case before the tax laws changed in 2002; luckily, we don't have to explain what 403(b)s used to be like!) But some 403(b)s are very different from 401(k)s because the employer isn't very involved. See the section "Understanding ERISA Versus Non-ERISA 403(b) Plans," later in the chapter, for more details.

403(b) plans may also give you the option of making after-tax Roth contributions.

What's in a name?

The name 403(b) comes from the section of the Internal Revenue Code that made these plans possible. You may have heard 403(b) plans referred to as tax-sheltered annuities (TSAs) or tax-deferred annuities (TDAs). These names come from the earliest retirement plans of this type — first created in 1958 — which allowed participants to invest in only annuities (see the section "Trekking Through Your Investment Options," later in this chapter, for details).

Stashing Away as Much as You Can: Contribution Info

Contributions to a 403(b) may come from the employee only, the employer only, or a combination of the two — for example, an employee contribution plus an employer matching contribution.

The 403(b) regular contribution limits and age-50 catch-up limit are the same as for 401(k)s. An individual can contribute up to $11,000 before taxes to a 403(b) in 2002; the limit rises by $1,000 a year until 2006. Additionally, contributions to the 403(b), including employer contributions, can't be more than 100 percent of pay or $40,000, whichever is less.

Workers who are age 50 and over could contribute an additional $1,000 as a catch-up contribution in 2002 if the plan was amended to permit this type of contribution; this limit rose by $1,000 a year until 2006.

Playing catch-up

Certain employees qualify for *another* type of catch-up contribution, often referred to as the "15 years of service" catch-up. (Guess how many years you have to work at your employer before you're eligible?) The following requirements apply:

✔ You must be employed by a qualified organization, such as a public school system, hospital, health and welfare service agency, church, or church organization.

✔ You must have at least 15 years of service with your employer (the years don't have to be consecutive, and you can get some credit for part-time work).

If you meet these conditions and you haven't contributed the full amount to your 403(b) in past years, you can contribute up to $3,000 extra per year. After you make contributions of this type totaling $15,000, you can't make any more. The formula for calculating how much extra you can contribute is complicated, so ask your employer or 403(b) provider to help you figure it out.

You're allowed to make both types of catch-up contributions in the same year if you qualify for both. After you exhaust the 15-years-of-service contributions, you can continue to make the age-50 catch-up.

Mix 'n match: Combining a 403(b) with other plans

Some employers offer a 403(b) along with another plan, either a 401(k) or a 457 (a similar plan for governmental and certain nongovernmental organizations).

If you're eligible for a 401(k) and 403(b), the most you can contribute to both plans, combined, is the federal maximum limit for a single plan (not counting catch-up contributions).

If you have a 403(b) and 457, though, the plot thickens (along with your retirement account, we hope!). You can contribute the federal maximum to *each plan*.

Trekking Through Your Investment Options

One big difference between 403(b)s and 401(k)s is the types of investments commonly offered. Many 403(b) plans offer only *annuities,* a type of investment sold by insurance companies. Annuities come in many different forms; 403(b) plans generally offer *variable annuities*. With variable annuities, your investment choices usually include either mutual funds or *separate accounts,* or *subaccounts,* which are like mutual funds but are run by the insurance company. Variable annuity accounts don't guarantee any return, nor do they necessarily guarantee your principal. You may have an option called a *fixed account* that guarantees your principal and a certain return. Annuity investments often carry higher fees than mutual funds outside an annuity.

Some 403(b) plans, called 403(b)(7) accounts, offer mutual funds. Mutual funds entered the 403(b) arena years after annuities did, so fewer employers have traditionally offered them. However, as more employees demand mutual fund choices, employers are increasingly looking for 403(b) providers to offer mutual funds.

You can't invest in individual stocks and bonds within a 403(b). You're allowed to invest in only mutual funds or an annuity contract.

Your 403(b) may have a fairly short list of providers that your employer pre-selects. Or it may have a laundry list of many providers that are not screened by your employer, offering dozens of possible investments. Either one is possible with a 403(b).

Research exactly what's available to you *before* you make a decision about what to invest in. Yes, we know that research takes time, but the saying "Act in haste, repent at leisure" couldn't be more true when it comes to 403(b)s. If you invest in the first option that comes along, you may spend a lot of time regretting it.

See Book IV for a lot more on investing.

Withdrawing Money: Watch Out for That Fee!

While you're working, withdrawal rules for 403(b)s are generally as restrictive as for 401(k)s. Getting your money out is difficult, but if you have a hardship, you may be able to take a hardship withdrawal. Some plans also allow loans.

With a hardship withdrawal, you generally owe a 10 percent early withdrawal penalty if you're under $59^1/_2$, in addition to the income tax.

If your 403(b) money is in an annuity, you may be charged an *exit fee* (or *surrender fee*) for withdrawing money, if you're even allowed to take it out. If you want to withdraw or transfer money from an annuity, find out how much the exit fee is. (Better yet, find out before you invest in the annuity!) Remember the cartoon character George of the Jungle? He always slammed into trees because he didn't look where his vine was swinging. Don't get caught in the same trap, slamming into fees because you don't look where you're investing.

After you retire, you may receive your money in one of several ways. Be sure to find out all your options.

✔ If you have an annuity investment, the insurance company offers you the chance to convert the annuity into a stream of payments. You should have a choice of how the payments are structured — whether they're for your lifetime, for yours and your spouse's jointly, and so on.

✔ Some annuities may offer a lump-sum payment or installment option, which you can roll over into an IRA. With a lump-sum option, you may have to pay a surrender charge; you can usually avoid this charge by withdrawing the money in installments. You can set up an annuity payment to last for your lifetime, but if you choose installment payments, the payments will end after a specific number of years. Confusing? You bet it is, which is why you may want to get help from a professional advisor before you make your decision. You usually can't change your mind after you pick your distribution method.

If you have a mutual fund account, your options at retirement should be similar to your options with a 401(k). You may be able to leave the money in the 403(b) and eventually set up a schedule of withdrawals from that plan, or you can roll the 403(b) into an IRA.

Taking Your 403(b) on the Road

In theory, 403(b) plans are as portable as 401(k) plans. When you change jobs, you can transfer your 403(b) money into an IRA or another employer's 403(b), 401(k), or 457 plan. As with 401(k)s, though, you can transfer a 403(b) into a new employer's plan only if that plan accepts rollovers.

Before 2002, you weren't allowed to roll a 403(b) into a 401(k) or 457 plan when you changed jobs. You could only roll it into an IRA or another 403(b). Because the 401(k) and 457 rollovers are relatively new, employers may be slow to adopt them. If you change jobs, be sure to ask your new employer whether it will accept a rollover of your 403(b). If not, you can always roll it into an IRA (see Book VI, Chapter 2 for more on IRAs).

If your 403(b) includes an employer contribution, you may be required to work for the employer for a certain period of time before the contributions vest. Vesting rules for employer contributions in 403(b) plans are the same as for 401(k) plans.

Understanding ERISA Versus Non-ERISA 403(b) Plans

Now comes the tricky part. One important point you need to know about your 403(b) plan is whether it is governed by the *Employee Retirement*

Income Security Act (ERISA). 401(k) plans are governed by ERISA, but not all 403(b) plans are. ERISA is the federal law that sets the standards that these plans have to follow.

ERISA: Employer + plan provider

Whether a 403(b) plan is governed by ERISA depends on the level of employer involvement in the plan. A 403(b) plan that is covered by ERISA is essentially an agreement between the employer and the plan provider, and it requires significant employer involvement. The employer selects a menu of investment options for participants to choose from, and it may make a matching contribution. If your 403(b) is covered by ERISA, it must follow ERISA rules. Your employer has fiduciary responsibility for running the plan in your best interests, you must receive an account statement at least once a year, and so on.

Non-ERISA: You + plan provider

However, a number of employers do not participate to this extent. Their plans are not covered by ERISA. Public schools often fall into this category. In this case, the 403(b) agreement is between you and the plan provider. Your employer simply agrees to send your 403(b) contribution each pay period to the plan provider that you've chosen. These employers give you a list of possible investments, but they aren't involved in preselecting the menu of investment options. The list often consists of simply 403(b) providers who've asked the employer to put them on the list. These providers may be (and often are) insurance agents selling annuities. (Companies can't just walk into a teacher's lounge and start signing up employees — they need the employer's permission.)

One disadvantage of the second type of plan is that it can be very hard to decide how to invest your money. The list may include dozens of names (or, in the case of the Los Angeles Unified School District, more than 100). A common criticism is that participants — usually lacking free time to research investments — may invest in a product simply because the vendor happens to hold a seminar on a day they can attend, or because a representative comes to see them at home. Frankly, that's no way to choose an investment.

If you're in this situation, you may want to first talk to coworkers to see what they've invested in. Don't run out and invest in the first one they mention, though; see if the same name comes up a few times. If so, it may be worth further scrutiny, particularly if your coworkers like the results.

Book VI

Retiring Comfortably

After you've narrowed your choices, do research as you would for any investment (starting, naturally, with Book IV).

If you're thinking of investing in an annuity, be sure that you find out all the fees you'll be charged, including the *surrender fee* if you eventually want out of the annuity. Get this information in writing — don't rely on verbal assurances from the salesperson.

You may be able to get your employer to add a provider you like to the list of choices, particularly with a non-ERISA plan. Then you can use that provider's investment options. In any 403(b) plan, definitely let your employer know if you're not happy with the investments. For example, if you want your plan to offer mutual funds, ask your employer. Mutual funds are becoming more common in 403(b) plans precisely because more employees are requesting them.

Finding Out Rules for Church Plans

403(b) plans offered by churches and church-related organizations aren't required to follow ERISA rules, and most don't. Furthermore, in addition to annuities and mutual funds, church plans can offer something called a retirement income account (RIA) that offers investment possibilities beyond what 403(b)(7)s offer. However, not all church plans offer RIAs. Churches may also offer 401(k) plans and may choose not to follow ERISA rules.

IRS Publication 571 contains a section explaining rules for 403(b) plans for ministers and church employees.

Why can't a (b) be more like a (k)?

Congress created 403(b)s for nonprofits in 1958 and extended them to educational institutions in 1961, long before the arrival of 401(k)s. Because annuities were their only form of investment for many years, 403(b) plans have a very different history than 401(k)s.

Insurance companies had a lock on the 403(b) business during the 1950s and 1960s. Other financial organizations didn't offer any competition — mutual funds were generally sold only to individuals for personal investing, and banks managed retirement money only for employer-run retirement plans, such as defined benefit pension plans.

The idea of employees saving for retirement through salary reductions actually started with tax-sheltered annuities (TSAs — the original 403(b)s) instead of 401(k)s. Making pretax contributions to a 401(k) gave employees of for-profit companies an opportunity similar to the one many employees of nonprofit employers had been enjoying for years, with a couple of significant differences:

The first distinction is the special nondiscrimination test for 401(k)s, linking the amount that highly compensated employees may contribute to the amount the non–highly compensated employees contribute. TSAs weren't subject to these tests because few, if any, employees of nonprofit employers were highly paid at the time. As a result, achieving a high level of participation was never an issue with TSAs. Today 403(b)s aren't subject to this test, either, although they have to fulfill other nondiscrimination requirements for employer contributions, employee after-tax contributions, and overall plan participation opportunities.

The second distinction involves investment products. Because 401(k)s weren't limited to annuities, insurance companies never controlled the 401(k) market. Certain products insurance companies offered, such as guaranteed investment contracts (GIC), were used whenever appropriate during the early days of 401(k)s, but mutual funds were also used. Senior-level managers also had a much higher level of interest in 401(k) investments than was the case with 403(b)s. One reason for this difference was the desire to achieve a high level of participation in a 401(k) to pass the nondiscrimination test. This desire to achieve high levels of participation led to better investment selections and, frequently, to employer matching contributions to help drive participation.

Things have changed in a number of ways. The need for employees to save for retirement is widely accepted, regardless of the type of employer. With the large number of employees who are now managing their own retirement savings, the level of investment awareness and knowledge is much higher than it was years ago. Competition among financial organizations to capture and retain retirement savings is intense. All these factors have resulted, and will continue to result, in better investment products for 403(b)s and 401(k)s. The 403(b) business is no longer limited to insurance companies. Their control will continue to decline as the investments under these plans move in the same direction as 401(k)s.

Book VI

Retiring Comfortably

Chapter 2

Retiring Your Way: IRAs

*Y*ou have many different ways to build the wealth that you'll need to retire in carefree comfort, with the financial horsepower to do what you want to do, when you want to do it. Would you like to take a trip around the world? Buy a vacation home near the beach? Do volunteer work in your community without worrying about getting a 9-to-5 job to pay the bills? You can do all this and more by regularly investing money as you approach retirement age. The more you invest, the sooner you do so, and the better your investments perform, the more relaxed and carefree your retirement years will be.

But how do you know what kinds of investments are the right ones — the ones that will grow enough to let you retire hopefully sometime before your 95th birthday? Of course, none of us has a crystal ball that works with complete, 100-percent accuracy (if you do, please mail it to us right away — ours is getting a bit cloudy), but the government has created a retirement investment option with a lot of financial horsepower: the *individual retirement account* (IRA).

In this chapter, we take a close look at this tax-favored retirement vehicle. First we explore retirement itself and then dig into IRA basics. We delve into traditional IRAs and consider a popular (and relatively new) IRA flavor: the Roth IRA. Finally, we tell you how to cash in your IRA when it's time to retire, or how to roll it over into another IRA if you change jobs or want to shift your investing approach. We also consider a variety of basic IRA investing strategies.

Why an IRA?

If you're reading this chapter, we think it's safe to assume that you're giving your retirement serious consideration. First of all, congratulations! Getting ready for retirement — no matter how many years away it might be — is one of the most important steps you can take in your own personal financial life and in the lives of your family and loved ones. Second, it's never too late to get started. Even if you're rapidly approaching your retirement years, you can take certain actions today to pave the way to a much more comfortable retirement than if you do nothing at all.

According to studies, fewer than 20 percent of baby boomers in the United States are putting away sufficient savings for their retirement. Even worse, about 25 percent of adults aged 35 to 54 *have not yet even started* to save money for their retirement. This is not good.

Why do some people fail to prepare for retirement? Some key reasons might include these:

- ✔ They think that it's too early to start planning for retirement. (Hint: It's not too early to start planning for retirement.)

- ✔ They think they don't make enough money to plan for retirement. (Hint: Anyone can afford to set aside even a modest amount of money for retirement.)

- ✔ Other priorities — job, school, vacation — get in the way. (Hint: If you've got time to watch TV for an hour or two every day, you've got time to plan for your retirement.)

- ✔ They think some financial windfall (lottery, Vegas/Atlantic City, insurance, inheritance) will come their way just in the nick of time. (Hint: Don't bet on it!)

- ✔ They think that Social Security will take care of them. (Hint: Although Social Security will help pay some expenses in retirement, it's unlikely to pay them all.)

Social Security is certainly better than nothing when you reach the age of retirement, and it can provide vitally needed disability and survivor benefits to a spouse or children well before you reach retirement age. If you earn the current maximum of $102,000 in annual income or more, you can expect to receive a monthly check (in current dollars) of slightly more than $2,000 when you retire, or about $25,000 a year — about 25 percent of your current annual income of $102,000. However, if your annual earnings are in the neighborhood of $50,000, you can expect to receive something more in the vicinity of $1,300 a month when you retire, or a bit more than $15,000 a year.

Considering that the poverty threshold in the United States — the annual income under which you are officially considered to be "poor" — is currently $10,499, you can see the importance of supplementing your Social Security payments.

When it comes to determining when you can draw Social Security payments, the words "when you retire" are key. The exact amount you'll receive each month depends on a complicated formula that takes into account how much you earned over your lifetime, how much you made during your highest-earning years, and the age at which you retire:

- ✔ If you were born before 1938, you can officially retire at age 65 and receive full benefits.

- ✔ If you were born after 1959, you have full retirement at 67.

- ✔ If you were born between 1938 and 1959, your full retirement is between 65 and 67.

You may also elect to take a reduced Social Security payment when you reach age 62, or you can defer taking Social Security payments until after your legally eligible retirement age, in which case your payments will be even higher. Widows and widowers can start receiving reduced benefits at age 60, and disabled individuals can start collecting at age 50.

If these rules sound just a bit complicated, believe us, they are. For an exhaustive rundown on the ins and outs of Social Security, be sure to visit the Social Security Administration Web site at www.ssa.gov.

Truth be told, Social Security is the sole source of income for 22 percent of elderly Americans. For 66 percent of elderly Americans, a monthly Social Security check provides them with at least half of their total income in retirement. But you want to do better than that when you retire — right? You want to do better than just getting along. You want to *really* retire when you retire and not worry about trying to find a job when you're 75 years old. And you want to have some peace of mind as you approach — and enjoy — your golden years.

That's where the magic of IRAs comes in.

The ABCs of IRAs

The *individual retirement account* — most commonly known by its abbreviation, IRA — is, according to the Internal Revenue Service, a "trust or custodial account set up in the United States for the exclusive benefit of you or your beneficiaries."

In plain English, an IRA is simply a tax-favored retirement plan/savings account. Created by amendments to the Internal Revenue Code of 1954 made by the Employee Retirement Income Security Act of 1974, IRAs allow you to set aside part of your pretax income each year in a special savings account at a bank, credit union, brokerage firm, or other financial institution of your choice. Annual contributions to the account are limited, and you must pay taxes when you make retirement withdrawals — typically starting when you reach age 59$\frac{1}{2}$.

According to the IRS, an IRA offers two key tax advantages:

- ✔ Contributions you make to an IRA may be fully or partially deductible, depending on the type of IRA you have and on your circumstances.

- ✔ Generally, amounts in your IRA (including earnings and gains) are not taxed until you make distributions. In some cases, amounts are not taxed at all if distributed according to the rules.

So why not just put your money into a regular, good-old-fashioned bank savings account? You can certainly do that — it's a free country. But because you aren't able to use pretax income to fund your regular savings account, you'll dramatically lessen the long-term bang you'll get for your savings buck. In addition, by directing all your savings into a regular bank account instead of an individual retirement account, you miss out on a legal way for you to lower your income taxes today — not an insignificant consideration. For example, if you're paying out 32 percent of your income between state and federal income taxes, a $6,000 contribution into an IRA would reduce your taxes by $1,920. The amount you save on your taxes will vary depending on your tax rate — the higher it is, the more you'll save. That's free money in your pocket.

As with almost any other government-created program that has implications for your income taxes, the rules governing IRAs are pretty complex. You need to first decide which kind of IRA is best for you and then understand when you can make contributions to your IRA (and in what amounts), and when you can start making withdrawals. In this section, we give you an overview of IRAs and how they work.

Types of IRAs

About 30 years ago, only one IRA — what is now called the *traditional IRA* — was available. Since then, many different kinds of IRAs have joined the ranks. Here we list some of the different kinds of IRAs you will encounter the next time you wander down to your bank or credit union or peruse an online investment brokerage Web site. We tell you more about the most common ones in later sections of this chapter.

- ✔ **Traditional IRA:** This is the basic IRA. Contributions are made with pretax cash, transactions and earnings within the IRA are not taxed, and most withdrawals at retirement are taxed as regular income.

- ✔ **Roth IRA:** Named for Sen. William Roth, this kind of IRA — which has gained in popularity in recent years — involves contributions made with after-tax cash. Transactions and earnings within the IRA are not taxed, and withdrawals are tax free, in most cases.

- ✔ **SIMPLE IRA:** This kind of IRA is actually a simplified employee pension plan, similar in some ways to a 401(k) plan, but easier and less costly to administer. With a SIMPLE IRA, both the employee and the employer can make contributions.

- ✔ **SEP IRA:** With a SEP IRA, employers can make contributions to a traditional IRA in the employee's name. Self-employed individuals and small businesses use this kind of IRA.

- ✔ **Self-directed IRA:** This kind of IRA allows you to control your investments yourself, instead of relying solely on the bank or other financial organization where your IRA resides to do all the work for you.

Book VI

Retiring Comfortably

So if you have to pay taxes on your money when you withdraw it in your golden years anyway, why bother with an IRA?

Here's why: Your taxable income is probably significantly higher during your prime working years — from 18 to 60 or so — than it will be after you retire and leave a full-time career behind. Thus, when you retire, the income taxes you pay will likely be assessed at a lower tax rate, because the tax rate you pay increases with higher incomes. By deferring the payment of income tax until retirement — when your income is presumably lower — the tax you pay will be less than if you paid it when you are younger and earning the income.

In addition, because you use pretax income, any contributions you make (except contributions to a Roth IRA) up to the allowable contribution limits (see the next section for more details on these limits) are removed from your taxable income for the year, lowering the taxes you pay that year. In addition, the returns on your IRA investments (any appreciation of assets, interest, and dividends) are allowed to compound tax free. Of course, you'll have to pay taxes when you withdraw your retirement funds (except in the case of the Roth IRA — more about that later in this chapter), but you'll have the benefit of all your IRA assets working hard for you as you grow older.

Basic IRA rules

Needless to say, plenty of rules and regulations govern individual retirement accounts and their care, maintenance, and use. But although each kind of IRA has its own unique rules and peculiarities — which change from time to time — a few basic rules and characteristics are common to most IRAs:

- The maximum allowable annual contribution for 2008 is 100 percent of earned income or $5,000, whichever is less, for individuals who are not yet 50 years old. For people 50 years of age or older, the limit is 100 percent of earned income or $6,000, whichever is less.

- In the case of a traditional IRA, you must fund your IRA before you reach the age of 70½. No such limit exists for Roth IRAs.

- IRAs must be funded with cash or cash equivalents. Using any other kinds of assets to fund your IRA negates its tax-advantaged status. However, after you have funded your IRA with the required cash or cash equivalents, you are allowed to use these assets to purchase other noncash assets, such as stocks, bonds, and mutual funds.

- However, in the case of transfers, conversions, and rollovers between IRAs and other kinds of retirement accounts, other noncash assets may be included.

- Some noncash assets are specifically prohibited from use in IRAs, including collectibles (such as rare coins and art) and life insurance.

- You are not allowed to borrow money from your IRA. Doing so strips your IRA of its favored tax status.

The U.S. tax code was not designed to be easy for mere mortals to navigate. It is an extremely complex and ever-changing set of rules and regulations. Dollar, income, and age limits change from time to time, and what was true last year may not be true this year — or the next. That said, the information used in this edition is current as of 2008. Refer to the IRS Web site (www.irs. gov) or to a competent tax accountant or attorney for late-breaking updates and changes. If there's one thing you can count on, it's that plenty of those changes will crop up.

Funding your IRA

After you set up your IRA — with a bank, a credit union, a stock brokerage, your employer, or wherever you decide — you need to take one more step to tap its benefits: You have to fund it. However, to set up and make contributions to an IRA, you must be under the age of 70½ in the case of a traditional IRA and have received taxable compensation during the year. According to the IRS, compensation is what you earn from working:

- Wages and salaries
- Commissions
- Self-employment income
- Alimony
- Nontaxable combat pay

However, compensation does *not* include the following:

- ✔ Earnings and profits from property

- ✔ Interest and dividend income

- ✔ Pension or annuity income

- ✔ Deferred compensation

- ✔ Income from certain partnerships

- ✔ Any amounts you exclude from income

So who can you give your IRA money to? According to the applicable IRA rules and regulations, you can set up an IRA with a variety of different financial organizations, including these sources:

- ✔ Bank, credit union, or other financial institution

- ✔ Life insurance company

- ✔ Stockbroker

- ✔ Mutual fund

The maximum allowable annual contribution for 2008 is 100 percent of earned income or $5,000, whichever is less, for individuals who are not yet 50 years old. For people 50 years of age or older, the limit is 100 percent of earned income or $6,000, whichever is less. In addition, you must make your annual contribution by the deadline, the due date for filing your tax return for that year, not including extensions. For example, if you want to make a contribution to your IRA for 2008, you must make the contribution no later than April 15, 2009.

Be aware of something else when it comes to making contributions to your IRA: *the retirement savings contributions credit.* This credit is currently up to $1,000 for taxpayers who are single, married filing separately, or widowed, and up to $2,000 for taxpayers who are married filing jointly. You are eligible for this credit if your 2008 adjusted gross income (AGI) for federal tax purposes is not more than these limits:

- ✔ $53,000 if your filing status is married filing jointly

- ✔ $39,750 if your filing status is head of household

- ✔ $26,500 if your filing status is single, married filing separately, or qualifying widow(er)

What's especially cool about the retirement savings contributions credit is that it is a true credit to your taxes, not just a deduction. Thus, you take the full amount of the credit right off the final amount of taxes you owe. Be sure to check the latest rules when you file for this tax credit. Like much of the rest of the tax code, income limits and actual credit amounts can and do change from year to year.

Withdrawing from your IRA

Generally, you can't withdraw money from your IRA before the age of 59^1/$_2$. Doing so triggers a tax penalty of 10 percent of the amount of the withdrawal. By the way, the IRS calls any withdrawal of cash from an IRA a *distribution*. In a number of circumstances, you *can* take distributions from your IRA without being penalized by the government. These exceptions include the following:

✔ You are allowed to make penalty-free withdrawals from your IRA if you are going to use the money to pay for expenses for a higher education for you or your immediate family (spouse, children, grandchildren). You'll need to attend an IRS-approved institution, however, which includes any college, university, vocational school or other post-secondary facility that meets federal student aid program requirements. Qualified expenses include tuition, fees, books, supplies, and equipment, as well as expenses for special-needs students. If the student is at least a half-time student, room and board are also qualified expenses. There is no limit on penalty-free withdrawals for qualified educational expenses.

✔ You may also make penalty-free withdrawals from your IRA to buy, build, or rebuild a first home (limited to a maximum total withdrawal of $10,000). This particular exception involves a lot of conditions, so be sure to look at IRS publication 590, "Individual Retirement Arrangements (IRAs)," for details.

✔ You can make penalty-free withdrawals from your IRA if you have unreimbursed medical expenses that exceed 7.5 percent of your income. In addition, if you suffer a disability, you may be able to make penalty-free withdrawals from your IRA, depending on your particular circumstances.

✔ You may not have to pay the 10-percent penalty for IRA distributions taken to pay for medical insurance for yourself, your spouse, or your dependents. However, all the following conditions must also apply:

• You have lost your job.

• You have received unemployment compensation paid under any federal or state law for 12 consecutive weeks because you lost your job.

• You received the distributions during either the year you received the unemployment compensation or the following year.

• You received the distributions no later than 60 days after you were reemployed.

✔ If you are the victim of any one of three hurricanes — Katrina, Rita, or Wilma — and your primary home is or was located in a qualified hurricane disaster area, withdrawals you made from your IRA in 2005 or 2006 are penalty free.

✔ Individuals who are military reservists (Army Reserve, Naval Reserve, Air Force Reserve, and so on) and were ordered or called to duty after September 11, 2001, and before December 31, 2007, may also be eligible for penalty-free IRA distributions.

✔ If you're the kind of person who enjoys working with numbers, you can make penalty-free withdrawals from your IRA before you reach age 59½ in another way: by setting up an *annuity*. In essence, you use an IRS-approved distribution method to determine a series of substantially equal payments for the rest of your life, based on your anticipated life expectancy at the time. This one can get kind of complicated, so be sure to consult with a CPA or tax accountant if you're going to give it a try.

WARNING!

It's usually best to avoid taking any distributions before you reach the age of 59½. Not only will you have to pay the 10-percent federal tax penalty (unless you're covered by one of the exceptions), but you also will likely pay a higher tax rate on this income than if you took the distribution when you were older.

Of course, sometimes you gotta "do what you gotta do" — you may have to take a distribution (and accept the tax penalty) when your financial situation dictates. If that's the case, try to take out the minimum necessary to get you through your financial pinch. The long-term growth and tax advantages of your IRA depend on the steadily growing funds in your account. Your IRA is a piggybank with a timer lock, which you should break open only when it's time — not before.

Traditional IRAs

Everything starts someplace. In the case of individual retirement accounts, that someplace is the *traditional* IRA — also commonly known as an *ordinary* or *regular* IRA. A traditional IRA provides you with the advantage of saving money for your retirement without paying taxes until you withdraw it. When you put money into a traditional IRA, your money grows tax free while your current taxable income is reduced.

REMEMBER

The traditional IRA has been around since IRAs were invented in 1974 and has some unique characteristics:

✔ The maximum allowable annual contribution for 2008 is 100 percent of earned income or $5,000, whichever is less, for individuals who are not yet 50 years old. For people 50 years of age or older, the limit is 100 percent of earned income or $6,000, whichever is less.

✔ In the case of a traditional IRA, you must fund your IRA before you reach the age of 70½.

✔ You can have a traditional IRA whether or not you have another retirement plan. However — depending on the other plan — you may or may not be allowed to deduct all your contributions to a traditional IRA.

✔ If both you and your spouse have earned income each of you can set up your own IRA. You cannot share an IRA with someone else, including a spouse.

✔ Although you can start withdrawing cash ("taking distributions") from your traditional IRA at $59\frac{1}{2}$, you are not required to do so before the age of $70\frac{1}{2}$. Withdrawals from a traditional IRA are taxable in the year of the withdrawal.

Generally, a traditional IRA appeals most to people who

✔ Expect to be in a lower tax bracket in retirement.

✔ Are most interested in a current tax deduction.

✔ Are not eligible to contribute to a Roth IRA.

How much will you need to retire?

A common question for people planning to retire is this: How much money will I need to retire comfortably? The simple answer is that you'll probably need to save more money than you expect.

Would you like to maintain your current standard of living after you retire? If so, then plan on maintaining a level of:

✔ 85 percent of your preretirement income if you're not much of a saver (4 percent or less of your annual income) and if you'll have a large mortgage or monthly rental cost.

✔ 75 percent of your preretirement income if you're saving a moderate amount of money (between 5 to 14 percent of your annual income) and if you'll have a small mortgage or monthly rental cost.

✔ 65 percent of your preretirement income if you're a big saver (15 percent or more of your annual income) or if you will own your home free and clear.

Whatever your situation may be, these numbers show that (1) it's never too early to get started planning for your retirement, and (2) you can never really save enough money. So what are you waiting for?

Roth IRAs: The New Kid in Town

Roth IRAs are a relatively recent take on the individual retirement account, and they appeal to savers for a variety of reasons. A Roth IRA gives you the advantage of withdrawing money from your retirement account *without ever paying taxes on it.* This is because you use regular, after-tax income to fund it. In addition, opening a Roth IRA involves no age restrictions. However, whereas contributions to a traditional IRA can be either deductible or not, depending on your situation, contributions to a Roth IRA are always non-deductible. So whereas traditional IRAs offer tax-*deferred* growth of your savings, Roth IRAs offer tax-*sheltered* growth of your savings. The one you choose depends on your specific savings goals and your unique personal situation.

The Roth IRA has its own unique characteristics:

- ✔ The maximum allowable annual contribution for 2008 is 100 percent of earned income or $5,000, whichever is less, for individuals who are not yet 50 years old. For people 50 years of age or older, the limit is 100 percent of earned income or $6,000, whichever is less.

- ✔ You can fund your Roth IRA at any age —no limits govern age.

- ✔ You are fully eligible for the Roth IRA if your income is below $95,000 a year for a single taxpayer, and below $150,000 a year for joint taxpayers. Above these amounts, limits increase. You are not eligible for a Roth IRA if your income is above $110,000 for a single taxpayer, and $160,000 for joint taxpayers.

- ✔ Contributions are not tax deductible.

- ✔ If your income is $100,000 or less, you can convert a traditional IRA into a Roth IRA.

- ✔ You can start withdrawing cash ("taking distributions") from your Roth IRA at 59^1/$_2$. These withdrawals are tax-free. Earnings withdrawn before the age of 59^1/$_2$ are generally taxable and subject to a 10 percent penalty (although this rule involves a number of exceptions).

Generally, a Roth IRA appeals most to people who

- ✔ Want tax-free distributions.

- ✔ Expect their tax bracket to be higher or essentially unchanged in retirement.

- ✔ Prefer tax-free income when they retire.

Rolling Over Your IRA

At some point between the time you open an IRA and you reach the age of retirement, you'll probably change jobs or want to move your assets from one IRA to a new one. Then what? If you're in this situation, it's time to talk about rollover IRAs. A *rollover IRA* is simply an individual retirement account that you move from one IRA into another. In most cases, people use a rollover IRA when they want to move assets from an IRA or 401(k) when they change employers or leave a job.

Here's the process:

- Contact your company's human resources department to initiate the rollover process. You'll need to obtain and complete a form for a *direct rollover.*

- Establish a traditional IRA at a bank, credit union, brokerage, or other eligible financial institution. This IRA will receive the rollover proceeds from your existing company plan.

- Request that your current employer transfer the funds electronically to the new IRA account. Although you can elect to receive a check for the funds that you can then deposit yourself, it's safer from a tax perspective to have the funds transferred directly into your new account.

- After you roll over the funds from your old IRA to your new one, you are allowed to invest them in almost any vehicle you like, including stocks, mutual funds, bonds, certificates of deposit, and more. Or you can simply hold your assets in cash.

Making the Most of Your IRA

So you've got an IRA or are serious about setting one up. That's great — you've taken a big step forward in your retirement planning. Now you've got a choice: You can sit back, forget about your IRA, and let it slowly but surely work its magic . . . or you can take a few more steps to tap its full potential.

If you're the kind of person who likes to play an active role in optimizing your investments and making the most of your IRA, here are a few tips for doing just that.

Direct your own investments

After you've made a cash contribution to your IRA, you are allowed to use this cash to buy other investments, such as stocks, bonds, and mutual funds.

By taking some time to study the financial markets and the performance of a wide variety of investments, you'll be able to set up a portfolio that will maximize growth. This strategy generally means including stocks or stock mutual funds in your IRA portfolio.

Consider a Roth IRA

Each kind of IRA offers its own unique set of advantages, so be sure to take a close look at the advantages of the Roth IRA and its potential to maximize your IRA savings. Remember, a Roth IRA is unique because (1) it doesn't require that you take required minimum distributions by any particular age, and (2) it allows tax-free distributions (because you use regular taxed income to fund it). Ultimately, you need to weigh the long-term impact on your savings of going with a Roth IRA versus the traditional IRA. If you're not sure, have an accountant or CPA get into the act and give you a full financial assessment of the pluses and minuses.

Do it — now!

Any time you invest money for retirement, the sooner you start a program of regular contributions, the better. As your contributions accumulate and generate interest, these savings compound — that is, the interest you generate from your savings gets added to your savings, which increases the amount of interest your account generates. The impact of this effect accelerates as time goes on.

Consider these two scenarios:

Scenario A

Let's say you're 25 years old. You've been working in your job for a few years, and you've already worked your way up to a salary of $35,000 a year. You know that you should start putting aside some of your salary for your retirement — your employer doesn't offer any sort of pension plan, after all — but you're still young and you'd rather have some fun with the money. However, you do decide to put $2,500 into a traditional IRA this year and gradually increase it to the maximum contribution over the next 30 or so years until you retire. As your contributions compound, your IRA is eventually worth more than $500,000 when you reach age 59.

Scenario B

After years of putting off setting up a retirement savings plan, you finally decide at age 54 to get serious about funding an IRA. You decide to go with the maximum contribution of $6,000 annually. However, because you can make contributions to an IRA only until age 59, you'll rack up total savings of less than $50,000, including interest.

Now, which one of these scenarios do you think would allow you to retire comfortably at an earlier age? Clearly, Scenario A would. The lesson is this: The sooner you set up and fund an IRA, the more money will accumulate in your account. Indeed, you can start an IRA at any age — not just as an adult — and get the savings clock ticking.

Chapter 3

Paychecks from Your House: Reverse Mortgages

· ·

In This Chapter

▶ Discovering the nuts and bolts of reverse mortgages

▶ Checking out loan choices

▶ Knowing who you have to deal with

▶ Receiving your money

· ·

You've probably heard a lot about reverse mortgages lately: They're quickly becoming a popular, safe, simple way to supplement seniors' retirement income. In this chapter, you can see the basics of modern reverse mortgages and get a feel for whether these loans are right for you or someone you love. By the end of this chapter, you'll be able to explain the rudiments of reverse mortgages to anyone like a pro.

Understanding Reverse Mortgages

People tend to shy away from the very idea of reverse mortgages, partly because of their former bad rap and partly because of all the scary terminology. If you're one of millions of people who are unfamiliar with real estate terms, when someone starts spouting off about how you can "utilize the equity in your home on deferred payments with a conversion mortgage," chances are pretty good you're going to tune it out.

In fact, that's why we wrote this chapter: to give seniors and their families facts and tips about reverse mortgages in language that's as approachable as a big-eyed puppy (unless you're a cat person — then just think of it as a little fluffy kitten). We want you to fully understand the benefits and disadvantages of getting a reverse mortgage. We want you to walk into that loan originator's office knowing exactly what you want. And most important, we want you to feel good about whatever decision you make for your financial future.

Checking out how it works

Reverse mortgages pay you to continue living in your home. You can think of your home as the Bank of You: You're borrowing money that you would have earned had you sold your house. You can then use the money for whatever you want. Anything your heart desires (and your wallet can handle) is yours for the taking, whether it's vacationing in Switzerland, moving your master bedroom to the first floor, or sending yourself to college!

The concept is kind of abstract if you've been paying a lender for the past 30 years or so, and it may be difficult to grasp at first. Take a look at the following quick reference points. When you get the gist of it, you can educate your friends and family about reverse mortgages. Next time you're at a cocktail party, holiday dinner, social lunch, or anywhere else reverse mortgages may come up in conversation, you can dazzle everyone with your knowledge.

Consider this quick rundown:

- You're a homeowner who owes little or nothing on your home. You decide you need more money to live the lifestyle you want, but your biggest asset is your home and you certainly don't want to sell it to get the money you need.

- A reverse mortgage lender figures out how much it can lend you based on your home value, your age, and interest rates, and lends you some percentage of the money you would have gotten if you'd decided to sell your home.

- You still own your home and continue to live in it, but now you're getting payments from the lender, so you've solved your cash flow problem.

- You pay back the loan (with interest) only when you don't live in the house full time anymore, usually when you move out or die.

- You never owe more than your home is worth, no matter how much you've accumulated in debt.

- You keep any leftover equity after the sale of the house; if you owe the lender $67,000 and your home sells for $200,000, you put the difference in your pocket and walk away smiling.

A reverse mortgage is sometimes called a *deferred payment* loan, for a very good reason. Instead of paying off the home loan as you borrow money, you put off (defer) the payments. Reverse mortgages can be such a good choice for seniors because, when you have a fixed income or are living off of your savings, it can help to have some extra cash in hand to supplement. Because payment is deferred, you are spending the equity in your home instead of earning it (as you would with a traditional forward mortgage). Because equity is an intangible value, you never feel the effects of the equity going down, but you sure feel the money flowing steadily into your checking account.

Being over the hill pays off

Society experiences a lot of ageism today, especially from employers and retailers. Even Hollywood starlets have a hard time finding work at a certain age. After a while, you may start to think that the only advantage to old age is the 10-percent-off discount on Tuesdays at the local Bar & Grille. But reverse mortgages operate for seniors only — whippersnappers need not apply. If you are a homeowner age 62 or older, you will probably qualify for a reverse mortgage and you won't need to worry about credit scores or income requirements.

Even better, the older you are, the more money you can usually get from your reverse mortgage. The reverse mortgage lenders (big companies such as the Department of Housing and Urban Development, Fannie Mae, and Financial Freedom) are playing the odds. If you're 86, chances are good that they won't have to service your loan for very long — you may need to move to assisted living or will die within only a few years, thus ending the loan. A 62-year-old, by contrast, probably has about 20 good years before the lender even needs to think about ending the loan. When has your age ever worked to your advantage like this?

Book VI

Retiring Comfortably

Getting rid of common misconceptions

Seniors often tell us that they were considering a reverse mortgage until a friend or relative said something like, "Reverse mortgage? Don't you dare! They'll take your house! Stay away!" We'd like to say that these fears are completely unfounded; unfortunately, they stem from a very old version of reverse mortgage (which is no longer done) that, in hindsight, wasn't such a hot idea. Today's reverse mortgages are safe, effective, and definitely in the best interest of the borrower. It's a whole new generation of loans. Although they were revamped and vastly improved in the past 20 or so years, people still tend to think of them as a poor choice for seniors. We're here to fix that. Take a look at these misconceptions and the truths that follow:

- ✔ **The lender gets your house.** This fallacy is by far the most widely misunderstood about reverse mortgages. In fact, you keep ownership of your home. The lender has no rights to your home and can't foreclose on you as long as you keep up with your taxes and insurance. Part of the confusion about this area stems from the fact that many reverse-mortgage borrowers choose to sell their homes to pay off the loan when they move. And it makes perfect sense — why do you need that house if you're not living there? But remember, you're selling to another regular buyer, not the lender.

- ✔ **You'll have no estate left.** This one is sort of up to you (see Book VII for more on estate planning). If you own anything when you die, you'll have an estate left. If you spent all your money on pinball machines and then donated everything else to charity, you won't. Many seniors are concerned that a reverse mortgage keeps them from leaving anything to their children. The fact is, the way you pay off your loan is up to you and your heirs. You also decide who you want to leave your estate to. Unless you form an emotional bond with your lender and leave your estate to it, your family or whomever you name in your will is the inheritor of your estate. Of course, they need to pay back the loan, but it's up to them how they carry out that responsibility.

✔ **You won't qualify because of poor credit.** If you have bad credit, or even moderate credit, you may have been turned down for a loan in the past. It's embarrassing, frustrating, and inconvenient. Reverse mortgages work differently: You can never be denied a loan because of bad credit — it's not even a consideration in your approval. The originator or lender runs a credit report, but it's only to make sure you don't owe the government any money (usually in back taxes). If you do, you have to use a portion of your reverse mortgage money to pay back those debts before you can start spending on yourself.

✔ **You must be debt free.** Although you are required to own a home to get a reverse mortgage, you don't have to own it "free and clear." One of the benefits of a reverse mortgage is that it can help pay off your remaining forward mortgage, leaving you without house payments for what may be the first time in your adult life. Here's how it works: The lender determines how much it can let you borrow and then deducts the amount you still owe from your available funds. That money pays off the first loan, and then you're free to do what you want with the rest of the money.

✔ **Only desperate people get reverse mortgages.** At one time, this assumption may have been true. However, today's reverse-mortgage borrower is more likely to get a loan out of want than need. In fact, a growing number of people who have no immediate need are taking out these loans because they like the security of having a financial cushion or are planning for future expenses. Take a look around and ask yourself if you could use several thousand dollars. Who doesn't? Don't let an antiquated stigma keep you from getting the money you want or need.

Knowing what it isn't

A reverse mortgage can be a lot of things: a way to make ends meet, a nice chunk of change for a rainy day, a fabulous dream vacation, or a remodeled kitchen. But it's definitely not free money. Reverse mortgages offer many wonderful benefits, but your loan must be paid back, just like any other loan (whether it's due when you move or upon your death).

The fees involved can include payments to the originator, the appraiser, postage fees, flood certificate fees, recording fees . . . the list goes on and on. Of course, these fees are the same sort you paid for the mortgage that bought you the home you live in now. You also have to pay interest on your loan, which is generally right around the interest rates on traditional mortgages. You pay interest only on what you borrow, so any money that you don't use from your pool of reverse mortgage funds isn't charged. People still get the idea, however, that lenders simply hand you checks every month out of the goodness of their hearts. Now, they're not bad people, but they certainly aren't looking to give away billions of dollars per year in reverse mortgages.

Because it's not a cheap loan, a reverse mortgage is also not the best way to pay off a small debt. Would you really want to spend several thousand dollars in fees and closing costs just to pay back a $900 credit card debt? You know that wouldn't make sense. But what if you owed the IRS $12,000 in back taxes? In most cases, a reverse mortgage is still too costly for this kind of debt. Okay, that's easy for us to say, and if it looks like the best option, then by all means take the first step and call a reverse mortgage counselor. If you're in a similar situation, you may also contact a financial planner who specializes in seniors' money. In fact, you can probably ask a reverse mortgage originator to refer you to someone. They love to hand out referrals.

Book VI

Retiring Comfortably

A reverse mortgage is also not a direct value-to-dollar loan. In other words, a lender won't lend you the actual value of your home; you'll get a percentage of that value, based on age, interest rates, and area. For example, a 66-year-old in a high-end county with a $500,000 home may expect to receive around $200,000 with a Home Equity Conversion Mortgage (depending on interest rates). Don't expect the full value of your home, or you'll be very disappointed. Before you make plans to spend money you don't yet have, go online to `www.reversemortgage.org` and click on the reverse mortgage calculator. This very cool tool gives you an estimate of what you may be able to borrow. Remember, you're not selling your home for the amount you're lent — you're simply borrowing equity that you already own.

Finally, a reverse mortgage is not a panacea or some kind of all-encompassing loan that's right for everyone. Just because you qualify by being a 62-year-old homeowner doesn't mean you're an ideal candidate. The next chapter lays out some questions to ask yourself to find out whether a reverse mortgage is right for you, but consider a few of the basics:

- ✔ Are you at least 62 and own your own home?

- ✔ Do you plan to be in your home for at least five years?

- ✔ If you're getting the loan to purchase or pay off something specific, have you looked into other options for financing those expenses?

- ✔ Are you comfortable with the terms of the loan?

The more of these questions you can answer "yes" to, the more ready you are for a reverse mortgage. When you feel you meet all of these suggested criteria, you're ready to seek out a reverse mortgage counselor.

Choosing a Loan Product

You can pick a reverse mortgage loan product in two ways:

- ✔ Throw darts at a list of mortgage products and see which one fate chooses for you.

- ✔ Talk to your counselor and originator, and let them lay out your options for you in an easy-to-understand, straightforward manner.

We suggest the last one. Besides, you could put an eye out with those darts.

Part of the reverse mortgage process involves using your best judgment and the tools at your disposal (the plethora of information your counselor and originator gives you) to make an informed and wise decision. No pressure, right? Actually, it can be a pretty easy choice to make when you see what each loan product has to offer and how each fits in with your goals and financial plans. Keep in mind that all loans have the same basic requirements, but they each have their little idiosyncrasies that may make one a clear choice for you.

Home Equity Conversion Mortgage

By far the most prevalent of the three main options, the home equity conversion mortgage (HECM, sometimes pronounced "heck-um") provides the most payment choices, low interest rates, and the added mental security of being insured by the Department of Housing and Urban Development (HUD), a government organization. Take a look at some of the main points of a HECM loan:

- ✔ The loan is calculated based on the age of the youngest qualified borrower.

- ✔ Eligible homes include most single-family homes, condos, townhouses, and manufactured homes built after 1976 (ask your originator about HUD guidelines and requirements for manufactured homes).

- ✔ Lending limits (the amount you can borrow, also called the principal) are lower than with other options, yet you can often get a higher principal than you would with others because of lower interest rates.

- ✔ Loans top out at $362,790 in high-home-value areas, $172,632 in lower-home-value areas (based on 2008 county lending limits).

- ✔ Interest rates can be based on monthly interest adjustments or annual adjustments (you don't pay anything until the loan is due — it just accumulates).

- ✔ Your money is easily accessible and payment options are very flexible.

Do these benefits sound like a good fit for you? If so, what the heck-um are you waiting for? Make an appointment with a reverse mortgage counselor today.

Home Keeper

Fannie Mae, America's largest loan funder, created two loans, but they both have the same basic foundation. The Home Keeper and the Home Keeper for Purchase were modeled after the HECM, so you may see a lot of similarities when you start to look more closely. However, some quirks separate these loans from the pack:

Book VI

Retiring Comfortably

- ✔ Home Keeper for Purchase lets you use a reverse mortgage to help buy a new home.

- ✔ Loan calculations are based on the combined ages of the qualifying borrowers, so married couples get less than singles.

- ✔ Eligible homes are single-family homes, condos, homes in planned unit-development projects, townhouses, or manufactured homes that meet Fannie Mae requirements.

- ✔ Lending limits are based on an adjusted property value, which is a national lending limit instead of a county limit.

- ✔ The national lending limit is $417,000 (based on 2008 lending limits).

- ✔ Home Keeper often costs less than HECM, but you'll probably receive less money in the long run.

Although Fannie Mae's Home Keeper loans may not bring you as much income as a HECM, their benefits (such as the ability to buy a new house with the reverse mortgage money) may make these the loans for you.

Figuring Out the People in Your Mortgage

Unlike most loans in today's Internet-crazy world, you can't simply go online and get a reverse mortgage from a pool of competing lenders. Reverse mortgages are highly personal, interactive loans, and several people make them happen and help you out along the way. Work closely with these people and let them help you. You know what's best for you, but they know reverse mortgages. Together you're an unstoppable equity-borrowing machine.

Counselor

Your first stop on the road to reverse mortgages is the counselor. These counselors aren't here to analyze your childhood or interpret your dreams; instead, they offer up sound advice and the information necessary for you to make an informed decision about your own loan. They are required to remain completely unbiased and can only give you the facts — they can never tell you what to choose or take away your power to make the best choice for you. It sounds great now, but come choosing time, you may want someone to just tell you what to do!

Even the most independent homeowners are required to seek the advice and educational offerings of an approved counselor. Typically, an "approved" counselor refers to "HUD-approved," but Fannie Mae and Financial Freedom have their own set of preferred counselors. Unless you know for a fact that you need the Home Keeper or Cash Account loan, it's usually best to see a HUD counselor. These professionals are acceptable for any of the major loans discussed in this book, and if you decide to get a HECM (even after you've been to a Fannie Mae or Financial Freedom counselor), you still need to make an appointment with a HUD counselor as well. You can save time and energy by going to a HUD-approved counselor from the start.

Many counselors (especially HUD counselors) operate free of charge, although because of the increased volume of requests for reverse mortgage counseling, HUD has now authorized "Borrower Paid Counseling" and have set the fee not to exceed $125. When you call the HUD-approved counseling agency that you choose, ask them what their policy is. The fee can be paid at the time of counseling, or many agencies will allow the fee to be financed into the reverse mortgage to be paid at closing with proceeds from the reverse mortgage.

During your counseling session, the counselor asks you all sorts of personal questions about your finances, your health, your family, your home, and your lifestyle. Don't withhold anything or stretch the truth even a little. Counselors have only about an hour with you and need all the information they can get in that time to show you the options that may work best for you. It can be a bit off-putting to spill the beans to a stranger, but it's necessary to make a smart decision regarding your loan. You can rest assured that counselor sessions are completely confidential — only you and your counselor have access to the information you provide, unless, of course, you bring someone with you to the meeting.

It's a good idea to bring along any trusted family members or friends who may be able to help you get a better perspective, supply information, ask questions you hadn't thought of, or just lend you some moral support. Counselors encourage families to come together, and you may find that you're glad to have someone else there. Bringing backup isn't a requirement, by any means, but consider it when you make your appointment.

Originator

Your originator is the person who sets your loan in motion. The originator meets with you to determine whether the loan you've decided on is really the best for your unique circumstances, helps you fill out the application, and submits it to the underwriters (who verify your information) and the lender (who actually signs your checks). You'll probably have at least two meetings with the originator: one to fill out the application and another to finalize details at closing. However, most people end up at their originator's office three, four, or more times over the course of their loan process. You may not choose a loan to apply to right away, you may have questions regarding your loan in progress, you may need to bring in additional information, or you may have a whole host of other reasons to visit. That's why you and your originator become such close friends before your loan is completed.

Time is money, and although originators don't charge by the hour, fees are involved for originators' services. Many of the fees you see on the Good Faith Estimate that originators are required to provide are additional closing costs unrelated to the originator's efforts. A Good Faith Estimate lists all approximate costs involved in getting your loan, from appraisal services to stamps. These fees can add up to several thousand dollars. That's a whole lotta cash to plunk down all at once, and the originators and lenders realize that it may present a burden. After all, if you had a few thousand dollars to spend, you may not need this loan. Thus, you can roll the amount of most, if not all, of your fees and closing costs into your loan. That way, the costs are absorbed into the reverse mortgage and become spread out over several years.

Keep these points in mind when you're narrowing the search for a reverse mortgage originator:

- Originators should be experienced in reverse mortgages. Don't pick a traditional loan originator because they probably don't have the expertise that a reverse mortgage originator has.

- Although it's not a requirement, you may feel better if your originator is a member of the National Reverse Mortgage Lenders Association (NRMLA). They have access to all kinds of resources and materials that others may not.

- Your originator should be patient, should never pressure you, and should encourage your family to attend your meetings (if you feel comfortable having them there).

- Most of all, you have to feel comfortable with your originator. If he or she doesn't feel like someone you can trust with your future financial well-being, trust your instincts. You won't hurt his or her feelings.

Straightening out the facts

Lending limits, loan value, and *home value* can be misleading terms. When your home is appraised, the value is not necessarily equal to the amount of money you can borrow. In fact, you'd have to be very, very old to get a loan for 100 percent of your home's value — we're talking born around the turn of the twentieth century. Lenders factor in your age, current interest rates (they change constantly — more on that shortly), and earned equity to come up with a percentage of the home value that they can lend. The younger you are (early 60s to early 70s), the less they will approve because they know that you will probably stay in the home longer than someone in their 80s or 90s. So although your home may be worth $250,000, they may lend you only $125,000.

Appraiser

Unlike the counselor and the originator, who hold meetings at their office, the appraiser comes to you. No matter which reverse mortgage product you decide on, an appraiser is required to come to your home to determine its value. Depending on home values in your area and the last time you had your home appraised, you may be pleasantly surprised to find out what your home is worth in today's market. Keep in mind that appraisals are largely subjective, and although they follow a certain protocol, appraisers have to simply use their best judgment to set your home's fair market value.

The appraisal visit is nothing to worry about, as long as you've kept up your home maintenance over the years. Either way, it can't hurt to do a bit of sprucing up: Clear your yard of any debris, clean your home the way your would if very special company was coming over, and fix any little things that you've been putting off if you can reasonably afford to do it. Also, gather up your home records — if you've ever had work done on the home (and who hasn't?), try to find those statements. The appraiser will be impressed by a home that's well kept, but he won't be impressed by receipts for granite countertops. Don't start waving your credit card statement under the appraiser's nose to prove how much you spent refurbishing the master suite. The money you put into a home never fetches an equal value when it's appraised.

Because you can't sway the appraiser's evaluation with cookies or compliments, the best thing you can do during the process is sit back and let him or her work. Be ready to answer questions, but don't hover or even follow the appraiser from room to room. If you need something to do, make a list of all the fabulous things you can do with your reverse mortgage income.

Getting Paid

Of course, what you're really interested in is the money. This is one time in your life when it's perfectly okay to be focused on material things. After all, that's what a reverse mortgage is all about — lending you the money you need to buy the things you want. This step is also the easiest part of getting a reverse mortgage: The lender determines how much you can borrow and you simply pick your payment option and start receiving money. No sweat. Still, you need to know some information about payments, your current financial issues, and the country's financial issues before you make a decision.

Figuring out how much you can get

Without sitting down with an originator, there's no way to tell you for sure what you can borrow from a reverse mortgage. We wish we could give you a simple formula, but one just doesn't exist. As we mention in this chapter (and elsewhere), the amount you can borrow is calculated using these factors:

- ✔ **Your age:** Generally, the older you are, the better off your loan situation is because the lender figures it won't have to work on your loan as long as if you were a spring chicken.

- ✔ **Your home value:** More equity equals more money available to borrow.

- ✔ **Your area:** Higher home values in the area means higher loan values for you if you choose a HECM or Home Keeper (which both use county medians to determine your loan principal).

- ✔ **Interest rates:** With this one factor, less is more — the lower the interest rates, the higher the principal.

If you can wait a few years to get your loan, the increased principal will make the wait worthwhile. Most people who wait at least five years are pleasantly surprised to find that their loan amount has gone up . . . to the tune of a few thousand dollars. Don't wait so long that you can't enjoy the cash flow — that trip down the canals of Venice will probably be a lot more fun at 68 than at 98 — but don't rush out and get a loan on your 62nd birthday if you don't really need it yet.

Also, each loan has its own system of determining loan value. For example, no matter what your home is worth, Fannie Mae's Home Keeper bases the amount available to you on a scale compared to the national lending limit ($417,000). On the other hand, the Cash Account has no set limit. It bases its principal solely on your age, your home value, and interest rates.

You can get an estimate of what each loan may be able to offer you using online reverse mortgage calculators. The NRMLA calculator (find it at www.reversemortgage.org) is a good indicator because it breaks down the entire loan, from what your estimated costs are to how much you get per month. However, they don't show you what you can get with a Cash Account — only HECM and Home Keeper. For a side-by-side comparison of all three loans, visit www.financialfreedom.com and take a spin on its reverse mortgage calculator.

Checking out payment options

Lottery winners get to choose whether they want their money in install-ments or one lump sum. Well, you may feel like you won the lottery when you decide how you want your reverse mortgage funds to arrive. Each loan has its own set of payment options (that's payment to you, from the lender). Listed here are the main payment options, along with which loans offer them. As you read down the list, think about which one fits best in your lifestyle.

- ✔ **Tenure** (HECM and Home Keeper): If you like the security of having stable, steady monthly checks deposited in your bank account, monthly tenure payments may be for you. The biggest advantage of this option is that no matter how long you have the loan (stay in your home), the lender continues to pay you — even if you've gone beyond what the lender originally agreed to lend you, and even if you live 30 years longer than anyone expected. The downside is that fixed monthly payments don't allow for sudden large expenses and don't adjust for inflation down the road.

- ✔ **Term** (HECM and Home Keeper): A monthly term payment has the security of getting equal monthly checks, as with the tenure plan, but you decide how long you continue to receive payments. The shorter the term, the more money you get per check. For example, if a lender sets your principal at $100,000 and you want to receive it over eight years, that's about $1,041 per month. If you decide instead to get your payments over five years, you're looking at $1,666 per month. That's a sizeable difference! But remember, when that term is up, you're out of money.

- ✔ **Lump sum** (HECM, Home Keeper, and one Cash Account option): Have you always dreamed of rolling around on a pile of money? Choosing a lump sum means you get the entire amount of the loan in one big check. It's up to you how you want to budget it per month, and it's up to you to make sure it lasts as long as you plan to live in your home. If you have a very large expense that you absolutely must pay in full, a lump sum could do the trick, although a better option is often a line of credit (see the next bullet).

✔ **Line of credit** (HECM, Home Keeper, Cash Account): A line of credit (also called a credit line) works very much like a savings account. You have access to the entire loan amount, but because you have to send in a form to get it, people are often more mindful of how they spend their money than they may be with a lump sum. In addition, depending on the loan, the line of credit can grow and you can have more available as time passes.

✔ **Combination** (HECM and Home Keeper): Can't decide? Maybe a combination of payment options is your best bet. You can choose how much you want to receive up front (through a lump sum, a line of credit, or both) and designate the rest to a monthly payment. Or work backward — figure out how much you need per month, multiply that by the number of months you expect to stay in your home, and leave the rest in a line of credit. The combinations are virtually endless because they're tailor-made for you.

Discovering the effect of the funds on your finances

Seniors, especially people who have gone through hoops trying to get their fair share of Social Security, pensions, Medicaid, and various other programs, are often concerned that a reverse mortgage may cancel out those benefits. People often ask us if they have to choose between those programs and a reverse mortgage. You should be glad to know that the answer is no. The income from a reverse mortgage has no bearing on your current benefits. What's better, it has no effect on your taxes because the IRS doesn't consider equity as income.

Of course, every rule has an exception. Although most people don't have any trouble maintaining their current benefits, some government programs (such as Supplemental Security Income) may include reverse mortgage payments in their income limits. If so, you can usually find ways around this. Talk to your counselor and originator about working out a system to circumvent this issue. If you want to err on the side of caution, talk to your tax advisor or financial planner about how your newfound income may impact your finances. In the vast majority of cases, the only effect is a positive one.

Dealing with inflation and interest rates

Any time you're investigating a mortgage, you're sure to have your eye on interest rates. In recent years, rates have been quite low, although they are slowly creeping back up again. What do interest rates mean for reverse mortgages? Just as in traditional mortgages, the lower interest rates are, the more money you can borrow. But unlike traditional mortgages, you don't pay a penny of that interest until the loan is over. It accumulates over time and is paid all at once when you repay the entire loan.

Aside from the initial closing costs and originator's fees, you can think of interest as the price of borrowing money. The longer you have your reverse mortgage, the more you pay over the years in interest. Rates will fluctuate up and down during your loan — you can drive yourself crazy trying to follow the trends and track rates. But there's really no point. When you have the loan, the best thing to do is forget about it. You can't control the market, and although you'll see your interest rate on your monthly or quarterly statement, you won't feel its effects until you end the loan.

One financial indicator that you may notice as the years go by is inflation. Think about the cost of your staple items 20 years ago — prices rise on an average of 1.5 percent per year. It may not sound like much, but when you consider it on a large scale, it makes a big difference. A loan worth $75,000 this year buys only $73,875 worth of goods and services the next year. Why is inflation important to reverse mortgage borrowers? Unlike income from a job, you don't get a raise for cost of living with a reverse mortgage. That means if you're on a fixed $900 per month payment option, that $900 won't go as far if you hold the loan for 10 or 20 years. A line of credit is a good way to beat inflation because, on a HECM loan, the amount available to you will grow and increase as you get older, which will help you keep up with rising prices.

The very savvy may see a great opportunity here to get the best of both worlds: stable monthly payments and an easy way to combat inflation. The solution is a combination of payment options. A HECM loan lets you set aside a portion of your principal for a line of credit and then receive the rest as monthly income. You can access the line-of-credit funds at any time, but by leaving them where they are, you build a greater equity savings.

Chapter 4

Managing Money in Retirement

In This Chapter

▶ Deciding when and how to take money out of your 401(k) after you retire

▶ Figuring out how much money to withdraw from your retirement savings each year

▶ Keeping taxes to a minimum when you withdraw money

▶ Making sure that you have enough money to last your lifetime (and then some)

*W*hen you retire, your investment job isn't over. In some ways, the job is just beginning. You have to convert your account balance (your nest egg) into a healthy income stream that will last the rest of your life. Thus, you have to decide not only how to invest your money, but also how and when to spend it.

It'd be great if you could invest the money in a way that would let you live off the investment income without touching the *principal* (the amount in your nest egg before withdrawing any money), but for most people this scenario isn't possible. You have to slowly spend the principal as well. Spending your account's principal is often referred to as *drawing down* your account. The trick is spending just enough to make life comfortable but not using everything up before you go to the great beyond.

This chapter helps you decide what to do with your 401(k) money when you retire from your job and how to manage it during your retirement, to give you comfort and peace of mind (and maybe even have a little something left over for your heirs).

Note: All the recommendations that we provide in this chapter are directed toward individuals, not couples. Both you and your spouse need to do your own retirement planning — unless you operate on a combined income. If you and your spouse have joint accounts and a "what's yours is mine" attitude, a combined plan is fine. But remember that, unless you have other resources, both incomes need to be replaced to maintain your lifestyle.

Decisions, Decisions: What to Do with Your 401(k) Money

One of your first decisions as a retiree is what to do with the money in your 401(k). You essentially have two choices:

- ✔ Leave it in the plan.
- ✔ Take it out of the plan.

Well, okay, the choices are a bit more complicated than that. On the first point, you can leave it in the plan if your vested balance is more than $5,000 and you haven't reached the plan's normal retirement age, usually 65. Leaving your money in your former employer's plan is probably fine if you like the 401(k) plan investments and if you won't need the money soon. However, remember that the employer can change the plan investments at any time, and you have to go along with it. Also, most plans won't let you take installment payments, so if you need to withdraw some money from the plan, it's all or nothing.

We now come to the second option — taking it out of the plan. When you take money out of a 401(k), you have to act carefully to keep taxes and penalties in check. The amount you take out has to be added on top of your other taxable income for that year. This additional income can push you into the highest tax bracket if you have a healthy account balance that you withdraw all at once. If your plan lets you take installment payments, you can arrange to take out what you need and pay income tax only on that amount each year. (This strategy works until you hit age $70\frac{1}{2}$, when you must start taking a *required minimum distribution* each year.) We explain these distributions in the section "Paying Uncle Sam His Due: Required Withdrawals," later in the chapter.

However, most plans have an "all-or-nothing" policy — either leave it in the plan or withdraw a *lump sum* (the entire amount). With all-or-nothing plans, the best solution is generally to transfer some or all of the money into an IRA, to preserve the tax advantage, and withdraw money periodically from the IRA as you need it. Again, you pay income tax only on the amounts that you withdraw, which works out to be less than paying tax on the entire amount all at once. (See Book VI, Chapter 2 for more on IRAs.) *Note:* Roth contributions and investment gains on these contributions will not be taxable if the distribution is a qualifying distribution.

What you decide to do, and when you decide to do it, should depend largely on two factors:

- ✔ Your age when you leave your employer
- ✔ When you plan to start using the money

Being older can save you money

Your age when you leave your employer is important because it determines whether you have to pay a 10 percent early withdrawal penalty on money you withdraw from the 401(k), in addition to taxes.

If you're at least 55 years old when you leave your employer, you don't have to pay the penalty on money withdrawn from that employer's plan. You still have to pay income tax on any non-Roth withdrawals, though.

The exemption from the 10 percent early withdrawal penalty doesn't apply to any 401(k) money you may still have with employers you once worked for but left before turning 55.

If you're under 55 years old when you retire, you *will* owe a 10 percent early withdrawal penalty on any 401(k) money you withdraw, other than qualifying Roth withdrawals, in addition to taxes. (We explain a few exceptions, called *72(t) withdrawals,* in the following section.) When you reach age 59½, though, you can withdraw your 401(k) money without a penalty, even if you retired from your employer before age 55. But the five-year minimum holding period still applies to Roth contributions.

Just to complicate matters, remember that your plan can refuse to let you withdraw money until you are the plan's "normal retirement age," which is often 65. Find out the rules for your plan before you do anything drastic, such as retire.

No matter how old you are, you can avoid the early withdrawal penalty tax by rolling over your 401(k) money into an IRA. Remember, though, that after it's in the IRA, you'll generally owe a 10 percent early withdrawal penalty on any money that you withdraw before you turn 59½. (The mysterious *72(t) withdrawal* exception, which we explain in the following section, applies here, too.)

Regardless of your age, you may also want to consider getting your money out of your employer's plan and into an IRA because things change. Companies are sold, human resources terminate, and so on. As a result, it can be difficult to track down the people who are responsible for overseeing the plan years after you leave your employer.

Foiling the dreaded early withdrawal penalty

But what if you need your money before age 55 or age 59½? Here's where the *72(t) withdrawals* (distributions) come into play — you can use them to avoid the early withdrawal penalty. These distributions are a list of exceptions to the penalty, such as being disabled or having medical expenses that exceed 7.5 percent of your income. However, anyone can use one of the exceptions, called a *SEPP.* (SEPP stands for substantially equal periodic payments.)

When you use SEPP withdrawals, you set up a schedule of annual payments that continue for five years or until you're 59$\frac{1}{2}$, whichever is longer. Each year, you withdraw the same amount. (You determine the amount using an IRS formula that is based on your life expectancy. Several approved methods exist. The simplest is the same one used to determine required minimum distributions, described in the section "Paying Uncle Sam His Due: Required Withdrawals.") You can set up SEPP payments with your 401(k) if your plan allows these periodic payments. If it doesn't allow periodic payments, you can roll your 401(k) balance into an IRA and take the SEPP payments from the IRA.

Use a SEPP to avoid the 10 percent penalty tax if you retire before age 55 and start withdrawals from your 401(k) before age 59$\frac{1}{2}$, or if you need to make withdrawals from your IRA before age 59$\frac{1}{2}$.

If you move your 401(k) money into an IRA, remember to have it transferred directly. Don't accept a check made out to you personally. If your employer makes the 401(k) check out to you, your employer must withhold 20 percent of the amount for taxes. You have to make up this difference when depositing the money in the IRA; otherwise, it counts as taxable income except for qualifying Roth contributions. Consider an example of a situation that requires SEPP withdrawals. Say you stop working at age 56 and leave your money in your 401(k). Everything is fine for two years, and then you decide that you need money from your 401(k). You don't have to worry about the 10 percent early withdrawal penalty because you were at least 55 years old when you left your employer. However, you still have to think about income tax. If you withdraw the entire 401(k) balance, you'll have a big tax hit. Your employer may allow you to take installment payments from your 401(k) in the amount of your choosing, which would solve your problem. However, if your employer lets you take only a lump-sum withdrawal, what do you have to do? (If you've read the earlier chapters, we expect you to belt out this refrain like a Broadway chorus by now.) That's right, roll over the 401(k) into an IRA to preserve the tax advantage.

You've got one complication, though. (There's always something.) If you take a distribution from an IRA before you're 59$\frac{1}{2}$, you have to pay the 10 percent penalty tax. It doesn't matter that you were older than 55 when you left your employer. To get the money out of the IRA without the penalty tax, you need to take a Section 72(t) distribution that must continue for at least 5 years — until you're 63, in this example.

An alternative is to take a partial distribution from your 401(k) for just the amount you need right away and then roll over the rest of the money into an IRA. For example, assume that you have $200,000 in your account and that you need to use $35,000 before you turn 59$\frac{1}{2}$. You can take $35,000 (plus enough money to cover the tax) from your 401(k) plan and transfer the rest of the money directly to the IRA. ***Note:*** Roth contributions may be rolled over into a Roth IRA, but this triggers a new five-year minimum distribution period.

After retiring, we recommend having the bulk of your savings in an IRA. IRAs give you greater withdrawal flexibility after age 59$^{1}/_{2}$ and more investment flexibility than a 401(k).

Leaving money with your former employer

If you don't need to use any of your 401(k) money for retirement income, and if your account exceeds $5,000, you can leave the money in your 401(k). Your employer can't force you to take the money out before you reach your plan's normal retirement age. Participants who are comfortable with the investments they have in their 401(k) and/or who don't like making decisions are more likely to leave their money in the plan. Participants who aren't thrilled with their 401(k) investments usually can't wait to get their money out of the plan and into other investments that they think are better.

No right or wrong decision exists here. Either arrangement is fine if your 401(k) investments are satisfactory. One point to remember is that money in a 401(k) may have somewhat greater protection from creditors than money in an IRA, depending on your state of residence, if you declare bankruptcy. (IRA protection depends on state law where you live, whereas 401(k) protection is afforded by federal law.)

On the other hand, an IRA offers much greater investment flexibility. An IRA also gives you greater flexibility in naming a beneficiary. (You don't have to get your spouse's approval before you can name someone else as beneficiary, as you have to with a 401(k).)

As you decide whether to leave your 401(k) money with your former employer, also consider the fact that the corporate landscape changes constantly. In a continuous merger-and-acquisition climate, we usually advise participants to get their money out of the 401(k) plan as soon as they can. Former employers can be elusive, and they can also change your plan investments at any time: Your employer can move your money from one set of investments to another without your approval.

Paying Uncle Sam His Due: Required Withdrawals

In the previous sections, we talk about when you're allowed to take money out of your 401(k). Now we switch gears and explain when you're *required* to withdraw money from your 401(k).

You must begin taking your money out of the 401(k) plan by the time you're 70¹/₂, unless you're still working for the employer that maintains the plan. (If you own more than 5 percent of the company, you must start taking distributions by age 70¹/₂, even if you're still working.) The government wants to collect tax on your money at some point, which is why you can't leave it in a 401(k) forever.

The amount that you're required to withdraw each year is called your *required minimum distribution,* or *RMD.* The first one you have to take applies to the year when you turn 70¹/₂, even though you have until April 1 of the following year to take the installment. You then have to take required distributions by December 31 of each year.

You have a few extra months to take your first required distribution (until April 1), but because that distribution is for the previous year, you still have to take a second required distribution for the current year before December 31 of that same year. Be aware that doing so increases your taxable income for that year. You may want to take your first withdrawal earlier.

Here's an example. If you turn 70¹/₂ in 2008, you have to take your first RMD by April 1, 2009. But you can take it sooner, in 2008, if you want. Why would you do that? Because you also have to take a distribution by December 31, 2009, for the year 2009. If you put off your 2008 distribution until 2009, you'll have a higher taxable income that year, all else being equal.

Calculating your RMD isn't terribly difficult if you have the right information available:

- **You need to know your account balance as of December 31 of the year before the one that you're taking the distribution for.** In other words, if you're calculating your 2008 distribution, you need to know your account balance as of December 31, 2007.

- **You also need to get hold of the IRS life expectancy tables that apply to you and find the correct number for your age.** You can find these tables in a supplement to Publication 590 for 2002, available at www. irs.gov/pub/irs-pdf/p590supp.pdf. Beginning in 2003, the tables have been included in Publication 590, which you can find on the IRS Web site (www.irs.gov). Use Table III if your spouse is less than ten years younger than you, if you're single, or if you're married but your spouse isn't your named beneficiary. Use Table II if your spouse is more than ten years younger than you. Don't worry about Table I — it's for beneficiaries who inherit an IRA.

For example, if you're 70 and married, and your spouse is 65, use Table III. On that table, the distribution period for a 70-year-old is 27.4. You divide your account balance by that number, and the result is your required minimum distribution. Say your account balance on December 31, 2007, was $500,000. Your required minimum distribution is $18,248.18 ($500,000 ÷ 27.4). That's how much you must take out the first year. For the following year, you do a new calculation with your updated account balance and the next distribution period number on the table.

If you think this calculation is complicated, you should've seen the rules before the IRS simplified them in 2001! You can always ask your plan provider or IRA custodian to calculate the RMD for you. In fact, IRA custodians are required to help you calculate it, so don't be shy about asking for help.

By the way, the rules for calculating required minimum distributions are the same whether your money is in a 401(k) or an IRA. And you can always take out more than the required minimum. However, if you take out less, the IRS will fine you 50 percent of the required amount that you didn't withdraw.

Strategizing to Deal with the Tax Man

You'd surely love it if taxes disappeared when you retired, but, unfortunately, they don't. The earlier sections of this chapter talk about minimizing taxes when you first move your money out of your 401(k), but you need to look at a few other situations, too.

Which comes first: Plucking the chicken or emptying the nest egg?

You most likely have some money saved in "taxable" (non-tax-advantaged) accounts as well as in your 401(k). Which should you spend first?

Historically, many professional advisors recommended keeping as much money as possible in a tax-deferred account, even during retirement. The rationale was that you would continue to benefit from the fact that no interest, dividends, or gains were taxable while the money was in the account.

But the game changed when Congress revised the tax rules regarding Social Security benefits. Although this tax-deferred advantage is still true, you also have to factor in taxation of your Social Security benefits. When you start receiving Social Security, your benefits are taxed if your income is more than certain limits. Distributions from a 401(k) or traditional IRA are taxable retirement benefits that are included in the income that must be counted to determine what portion, if any, of your Social Security benefits are taxable. So if you take money out of your 401(k) or IRA when you start receiving Social Security benefits, you may have to pay tax on your Social Security benefits. Do some basic planning before you decide on withdrawals. For up-to-date rules, contact a tax attorney and look at the Social Security Administration Web site at www.ssa.gov.

If you retire a few years before you take Social Security benefits, you may want to use up your tax-deferred accounts first instead of your other savings.

Consider an example. Assume the following:

✔ You retire at age 60.

✔ You plan to start receiving Social Security benefits when you reach 62.

✔ You have $100,000 of personal savings.

✔ You have $250,000 in your 401(k) account.

✔ You will need $35,000 of income (after taxes) each of your first two years of retirement (before Social Security kicks in).

You could either use your personal savings or withdraw approximately $40,000 from your retirement account during each of these two years. (We're assuming that a $40,000 withdrawal leaves you about $35,000 after paying taxes. If you have other taxable income, your tax rate may be higher.) Withdrawing the money from your 401(k) right away reduces the size of the taxable distributions you'll receive after you become eligible for Social Security. It reduces your taxable income after you start to collect Social Security benefits, so perhaps you won't have to pay as much, or any, tax on your benefits. This situation may be a better tax deal than the tax break you receive by keeping more money in your retirement account. And you'll still have your personal savings available, which have already been taxed.

You need to do some fairly complex calculations to see what's better in your situation, so we strongly encourage you to consult an experienced tax attorney or other qualified advisor who does this type of planning.

More on that darned company stock

You also need to consider taxes when you decide what to do with the company stock you may have accumulated in your 401(k) account or other employer-sponsored plan, such as an employee stock ownership plan (ESOP). You get a special tax break when you receive company stock as a distribution. You pay tax only on the value of the stock when it was credited to your plan account, not on its current value. You pay a capital gains tax on the difference whenever you eventually sell the stock. These capital gains taxes are lower than the income taxes you would otherwise pay. Finally, if you pass the stock to your heirs when you die, they won't pay tax on any gains that occurred before it was given to them. This type of estate planning is feasible only if you don't expect to use the stock during your retirement and you're willing to take the risk of having a chunk of money tied to one stock for many years.

Holding stock in an individual company is much riskier than investing in a number of different investments.

If you roll your company stock into an IRA, you can sell it and diversify into other investments. You will have to pay income tax on your eventual withdrawals. If you take your distribution of stock, you must pay tax on the value of the stock when you received it in the plan. You can then sell the company stock, paying only capital gains tax on the gain, and use the money to invest in more diversified mutual funds or a portfolio of stocks. However, returns on these "taxable" investments are subject to income tax every year. Still, the benefits of diversification probably make either one of these strategies more palatable than holding on to the company stock, unless you really won't need the money during your lifetime.

Don't let the tax tail wag the dog. Passing company stock on to your heirs is tax planning for them that hampers good investment planning for you.

Book VI

Retiring Comfortably

Managing Investments in Retirement

Investing to build up an adequate retirement nest egg takes most people an entire working career. But, believe it or not, managing your investments is even more critical *during* your retirement years because what took many years to build can go "poof" in an instant. When you're younger, you can do some really dumb things and still have time to recover. If your investments lose 20 percent or more when you're 30, it's a nonevent. When you're 70, it can be a disaster. As a retiree, you really have to pay attention to your investments so that you can convert your retirement account and other resources into an income stream that will last for the rest of your life.

As you decide how to manage your nest egg during retirement, we can't emphasize enough the importance of consulting a professional. Seeking professional advice is probably the best investment you can make for your retirement. Ask coworkers, friends, or family members for recommendations on financial professionals. A couple good resources are www.napfa.org, the Web site of the National Association of Personal Financial Advisors, and www.fpanet.org, the Web site for the Financial Planning Association. You can also try the Advisor Finder from Dalbar, Inc., at www.dalbar.com/.

Live long and prosper

Maintaining an income stream that will last for the rest of your life is more difficult now than it used to be. A generation or two ago, retirees commonly converted all their available funds into *income-producing investments*. For most retirees, this scenario meant converting their funds into bank certificates of deposit (CDs). People who owned stocks typically stuck to the ones that were popular for widows and orphans — in other words, stocks such as utilities that paid high dividends and had a history of steady income with low price fluctuation and modest long-term growth. Keeping up with inflation wasn't a big deal when the average retiree lived for only 10 to 12 years after retiring. A 3 percent inflation rate reduced the amount of income a retiree could spend by only 23 percent after ten years.

Today, if you retire during your 50s or early 60s, you need to plan for at least 30 years of retirement income. Your buying power will be reduced by 58 percent after 30 years of inflation at 3 percent. You've probably read that you have to keep some money invested in stocks during your retirement years to help offset the impact of inflation. This advice makes sense because stocks have produced an average higher level of return than other investments over 20- to 30-year time periods. But how much stock, and which types of stock?

When you do your retirement planning, don't expect an annual 15 percent or higher return. Too many 401(k) investors came to expect just that during the high-performance 1990s. But as the market plummeted in the early 2000s, these investors learned the hard way that the stock market has never produced a return in this range for more than a few years. Expect your return to average 6 to 7 per year during your retirement years — even with stock investments.

Be realistic about your expectations

In the previous section, we tell you what *not* to expect. Now, to help you plan, we give you some rules about what investment return to expect. In general, stocks have produced about a 9 percent average return, and fixed income about a 5 percent average return over a 20- to 30-year period. The return for your overall portfolio depends on your mix of stocks and bonds. For example:

- ✔ If 75 percent of your money is invested at 5 percent and 25 percent is invested at 9 percent, expect an average portfolio return of 6 percent.

- ✔ If your money is split 50/50, expect an average return of 7.0 percent.

- ✔ If 25 percent of your money is invested at 6 percent, and 75 percent is invested at 10 percent, expect an average portfolio return of 9 percent.

Remember that these guidelines simply intend help you establish realistic investment expectations for your retirement years and decide how to split your money among different types of investments. They outline *average returns* that you can expect during a *20- to 30-year period.* The year-to-year returns will vary when you have a large amount invested in stocks. You also have to consider the fact that these numbers are average long-term expectations. You won't get these returns every year. Your return may be higher some years and lower other years; it may even be negative some years.

You can expect an average return in the range of 6 to 7 percent if you follow the most commonly recommended mix of stocks and fixed-income investments for retirees. This mix includes a stock allocation of around 25 to 50 percent, depending on your age and risk tolerance. For example, a 50 percent stock allocation may be appropriate during the early years of your retirement, but in most cases, you should reduce the percentage as you age.

A very good alternative to deciding how to mix your investments is to put all your money into a Target Maturity Fund with one of the top mutual fund companies. These funds are typically identified by the year when distributions for retirement are expected, such as 2005, 2010, 2015, and so forth. Somone retiring today should use the 2010 fund.

Managing Risk and Maximizing Return

Why so much talk of risk during your retirement years? After all the years you worked hard to reach your retirement goal, you probably want — and deserve — a break that's free of investment stress. We wish we could tell you how this sort of break is possible, but we can't — because it's not. At this point, you need to withdraw money from your account to live. The combination of a low or negative return for a couple of years and regular withdrawals can really disrupt your carefully laid plans.

Imagine you have a retirement nest egg worth $250,000. You withdraw 6 percent, or $15,000, for living expenses the first year. The next year, you withdraw $15,450 to keep up with 3 percent inflation. Now say the value of your investments drops 10 percent the first year and 4 percent the second. And assume you based your plan on an 8 percent return during retirement.

An 8 percent return may have looked like a certainty when you retired, but the market hasn't done well during the first two years of your retirement. Table 4-1 shows how much the value of your nest egg drops after two years of retirement, and where you are compared to your original investment plan.

Table 4-1	How Actual Results Can Differ from Your Plan		
	Your Plan (Assumes 8 % Return)	Your Results with 100% Stock	Your Results with 50/50 Split Stocks/ Bonds
Beginning amount	$250,000	$250,000	$250,000
Withdrawal year 1	$15,000	$15,000	$15,000
Withdrawal year 2	$15,450	$15,450	$15,450
Investment gain (or loss) year 1	$19,400	–$24,250	–$4,850
Investment gain (or loss) year 2	$19,734	–$8,121	$2,224
Ending balance year 1	$254,400	$210,750	$230,150
Ending balance year 2	$258,684	$187,179	$216,924

This example assumes that you withdraw money monthly. Although no one can predict when the market will go up and down, you need a predictable stream of income during your retirement years. But withdrawing money when the value of your investments is declining can be gut wrenching.

One way to avoid having to sell stocks when they're down is to invest about 20 percent of your nest egg in low-risk, fixed-income investments, such as a money market or short-term bond fund. Hold these investments in your regular IRA or a separate IRA. Use this money as a special cash reserve fund during down periods. You can tap this fund instead of selling stocks when their value is down. Or invest in a target maturity fund. These funds make withdrawals easy because your money is all in one fund. You decide how much to take out each month, and the fund manager automatically rebalances your stock/fixed income investments periodically. The fund manager also reduces your risk as you grow older by cutting back on the stock allocation.

You can reduce the risk of a loss in any retirement year by increasing the amount you invest in bonds and other fixed-income investments. In the example Table 4-1 illustrates, if you had invested 50 percent in stocks and 50 percent in bonds instead 100 percent in stocks, the overall loss in the first year would've been only 2 percent; you actually would've gained 1 percent in the second year. This amount would still be different from your target, but it would substantially soften the blow.

We can hear you asking why you shouldn't simply put your entire account into fixed-income investments during your retirement years. The answer is that dreaded "I" word: *inflation*. In the example in Table 4-1, the amount of money that you need to withdraw during the 20th year of your retirement will have increased from $15,000 to $26,300. (That's assuming a 3 percent inflation rate, which is on the low side, historically.)

If you're particularly thrifty, you may think that you don't need to adjust for inflation. Don't fool yourself. You're not living on the same income now that you had 20 or 30 years ago, and you won't want to live on today's income 30 years from now. Some argue that, despite inflation, expenses decrease during retirement years. That's true for some expenses, but medical expenses usually increase, and you may ultimately need to cover the cost of an assisted-living facility. Keeping some of your investments in stock should help you make up the gap that inflation causes.

Living within Your Means for Life

Some people think that they'll never run out of money if the amount they withdraw from their retirement account each year never exceeds their investment return. But how can you do this in years when your return is low or negative? Would you be able to live on 1 percent of your account? (Even with an account of $500,000, that would be $5,000 for the entire year.)

Achieving an investment return such as 7 percent is not a given every year. Stock returns can be almost nonexistent even during extended periods. Living through one of these longer-term market funks when you're building your nest egg isn't easy — but it's much more painful when you're retired and watching your account shrink. In addition to good planning, a favorable economy during most of your retirement years will certainly help — but, of course, you can't control that.

If you have a $500,000 nest egg, a realistic amount to withdraw each year to avoid running out of money is around $30,000 per year (adjusted for inflation). If you find that hard to believe, look at Table 4-2, which shows the effect of those annual withdrawals on the account. After 25 years, you've got enough left for only two more years. That amount isn't a very big cushion.

Table 4-2	**Managing Your Nest Egg During Your Retirement Years**			
No. of Years	*Beginning of Year Balance*	*Annual Withdrawal (Assumes 3% Inflation)*	*Investment Return (7%)*	*End-of-Year Balance*
1	$500,000	$30,000	$33,950	$503,950
2	$503,950	$30,900	$34,195	$507,245

(continued)

Table 4-2 *(continued)*

No. of Years	Beginning of Year Balance	Annual Withdrawal (Assumes 3% Inflation)	Investment Return (7%)	End-of-Year Balance
3	$507,245	$31,827	$34,393	$509,811
4	$509,811	$32,782	$34,539	$511,568
5	$511,568	$33,765	$34,628	$512,431
6	$512,431	$34,778	$34,653	$512,306
7	$512,306	$35,822	$34,610	$511,094
8	$511,094	$36,896	$34,485	$508,683
9	$508,683	$38,003	$34,278	$504,958
10	$504,958	$39,143	$33,977	$499,792
11	$499,792	$40,317	$33,574	$493,049
12	$493,049	$41,527	$33,060	$484,582
13	$484,582	$42,773	$32,424	$474,233
14	$474,233	$44,056	$31,654	$461,831
15	$461,831	$45,378	$30,740	$447,183
16	$447,183	$46,739	$29,667	$430,111
17	$430,111	$48,141	$28,423	$410,393
18	$410,393	$49,585	$26,992	$387,800
19	$387,800	$51,073	$25,358	$362,085
20	$362,085	$52,605	$23,505	$332,985
21	$332,985	$54,183	$21,413	$300,215
22	$300,215	$55,809	$19,062	$263,468
23	$263,468	$57,483	$16,431	$222,416
24	$222,416	$59,208	$13,497	$176,705
25	$176,705	$60,984	$10,236	$125,957

If that's not enough to convince you, and you want more information on this topic, you may want to look at a widely reported study by three finance professors at Trinity University in San Antonio, Texas (the "Trinity Study").

The study showed that portfolios with a stock/bond mix, rather than 100 percent stocks or 100 percent bonds, are most likely to provide an income for the longest period of time. It also found that withdrawing more than 6 to 7 percent of your retirement account per year substantially increases the chance that you will outlive your savings. Your chance of *not* running out of money is even better if you withdraw only 3 to 4 percent each year.

Generating Predictable Income

When you're living off your retirement accounts, you need to come up with a strategy to provide a stream of income that's as predictable as your paycheck was. You'll have expenses that need to be paid, trips you want to take, and activities you want to participate in, and they will all cost money. You can structure your retirement account in ways to provide predictable income.

Book VI

Retiring
Comfortably

IRA withdrawals

One way to develop a monthly stream of predictable income is to take monthly withdrawals of a specific amount from mutual funds held in an IRA. You can even have the money automatically deposited directly to your checking account.

For example, assume that you have $250,000 in your IRA, and you want to withdraw a total of 6 percent per year. This amount is $15,000, divided into monthly payments of $1,250. If your investments are split evenly between a bond fund and a stock fund, you can ask to have $625 transferred from each account into your checking account every month.

When you invest in mutual funds, you may receive dividends, interest, and realized capital gains (gains on stocks that the mutual fund sells). You can elect to have these amounts paid directly to you, but having them reinvested into new mutual fund shares is easier. The mutual fund company sells enough shares each month to generate the payment you've requested.

You can increase or decrease your withdrawal amount if you absolutely have to, but try hard to stick with your plan. Remember that your nest egg doesn't provide a guaranteed lifetime income stream: The checks stop when your account balance hits zero. For example, you can increase the amount you withdraw annually by 3 percent, or whatever inflation rate you've built into your plan; however, it's wiser to keep the withdrawal amount at the same level until you really need the additional income.

Keeping your withdrawal amount steady gives you a cushion for later. Your plan for managing your nest egg during your retirement years includes many variables, including a "guesstimate" of when you will exit your earthly existence. It's highly unlikely that everything will happen exactly as you plan. Living somewhat more frugally during the early years of your retirement reduces the potential that you'll outlive your nest egg.

The annuity option

Another way to get a monthly check in retirement is to purchase an *immediate annuity,* a financial product that protects you if you live beyond a normal life expectancy. To buy an immediate annuity, you pay a lump sum (which you can roll over from a 401(k), for example); in return, you are guaranteed income for life — no matter how long you live. How much income you receive depends on the terms of your annuity. An annuity is a good option if you have a limited amount of money that has to last you for many years.

Evaluating the pros and cons

A major disadvantage of an annuity, besides additional fees, is the fact that, depending on the terms of your annuity, the insurer may keep your money if you die sooner than expected. You can guarantee payments for a certain number of years beyond your death or for the life of another beneficiary, but doing so reduces your monthly payments while you're alive. Financial organizations that sell annuities aren't in the business of giving money away. To put it bluntly, annuity-holders who die early pay for the ones who live longer than expected.

Another risk of an annuity is that the insurer that is guaranteeing the annuity may fail. Buy an annuity only from a company that has a top rating. Companies that rate insurers include A. M. Best (www.ambest.com), Standard & Poor's (www.standardandpoors.com), and Duff & Phelps (www.duffandphelps.com).

If you like the guarantee that an annuity offers, one solution is to split your retirement money between an annuity and other investments. This solution can be the best of both worlds for some people — they can count on a certain amount of life income from the annuity, plus a monthly withdrawal from the mutual funds or other investments that they make outside the annuity.

After you buy an annuity, you may not be able to change the payment structure for some unexpected need. Some annuities are now being offered that provide more flexibility than used to be the case with annuities. This is good, but it's also made it harder to know just what you are getting. therefore be sure you understand the terms of the annuity before you purchase it.

Varying your annuity

Immediate annuities exist in *fixed* or *variable* types. With a fixed annuity, the insurance company guarantees you payments of the same amount each year. Your payments don't increase to keep up with inflation. A variable annuity lets you invest in mutual funds to try to boost your payments and keep up with inflation. However, investing in these mutual funds through a variable annuity is more expensive because of the income guarantee. Plus, your payments may drop if your investments don't do well.

If you do buy a variable annuity, choose one that gives you access to mutual funds that you prefer. You can buy an annuity directly from most mutual fund companies. Remember to split your annuity investment between stocks and fixed-income investments, as you do with the rest of your portfolio.

A word of caution: Consult a trusted financial planner or other professional advisor to make sure that either type of annuity is right for you. Getting out of an annuity after you've bought it is very difficult, if not impossible.

Your home is your asset

When you consider financial resources to fund your retirement, you may also wonder whether you should convert your home into an income-producing asset. In some cases, selling the house makes sense, but many people are emotionally attached to their family home and don't want to sell it. You may have to try to take a less-emotional look, however, because you may need the equity from your home to achieve a comfortable level of retirement income.

A better option may be to sell your home and use the proceeds to generate income, and then find a place to rent. Why rent if you own a home without a mortgage? A home is indeed an asset, but it doesn't produce money — it eats it. Even if you don't have a mortgage, living in your home costs a lot. Assume that you own a $250,000 home. The real estate taxes are probably in the $3,500 range. Your routine annual maintenance costs are probably in the $2,000 to $3,000 range. (Check all your expenditures for a year if these estimates seem high.) You also have to factor in major periodic repairs, such as a new roof. You probably spend at least $5,500 to $7,500 per year for the privilege of owning your $250,000 home — even with the mortgage fully paid. This additional expense is okay if you have adequate retirement income, but it's not wise if your retirement resources are limited. You need assets that generate income, not one that takes substantial money to maintain.

You can probably find a nice place to rent for $1,000 per month near your $250,000 home. The rental will cost you $12,000 a year compared to the $5,500 to $7,500 it may cost to live in your present home. You're paying more, but without the hassle of home ownership. Most important, you can reinvest the money from the sale of your home and make up the difference.

Assume that you have $225,000 left after you sell your home and move. (Also assume that you don't owe capital gains tax.) You can reinvest this money in a 50/50 stock and fixed-income portfolio that may generate an average 7 percent investment return of $15,750. You could use $4,500 to 6,500 of this "profit" to make up the difference between the rent you pay and the housing expenses that you've eliminated. You then have the remainder for additional annual retirement income that may enable you to do some things that would not otherwise be possible. You also have access to the $225,000 for emergencies. The same logic applies if you live where housing costs are very high. If you have limited retirement resources, relocating to a lower-cost area makes sense so that you can unlock the equity in your expensive home.

Chapter 5

Online Retirement Planning

*M*any people expect their retirement years to be the best years of their lives. That expectation is what makes retirement planning more than just investing and saving for the future. Retirement should be about enjoying your life, not being constrained by economics and worry. Give plenty of thought to how you're going to spend your time when you're not at work.

Saving for your retirement requires discipline. Retirement often is 40, 30, 20, or even only 10 years away, but it just doesn't seem like it's going to happen anytime soon. A study by Hewitt Associates, a benefits consulting firm, shows how difficult it is for individuals to visualize their retirement years. The study indicated that about 49 percent of workers surveyed said they didn't think they were saving enough; another 18 percent just weren't certain.

This chapter is about how you can use the Internet to help you get ready for retirement. In this chapter, you find out how to use online tools provided by the Social Security Administration to determine how much you can expect in Social Security benefits. And you discover a breakdown of average retiree expenses so you can start calculating how much money you need for retirement. This chapter shows how you can use the Internet to develop an online retirement plan. We provide an example of how you can fill the gap between your retirement income and expenses, and we tell you about a few places online where you can create "what if?" scenarios to maximize your retirement savings. Best of all, this chapter helps you explore the Net for the optimal ways to save for your retirement.

Pop Quiz: How Ready Are You for Retirement?

Everyone needs a game plan, a strategy for retiring. Individuals who write down their retirement plans have a better chance of achieving their goals than folks who keep putting off the task of taking a good look at what they need to do to secure their retirement. Bear in mind that crafting your retirement plan is similar to creating a business plan. To get started, you need to know this information:

- ✔ **Your current needs:** If you haven't calculated how much you need to keep your head above water, you must figure it out now. Knowing your current expenses helps you compute your future expenses.

- ✔ **How much you need to retire:** Many people want to move to another state or travel to all the places they were too busy to see when they were working.

- ✔ **Your retirement time frame:** When do you plan to retire? What activities do you plan to participate in? Will your mortgage be paid or will you have children in college?

- ✔ **Your retirement expenses:** Determine your fixed expenses. How much income overall will you need? How much do you expect to receive from Social Security? What about your company pensions and your own retirement savings?

Also consider a few tips for the road ahead:

- ✔ **Get the most out of your 401(k) plan.** Taking full advantage of your employer's 401(k) plan today may make a huge difference in your retirement lifestyle.

- ✔ **Take advantage of other savings plans.** Most folks have a gap between their expenses in retirement and the retirement benefits they'll receive. You can compensate for this deficit with IRAs, Roth IRAs, SEP-IRAs, and other savings plans.

- ✔ **Don't ignore your retirement investments.** Monitor your savings and investments. Compare your financial status with your retirement plan. Do you see any problems?

- ✔ **Plan your quitting-time strategy.** Set a reasonable withdrawal rate from your nest egg. Manage your money so you don't run out of money before you run out of time.

✔ **Periodically revise your long-term plans.** Update and rebalance your plan as necessary. If you decide you want to travel more in your retirement years, you may have to increase your savings.

✔ **Be passionate about your retirement planning.** Give some real thought to how you want to spend your retirement years. Apply this enthusiasm to your retirement planning. Remember, each person gets only one retirement.

The Internet provides many online tutorials to help you become skilled at planning for your retirement. A few examples include the following:

Book VI

Retiring Comfortably

✔ **About.com Retirement Planning Tutorials** (`http://retireplan.about.com`) offers tutorials and links to online resources for information about investing in 401(k) and 403(b) plans.

✔ **University of Illinois Extension How to Guide for Planning Well and Retiring Well** (`www.retirewell.uiuc.edu`) explores how your savings can grow between now and retirement. Catch up on the basics of investing and how to get the most out of your tax-deferred retirement plans. Calculate where you are now, and how much you will need to save for the retirement you want.

✔ **Retirement Planning for the Golden Years** (`www.retirementplanninggoldenyears.com`) offers a broad look at how retirement planning and the lack of retirement planning can affect your "Golden Years." This Web site provides a collection of 13 easy-to-understand articles about retirement planning.

✔ **Prudential Financial** (`www.prudential.com`) offers an online retirement-planning tutorial. On the home page, click Retirement Planning. You'll discover retirement planning articles, calculators, guides, and answers to common questions.

Developing a Retirement Plan

If you don't have a retirement plan, create one. If you have a retirement plan, review it and put more into it. Most Americans know they're not saving enough for their retirement. Many individuals aren't saving because they've been shaken by recent stock market losses, and others just let life get in the way of saving.

Whether you have a traditional pension plan, a 401(k) plan, or no retirement plan, the Internet can help you develop a do-it-yourself plan. The Net provides many sources, tools, and resources to help you build your retirement plan. In many cases, the Internet even does the math for you. The following are a few examples of Web sites that can assist you with building your retirement plan online:

- ✔ **Investopedia** (`www.investopedia.com`) offers an online introduction to retirement planning. Discover how much you need, the different types of retirement plans, and how taxes affect you and your retirement.

- ✔ **Morningstar.com** (`www.morningstar.com`) provides an online retirement planner to help you plan for your golden years. It requires Premium membership, which costs $16.95 per month.

- ✔ **SmartMoney.com** (`www.smartmoney.com`) supplies one of the Internet's best retirement-planning tools. You can get worksheets, information about how long your money will last, and more, without having to register or pay a dime. On the home page, click Personal Finance and then Retirement, or go directly to `www.smartmoney.com/retirement`.

- ✔ **The Motley Fool** (`www.fool.com/retirement/retirementplanning/retirementplanning01.htm`) offers an online retirement primer to get you started with planning your retirement.

- ✔ **The *Wall Street Journal*** (`www.wsj.com`) provides Personal Finance News and Tools to assist you with your retirement planning. It's powered by the SmartMoney's Retirement Worksheet Calculator. Online-only subscriptions are $99 per year with two weeks free. You can also purchase a print and online subscription for $125 per year with four weeks for free.

The foundations of many people's retirement plans are their pensions and Social Security benefits. The following sections discuss both.

Pensions

Pension plans are defined as a promise by a sponsor, usually a company or a union, to pay a pension to the plan member. A variety of pension plans are in place. Consider two examples of traditional pension plans:

- ✔ **Defined benefit plan:** In a defined benefit plan, the promised pension is based on a clearly defined formula, such as years of service or hours worked.

- ✔ **Defined contribution plan:** In a defined contribution plan, the sponsor or company makes contributions to an investment fund in the plan member's account. The plan member's account grows with the contributions and with the investment earnings from the fund. At retirement, accumulated funds are used to purchase an annuity or similar financial product that pays the retirement income.

For more about different types of pensions, see the U.S. Department of Labor Web site at `www.dol.gov/dol/topic/retirement/typesofplans.htm`. You'll discover descriptions of various pension plans and find out what you need to know about pension plans and your rights.

Social Security benefits

In 1935, Social Security was enacted to provide a safety net for America's older citizens. About 164 million workers are earning Social Security protection, and about 34.5 million people receive retirement benefits from Social Security. Almost 9 million workers and family members get disability benefits, and about 6¹/₂ million people get monthly survivors benefits. That's a total of 50 million people who receive a Social Security check each month. Social Security taxes cover five categories: retirement, disability, family, survivors, and Medicare. At this time, workers with earnings of less than $102,000 per year pay 7.65 percent of their income to Social Security. (Employers match workers by paying in the same amount.) The self-employed pay a total rate of 15.3 percent of income less than $102,000 per year.

As you work, you earn credits toward your retirement. People born in 1929 or later need at least 40 credits to receive retirement benefits. Your actual earnings determine the amount of Social Security benefits you receive. Full retirement age gradually is increasing, depending on the year of your birth. You can receive benefits at age 62, but they're reduced. The average age of retirement is 65. If you hold off until age 70, you get a larger benefit check.

Your Social Security statement details all three scenarios. Since 1999, the law requires the Social Security Administration (SSA) to send a Social Security Statement every year to all workers who are 25 and older who aren't receiving Social Security benefits. If you don't automatically receive your statement, you can request one online at www.ssa.gov/online/ssa-7004. html or call toll-free 800-722-1213 and request that form SSA-7004 be mailed to you. You'll receive your statement in the mail in about two to four weeks after your online request.

If you're uncertain about when to cash in your Social Security benefits, refer to the Social Security benefits calculators located at www.ssa.gov/ planners/calculators.htm. You'll find three styles of calculators:

- ✔ **Quick calculator:** This quick-estimate calculator uses your date of birth and years of earnings. To use this calculator, you must be older than 21 years old and younger than 65 years old.

- ✔ **Online calculator:** This online calculator requires your date of birth and complete earnings history, and it projects your future earnings. This calculator is similar to what's shown on your Social Security statement — the one you receive on a regular basis from the SSA.

- ✔ **Downloadable detailed calculator:** The third calculator is a free downloadable program that provides the most precise and detailed estimates. Keep in mind that your Social Security records are private.

For more information about your Social Security benefits, check online at one of these sites:

- ✔ **AARP** (www.aarp.org/socialsecurity) maintains a Social Security Center on its Web site. You can find answers to some commonly asked questions about Social Security.

- ✔ **Fairmark** (www.fairmark.com/retirement/socsec) explains key facts about the retirement benefit provided by the Social Security program. These articles are designed to provide you with a better general understanding of this benefit, and to help you make informed decisions about your benefit, such as when to stop working and when to begin taking benefits. The choices are important because they can affect the amount of retirement benefits you receive for the rest of your life.

- ✔ **How Stuff Works** provides an introduction to how Social Security works, defines what retirement benefits are, provides a brief history of Social Security, and has lots more.

Using the Internet to Determine How Much You Need to Live On

What expenses will you have in retirement? Table 5-1 shows how the average percentage of income is allocated for most retired people. Table 5-1 indicates that you still can expect to pay taxes and will be required to save well into your retirement years.

Table 5-1	Retirement Expenses
Expense	*Average Percentage*
Housing	20%
Groceries	11%
Personal care	5%
Automobile	9%
Unreimbursed medical expenses	4%
Insurance	4%
Recreation	5%
Gifts to charity and others	2%
Interest on consumer loans and credit cards	4%
Other items	8%
Taxes and savings	28%
Total	**100%**

Knowing how much your expenses will be in retirement is important. Many financial planners believe that retirees will need 80 percent of their current income. Many retirees require more income in their retirement years than when they're working. Some retirees cruise around the world. Other retirees take up expensive hobbies. Many retirees just travel to visit their children and grandchildren. Regardless of how you envision your retirement years, you need to know the costs in advance. A few Web sites can help you focus on retirement expenses:

- ✔ **Argone Credit Union** (`http://hffo.cuna.org/story.html?doc_id=491&sub_id=14953`) supplies an easy-to-understand article about how you can quickly and easily calculate your retirement needs.

- ✔ **Yahoo! Finance** (`http://finance.yahoo.com/calculator/retirement/ret-05`) provides a calculator for determining the impact of inflation on your retirement income needs. For example, an anticipated 3 percent inflation rate could radically change the quality of your retirement years.

- ✔ **Living to 100** (`www.livingto100.com`) offers an online calculator to assist you with planning for your retirement. Fill out the Web site's questionnaire, and you'll even discover your life expectancy. The longer you live, the more savings you require.

- ✔ **AXA Equitable** (`www.axa-equitable.com/learning-center/tools-and-calculators.html`) offers a Life Expectancy Calculator. Estimate your life expectancy based on your current age, smoking habits, gender, and several other important lifestyle choices. Just click on the link titled Life Expectancy Calculator.

Figuring out how much to save: A real-world example

Choose to Save (`www.choosetosave.org`) is a not-for-profit Web site that is completely devoted to financial education. Choose to Save provides articles and calculators for thinking about many money-related situations. You'll also find an example of how to get a "ballpark" estimate of your retirement needs. Let's say Jane is a 35-year-old woman with two children, earning $30,000 per year. Jane has determined that she will need 70 percent of her current annual income to maintain her standard of living in retirement. Seventy percent of Jane's current annual income ($30,000) is $21,000. Jane would then subtract the income she expects to receive from Social Security ($12,000 in her case) from $21,000, equaling $9,000. This is how much Jane needs to make up for each retirement year. Jane expects to retire at age 65 and if she is willing to assume that her life expectancy will be equal to the average female at that age (86), she would multiply $9,000 by 15.77 for a result of $141,930. (See Table 5-2 for details.)

Table 5-2	Determining How Much You Need to Save	
Age You Expect to Retire	Male 50th Percentile (age 82): Multiply Annual Need By	Female, 50th Percentile (age 86): Multiply Annual Need By
55	18.79	20.53
60	16.31	18.32
65	13.45	15.77
70	10.15	12.83

Jane has already saved $2,000 in her 401(k) plan. She plans to retire in 30 years, so she multiplies $2,000 x 2.4, equaling $4,800. (See Table 5-3 for details.)

Table 5-3	Multiply Savings to Date by the Factor
If You Plan to Retire in	Your Factor Is
10 years	1.3
15 years	1.6
20 years	1.8
25 years	2.1
30 years	2.4
35 years	2.8
40 years	3.3

She subtracts that from her total, making her projected total savings needed at retirement $137,130. Jane then multiplies $137,130 $\times$ 0.020 = $2,742. (See Table 5-4 for details.)

Table 5-4	Multiply the Total Amount by the Factor to Determine Annual Savings Needed
If You Plan To Retire in	Your Factor Is
10 years	.085
15 years	.052
20 years	.036
25 years	.027
30 years	.020
35 years	.016
40 years	.013

The amount Jane will need to save in the current year for her retirement (assuming the annual contribution will increase with inflation in future years) is $2,742. ***Note:*** It is important to mention that the calculation assumes Jane would have an average life expectancy for a female already age 65. However, this will produce an amount that is too low in approximately half of all cases. If instead Jane wanted to have a sufficient amount for three quarters of cases, she would base her calculations on a life expectancy of 92. This would necessitate multiplying $9,000 by a factor of 18.79 for a result of $169,110. All the remaining calculations would be similar and the contribution for the first year would increase to $3,286.

Let the Internet do the heavy lifting

Book VI

Retiring Comfortably

The Internet provides many online calculators to assist you in determining your specific retirement savings needs. American Funds (www.american funds.com/retirement/calculator/index.htm) provides a quick analysis. All you have to do is answer four questions (this takes about five minutes). This version makes assumptions about your situation, including your retirement age and length, taxes, Social Security benefits, investment growth rates, inflation, and raises. The detailed analysis is 15 questions (and takes about 15 minutes to complete). You'll be able to enter your investment information in 17 subcategories. The results are customized by allowing you to enter more details about your financial situation.

The results of the Retirement Planning Calculator indicate whether your savings will provide what you need in retirement. You can make adjustments to your savings plan and recalculate by increasing your future annual contributions. Enter the higher amount where indicated and click Recalculate to see what effect this change may have.

The Retirement Planning Calculator results provide a chart that compares your projected savings to your retirement goal. Try different scenarios to see how changes in your savings affect your results. You can click on each question for help or additional information. Revisit the calculator when your financial situation or goals change. ***Note:*** The Retirement Planning Calculator is for illustrative purposes only and is not intended to provide investment advice or portray actual investment results.

For more information on this topic and to avoid having to calculate the math to determine how much you need to save if you have a shortfall, the Internet can do the work for you with online calculators that take the guesswork out of retirement planning. Here are a few of the best, to help you get started:

✔ **PA Directory** (www.cpadirectory.com/calculators/java/RetirementPlan.html) offers a calculator that you can use in two ways. To calculate how much you can save, enter your current savings and leave the amount to deduct from earnings field blank. Second, to determine how much you need to achieve a certain goal leave your current savings and the percent to deduct from income fields blank. Click Compute to calculate the results.

✔ **Kiplinger.com** (www.kiplinger.com/tools/retirement-savings-calculator.html) provides an estimate of how much you need to save initially each month to match your retirement nest-egg goal. You'll discover whether you're saving enough each month or if you need to increase your savings in the future to keep pace with inflation. Results assume 3 percent inflation and 2 percent annual home appreciation.

✔ **Investopedia** (www.investopedia.com/calculator/PVAnnuityDue.aspx) offers an easy-to-use online calculator that shows, for instance, exactly how much money you need to have today if you want to retire with a steady stream of income per year.

Using "what if?" scenarios

You can prepare for your retirement in many different ways. Some industry experts say your retirement nest egg must be limited to 5 percent withdrawals per year. Therefore, if you expect to live for 20 years after you retire and plan to deduct $30,000 per year from your nest egg to supplement your pension, Social Security, and other sources of income, your nest egg needs to be $600,000.

Although this plan is one way to make certain your money lasts, you can try other scenarios. The Internet is a no-fuss, no-muss way to help you try a wide variety of "what if?" scenarios. This experience can help you gain a better understanding of the possible outcomes of what you do today so you can maximize your retired tomorrows. Consider a few examples:

✔ **About.com** (http://retireplan.about.com/cs/calculators/a/calculators.hrm) offers an online retirement calculator and retirement workshop for online retirement planning.

✔ **Choose to Save** (www.choosetosave.org/ballpark/index.cfm?fa=interactive) is an easy-to-use, one-page worksheet that helps you quickly identify approximately how much you need to save to fund a comfortable retirement. The Ballpark Estimate translates complicated issues such as projected Social Security benefits and earnings assumptions on savings into easily understandable language and mathematics.

✔ **Financial Engines** (www.financialengines.com) is often considered the Cadillac of online planners. Developed by 1990 Nobel Prize-winning Stanford University professor William Sharpe, Financial Engines is costly ($39.95 per quarter or $149.95 per year, but it's worth every penny). With your Total Retirement Advice subscription you receive a personalized retirement forecast, monitoring of your portfolio, and Investor Central financial and investing information. You receive advice on all your tax-deferred accounts. You can also forecast for your employee stock options and for your non-retirement financial goals.

Book VI

Retiring Comfortably

Saving for Retirement

The number of traditional retirement plans has continued to decline, and many employers are replacing them with more conventional retirement options, such as 401(k) plans. Doing so takes much of the burden off the employer and gives employees greater control over their accounts. However, many participants forget the purpose of the 401(k) plan and cash out when they change jobs. In other words, they unnecessarily incur taxes and a 10 percent penalty (if the participant is younger than $59^{1}/_{2}$ years old).

If you accumulate $10,000 in a 401(k) plan, for example, and you cash out at age 25, you pay a big chunk of the money you receive in income taxes to Uncle Sam and you pay an early withdrawal penalty that amounts to $1,000. If, on the other hand, you didn't touch the funds until you turned 65 years old, and that $10,000 was earning an average 8 percent annual return, you'd have $217, 000 for your retirement. Granted, you couldn't buy a yacht, but you could get a pretty decent sailboat.

The joys of 401(k) plans

The Revenue Act of 1978 created new options for employee retirement plans. Instead of traditional pension plans, employers can offer workers 401(k) plans. Eligibility for most plans is set for employees of a certain age (21 years old, for example) and for a predetermined number of hours of annual service (more than 1,000 work hours per year, for example). Workers can make contributions to the plans in four ways:

✔ After-tax dollars (the "thrift plan").

✔ Worker contributions that the employer matches. For example, a worker contributes 10 percent of his or her paycheck, and the employer provides a 5 percent matching contribution, so the employee ends up with 15 percent.

- ✔ Nonelective contributions, which are automatically deducted and placed in the plan.

- ✔ Worker-elective pretax contributions, in which you can sock away part of your salary each year for your retirement.

For more information about 401(k) plans, check out Book VI, Chapter 1, along with these Web sites:

- ✔ **About.com** (http://etire.about.com/cs/401k/a/401k.htm) offers more information about 401(k) plans.

- ✔ **SmartMoney.com** (www.smartmoney.com) provides a 401(k) planner. Discover how increasing or decreasing your 401(k) contribution affects your take-home pay and the amount of money you'll have for retirement.

- ✔ **The-Adviser.com** (www.the-adviser.com/Questions/401kplans. htm) offers all the information you want about withdrawals, jobs changes, retirement, and minimum required distributions.

- ✔ The *Wall Street Journal* (www.wsj.com) offers the Money Toolbox. Financial/retirement-planning tools include an online retirement-planning worksheet, a 401(k) planner, and a 401(k) contributions calculator. Subscriptions cost $3.95 per month or $39 per year.

Employees of nonprofit organizations can have 403(b) plans, which are similar to 401(k) plans.

Individual retirement accounts (IRAs)

When you open an individual retirement account (IRA), you must decide whether you want a traditional IRA, a Roth IRA, or an education IRA (now called Coverdell ESAs). Each type of IRA has its own advantages and limitations. Book VI, Chapter 2 covers IRAs in detail, but here's some basics:

Traditional IRAs

Congress created traditional IRAs in 1974 as a means of saving for retirement without having to pay taxes on the money you earn in your account until you start withdrawing the funds during retirement. You may also be able to deduct your annual contribution to a traditional IRA from your yearly income taxes. Being able to do so depends on how much you earn.

In 2008, the maximum annual IRA contribution is $5,000. It is important to mention that this maximum is the contribution limit of all your IRA accounts. Beginning in 2009 the contribution limit will adjust annually for inflation in $500 increments. If you are 50 or older you can take advantage of the "catch-up" contribution of $1,000. In 2008 for single tax filers with an employer-sponsored retirement plan, an IRA contribution is fully tax-deductible if your income is below $53,000. It is then prorated between $53,000 and $63,000. If your income is over $63,000, and you have an employer-sponsored retirement plan, such as a 401(k), you receive no tax deduction. For married couples, the same rules apply except the deduction is phased out between $83,000 and $103,000.

Several rules affect withdrawals from traditional IRAs. For instance, you can't begin withdrawing funds without penalties until you reach age 59½. If you withdraw funds before that time, you pay a tax penalty. In addition, you must withdraw funds when you turn 70½, which is when you no longer can contribute any more money to the IRA. Expect to pay taxes on any funds that you withdraw. As such, spreading your withdrawals across as many years as possible is a wise choice so you won't be hit with a large tax bill when you're older than 70.

Roth IRAs

Roth IRAs were created in 1997. Roth IRA contributions are limited for higher incomes. If your income falls in a "phase-out" range, you are allowed only a prorated Roth IRA contribution. If your income exceeds the phase-out range, you do not qualify for any Roth IRA contribution. The income phase-out ranges for Roth IRAs are as follows: For married filing jointly or head of household the 2008 income phase-out range is $159K to $169K. For singles, the 2008 income phase-out range is $101K to $116K. For those married filing separately, the 2008 income phase-out range is $0 to $10K.

Roth IRA withdrawals are tax-free if you hold the account for five or more years and you're 59½ or older. Withdrawals also are tax-free if you become disabled, if you're purchasing a home for the first time, or if the account holder dies. Keep in mind that as long as you have earned income, you can contribute to a traditional IRA until you turn 70½. Investors older than 70½ can't contribute to a traditional IRA but can contribute to a Roth IRA. If you don't have earned income but are married and file a joint return, you still can contribute to an IRA based on your working spouse's income.

For more information about Roth IRAs, see these Web sites:

- ✔ **Employee Benefit Research Institute** (www.ebri.org) is a nonprofit, nonpartisan organization that provides information and education about employee benefits. Here you can find the latest information about IRAs.

- ✔ **Kiplinger.com** (www.kiplinger.com/basics/managing/retirement/roth1.htm) provides a large online retirement center that includes articles, resources, and online calculators.

- ✔ **Roth IRA home page** (www.rothira.com) offers technical and planning information about Roth IRAs to practitioners and consumers.

Book VI

Retiring Comfortably

✔ **The Motley Fool** (`www.motleyfool.com`) provides "The 60-Second Guide to Opening an IRA Account." This online guide offers step-by-step guidance for opening an IRA and a calculator to determine what type of IRA account is best for you. You'll also find suggestions about where to invest your cash and brokerage comparisons.

Online calculators for determining the best IRA account

Several kinds of IRA accounts are available. The Vanguard Group (`https://personal.vanguard.com/us/planningeducation/retirement`) has a Retirement Center that offers an online calculator that can help you determine what kind of IRA is best for you. At the Retirement Center, click "I'm already saving or just starting to save for retirement" and then click "Which IRA is best for me?" You'll discover whether you can contribute to a traditional or Roth IRA, find out whether you're eligible to deduct your traditional IRA contribution, calculate your maximum allowable contribution, project the long-term returns of each type of IRA, and then compare your options.

Find other online IRA comparison calculators at these Web sites:

✔ **Morningstar.com** (`http://screen.morningstar.com/ira/ira-calculator.html?tsection=toolsiracal`) provides an IRA calculator to help you make better IRA decisions. Discover your eligibility, determine your contributing limits for Roth or traditional IRAs compare various scenarios to uncover which IRA is best for you, and discover whether you need to convert your traditional IRA to a Roth IRA.

✔ **CCH Financial Planning Toolkit** (`www.finance.cch.com`) offers a number of useful online calculators. Several of our favorites are the Traditional IRA Calculator, The Roth IRA Calculator, and the Traditional IRA Versus Roth IRA calculator. At the home page, click Financial Calculators in the left margin.

Retirement plans for small businesses and the self-employed

Simplified employee pensions (SEPs) frequently are best for business owners who have high incomes. These individuals want to maximize their contributions, keep their plans simple, and pay low fees. You can contribute up to 20 percent of your compensation if you're unincorporated, and if you're incorporated, you can contribute up to 25 percent of your compensation, up to $46,000 per year in 2008, whichever is less. Keep in mind that if you have employees, you must contribute the same percentage of compensation for your employees that you do for yourself. The following Web sites offer a few examples of more online information:

✔ **Internal Revenue Service** (www.irs.gov/retirement/content/0,,id=97203,00.html) offers a full menu of high-quality articles about retirement plans for small businesses and the self-employed.

✔ **Retirement Planner** (www.retirementplanner.org/index.html) offers a full menu of retirement advice. Discover how to safeguard your 401(k) plan, IRAs, and annuities.

✔ **Human Resources Executive Online** (www.workindex.com) offers links to retirement benefits and services sites on the Internet. Enter "Retirement Benefits" in the search box on the home page.

Other retirement options

If you're shut out of a 401(k) plan for some reason and can't qualify for an IRA account, you may want to consider investing in a variable annuity. You can purchase a variable annuity that guarantees a 6 percent return. In other words, you're guaranteed to earn at least 6 percent annually and you may earn a higher return. Say you invest $200,000 with a 6 percent guarantee. In ten short years, your investment grows to be worth a minimum of $360,000. During this time, the stock market hits a high and your investment is worth $500,000. The stock market also hits a low and your investment is worth $300,000. When you begin to make monthly or annual withdrawals from your guaranteed annuity, your payments will be based on the high of $500,000. For more information about annuities, see these Web sites:

✔ **Annuity.com** (www.annuity.com) offers a broad spectrum of information about annuities, including definitions, rates, quotes, and online calculators.

✔ **About.com** (http://banking.about.com/od/annuities insurance/Annuities_Insurance_Products_in_Banks.htm) shows how banks offer a variety of ways to save money and features annuities. Annuities have been one of the most popular investment alternatives for a variety of reasons. This page offers essential annuity information and explains why banks offer annuities.

✔ **Money Instructor.com** (www.moneyinstructor.com/art/annuities101.asp) shows an overview of how annuities may seem like something for the very wealthy but may be a great savings option for anyone who would like to make the most of their long-term savings.

Book VII
Planning Your Estate and Will

The 5th Wave   By Rich Tennant

"That? That's form 1040DTX. In the unlikely event that anyone ever does figure out how to 'take it with them,' the federal government has in place a form and instructions on how to send back the appropriate amount of taxes due."

In this book . . .

It's true you can't take it with you, but it's also true that you can fail to plan for what will happen to your estate and end up not passing on what you thought would be passed on to your beneficiaries. By taking some time now to plan your estate and write your will, no matter your age, you will save yourself and probably your loved ones a lot of grief down the road. This book is where we discuss these important but often neglected matters.

Here are the contents of Book VII at a glance.

Chapter 1

Fundamentals of Estate Planning

The protection and control that you need. No, this phrase isn't the marketing slogan for a new deodorant. Instead, it expresses the two most important reasons for you to spend time and effort on your estate planning:

✔ After you die, the government will try to take as much of your estate as possible, so you want to protect it to the greatest extent that you can.

✔ For the portion of your estate that you are able to protect from the government, you want to have as much control as possible over how your estate is divided up. Basically, you want to decide what will happen to your estate instead of having a set of laws dictate who gets what.

Before you can plan your estate, you need to understand what your estate really is. Many people think that estate planning involves only two steps:

✔ Preparing a will

✔ Trying to figure out what inheritance and estate taxes — the so-called "death taxes" — apply (and if so, how much money goes to the state and federal governments)

But even though wills and death taxes are certainly important considerations for you, chances are your own estate planning involves much, much more. This chapter presents the basics of estate planning that you need to get started on this often-overlooked topic of your personal financial planning. Here you also discover that estate planning is every bit as important as saving for your child's college education or putting away money for your retirement.

What Is an Estate?

In the most casual sense, your estate is your *stuff,* or all your possessions. However, even if your only familiarity with estate planning comes from watching a movie or television show on which someone's will is read, you no doubt realize that you aren't very likely to hear words such as, "I leave all of my stuff to. . . ." Therefore, a bit more detail and formality is in order.

The basics: Definitions and terminology

What's that, you say? You don't own a house or any other real estate, so you think you don't have any property? Not so fast! In a legal sense, all kinds of items are considered to be your property, not just real estate (more formally known as *real property,* as discussed later in the' "Property types" section):

- Cash, checking, and savings accounts
- Certificates of deposit (CDs)
- Stocks, bonds, and mutual funds
- Retirement savings in your individual retirement account (IRA), 401(k), and other special accounts
- Household furniture (including antiques)
- Clothes
- Vehicles
- Life insurance
- Annuities
- Business interests
- Jewelry, baseball card collection, autographed first edition of *Catcher in the Rye,* and all the rest of your collectibles

Your estate consists of all the preceding types of items — and more — divided into several different categories. (For estate-planning purposes, these categories are often treated differently from each other, but we cover that later.)

The types of property listed almost always have a *positive balance,* meaning that they are worth something even if "something" is only a very small amount. Of course, an exception may be your overdrawn checking account, which then is actually property with a negative balance. In the case of an overdrawn checking account, the "property" is the amount that you owe a person or company (your bank, in this case). So your estate also includes *negative-value* property:

✔ The outstanding balance of the mortgage you owe on your house or a vacation home

✔ The outstanding balances on your credit card accounts

✔ Taxes you owe to the government

✔ Any IOUs to people you haven't paid yet

Basically, all the debts you have are as much a part of your estate as all the positive-balance items.

In addition to understanding what your estate is, you need to know what your estate is worth. You calculate your estate's value as follows:

1. **Add up the value of all the positive-balance items in your estate** (banking accounts, investments, collectibles, real estate, and so on).

2. **Subtract the total value of all the negative balance items (remaining balance of the mortgage on your home, how much you still owe on your credit cards, and so on) from the total of all the positive-balance items.**

The result is the value of your estate. In most cases, the result is a positive number, meaning that what you have is worth more than what you owe.

(If calculating a *net value* by subtracting the total of what you owe from the total of what you have seems familiar, you're right! In the simplest sense, calculating the value of your estate involves essentially the same steps that you follow when you apply for many different types of loans: mortgage, automobile, educational assistance, and so on.)

However, in many cases — including perhaps your own — determining what the parts of your estate are, and what they are worth, can be a bit more complicated than simply creating two columns on a sheet of paper or in your computer's spreadsheet program and doing basic arithmetic. If you are a farmer, for example, you need to figure out the value of your crops or livestock. If you own a small one-person business, you need to calculate what your business is worth. Or perhaps you and six other people are joint owners of a complicated real estate investment partnership; what is your share worth?

For now, another point to keep in mind is that, in addition to what you have right now, your estate may include other items that you don't have in your possession but will have at some point in the future:

✔ Any future payments that you expect to receive, such as an insurance settlement or the remaining 18 annual payments from that $35 million lottery jackpot that you won a couple of years ago

✔ Future inheritances

✔ A loan that you made to your sister to help get her business started, and when she plans to repay you

Book VII

Planning Your Estate and Will

When you're figuring out what your estate contains and what your estate is worth, you also need to include your own personal *accounts receivable* — a business and accounting term that refers to what people or businesses owe you — along with your banking accounts and home.

One final term to cover is estate planning. By definition, *estate planning* means planning your estate. (Duh!) More precisely, you need to follow a disciplined set of steps that we discuss later in this chapter. Why? You want to protect as much of your estate as possible from being taken away, and you (not the government or a scheming family member) want to control what happens to your estate after you die.

Your estate plan typically includes the following components:

✔ Your will

✔ Documents that substitute for your will

✔ Trusts

✔ Tax considerations, with the idea of minimizing taxes

✔ Various types of insurance

✔ Items related to your own particular circumstances, such as protecting your business or setting aside money to pay for your healthcare costs or a nursing home in your later years

We discuss all of these aspects of estate planning in this book. If this collection of estate-planning activities seems a bit overwhelming, think of estate planning as parallel to how you plan your personal finances and investments. Your investment portfolio may be made up of individual stocks, bonds, and mutual funds, along with bank CDs or other savings-related investments. Then within each type of investment, you have further categories (for example, different types of mutual funds) that you may want to use.

Your investment objective is to sort through this menu of choices and put together just the right collection for your needs. You must also do the same with your estate plan. You need to have the right will and insurance coverage, possibly accompanied by trusts, if they make sense for you and your family. Furthermore, you may need additional estate-planning activities and strategies particular to your own needs.

Property types

You can have several types of property within your estate. Make a distinction between these types of property because various aspects of your estate planning treat each type differently. For example, in your will (see Book VII, Chapter 2), you can use different legal language when referring to various types of property, so remember to keep these distinctions straight.

We already mentioned one type of property — *real property* — and noted that real property refers to various types of real estate:

- ✔ Your home (a house, condominium, co-op apartment, or some other type of primary residence that you own)

- ✔ A second home, such as vacation property on a lake or near a ski resort

- ✔ A "piece" of a vacation home, such as a timeshare

- ✔ Any kind of vacant land, such as a building lot in a suburban development or even agricultural land that you may own next to your "main" farm

- ✔ Any investment real property that you own either by yourself or with anyone else, such as a house that you rent out or your share of an apartment building

In addition to the actual real property itself, your estate includes any improvements that you can't even see. For example, if you and three of your friends bought 200 acres of land with the intention of turning that land into a subdivision and you have spent loads of money on infrastructure — water lines and hookups, sewer lines and hookups, in-ground electricity and cable, and so on — those improvements (or, more accurately, your share of those improvements) are also considered to be part of your estate, along with the original real property itself.

Your estate also includes *personal property,* which is further divided into tangible and intangible personal property. Your *tangible personal property* includes possessions that you can touch, such as your car, jewelry, furniture, paintings and artwork, and collectibles (baseball cards, autographed first-edition novels, and so on).

Your house is considered to be real property, not tangible personal property, even though you can touch it. Why? Because your house is permanently attached to (and thus made a part of) the land upon which it is built.

Your *intangible personal property* consists of financially oriented assets such as your bank accounts, stocks, mutual funds, bonds, and IRA. Of course, you can hold a stock certificate or mutual fund statement in your hand, but the stocks or mutual funds are still considered intangible personal property.

Technically, that stock certificate or mutual fund statement isn't actually what you own; it represents your portion of the ownership of some company (in the case of the stock certificate) or your portion of that mutual fund in the companies' stocks in which it invests. Financially oriented paper assets are typically intangible personal property, whereas actual possessions are tangible personal property. If you have any doubt about what category any particular item of your possessions falls into, just ask one of your estate-planning team members who we discuss later in this chapter.

Types of property interest

For each of the three types of property in your estate — real, tangible personal, and intangible personal — you also need to understand what your interest is. "Of course I'm interested in my property," you may be thinking; "After all, it's my property, isn't it?"

In the world of estate planning, *interest* has a somewhat different definition than how that word is used in everyday language, or even how the word is often used in the financial world (interest that you earn on a certificate of deposit or that you pay on your mortgage loan). More important, the specific type of interest in any given property determines what you specifically need to be concerned about for your estate planning.

Property interest is an essential part of almost all of your estate planning, from the words that you put in your will to how you may set up a trust, for two very important reasons:

✔ You need to clearly understand what type of interest you have in your property so that you can make accurate decisions about how to handle your property when you plan your estate.

✔ As you decide what to write in your will and perhaps also set up trusts as part of your estate plan, you need to make decisions about what type of interest in each property you want to set up for your children, your spouse, other family members, or institutions such as charities.

The two main types of property interest are legal interest and beneficial interest. If you have only a *legal interest* in a property, you have the right to transfer or manage that property, but you don't have the right to use the property yourself. By way of a very brief introduction to that topic, when you set up a trust, you name a *trustee,* a person who manages the trust.

Suppose that you set up a trust for your oldest son, Robert, as part of your estate plan, and you name your brother-in-law, Charlie, as the trustee. Charlie isn't allowed to use Robert's trust for his (Charlie's) own benefit, such as to withdraw $10,000 for a trip to Paris. That's called "Uncle Charlie goes to jail for stealing!" Assuming that Charlie does what he is supposed to do — and, more important, doesn't do what he's not supposed to do — Charlie has a legal interest in your son's trust as the trustee.

Unlike his Uncle Charlie, Robert has the other type of property interest in his trust: a *beneficial interest,* meaning that he does benefit from that trust. Basically, you set up that trust to benefit Robert.

Now, to complicate matters a bit more, two "subtypes" of beneficial interest exist: present interest and future interest. If you have a *present interest* (remember, that means "present beneficial interest"), you have the right to use the property immediately. So if Robert has a present interest in his trust his Uncle Charlie manages, Robert may receive payments from the trust of some specified amount — say, $30,000 every three months, for this example. After Robert receives the money, he can do whatever he wants with it; the money is his to use, with no strings attached.

The other type of beneficial interest — *future interest* — comes into play when someone with a beneficial interest (that person is allowed to benefit from that property) can't benefit right now, but instead must wait for some date in the future.

For example, you can set up the trust described to benefit not only your oldest son, but also your other two sons, Chip and Ernest. But you decide to take care of your three sons differently within that same trust. Suppose that after Robert receives his quarterly $30,000 payments for five years, his payments stop, and Chip and Ernest each begin receiving $30,000 quarterly payments at that point. Essentially, Chip and Ernest have a future interest in the property (the trust) because they can't benefit right now; they benefit in the future.

Complicating factors just a bit more (last time, we promise!), someone with a future interest in property can have one of two different types of future interest: vested interest and contingent interest. If you have a *vested interest,* you have the right to use and enjoy what you will get from that property at some point in the future, with no strings attached.

In the world of estate planning, the word *vested* means basically the same as it does in the world of retirement plans, stock options, and other financial assets. When you are vested in your company's retirement plan, you have the right to receive retirement benefits according to the particulars of your company's plan, even if you leave your job. Similarly, if you have stock options that have vested, you have the right to "exercise" those options and buy your company's stock at your "strike price." Furthermore, if you want, you can immediately sell those shares for a quick profit if your company's stock price has gone way up. (Unless you worked at Enron, but that's basically the same story. . . .)

However, if you have the other type of future beneficial interest — *contingent interest* — you have to deal with some "strings attached" other than the simple passage of time. For example, you may set up that trust for your three sons in such a way that, for Chip and Ernest to *realize* that future benefit, each must graduate from college and spend two years in the Peace Corps.

(Or you may set up the trust so that Chip receives his future benefit only if he marries and his wife gives birth to a set of triplets, if the earlier example reminds you of the old television show *My Three Sons.*)

Book VII

Planning Your Estate and Will

Why You Need to Plan Your Estate

Of course, you can decide to leave what happens to your estate after you die totally up to chance (or, more accurately, the complicated set of state laws that will apply if you haven't done the estate planning that you need to do). But because you're reading this book, chances are, the two fundamental goals of estate planning at the beginning of this chapter — protection and control — are uppermost in your mind.

But going beyond the general idea of protecting your possessions and being in control, you have some very specific objectives that you're trying to accomplish with your estate planning:

- ✔ **Providing for your loved ones:** You have people, including your spouse or significant other, children, grandchildren, and parents, who may rely on you for financial support. What will happen to that financial support if you died tomorrow?

  Even if you have a "traditional" family (that is, the kind of family typically shown in a 1950s or early 1960s situation comedy that is in perpetual reruns on TV Land or some other cable network), financial and other support for family members after you die can get very complicated if your estate isn't in order. But if your family is one that may be described as (quoting Nicholas Cage in the movie *Raising Arizona*) "Well, it ain't *Ozzie and Harriet,*" you absolutely need to pay attention to all the little details of protecting your family members if you die. Specifically, if your loved ones include former spouses, children living in another household, stepchildren, adopted children, divorced and remarried parents, or an unmarried partner, you have a lot of decisions to make regarding your estate and who gets what.

- ✔ **Minimizing what your estate will have to pay in estate taxes:** Yes, we know, we said that estate planning involves much more than the inheritance and estate (death) taxes, but make no mistake about it: Death taxes are certainly a consideration. Why pay more than you have to? You can take several steps — such as giving gifts while you're still alive — to reduce the value of your estate and, therefore, reduce the amount of death taxes that will have to be paid.

- ✔ **Protecting your business:** Politicians love to talk about the small business owner or the family farmer when describing how they are "a friend of the little guy." Still, if you own a small- or medium-scale business, such as a retail store or a farm, that business can be turned topsy-turvy if you die without a solid estate plan in place. (So actually, you want to make sure that, if you're a farmer, your farm is protected after you've "bought the farm.")

Sure, it's human nature to just let things happen. You're very busy with your career and your family. After all, do you really want to dwell on morbid thoughts, such as your own death? Because you really can't take any of your property with you, you do leave behind people and institutions (charities, foundations, and so on) that you care about along with all of your possessions. Why wouldn't you want to take the time to appropriately match up your property with those people and institutions?

Besides, estate planning is as much (if not more) about what you do during your life to manage your estate than it is about what happens after you die. Sure, it makes good theater to have a deathbed scene where the aged family patriarch or matriarch dictates what will happen to the vast family fortune, but the place to begin your estate planning isn't on your deathbed! That last-minute approach usually opens up the probability of one or more disgruntled family members trying to overturn your dying words. More than likely, your lack of estate planning will leave your estate dwindling away through more legal fees and taxes than what should have been paid.

(And not to be morbid, but if you die suddenly and unexpectedly, you may not even have the "opportunity" for that dramatic deathbed scene. If you haven't done your estate planning, chances are, nobody in your family will have any idea of what you want to happen to your estate.)

Need more? How about the game that the U.S. Congress is playing with the federal estate tax? As part of the estate tax laws, you have an *exemption* — an amount that you may leave behind that is free of the federal estate tax. (The estate tax doesn't kick in until your estate exceeds the exemption amount).

As part of Congress's latest overhaul of the tax code, the federal estate tax exemption will rise each year, to $3.5 million in 2009. Then, in 2010, the federal estate tax goes away entirely, but only for one year! In 2011, the estate tax not only "comes back from the dead" (appropriately enough, huh?), but the exemption also becomes $1 million, or $2.5 million less than it was only two years earlier.

For federal estate tax purposes, your estate planning is actually a moving target between now and 2011. If you die between now (the time you're reading these words) and 2011, the amount of federal estate tax could be all over the map if your estate is very valuable. If you die in 2010, under the current law, you won't owe any federal estate tax; however, if you die in 2011, you could owe a lot. Now, most people won't try to work "die in 2010" into their estate plans for the sole purpose of saving money on federal estate taxes, but the point is that you really need to stay on top of your estate-planning activities to try to minimize the amount of those taxes.

Book VII

Planning Your Estate and Will

Another reason to plan your estate deals with a mistake that many married couples make with their respective estates. Regardless of the federal estate tax and varying exemption amounts we've already discussed, you can leave an unlimited amount of your estate to your spouse, free of federal estate taxes.

However, sometimes you're better off not leaving your entire estate to your spouse, especially if your spouse also has a sizable estate (not only property jointly owned with you, but personal property that only your spouse owns). Why? Because then your spouse (assuming that you die first) now has an even larger estate, which is then subject to a potentially larger tax liability than if you had done something else with your estate. Basically, your children or whomever else you and your spouse are leaving your respective estates to will likely be stuck with paying more in federal estate taxes just because you decided to take the easy step with your estate and leave it all to your spouse.

Many states also impose inheritance and estate taxes, which your estate pays in addition to federal estate taxes. The answer? You need to proactively conduct your estate planning, consider all the matters in this section, and create a personalized estate plan.

Why Your Estate-Planning Goals Differ from Your Neighbors'

You are a unique individual.

No, not as part of the latest feel-good pop psychology designed to boost your self-esteem (not to mention make tons of money for the guru with seminars and videotapes). It's a statement to stress why you need to take time to create an individualized estate plan for your own situation.

Many people finally and grudgingly acknowledge that they need to worry about their estate plans, but then they take a haphazard, lackadaisical approach to estate planning: a generic fill-in-the-blank will purchased in a stationery store, a cursory review of active insurance policies, and a check to see whose names are listed as beneficiaries on the retirement plan at work. But that's all; everything else will fall into place, right?

Besides, is it really worth putting in any more time and effort beyond those basic tasks? After all, you're the one who will be dead. Why make all that effort for a series of events that will take place after you've died?

However, consider all the factors that make up many different aspects of your life:

- Your marital status: married, divorced, separated, single, widowed (or "widowered"), or maybe unmarried but living with someone

- Your age

- Your health (Not to be excessively morbid, but if you know that you have a potentially fatal condition or illness, or are in generally poor health, time is of the essence for your estate planning.)

- Your *financial profile,* such as the property (real and personal) you have and what that property is worth

- Any potentially complicated business or financial situations that you have, such as investment partnerships

- Any money that you expect to receive — particularly large sums — such as an inheritance, a lawsuit settlement, or severance pay from a job you are leaving

- Insurance policies you have, and the type and the value of each

- Information on whether any of your assets are particularly risky, such as stock or stock options in a start-up company that, on paper, are worth millions of dollars but that you can't do anything with, for some reason (for example, your stock options haven't fully vested)

- Details on your children, if any, including their ages, their respective financial states, and their respective marital statuses

- Details on your grandchildren, if any, and whether you want to explicitly take care of them as part of your estate planning or, alternatively, leave it to your children to take care of their own children as part of their own estate planning

- Details on your parents, if they are still alive, and whether they are still married to each other, whether either has remarried, their financial status (together or, if divorced, separately), and whether you need to take care of them

- Details on your brothers and sisters, and if whether you want or need to take care of them as part of your estate planning

- Information on any other family members (cousins, aunts, uncles, and so on) or even friends that you want to include in your estate planning

- Charities and foundations that you support

Just consider the items in this list — not to mention dozens of others that you can probably think of — and the answers for you and your life. Sure, somewhere in the United States, you can probably find someone else with more or less the same profile as yours, but the point is that no estate plan is a one-size-fits-all plan that you can effortlessly adapt to your situation.

Book VII

Planning Your Estate and Will

Additionally, even a canned plan that seems to be suitable for your situation may actually be a poor choice when you really dig into the details. Think of the man's suit or woman's evening dress that looks great in a magazine advertisement or even on a store mannequin. It may seem to be bodily proportional to your own, but when you try on that suit or dress, something may not look or feel right.

We strongly recommend that you make your credo for estate planning "No short-cuts allowed!" The time and effort, and even expense, that you put into developing a solid, comprehensive estate plan will be well rewarded. True, you won't necessarily be alive to fully see the benefits of your efforts, but the people you care about enough to include in your estate plan likely will be grateful.

The Critical Path Method to Planning Your Estate

Estate planning is a process that we can further divide into multiple steps or activities (or, for you computer and business types, *subprocesses*). In business, building computer applications, or even life itself (weddings, for example), most processes tend to take days, weeks, months, or even years from start to finish; rarely does any process happen overnight.

Treat your estate-planning activities as a process. The process includes a disciplined method created from a set of steps that lead you from a state of *estate-planning nothingness* (that is, you have no estate plan) to the point at which you have a well-thought-out estate plan in place. We recommend using the *critical path method* to planning your estate.

If you've taken a college business class in operations research, quantitative methods, or a similar topic, you may already be familiar with the critical path method, which is defined as the most effective way through a series of steps to reach your objectives. In other words, even when you have a seemingly infinite number of possible paths in front of you, you can find one particular path that is the most effective and efficient.

In estate planning, you often face many side roads when working on your will or setting up a trust. Before you know it, the side road has turned into a detour and your estate plan is in a state equivalent to your car being stuck up to its lugnuts in mud. (For the automotively challenged, the previous sentence means you aren't going anywhere anytime soon.)

If the terms *operations research* and *quantitative methods* cause you to draw a blank stare or if those terms cause shudders and tremors as you flash back to long-forgotten, hated college courses that you barely passed, simply think of the critical path method as a map. If you're standing on a corner in Winslow, Arizona, and you want to go to Phoenix, Arizona, you can get in your car and, after checking a map, drive approximately 190 miles of inter-state highway. Or maybe you don't know the area very well and you're one of those I-never-check-a-map kind of people, so you get in your car and just start driving. First, you head to Los Angeles, then drive up to San Francisco, then maybe go over to Chicago, drive back to Denver, and then drive toward Phoenix. ("By the time I get to Phoenix, she'll be on Social Security.")

Anyway, the critical path method is fairly straightforward and includes the following steps:

1. **Define your goals.** Before you begin your estate planning, decide what you're trying to achieve. Are you trying to make sure that your spouse has enough income for some period of time (say, five years, or maybe longer) if you died suddenly? Are you trying to make sure that your children have enough money for college after you're gone? Is your estate worth more than $10 million, and are you trying to protect as much as possible from the eventual federal estate tax bite?

    As we mention earlier in this chapter, your estate-planning goals are almost certainly different than anyone else's that you know, so make sure that you take the time to define those goals.

    Write down your goals; don't just think about them. Often by actually writing down your goals instead of just visualizing them, you get a better handle on how your goals relate to one another, and you make sure that you haven't forgotten anything.

2. **Determine which estate-planning professionals you want to work with.** Financial planners, insurance agents, attorneys, and accountants (all of whom we discuss in the next section) can provide valuable guidance and service to you. You need to determine which professionals best help you meet your goals. For example, have an attorney work with you on your will to be sure you meet all of your own state's requirements for the will to be legally binding. You may also decide to work with other professionals, depending on the complexity of your estate and the par-ticular goals you defined in the previous step.

3. **Gather information.** Whether you work with professionals or not (more on this particular decision point in the next section), you need to have as much available information as possible so that you know where you are currently in your estate-planning process. Ask yourself the following questions:

    1. Do you have a will right now? If so, when did you prepare that will?

    2. What in your life has changed since you created that will?

    3. What insurance policies do you currently have?

    4. Have any insurance policies expired?

    5. Perhaps most important, what property is in your estate and what is the value of that property?

4. **Develop your action plan.** Basically, get ready to do the many different activities we discuss in this book: Work on your will. (Create your will, if you don't have one, or perhaps update your will if the will is outdated.) Decide whether trusts make sense for you and, if so, choose which ones. Figure out what you need to do to protect your business, and so on.

5. **Actually conduct your action plan.** People often trip up on this step during their estate planning (or anything else they like to procrastinate on). Actually do the plans that you developed in Step 4. If you die without a will, complications may arise even if someone in your family finds a sheet of paper on your desk that reads "Step 4: Prepare my will."

6. **Monitor your action plan.** You may like going through all the previous estate-planning steps, finishing them, and then just forgetting about them all. But in estate planning, you never really finish. You periodically need to resynchronize your estate plan with any major changes in your life. For example, have you gotten divorced and remarried? You had better get cracking on those updates! Even-less dramatic changes in your life can trigger changes, so your best bet is to double-check everything in your estate plan once each year so you can make sure that your estate planning reflects all changes to your life, great and small, in a timely fashion. You can even tie your "checkup" to an annual occurrence, such as your birthday, or the beginning or end of daylight saving time (unless you live in one of those places like Arizona that doesn't "spring ahead and fall back" each year), or to some other occasion that you won't easily forget.

By following these steps and staying on the critical path, you greatly reduce the chances of taking all kinds of unnecessary and potentially serious detours with your estate planning, and you can typically get through the tasks with minimal stress.

Take the initiative to meet with each member of your estate-planning team annually. Or ask someone on the team to remind you annually to review your estate plans — the way your dentist reminds you to come in for a checkup.

Getting Help with Your Estate Planning

You can do all of your estate planning by yourself, but you don't have to. Even more important, we don't recommend that approach. But can you turn to someone with a job title along the lines of Professional Estate Planner for help?

Not exactly. As we mention several times in this chapter, estate planning actually consists of several different specialties or disciplines. If you want, you can work with one or more people in each of those specialties as part of your estate planning.

The number of people with whom you work largely depends on two main factors:

- ✔ How comfortable you are with the overall concepts and mechanics of estate planning
- ✔ How complicated your estate is

The material covered in this book can go a long way toward helping you with the first of those two factors. But even if you thoroughly understand little nuances of the clauses to include in your will or the basic types of trusts, you may still want to tap into a network of professionals if your estate is particularly complicated. Sure, you'll spend a bit more money on fees, but in the long run, you are more likely to avoid a horrendously costly mistake (financially, emotionally, or both), particularly if your estate is rather complicated.

How to make sure your team of advisers is "FAIL" safe

So whom do you work with? Use the FAIL acronym to help you remember the people you need to think about for your estate-planning team:

- ✔ Financial planner
- ✔ Accountant
- ✔ Insurance agent
- ✔ Lawyer (or attorney, the more familiar word we use in most places in the book)

The order of the professionals in this list doesn't indicate any type of priority (that is, your financial planner isn't more important than your accountant) or any type of sequence (you don't have to work with your accountant before you work with your insurance agent). The order shown is solely for the purposes of the FAIL acronym, to help you remember these different professions and how they may help you.

 You don't necessarily need a full slate of estate-planning professionals on your team. For example, you may work with your attorney and accountant. But if you've decided that insurance is only a minimal part of your overall estate plan, you may not need to work with an insurance agent. Or if you are well versed in investments and financial planning, you can handle that aspect of your estate plan by yourself and work with team members from the other specialization areas.

Straight talk

Talk candidly and honestly about personal and sometimes sensitive — or even painful — matters with your estate-planning team. The last thing you want is for your insurance agent to recommend a certain type of insurance policy that the issuing insurance company could invalidate because you hid some important fact. And your attorney needs to thoroughly understand all aspects of your relationships with your family, to help you create a will that accurately reflects your wishes. For example, if you really want to cut someone out of your will and leave that person nothing, make sure your attorney knows so that you can construct your will appropriately.

The best professionals sometimes set things into motion that can have unintentional and less-than-desirable consequences if another member of your estate-planning team isn't aware of what was done. For example, you need to be certain that you understand all the tax implications — federal income, state income, gift, estate, and so on — of a trust that your financial planner recommends and that your attorney sets up. Therefore, your accountant needs to work side by side with your attorney and your financial planner before the trust is created, to be certain that no unpleasant tax surprises pop up.

Working with Certified Financial Planners (CFPs) and other professionals

Because a significant portion of your estate likely involves your investments and savings, consider working with some type of financial planning professional. You can work with a financial planning professional solely on an advisory basis. If you want, you can make your own decisions about your investments and savings after consulting with a professional. Your financial planning professional also can play a much more active role, such as making major decisions for your financial life (with your consent, of course).

All financial-planning professionals aren't created equal, nor do they necessarily have the same background and qualifications. In the following paragraphs, we provide a brief overview.

Before you decide to work with any financial-planning professional, you need to understand just who these people are, what type of formal training and credentials they have, and how using them relates to your estate planning.

Other financial-planning professionals

If your financial life is particularly complicated, you may need to work with several types of financial-planning professionals in addition to a basic financial planner (who may or may not be a CFP).

Two other types of financial-planning professional are the *Investment Adviser* (*IA*) and the *Registered Investment Adviser* (*RIA*). IAs and RIAs specifically advise their clients about securities (stocks, bonds, and so on). Any IA who manages at least $25 million in assets must register with the Securities and Exchange Commission (SEC). You can check out this information at www.adviserinfo.sec.gov.

Chartered Financial Analysts (*CFAs*) are typically portfolio managers or analysts for banks, mutual funds, or other institutional clients (in Wall Street lingo), but some CFAs also advise wealthy individuals and families who have particularly complicated investment situations. CFAs take a series of examinations covering portfolio management, accounting, equity analysis, and other subjects, and must have at least three years of professional experience in investments. CFAs are also required to sign an ethics pledge every year.

A *Certified Investment Management Consultant* (*CIMC*) works with the wealthiest of the wealthy — high-net-worth private clients. A variety of examinations and continuing education, plus at least three years of professional experience, is required.

A *Certified Fund Specialist* (CFS) works with clients on mutual funds. (Some CFSs also provide general financial-planning services.) Examinations and continuing education are required to retain CFS status.

Certified Financial Planners (*CFPs*) provide financial-planning services and general financial advice on a wide range of topics, from investments to taxes and from estate planning to retirement planning. CFPs are required to pass college-level courses in a broad range of financial subjects and then must pass a two-day, ten-hour examination. CFPs must also have either a bachelor's degree and at least three years of professional experience working with financial planning clients, or. without a degree. at least five years of experience doing financial planning.

You can check with the Financial Planning Association at www.fpanet.org or search for planners by state, city, or zip code, or call 404-845-0011 (toll-free 800-322-4237). You can find financial planners who have the CFP credentials. You can then verify a planner's CFP status with the CFP Board of Standards at www.cfp-board.org.

You can regularly check *Money* magazine, *Smart Money,* and other personal finance publications for the latest information, even problems and scandals in the profession.

Make sure you clearly understand how your financial-planning professional — CFP or otherwise — gets paid. Some financial-planning professionals get paid on a "fee-only" basis, meaning that they don't receive any commissions for selling you financial products; they are compensated only for advice (basically, they're consultants).

Fee-based financial-planning professionals not only earn fees from the advice they give you, but they also earn commissions for selling you financial products. Commission-based financial-planning professionals make money only from the products they sell you.

You can certainly find both ethical and unethical people (not to mention competent and incompetent ones) in any of these three categories. However, pay particular attention to recommendations from fee-based or commission-based financial-planning professionals. Perhaps those investment choices are the perfect match for you, but you need to make that decision, not your financial-planning professional who stands to benefit financially from selling you some type of product.

Knowing what to expect from your accountant for your estate planning

Your accountant can do a lot more for you than fill out your tax returns for the previous year. Businesses use accountants for planning purposes, trying to steer what happens in the future for tax purposes by doing certain steps today. Plan on working with an accountant on your estate planning for those very same reasons, even if you do your own income taxes and haven't really worked with an accountant before.

Make sure the accountant on your estate-planning team presents you with scenarios of what can likely happen, based on recommendations from other members of your estate-planning team. If your CFP recommends certain investments or insurance products, what are the tax implications when you die? What are the tax implications if you die tomorrow versus dying ten years from now?

Your accountant can also have a more active role in your estate planning, suggesting certain tactics with an eye toward reducing your overall estate tax burden (giving gifts, in particular).

Never do any financial gift-giving (as contrasted with birthday gift-giving or holiday gift-giving) without consulting an accountant for tax implications.

Seek out an accountant who is a Certified Public Accountant (CPA), meaning that the accountant has passed the American Institute of Certified Public Accountants (AICPA) examination.

You may also consider combining two of the roles on your estate-planning team — the financial-planning and accounting specialists — by working with someone who is a Certified Public Accountant/Personal Financial Specialist, (CPA/PFS). In other words, this person is a CPA who also provides overall financial planning and has passed the PFS exam. Check out www.cpapfs.org.

Working with your insurance agent

Depending on your particular estate-planning needs, various forms of insurance (life, disability, liability, and other types) may play a key role. Most people who have dependents (particularly a spouse and children) wind up working insurance into their estate plan to meet the "protection" objective of estate planning.

Therefore, consider your insurance agent a part of your estate-planning team. For example, when you discuss life insurance and make decisions about different types of life insurance policies, make sure that your insurance agent is aware of any estate-planning strategies, such as trusts, so that you can have your policy beneficiaries listed correctly.

Some insurance companies are *agentless,* meaning that, unlike traditional insurance companies, in which you have an assigned insurance agent, your contact with the company is through any one of hundreds or even thousands of customer service representatives, almost always over the phone or the Internet. In these situations, ask one of the customer service representatives whether you can speak with or even work with anyone at the company on estate-planning matters. Chances are, the representative will say yes, so even though you don't technically have an insurance agent, you may still have access to short-term estate-planning assistance when you need it.

Working with your attorney

Even though your attorney is last on the list of the members of your estate-planning team (courtesy of the "L for Lawyer" that we used in our FAIL acronym), he or she may quite possibly be the most important member, for one simple reason: Your attorney keeps you from inadvertently making very serious mistakes.

All kinds of problems can trip you up and cause serious headaches in the future — well, not headaches for you, because you've already died, but for someone else. For example:

✔ How should your will read to make sure that your significant other, to whom you are not married, receives what you want out of your estate?

✔ How should the deed to your home be written to make sure that your unmarried significant other isn't forced to move if you die first?

✔ If you have an elderly parent who needs to go into a nursing home, what are the implications to your parent's estate and your own?

Basically, think of your attorney as your "scenario-planning specialist." Your attorney considers all kinds of information about you and your estate. He or she then presents you with options, based on various scenarios, such as you dying suddenly next week (morbid, but definitely an eye-opener for many people when first doing their estate planning) versus you dying at the ripe old age of 134 (courtesy of advanced biotechnology), having outlived everyone else in your family.

Beyond the scenario planning, make your attorney your primary advisor for your will, trusts, legal implications for your business, and pretty much any other legal matter that directly or indirectly relates to your estate planning.

Chapter 2

Where There's a Will

*Y*our will is the Number 1 legal weapon you have at your disposal to make sure that your estate is divided and distributed according to your wishes after you die. Basically, think of your will as your voice from beyond the grave to prevent the government from grabbing too large a share of your estate, to make it absolutely clear who will receive your assets, and to prevent unintended and unpleasant side effects to your well-thought-out estate plan.

But sometimes the best-laid plans of mice and men (well, make that women and men — we've never seen a mouse that has a will) are thwarted by selecting a type of will that is inappropriate or inadequate for the particulars of a given estate, or by leaving out key wording that is necessary to make a will valid. And sometimes your will can be 100 percent perfect for you and your estate at one point in your life, but you neglect to keep your will up to date with changes in your life. If you don't keep your will updated, your estate and the people you want to take care of after you die can have serious troubles.

You must also take care to keep your will very "matter of fact." You may have seen movies or television shows in which someone uses a will as a from-the-grave statement of love, hate, indifference, generosity, stinginess, or some other emotion. If you use your will in that fashion (something like "To my eldest son, who has always disappointed me his entire life, who never sent me any cards, who married someone whom I despise, I leave absolutely nothing"), you open the door to all kinds of problems. You can make a mistake in your wording choice that can cause your will to be invalid. Even if your will is letter-perfect, you can open emotional wounds and cause psychological scars that could take years (and a lot of expensive therapy!) to overcome. So in your will, stick to — like the detectives on *Dragnet* used to say — "just the facts!"

Getting technical with terminology

One of the primary purposes of creating a will is to take care of your *beneficiaries.* However, if you fail to properly prepare your will, your *heirs* may wind up with less than expected, or maybe with nothing at all. Legal double-talk? Not exactly. People (such as your family members and friends) and institutions such as charities that you take care of in your will are called *beneficiaries.* However, if you don't have a will — or don't have a valid will, as we discuss later in this chapter — the individuals who benefit from your estate are determined by state law and are usually called *heirs* (or *heirs at law*). In layman's language, the terms *beneficiary* and *heir* are often used interchangeably. However, the two words technically have a significant distinction.

In this chapter, we focus on the basics of wills necessary to ensure that your will is the most appropriate for your wishes and needs, and to be sure that your wishes are carried out.

Planning for Your Will

We advise that you work with your attorney to create and take care of the technical and legal details of your will. Even the simplest, most straightforward wills are filled with legal terminology. Your attorney has likely prepared hundreds or thousands of wills. Why not leave the details to someone for whom the legal-speak and technicalities are second nature?

But before your attorney starts putting anything on paper for your will, you need to consult with him or her to determine your major objectives. You need to specifically discuss the following items:

✔ What your *tax exposure situation* is, based on your estate's value. Your estate may have to pay federal estate tax and any state estate or inheritance tax if your estate is worth more than the allowance at which taxes are owed. Your will needs to reflect your overall estate planning, including your tax planning, so both you and your attorney need to clearly understand all tax implications to your estate.

✔ Who you want to explicitly take care of, as we discuss later in this chapter. You can write your will in many different ways to reflect the people to whom you want to give what portions of your estate. However, you need to have a general idea of which family members you want to take care of, such as the following

- Your spouse and your children

- All your children (including adopted children and stepchildren), but only your children

- Only some of your children

- All your children and all your grandchildren

- All your children and your brothers and sisters

- Your parents and your brothers and sisters

- Only two of your four children and all except one of your sisters

✔ You also need to decide whether you want some part of your estate (or even all your estate) to go to one or more charities, foundations, or other institutions. Later in this chapter, we discuss different ways in which you can divide up your estate among the people you want to include in your will.

The first time you sit down with your attorney, make sure you talk about all three items — the value of your estate and your tax situation, the individuals (family members and others) and institutions you want to leave your estate to, and nursing home concerns — so that your attorney clearly understands your motivation and can help you prepare a will that accurately reflects your situation and preferences.

Book VII

Planning Your Estate and Will

Getting to Know the Different Types of Wills

Before you even think about what wording to put in your will, you must decide which of several types of wills is right for you. The good news is that you can usually stop your search for the perfect type of will with the first type we discuss, the simple will. However, you need to be familiar with the other types, in case your attorney advises that some unique aspect of your estate makes one of these other types more appropriate.

Simple wills

Almost always, a *simple will* is the will of choice for you. A simple will is a single legal document that applies only to you (unlike a *joint will* for you and your spouse, which we discuss briefly in the next section).

A simple will describes the following:

- ✔ Who you are, with enough information to clearly identify that document as your will.

- ✔ The names of your beneficiaries, both people — whether those people are family members or not — and institutions, such as charities, and enough information about the beneficiaries, such as their addresses and birthdates so whoever is reading your will can figure out whom you are referring to.

- ✔ The person you're appointing to be the *executor* of your will. The executor is the person who is legally responsible for making sure that your directions are carried out. You also need to appoint a backup executor — or maybe even a backup to the backup — if, for any reason, your designated executor is unable to perform the official duties.

- ✔ Always check with whomever you specify as an executor or backup executor in your will before you put that person's name in your will. You want to avoid unnecessary complications that may arise if that person is unwilling or unable to serve as your will's executor.

- ✔ Your directions for who will care for your children or for anyone else you are legally responsible for.

- ✔ How you want your assets distributed, and to whom, after you are gone.

Your simple will should be *typewritten* — a term that comes from the days of old-fashioned typewriters but that also applies to a printed and produced document by a computer and printer. Other forms of your will, such as written in your own handwriting or spoken (we discuss both forms briefly in the next section), are usually filled with problems and shouldn't be used.

Other types of wills

You do have options for your will other than the simple, typewritten will we discuss in the previous section. Consider these other choices, along with the drawbacks of each:

- ✔ A *joint will,* which is a single legal document that applies to two people (you and your spouse, for example). Some married couples mistakenly think that they're required to have a joint will or that a joint will is better for them than two simple wills. Indeed, a single joint will may be less expensive to have prepared than two simple wills. However, joint wills are usually a bad idea. The primary problem is that most courts treat a joint will as a form of a *contractual will,* which is a will or contract that is irrevocable and can't be changed after one party dies. Therefore, if your spouse dies first and you want to revise the contents of your joint will for estate planning or tax purposes, you probably can't. Don't even think about a joint will unless your attorney suggests that some particularly unique aspect of your situation makes a joint will advisable, and then ask your attorney to explain, explain, and explain some more!

✔ A *mutual will,* which you can use to coordinate your estate planning with someone else, such as your brother. For example, suppose that you and your brother want to leave a substantial amount of money to be split among two charities — Charity No. 1 and Charity No. 2 — that both of you have supported for many years. You can create mutual wills that state the following:

  • No matter which one of you dies first, 75 percent of either your estate or that of your sibling goes to Charity No. 1, with 20 percent going to Charity No. 2 and 5 percent going to some other beneficiary.

  • When the other one of you dies, 50 percent of that person's estate goes to Charity No. 2, with 30 percent going to Charity No. 1 and 20 percent designated for some other beneficiary.

  Basically, because you don't have a crystal ball to tell you and your sibling which one of you will die first (and even if you did, would you really want to know?), you both have set things up so that, no matter what happens, Charity No. 1 receives a larger amount of money first than Charity No. 2 does. If you think that a mutual will is particularly suitable for some unique aspect of your estate, ask your attorney and then proceed with caution.

✔ A *holographic will,* which is a handwritten will. A holographic will is handwritten and signed by you. A handwritten will doesn't require an attorney to be involved when you prepare this form of will. However, only some states recognize a holographic will as valid, which means that you may think you have a valid will, but you actually don't.

✔ A *nuncupative will,* a technical term used to describe a spoken will and has nothing to do with Sister Maria or any of the other nuns from *The Sound of Music.* (Everybody sing along: "How do you solve a problem like Maria's estate planning?") Even though creating a nuncupative will is extremely easy — all you have to do is talk and have someone present to listen — you have many complications and limitations. Some states allow only persons who are on their deathbed (literally!) — about to die any minute — to use a nuncupative will for a last-minute expression of what they want done with part of their estate. Some states allow only certain types of property or only property up to a certain dollar amount to be transferred with a nuncupative will.

Book VII

Planning Your Estate and Will

Don't use any of the preceding nonstandard types and forms of wills except in extraordinary circumstances.

Choosing Your Will's Contents

Your will is composed of a number of *clauses* that, when put together into a single legal document, accurately and precisely represent your wishes for your estate. The clauses in your will fall into three categories:

- ✔ **Opening clauses:** These clauses provide basic information about you and also lay the groundwork for the other clauses in your will that follow.

- ✔ **Giving clauses:** These clauses follow the opening clauses and comprise the main body of your will, which specifies your who-gets-what-part-of-my-estate strategy.

- ✔ **Ending clauses:** These clauses help to make your will valid by ensuring that all statutory requirements have been met.

How about a preprinted, ready-to-fill-in will?

Many do-it-yourself preprinted will forms are available, and some people use them to save money (as compared to meeting with an attorney and having a will created from scratch). Chances are, though, your individual needs most likely require you to customize your will, to some extent. Thus, in most cases, preprinted will forms won't be quite right for you, even though many of these will forms are advertised as suitable for complicated situations.

You most likely will have to do at least some customization if you use a preprinted will form. As soon as you begin customizing, you open up the possibility of all kinds of problems. Why? First, you need to be sure that you're satisfying legal requirements specific to your own state; otherwise, your will may not be valid. If you're going to put the time and effort into preparing your will, you certainly want the finished result to be legally binding.

Second, you're better off starting your will with a clean slate than using preprinted boilerplate language; doing so actually forces you to decide what to include in your will.

However, if you think that your specific situation is so uncomplicated that a preprinted will form may do the trick — and you really are trying to spend as little money as possible on your will and your estate planning — then we recommend that you at least get an attorney to look over your filled-in will form after you're completed it, to advise you on whether the finished document may incur any problems. If you have limited financial resources, you can usually obtain low-cost or even no-cost basic legal assistance within your community; just check around.

However, just as you put together a bicycle, bake blueberry muffins, or do anything else in which you need to combine parts or ingredients, you need to make sure of two things:

1. That you select the right parts or ingredients — or, in the case of your will — the right clauses

2. That you put together those parts, ingredients, or clauses in the right order, with the right number of each, to make sure that the finished product is what you intend it to be

If you leave out or mess up just one essential clause, you can completely change your intentions or even make your will invalid. And because clauses can get very technical with all kinds of legal terminology, have a professional, such as your attorney, prepare your will for you. (See the sidebar "How about a preprinted, ready-to-fill-in will?")

Opening clauses

Think of the opening clauses of your will as a preamble in which you provide some basic information to set up the giving clauses that follow. Your will's opening clauses include the following:

- An introductory clause that

  - Clearly identifies you as the maker of the will.

  - Explicitly states that you created this document of your own free will (this part is where you write "being of sound mind," as in the movies).

  - Explicitly states that any wills you previously created are no longer valid.

- A family statement clause, which introduces your family members referenced later in your will.

- A tax clause — the structure of your will needs to align with your overall tax strategy for your estate. You can include a tax clause to specifically state how you want taxes to be paid — often out of the *residuary* (everything else) part of your estate, as we discuss later in this chapter. But if you want to specify some other tax strategy in your will, you use the tax clause to state how you want taxes to be paid, by whom, and from what part of your estate.

Your attorney likely has a favorite way of preparing opening clauses, based on hundreds or thousands of wills he or she has prepared. Still, before your attorney starts writing anything for your will, make sure that you discuss your overall strategy.

Book VII

Planning Your Estate and Will

Giving clauses

The heart of your will may contain the giving clauses in which you specify as precisely as possible how your estate is to be divided among your beneficiaries. In general, you can take one of three different approaches to how you want your estate divided and how the contents of your will's giving clauses will be written.

- ✔ You can be extremely general.
- ✔ You can be extremely explicit and detailed.
- ✔ You can be very explicit about part of your estate and very general about the rest of your estate.

The simplest approach you can take for your will is to basically lump all or almost all of your property together, identify the beneficiaries who will share that property, and simply leave all that property to the entire group of beneficiaries to be divided up equally. For example, if you have an estate worth $500,000 that consists primarily of bank accounts and stock, if your spouse has died before you, if you live in a rented apartment and no longer own a home, and if you want to divide your estate equally among your four children, all of whom are still alive, you can be extremely general and just leave that $500,000 worth of property to all your children, each of whom gets an equal share of your estate.

But suppose that you have an estate worth $3 million, a significant portion of which is made up of collectible cars and several vacation homes? And suppose that you have not only two living children from your third (and current) wife, but also seven living children from previous marriages, not to mention several stepchildren? And what if you want not only all of these children and stepchildren to share in your estate, but also your two sisters — but not your two brothers?

In this example, you must be as explicit as possible in your will about who will receive specific property from your estate. Which child will receive the 1955 Thunderbird? Who gets the 1967 Corvette, and who gets the 1965 Pontiac GTO? Should your sister who works at IBM get your IBM stock and your other sister who still works at General Motors get your GM stock, or should you give your IBM stock to your sister who works at GM and your GM stock to your IBM-employed sister, to help each sister diversify their respective portfolios?

The third strategy for your giving clauses — somewhere in between very explicit and very general — can be useful if you want to divide most of your estate equally among your children, but you still want to explicitly leave other smaller amounts of your estate to your grandchildren, parents, brothers and sisters, a favorite niece or nephew, or a charity.

So regardless of which of the three strategies you want to follow, how do you use your will's giving clauses to make it all happen? You can use three types of clauses:

- ✔ Real property clauses
- ✔ Personal property clauses for intangible and tangible property
- ✔ Residuary clause

Real property clauses

Your real property — for most people, their home — is often the most significant asset in terms of dollar value that you leave to your loved ones, quite possibly far more valuable than all your personal property put together.

If you want to explicitly leave real property to one or more beneficiaries, you use a *real property clause,* which is a straightforward statement that reveals who is to receive your real property, identifies the property to which you're referring, and names who is to get that property.

Personal property clauses

If you're following the be-very-explicit strategy for your will, your will must contain personal property clauses specifying what will happen to both your intangible and tangible personal property. In the case of your intangible personal property, such as your stocks and bonds, you can specify who gets your IBM stock, who gets your GM stock, and who gets your Enron bonds (just kidding about that last one!).

Even though you plan to use the partly-general-and-partly-explicit will strategy, you can still use a personal property clause to identify some stock or other intangible personal property that you want to give to someone different. For example, if you want to divide most of your $750,000 estate among your children, but you want to leave each of your five grandchildren $10,000, you can use this strategy.

For your tangible personal property, you can divide your personal items among your beneficiaries. Very often, you want to specify what will happen to sentimental items that are small in monetary value but large in heart value, such as your grandmother's antique quilt or your great-great-great-great-grandfather's diary that he carried through the Civil War.

The residuary clause

Technically, your will's *residuary clause* covers the leftovers in your estate that you didn't explicitly mention in real property clauses or personal property clauses. The residuary clause gives you and your will a safety net, in case you forget to specifically identify some part of your estate in your will. Remember that your estate can change over time, and if you haven't updated

Book VII

Planning Your Estate and Will

your will lately, you may have forgotten to account for some particular item (often tangible personal property, such as a valuable painting you may have recently acquired).

However, you can use your will's residuary clause for far more than just the leftovers — actually, your entire estate or the majority of your estate — if your will strategy is to be as general as possible. You simply don't use any other giving clauses to explicitly mention real or personal property as we describe earlier, which forces your estate into being covered by the residuary clause.

Or if you want to take that in-between approach to your will — partly explicit and partly general — you use specific giving clauses for whatever real property and personal property you explicitly want to give to someone. You use a residuary clause to cover everything else.

No matter what your will strategy is, don't forget to include a residuary clause! Even though you may want your will to be as explicit as possible, you will almost always have property in your estate that falls into the leftovers category. Be sure to designate one or more beneficiaries to receive those leftovers.

Appointment and fiduciary powers clauses

The section of your will that includes your giving clauses also contains some additional clauses that actually don't have anything to do with how your estate will be divided. You use the *appointment clause* to name the person you have chosen to manage your estate. At the time you prepare your will, you need to decide who you feel is the best person to handle your estate and act as your *personal representative* after you die.

The *fiduciary powers clause* is a companion clause to the appointment clause that gives you the ability to provide your personal representative with powers beyond what may be available in your state regulations. For example, use the fiduciary powers clause to specify that your personal representative will provide your children with some amount of income on an interim basis until your estate is settled. Another way you can use the fiduciary powers clause is to allow your personal representative to continue operating your solely owned business that still provides income to your estate.

Ending clauses

After you complete the most difficult part of your will — the giving clauses portion, which reflect your overall will strategy — you need to finish up your work with your ending clauses, which include the *signature clause*. You date and sign your will in the signature clause.

For fans of *L.A. Law* and *The Practice*

We've taken great care to use plain English in discussing your will and the clauses that make up its contents. But if you're one of those people who can't wait for the next John Grisham novel, and if you counter your son's dinnertime complaints with either "I object!" or "You're out of order!" you may be interested in the legal-speak of wills. Take a look at some of the legal terms you may come across:

✔ *Exordium clause:* The introductory clause in your will, in which you state "I, John Doe, of the City of Tucson, County of Pima and State of Arizona, being of sound mind and under no undue influence . . ." and all the rest of the beginning of your will.

✔ *Dispositive clauses:* The technical term for your will's giving clauses, in which you specify who is to receive various parts of your estate.

✔ *Devise and devisee, bequeath, bequest, and legatee:* Technically, you devise (give) your real property to your devisee, and your personal property is a bequest (also called legacy) given to your legatee. For bequests, you use the word *bequeath* instead of *devise* to mean "give." However, these types of property and the associated language have blurred over the years. According to www.dictionary.law. com, "The distinction between gifts of real property and personal property is actually blurred, so terms like *beneficiary* or *legatee* cover those receiving any gift by a will." Likewise, the same Internet site describes *devise* as "an old-fashioned word for giving real property by a will, as distinguished from words for giving personal property."

✔ *Testamonium clauses:* The technical term for your will's signature clauses.

Your will's witnesses also sign the will, along with appropriate language that indicates that they witnessed you signing your will and that you executed the will voluntarily and did so of your own free will. (In other words, you weren't coerced or perhaps unconscious, with a devious family member putting a pen in your hand to make you "sign" your will.)

Most states recognize that a will can be *self-proved,* which is a method of avoiding the requirement of producing witnesses at the time of probate to prove the validity of the signature of the decedent (the person who died). In the usual case (with a "non-self-proved will"), the person making the will simply signs the will in the presence of witnesses, who also then sign their names as witnesses. In a self-proved will, however, the signature of the person making the will is acknowledged in addition to being witnessed, and the witnesses also execute affidavits. Doing so avoids the necessity of providing witnesses at the time of probate.

Book VII

Planning Your Estate and Will

Safeguarding Your Will

Take this quick quiz: On what single point about wills are estate-planning professionals more likely to passionately disagree?

The answer may surprise you: whether you to keep your will in a safe-deposit box.

Some contend that you must keep your original, signed will in your safe deposit box, and that you must also make several copies of your will (or have your attorney make several copies) and give a copy to your personal representative. You must also give copies to certain family members or friends (different people than your personal representative), such as your children or your brother or sister.

Others argue that you must keep your will not in a safe-deposit box, but in a safe at your attorney's office or a fireproof safe at home. These people contend that, after you die, your safe-deposit box may be sealed until probate (depending on what state you live in) or at least may be subject to highly restricted access. For example, your safe-deposit box may be accessible only by a person whom you designated on the signature card when you opened the box, and only during a visit supervised by a bank official and possibly audited by your attorney or the taxing authorities. And in some states, the only items that can be removed from the safe-deposit box are your will and burial plot deed.

Our suggestion: Ask your attorney what he or she recommends and follow those directions. If you live in a state where safe-deposit boxes aren't sealed, your attorney may advise you to keep your signed will in your safe-deposit box. But if you live in a state that does seal safe-deposit boxes, you may be advised to keep your signed will with your attorney or at home.

 Keep your will at home only if you have a fireproof safe. That stack of to-be-filed receipts, to-be-replied-to letters, and candy bar wrappers on your desk in your den or a corner of the family room is no place for your will!

Also, regardless of where you safeguard your original will, you must also keep an unsigned copy of your will for yourself so you don't need to touch the original signed copy in your safe-deposit box. If you want to double-check whom you left a particular item to or some other detail on your will, or scribble a possible change that you want to ask your attorney about, you won't risk invalidating your will by damaging or defacing it.

Also give unsigned reference copies of your will to key family members and others so that your family can start planning for what will happen to your estate.

(Of course, if you have a flair for the dramatic and don't want anyone to know what's in your will until after you're dead, you can always do the bad movie-plot version and give no one a copy, but we strongly advise against that approach!)

Changing, Amending, and Revoking Your Will

Now that you have completed your will, you may assume that you're done with it. Even though you have completed the tough process of formally expressing what you want to be done with your estate, you must keep it up to date. Often, working on your will can be an emotional process for you as you decide who will get your best dishes when three different children and grandchildren have explicitly expressed their interest with comments such as "Boy, I sure do love those plates" at your family dinners. Nevertheless, you have finally made your tough decisions, you want to put the whole process behind you, and you're tempted to simply put your will in a safe place so that someday in the future your "wishes for your dishes" will be carried out.

Don't make the mistake of putting away your will and forgetting about it. You must make sure that, at all times, the details of your will reflect changes in your life that occurred after you initially executed your will.

Book VII

Planning Your Estate and Will

Why you may need to change your will when something happens

Your will is a dynamic, living document. Ironically, although a will's intent is to provide for what happens to your estate after you die, the reality is that your will needs to change as your life changes. Think about the climactic last scene of some old black-and-white movie in which the stoic attorney reads the deceased's will aloud as the family members gather around to see what rich-oil-magnate Grandfather has left them. In that last scene, almost everyone is surprised to find out that Grandpa made changes to his will as family members drifted in and out of favor, and at the time of his passing, family members who were out of favor received nothing except a token amount of cash and a stern from-beyond-the-grave lecture (whereas family members Grandpa favored the last time he updated his will are all smiles).

This classic movie scene can remind you that those shocked family members were probably blindsided because of some change made to the will that they weren't aware of. Keep this scenario in mind because your life does change — marriages, children, divorces, increases in your estate value, and so forth — and your will may need to change with these life changes.

The reasons you need to change your will vary. The following are typical reasons to change a will:

- ✔ **After a marriage:** You now need to include your new spouse in your estate plan.

- ✔ **After a divorce:** You most likely want to absolutely, positively, and certainly make changes to the list of what you had previously been planning to leave to your now ex-spouse.

- ✔ **After your spouse's death:** Most likely, you left a significant portion — or perhaps all — of your estate to your spouse in your will. Now that your spouse has died, you need to update your will to adjust whom you now want to leave your assets to.

- ✔ **After the death of one of your heirs or dependents:** Suppose that your will specifies that a particular person is to receive a specific asset. If that person dies before you do, you need to update your will to reflect another person to receive that asset.

- ✔ **After you experience a significant change in your estate's value:** For example, your stock holdings may go way up (or way down!). You may now reevaluate who gets what and how much.

- ✔ **After any other change in your life that causes you to reevaluate to whom you want to leave something:** For example, you become passionate about a specific cause and decide that you want to leave a large portion of your estate to some charity that champions that cause.

If the change to your will is triggered by an emotional event, such as being extremely angry with a family member and wanting to write that person out of the will, allow yourself some time to clear your head before you act. Make changes or amendments to your will after life changes, not after an emotional reaction that may dissipate over time.

Ways to change your will

You can change your will in one of two ways:

- ✔ You can create an entirely new will that supersedes your current will.

- ✔ You can change or delete specific parts of your current will, or add new parts, while leaving the rest of your current will unchanged. You do so through a new, separate document (we explain this document in a moment), not by directly altering your original will itself.

Each of the two methods listed has advantages and disadvantages. In most cases, you want to simply create an entirely new will with the changes, additions, and deletions. Creating an entirely new will is relatively straightforward, especially in these days of computer files and printers. (Your attorney doesn't need to have an entirely new will typed from scratch, as in the old days before personal computer).

However, you can add, change, or delete specific parts of your current will without creating an entirely new will through a form called a codicil. A *codicil* is a separate document that adds to your original will.

Codicils are often expressed in the context of specifically referenced portions of your will. Because a codicil needs to clearly reference a specific portion of your will that it's amending, ask your attorney to prepare any codicils instead of trying to do them yourself, no matter how simple it may seem to just write or type a couple of lines of text. If you mess up, your codicil most likely won't be valid.

When do you use a codicil?

- ✔ When your original will is very long and you want to make only a few, minor changes.

- ✔ When your competency at the time of executing the codicil may be challenged. If someone successfully argues that you were losing your grip in later years, the codicil may be overturned without affecting the will itself.

Protecting Your Loved Ones from Your Unloved Ones

Perhaps your family bears an uncanny resemblance to an episode of *The Waltons* (still showing in reruns on cable!) or maybe a family scene from a Norman Rockwell painting. Everyone gets along most of the time and every holiday dinner creates new lifelong memories.

On the other hand, maybe your family is more like an episode of a particularly nasty soap opera: lots of bickering and arguing, one family member not speaking to another for years — you know the story. Quite possibly, your family consists of loved ones and "unloved ones." Suppose, then, that you decide that your unloved ones will receive little or nothing from your estate. If you have made that decision and are willing to live with it (so to speak, because they may not find out your decision until you've died), you need to be concerned with more than just figuring out how to leave those individuals out of your will. You also need to be concerned with protecting other family members — your loved ones — so that they justly get what you want them to receive without interference from the others whom you decide to leave nothing.

You may think that the most logical way to not leave anything to unloved ones is to simply leave them out of your will (basically, not to mention them at all), but that may be the worst thing you can do. Why? Because doing so leaves the door wide open for the unloved ones to contest your will by saying they were excluded by accident. ("You know, he was always so distracted, he obviously forgot to mention us. After all, we're blood relatives — why wouldn't we be in his will?")

Therefore, you need to explicitly state your intentions for your unloved one in your will, no matter how painful it may be to form those words and commit them to paper. Your attorney can help you with the language to include, as well as help you to keep those words as factual and unemotional as possible.

A simple way to handle the wording problem is to mention the unloved ones in your will, but to leave them only a small or token sum. That way, they can't claim that you overlooked or forgot them, and you don't have to explain in your will why they are otherwise excluded.

Still, after you die, those unloved ones may try to overturn your wishes to receive what they feel they rightly deserve from your estate.

Figuring Out Your Will Status

When you die, you have one of three *will statuses,* depending on whether you have a complete valid will:

- ✔ *Testacy:* All your assets are covered by a valid will, and you're in pretty good shape.
- ✔ *Intestacy:* You die without a valid will.
- ✔ *Partial intestacy:* Your estate is in "no man's land" (or maybe purgatory?) because only some of your assets are covered by a valid will.

Testacy: When you've nailed everything down

If you have a valid will, you are said to die *testate.* Basically, you have spelled out your intentions completely and legally in your last will and testament, and you have attained one of your two primary objectives of estate planning, as we mention at the beginning of Book VII, Chapter 1: control. (Your other primary estate-planning objective is protection.) Not to sound like a television commercial for a funeral home or life insurance policy, but when you die testate, you at least die with some peace of mind knowing that your wishes will be followed through, courtesy of the legal system.

Intestacy: When you die with zero "will power"

Intestacy: the dark side! Being *intestate* means that you die without a valid will. Depending on your particular circumstances, the implications of your intestacy can be far-reaching. Most important, dying intestate results in your estate being distributed through the *laws of intestate succession* (commonly referred to as the *intestate law*) — a technical way of saying that the legal system decides how your estate is distributed. Essentially, your state writes a will for you — not an actual on-paper, physical will, but (for any computer and technical readers out there) sort of a virtual will, made up of your state's default clauses that apply to the particulars of you, your family, and your estate.

Now you have no say whatsoever in how your estate is distributed and who receives it. The intestate succession laws vary by state but are usually similar in terms of the primary purpose: basically, to determine who receives your estate. The intestate law establishes a particular priority for distributing your estate. Did you have a spouse? Did you have children? What other relatives are in the picture?

But what about other people — specifically, those people who aren't related to you — that you had wanted to take care of? Most likely, they're out of luck if you die intestate. Suppose, for example, that you had wanted to leave $100,000 worth of IBM stock to the family housekeeper, who has been with you for years and even worked for your parents. Without you having a valid will specifying that desire — and thus being intestate — your housekeeper will most likely never receive anything from your estate.

(Of course, whoever does wind up with that $100,000 worth of IBM stock according to the intestate succession laws may later transfer that stock to the housekeeper, as you wanted, but don't count on it!)

Also, if you don't have any living family members covered by the state's intestate laws, depending on the state where you live and your particular circumstances, the state's intestate laws could make your state your only beneficiary! Unless you really want to leave your estate to the state where you live, make sure you have a valid will so you don't die intestate.

Partial intestacy: When the vultures start circling

No-man's land. Purgatory. Between a rock and a hard place. *Partial intestacy* — when part of your estate isn't covered by your valid will — is an in-between will status, not quite testacy but not quite intestacy, either. Very often, forgetting to include a residuary clause (we discuss this clause earlier in this chapter) in your will causes you to be considered partially intestate when you die.

If you have followed all the steps we discuss in this chapter and you've prepared your will, you may be tempted to think that you no longer have to worry about being intestate or partially intestate. Wrong! You may have overlooked some little item in your will that could negate your will completely if a disgruntled family member contests your will's validity.

If that disgruntled person is successful, you may be *rendered* (basically, switched) into intestacy if your will is declared invalid, resulting in your estate being distributed through intestate succession laws — which you wanted to avoid in the first place by having a will! Or maybe you forget to include the all-important residuary clause. What happens to your collection of 1930s-era baseball player autographs that you neglected to specifically bequeath to someone? Because you are intestate with regard to those autographs, they will pass to your heirs at law under the intestate law.

Be sure to periodically consult with your attorney to make sure that your will is complete, is current, and has been properly signed and witnessed, to increase the likelihood of your will status being testate (remember, that's good!).

Chapter 3

Limitations of Wills: What You Can and Can't Do

In This Chapter

▶ Understanding the laws that affect or interpret your will

▶ Grasping the laws that your will can change and what you must do about them

▶ Comprehending the laws that your will can't change

*W*e've slightly altered an old saying: "Where there's a will, there are all kinds of laws you need to worry about." (Well, it could be an old saying in legal circles, anyway.)

Even though your will provides you with a fantastic tool to direct what happens to your estate after you die, you don't exactly have a free hand in what you can make your will do for you. A number of state statutes affect or interpret your will and, consequently, the way you transfer assets to others. If you know what these laws provide, you can include appropriate language in your will to amplify or diminish the effect of those statutes.

In this chapter, we discuss those statutes. Keep in mind that because state law — not federal law — governs your will, some of the statutes we discuss in this chapter may not apply to you simply because of where you live. But because you're working with your attorney to create your will (see Book VII, Chapter 2), don't worry; your attorney is well aware of the particular provisions that affect your will.

Making Your Peace with Statutes That Affect Your Will

Before you start grumbling about those laws or statutes, remember that many of them protect your beneficiaries, particularly your spouse and children, so they're not necessarily bad for you and your estate. Think of these statutes as playing cards: You have to play the hand you're dealt, but if you really know your game, you can give yourself an advantage.

For example, what happens if your will specifically states that $100,000 must be left to each of your two children (a total of $200,000), but when you die, your estate is valued at only $150,000? A statute called the *abatement statute* (which we discuss in the next section) specifies what happens then.

After you die, who is responsible for paying any death tax that is due? Again, a statute is waiting in the wings to say exactly what happens.

As you figure out what you want to write in your will (see Book VII, Chapter 2 for a discussion about the basics of wills), you need to keep the list of the statutes we discuss in this chapter handy, for easy reference.

Some statutes that affect or interpret wills are complicated, especially when the fine print kicks in. Furthermore, the particulars of these statutes vary from one state to another, so you really need to work with your attorney when you prepare your will instead of using a general fill-in-the-blank form that quite possibly doesn't address the impact of these statutes on your estate.

Identifying Statutes That Your Will Can Change

You can write your will in a certain way to address the following statutes:

- **Abatement statutes:** What happens when your estate isn't worth enough to provide what you want to leave your beneficiaries and to meet any debts you have remaining when you die?

- **Ademption statutes:** What happens if some of your property is missing when you die?

- **Antilapse statutes:** What happens if certain beneficiaries die before you?

- **Divorce statutes:** Well, these statutes are fairly self-explanatory.

- **Simultaneous death statutes:** What happens if you and someone else die at the same time?

Abatement: There's not enough in the cupboard for everyone

In Book VII, Chapter 2, we discuss how you can use that information to specify in your will how much of your estate will go to various beneficiaries. But what happens if you die and, for whatever reason, your estate isn't worth enough to give everybody what you want them to get? Your state's *abatement statutes* come into play.

Abatement is defined as the process of reducing or lessening something, so you can think of abatement statutes as those laws that say, "Hold everything, folks! Because your estate doesn't have enough value to go around, here's what we're going to do." Abatement statutes typically provide for a distribution priority if the assets in your estate are not sufficient to pay all of your creditors and to make a full distribution to each of the beneficiaries named in your will. The abatement statutes specify, for example, that property in your estate's *residue* (your "leftovers") may abate — that is, be reduced — before other property you specifically mention in your will.

Check with your attorney to determine how your particular state's abatement statutes work. However, if you're not satisfied with your state's statutory method of abatement, don't panic! Usually you can make specific provisions in your will to specify how (and in what order) your assets should abate if your estate is not large enough to provide for the payment of all debts (including taxes) and to then carry out your directions for leaving specific dollar amounts or specific items to your beneficiaries.

Your best strategy to avoid your estate being affected by your state's abatement statutes is to use percentage amounts instead of actual dollar amounts whenever possible in your will.

Suppose that you calculate the value of your estate at $200,000, and you want to split that amount equally between your two children. One way to do so is to specifically state in your will that each child receives $100,000.

However, what happens if your estate doesn't grow at all, and instead shrinks? Maybe some stock you own has declined significantly in value, or maybe you had a large amount of medical expenses. No matter what happens, if your estate is now worth $150,000 and you haven't updated your will to reflect the reduced value of your estate, you have a problem!

But if you had used percentage amounts instead of dollar amounts in your will, specifying that 50 percent of your estate goes to each child, you can avoid abatement statutes coming into play, even though your estate's value has shrunk.

Abatement statutes also arise even if you have enough assets in your estate to cover specific dollar amounts you've specified for your beneficiaries, but you have outstanding debts that need to be settled when you die. For example, suppose that you still have $200,000 worth of cash, stock, and other assets when you die, but you also have $50,000 outstanding on a variety of credit cards and other debts. Your estate isn't worth $200,000 at all, but rather $150,000 — your $200,000 in assets minus the $50,000 in debts.

Can't your family just, shall we say, forget about what you owe? After all, you're dead, right? Sorry. In the probate process, valid creditors' claims must be paid.

You need to tally up your debts as well as your assets when you're figuring out what your estate is worth. Don't forget — otherwise, you may be way off in your calculations of your estate's value, compared with what your estate is really worth. Be sure to consider an estimate of probate costs and death taxes as parts of your estate's "debt" because those items will also diminish the amount of your estate that is available to distribute to your beneficiaries.

But what happens if the way you write your will (typically, with specific dollar amounts used throughout) causes abatement statutes to apply to your estate? Basically, the abatement statutes determine how your will's property transfers to your beneficiaries are reduced, and by how much. In the worst case, some of your property transfers may actually disappear because of a lack of funds available to pay them. That $25,000 to your cousin Jane? Sorry, the money is gone! But why?

State law, not federal law, regulates property transfers in wills. States greatly vary in the laws or statutes that affect these transfers. Some states follow the Uniform Probate Code (UPC) regarding wills. More than half of the states in the United States have adopted the UPC, in part or in whole. The adoption of the UPC results in some uniformity of statutes among states, including abatement statutes.

In Book VII, Chapter 1, we mention that one of the primary roles of your attorney on your estate-planning team is to help you with the "what if?" scenarios and to help you prevent problems from occurring. When you're working with your attorney on your will, ask about the abatement statutes that apply in the state where you live and what may happen to your property based on those statutes. While you're asking, specifically question your attorney to help you prepare your will so abatement statutes won't come into play at all.

Ademption: Some property is missing

Cataloging and valuing your tangible personal property (jewelry, antiques, collectibles, furniture, and so on) can be tedious and frustrating, but you need to take the time to do it as part of your estate planning.

In your will, you can explicitly leave items to someone through a *specific bequest.* For example, you can leave your valuable collection of 1950s and 1960s baseball cards to your baseball-crazy oldest son, and your collection of autographed first-edition novels to your other son, who is working on his Ph.D. in English literature.

But what happens if you die and the baseball cards or the novels — or maybe both — are no longer part of your estate? You maybe had to sell some of your property to pay for medical expenses. Or maybe you already gave your baseball cards to your son as a gift, with the appropriate gift tax implications, while you were still alive, meaning that you already transferred that property from your estate to his.

Regardless of the reason, if your will refers to property that isn't part of your estate when you die, that property is considered to be missing, or *adeemed,* and the *ademption statutes* apply.

Ademption statutes concern whether the specific asset in question is in existence when you die. In general, the statutes provide that your "who gets what" direction will fail if you are not the owner of the asset when you die. However, exceptions to the rule may apply in your case, including what happens if you dispose of an asset while incompetent but receive another asset in exchange. Ask your attorney to walk you through the various scenarios that specifically relate to your estate's property.

Ademption statutes vary from state to state and determine whether the beneficiary who can't receive the specific bequest from your will is allowed to still receive something from your estate and, if so, what that beneficiary will receive.

So what can you do to keep ademption statutes at bay? You can include *backup property* for some or all beneficiaries in your will. For example, you can specify that if your baseball card collection worth $50,000 is no longer part of your estate, your son is to receive $50,000 in cash instead. Beware, though: Including backup property in your will can be complicated and can have unintended side effects, so work carefully with your attorney on what backup property to use and what wording to use in your will.

Antilapse: Someone dies before you do

Antilapse sounds like a doddering old relative. Actually, antilapse occurs when somebody named in your will dies before you do. To cover yourself, consider naming a *contingent beneficiary* (your backup beneficiary) for any property distribution in your will by including words such as the following:

"In the event that my named beneficiary for the property listed herein does not survive me, then I hereby direct that that my bequest be given to John Doe."

If you don't make your own provisions for contingent beneficiaries, and if your state has an antilapse statute, that law dictates who receives the property that is in limbo because of your beneficiary who died. If your state doesn't have an antilapse statute, typically the in-limbo property goes to the beneficiaries you name in your *residuary clause* (that statement names the beneficiaries who get anything you haven't explicitly mentioned in a giving clause). Sometimes, though, that is exactly what you want. Be sure to work with your attorney to determine whether naming a contingent beneficiary makes sense.

Divorce: High noon in Splitsville

Nearly everyone has heard the statistic again and again: Approximately half of all marriages end in divorce. With that large of a target audience, no wonder states have divorce statutes that you need to be aware of for your estate planning.

Your spouse automatically has a claim on part of your estate after you die. If you live in a common law state (we cover these states later in the chapter), your spouse is entitled to claim a percentage of your assets. If you live in a community property state (we also cover these states later in the chapter), your spouse generally owns half of your property.

You may not want to change your will right away after you divorce. For example, you may not have initiated the divorce and you subconsciously think that changing your will is equivalent to acknowledging that your marriage has ended. Therefore, estate-planning procrastination is a natural reaction for the recently divorced.

The good news: In many states, if your marriage has ended but you resist changing your will to reflect this fact, your estate is protected from claims by your ex-spouse. As a result, typically your ex-spouse isn't allowed to claim a share of your estate if you die after you are officially divorced but before you change your will. But be careful!

Even with the protection provided by such statutes, you still need to change your will as soon as possible after a divorce, to clarify your intentions of who your beneficiaries are. If your ex-spouse isn't one of them, make sure your will reflects that intent.

Simultaneous death: Sorry, but we have to talk about it

Estate planning can sometimes be a depressing topic because it revolves around the subject of death, and the statutes dealing with simultaneous death are particularly depressing. However, you need to understand these statutes' implications for your estate if you want to be as comprehensive as possible.

The simplest way to understand simultaneous death statutes is to consider the following situation:

- You and your spouse both die.
- The order of your deaths can't be established. (For example, you and your spouse both die in the same fatal car accident, and the order of death can't be determined.)
- Your state law determines the order of death for inheritance purposes.

All states have adopted a form of the *Uniform Simultaneous Death Act* to deal with simultaneous death situations. This act is based on the assumption that when the transfer of property depends on the order of death, the estate is distributed as if each person had survived the other person. For example, if a childless married couple dies in an accident, the wife's estate is left to her relatives and the husband's estate is left to his relatives. Why? Because each person is assumed to have survived the other, the act treats the estate distribution as if the other spouse had already died, which is actually good news (if you can consider any news in this type of situation as "good news"). The same assets don't pass through probate twice (once for each spouse), quite possibly subjecting the estate to double estate taxation and twice as much complication.

To be on the safe side, include a *survival clause* in your will to either confirm or change your state's version of the Uniform Simultaneous Death Act, according to what you and your attorney decide makes sense for you.

A survival clause is important in "closely related death" (though not simultaneous death) situations. You effectively "void out" a directive you made in your will to leave property to someone if that person dies very soon after you do.

For example, suppose that the same childless couple is critically injured in an accident, but one spouse dies five days before the other. Without a survival clause, property from the spouse who dies first transfers to the surviving spouse and goes through probate, possibly being subjected to death taxes. When the other spouse dies only a few days later, that very same property can once again be subjected to estate taxes. In effect, the estate goes through double taxation that wouldn't have occurred if that couple had died simultaneously.

Book VII

Planning Your Estate and Will

To help prevent these complications, specify in your will that your beneficiary must survive for some period of time — 30 or 60 days, for example — after your death before receiving the assets you've specified in your will. If that beneficiary dies very soon after you do, your property will skip over that person and go to someone else, avoiding double probate and possible double estate taxation.

Living (And Dying) with the Laws That Your Will Can't Change

If you prepare a will that conflicts with certain statutes, you risk spending a lot of time and effort only to find out that you've created a will that may not be effective or valid. If you decide to treat your will and your estate like a bad soap opera plot and leave as little as possible to your spouse and children (and possibly leave them in serious financial trouble), your state's statutes may come to the rescue and provide some amount of financial protection for your family.

But even if you aren't deliberately and maliciously trying to hurt your family with what you specify in your will, you still need to be aware of what your state's laws say about what may happen with your estate. Otherwise, you stand a very real possibility of preparing what you think is a valid will, but because you've accidentally run aground of one or more of your state's statutes, your will isn't valid at all.

Read through the following descriptions of statutes so that you know what you're dealing with.

Community property

If you live in a *community property* state, any property that you acquire and income that you make while you're married is considered to be owned 50 percent by you and 50 percent by your spouse. More important for estate-planning purposes, you're required under those states' community property statutes to leave half of your community property to your spouse.

Eight states are community property states: Arizona, California, Idaho, Louisiana, Nevada, New Mexico, Texas, and Washington. Wisconsin has a system similar to community property, called marital property, and for purposes of our discussion, we lump Wisconsin in with the other eight community property states.

A complicated community

Community property laws can be very complicated. For example, property that you own before you marry in a community property state is still considered to be your own. However, income that you earn on your own property after you're married may be considered community property. For example, if you inherit a farm from your parents before you get married, and then marry and live in a community property state, income from that farm may be considered community property.

Additionally, you need to be aware of what happens to your estate if you married in a community property state but later moved to a noncommunity property state, or if you purchased investment property in a community property state but live elsewhere.

You absolutely need to consult with your attorney to see if community property statutes apply to any part of your estate and, if so, what those statutes mean to your estate.

If you live in a community property state, all property acquired while you're married is considered community property, except for property that you personally receive by a gift or by inheritance, which is considered to be your sole and separate property. For example, your grandmother's inherited wedding ring or the $10,000 cash gift from your aunt to you isn't part of your community property. Additionally, property that you owned before you were married is exempt from being included in community property.

Keep your noncommunity property separate from your community property. You can actually override the "separate stuff" aspect of your noncommunity property by either specifying in writing that you want that property (again, a gift or inheritance) to become part of your community property with your spouse or intermixing your noncommunity property and your community property. For example, say that you put your $10,000 cash gift from your aunt into a joint savings account that you and your spouse have. If you turn your noncommunity property into community property, either accidentally or on purpose, you lose your sole control over that property, and the community property statutes take over.

Book VII

Planning Your Estate and Will

Spousal elective shares

What if you reside in one of the other 41 states that aren't community property states? You live in a *common law* state, and your spouse still has a claim to some part of your estate, although not the automatic half specified by community property statutes. In almost all common law states, your spouse is provided for through *spousal elective shares,* or the law that permits your spouse to claim some part of your estate.

The one exception is Georgia, which uses the old English concepts called *dower* and *courtesy,* which we discuss in the section "Homestead allowance — keeping a house for kiddies and spouse," in this chapter. In all other common law states, spousal elective shares have replaced dower and courtesy.

Your spouse has the right under spousal elective shares to claim a portion of your estate, with the amount depending on your own state's spousal elective shares statutes. But what about your will? Spousal elective shares are sort of like flipping a coin and calling "Heads, I win; tails, you lose."

Your spouse basically gets a choice between accepting the amount you specified in your will or the amount specified in your state's spousal elective shares. If your will specifies that your spouse is to receive more than your state's spousal elective shares specify, your spouse can accept that higher amount. But if your will specifies a lower amount than your state's spousal elective shares, your spouse can opt for the higher amount specified by law. In doing so, your spouse can cause all kinds of complications to your will.

Spousal elective share amounts vary among states. Under some statutes, your spouse's share is a percentage amount that ranges from 3 to 50 percent of your estate, based on how long you were married. Other states' statutes specify an amount equal to some flat percentage of your estate, regardless of how long you were married.

In some states, spousal elective shares are based on an *augmented estate* amount instead of your actual estate amount. Basically, certain property that isn't technically part of your estate is added back to your estate's value, and the spousal elective percentage amount is based on this higher, augmented value instead of your estate's actual value at the time of your death. What's the deal? States that use augmented estate amounts are trying to protect a surviving spouse from that person's husband or wife deliberately trying to reduce the value of an estate and leaving as little as possible to the surviving spouse.

For example, property transfers that you made within a certain period of time before your death may be added back to your estate, along with certain property in which you have ownership with right of survivorship and sometimes life insurance proceeds, retirement benefits, and annuities. When you work with your attorney, make sure you understand the spousal elective share laws in your estate and ask if augmented amounts apply to your estate.

If you really don't like your spouse, don't use your estate plan to try to punish him or her by trying not to leave anything as part of your estate. Your estate-planning attorney isn't the person you should be working with on this problem; try a marriage counselor, or if that doesn't work, ask your estate-planning attorney for a recommendation for a good divorce attorney! Don't complicate or even trash your estate planning by trying to give your spouse a raw deal and make some kind of point. Your entire estate plan may be defeated if your spouse makes that spousal election after your death!

Homestead allowance: Keeping a house for kiddies and spouse

Just as Dorothy discovered in *The Wizard of Oz,* there's no place like home. You definitely want your home to be protected after you die. Fortunately, the *homestead allowance statutes* may take care of your home. Unfortunately, though, only a few states have these statutes.

The purpose of homestead allowance statutes is to make sure that your spouse and any minor children (under 18 years of age) have a place to live after you die. Your homestead is typically defined as your house and may also include a certain amount of adjacent land. (The legal term you may run across is *curtilage.*) The land aspect of homestead allowances is very important if you live on a farm or any property with many acres.

Homestead allowance statutes come from the old English common law concepts of *dower* and *courtesy,* and you may come across those terms. (We discuss in an earlier section that Georgia law uses dower and courtesy instead of spousal elective shares or community property statutes.) The purpose of dower and courtesy was to give a surviving spouse an interest for the rest of his or her life in the real property owned by the spouse who died, therefore giving the surviving spouse somewhere to live. *Dower* is the word used for a wife's interest, whereas *courtesy* refers to a husband's interest.

Homestead exemption: How the law protects your house from your creditors

Homestead exemption statutes are closely related to homestead allowance statutes and apply if your estate needs to pay debts you owe to creditors. If not enough cash is available, the estate is forced to sell off property — real, personal, or perhaps both — to get enough money to pay the creditors. If your estate owes a lot of money for debts, selling off a single high-value item, such as your house, is often easier than trying to sell a lot of smaller items.

So the homestead exemption statutes are intended to prevent your surviving spouse and minor children from being kicked out of your home if property must be sold to pay creditors.

Even with homestead exemption statutes, your home can be subject to a forced sale. Think of these statutes simply as a first line of defense rather than a 100 percent guarantee that your spouse and children can remain in your home if your estate owes a lot of money and money can't be raised by selling other property from the estate. Therefore, you need to consider the other parts of your overall estate planning, such as life insurance, to help the homestead exemption statutes and protect your family and your home.

Exempt property: How the law protects your personal property from creditors

Your estate consists of various types of property: real property and personal property, including both tangible personal property and intangible personal property.

The two types of homestead statutes that we discuss earlier — homestead allowance and homestead exemption — help to protect part of your real property (your home). However, the vast majority of your intangible personal property (stocks, bonds, and so on) isn't covered by protective statutes and, therefore, may be forcibly sold to satisfy claims from your estate's creditors.

The good news: Some of your tangible personal property (your car, collectibles, jewelry, and so forth) may be protected through *exempt property award statutes*.

With the homestead statutes, exempt property award statutes vary among states, so you need to consult with your attorney about what types of tangible personal property your state's statutes protect and how that relates to your estate plan.

Family allowance: Drawing from your estate to protect your family

Your spouse and children may rely on you as the family's breadwinner. Even if you aren't the sole breadwinner, the income that you provide to your family may cover a substantial portion of basic care, such as food and shelter, for your family. Therefore, your unanticipated death may create an immediate financial crisis for your family. But you have several assets and your will specifies what goes to your family, so you don't have this problem, right?

Not necessarily! Your estate may be tied up in the probate process for an extended period of time. Typically, your estate can't make any distributions to your beneficiaries until all debts to your creditors have been paid. Therefore, your family's immediate financial needs, such as the mortgage payment and even utilities and food costs, may be in jeopardy!

Fortunately, *family allowance statutes* enable the probate court to provide money for support of your spouse and minor children during the probate process. In fact, family allowance statutes are one of the only distributions that can be made from your estate without risk before the claims of your creditors are paid.

The amount of your family's allowance under your state's law may depend on a number of factors, including your estate's size and your family's living expenses. Ask your attorney to inform you of the likely allowance so you can factor that into your overall estate plan. For example, you may want to set up your gift-giving strategy to transfer enough cash while you're alive to your beneficiaries that they can use to help cover living expenses during the probate process.

Oops! Taking care of VIPs who aren't in the will

You must continually update your will as circumstances in your life change, particularly when you get married, give birth, or adopt.

But suppose that you get married or have a child and you don't update your will before you die. Are family members who aren't mentioned in your will totally out of the picture when your estate is distributed? (In legal-speak, a spouse or child not included in your estate is called a *pretermitted* or *omitted* heir or beneficiary.)

Pretermitted or omitted heir statutes help to protect certain family members that you don't mention in your will, but they apply only to your spouse and children. These statutes, which (as you probably expect us to say) vary from one state to another, govern what part of your estate must go to your spouse and children if you procrastinate and don't keep your will up to date.

Book VII

Planning Your Estate and Will

Chapter 4

Estate Planning Online

*E*state is a legal term, but its meaning is more personal. An estate, regardless of how large or small, planned or not, is simply how folks refer to or describe what you've accumulated throughout your life. People always have plenty of excuses to put off planning their estates, including "I'm too young and much too busy," or "It's depressing to think about what will happen when the inevitable happens," or "All my relatives are insincere ingrates and don't deserve my time and consideration." Adding fuel to these burning embers, estate tax rules change every year (at least through 2010), creating even more reasons to avoid estate planning. However, in spite of all the Congressional wrangling, flexible estate planning is becoming more important than ever.

This chapter focuses on estate planning, which can include life insurance policies, financial planning, and retirement planning. It deals with what's important to include in your estate plan and how the Internet can solve the mysteries and ease the dread of determining who gets what from your estate.

Calculating Your Estate's Value Online

Knowing the value of your estate can help you determine how to plan to distribute your estate. A wide variety of online calculators can assist you in determining its value. You may find a few of these calculators useful:

- **Charles Schwab** (www.schwab.com) offers an online estate tax and probate calculator. You can use this Internet calculator in one of two ways: One is for detailed calculations about your asset values, and the other is for a quick calculation. To find the online estate-planning calculator, go to Schwab's home page and click Planning, then Tools, and then Estate Tax and Probate Calculator.

- **Smart Money** (www.smartmoney.com/estate/index.cfm?story=estatetax#worksheet) uses what it calls an Estate Tax Exposure Meter to show you how to take advantage of higher exclusion amounts. Higher exclusion amounts and good estate planning can help you reduce or even avoid estate taxes. The calculator assesses how much you'd owe today.

- **Fidelity** (http://web.fidelity.com/EstatePlanning/tools/tax/taxM1.jhtml?_requestid=421673) provides an online federal estate tax calculator. Enter your personal data to project your estate, and allow the calculator to estimate your potential federal estate tax burden based on current tax laws. Additionally, you can consider your potential future estate-tax estimates. At the home page, click Retirement and Guidance in the top header and then Estate Planning. Next, click Estate Tax Calculator.

Understanding Wills and Trusts

The most accepted way of transferring assets to survivors and beneficiaries is through a will or a trust. A *will* is defined as a legal document that describes how you want your resources to be distributed after your death. The distribution is controlled by a legal process called probate. *Probate* is Latin for "prove the will." If one or more of your heirs contest your will (or if there's a lack of agreement among your heirs), a supervised probate is required. Supervised probates need formal reports from appraisers, accountants, and attorneys. The court reviews these documents at each stage of the proceedings. All court actions, including the presentation of the facts and figures from the formal reports that relate to your estate, are conducted in open court. As a result, nothing is private. After the probate process begins, your family no longer controls your estate; the court, probate attorneys, and named executors are in control of all your assets. For individuals who are incapacitated due to illness or injury, probate is good. For widows with children, probate can cause a delay in the payment of living expenses.

A *trust* is a document that enables you, the *grantor* (a fancy word for the owner of the estate), to establish a separate entity (much like a corporation) to hold, manage, and eventually distribute your assets in the manner you desire to your beneficiaries. A chief benefit of establishing a trust is that it's not a public document that goes through probate. A trust offers your heirs an element of privacy. However, establishing a trust (or trusts) frequently is more costly than creating a will.

Book VII, Chapters 1 and 2 cover this area in lots of detail. For now, though, you can find more information about estate planning at these Web sites:

- **Federal Citizen Information Center** (`www.pueblo.gsa.gov/cic_text/money/estateplan/planning.htm`) provides an online pamphlet about estate planning.

- **Prudential Financial** (`www.prudential.com`) provides an easy-to-understand overview of estate planning. On its home page, click Financial Planning and then Estate Planning Overview.

- **Kiplinger.com** (`www.kiplinger.com`) offers suggestions for starting your estate planning and articles about the top estate-planning issues and tools. On the home page click Planning and then Estate Planning.

Where there's an online will, there's a way

Creating a will is one of the easiest estate-planning tools you can use to help your family. Unfortunately, as many as 70 percent of all Americans don't have a current and valid will. Wills describe to members of your family how you want your estate to be distributed. Dying *intestate,* or without a will, can cause additional work and expense for your survivors. Although a qualified estate-planning attorney is recommended, it isn't required. Many courts accept handwritten wills, drawn up without legal counsel. You can even put together a will online. A proper will usually includes these components:

- How you want your property to be distributed among your heirs. Remember to avoid vague instructions that can lead to costly legal bills and squabbles among your beneficiaries.

- The name of the executor (or personal representative) of your estate.

- How the costs incurred in settling your estate will be paid.

- Who you're designating as guardian for your minor children and the name of a trustee to protect any money they inherit.

If the will is proven invalid, the estate is considered *intestate* (without a will). At that point, the probate court uses all the preset formulas for distributing assets. If no living relatives are found, the estate reverts to the state.

Avoiding probate

Probate is a legal process that identifies and catalogs all of your property, appraises the property, pays all debts and taxes, and distributes the remaining property to your heirs according to your instructions.

Book VII

Planning Your Estate and Will

Good will hunting

All your estate planning goes to waste if your survivors don't know where you keep your will or trust documents. Sometimes these documents aren't stored in obvious places, such as a desk drawer, file cabinet, or home safe. For example, some folks actually wrap these documents in foil and store them in their freezers.

When you can't find the documents at home, check the person's safe-deposit box. Also don't forget to check desk drawers and file cabinets at the person's place of business, or look for the lawyer's name and contact information. Note: You'll need a key to the safe-deposit box and an official death certificate.

Probate often takes several months to complete, is frequently cumbersome, and can be expensive. All probate records are open to the public. These records are exposed to con artists who view grief-stricken family members as easy targets and can use the information they gain from public records to prey on survivors. Probate records aren't private; relatives, friends, and associates can view these public records and petition the court for a share of your estate. For that reason, avoiding probate can prove valuable to many people.

If you're executing any of the fiduciary duties associated with someone's will, it's a good idea to get more than one copy of the official death certificate. Many of the agencies that you run into will ask for an official copy of the death certificate. Therefore, obtaining a half-dozen or more is often a good idea and a timesaver in the long run.

These Web sites about wills are a few of the best available:

- ✔ **Legalzoom** (www.legalzoom.com) helps you create a will that's valid in any state without ever leaving your computer. In just three steps, you can complete your will and have it reviewed for the most common mistakes, with delivery in 48 hours. The Standard package costs $69 including a comprehensive customized Last Will and Testament, reviewed by a LegalZoom specialist and advanced provisions, such as credit shelter trusts to protect every member of your household, plus it is printed on archival paper and you receive free revisions for 30 days. The Gold package for $99 adds free unlimited revisions for five years. For $119 the Vault package adds secure electronic storage for five years, same-day preparation, and express email delivery.

- ✔ **Probate FAQ** (www.nolo.com) provides you with the basics of probate, who is responsible for handling probate, and how you can avoid it. On the home page, under Browse the Law Centers, click Wills & Estate Planning and then Living Trusts and Avoiding Probate.

✔ **SaveWealth** (www.savewealth.com/planning/estate/probate) provides useful guides to how the probate process works in California, Colorado, Florida, Georgia, Hawaii, Illinois, Indiana, Maine, Massachusetts, Mississippi, Ohio, Pennsylvania, Texas, and Virginia.

✔ **The Funeral Directory** (www.thefuneraldirectory.com/planit yourway/samplewill.asp) offers a fill-in-the-blank sample will that serves as an easy-to-understand outline of what needs to be included in a will.

✔ **Wills FAQ** (www.nolo.com), at NOLO Law for All, illustrates what happens if you die without a will and covers the validity of handwritten wills and what makes a will legal. On the NOLO home page, click Wills & Estate Planning and then Wills. Scroll to Wills FAQ and click it.

Getting the Basics of Trusts

Trusts (excluding a living trust that replaces a will) can be flexible and valuable tools for allocating your assets. Trusts come in several flavors and can be created and funded during the grantor's lifetime or by the terms of a will. The terms of the trust may allow for the grantor to make changes or even revoke it in its entirety. By contrast, the terms of the trust may be fixed or irrevocable on the date it's conceived. Although several types of trusts can be administered, each involves the following three factors:

✔ **Grantors transfer (or arrange for transfer of) ownership of their assets to a trustee during their lifetimes.** Trusts often aren't expensive to maintain. Therefore, grantors don't have to be wealthy to have a trust.

✔ **A trustee holds the resources defined by the trust for the benefit of the inheritors.** A trustee can be an attorney, banker, financial planner, family member, or trusted friend.

✔ **The beneficiaries or inheritors receive the assets as intended by the grantor.** Trusts provide flexibility and need not alienate inheritors from the decision-making process.

Table 4-1 compares wills to trusts in terms of benefits and limitations. A will or a trust can be the best way for you to protect your assets, but bear in mind that estate planning often includes more than just one of these approaches. Your plan needs to cover all unforeseen events that you may encounter.

Book VII

Planning Your Estate and Will

Table 4-1	A Comparison of Wills and Trusts
Wills	*Trusts*
Wills implement your estate plan.	Trusts provide continuity to the management of your assets upon your death or disability.
With a supervised probate action, several weeks may pass before the court appoints an executor who is authorized to deal with income and expenses of your estate.	Upon the grantor's death, trustees can distribute assets more quickly. A more-rapid distribution of assets may be important for a surviving spouse or beneficiaries.
If you suffer any physical or mental incapacity, a court proceeding may be required to determine conservatorship of your assets. (Conservatorship is a process in which the court appoints a person to make certain legal decisions to protect them from neglect, financial abuse, and isolation.)	A trust protects the grantor against mismanagement or nonmanagement of his or her assets during physical or mental incapacity.
Probate is often expensive. For their fees, probate attorneys receive 2% of the first $1 million and 1% of the next $9 million of assets passing through probate.	To reduce costs, a family member or close friend may be appointed as trustee or executor.
Open-court probate records are available to the public.	Trusts, for the most part, are not open to the public.
Death tax returns and the payment of death taxes must be completed.	Death tax returns and payment of death taxes must be completed.

Adapted from "Estate Planning Basics" by the National Association of Financial and Estate Planning (1999 and 2001). Available online at www.nafep.com.

Alternatives to probate are frequently used for small estates with assets of less than $100,000 and for property that passes outright to the surviving spouse. These alternatives generally are inexpensive but effective. When planning your estate, you need to keep these alternatives in mind.

Trusting in Living Trust to Avoid Probate

A *living trust* is a fictitious entity created for the purpose of owning an individual's assets during that person's lifetime and for distributing those assets after his or her death. The individual who creates a living trust is called the *grantor* and names a trustee. The trustee follows the instructions of the grantor after he or she dies. While the grantor is living, the trustee may administer the living trust and control the assets even though they belong to the living trust. Living trusts are active during an individual's lifetime. A will does not spring into effect until after death. During your lifetime, you transfer ownership of your assets to the living trust, called *funding the trust.* Keep in mind that merely executing the living trust doesn't automatically cause the living trust to be funded. For example, the grantor has to transfer titles of any bank accounts, stock certificates, or real estate into the living trust.

As part of the funding process, if you're transferring mortgaged real property to your living trust, the mortgage company must consent. You will sign a new deed, showing that you now own the real property as trustee of your living trust. The mortgage lender may require that the living trust be recorded, along with the deed, in the county clerk's office. At that point, the living trust can become part of the publicly accessible records.

Often a living trust enables you to bypass probate if you fund your trust while you're alive. The trust then owns all your assets, and no assets are held separately outside the trust for the probate court to administer. Upon your death, ownership of your assets passes to the successor trustee of your living trust, who then distributes your resources according to your instructions.

The living trust can be revocable or irrevocable:

- ✔ **Revocable trusts** enable the grantor to keep the right to change how he or she manages their assets and allows the grantor to change the trustee at any time.

- ✔ **Irrevocable trusts** cause the grantor to give up control and ownership of the property that's placed in the trust but offer tax advantages for grantors with estates that exceed the federal estate tax exclusion and gift-tax credit.

Keep in mind that a will doesn't spring into effect until you die. A living trust can assist you during a lifetime of planning. That is, a living trust can preserve and increase your estate while you're alive, yet still offer you protection if you become incapacitated or mentally disabled.

For more information about trusts, check out these resources:

- ✔ **CNN Money 101** (http://money.cnn.com/pf/101/lessons/21) illustrates how trusts aren't just for the superwealthy. You'll discover whether creating a trust is the right type of estate planning for you or whether you don't need to worry about it.

- ✔ **American Bar Association** (www.abanet.org/publiced/practical/ books/wills/home.html) offers an online book titled *ABA Guide to Wills and Estates.* The book includes information about getting started, transferring property without a will, making a will, trusts, living trusts, common estate planning situations, special considerations, death and taxes, changing your mind, choosing an executor or trustee, planning how to make things easier for your family, and what to do if you can't make a decision. The online book includes an Estate Planning Checklist and a Health-Care Advance Directive.

Book VII

Planning Your Estate and Will

✔ **Living Trusts on the Web** (www.livingtrustsontheweb.com/pages/faq.thml) is a large collection of frequently asked questions about living trusts.

✔ **NOLO** (www.nolo.com) introduces you to living trusts and shows why they're a popular way of avoiding probate. At the NOLO home page, click Wills & Estate Planning and then click Living Trusts and Avoiding Probate. The Nolo Web site supplies authoritative information that is easy to understand.

✔ **The Assets Protection Law Center** (www.rjmintz.com/funding-living-trust.html) provides an online asset-protection law library. Discover how to fund your trust and more at this Web site.

Joint Tenancy and Beneficiary Arrangements

Not everyone's family fits into a standardized model. Today many families are blended, meaning that they include first and second spouses and children from a new spouse's former marriage. Additionally, because people live longer, seeing widowed senior citizens getting married isn't uncommon. These situations require some more complex thinking and considerations when it comes to estate planning.

Joint tenancy enables two or more people to be listed as owners of a property. As a result of this joint ownership, upon the death of one of the owners, the property immediately transfers to the other owner without having to pass through probate court. Using rights of survivorship, individuals A and B jointly own the property and agree to pass title to the property to the other when one of the joint owners dies. However, if one of the joint tenants becomes incapacitated, the property can be held in limbo for years.

Beneficiary arrangements are situations in which assets transfer to heirs without the benefit of legal instruments such as a will or trust. For example, a beneficiary may be specified in a pension plan, insurance policy, annuity, or investment account. When the original owner dies, the assets remaining from these financial arrangements can transfer to the specified heirs without having to go through probate. Several drawbacks to this type of transfer exist. For example, beneficiary distribution can be subject to any lawsuits, bankruptcies, and divorce problems that the inheritor experiences.

The Internet provides many online courses estate planning, including:

✔ **AARP** (www.aarp.org) provides sound advice for estate planning. On the home page, click Money and Work, and next click Financial Planning. In the left margin, click Estate Planning. Click Estate Planning Guide.

✔ **American Law Institute, American Bar Association** (www.ali-aba.org/index.cfm) allows free registration, and you can receive free information or purchase information about estate planning. In the left margin select the Estate Planning practice area. You'll discover information about estate planning live courses, Webcasts, MP3 and CD-ROMs, DVD videos, periodical articles, printed course materials, digital course books, coursebook papers, and books. Prices vary from a few dollars to several hundred dollars.

Filling out a few forms sometimes can eliminate extra costs, arguments between family members, and plenty of pain and suffering. Signing a *durable power of attorney form* (which isn't the same as giving someone power of attorney) designates someone as your agent in case you're incapacitated and thus enables that agent to make financial decisions on your behalf. Book VII, Chapter 5 covers durable power of attorney.

Signing a *healthcare proxy* also can eliminate much of your family's pain and suffering if you become terminally ill or are injured in an accident and don't want to live by artificial means. A healthcare proxy enables your agent to make healthcare decisions for you when you're unable to make them for yourself. For example, your healthcare proxy does the following:

✔ Provides specific medical guidelines for your healthcare representative

✔ Permits your agent to take your religious and moral beliefs into consideration when making a decision about your care

✔ Permits you to name an alternative representative if your first-choice representative is unavailable or refuses to serve as your agent

Whenever you hire an attorney to draw up your will or trust, he or she probably will include documentation for a durable power of attorney and healthcare proxy either for free or for a minimal charge.

You can pick up the forms for designating durable power of attorney and initiating a healthcare proxy from most stationery stores. Or save yourself that trip to the mall by going online and downloading those same forms for free. These forms are available at several Web sites, including these:

✔ **CCH Financial Planning** (www.finance.cch.com/tools/poaforms_m.asp) offers free online state healthcare proxy forms. Just click on the link for the state in which you live. Keep in mind that some forms are guidelines and may enable you to make modifications that suit your individual needs. Other forms may have to be completed as is.

✔ **Family Care Givers Online** (www.familycaregiversonline.com/legal-medical.html#Power%20of%20Attorney%20Forms) offers easy-to-use online education and information resources for anyone helping older adults. The site has free downloadable durable power of attorney forms.

The Funeral Directory (`www.thefuneraldirectory.com/planit yourway/livingwill.asp`) provides a free downloadable medical directive form that's invaluable for getting organized in a hurry.

Not all heirs are created equal

If you don't have any heirs and your personal situation fits into the formula for settling an estate in your state, you may not need a will, trust, beneficiary arrangement, or joint tenancy. However, most people live in a complicated world of blended families and ties that go beyond the narrow limits of probate court. Therefore, if you want to have some say in how your assets are allocated among your heirs, you need to do a little planning.

If you write a will and own property in your name, your estate probably will have to go through probate court. All court proceedings are open to the public. This situation exposes your estate to public scrutiny. A living trust is a good way to avoid the rigors of probate and the prying eyes of potential swindlers. The trustee of your living trust can quickly and easily transfer your assets to your heirs. Beneficiary arrangements can be used to transfer assets, particularly pension plans, retirement accounts, insurance policies, annuities, bank accounts, and brokerage accounts. Some married couples (or unmarried couples) use joint tenancy with rights of survivorship to hold a title together.

Don't keep your estate plans hush-hush

Many of the items you own have sentimental value to your children. Sometimes more angst besets the question of who gets the gravy bowl than just about anything else. And surprising your beneficiaries isn't a good idea, either. Make certain that everyone knows who gets what and why. That way, no one feels left out or mistreated.

Divorce causes a blending of families and tends to complicate estate planning. Teen or adult children from first marriages and young children from second marriages need to be provided for in different ways. Sometimes using the benefits of a life insurance policy can ensure that your children actually receive what you want them to have, thus keeping the money out of the hands of an estranged former spouse. However, you must decide whether you want your children to have a large lump sum (that can be swallowed up if the child divorces) or graduated payments, to minimize bad money-management habits.

Frequently, the family doesn't know what type of funeral and burial plan a relative wants, so writing down funeral instructions for survivors is important so that they can carry out your last wishes.

Customizing Estate Planning for All Ages

As you progress through the cycle of life, you need different types of estate plans to cover different situations. I have divided estate planning into three distinct categories, based on age. Each age-based estate plan may not meet your exact needs, but it provides you with the basics for getting the right plan for the right time. Several estate planners available online can help you get started. A few of the better ones include the following:

- ✔ **Charles Schwab** (www.schwab.com) determines an estimated value of your estate and the amount of taxes you may incur. At the home page, click on "Planning," then "Planning Your Estate," and then "Estate Planning Steps." Return to the Estate Planning home page and click on "Alternatives" to see which estate-planning approach is best for you.

- ✔ **CNN Money** (money.cnn.com/magazines/moneymag/money101/lesson21) offers a full course on estate planning, starting with the top ten points you need to know, followed by how to assess your assets and the differences between wills and trusts. The online course includes a glossary and quiz.

- ✔ **Fidelity** (http://personal.fidelity.com/planning/estate/) has an online Estate Planner that's designed to help you illustrate potential planning strategies. It provides descriptions of various estate-planning techniques based on your inputs and various assumptions. Your particular circumstances are unique and affect actual planning done by an estate-planning professional; however, you can use the online Estate Planner to point you in the right direction. *Note:* All examples are hypothetical and are intended only for illustrative purposes.

Your estate-planning priorities will change as you grow older. College-age students don't have the assets or responsibilities of older individuals. Older individuals may want to donate to charities or give gifts to fund the college educations of their grandchildren. Overall, estate planning is a family issue. It can be simple or complex, depending on your personal situation. We've divided estate planning into these three life stages:

- ✔ Young singles and adults with children

- ✔ Middle-aged adults who have accumulated a few assets

- ✔ Seniors or retirees who are conserving personal wealth for their retirement or offloading assets so their heirs pay minimal estate taxes

These suggestions cover the top issues and may not fully address your needs.

Under 30 and loving it

When you're younger than 30, the likelihood of dying is remote. Your estate plans can be short and sweet, unless, of course, you have a dangerous job that places you in hazard's way on a regular basis. If you're just starting out, the value of your estate probably comes in under the radar of your state's requirement for going to probate court. If you're a wealthy young person, you can write a will and leave your possessions to your favorite cause or relative. If you don't write a will, the state gives your assets to your surviving parents.

If you have a significant other but aren't married (some exceptions exist), your closest relatives inherit everything. One alternative to this scenario is owning big-ticket items, such as your house, car, boat, and so on, in joint tenancy; the surviving joint owner then automatically owns the property. However, joint tenancy has its own perils, so read the fine print. For example, if you or your spouse becomes incapacitated, the ownership of jointly held assets gets really messy and usually ends up in court.

If you're married with young children, you have plenty to think about. You need to identify your future goals and concerns for you, your spouse, and your children. You may want to consider the following:

- ✔ Writing a will that leaves your property to your spouse (or a designated person) and names a guardian for your children. Remember, if you don't have a will, probate court may give half of your assets to your spouse and the other half to your children. If your spouse needs money for the children, he or she has to go to court.

- ✔ Determining the future cost of tuition and finding the best way to reach your goal of providing for your children's educations. For more on saving for college, see Book IV, Chapter 4.

- ✔ Completing healthcare proxies and durable powers of attorney so that a family member can direct the healthcare and financial decisions of the family if you and your spouse are out of action at the same time.

  A durable power of attorney enables the person you select to represent you, in case you become incapacitated and cannot represent yourself. For more information about a durable power of attorney, go to the ExpertLaw Web site at `http://expertlaw.com/library/pubarticles/ Estate_Planning/durable_power_of_attorney.html`, which offers a free durable power of attorney form. This sample form covers the general provisions of establishing a durable power of attorney. Have an attorney review your durable power of attorney form to make sure it meets your legal needs and is valid in the jurisdiction where you live.

- ✔ Creating an estate plan that minimizes estate taxes and maximizes the accumulation of wealth. It's never too early to purchase life insurance (Book V, Chapter 5) and consider retirement planning (Book VI) to round out your estate planning.

Grooving in your midlife

If you're middle-aged and just hitting your stride, you've probably accumulated a few assets. Wanting to keep court and legal costs to a minimum, you may want to consider a revocable living trust as a way to distribute your assets to your heirs. Living trusts don't affect your current lifestyle and generally are easy to set up, and they enable your assets to be quickly transferred to your beneficiaries upon your death. The trust can be revoked at any time while you're alive.

Some families get caught in what we call the "boomer sandwich" — when they're shelling out money for their children's college education, paying for assisted living for their parents, and trying to save enough for their own retirement. As a result, their estate plans must maximize every dollar.

For more information on gift taxes and charitable trusts, see these resources:

- ✔ **NOLO** (www.nolo.com) provides an easy-to-understand "Estate and Gift Tax FAQ" section for estate planning. According to the NOLO Law Center, most estates don't owe taxes. However, it pays to be informed. Answers to FAQs about estate taxes and gift giving to reduce taxes are written in a way that clears up any misunderstandings you may have about complex estate planning. On the home page, go to Browse the Law Centers and click Wills & Estate Planning, then click Estate Taxes.

- ✔ **A Guide to Planned Giving** (www.giftlegacy.com/members/ Planned_Giving_for_Beginners.pdf) is a 12-page tutorial about how to incorporate charitable giving into your personal financial plan. You'll need Adobe Reader for this tutorial.

- ✔ **Charity Navigator** (www.charitynavigator.org) provides independent evaluations of the financial health of over 5,300 of America's largest charities. Click Tips and Resources for intelligent tips and resources to assist you in your personal gift giving.

Book VII

Planning Your Estate and Will

Retired and enjoying the good life

Retirement often is a wake-up call for getting your estate plan in order. Some folks play golf or bridge for years, and other retirees may suddenly become ill. Either way, now is the time to get going and make your estate plans. One of the most important decisions you need to make involves healthcare. You may want to consider assigning someone in your family the task of making your healthcare decisions for you if or when you become incapacitated. After all, a doctor or the court doesn't know you the way members of your family do. A family member needs to have your durable power of attorney (he or she doesn't have to pass a bar exam to do it) to act as your agent. You can stipulate that the durable power of attorney doesn't go into effect unless you're incapacitated. Don't forget to have the form signed and notarized.

Folks near retirement and retirees need to consider the best way to provide growth potential for their assets and preserve capital. One protective strategy is a charitable remainder trust. A *charitable remainder trust* offers an immediate tax reduction and can help reduce capital gains. Estate planning dictates that you must understand that you can't take it with you.

- ✔ **Contributing to the grandkids:** If you can afford it, you can give the maximum amount of money allowed each year to your grandchildren's Uniform Gifts to Minors (UMG) accounts or set up a Section 529 plan to supplement their education funding while using the tax advantages.

- ✔ **Disbursing money to your favorite charities:** Doing so reduces estate taxes. Don't forget, charities also can be named as trust beneficiaries.

- ✔ **Transferring the benefits of your existing life insurance policy to a trust, to protect your heirs:** If you're a business owner or are self-employed, transferring the benefits of your insurance policy (or policies) to your trust may be valuable to your heirs. This estate-planning technique can protect the inheritance of your heirs in case of bankruptcy, divorce, or some other unforeseen event.

Selecting an Estate Planner

Although the Internet can point you in the right direction and provide the basic education you need to understand different approaches to estate planning, an estate-planning attorney is necessary to make sure your beneficiaries don't run into any unpleasant surprises. Finding a qualified attorney can be difficult. You may want to start by asking friends and family for recommendations. Your broker or accountant may be able to recommend a good estate-planning attorney.

Keep in mind that financial planners also can provide advice for investments, insurance, taxes, wills and trusts, and mortgages. The following Web sites can help you locate someone who is an expert in estate planning, elder law, post-mortem services, and financial services:

- ✔ **American Academy of Estate Planning Attorneys** (www.aaepa.com) is a professional association that educates estate-planning attorneys and provides consumers with valuable information. Search on "Estate Planning" and click on "Other Academy Links." The Center can assist you in finding a trusted attorney and protecting your personal wealth.

- ✔ **Estate Planning Law** (www.estate-planninglaw.com/#lawyers) offers a listing of estate-planning attorneys by name. All the attorneys listed have Web sites so that you can view their major practice areas, estate-planning approaches, and attorney profiles.

✔ **National Directory of Estate Planning, Probate & Elder Law Attorneys** (www.search-attorneys.com) can assist you in finding an attorney in your area who focuses on estate planning. You can search the national directory by location, firm name, or attorney.

✔ **LegalMatch** (www.legalmatch.com) enables you to anonymously describe your estate-planning concerns online to qualified, prescreened local lawyers for free. Lawyers respond to your case with an offer. You can access detailed information about each attorney and then choose the one with the experience, consumer ratings, and fees that you like best. Try using the online demo to find out how it works.

Preparing to Meet Your Estate Planner

Your first meeting with your estate-planning attorney needs to be a working meeting, which means that you need to bring a file that includes copies of bank and brokerage statements and your existing will or trust (if you have one). If you're prepared, such a meeting can be a time to review your personal information and discuss fees. The following quick checklist gives you an idea of what you need to prepare before the meeting with your estate-planning attorney. Use the Internet to help you gather the documents you'll need:

✔ An inventory of your assets. You can use the online estate-planning calculators we mention shortly to help you get started.

✔ Copies of auto titles, home deeds, and other assets in your inventory.

✔ A printed copy of your most recent brokerage account statement.

✔ Copies of your insurance policies. If they're locked up in your safe-deposit box, bring copies of your paid insurance policy invoices.

✔ Copies of your pension plans. You may want to contact the Social Security Administration (SSA) for your latest statement.

✔ Copies of paperwork for large debts. For example, go online and print a copy of your most recent mortgage and credit card statements.

✔ Copies of any existing wills or trusts and previously filed gift tax returns that you may have. The status of these documents may determine whether your estate plan stays the same or whether you haves to start over.

✔ Copies of any powers of attorney or letters of intent or last instructions that you may have completed and signed.

✔ Social Security numbers of members of your family.

✔ Copies of all family members' medical insurance cards. This information may be used to clear up any misunderstandings that may occur.

Book VII

Planning Your Estate and Will

For online information about preparing to meet with your estate planner, check out the online sources in the following list. Although these Web sites promote the services of different organizations, they also include valuable estate-planning information and data sheets.

- ✔ **eXtension.org** (www.extension.org/pages/Getting_Ready_for_ Estate_Planning_Lesson) is an interactive learning environment for researched knowledge from land-grant university minds across America. eXtension offers a full estate planning tutorial. In Step 2: Take Stock of the Present, you'll uncover downloadable estate-planning checklists. Completing the checklists before your first visit to an estate planner can save you time and money.

- ✔ **Deloitte** (www.deloitte.com) provides timely articles, tools, and advisors to ensure that your plan addresses your family's values and long-term goals. On the Deloitte home page, pull down the Global Site Selector menu and choose United States. Next, click Services, click Tax, then Private Client Advisors. On the Client Advisors page click on the link to the Essential Tax & Wealth Planning Guide for 2008. This 56-page guide provides information about how to review current personal tax and wealth-planning situations. You'll gain an understanding of the current tax environment and recent regulatory changes, see how these changes may affect your tax situation this year and in the future, and get a grip on what steps you can take now before year-end.

- ✔ **Prudential** (www.prudential.com/view/page/public/14331) offers an online estate preservation calculator. This calculator can assist you in quickly and easily forecasting your gross estate for 10, 20, or 30 years and calculate your estate taxes in the privacy of your home or office. You'll need to provide a summary of your assets with appropriate growth rates, information about existing life insurance, and answers to a few simple questions.

Chapter 5

Taking Care of Aging Parents with Durable Power of Attorney

*P*arents who have Alzheimer's, dementia, or other mental incapacities may be physically able to stay in their homes and may want to remain where they are. In fact, many seniors with mental dysfunctions are unnecessarily agitated by being moved. A reverse mortgage, for example, can help aging parents enjoy life in the home they love, even if they aren't quite lucid.

One of the most common ways to secure a reverse mortgage for your parent is with a durable power of attorney. When you get durable power of attorney over a parent as an adult child, you are entitled to make large-scale financial decisions on your parent's behalf unless the written durable power of attorney says otherwise. This way, you can help your parent receive the benefits of a reverse mortgage without tearing your hair out trying to make him or her understand the concepts. In this chapter, we give you tips for recognizing mental incapacity, explain what your durable power of attorney allows, and offer advice on how to get the help you and your parent need.

Understanding Power of Attorney

One of the unofficial requirements for a reverse mortgage is that borrowers must understand the basic principles of the loan and all of the implications that go along with it. In short, the borrowers have to know what they're getting into. The loophole that allows you to give your parent the comfortable life he or she deserves is a durable power of attorney. By definition, a *power of attorney* is written permission for someone else to act on another's behalf.

Almost every state in the country requires that a power of attorney be *durable,* which means that it goes into effect when the papers are signed (or on a date specified in the official paperwork) and that it stays in effect if your parent becomes incapacitated. The only way it is revoked is if your parent revokes it or if the paperwork specifies a date on which the powers are revoked. Your parent can specify what powers the durable power of attorney actually covers.

Whenever we talk about power of attorney in this chapter, we use the term *durable power of attorney* because it's not only required by most states, but it's also the safest and smartest way to go. We're also assuming that you're looking for durable power of attorney for your parent, but the same rules apply no matter whose affairs you're looking to manage.

 When dealing with durable power of attorney proceedings, you may also hear the term *springing power of attorney.* This document is another kind of durable power of attorney, but with one key difference: The springing power of attorney doesn't go into effect *until* your parent is incapacitated. A springing power of attorney can be good for seniors who want to retain independence until their last synapse pulls in at the station, and at the same time takes some of the pressure off you because you have time to get used to the idea before you have to jump in with both feet. But take heed; we don't recommend a springing power of attorney in many situations, particularly because it's not always clear that a senior is, in fact, unable to take care of him- or herself. As a result, you may find that many institutions don't accept the power of attorney without additional documentation, which just means a headache for you. In addition, unless your parent becomes suddenly or completely unquestionably incapacitated, a springing power of attorney could land you in a battle with other family members who disagree that Mom or Dad is unable to care for him- or herself anymore.

Assessing what your power may cover

When you hold durable power of attorney, you often have more control of your parent's life than you ever thought you would (or ever wanted). Any major decisions your parent made are now yours to make. If you're getting durable power of attorney expressly to apply for a reverse mortgage, consider whether you want this power to be exclusive to the loan or across the board for all financial and real estate matters (not to mention medical decisions). A durable power of attorney that covers all aspects of finances gives you the power to do the following:

- ✔ Apply for a reverse mortgage
- ✔ Oversee and sign tax forms and returns
- ✔ Open a bank account
- ✔ Make donations

✔ Pay yourself

✔ Manage existing accounts, pensions, insurance, and healthcare

You or your parent may be uncomfortable with all that power. After all, you're pretty much taking over another person's life. In this case, you also have the option to do a limited durable power of attorney, which specifically includes or excludes certain privileges.

Without a limitation clause, the durable power of attorney pretty much allows you to do whatever you want. The laws are very broad and far reaching in most states. Whether you choose a general or limited durable power of attorney, be as specific as possible in the wording. An elder law attorney (see "Finding an Elder Law Attorney," later in this chapter) can guide you through spelling out your and your parent's wishes.

Knowing your responsibility

We would never accuse you of being selfish. After all, if you're reading this chapter, you obviously care about the well-being of your parent. But you may be wondering what your role is in the durable power of attorney and how your parent's loan affects you if you are the one who initiates and executes it.

First and foremost, you can't be held personally responsible for your parent's debts, even though you are the one with durable power of attorney, because you are signing on behalf of your parent's estate. When you sign anything for your parent, including the reverse mortgage documents, you sign Chelsea Child as "an agent" for Susie Senior, or Susie Senior, as Chelsea Child, "attorney in fact."

A few variations on the signature format exist, but the idea is the same; as long as your reverse mortgage originator accepts the signature, you're good to go. This "dual" signature absolves you of the responsibilities incurred in your parent's name, but it does not give you license to sign off on treats for yourself all over town, using your parent's name. Okay, technically it may leave you open to that sort of debauchery, but don't do it. You'll land yourself in a heapin' helpin' of legal trouble.

Bigger than the signatures, of course, is the knowledge that you have a tremendous level of power over your parent. If this thought makes you rub your hands together like an evil villain, you are not the person for the job. You need to have the patience, time, morals, basic legal understanding, and mental stamina to take responsibility for your parent. You will be the one who signs off on the loan documents, manages your parent's budget, keeps an eye on any investments, staves off senior scam artists, doles out birthday money — in short, everything you do for yourself times two.

If all else fails and you decide that you really aren't cut out to hold a durable power of attorney, your wingman can take your place. Most durable powers of attorney name an agent (you) along with a "just in case" successor. This successor covers you if you want to step out of the equation or if you become incapacitated in some way yourself, which just may happen if you let all these reverse mortgage transactions drive you crazy.

Determining Necessity

Many people find it heartbreaking to look honestly and candidly at a parent who raised them — who kissed their scraped knee, helped them with their homework, and embarrassed them in front of their friends — and know deep down that Mom or Dad is no longer able to take care of him- or herself. It's hard, it's sad, it's scary, and it's easy to settle into denial about the whole situation. Not facing the facts doesn't help anyone and can make the situation worse for a parent who needs some extra care.

If your parent has gone to a reverse mortgage counselor who feels that Mom or Dad was unable to understand the basics, or if you already know that there's no way you could explain declining equity to your parent, your durable power of attorney may be the ticket to your parent's financial security. By using the money from a loan, your parent may be able to afford in-home care or a paid companion who can just hang out and make sure no one leaves the stove on overnight.

Going through a behavior checklist

We all have odd moments when we realize we've just put the milk in the cupboard and the cereal in the fridge. Everyone loses their keys and discovers them someplace completely random, and everyone has spent 45 minutes looking for their eyeglasses, only to find them sitting conveniently on their own head. These moments aren't signs of incapacitation — that's just life. But you can't ignore some clues. Look at the following list of common mental incapacity traits with an open mind; not every point is an indicator of diminished mentality, but add a few together and you need to seek professional guidance.

As you go down the list, try not to make excuses such as "She's always been that way" or "He doesn't do it that often." Being honest with yourself about your parent is the best way to help Mom or Dad on the road to getting a reverse mortgage.

Understanding that patience is a virtue

Dealing with a senior who has mental incapacities (full or partial) can be trying. It's hard enough to come to grips with an aging parent, but when that parent's behavior starts to send you over the edge, try to remember that this person is still your parent. Seniors with dementia or other mental illness may not always know exactly what's going on, but they do know when things are going well and when something isn't quite right. They still have feelings and emotions. They're not trying to aggravate you on purpose. When they ask two dozen times where you got your sweater, it's not to be annoying and it's not to get attention.

Most important, it's not their fault. No one asks to lose their mental faculties. It can be just as scary for them to experience as it is for you to watch. Summon all your kindness, patience, and composure, and try your hardest to listen, smile (or whatever the appropriate expression is), and help them feel at ease. Remember not to lash out at your parent — getting angry only knocks down your parent's trust in you and could ignite an undesirable reaction. Just keep saying to yourself, "It's not his/her fault."

Review these indicators:

- ✔ Poor memory that just keeps getting worse
- ✔ Asking the same questions over and over
- ✔ Initiating the same conversation over and over
- ✔ Making bad decisions that could be harmful, such as walking 5 miles to the grocery store in the rain at night
- ✔ Having a sudden change in personality, good or bad
- ✔ Misplacing money
- ✔ Buying the same item several times (before it's needed again)
- ✔ Being unable to make a decision, or having a blasé attitude
- ✔ Being often confused about place and/or time
- ✔ Being unable to plan for the future, even a day or a few hours in advance
- ✔ Forgetting basic personal hygiene and/or not taking interest in appearance

If your parent is exhibiting a few of these signs, schedule a doctor's appointment and then, if necessary, take the next step and get a durable power of attorney. With the income from a reverse mortgage and you at the helm, you can ensure a safe and comfortable life for your parent, even if he or she doesn't seem to realize it.

Book VII

Planning Your Estate and Will

Taking the first steps

When you've determined that your parent needs a little (or a lot of) help, your first move should be to get an elder law attorney. Sit down with your parent and the lawyer to discuss what level of durable power of attorney you need. Talk to your parent ahead of time so that he or she isn't taken off guard. Many seniors are less than receptive to the idea of someone else taking over their lives, but honesty really is the best policy here. If your parent is extremely resistant, go alone and get all the information you can without your parent present, and then explain it all in a more secure setting (like Mom or Dad's own living room). It's not ideal, but if you're not getting anywhere with firm yet gentle insistence and you don't want to carry your parent there, making the first visit alone is a good alternative. For heaven's sake, don't tell your parent that you're taking them to the ice-cream parlor and then pull up in the attorney's parking lot. It's not just a mean trick, but it also starts to destroy trust — which you need plenty of if you're going to convince your parent that you need to have durable power of attorney.

Never explain that you're going to "take care" of your parent or that you "know what's best." Your parent probably won't take kindly to being treated like a child and may (ironically) rebel, just like a child would. Instead, use phrases such as "help manage your loan," "give you a hand with your checkbook," and "protect your money." These phrases are much less threatening, and your parent may receive them more positively.

Afterward, contact a reverse mortgage counselor and set up an appointment to meet. Explain on the phone that you have durable power of attorney, although the counselor will probably still want to speak to your parent on the phone before making the appointment. If you have durable power of attorney, you must be present for the counselor meeting.

If you look over at your parent during the meeting and he or she seems to be staring out the window, try to focus your parent's attention back to the topic at hand. Do this three times. If your parent can't seem to pay attention or isn't grasping the concepts enough to take interest, just let him or her be. Don't try to oversimplify the ideas of a reverse mortgage because it may come off scarier than it actually is. If you have full durable power of attorney, your parent can flip through a magazine for the whole session and it won't make any difference. However, if your parent seems to be trying to understand the reverse mortgage concepts, your counselor will be able to break down the ideas into easy, mentally digestible pieces. We don't have to tell you that if your parent seems to understand the basics of a reverse mortgage and is ardently against it, don't proceed. Your counselor can also help you assess your parent's reaction and direct you on how to go from there.

Remember that, as the durable power of attorney agent, you must be present at all meetings so you know what's going on at all times. If you could send your parent alone, you probably wouldn't need to have durable power of attorney.

Finding an Elder Law Attorney

Although the law doesn't require you to have an elder law attorney prepare your durable power of attorney documents (and preparing one on your own can save some cash in the very short term), lacking the legal knowledge to create a durable power of attorney for property management can cost you thousands, if not more, because of common mistakes or loopholes. A durable power of attorney must be tailored to your specific circumstances to be the most effective document possible. We don't recommend that you draft your own durable power of attorney, and we hope that you consider carefully the potential problems with do-it-yourself forms and kits.

Most lawyers don't specialize in serving a particular type of person. Criminal lawyers may have a knack for people with similar hobbies — say, knocking over liquor stores — but they don't focus on a precise segment of the population as an elder law attorney does. You may be tempted to use your own lawyer to oversee the durable power of attorney, but this decision is usually not the best choice. Consider why:

✔ General-practice attorneys may buy into the myths that go along with old age. They may patronize a perfectly aware senior, talk loudly for no reason, or ignore them altogether.

✔ Elder law attorneys have connections in the world of senior citizens, from in-home assisted living providers to gerontologists (senior doctors), senior-care psychologists, government program information, and more.

✔ General-practice attorneys may not be familiar with all of the subtle aspects of a durable power of attorney, especially in relation to a reverse mortgage.

Your general family lawyer will probably be able to refer you to a good elder law attorney, however, so don't scratch him or her out of your phonebook quite yet.

Book VII

Planning Your Estate and Will

Knowing what to look for

Part of what makes finding a good elder law attorney somewhat difficult (besides the fact that you may not have one in your area if you live in a small town) is that so many fields of elder law exist. Different elder law attorneys specialize in all sorts of areas: medical claims, Social Security issues, estate planning, elder abuse, age discrimination, nursing home problems, and elder fraud, just to name a few. When you call around, be sure to explain up front that you're looking for someone who has experience in creating durable power of attorney authorizations and who is also knowledgeable about reverse mortgages.

Speaking of that first call, now is a good time to ask some preliminary questions. You may be speaking with a receptionist or assistant, but it's okay — that person should be able to spout off the answers without missing a beat.

Some good first questions to ask include the following:

✔ How long has the attorney practiced elder law?

✔ What associations is he or she a member of?

✔ What should I bring with me when I come in?

✔ What is the fee structure? Does that include the first consultation?

In fact, ask anything you want; just remember that the person answering the phone probably isn't a lawyer, so it's best to save detailed questions for the attorney. When you're in and have explained your reason for coming, lay on the more difficult questions. Start with "Have you ever done a durable power of attorney for a reverse mortgage?" Don't be shy — if you don't understand something the first time, just keep asking until you do. You're on the clock, but it's worth it to get a satisfactory answer.

Some sample questions to take with you may be the following:

✔ What are the downsides to getting durable power of attorney in our particular situation?

✔ What provisions do you recommend to the written durable power of attorney?

✔ Judging by our conversation, do you think we have any better alternatives to getting durable power of attorney that we haven't thought of?

✔ After seeing my parent in person, do you feel that a durable power of attorney is appropriate?

✔ How long does it take before the durable power of attorney goes into effect? (Timing may depend on who draws up the paperwork and the office's turnaround time.)

✔ How often should we revisit the durable power of attorney documents?

Because the answers to these questions can vary from family to family, we can't give you definitive answers here; it's important to discuss these issues (and any others you can think of) thoroughly with an elder law attorney.

In addition, your elder law attorney must possess the same qualities that a good reverse mortgage counselor or originator has: patience, respect for seniors, and superb communication skills. Just as you would with an originator, you and your parent need to feel that you can ask questions, get results within the promised timeframe, and receive personal attention that shows that the attorney cares about you beyond your checkbook.

Elder law attorneys (as with any other lawyers) usually charge by the hour or part thereof, plus whatever expenses they incur on your behalf (such as making copies or mailing something). Fees vary from office to office but can run as low as $50 an hour at very generous offices with senior finances in mind, to as high as a few hundred dollars an hour. Discuss your financial situation with your attorney right off the bat. If you can't afford their high fees, many elder law attorneys may very kindly lower their rates or reduce the billable hours. When your attorney tells you the rate and gives you an estimate of how much the total cost will be, level with him or her — say how much you can spend and ask nicely if the attorney can help you stay within your budget. Most attorneys will, but many won't assume you even have a budget unless you say something.

You can make the experience of creating a durable power of attorney a positive one by being sure to bring all of the documents, statements, and other items that the elder law attorney requests of you. If your parent has already gotten a reverse mortgage, bring all the loan documents, including the loan agreement, which lays out all of the terms of repayment. You can also ask the reverse mortgage originator you're working with (or plan to work with) for sample copies to take with you so that the elder law attorney knows all the details of the loan.

Finding a good elder law attorney

Beyond flipping through pages of "Call for a free estimate" ads that make your legal issues sound like a broken-down car, countless resources available to you can help you find a highly regarded elder law attorney in your area. Remember, you don't have to go with the first attorney you talk to, and you don't have to worry about hurting an attorney's feelings if you choose someone else. At upward of $250 an hour, attorneys can use their wads of cash to dry their tears.

Some great places to start searching include the following:

- **National Association of Elder Law Attorneys (NAELA):** It may come as no surprise that the NAELA Web site is a great place to start when you're looking for an elder law attorney. Its "Locate an Elder Law Attorney" database has listings of NAELA members all over the country, some with information such as law specialties and links to their own Web sites where you can find out more about each attorney. Visit the site at www.naela.com or call 520-881-4005.

- **American Bar Association (ABA):** The Senior Lawyers Division of the ABA provides a directory of state and city senior lawyer groups in the United States. The ABA Web site also has an option to search for lawyers by specialty. You can find the ABA's senior groups at www.abanet.org/srlawyers/.

✔ **Alzheimer's Association:** Not only will you find incredible and up-to-date information about Alzheimer's tips and recent research on its Web site, but you can also contact your local chapter, which can most likely give you a referral to a competent elder law attorney. Visit www.alz.org or call 800-272-3900.

✔ **AARP:** AARP is an excellent resource for all facets of aging, and here you can find that AARP really shines. Log on to www.aarp.org/money/legalissues/ to discover a "Find a Lawyer" link, plus an option to receive 30 minutes of free legal advice from one of AARP's network attorneys. If your parent is an AARP member, he or she can receive additional reduced-fee services. While you're at the site, check out the reverse mortgage links.

✔ **Children of Aging Parents (CAPs):** This nonprofit organization has resources for many aspects of managing your parent's affairs. Its chapters are in only about 15 states, but this organization may be able to help you contact a similar group in your own area. Call 800-227-7294 for support and suggestions.

Using a Living Trust as an Alternative

A durable power of attorney isn't right for everyone. Some people just aren't cut out to manage other people's lives; some can barely manage their own. This huge undertaking takes a lot of dedication. Now, everyone loves their parents, even if it's way, way deep down. But if you're feeling like durable power of attorney is a bit too committal for you, you have other options (we can talk about your commitment issues later).

You may have heard about wealthy spoiled kids who have a trust fund waiting for them when they turn 18. Granted, this scenario happens more often in the movies than in real life, but trusts can be a useful tool in managing another person's finances. For our purposes, we focus on the living trust (also called *intervivos*). A living trust is the only kind that can help you in getting a reverse mortgage for your parent because it's the only one that guarantees that the trust was created during your parent's lifetime (hence the name *living trust*).

Generally, a living trust allows one person (the trustee) to handle the property title for another person (the beneficiary). The language of living trusts is confusing because, unlike your parent's will, which names beneficiaries who are usually the heirs, such as you or your other family members, you are the trustee in this instance and your parent is the beneficiary. It's a financial doppelganger.

What's not confusing is the basic benefit of a living trust: Your parent can be both the trustee and the beneficiary (which means that your parent has control over everything on his or her own) until your parent becomes incapacitated; then you or another named trustee can step in and take over. You don't have to worry about having too much control while your parent is still fully mentally functional. In this way, a living trust is similar to a springing power of attorney, but it has one big advantage: Living trusts are a respected part of the financial world. Whereas people are often suspicious of a springing power of attorney, a living trust almost never causes problems. Living trusts are widely accepted as legal and reputable.

A living trust may be set in stone (irrevocable), changeable, or even revocable (in other words, it can be canceled). The format that you and your parent choose depends on your individual situation, but keep in mind that things change. You may decide after a few years that a durable power of attorney is the best path after all, or your parent may decide that your sister is really the one who should be in charge of the house. Talk to a professional about the benefits and potential pitfalls of both options.

Setting up a living trust is fairly simple, but it's not the kind of thing you can do yourself, just as it's not a good idea to set up a durable power of attorney on your own. Too much legal mumbo jumbo and too many considerations are involved, such as what effects the living trust has on your parent's other financial areas. The property in a living trust can sometimes (but not always) have an effect on your parent's taxes and government aid, such as Medicare. You don't want to go to all the trouble of setting up a living trust and getting a reverse mortgage just to find out that it has negative implications for your parent's taxes. The same elder law attorney you scouted out for the durable power of attorney can help create a living trust (see "Finding an Elder Law Attorney," earlier in this chapter). Your regular attorney can help you with this, as long as he or she has some background in living trusts and other aspects of estate planning.

Part of the reason a living trust is so easy to do is that you pay someone else to do it — a lot. You have to pay legal fees, processing fees, transfer fees, attorney-needs-a-vacation fees — you get the idea. If you haven't already, skip back to the section "Finding a good elder law attorney," earlier in this chapter, and start looking for a good attorney who won't charge you an arm and a leg. Again, your parent's financial planning isn't the time to skimp on costs, but you may have some options for reduced-cost elder law attorneys.

One of the downfalls of a living trust is that even when your parent is incapacitated and you're managing the trust, a living trust gives you power only over the property. In most cases, that's as far as you can go with it. You can get a reverse mortgage on the property, sell it, bulldoze it, paint it purple, whatever you want. But you have no control over the rest of the assets unless the living trust expressly lays them out and transfers them to you. So if you are the trustee but forgot to mention that you will eventually need control over the rest of the estate (bank accounts, other property, family heirlooms, and so on), you're out of luck. You need to have a capable attorney helping you tie up any loose ends.

Book VII

Planning Your Estate and Will

Index

• B •

Notes

Notes

Notes